Music Ways of Listening

Music Ways of Listening

Elliott Schwartz
Bowdoin College

Holt, Rinehart and Winston
New York Chicago San Francisco
Philadelphia Montreal Toronto London
Sydney Tokyo Mexico City
Rio de Janeiro Madrid

Acquisitions Editor Thomas W. Gornick
Project Editor Ellen Small
Production Manager Nancy Myers
Art Director Lou Scardino
Text Design and Cover Caliber Design Planning

Library of Congress Cataloging in Publication Data

Schwartz, Elliott, 1936–
Music: Ways of Listening.

Includes index.
1. Music—Analysis, appreciation. I. Title.
MT6.S354M9 780'.1'5 81-20327
ISBN 0-03-044676-7 AACR2

Address correspondence to:
383 Madison Avenue
New York, N.Y. 10017

Printed in the United States of America
Published simultaneously in Canada
2 3 4 5 032 9 8 7 6 5 4 3 2 1

CBS COLLEGE PUBLISHING
Holt, Rinehart and Winston
The Dryden Press
Saunders College Publishing

To Grandma Pearlie,
Grandma Rosie,
and Grandpa Meyer

Preface

Music: Ways of Listening is intended for use in introductory college courses for students with little or no prior background in music, and is focused upon the development of perceptive listening skills and a broad survey of the Western concert literature. In writing this text, I have emphasized the primacy of the student's ***listening*** experience—relating new concepts and terms to aural perceptions, so that factual information "about" music grows naturally out of one's absorption in a body of compositions being studied (rather than using pieces offhandedly to illustrate abstract points). In this regard, I have been especially concerned about the development of listening skills even at the earliest stages of discussing musical elements. Accordingly, most of the material of Part 1 (which introduces concepts of melody, polyphony, rhythm, and the like) is presented aurally, linked to fifteen musical examples for listening available on an individual long-playing record.

Secondly, I have tried to offer a historical survey—Part 2 of the book—that stresses ***style*** distinctions, forms and genres as they have evolved through the years, and an overall approach to music as a ***social*** phenomenon related to matters of politics, economics, social class, taste, technology, literature, and the other arts. Here, too, the text is drawn from concentrated aural absorption in a body of compositions: ***listening,*** as an active, creative venture. In fact, the book's major premise is that the experience of hearing music cannot be thought of as "passive"; on the contrary, it is a wonderfully challenging, stimulating activity for the spirit and the intellect. Ideally, ***listening*** can (or should) trigger the widest kind of ***thinking,*** whether about musical materials and sonic patterns themselves, or the broader dimensions of social history, biography, expressive statement, or style comparison.

Other features of ***Music: Ways of Listening*** have grown out of the assumptions noted above, and include:

1. The five brief "Interludes" located at key junctures in the book. These are meant to pose questions rather than answer them: thought-provoking essays on a variety of topics, placed at points within the text where these topics might naturally arise.

2. Integration of non-Western musical concepts into the study of the Western tradition, especially throughout the Part 1 discussions of musical elements. I find that approach to non-Western culture preferable to the isolated chapter or two exclusively devoted to this area, which when time presses may be skimmed over or omitted entirely by students and instructors. ***Music: Ways of Listening*** is a book mainly about Western art music, but it is not meant to be ethnocentric. Just the opposite, in fact: I hope the book helps listeners reconcile many cultural traditions more easily, perceive the common denominators of style in various cultures, and approach Western music—with its own unique, striking traits and assumptions—from something of a world perspective.

3. Now that our century has almost ended, it seems especially crucial that we bring introductory music students into greater contact with the wide variety of twentieth-century styles. In this respect, even the early chapters of Part 1 draw upon contemporary examples: five of the fifteen selections for listening (Penderecki, Webern, Babbitt, Terry Riley, and Bessie Smith) are of our century. And the historical-stylistic survey of Part 2 goes beyond a discussion of contemporary "classics" into the more uncharted domain of recent experiments.

4. The text has been designed for the student who does not read music, and for a course in which music notation is not taught; in fact, this book was intentionally designed with fewer illustrative examples in staff notation than most competing "appreciation" books. On the other hand, ***notation itself*** (as a social and cultural phenomenon, as a mirror of stylistic priorities, and as a graphic tool for composers and performers) receives special attention in Part 1. There is no attempt made to teach students the written "language" of Western music, but, rather, an introduction to the "linguistics" of written symbols in all musical cultures.

5. In addition to the basic record containing the fifteen selections which dominate Part 1, we have prepared 6 more records, on which can be found a great many of the compositions discussed in the text. It is possible to obtain the single record for Part 1 separately, or an album of the complete set of 7 records.

A great many people have helped see this book through its various stages of initial writing, revision, and eventual publication; I am indebted to them all. Those who commented upon the manuscript in progress include Donald Aird, Robert Beckwith, Steven Cerf, Barney Childs, Robert Erickson, Vivian and Robert Folkenflik, Benjamin Folkman, Tom Johnson, Jonathan Kramer, William Matthews, John Rucker, George Michael Schelle, Bertram Turetzky, and Julia Walkling. Colleagues who reviewed the manuscript include Wayne C. Wentzel, Petter Juel-Larsen, Leo Kreter, Barbara Garvey Jackson, John Schneider, and Francis T. Schuessler. My Bowdoin College colleagues Gabor Brogyanyi and Steven Cerf prepared translations of French, German and Italian texts; James Roy and Barbara Peterson of BMI helped locate photographs. Invaluable aid in steering the manuscript through various storms into final publication was provided by Ruth and Seymour Drescher, John Howland, Philip Isaacson, Vreni Keller, Michael Nebe, David Rice, and Mel Simensky. Among the editors at Holt, Rinehart and Winston who helped shape the finished work, Roth Wilkofsky, Tom Gornick, Tom Hitchings, and Susan Katz merit thanks, and Ellen Small very special thanks. Laura Harth and Liz Nealon of CBS Special Products were extremely helpful in assembling the accompanying record package.

A sabbatical leave from Bowdoin College, partially supported by a grant from Bowdoin's Faculty Development Fund (acknowledged here with much appreciation), provided the impetus for ***Music: Ways of Listening.*** The manuscript was initially written during that leave and my year-long residency at the Center for Music Experiment of the University of California San Diego; I am grateful for the time provided by the Center, and the generous use of the facilities at the La Jolla Athaneum. Extensive revisions were made during another residency, a year later, at the Rockefeller Foundation's Villa Serbelloni (Bellagio, Italy) while I was also engaged in composing a string quartet. The fellowships in California and Italy offered me the freedom and stimulus to write amidst some of the most gorgeous natural surroundings on earth, and I cannot be too thankful.

Finally, I have been aided immeasurably by my wife Dorothy throughout the duration of this entire project. She has always been present when I've needed her—for imaginative insight, comfort, criticism, wise counsel, or sharp proofreading—and is singlehandedly responsible for the photo research and selection of the book's illustrative material. She is also awarded Grand Prize for Patience (as always).

E.S.
Brunswick, Maine
September 1981

Contents

Music Ways of Listening

1

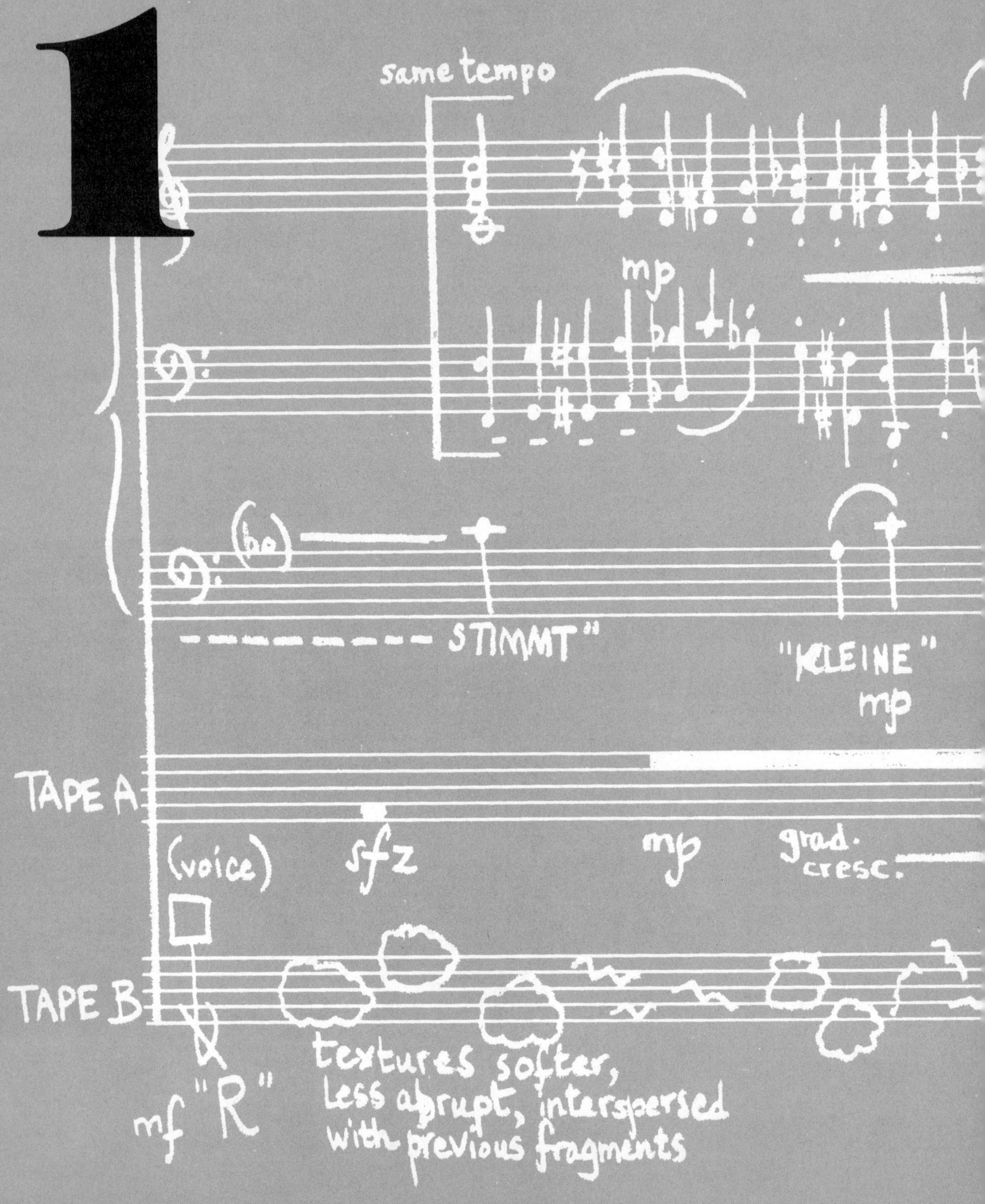

same tempo
mp
STIMMT"
"KLEINE"
mp
TAPE A
(voice)
sfz
mp
grad. cresc.
TAPE B
mf "R"
textures softer, less abrupt, interspersed with previous fragments

Musical Elements

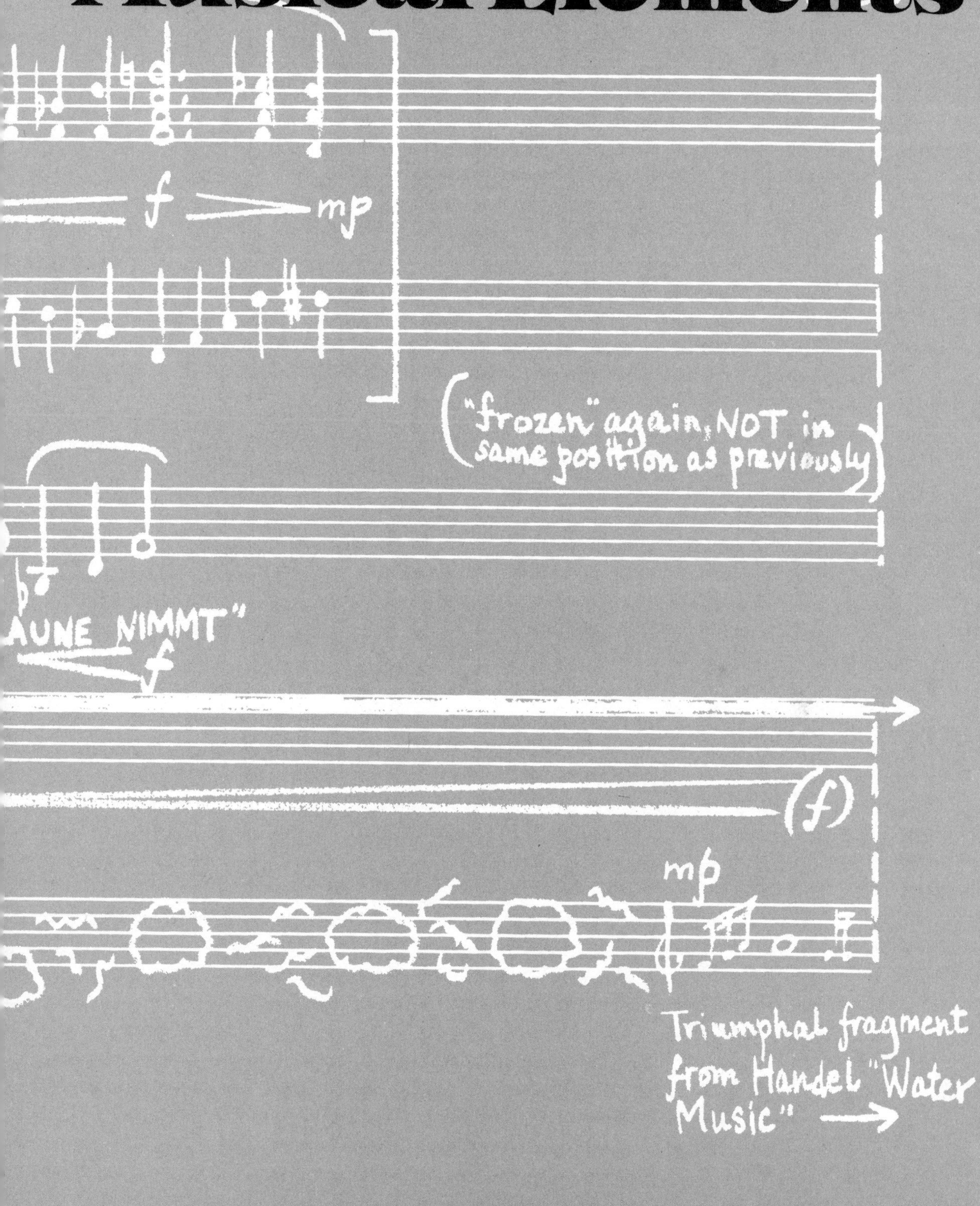

("frozen" again, NOT in same position as previously)

"...AUNE NIMMT"

Triumphal fragment from Handel "Water Music" →

Overture: Ways of Listening

Music is such a familiar component of our daily lives, essential to the ceremonial and emotional fabric of every civilization on earth, that it seems unnecessary to read (or write) a book about it. After all, isn't it called the "universal language"?

Yes and no. In reality, the styles, instruments and actual sounds of music vary so greatly from one culture to another that the term "universal language" is hardly appropriate: a Beethoven symphony is quite different from an African drumming ritual or the music of the Japanese court. To be sure, the person who first applied the phrase "universal language" to music was most likely thinking only of the Western European tradition. In that context, the phrase was meant to refer to a universality of feeling: the "expressive" content of music, or—to quote another familiar catch-phrase—music as the "language of the emotions."

But the truth is that music presents us with many paradoxes. It may indeed be a major vehicle for emotional utterance, but it can also be aggressively anti-expressive. It can be, perhaps next to architecture, the most scientific and mathematical of the arts, since it often deals with measurements, proportions and acoustic properties. But in performance it offers the most immediate, sensual and perishable of experiences: a few fragments of sound in the air, heard and then gone. Music has often been associated with rigorous logic and precision, but it has also played a vital role in our celebration of the irrational and unknowable: consider its importance in magical and theatrical ceremonies. Music suffers from the stigma of an elitist calling, whose mysteries are penetrable only by those possessing special skills; on the other hand, it is the most accessible and popular of the arts, capable of evoking a response in every one of us no matter what our level of experience. In fact, we are all *surrounded* by music, bombarded by all kinds of musical stimuli every day: transistor radios, electric guitars, church choirs, the canned Muzak that greets us in elevators and shopping centers, concerts witnessed in the flesh and concerts preserved in recorded form.

It's very likely we aren't listening to much of this; we tune out most of it. (A good thing, too: if we didn't have the ability to cope with an overload of sensory information, we would be driven mad.) Of course, much of the music around us is meant to function in the background. We are not supposed to perceive it for its own sake, or focus upon it at all. Unfortunately, we may find it hard to concentrate upon music meant to dominate the *foreground* of our consciousness. When we have spent our lives learning to "tune out" musical impulses, it may be challenging to switch gears and do just the opposite. In studying music, that is just what we will be doing: developing an active, attentive kind of perception, focusing in rather than tuning out.

Listening in this heightened, concentrated way may seem difficult at first, but it will be much less so if we know what to listen for. The process will also become easier as we gain more confidence in our own listening powers. Even now, we are ***all*** discriminating listeners, beginning students included; we have all developed the ability to screen out some sounds and respond to others, and we all have confirmed tastes in music, whatever they may be.

The Enraged Musician by William Hogarth, 1741.

Suggestions for Listening

Perhaps we can use that last statement as a point of departure. We might ask ourselves why we like one kind of music and not another, and what features we find most enjoyable in the music we prefer. As we examine our responses, we find that we probably listen to music in a special way, different from the way we hear conversation or street noises. The *expressive* references of musical sounds, or their sensuous effect as sheer *sonority,* may occupy our attention. We become aware of relationships between sounds, so that a quality of *organization* becomes apparent. Even though a composer may have created that organization, and a performer may have articulated and clarified it, we contribute to the organizing process, too, by recognizing it. Listening in a special fashion, then, is an important component of the esthetic experience.

The nature of our listening changes as the music does; for example, we are more conscious of the rhythmic element in dance music than in solemn liturgical chant. "Abstract" music advancing an extended pattern or argument in sound differs in listening challenges from "program" music, which attempts to tell a story or paint a picture in sound, or from vocal music in which sung words make meaning explicitly clear. We also alter our listening responses when switching from a seventeenth-century piece to a nineteenth century one, or from German style to French. So the special way in which we hear music is not one skill, but a collection of many.

Every listener, even the least experienced, has a good number of these skills already. Other skills, dulled by our built-in twentieth century habit of tuning out, need to be developed. We can each begin by considering the following suggestions, concerned with aspects of perceptive listening:

1. Develop your *sensitivity to sounds.* Try to respond esthetically to *all* sounds, from the hum of a refrigerator motor or the paddling of oars on a lake, to the tones of a cello or muted trumpet. When we really hear sounds, we may find them all quite expressive, magical and even "beautiful." On a more complex level, try to relate sounds to each other in patterns: the successive notes in a melody, or the interrelationships between an ice cream truck jingle and nearby children's games.

2. As we will see in future chapters, *time* is a crucial component of the musical experience. Develop a *sense of time* as it passes: duration, motion, and the placement of events within a time frame. How long *is* thirty seconds, for example? A given duration of clock-time will feel very different if contexts of activity and motion are changed.

3. Develop a *musical memory.* While listening to a piece, try to recall familiar patterns, relating new events to past ones and placing them all within a durational frame. This facility may take a while to grow, but it eventually will. And once you discover that you can use your memory in this way, just as people discover that they really can swim or ski or ride a bicycle, life will never be the same.

4. If we want to read, write or talk about music, we must acquire a working ***vocabulary.*** Music is basically a nonverbal art, and its unique events and effects are often too elusive for everyday words; we need special words to describe them, however inadequately. Many new terms will be introduced during the course of this book, each related directly to the listening experience.

5. Try to develop musical ***concentration,*** especially when listening to lengthy pieces. Composers and performers learn how to fill different time-frames in appropriate ways, using certain gestures and patterns for long works and others for brief ones. The listener must also learn to adjust to varying durations. It may be easy to concentrate on a selection lasting a few minutes, but virtually impossible to maintain attention when confronted with a half-hour Beethoven symphony or a three-hour Verdi opera.

Composers are well aware of this problem. They provide so many musical landmarks and guidelines during the course of a long piece that, even if listening "focus" wanders, you can tell where you are. The opera provides other reference points as well: words, stage action, lights, scenery. Very often a large whole is divided into smaller, more manageable units: the symphony into its movements, the opera into acts and scenes. Of course, neither Beethoven nor Verdi (to use our two examples above) ever envisioned a recorded performance heard over loudspeakers or headphones. Listening to records may entail an extra ounce of concentration, if only to compensate for the missing visual stimuli and pageantry of the live performance; on the other hand, recordings can aid and build concentration, by allowing you to hear passages again and again.

6. Try to ***listen objectively and dispassionately.*** Concentrate upon "what's there," and not what you hope or wish would be there. At the early stages of directed listening, when a working vocabulary for music is being introduced, it is important that you respond ***using that vocabulary*** as often as possible. In this way you can relate and compare pieces that represent different styles, cultures and centuries. Try to focus upon "what's there," in an objective sense, and don't be dismayed if a limited vocabulary restricts your earliest responses. If a beginning listener hears a particular passage and states, "all the notes are bunched together, very high, with the volume alternating between very loud and very quiet states," he or she has said a lot about that passage—a lot more, in fact, than any of the following comments (which convey no information at all):

> "I really love that."
> "It reminds me of fairies dancing in the moonlight."
> "My girl friend used to play that on the piano."
> "It sounds like background music for a horror movie."

There's nothing actually wrong with such responses. Your own memories and associations are important factors that you, as an individual, bring to the listening experience. But they say very little about the passage itself. If we try to imagine the music being described in these terms, nine times out of ten we cannot; you might be referring to a loud passage or a quiet one, a piece of Mozart or one by Scott Joplin. Such comments resemble the syrupy program notes for symphony audiences, or inspirational guides to "appreciation," that flourished at the turn of the century. On reading the following example it would take a great deal of prior knowledge, and luck, to guess that the subject of the essay is Beethoven's Ninth Symphony. And there is *no* useful information—historical, structural or biographical—being conveyed about the piece or its composer!

> . . . He (the composer) descends to realms of darkness . . . calls up ghosts of the past, and, lifted above the grasp of fate, remembers the despairing conflict in which his will once wrested for earthly joy . . .

A Youth Playing Pipes by Thomas Eakins, 1883. Hirshhorn Museum and Sculpture Garden, Smithsonian Institution

Listeners need to develop musical responses that are unencumbered by such visual or literary images, particularly because a large body of concert music stands on its own without the need for such imagery. Objective listening helps to develop attentive, focused hearing skills; stress upon "what's there" will also help listeners acquire a working vocabulary for music.

7. ***Bring experience and knowledge*** to the listening situation. That includes not only your concentration and growing vocabulary, but information about the music itself: its composer, history and social context. Such knowledge makes the experience of listening that much more enjoyable.

There may appear to be a conflict between this suggestion and the previous one, in which listeners were urged to focus just on "what's there." Ideally, it would be fascinating to hear a new piece of music with fresh expectations and truly innocent ears, as though we were Martians. But such objectivity doesn't exist. All listeners approach a new piece with ears that have been "trained" by prejudices, personal experiences and memories. Some of these may get in the way of listening to music. Try to replace these with ***other*** items that might help focus upon the work, rather than individual feelings. Of course, the "work" is much more than the sounds heard at any one sitting in a concert hall; it also consists of previous performances, recorded performances, the written notes on manuscript paper, and all the memories, reviews and critiques of these written notes and performances, ***ad infinitum.*** In acquiring information about any of these factors, we are simply broadening our total awareness of the work itself.

On the other hand, rest assured that an introductory music course does not emphasize theory or history—or the ability to play an instrument. Any beginning course in listening should stress the ***sounds*** of music: audible patterns and gestures, rather than facts about music that might be important for professional specialists. As for playing skill, bear in mind that many highly perceptive listeners have little or no practical experience in music-making. It is not necessary to read music to become aware of patterns, forms and historical styles. Students with performing experience often discover that, as ***listeners,*** they are at the same beginning level as everyone else. They, too, have unconsciously learned to tune out sounds, and they haven't necessarily heard a wide variety of music beyond that which they were specially trained to play. Listening to music is a skill and art of its own, not dependent upon the ability to read music or perform.

Remember, though, that we listen with more than our ears. We listen with our experiences, expectations, and a fine sense of relating many factors. The more knowledge we bring to bear upon the sounds, the more complete our listening will be. Awareness of the way music is made, and of its cultural context, is as much a part of the listening experience as a set of healthy ears.

1

Listening to Music

Music is the house that sounds live in.

Six year-old Navarana Smythe, as told to David Reck

A Definition for Music

frequency/pitch

Music, of course, deals with sounds. According to the science of physics, sound occurs when a vibrating object, such as the reed of an oboe or a violin string, sets up similar vibrations in the air. The atmospheric vibrations, called sound waves, eventually cause a similar vibration in our ear drums. The speed of vibration, or ***frequency,*** determines the ***pitch*** of the sound, with a higher (faster) frequency resulting in a higher pitch. The sound waves assume various shapes when visually observed on an oscilloscope.

Figure 1.1 shows the regularity of a simple frequency produced by an electronic synthesizer, the more complex wave-form of an instrumental tone (possibly oboe or trumpet), and the irregular mass of a sound that we might call noise—perhaps a rock striking a tree.

Figure 1.1

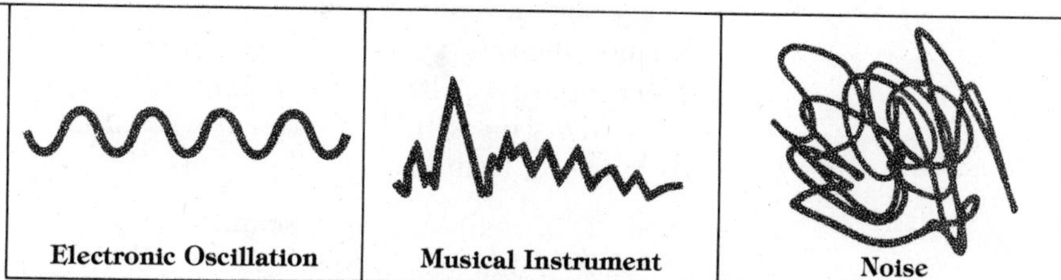

On another level, we know about sounds through our daily experience with them: thunder, the rustle of wind, a barking dog, human speech, or song. We make use of these sounds in countless ways, by responding to instructions or warning signals, and by communicating pleasant or angry feelings to each other. Furthermore, we do this while immersed in a constant bath of background sound, usually so familiar that we ignore it. Apparently we only hear background sound if we make a conscious effort to perceive it, or if we find ourselves transported to a totally foreign sound-world (a boiler factory, or tropical rain forest) where the background is new and fresh.

Most of us agree that there is a difference between music and sound: we may assert that music is "prettier" or "more meaningful" than mere sound, and we might dismiss music we don't like as "just sounds." Similarly, a mid-Victorian definition of music would have stressed its reliance upon pleasing *tones* or *notes* (which have specific frequencies) rather than mere sounds. On the other hand, some of our greatest composers have used such "noisy" instruments as cannons, cymbals, anvils and bass drums; twentieth century music and the music of non-Western cultures abound in the sonorities of bells, gongs, drums and other percussion instruments—sounds which could be considered acoustically complex "noises." In fact, *all* sounds can be the building blocks of music. Most modern dictionaries have taken this into account. Here are two typical definitions:

> Music: an arrangement of, or the art of combining or putting together, sounds that please the ear.
> Music: a succession or combination of sounds pleasing to the ear.

There is a problem with the stress on "pleasing the ear" found in such definitions. A great deal of music is not meant to be pleasing; rather, it may seek to express or evoke feelings of anger, pain, terror, sadness, or brutality. However, we can agree with the dictionaries that music uses *sounds* in certain *arrangements* or *combinations.*

Let us alter the typical dictionary definitions in two ways. First of all, an "arrangement" might be conscious or unconscious, planned or accidental. But most of the world's music has been the result of conscious, human *organization;* we should use that term instead. Secondly, our typical dictionary definitions say nothing about *time,* the crucial dimension through which sounds inevitably must pass. The relationship between *time* and *sound* is the most important in music. It is that relationship which, in fact, becomes "organized" as a piece of music takes shape.

Here, then, is a simple working definition: *Music is the organization of sound and time.* The three components of that definition can be regarded as three areas on which to concentrate, either singly or in combination, while listening to music.

1. What kinds and variety of *sounds* are there?
2. In what manner does *time* seem to pass?

Cycladic Syrinx Player, 2600–2000 B.C., yellowish marble. (H. 10 1/2″)
The Detroit Institute of Arts, Bequest of Dr. Lester W. Cameron.

3. What sort of *organization* unites those two elements? Are there discernible *patterns* emerging as the time and sounds pass by?

Let us begin by listening to five musical selections. Plan on listening to each a number of times: at least once for an overall sense, then with attention to details, and finally in a comparative way that relates and contrasts pieces with each other. The five selections are:

An example of Gregorian chant (Antiphon, *Laus Deo Patri:* Psalm 113, *Laudate pueri*)
Hector Berlioz: 4th movement ("March to the Gallows") from the *Symphonie Fantastique*
An example of Indian Raga (sitar, tabla, tamboura): *Raga Abhogi,* performed by Ravi Shankar
Henry Purcell: "Dido's Lament" (aria) from *Dido and Aeneas*
J. S. Bach: Prelude and Fugue in C Minor; from the *Well-Tempered Clavier,* Book I (performance on the harpsichord)

Listening for Sound

Our own everyday experience can lead to a number of observations about sound. They may have occurred to us before, and may even seem overly simple, but they are still useful as points of departure.

Sounds May Be Higher or Lower

There is a relationship between frequency (the number of vibrations per second) and the "highness" or "lowness" of sound. This sense of high and low is called *register;* the higher the frequency, the higher the register.

register

Listen to the openings of the Berlioz march, the Purcell aria (before the voice enters) and the Gregorian chant, and notice that they all occupy a relatively low register. But note as well, in each example, a succession of pitches (a "line") *within* that register, a contour with its own high and low points. We might speak of the high note of the opening Purcell melody, even though the entire melody occupies a low register. The high and low points of that total contour define the *range* of a passage in relative degrees of width

range

Figure 1.2

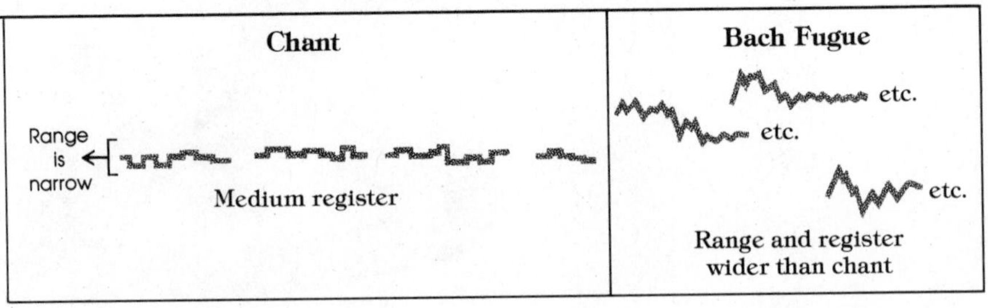

Figure 1.3

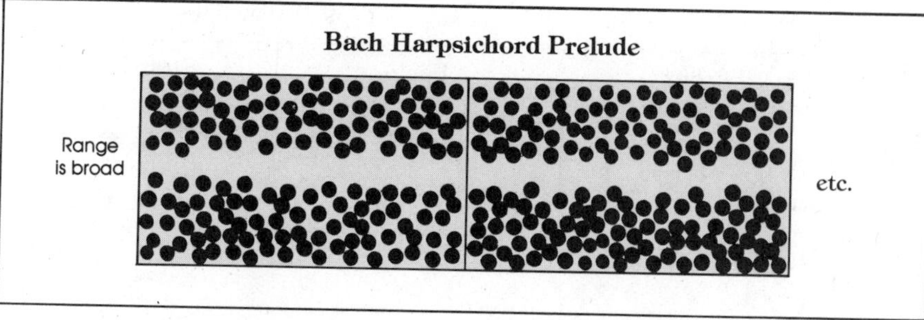

or narrowness. Listen to the entire Gregorian chant this time, and note that the range is rather narrow, with the individual pitches staying fairly close to one another. Imagine the chant being sung by a chorus of very high sopranos or very low basses; in either case the register would change drastically, but the range of the example would be maintained. That narrow range is suggested in Figure 1.2. (Note the comparison with the wider range and register of the Bach Fugue opening.)

The range and register of the chant, once begun, change very little over the course of the work. In the Purcell and Berlioz selections noticeable changes take place. They are gentle in "Dido's Lament," as new layers of sound are added in a higher register, but quite sudden in the Berlioz: notice the loud crashing chord at the climax of a drum roll. Much Western European music of the last few hundred years uses contrast and change of register for expressive or organizational purposes and employs a wider total range than the Gregorian chant.

Music from outside the Western tradition also employs patterns of range and register. Listen to the opening minutes of the Indian Raga. At first, the fixed range and relatively static middle register may seem similar to that of the chant; but then notice a subtle unfolding, closer to the Purcell example, as the music grows from a single drone to the sitar's long melody and then the superimposition of a rhythmic drumming pattern.

If we turn to the beginning of the Bach Prelude, we hear music that is basically middle register, but a "middle" that extends higher and lower to form a broad total range. The massive "wall" of sound heard at the very opening of the Prelude (Figure 1.3) reveals this broad range immediately.

Sounds May Be Louder or Softer

This statement is easily illustrated by the Berlioz "March," in which hushed murmurings are explosively contrasted with sudden bursts of volume. Now compare this selection with the Raga or the chant. The Raga grows louder and softer in a graceful, flowing arc. Volume changes within the chant are even more refined: they seem to represent two states of quiet, one associated with the choir and the other with the solo voice.

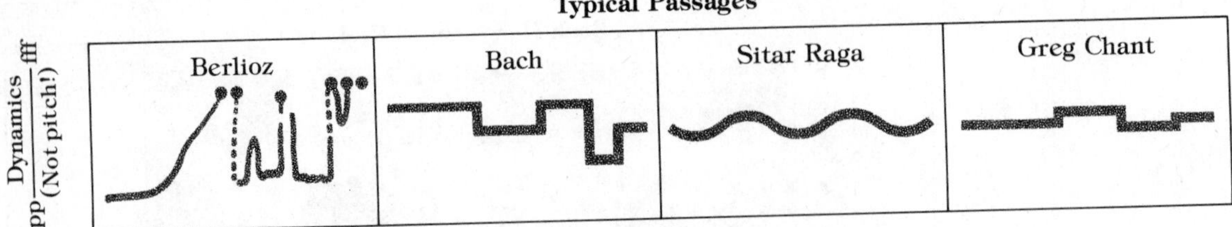

Figure 1.4

dynamics

The term ***dynamics*** refers to the dimension of musical volume. Western musicians traditionally indicate ***dynamic*** range by a series of Italian terms and their abbreviations, suggesting stages of comparison. These terms are fairly flexible in their interpretation (unlike the notated symbols for pitch, which are related to specific frequencies).

dynamic levels	ppp	extremely quiet	pianississimo (!); triple piano
	pp	very quiet	pianissimo
	p	quiet	piano
	mp	moderately quiet	mezzo-piano
	mf	moderately loud	mezzo-forte
	f	loud	forte
	ff	very loud	fortissimo
	fff	extremely loud	fortississimo (!); triple forte
important effects	<	growing louder	crescendo
	>	growing softer	diminuendo (or decrescendo)
	sfz	suddenly loud	sforzando
	sub pp	suddenly quiet	subito piano

Of our five examples, only the Berlioz and the Purcell employ frequent changes of dynamic level (***crescendo*** or ***diminuendo***). The sudden ***sforzando*** (*sfz*) crashes of the Berlioz are also noteworthy; they gather strength as the music proceeds, exploiting dynamic contrasts for vivid shock effect. Subtle changes and inflections of volume occur within the Raga and the chant, swelling and receding in gentle waves—unlike the thrusting and punching of the Berlioz. The Bach harpsichord selections seem to maintain fixed levels, which then change abruptly: for example, from steady *p* to steady *mp* and then back again. This practice was an accepted part of instrumental performance during the century in which Bach lived (see Chapter 10). Figure 1.4 suggests a few of these comparisons.

Sounds Have Specific "Colors"

timbre / tone color

There are special qualities to sounds, enabling us to recognize their source. Each sound source, from oboe to drum to voice to electronic synthesizer, possesses a unique ***timbre*** or ***tone color,*** which composers use singly or in combination with other timbres. This aspect of music will be discussed more fully in Chapter 6.

Sounds Convey Density

density

In the Gregorian chant there is a difference between the passages sung by full choir and those for the soloist. The subtle distinction may be heard as one of timbre, or of dynamic level, but it is unmistakable: the same phrase takes on a thicker, heavier *density* when sung by a group. An even more complex situation develops when we have more than one line or event at any point in time. For example, the Indian Raga can be heard on three levels: the continuously unfolding melody of the stringed sitar, the drumming patterns of the tabla, and the unshakeable drone of the tamboura. Each of these could, if heard alone, provide a fascinating listening experience. Hearing all three together, allowing our minds and ears to separate and recombine them as the performance takes place, is a much more challenging activity.

In listening for *density,* concentrate on the distinctions between weighty and light sounds, few performers and many, the heaviness of certain timbres as opposed to others. For example, notice the brilliant way in which Berlioz juggles different "weights:" thick chords, percussive crashes, single lines performed by a number of players, and the plaintive solo woodwind melody that is abruptly cut off just before the ending.

Giacomo Balla, *Plastic Construction of Noise and Speed.* 1968 reconstruction of original, 1914–15. Aluminum and steel relief, 40 x 47 x 8″. This three-dimensional wall relief conveys a sense of great density through its use of bent shapes at many lines and angles. As the title suggests, a "musical" idea underlies this visual projection. Hirshhorn Museum and Sculpture Garden, Smithsonian Institution.

The Bach Prelude and Fugue are fascinating studies in density. We have already noted the opening solid-wall effect of the ***Prelude;*** later on, notice Bach's use of a single line suddenly emerging from that dense sound mass, near the Prelude's end. The ***Fugue*** begins with a single-line melody, to which is added a second and then a third line. Each line begins with a statement of the original tune, creating an effect something like that of a round. In Purcell's aria there is a comparable growth of density, from the initial (low) melodic line to a larger mass. Note, though, that Purcell's low line keeps ***repeating itself*** again and again. It functions, in this respect, as a kind of "drone," somewhat like the tamboura part of the Raga.

Silences May be Just as Important as Sounds

Silence does not just mean the absence of sound; it plays a much stronger and more positive role than that. It is, in fact, an integral component of music, providing dramatic and structural articulation and emphasis. Without the subtle breaths, pregnant pauses, or sudden gaps in the musical fabric, much of the drama of the Berlioz and Bach works would be missing, and the recurrent phrases of the chant could not be separated.

Silence has this positive force only if we tune out the everyday world and focus upon a defined musical situation (such as a concert). If, on the other hand, silence itself becomes the object of our focus, then "silence" ***ceases to exist.*** It is, rather, simply teeming with sound. One need only to perceive it attentively, with an appropriate musical attitude, to respond to the sounds within it. The American composer John Cage teaches us this much in a composition entitled ***4′33″.*** The work consists of 4 minutes and 33 seconds during which no intentional sounds are made by the performer; it takes music from the domain of planned sounds into the realm of natural, accidental sounds—coughs, the rustle of paper, an airplane passing overhead—that are always with us.

Cage's brief piece also forces us to consider the possibility that music is primarily a ***time*** art, rather than a ***sound*** art. Time is the dimension in which sound and (so-called) silence exist; through a mixture of sound and silence called music, the passage of time is made meaningful. This view is hardly acceptable to everyone, but it does enable us to turn our attention now to ***time.***

Listening for Time

Time may appear to be "driving," conveying a strong sense of forward motion, or it may be durational canvas upon which sounds and silences are placed. Most Western music of the past 300 years pushes forward, driving towards a series of goals very much as speech patterns group around commas, periods, paragraphs and other points of arrival. The Bach, Purcell and Berlioz examples drive forward very positively, but the Indian Raga is less concerned with "going somewhere" than with the elaborate unfolding of a single, leisurely idea. The Gregorian chant is even more static, lacking the easygoing flow of the Indian tabla (drum) beat or the strong accents of the Bach and Berlioz.

These overall effects are the product of many converging elements: choices of register, pitches, dynamic levels, density contrasts and so on. Nevertheless, our immediate responses are often couched in terms of "motion." Music is often perceived as hurried, relaxed, fidgety, soothing, motionless, or yearning towards a goal.

Musical "Motion" May Have Various Qualities

tempo

The speed at which music moves is called its *tempo.* A particular tempo may suggest a special mood or energy level. Compare the brisk, active tempo of the Bach Fugue with the gracefully cascading rhythms of the Raga or the calm stillness of the chant. The scurrying patterns of the Bach Prelude may seem extremely active, but beneath the surface of busy note-spinning the music's inner flow is steady and deliberate; it is, in fact, no faster than the jogging pace of the Berlioz "March."

meter

In Purcell's aria, the even flow of the tempo is measured out in periodic pulses and accents; one feels an underlying "beat" in such music, with an accent invariably occurring after a set number of beats. This grouping of pulses into regular accents and beats is called *meter.* There is a periodic meter in the Bach, Berlioz and Purcell examples. In the Purcell "Dido's Lament," that regular accent occurs every third beat; it is therefore an example of *triple meter.* The Berlioz and Bach examples fall into patterns with accents on every second or fourth beat: *duple meter* (see Figure 1.5).

Regular meter does not necessarily guarantee smoothly flowing motion. The Berlioz "March" and Bach Fugue both move at a steady tempo and duple meter. Yet they stress angular patterns and sudden, unpredictable accents; time seems to bounce rather than flow. The Gregorian chant, on the other hand, is apparently lacking in meter. Its rhythms are not grouped into regular patterns, but seem to follow the declamation of the Latin text,

Figure 1.5

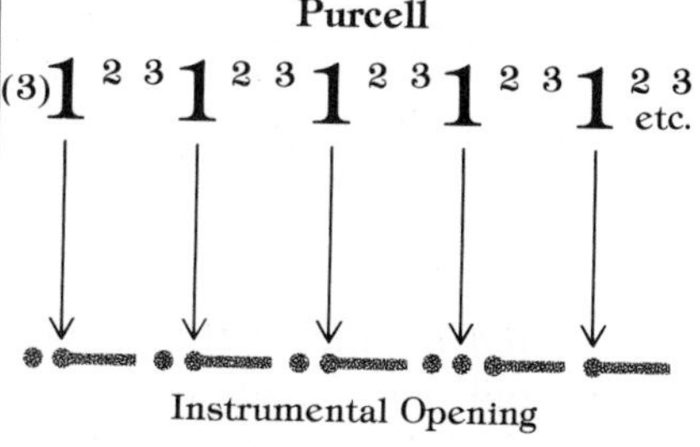

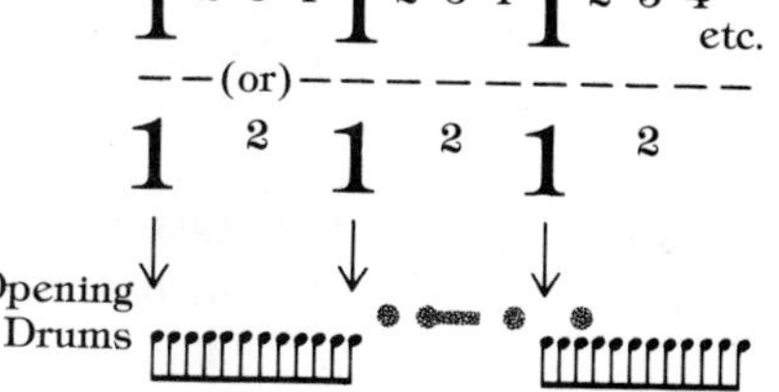

Figure 1.6

syllable by syllable. The combination of speech rhythm and a steady even tempo with no meter creates a uniquely ambiguous time sense.

Musical works of complex density may also offer different layers of time organization. As noted in Figure 1.6, one could hear the furious fingerwork of the Bach Prelude as extremely rapid groupings every two beats, or a grouping of every four or eight: each larger grouping presupposes a slower pace for the whole. All listeners would agree that the music moves in a steady duple meter, but might disagree on the tempo and the number of beats within each metric group.

Musical Time Implies Change

As time passes by, events change: this is a fact not only of art, but of our lives. As a uniquely time-centered activity, music constantly deals with qualities of change—growth, development, reappearance, memory and flashback. We, as listeners, cannot simply perceive the musical components (such as register or dynamics) of any given moment. We must assume that the moment may be altered even as we become aware of it. Listening takes place *in time,* just as the musical performance does.

In certain non-Western styles and recent experimental twentieth century pieces, very few changes, if any, may seem to take place. As we listen to the Indian Raga excerpt, for example, we may be struck by its leisurely quality. In contrast to the thrust of Western forward moving time, the Raga seems more concerned with "inner" time, or the frozen time of deep ritual. Those who create and perform such music are not unaware of change as a process; rather, they have chosen to rechannel its artistic operation. And all of us who experience music—composers, performers and listeners—must inevitably confront the passage of time.

Musical Organization

The *organization* of sound and time is the most complex subject of all; it is a matter of processes and not of materials. Even the beginning listener, however, can detect some of these processes at work. Start by observing the ways in which a composer uses various factors so that they contribute to a total effect. Listen for elements of sound and time as they relate to one another.

Listen Carefully to Beginnings and Endings

In the earliest stages of listening for musical organization, it may be useful to concentrate upon the very opening moments, and the final closing gestures, of pieces. First of all, they are obviously *there,* located at the only two places in the music's shape that are impossible to miss. Secondly, beginnings and endings are often planned with special care on the composer's part; the initial gesture that cuts into the silence, and the point of taking leave, often have a unique importance within the total shape. Thirdly, on repeated hearing the focused attention given to opening and closing moments will spill over in both directions, to the opening and closing few *minutes,* and eventually embrace an entire movement.

This is not the way a piece of music is meant to be heard, of course, but it is the way many people read novels. Meanderings of this sort would have been impossible a century or so ago, when live performances were the only means of hearing music, but they are now quite easy, thanks to recording technology.

Compare Pieces: Listen for Dominating Patterns

A great deal may be learned from making comparisons. It would be interesting, for example, to compare the openings of our five pieces: the Bach Prelude plunging directly into the business at hand, the eerie drumming of the Berlioz, the gentle drone of the Raga (which gives the impression of having begun before our arrival). And what do these beginnings lead to? The Berlioz "March" proceeds from its tentative opening to a brilliant *fortissimo* climax. Purcell's aria begins at a measured, deliberate pace, with instruments alone; note how the ending, also entirely instrumental, rounds off the shape of the piece. A few of the endings in this group of selections are not really "endings" at all. (The Bach Prelude leads directly into the Fugue, and as "Dido's Lament" reaches its final note another section of Purcell's opera immediately begins. The Berlioz "March" is a movement of a symphony, and leads to another movement. One would hear the Gregorian chant, of course, as part of a much larger service of worship.) Thinking about music in such ways will often provide insights into its organization.

Listen for important *patterns:* gestures or ideas that dominate a work. These may be melodies, as in the Purcell, distinctive approaches to dynamics and register (Berlioz), or a characteristic use of density (the Bach Prelude). A consistent, unified approach to melodic contour, register or time flow, as in the Raga, may also command our attention.

The five pieces just discussed will be referred to in future chapters as we investigate musical elements and their relationships. We will now add ten new listening selections:

Joseph Haydn: String Quartet Opus 76, no. 3 (''Emperor''). 2nd movement
An example of African drumming: Djerma Dundun drummers
Milton Babbit: ***Composition for Synthesizer*** (excerpt)
Franz Schubert: ''Gretchan am Spinnrade'' for voice and piano
Krzystof Penderecki: ***De Natura Sonoris I*** (excerpt)
Frederick Chopin: Prelude in C Minor and A Major (piano solo)
Terry Riley: ***In C***, for mixed ensemble (excerpt)
Anton Webern: ***Variations for Orchestra,*** opus 30
Wolfgang A. Mozart: Concerto no. 3 for horn and orchestra (movement III)
An example of Blues: ''Mean Old Bedbug Blues,'' sung by Bessie Smith

This will now give us a total of fifteen listening excerpts. During the remaining chapters of Part I, these fifteen will be referred to many times, often in ways that ask you to compare one excerpt with another. It's *not* necessary to memorize the pieces so that you recall their details when reading about them. On the contrary, try to read about an excerpt first and *then* listen to it, ''confirming'' the concepts under discussion with your own ears. Or try listening and reading simultaneously.

The fifteen recorded examples will be used as familiar reference points, as we introduce new concepts and terms during the coming chapters. On another level, we also hope that the fifteen examples themselves will take on heightened meaning, as they are re-heard with new perspectives and in changing comparative contexts. As we continue to bring more to the listening experience, the more exciting that experience becomes.

2

Exploring Sound

> The object of music is sound.
> Its purpose is to give pleasure . . .
>
> *René Descartes*

Intervals

A musical ***pitch*** is the audible result of a vibration in the air around us. Certain vibrations may be so low or so high that we cannot hear them as sound; for example, a dog whistle produces a frequency too high to be perceived as sound by people, but it is perfectly audible to animals. The ***audible range*** for human beings extends from a low of about 20 cps (cycles per second) to about 20,000 cps. Frequency can be measured and calibrated, so that a particular musical tone corresponds to a specific rate of cps. When an orchestra tunes up, all the players match their pitches to a note given by the orchestra's oboe player. That note is called "A" (the A above middle C, to be exact), and its frequency is 440 cps.

That same note A (440 cps) can be found at the piano keyboard, by studying the arrangement of black keys in alternating groups of twos and threes. Look for the white key between black keys 2 and 3, in the middle of the keyboard. By moving along the keyboard either to the left or right, another note A can be found; it will occupy the same relative position—the white key between black keys 2 and 3—as A-440. Note that it sounds remarkably like A-440, but is either lower than A-440 (if to the left of it) or higher (if to the right). The distance between the original A and the new A on either side of it is called an ***octave***. The frequencies of pitches an octave apart are related by doubling or halving. Figure 2.1 shows pitches A at 110 cps, 440 cps and 880 cps.

octave

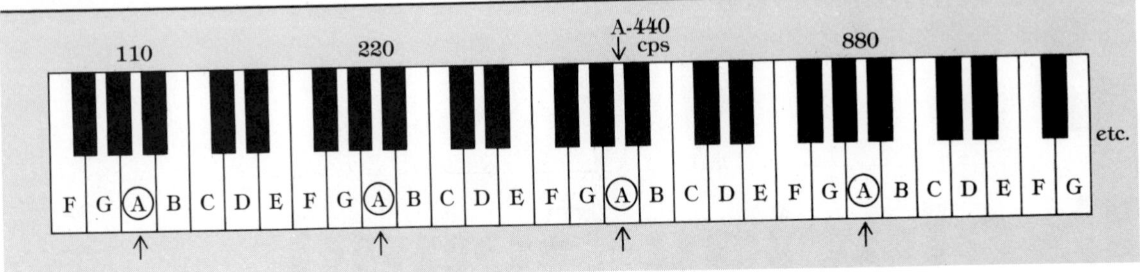

Figure 2.1

The octave is a familiar, comfortable distance. Two notes an octave apart are easy to sing or recognize: for example, the first two pitches of "Over the Rainbow." "Rock-a-Bye Baby" covers an octave within its first three pitches; and "The Star-Spangled Banner" has two octave spans in its opening line (see Figure 2.2).

interval

The distance between two pitches is called an ***interval.*** The octave is one example of an interval, and we recognize it as a fairly broad span. The contours of melodies are made up of various intervals, large and small, arranged in a particular order. In Figure 2.3, we can observe the contours of three familiar tunes drawn from our fifteen listening examples. Note that the Berlioz melody (beginning immediately after the drum crescendo) starts

Figure 2.2

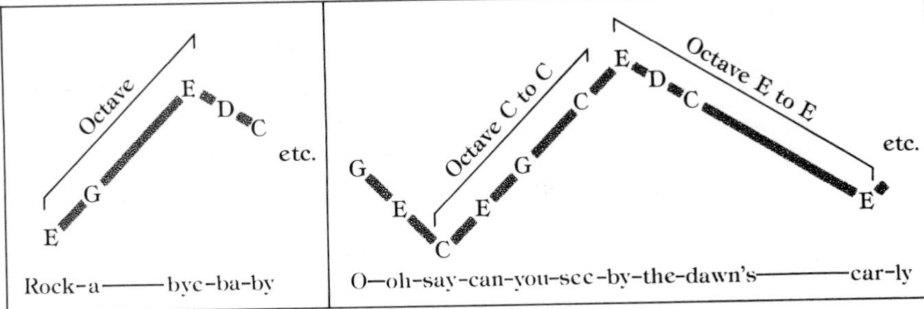

Figure 2.3

Intervals, Large and Small

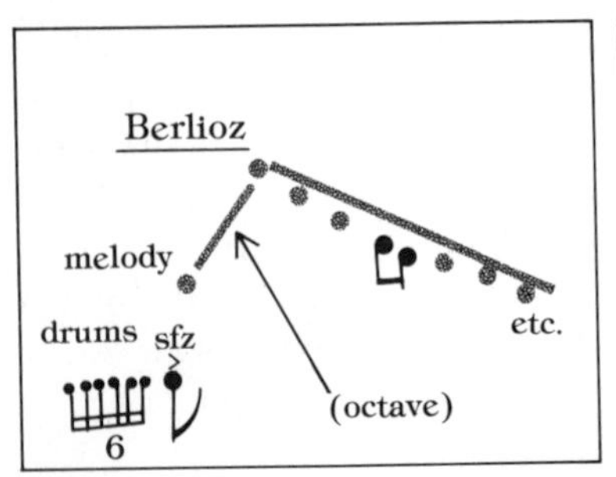

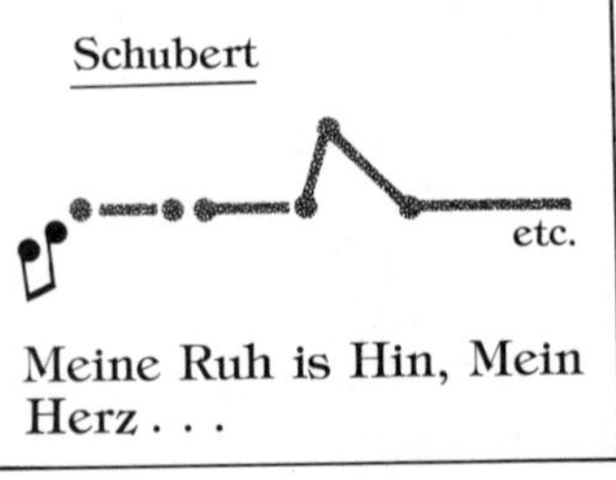

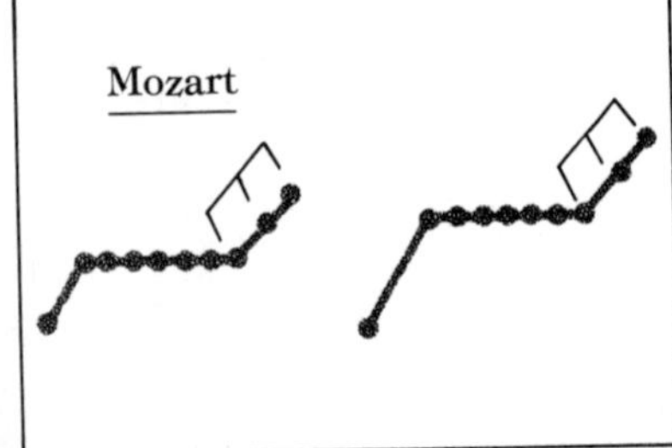

Figure 2.4

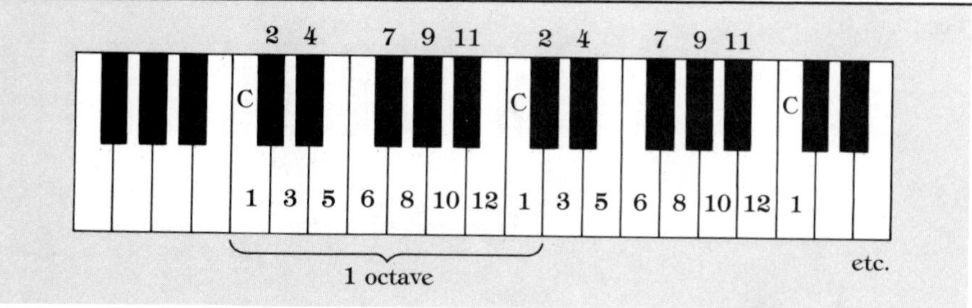

Figure 2.5

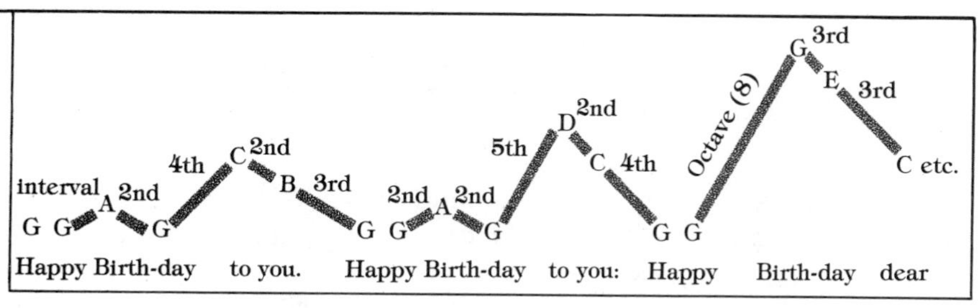

with an octave jump. The tune of the Mozart concerto excerpt opens with a fairly broad intervallic skip, and then repeats the same pitch seven times. When that pitch changes, it does so in a succession of very small intervals (bracketed in the example): in fact, the smallest interval commonly used in Western music. This interval is called the ***half step.*** In Western music there are twelve such half steps within the octave, creating twelve distinct pitches as well. These can be observed at the keyboard as the succession of all keys, black and white, beginning on any pitch and ending an octave away. In Figure 2.4 we move from note C to C. The new C, an octave higher, is the thirteenth pitch in the series; the distance between any two adjacent pitches is a half step.

half step

whole step

The interval of two half steps is called a ***whole step*** or whole tone; it could also be called a 2nd. (Wider intervals are invariably called 3rds, 4ths, and so on.) A melody can be regarded as a succession of pitches, *or* as a succession of intervals. In Figure 2.5 we have indicated both ways of thinking about "Happy Birthday to You."

Scales

scale

Musical cultures can be characterized by the way in which the octave is divided into particular pitches. A collection of such subdivisions, grouped in a succession from one pitch to its octave, is called a *scale;* obviously, this collection contains not only pitches but intervals as well. In many cultures, certain pitches are considered more important than others, and they act as

Figure 2.6

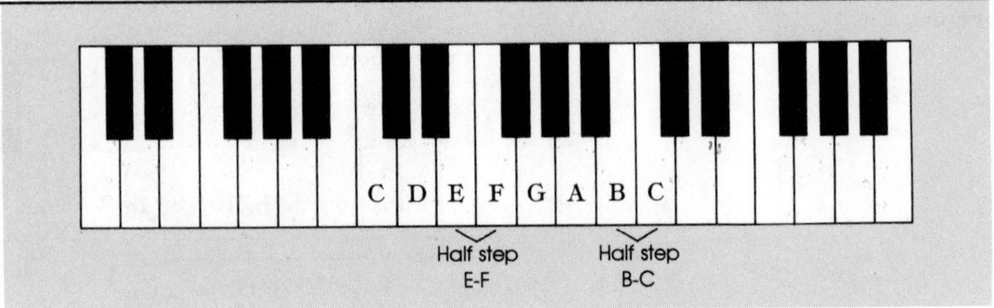

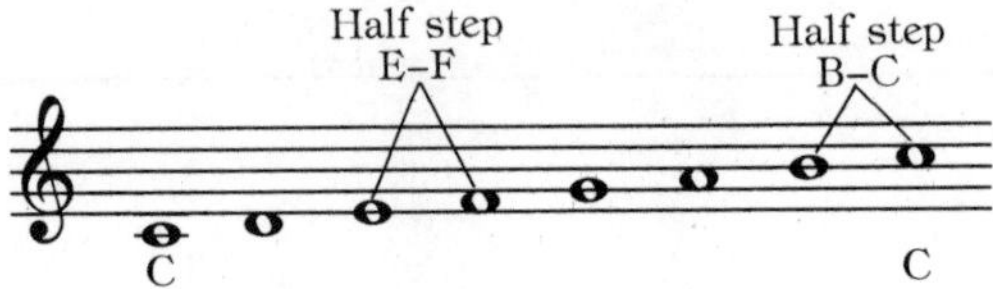

focal points towards which other pitches move. Figure 2.6 presents an example of the ***major scale,*** the most widely used scale in Western music. This example begins on C and moves to the C an octave away, using only the white keys of the piano keyboard.

major scale

The symbols for pitches occupy lines and spaces on a five line ladder called a ***staff.*** The symbol at the far left of the staff, called a ***clef,*** assigns the lines and spaces to a specific register; therefore the first pitch above is not just any C, but middle C. As the scale ascends, the pitch symbols move from line to space to line, and so on. Note, too, that the lines and spaces correspond to the white keys of the piano.

staff/clef

Although there are eight pitches in the major scales, only seven of them are different: pitch 1 is duplicated an octave away as pitch 8. The pitches of the major scale are grouped in a unique ordering of intervals: a half step between pitches 3 and 4, a half step between 7 and 8, and whole steps between all the others. Pitch 1 (or 8) is the focal point about which all the others revolve, and towards which they move. In Figure 2.6, that focal point is the note C; this collection of pitches is not just a major scale, but, specifically, a ***C-major scale.***

Major scales built on other pitches would also need eight notes, with half-step intervals between notes 3–4 and 7–8. But we could not construct other major scales simply from the pitches of C major. For example, in creating a ***G-major scale*** the note F would have to be replaced by the black key to its immediate right at the keyboard. This new pitch is called F-***sharp,*** indicated by the symbol F♯. The main tune of the Haydn string quartet movement uses the notes of the G-major scale, as seen in Figure 2.7.

sharp

Major and Minor

The other scale form most often used in Western music is called the ***minor.*** Like the major, the minor fills an octave with eight tones: seven

Figure 2.7

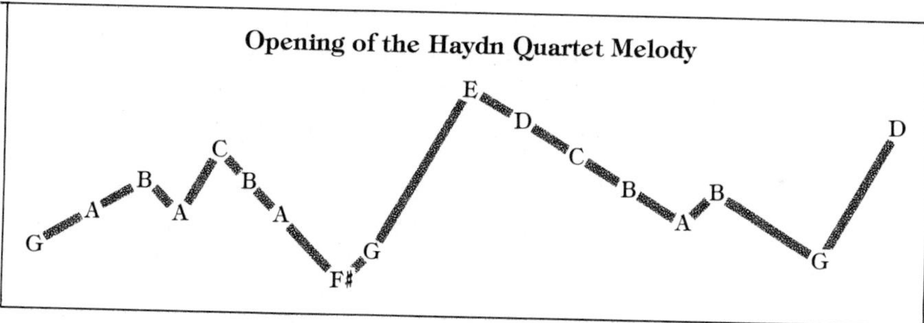

different ones plus a duplication of pitch 1 at the octave. The selection is slightly different, providing another vocabulary of pitches and a new ordering of intervals. The C-major scale will be converted to ***C minor,*** for example, if notes 3 and 6 are lowered one half step. (See Figure 2.8.) At the keyboard, E and A are replaced by the black keys immediately to their left, called E-***flat*** and A-***flat.*** (The symbol for flat is ♭.) Note 7 of the scale—the note B of a C scale—is often "flatted" one half step as well, although not as frequently as pitches 3 and 6.

flat

The Bach Fugue melody uses the C-minor scale. "Dido's Lament" by Purcell, and the opening moments of the Berlioz "March," are also composed with minor scales. Some people believe that the major scale signifies bright, cheery feelings, while the minor scale expresses the gloomy and the sombre. On the other hand, there are many gay, festive folk dances that use the minor scale: the Italian tarantella, Jewish hora, and Polish mazurka. And the Bach C-Minor Fugue is really rather brisk and businesslike—anything but mournful.

Admittedly, striking changes of mood take place in compositions where a tune previously heard in the minor form reappears in the major, or ***vice-versa.*** That sort of vivid contrast can be heard in the opening movement of Schubert's String Quartet no. 13 (discussed in the section on Schubert's work, Chapter 13). The main theme of the movement, originally stated in A ***minor,*** takes on a brighter quality when restated in A ***major.*** On the other hand, Schubert's "Gretchen am Spinnrade" is consistently minor.

Figure 2.8

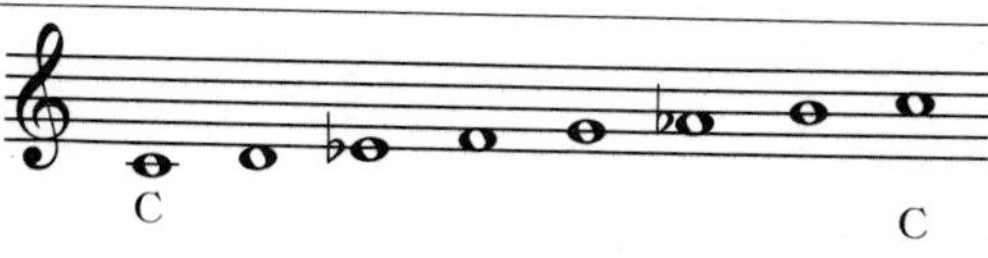

The words of the love-struck girl at the spinning wheel, and the music that surrounds the words, evoke her feelings of yearning, her melancholy, and the tedium of her spinning. The words and music of Purcell's operatic aria project a different sort of sadness: Dido's "lament" is one of heroic resignation.* The Berlioz "March" is as brutal and stark in the area of major-minor contrast as in that of dynamics, register, or timbre. There is a haunting juxtaposition at the very end of the movement; a plaintive solo woodwind melody in the major scale suddenly emerges from a furious passage in the minor scale, and is then abruptly ended.

Diatonic and Chromatic

chromatic

diatonic

The C-major scale illustrated earlier uses seven different pitches, drawn from the twelve pitches available within the octave. The other five pitches are called ***chromatic*** with respect to that scale. C♯, D♯, F♯, G♯, and A♯, the black keys of the piano, would be considered chromatic if heard in a passage predominantly based on the C-major scale. The seven different pitches that comprise the "pure" major scale are called ***diatonic***.

In "Dido's Lament" by Purcell, the voice enters with a phrase in G minor. At the sixth note, however, there is an upward "inflection" to a pitch not found in the G-minor scale (see Figure 2.9). Similarly, the opening tune of the Mozart horn concerto excerpt begins in the E♭-major scale. The repeated E♭s move upward to a note that doesn't belong in the diatonic scale.

natural

chromatic scale

In each case, the chromatic note (B for the Purcell, E for the Mozart) needs a special symbol to show that it is ***not*** the B♭ or E♭ expected within its scale. The pitches have been notated, therefore, as B-***natural*** and E-natural, using the symbol ♮. Listen again to the instrumental line, preceding the vocal entrance, with which the Purcell aria begins. Its first six pitches move steadily downward by half steps. Not only are some of the notes chomatic with respect to the G-minor scale, but that entire series of half steps illustrates a fragment of the ***chromatic scale*** (the complete collection of pitches within the octave, as illustrated earlier in Figure 2.4).

Composers use the five chromatic tones to lend inflection, "color" or heightened expressivity to the seven diatonic tones. The added tones may

*See Appendix E for texts of Schubert song and Purcell aria.

Figure 2.9

Purcell-Vocal Melody (opening)

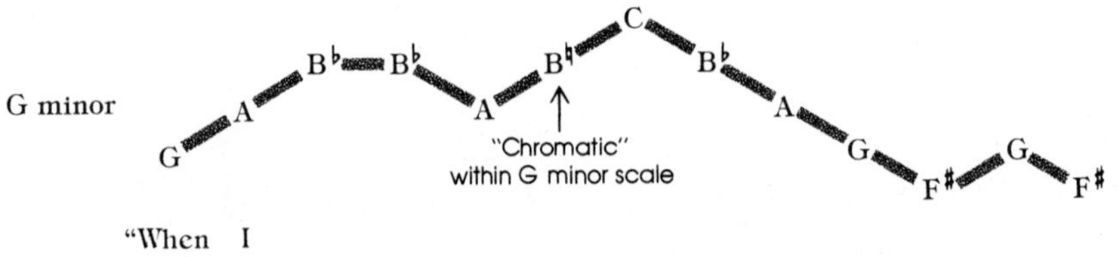

G minor

G A B♭ B♭ A B♮ C B♭ A G F♯ G F♯

"Chromatic" within G minor scale

"When I

appear in the melody, as in the Purcell and Mozart examples, or in the background texture. If chromatic tones are used frequently, then a given passage or work might be regarded as ***chromatic. Chromaticism*** is often an important feature of a composer's music, or of entire national styles or historical periods.

Other Scales; Modes; Ragas

Although the major and minor scales dominate Western music, most of the world's people make music with scale patterns very different from ours. Western European music composed many centuries ago also offers unusual scales. The Gregorian chant example, dated earlier than 1,000

mode

A.D., uses a particular kind of scale called a ***mode.*** The modes are easy to locate at the keyboard: they are eight-note successions of white keys only, from any pitch to its octave. Each mode has a unique sequence of whole and half steps. We find modes not only in liturgical chant, but in ancient folk tunes ("Greensleeves"), carols ("God Rest Ye Merrie, Gentlemen"), and the present-day folk music of many European cultures.

Like the Gregorian chant, the Indian and African excerpts offer unusual intervals and scale patterns. African chanting uses a limited number of pitches, concentrating upon them in repeated patterns. One or two strong tones are decorated by a few satellite tones. Note, too, that the intervals seem smaller than Western half steps and whole steps: in this system the octave has *not* been divided into twelve equal parts. Our Western system is only one of many possible subdivisions of the octave. (A siren passes through a virtual infinity of divisions!)

For example, the performance of Indian Raga uses a collection of

raga

pitches drawn from a twenty-two part division of the octave. The title ***raga*** does not refer to a set composition, but to a melodic formula related to each pitch collection, and to the elaborate improvised performance based on the given material. The complete "scale" is often introduced at the beginning of a performance; what follows is a gradual unfolding, patiently and elaborately, of this opening material. Indian musicians may perform for hours, using a particular raga as their source, very much as Western jazz players spin countless variations on a well-known tune.

intonation

Any method of tuning or dividing the octave is known as an ***intonation*** system; obviously, the intonation of Indian raga differs from that of Western music. For this reason, certain pitches in the raga performance may sound "flat" or "bent" to Western ears. We might automatically assume that these pitches are merely inflections, or "decorations," of the familiar twelve-note Western octave. In the case of the raga, our assumptions would not be correct. But at times Western performers do use intervals smaller than a half

microtones

step (***microtones,*** as they are often called) for expressive purposes, within our own twelve-note intonation system. Jazz saxophonists, operatic sopranos or country fiddlers may all delight in such subtle intonation changes. Listen to Bessie Smith's blues excerpt: there are so many embellishments in

Figure 2.10 **"Blues" scale built on C**

the melody, typical of the blues generally, that musicians often speak of a "blues scale" that has major and minor elements simultaneously (see Figure 2.10). Microtonal inflections abound as well.

Tonality

tonality

In most music there will be one preeminent pitch about which the other pitches group themselves. When we refer to the Bach Prelude and Fugue in C-Minor, this indicates more than the use of the C-minor scale; it also implies that the pitch C is the *tonal center* of the music. To say that a piece is in a certain "key" indicates not only scale but ***key center.*** This phenomenon is called ***tonality.***

Ravi Shankar playing the sitar.

Tonality in its strictest sense is related to the major-minor scale system, but the broader concept of "focal point" or "center" is almost universal. In the Gregorian chant, for example, a single pitch is sung more frequently than its neighbors; that pitch is often returned to at points of repose when the musical motion temporarily stops. (Notice that a different focal point takes precedence later, followed by a return to the original center.) The Indian Raga excerpt also offers a strong "center." The Raga melodic formula itself specifies certain notes as being more important than others: we can hear the sitar soloist bringing out these strong pitches. Moreover, the very first sound of the performance is a sustained drone, played by the tamboura. The continuing drone exerts a gravitational pull of its own upon the sitar's pitches, so that we relate the total melodic pattern to a constant center. And in the African chanting and drumming there is a similar series of repeated pitches, like a drone, providing a central focus.

Most Western music since 1600 is composed in the major-minor scale system, and is ***tonal*** by definition. But not all pieces or all styles are equally clear about their tonality. Composers may wish to cloud our sense of key center, or toy with our expectations; they may delight in ambiguity, heightened tension, or playful surprise. A sudden change of key center may be effective, or the music may have a highly ***chromatic*** character, in which the increased use of all twelve pitches confuses the listener's sense of tonal direction. In the Berlioz "March" different key centers are set against one another; Schubert's "Gretchen am Spinnrade" uses chromaticism to indicate the character's growing emotional tension.

atonality

The Babbitt, Webern and Penderecki excerpts are examples of music ***without*** key center. This situation is called ***atonality,*** and such works are referred to as ***atonal.*** The Webern and Babbitt pieces are each based upon a different ordering of the twelve chromatic pitches, known as a "row," which suggests intervals, melodic contours and other combinations. (In this respect the rows are closer to ragas than to traditional Western scales.) Many composers of our century have used tone rows in their work, to retain a sense of logical structure while abandoning the familiar "logic" of tonality. Penderecki's ***De Natura Sonoris I*** offers still another approach, in that it often shows no concern for specific pitches or note-to-note relationships. Instead Penderecki takes large bunches of adjacent pitches, perhaps all the half steps between C and F♯, and uses the resulting ***cluster*** as a single band of sound mass. This technique concentrates upon contrasts of density, register, and instrumental timbre, rather than pitch relationships.

If major-minor ***tonality*** corresponds to a hierarchy of satellite pitches grouped around a central "sun" (the key center), then Babbitt's use of a twelve-tone row could be represented as a collection of many small interval (or pitch) groups, independent and yet interrelated. Penderecki, on the other hand, allows single pitches to be swallowed up within dense sound clusters, so that individual tones often cannot be heard.

Composer Milton Babbitt seated at the RCA Synthesizer.

Melodic Patterns

Most people would agree that the Penderecki excerpt is lacking in "melody." There might be disagreement about the degree of melody in the Babbitt piece, but little argument about the Schubert or Haydn selections: virtually ***everyone*** considers the latter works highly "melodic." That is, their pitches make recognizable ***patterns,*** when heard in succession. Although rhythms and durations greatly contribute to melodic character, a pitch contour can be distinctive in its own right. It is not necessary to know the rhythm of the tune outlined in Figure 2.11 in order to recognize it: the example is the opening of "Mary Had a Little Lamb," in the key of F major.

This familiar contour is not dependent upon any one collection of pitches; the order of intervals is of far greater importance. In fact, we can

Figure 2.11

in F Major														C	C
	A				A	A	A				A				
		G		G				G	G	G					
			F												

transposition

cadence

dominant

tonic

phrase

move the passage from one key center to another, retaining the intervals while changing the pitches. This process is called ***transposition.*** In Figure 2.12 the complete "Mary Had a Little Lamb" has been transposed to G major and written as notes on a staff (but without rhythm). We can see that the tune divides into two sections, beginning exactly the same but coming to rest at respectively different points.

Each place of rest is called a ***cadence.*** Note that the first cadence falls on pitch number 5 of the scale, called the ***dominant,*** while the second cadence—which seems much more final and decisive—falls on pitch number 1, or the ***tonic.*** (The tonic is, of course, the most important pitch of the scale, and the dominant is second only to it in the scale hierarchy.) Each of the two sections is called a ***phrase.*** Many simple tunes consist of symmetrically balanced groups of phrases, usually leading to a final cadence on the tonic note of the key. This succession of temporary cadences and eventually a final one, is like the series of phrases and clauses, punctuated by commas, semicolons and periods, that make up sentence structure.

By looking within each of the phrases, we can observe certain patterns of pitches. These are arrived at by some combination of three basic possibilities: repeated note patterns, stepwise scale motion, and skips of various widths. In this example, repeated notes and scale motion are much more important than skips. Compare this with the initial melody of the Bach fugue (Figure 2.13), which attracts the listener's attention with its many skips of large, striking intervals. Note that the skip of a 4th returns as a 5th and then a 6th. In between, the little C-B-C figure, with its own characteristic rhythm, offsets and punctuates these ever-widening excursions.

Figure 2.12

Mary Had A Little Lamb

Notice the repeated-note patterns throughout, and the identical rhythms of the three bracketed groups.

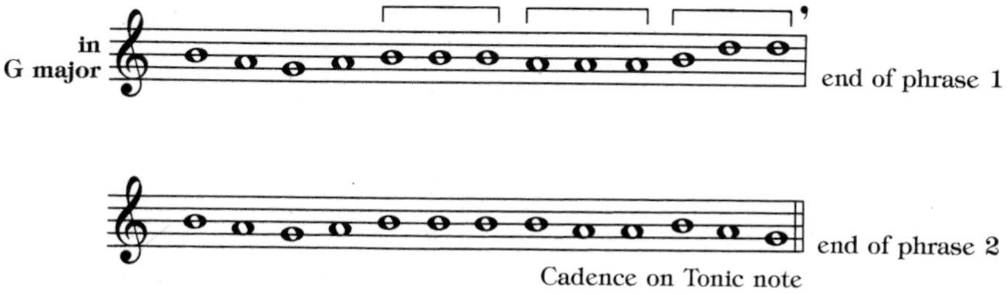

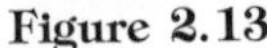

Figure 2.13

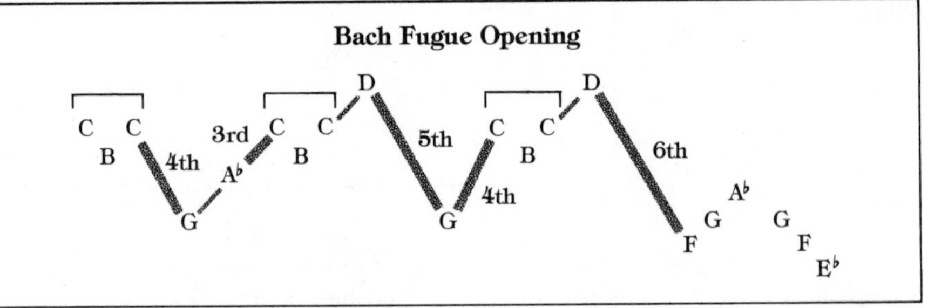

Sequences

sequence

Within a melodic contour, a pattern may be heard on one pitch level and then immediately repeated at another level—that is, beginning on another note. This procedure is known as ***sequence.*** In Figure 2.14 we can observe sequences in the beginnings of two well known compositions; note, also, the sequentially balanced phrases of the Chopin C-Minor Prelude, one of our fifteen listening selections.

The theme of the Haydn selection (Figure 2.15) presents us with a number of phrases. Note the gradual increase in range as the melody proceeds; low D is added at the third phrase. It climbs one octave to a higher D by the end of the phrase, reinforcing the intensity of the ascent with the chromatic C♯. As the fourth phrase begins the highest note of the tune (high G) is heard, and the phrase gracefully descends via a ***sequence*** to the lower G.

A traditional tune might end here, at the conclusion of phrase four. But Haydn elects to repeat the final phrase, creating an asymmetrical grouping of five phrases. Perhaps this is because each of the first three phrases has come to rest on the dominant (D). After three tries, so to speak, the listener may unconsciously feel the need for resolution to the tonic G. That

Figure 2.14

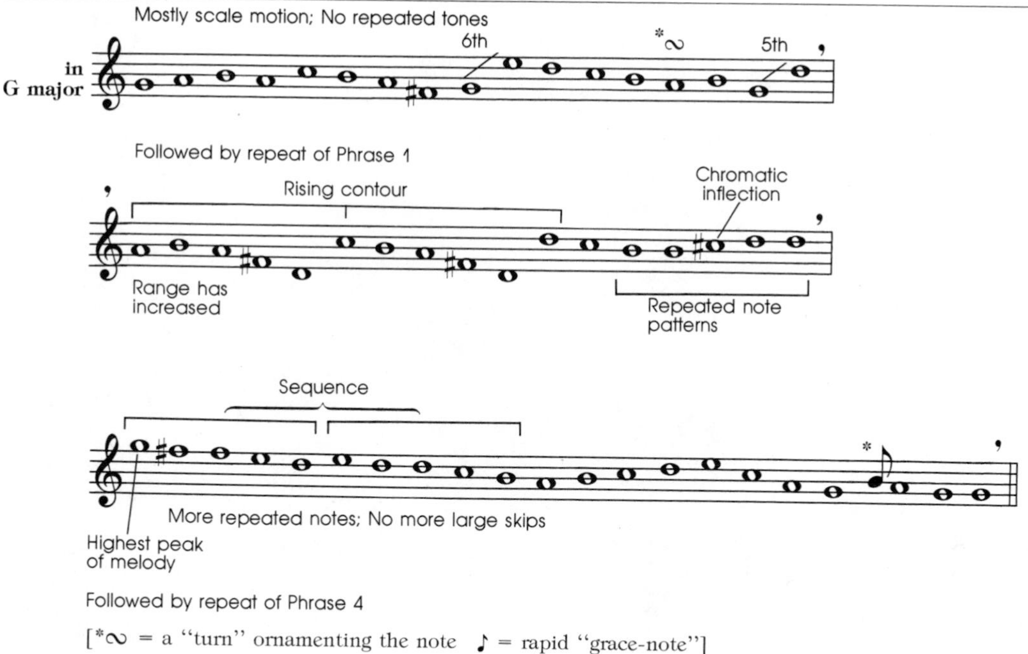

Figure 2.15

is the essential wonder—aural, structural, and psychological—of tonality. The high G at the start of phrase four breaks the tension, and leads to a strong cadence; the sense of repose and resolution is enhanced and confirmed by the repetition of that final phrase.

Melodic Profiles

Every melodic line has its particular contour, or profile. It may be jagged and angular, or smoothly flowing. For example, the most obvious feature of the Purcell opening, apart from its low register and deliberate tempo, is its single-minded sense of downward direction. Schubert's opening vocal line for "Gretchen am Spinnrade" has a less extroverted contour than the Purcell selection; it hovers about the dominant and the tonic notes A and D. As Gretchen's memories become increasingly agitated, the line becomes more jagged as well as more chromatic.

There are, in fact, as many melodic profiles as there are pieces of music. The angular motivic cells of Babbitt's electronic excerpt are far removed from the undulating rise and fall of the Gregorian chant. Compare the chant, in turn, to the African selection. They are alike in one respect: the formal interplay between vocal soloist and larger body. One echoes the other

The rhythms of African music are often additive in nature.

in a question–answer format referred to as "call and response." The African melodic profile, even more than the Gregorian contour, is a fixed pattern of pitches in a static frame of repetition. The use of a deliberately "frozen" contour in this way is a feature not only of African music but of a variety of folk idioms throughout the world: the twentieth century composer Igor Stravinsky, drawing upon his Russian heritage, made great use of it.

The Indian Raga performance creates the opposite effect: a wealth of melodic variety as pitches and phrases are decorated, ornamented, and restated differently each time they return. The sitar virtuoso Ravi Shankar refers to his native music in terms of "melody that has been developed and refined to a very high degree, with an infinite variety of subtleties."

Melody, Tune, Theme and Motive

Phrase lengths in raga performance are often *long,* spanning a great many pitches; they are less likely to be joined in symmetrical groups than their Western counterparts. Similarly, the African vocal patterns may be considered too ***brief*** to function as phrases in the Western sense. One might also distinguish between symmetrically balanced lines of two or more phrases (the Haydn or Berlioz), and brief "profiles" stated in a single phrase, such as the Bach Fugue subject, or Purcell's descending instrumental line.

tune
motive

subject
themes

A symmetrically balanced phrase group could be referred to as a ***tune.*** A ***motive*** is likely to be brief, perhaps only a single phrase or fragment of phrase used as the generating material for long, complex compositions. (The generating material for a fugue is called a ***subject.***) Symphonies, concertos, and sonatas are often discussed in terms of their ***themes.*** A theme may be as pithy as a motive or as well-rounded as a tune. In a large-scale work it undergoes alterations and transformations as it is fragmented and reassembled in various guises.

The Uses of Melody

There is no such thing as a good melody or bad melody ***per se;*** every profile can be effective and expressive within the right context. Composers occasionally have fun by constructing melodies from the "profile" of the New York City skyline or a graph of the stock market's daily fluctuations. In the world of popular music, an entertainer like Steve Allen will invent tunes from audience telephone numbers and license plates. Although it may be tempting to dismiss some of our examples as having "no melody," remember that each does offer a distinctive contour. A profile does not necessarily need the balanced phrases of a "tune," or the narrow range of the singing voice. And it need not be "pretty" to be useful. As David Reck notes in his admirable book ***Music of the Whole Earth,***

> Beauty may not even be a factor in many societies' judgments of melody and songs: the Navaho . . . may be more concerned with a song's power. Its usefulness or function in a work or ritual situation can also be a factor . . .

Finally remember that ***pitch*** or frequency is only one of the four main attributes of sound. There are also ***dynamics, duration*** and ***timbre*** to be considered. A melodic contour takes on life when it is heard as sound: a sweeping curve that grows in volume, an alteration of loud and quiet patterns, the unique tone color of a viola or muted trombone. As sound, every kind of profile has a function and beauty of its own.

3

Exploring Time

> Music is the best means we have of digesting time.
>
> *W. H. Auden*

Rhythmic Profiles

rhythm

As noted previously, an important attribute of sound is *duration.* Each sound in a piece of music has its own duration, whether long or short. The succession of these durations (for example, short-short-long) forms a pattern called *rhythm.* Just as there are melodic pitch profiles, there are distinctive rhythmic profiles: striking and easily recognized. A familiar rhythm can often retain its individuality, regardless of specific pitch or timbre: we all recognize the pattern · · · –, whether tapped out in Morse Code or played by an orchestra, as the "motto" rhythm of the Beethoven Fifth Symphony. For example, a pattern of six equal durations followed by another one twice as long as one of the six is easily recognized as "Twinkle, twinkle little star" (long). On the other hand, a group of two short durations, three that are each twice as long, and one that is four times the original duration might bring to mind "Happy Birthday to *You.*" (♪ ♪ ♩ ♩ ♩ 𝅗𝅥) But it could *also* be

Figure 3.1

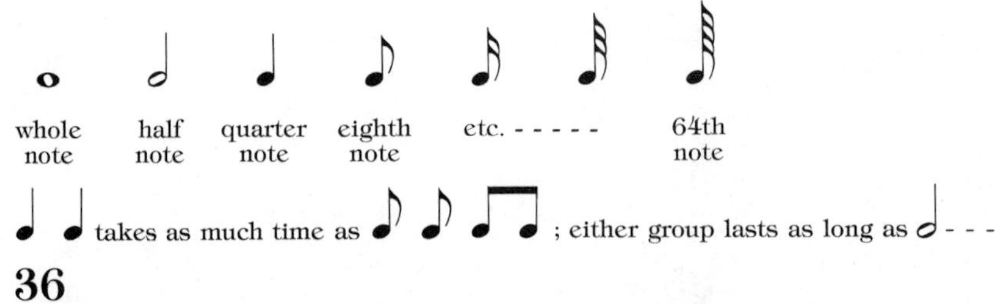

Figure 3.2

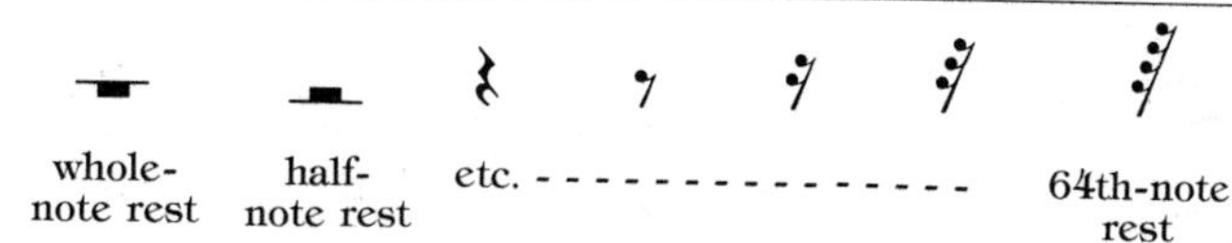

"O-oh say can you *See.*" In this case, the complete tune results from a combination of pitch and rhythmic profiles, one reinforcing the other.

As the examples above indicate, many rhythmic patterns in Western music involve successive durations being related to each other by doubling or halving (or a multiple of these). This is reflected in the written symbols for rhythm, which stand for ***relative durations.*** In Figure 3.1, reading from left to right, each note lasts half as long as the one immediately preceding it. When these relative durations are combined in a pattern, such as ♩ ♩ 𝅗𝅥, a rhythm results. Since the symbols are relative, there is no way of knowing how long ♩ ♩ 𝅗𝅥 will take in clock time unless the ***tempo*** is indicated. And with relative symbols it is possible to indicate the same relationship—or rhythm—in different ways. For example, ♩ ♩ 𝅗𝅥 and ♪ ♪ ♩ could both represent the opening notes of "Jingle Bells" at a specific tempo.

rests

There are also symbols that represent ***silence:*** relative durations, during which a performer makes no sound. These are known as ***rests*** (see Figure 3.2). Rests and notes of various relative values may be combined to produce complex rhythms (for example ♩ ♩ 𝄽 ♪ 𝄾 𝅗𝅥 ♩ 𝄽) made up of sounds and silences.

tie/dot

Two other rhythmic symbols of special interest are the ***tie*** and the ***dot.*** In the opening rhythm for "Mary Had a Little Lamb," the syllable "Ma-" lasts three times as long as "ry." By using a ***tie*** (a curved line extended between two note heads, as in Figure 3.3), we can add two rhythmic values together; a relative duration of "3" will result from the addition of "1" plus "2." The relative durations of 3 plus 1 (as in "Ma-ry") form a particular rhythmic pattern of their own—perhaps the sense of two beats "leaning" so that one becomes elongated and the other shortened. A special symbol has evolved to deal with this special pattern: a ***dot,*** placed directly to the right of a note-head. The dot extends the relative value of that note by one half, so that 𝅗𝅥. = ♩ + ♩ + ♩. As we can see in Figure 3.4, "Mary Had a Little Lamb" may be notated with the aid of the dot.

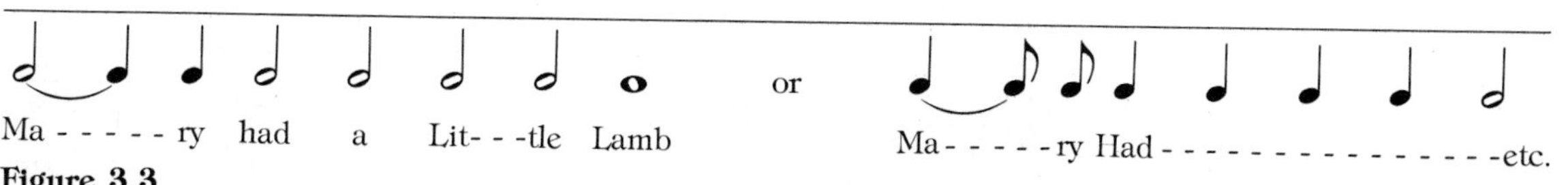

Figure 3.3

Figure 3.4

dotted rhythm

The rhythmic pattern ♩. ♪ (or ♩. ♬, etc.) is often referred to as a ***dotted rhythm.*** The opening of "The Star-Spangled Banner" can be rather stately if sung in equal values, but some prefer the spirited swing and vigor of a dotted rhythm, as shown in Figure 3.5.

Figure 3.5

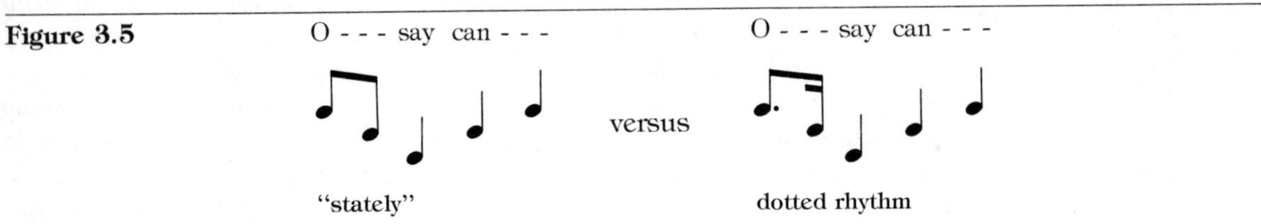

Figure 3.6 provides two familiar examples of dotted rhythm, drawn from our fifteen listening selections, plus a well-known example in which both dot and tie are used. There are no dotted rhythms in this last excerpt, merely extended durations.

Figure 3.6

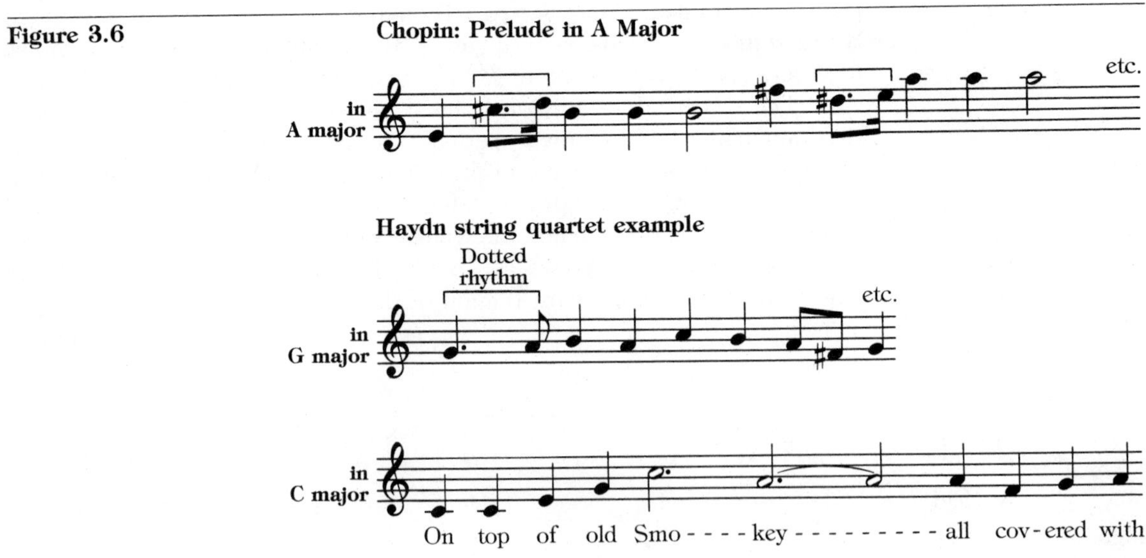

Figure 3.7

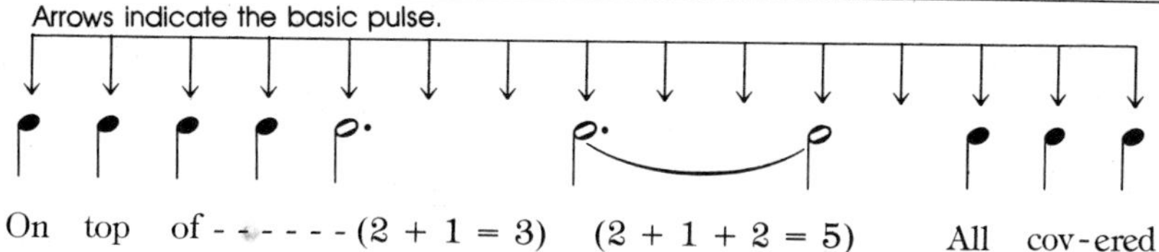

Meter and Pulse

In counting ***through*** the long durations for "Smo---key---" in the above example, we become aware of the tune's basic ***pulse.*** There is a regular periodic "heartbeat," creating a standard unit of movement against which the surface rhythms occur. The basic pulse here (see Figure 3.7) corresponds to the durations for the words "On top of old." In this case the durations of individual rhythms are extended beyond the basic pulse. But note values can also subdivide the pulse into faster (shorter) articulations, as seen in Figure 3.8.

accent

The underlying pulse will often be referred to as the music's "beat." There will also be an ***accent,*** or stress upon one beat more than others. In almost any series of regular beats, some will appear to be stronger. Accents may even be inferred where they don't exist! Listen, for example, to the steady clicking of a clock: the neutral tick-tock may begin to sound like ***Tick***-tock, ***Tick***-tock, or perhaps ***Tick***-tock-tock, ***Tick***-tock-tock.

A periodic, regular series of accents creates the sense of ***meter*** (noted previously in Chapter 1). The strong accent for "America" falls on every third beat, whereas in "Baa-baa Black Sheep" it occurs every four beats. These tunes are therefore examples of ***triple meter*** and ***duple meter,*** respectively. Some meters subdivide regularly into triple patterns: for example, a duple meter with consistent triplet rhythms might be written as $\frac{6}{8}$. Although there seem to be six beats per measure, there are really only two basic pulses. Meters with regular triple patterns, such as $\frac{6}{8}$, $\frac{9}{8}$ and $\frac{12}{8}$, are called ***compound meters.***

bar line

measures

In writing out music, a vertical line is drawn just to the left of each principal accented beat; this is called the ***bar line,*** and it divides the rhythmic flow into separate ***measures,*** each with the same number of beats. Meter is indicated by a written symbol of two numbers (such as the $\frac{6}{8}$ mentioned

Figure 3.8

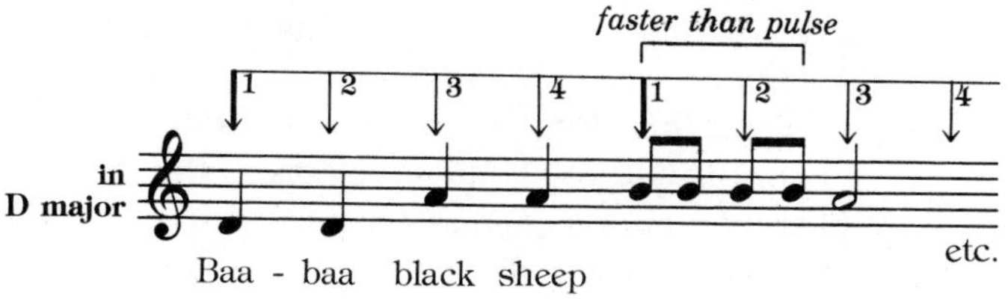

faster than pulse

1 2 3 4 1 2 3 4

in D major

Baa - baa black sheep

etc.

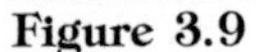

Figure 3.9

above). The upper number symbolizes the number of beats per measure, and the lower number represents the note value receiving one beat—a number 8, for example, standing for an eighth note. In Figure 3.9 we see rhythmic patterns drawn from three of our fifteen listening selections: the Chopin C-Minor Prelude (duple meter), "Dido's Lament" by Purcell (triple meter), and the Mozart concerto movement (compound duple meter).

The Schubert "Gretchen am Spinnrade," like the Mozart, is written in compound $\frac{6}{8}$ meter. One particular rhythmic pattern, heard in the piano part at the very outset, dominates the entire song. Note the steady configuration of sixteenth notes $\frac{6}{8}$ in a circular melodic design, set against a curiously halting pattern of beats and rests $\frac{6}{8}$. The lyric vocal line presents a third level of rhythmic activity, more impetuous and unpredictable, superimposed upon the other two.

Unusual Meters and Rhythms

Regular, periodic beats and steady meters are typical of most Western music, but they hardly represent the total range of possibilities. Accents can occur at intervals that are irregular rather than periodic: ***changing meters*** are featured in many twentieth century works. Our listening excerpt by Anton Webern, for example, contains successive measures of $\frac{3}{8}$, $\frac{3}{16}$, $\frac{5}{8}$, $\frac{2}{4}$, $\frac{3}{4}$, $\frac{2}{8}$, and $\frac{3}{8}$. There are also pieces built on asymmetric meters: a steady accent every five (or seven, or eleven) beats. Examples of a quintuple meter include the Tchaikovsky ***Pathetique*** Symphony (movement II) and the well-known jazz piece ***Take Five*** by Dave Brubeck.

In the Gregorian chant selection, the pitches move in a series of long and short durations and at a steady tempo, but ***without*** any sense of meter. There are subtle points of stress which might be considered accents; generally these are the pitches of the longest duration. But they do not move the music forward; in fact, they occur at points of rest. The Babbitt ***Composition for Synthesizer*** might appear to be equally meterless, but it actually offers many strong accents and pulses. These often overlap in simultaneous lines and change unpredictably; in the flexible continuum that results, periodic accent plays a small role.

additive rhythm

There are also interesting features in certain non-Western rhythmic practices. Western rhythms are apparently arrived at by ***dividing*** large durations into smaller ones—measures into beats, whole notes to half notes, and so on. Other musical cultures practice ***additive rhythm,*** in which patterns are built by taking a small durational unit and adding such units together. Imagine a high-speed clock ticking in a pattern of unpredictable accents: ***Tick***-tock / ***Tick***-tock / ***Tick***-tock-tock / ***Tick***-tock / ***Tick***-tock-tock, then the entire series repeated again and again. This would be a simple sort of additive rhythm. If the pattern is repeated often enough, it establishes a regular meter, but one with asymmetrical internal subdivisions.

polyrhythm

Listen to the patterns of the tabla (drums) in the Indian Raga performance, based upon a subtle additive rhythm; note that the rhythms of the sitar melody may contradict the additive patterns of the tabla. Two or more rhythmic profiles heard simultaneously create ***polyrhythm.*** In the African drumming example, a number of additive rhythms are superimposed in polyrhythms. These are executed at great speed and with staggering precision, so that the listener at first only hears a single metric accent subdivided into a flurry of rhythmic patterns. But subtle relationships reveal themselves as the total fabric repeats: for example, the subtle interplay between the drummers and the equally complex vocal call-and-response.

The Up-Beat: Beginning with Silence

upbeat/downbeat

A composition does not have to begin on the accented downbeat. "Home on the Range," "The Farmer in the Dell," and the Purcell aria all start on the weak beat of the measure, just before the bar line. This weak point, called the ***upbeat,*** then leads directly to the ***downbeat*** across the bar line. In most cases the listener will not mistake the opening beat for a strong accent: the true meter and pulse are discerned within split seconds.

Other rhythmic patterns begin neither on an upbeat nor on a downbeat, but at some point within the measure that may be difficult to place metrically. As seen in Figure 3.10, the Bach Fugue subject opens with a rest (silent beat) on beat 1.

Figure 3.10

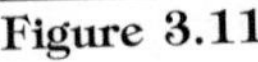
Figure 3.11

Syncopation

Perhaps seeing the Fugue subject (Figure 3.10) may explain its forceful, driving quality. The striking melodic profile of the subject has already been mentioned earlier, but now notice the distinctive ***rhythmic*** shape, and the way both pitch and rhythm fit into a ***metric*** context. The repeated C-B-C figure has a catchy ♫ ♩ rhythm; this rhythm appears on beat 2 in every measure but the last (when it is displaced and takes on different pitches). At the opening of measure 4 the broadest skip reaches the lowest pitch (thus far) of the subject, and immediately rebounds upward to the note of longest duration ***and*** most unexpected pitch (A♭). The strongest accent and point of greatest tension, therefore, have settled in an unlikely place: beat 2.

syncopation

A strong accent at a normally weak spot in the meter is called ***syncopation.*** In $\frac{4}{4}$ time, the strongest accents should fall on beats 1 (primary) and 3 (secondary); in triple meter a single accent usually occurs on beat 1. To place a strong accent somewhere else would generate a particular kind of tension and rhythmic activity, as seen in Figure 3.11. Although syncopation is often associated with American folk and popular music, it can be found in cultivated European "art" music as well: the Berlioz "March" is overwhelming in its many off-beat accents. Many European folk dances have strong syncopations, which composers retained in their refined versions for the concert hall and parlor piano.

If syncopated accents occur regularly, they can set up a fascinating cross-talk between two levels of metric stress, as in Figure 3.12. Many folk tunes, spirituals, and popular songs (such as "Tea for Two") naturally lend themselves to such treatment.

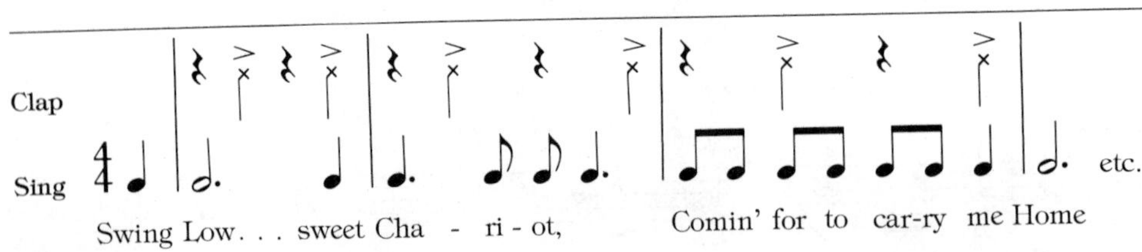

Figure 3.12

Tempo

tempo

Tempo refers to the rate at which music moves through time—the speed at which rhythms and metric pulses operate. If a metronome is used to set tempo, the rate is measured against a clock: metronomic markings refer to the number of beats per minute, a setting of 60 therefore indicates one beat each second. A modern composer wishing to specify exact tempo might write "♩ = 108." But this luxury was not available before the nineteenth century; our Gregorian chant and Bach excerpts have *no* tempo markings (and no indications for dynamics or phrasing, either). Performances of chant are based upon modern interpretations of ancient church tradition, and performance of Bach's music are based upon writings, theories and clues in the printed scores.

During the later eighteenth century, the use of Italian phrases to signify tempo became widespread, and are still familiar to musicians. Twentieth century composers may be inclined to write tempo instructions in their native tongues, rather than in Italian. But more than a century ago the German Beethoven wrote ***Allegro con brio*** at the beginning of his ***Eroica*** Symphony. The Frenchman Hector Berlioz specified ***Allegretto non troppo*** for the "March to the Gallows," and our string quartet movement by the Austrian Haydn reads ***Poco adagio; cantabile.*** Many of these traditional terms indicate mood as well as speed. (The more commonly used terms are shown in the accompanying table.) A performer or conductor has great latitude in interpreting such flexible instructions. Three equally distinguished conductors might interpret a Haydn minuet marked ***Allegro molto*** with drastically different results.

Andante (walking)	Allegro (rather fast)
Largo (broad, stately)	Presto (very fast)
Adagio (moving slowly)	Moderato (moderate)
Vivace (brisk, lively)	Non troppo (not too much)
Poco (a little)	Con brio (with spirit)

Varying the tempo is not as significant a factor in the music of other cultures as in our own. The Raga performance proceeds at a very steady pace, and the African drumming excerpt, although it appears to have a slower section at its midpoint, maintains its single beat unit throughout. Density and complexity may change, but the rate of movement is generally unchanging. Fixed ritual tempos are passed from one generation to another, from master drummer to disciples. Consider, too, the unvarying tempo—slowly unfolding, although articulated by rapid surface rhythms—of Terry Riley's ***In C.*** The Riley work, which will be discussed more fully in the next few chapters, has been strongly influenced by non-Western models.

The European tradition, however, often exploits contrasts in tempo. Nineteenth century composers delighted in sudden tempo changes, an example being the slow, lyric solo near the end of the Berlioz "March." Subtle fluctuations in the basic pulse of a piece were also common in the nine-

Ethiopian priests dancing to the accompaniment of native instruments.

teenth century. ***Accelerando*** (speeding up), ***ritardando*** (slowing down) and ***rubato*** (stretching and contracting rhythms) were important expressive devices to composers such as Chopin. Such alterations are less frequent in performances of J. S. Bach, since many scholars assume the practice was not prevalent during Bach's lifetime.

Is there a set tempo for either the Penderecki or the Babbitt? The Penderecki may not seem to move forward in the traditional sense—at least not during its initial moments. But changes do occur: subtle ones at first, followed by a series of striking, explosive punctuations. If there is a rate at which the excerpt moves, it is clock time, since that is the literal standard of the printed score. The duration of events is indicated by reference to ***seconds,*** not by traditional rhythmic symbols and tempo markings. Babbitt's ***Composition*** exists solely on magnetic recording tape or phonograph disc, and therefore has no printed score. The excerpt offers an interlocking network of individual lines, each apparently moving at its own tempo. Note that the same melodic-rhythmic profile is often presented in multiple simultaneous levels, each at a different speed, register and timbre. The total effect is not that of a steady rate, but a dazzling assortment of intervals, speeds, rhythms and colors colliding and intersecting in the free space of clock time.

Interlude 1
Thinking About Music

This is a good place, after a heavy concentration of new concepts and terminology, to pause in our narrative to consider some general questions. To begin, note that the elements of music introduced in the preceding chapters, and those that will follow, are most valuable when they alter the act of *listening*. They are not so much facts to be memorized as relationships that—eventually—can be *heard*. It may take time before the ear "knows" what the mind has absorbed as factual information—certainly more time than that spent in reading a chapter of a book or listening to assigned pieces. But after a while the ear and mind, working together, will recognize patterns and relationships in the collections of sounds we call "music."

Fifteen musical selections have been assigned for repeated listening so far; they will be referred to extensively during the next four chapters. These examples represent a fairly broad cross section of the musical literature. Two of them are non-Western; the Gregorian chant, which may seem equally exotic to some listeners, represents a very early period—well before 1,000 A.D.—in the history of Western music. Purcell's aria comes from the late seventeenth century and Bach's harpsichord music from the mid-eighteenth century; both works belong to the Baroque period. The Haydn and Mozart examples stem from the late eighteenth century (the classic period), while Berlioz, Schubert, and Chopin represent the nineteenth century romantic movement. The remaining five works—Babbitt, Penderecki, Webern, Riley and the Blues—are all products of our century; the earliest of the five, the Blues selection, was recorded in the 1920s, and the Webern was composed in the 1940s. The other three were created after the end of World War II.

It may seem unusual that fifteen unrelated pieces, drawn from a wide range of time and places, would have so much in common. Precisely so: large musical concepts cut across stylistic and cultural lines. Revealing comparisons might easily be made about any diverse collection of examples. More important than the individual works, surprisingly, is the level of curiosity and perception brought to the listening experience: the fact that listeners are *thinking* about music. Audiences attending a concert may also be hearing a collection of unrelated pieces, representing a wide range of styles. It would be ideal if they, too, would respond by thinking, comparing, relating, listening intently. Unfortunately, many people use music as an excuse for *not* thinking. They sit in the audience in a state of dreamlike bliss, only rarely bringing their rational faculties to bear upon the experience. They may not realize it, but they are missing half the joys of listening.

In the concert hall a listener may have to digest a lot of new information on only one hearing. That special challenge is probably balanced, in a typical program, by the presence of a familiar work. Both kinds of experience have their rewards; the first hearing provides the sheer excitement of the sounds and patterns, the surprises and contrasts, the thrill of confronting the unexpected. The familiar piece, on the other hand, often reveals unexpected dimensions and relationships on repeated hearings. And even an old favorite becomes fresh and new again, in a different performance, an unfamiliar recording, or another location. The human capacity for discrimination, responsiveness and growth is remarkable.

A number of musical terms have been introduced in the preceding three chapters. Most of these terms are clear-cut; that is, we can generally be sure that each has but one meaning. There are a few other terms, however, that are ambiguous. Unfortunately, some of these are among the most commonly used musical terms. Be particularly careful of the following:

1. *key,* which might mean that part of an instrument (piano, flute and so on) pressed by a performer's finger, *or* a tonal center (for example, the "key of G major");
2. *note,* which could be a written symbol on the musical page, *or* the sound (tone) indicated by the written symbol. The "note C" could be either of these or both;
3. the word *chromatic,* used to represent the five pitches not in a given diatonic scale, has a different meaning from *chromatic scale*: the latter is the collection of all twelve tones within the Western octave;
4. *phrase,* used as a noun, refers to part of a melody—a group of pitches leading to a cadence. When used as a verb ("to phrase the passage a certain way"), or changed to *phrasing,* the term denotes articulation and dynamic gradations: for example, smoothly connected pitches versus brief, detached ones;
5. *mode* may refer to one of the early scales that flourished during the Middle Ages and Renaissance (as exemplified by our Gregorian chant), *or* either of the two scale forms used in more recent Western music ("This passage in the key of F moves from the minor mode to the major");
6. the *pitch* intervals called *whole step, whole tone, half step* and so on, should not be confused with the *rhythmic* values of *whole note, half note* and the like.

The next two chapters will deal first with a fairly specific term—*texture*—in some detail, and then with a very broad musical concept, *form,* which will require further elaboration later in Part 2.

4

Texture

Do you know that our soul is composed of harmony?

Leonardo da Vinci

Texture, Fabric and "Density"

As noted earlier, *density* is the quality which leads us to describe sounds as thick or thin, heavy or light, transparent or opaque. Many factors contribute to this quality: register, dynamic level, and the number of instruments or voices, to mention a few. A simple C-major chord (the pitches C, E, and G sounded simultaneously) would create one sort of density if its three notes are close to each other, but a very different effect if the notes are spaced far apart. Playing the chord at the lowest register of the keyboard, or the highest, alters the density in another way; if the chord were to be played by trombones or violins, rather than the piano, other aspects of density would change. The Penderecki and Webern examples are quite provocative in their respective approaches to density: the former with its broad washes of sound and massed clusters, the latter transparent in its kaleidoscopic array of isolated colors.

The term *texture* refers to the "fabric" of density, the way in which different sounds are combined either at a single moment or over a span of time. Generally, matters of musical texture are concerned with two questions: How many sounds, or events, or "lines," are heard at one time? How are they related to one another? The analogy of musical texture with fabric is a useful one, because the different threads (sounds) of music can be "woven" in different ways; they may be tightly or loosely connected, contrasting or similar, horizontal or vertical. The concept of *texture* is related to

Ben Shahn, ***Silent Music.*** 1951. Both the silk screen and the etching (opposite) take their inspiration from musical subjects, but beyond that they are remarkably contrasted in their use of line to create texture. Philadelphia Museum of Art. Purchased: The Harrison Fund.

styles of weaving—the way in which different sounds contribute to a larger fabric.

The pitches C, E, and G sounded together can yield an astonishing variety of ***densities,*** as noted earlier. But from the standpoint of ***texture,*** that collection of pitches is simply regarded as a C-major chord. The concept of "chord" is, in a sense, a textural model. An almost limitless variety of densities in the real world of sound could fit the model.

Music of the Western tradition offers an exceptional range of textures. Other cultures may stress highly sophisticated rhythms, scales and intonation systems; by contrast, Western music relies largely upon two scale forms and a fairly simple approach to duration and rhythm. Much of our creative evolution has been in the area of texture, varied combinations of timbre, and the development of large-scale forms. (See the next chapter for an introduction to the concept of form.)

Monophonic Texture

monophonic

A *monophonic* (one sound) texture occurs when a single melodic line is stated. The unaccompanied line of Gregorian chant is a perfect example of monophony. This texture characterizes work for unaccompanied instru-

Henri Fantin-Latour, *A Piece by Schumann.*

ments as well. A good deal of non-Western music is monophonic; in certain cultures a single melodic line is surrounded by other levels of activity, perhaps a percussive rhythmic background. The African vocal chant is set against the complex additive rhythms of ceremonial drummers, while the ornate sitar melody of the Indian Raga (see Figure 4.1) is heard against rhythmic tabla patterns ***and*** an unchanging background drone. Some might claim that this latter texture is too complex to be monophonic, but all would agree that the elaborate texture has grown from a single line. In any case, varieties of density can exist within monophonic texture. Different levels can be heard in the Gregorian chant performance, or in any piece for solo instrument, when register and dynamics are altered.

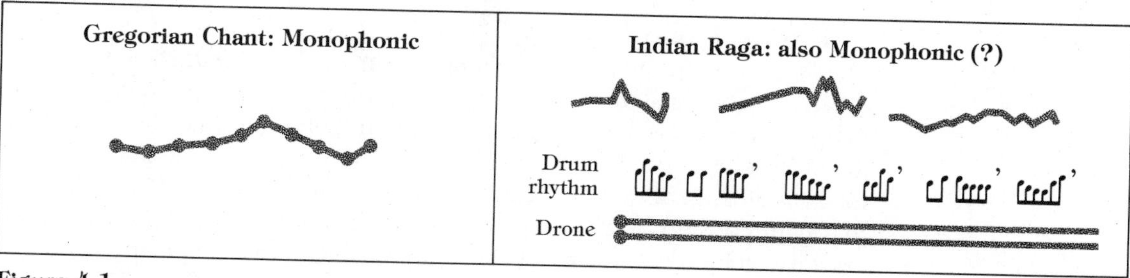

Figure 4.1

Monophonic
tune

Heterophonic
version

Figure 4.2

To return briefly to the chant: if the choral passages were sung by a group of men and women, or men and boys, the differences in vocal range could produce a passage sung in *octaves.* Performing the same line on different levels, an octave apart, is a common occurrence whenever people get together to sing. This sort of texture is still considered monophonic. There is only one independently moving part; the other is an exact duplicate of it.

Heterophonic Music

heterophony

The texture that occurs when a single line is elaborated upon by a group of performers is called *heterophony* (see Figure 4.2). In heterophonic music all musicians perform the same basic melody, with one or more performers adding their own melodic embellishments, variations, and rhythmic deviations. This is often produced intentionally within non-Western performance traditions, as in our African excerpt. Heterophonic texture may also come about accidentally, when a number of amateurs attempt to perform a single line: a crowd singing the national anthem before a baseball game, or the congregation joining the performance of a hymn at the local church.

Polyphonic Texture

polyphonic

A *polyphonic* texture consists of two or more independent, active melodic lines: not "shadows" of each other in parallel, but separate lines heard simultaneously. The word polyphony is often considered a synonym for *counterpoint,* although the two have slightly different meanings: counterpoint is a compositional technique for putting tones together in certain ways, and polyphony the product of that technique.

Imitative Polyphony

imitation

The most easily recognized polyphonic texture is that of *imitation.* Here the different lines are actually variants or duplicates of the *same* contour, with their entrances staggered to begin at different points in time. This practice might have originated when, during group performances of a single line, a few participants decided to begin slightly later than the rest. Something of this nature occurs in the recorded African example. During the call-and-response echoing between soloist and group, the two frequently overlap, resulting in momentary imitation.

Figure 4.3

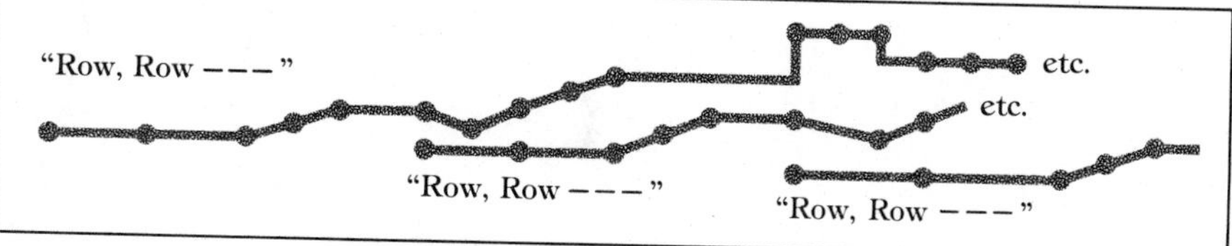

canon

round

When each melodic contour exactly duplicates that of its neighbors, the resulting imitative texture would be called *canon.* One familiar variety of canon is a *round.* For many listeners, such rounds as "Three Blind Mice" or "Row, Row, Row Your Boat" (see Figure 4.3) are a delightful musical memory of childhood.

Imitative polyphony plays an important role in the selections by Babbitt and Webern. Instead of organizing their music around sweeping lyric themes or tonal centers, both composers concentrate on the manipulation of brief melodic cells. They often vary their presentation of these basic cells by stating them in overlapping contrapuntal imitation. Imitative fragments often occur simultaneously at different speeds. In the opening of the Babbitt *Composition for Synthesizer* a twelve-note tune, with a characteristic jaunty rhythm, is heard at the very outset as a solo line. Listen to that tune as it repeats in a series of imitative statements, each line moving at a different speed. A greatly slowed-down version can be heard in the low register, while the tune is stated quite rapidly in the highest register. Webern also uses motivic fragments in imitation, colliding and interacting with abrupt changes of timbre, register, speed and dynamic level.

The opening minutes of *In C* by Terry Riley will provide an unusually static-sounding group texture, one in which repetitive patterns appear to be "frozen" as in the African recording. Actually, the Riley texture is undergoing very gradual change, noticeable only over a substantial time span: each player in the ensemble is contributing to a massive, slowly unfolding *canonic* texture. There is only one single "line" and as many randomly staggered entrances as there are players.

In a familiar round, as in Riley's *In C,* a canonic texture is sustained for an entire piece of music. But a canon may also be used as part of a larger piece, along with other textures.

The Fugue

fugue

A fugal texture is also imitative, but it has very special characteristics of its own. Like the round, a *fugue* begins with a single line, to which new lines are added one by one. But the subject's second entrance must occur at the interval of a 5th from the opening note. In the Bach Fugue in C Minor, the starting pitch C is answered by a G in the second entry. When the third voice enters, its initial pitch is once again C. This duality between imitative state-

Figure 4.4

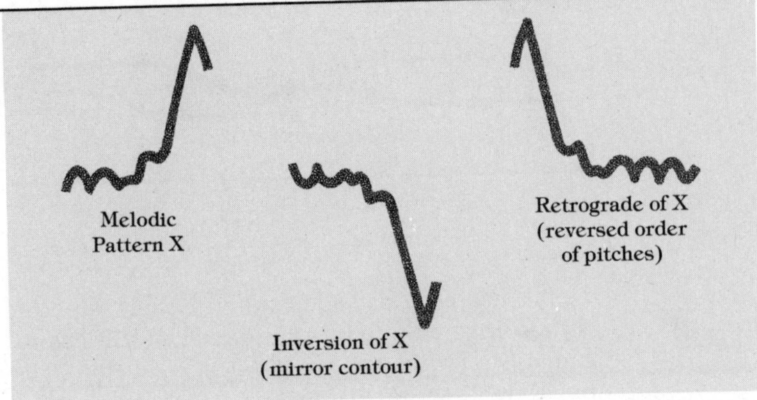

ments on the tonic and dominant was an essential component of fugal thinking from the time of Bach until our own century.

Fugal imitation is not carried through literally in the canonic sense. Only the theme, or subject, is imitated exactly, while the original line veers off with entirely new free counterpoint of its own.

Rhythmic variants of the basic material can be found in fugues as well as canons. The fugal subject may also appear with its *pitches* in reverse order, or with its melodic contour inverted so that upward motion has become downward (see Figure 4.4). In some fugues the original subject might be stated in one voice, while its inversion or rhythmic variant is heard simultaneously at another level. Listen for these imitative devices in the Babbitt and Webern selections.

Fugues, like canons, do not necessarily constitute entire pieces. A fugal passage might occur as part of a larger composition. Examples include the brisk *"Fugato"* (short final section) in the Beethoven Fifth Symphony, movement III, and the sombre opening of the second movement of Stravinsky's *Symphony of Psalms.* (Both works are discussed during Part 2.)

Ostinato Patterns; the "Ground"

The opening sitar and tamboura relationship of the Raga excerpt can be found in the music of many cultures. It consists of a single melodic line and a constant drone: a monophonic texture just on the verge of becoming poly-

Figure 4.5

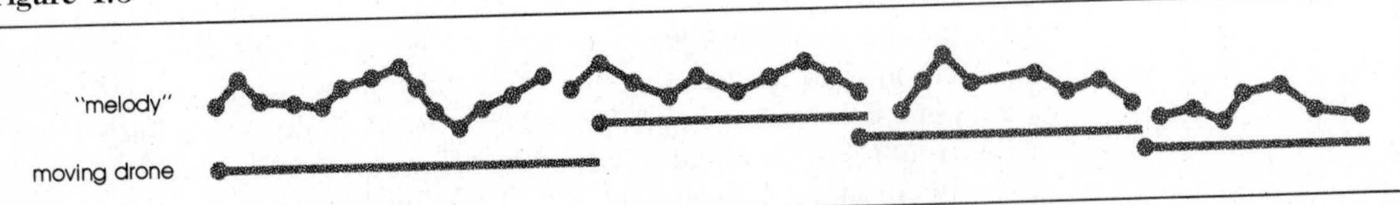

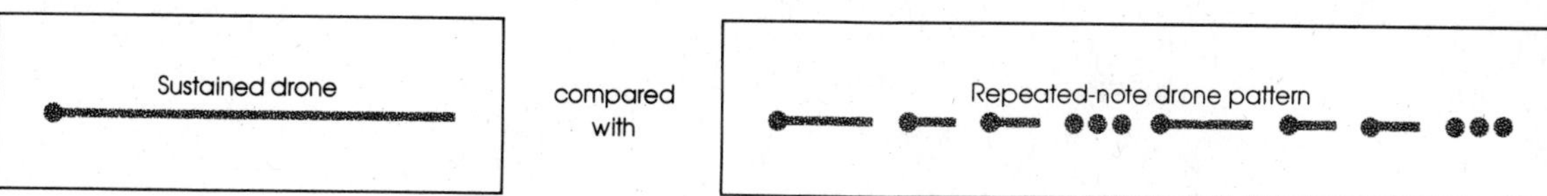

Figure 4.6

phonic, so to speak. The monophonic quality prevails if the drone stays in the background, providing nothing beyond sustained resonance and pitch "center." This is generally true of Indian raga, country fiddling, or Scottish bagpipe music. But a drone will take on independent foreground status if it changes pitch every now and then (Figure 4.5), and it may assume prominence within a texture if it is stated *rhythmically.* Even if the drone's pitches do not change, it can enter the foreground of a listener's attention (Figure 4.6) if it has a pattern of beats and pulses. If such a rhythmic pattern is repeated a number of times, *and* associated with a series of different pitches, then the simple drone has become a melodic motive in its own right—a fixed, continuously repeated contour rather than a single sound. This is called an *ostinato* (an "obstinate" figure). *Ostinati* vary widely from the repeated polyrhythmic patterns of the African drumming excerpt (Figure 4.7), to the "tape loop" created in an electronic music studio, or the repeated melodic contour that dominates "Dido's Lament" by Henry Purcell.

ostinato

The Purcell aria, with its flowing vocal melody set against a fixed melodic pattern in the lower register, provides two levels of polyphonic interest. With each restatement of the basic ostinato melody the polyphonic context changes as well; there is, in fact, a miniature set of variations over a repeated ostinato. Purcell referred to this format as "variations upon a ground."

Free Polyphony

In both kinds of polyphony studied thus far, there is a minimum of thematic material: imitation is concerned with the elaboration of a single basic motive, and the ostinato provides a fixed level against which other material

Figure 4.7

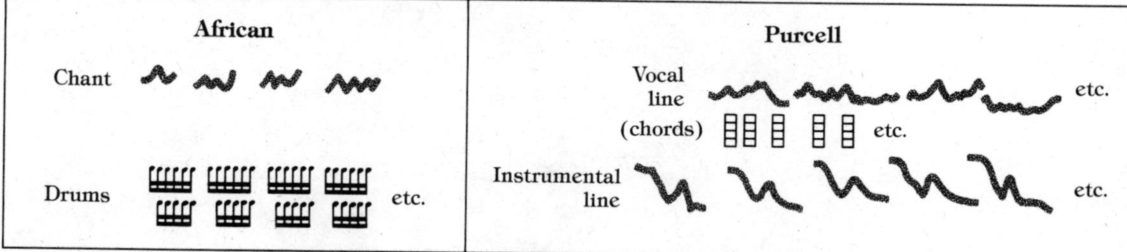

may move. Another sort of polyphony occurs when the different parts are independent, nonimitative, and equally active. Certain tunes which are not intentionally related may sound pleasing when performed simultaneously. An example of independent "free" polyphony can be heard in the early Dixieland style of jazz, where a number of soloists compete and interact at the same time, against a keyboard accompaniment of background chords. The exact same texture might be found in a Baroque Trio Sonata of the eighteenth century, although there would be obvious differences in rhythm, melodic styles, and instruments.

Vocal music for the theatre is an ideal vehicle for florid, nonimitative polyphony. An opera or operetta may feature one or more ensemble numbers, in which several characters sing very different melodies at the same time. There may be different emotional states or dramatic motives being projected as well. Examples might include the quartet from Verdi's opera ***Rigoletto*** (see Chapter 14), or "I Hear Music but There's No-One There" Irving Berlin's ***Call Me Madam.*** In extended works of instrumental music, composers may combine a number of melodies heard previously in a new contrapuntal "mix," perhaps at the climactic point of a movement. There is a unique excitement in hearing themes that were stated earlier, now sounding together.

Pootagook, stonecut.

Throughout the world, music reveals a great range of texture: an Eskimo woman and her bowed instrument (opposite), a Japanese ensemble of Kotos and shakuhachis (right), and a Western string quartet (below).

Homophonic Texture; Chords and Harmony

Melodies, lines, and polyphonic voices might be termed the "horizontal" dimension of music, moving with the time flow and relating sounds in linear succession. In responding to the horizontal aspect of texture, the listener recognizes phrases and melodies, or perhaps a number of lines heard simultaneously. There is also another musical dimension, often referred to as the *vertical.* (Of course, such words are more related to the way music looks on paper than the way it sounds!) Here the listener stops the time flow, however briefly, and focuses upon everything heard during a given instant. If during that moment we hear one sound made up of different notes, we can refer to it as a *chord.* A chord contains at least three pitches, and should register on our consciousness as an independent object in its own right—a single unit, rather than a collection of many particles.

chord

Responding to the vertical dimension of music, then, means "thinking chords." This is often dependent upon the way a listener chooses to hear a given mass of sounds, and in that sense the difference between one textural dimension and the other is one of degree. If any single moment of the Bach Fugue or "Three Blind Mice" were frozen in time, a chord would be heard. The entire fugue or round could be perceived as a series of chords, rather than an interaction of lines. To consider a different situation, a series of chords could be sung by a choir, as in Figure 4.8. A person in the choir who sings the circled notes regards those notes as a line—perhaps even an inner melody. If that person had an obtrusive vocal timbre, or missed a cue and sang louder than anybody else, the *audience* would become equally aware of that inner part as a line in its own right.

The distinction between horizontal and vertical texture can be a very fine one. On the other hand, the music itself offers clues, leading the listener to one interpretation or the other. In Western music, certain kinds of chords are traditional, familiar objects to our ears. Composers know how to use rhythm, register and timbre to bring these chords to our attention. Or, they can stress the linear dimension through their handling of melodic profile and other elements.

The terms *chord* and *harmony* are often confused. Strictly speaking, a chord is an entity of various pitches sounded at one time. Harmony refers to an ordering of successive chords: the way chords relate to each other over a time span. Finally, there is the concept of *homophonic texture,* in which harmony and melody create an interesting foreground–background relationship. Each of these terms will be discussed in turn.

Figure 4.8

Chordal textures are frequently produced by the bells and gongs of the Indonesian gamelan.

Chords

In any culture, chords and melody are built from the same scales. (This is not only true of Western music, but of societies that use other scale systems and intonation patterns.) Therefore, the chords of Western music, like the major and minor scales, assume an octave divided into twelve tones. Most Western chords are built in 3rds, using the pitches found in certain scales. For example, a chord may be built on the note F by moving up from F in 3rds (F, A, C). The resulting "object" is called an F-major chord. As it consists of three notes, it is also called an F-major ***triad.*** This particular triad would most likely be heard in a piece of music that used a scale with the notes F, A and C: the keys of F-major or C-major, to name only two. An F-***minor*** triad would contain an A♭, rather than A, corresponding to the A♭ of

triad

Figure 4.9

the F-minor (as opposed to major) scale. (Figure 4.9 shows F-major and F-minor triads.)

Major and minor triads are possibly the most familiar sounds of Western music. Listeners have heard them in countless nursery tunes, hymns, symphonies, operas, folk tunes, popular songs, and dances. Chords may be built on other intervals as well, creating sounds that are less familiar. By piling 4ths upon each other composers can create objects with a "spacious" or "hollow" quality. The opposite effect—a dense cluster—results from building chords in 2nds. Both kinds of sonorities have aroused interest during the twentieth century. Thickly clustered bands of massed 2nds are often found in Penderecki's music. A number of examples will be found in *De Natura Sonoris I* excerpt.

Harmony

harmony

Western *harmony* is a system of relating triads to each other, creating a sense of directional, forward-driving motion to the goals of cadence and tonality. The greatest goal of all is the *pitch* that has given its name to the given tonality, and the *triad* built on that pitch: for a typical piece in the key of G major, these would be the note G and the G-major chord. To reach these goals, the practice of harmony assumes that some triads are more important than others. The chord built on the key center itself (pitch 1 of the scale) is obviously the most important, and it is followed in order by the chord built on pitch 5 and that built on pitch 4. These are called, respectively, the tonic, dominant and subdominant chords—or, as musicians often label tonal relationships with Roman numerals, the I, V and IV chords. Figure 4.10 shows these important chords as they might appear in the key of C major.

Certain successions of chords, such as I-IV-V-I, project a convincing sense of forward motion: digression from the tonic, and then return to it. A grouping of chords in a particular order is called a ***chord progression.*** The sum total of such progressions in a given work, suggesting various states of "movement" and "rest," constitutes its ***harmony.*** Many simple tunes can

Figure 4.10

Chords built on the 1st, 4th, and 5th pitches (or I, IV, V chords) are shown above.

Figure 4.11

be harmonized with nothing more than progressions of I, IV and V chords. A more complex piece might use an elaborate hierarchy of many chords. But in either case, tonal harmony is one of the great organizing forces of Western music.

Harmonic progression does not necessarily exist in all music. Indonesian and Japanese styles use chords, but in ways that do ***not*** create tension, resolution or the forward drive towards a "goal." Twentieth century composers have been influenced by such non-Western precedents (as we will note in the latter chapters of Part 2). In this vein, consider the striking use of triads in Terry Riley's ***In C,*** in ways that highlight their sonority but minimize their need to "push on" in progressions.

Consonance and Dissonance

consonance / dissonance

In Western tonal harmony, with its strong sense of direction, chord progressions are the chief vehicle for creating "tension" and "resolution." The dominant (V) chord, generating tension, is considered ***dissonant*** when compared to the release afforded by the ***consonant*** tonic (I) chord that follows. The terms ***consonance*** and ***dissonance*** are relative. When confronted with just one chord out of context, as in Figure 4.11, the listener has no way of knowing whether the chord is consonant or not. *If* the chord exists within a tonal, goal-directed grammatical series, and if the other members of the series are known, then the context becomes clear, and relative consonance–dissonance levels can be judged.

Listen to some familiar recorded examples, with special attention to their harmony. The Haydn String quartet theme consists of five phrases, and begins and ends in the key of G major. Each of its first three phrases ends on the dominant (V) chord, creating an unresolved, ***dissonant*** state. But there is an affirmative tonic chord at the beginning of the fourth phrase: a feeling of consonance leading to a relaxed cadence (with its own little V-I tug of tension and release).

The rapidly articulated sound-masses of the Bach harpsichord Prelude are basically "broken chord" outlines, following a fairly taut, dissonant progression. In fact, the opening of the Prelude consists of nothing ***but*** chordal figurations: rhythm, meter, density, register and dynamics are all static by comparison. In this sense, all the excitement of the piece is being generated by the continuum of ***harmonic*** tension and release.

Now turn to the Chopin Prelude in A Major. This piece contains a symmetrical grouping of phrases, all but one ending in a cadence on the dominant or tonic chord. The ending of the sixth phrase, marked with an

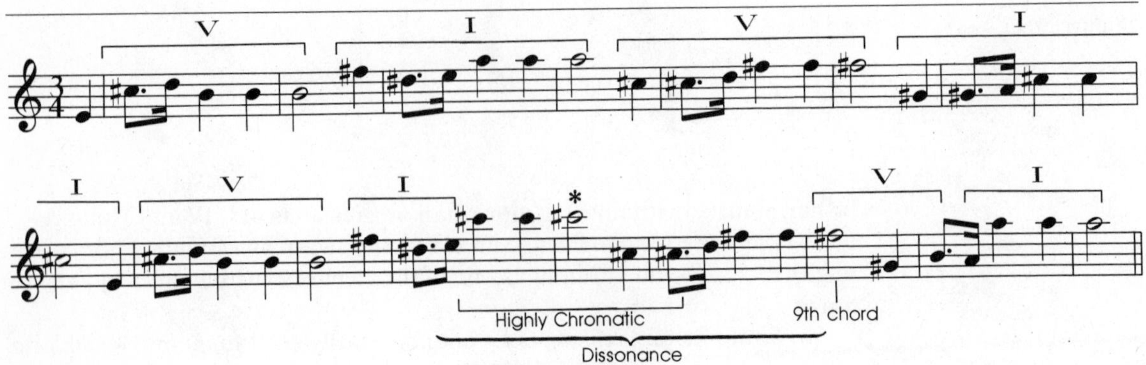

Figure 4.12

asterisk, in Figure 4.12, stands out as the structural and expressive high point of the work. The chord harmonizing this high point is a strikingly dissonant ***chromatic chord***; that is, it contains pitches that are not in the diatonic scale of A major. Chromatic harmony, as practiced by nineteenth century composers such as Chopin, was a powerful tool for generating dissonance, strong forward motion, and expressive intensity.

Finally, consider the blues selection sung by Bessie Smith. Here we have a constant background of triadic harmony (the progression I-IV-I-V-I repeated again and again), against which the soloist weaves an elaborate melodic line. The melody, often quite chromatic in its inflections, is based on one of the complex scales of the blues performance tradition—just as the performance of Indian raga draws upon *its* stylized, traditional materials.

Homophonic Texture

homophonic texture

Mention of the crucial word background leads us to one more important texture, ***homophony,*** in which melodic line and accompaniment function on two distinct levels. A ***homophonic texture*** usually consists of a single melody and a harmonic background. At the simplest level, we might think of it as a tune and chords. A number of familiar examples may come to mind: a Church hymn, patriotic song, the Chopin A-Major Prelude of our listening, Bessie Smith's blues excerpt.

The background level of a homophonic texture is not necessarily simple; the accompaniment figuration of Schubert's "Gretchen am Spinnrade" is quite intricate, as it evokes images of the spinning wheel and the singer's uneasy thoughts. In fact, the many possible accompaniment patterns of homophonic music are fascinating in their variety. There are the broken-chord figurations of Mozart and Haydn, the "oom-pah" of the marching band and Italian opera, and countless permutations of chordal accompaniment heard in jazz, country music, and Viennese waltzes. Sometimes the lowest accompaniment notes form a secondary melody with a profile of its own; this is called the bass line. Because the low bass line is so important to the grammar of chord progressions, some homophonic music may sound like a duet between melody and bass, with accompaniment figuration acting as a third element.

Is such music really homophonic or polyphonic? Do linear aspects take precedence over the chordal? Are all strands of the texture equal, or does one stand out? These differences are often ones of degree; they are not opposites, but interrelated stages along a sliding scale. For example, Terry Riley's ***In C*** may present us with a different textural message each time we hear it. The work consists of an extended canon (polyphonic) for all the players, but also produces a very slowly moving chord series—basically triadic, but not goal-directed. Note, too, that the foreground–background relationship keeps changing as solo colors emerge from the overall fabric. Ambiguities such as this are no cause for alarm. On the contrary, ***any*** work we enjoy will reveal new facets on repeated hearings.

5

Musical Form

> A sound lasts as long as we remember it. . . . Unforgettable sounds, like unforgettable stories, give rise to mythology. The affectionately remembered sound joins hands with the anticipation of new sounds to form a loop. . . .
>
> *R. Murray Schafer*

An Introduction to Form

As music is a time art, its sounds occur not only simultaneously, creating texture or density, but successively as well. *Form* is the shape given to the passage of time, by the organization of the musical events within it.

In this chapter we will discuss some general principles of form. During the past few centuries, these general principles have led to very specific, stylized models. When Western musicians speak of "form," they often refer to one of these stylized models such as the Rondo or Sonata. Models like these will be discussed during Part 2 of this book. Many people confuse form and genre; the great Western genres—symphony, concerto, opera and so on—will also be examined in Part 2. ("Genre" and "form" are really not the same. A typical symphony may be constructed with many possible forms as models.)

For the listener, being able to grasp the music's "shape" is a great asset, especially in dealing with compositions that last longer than a few minutes. In fact, a lengthy work brings some complex listening skills into play. Although we experience the piece moment-by-moment, we must also relate each momentary detail to the whole (or what we expect the whole to be). That is, we rely upon memory of the past and anticipation of the future.

Fortunately, many pieces will provide their own guidelines: important themes that disappear and then return in significant places, vivid tempo contrasts, or the use of costumes or architectural space in theatrical works. Even so, the listener has to fit each passing moment into an overall context of proportions and relationships. (We need hardly stress that music is an art of proportions! Ratios determine the way scales are built from intervals, or rhythmic patterns from durations. In writing a thirty-minute symphony, or listening to one, we also deal with proportions.) Almost everyone performs this sort of operation quite easily when using written and spoken language. We can follow the thread of a story, including complex subplots, and we associate names, personalities and character traits. (Rarely in a theater audience would anyone ask, "Which one up there is Hamlet?") We respond to the grammatical curve of sentences, prepare for endings before they arrive, and often predict what the last word will be. In dealing with lengthy musical shapes it is essential to apply the same skills. Otherwise the ear cannot relate momentary impressions to a larger shape. Without those skills the listener would be like a tiny fly wandering across the surface of the ***Mona Lisa,*** or someone driving a car through the countryside who does not read a map, use a compass, or ask for directions.

At this point someone will invariably ask, "Does it make your trip more enjoyable to have a map?" There are people who will argue to the contrary. For them, knowing "where you are" is secondary to the delight of viewing the horizon, savoring the air, and looking across the meadows. Similarly, one could find great pleasure in ***certain*** kinds of music by blissfully melting into each gorgeous sound as it comes along. But there are other kinds of journeys that call for different habits. In many works of Western music, shape or argument may be more important than sheer beauty of sound. Beethoven's music is not always as pretty as Debussy's, and a fugue may not have the sensual appeal of the Gregorian chant; the listener's ear should be adjusted accordingly. Miraculously, the human ear does adjust, shifting automatically from the larger "form" to the sensory "moment" and back again. Be thankful that we do not listen to music in the manner of Figure 5.1. Instead, we allow individual moments to accumulate, so that proportions, directions and shapes begin to emerge, as in Figure 5.2. Imagine how complicated it would be if painting really were viewed in this manner. Painting would then be a ***time***-art. To a certain degree, it already is: viewing a picture certainly takes time, and a painting is "read" for its information very much as we read a book.

Another very important element in the composition of a painting, as shown in Figure 5.3, is its frame. Viewers often ignore the frame, but it represents the physical context, the boundary, within which various elements have been arranged. There is no exact musical equivalent for the visual frame, but a number of analogous factors are worth considering. One of these is the ***time dimension*** itself: the duration of minutes and seconds against which the sound events are placed. Another is the ***setting*** and social

Figure 5.1

(Time moving in this direction) →

context for which the music was originally composed: church, garden, salon, factory, and so on. Finally, consider the situation of any given performance, the musical space on either side of the work's own time: that is, which pieces will precede it on a concert program and which ones will follow it. All of these factors influence the way we listen.

Figure 5.2

Figure 5.3

Form, Motion, Balance and Narrative

Although music occupies time, it does not have to move forward in any directional sense. As we have noted, certain musical elements favor goal-oriented, forward-driving motion. Other approaches, especially outside the Western tradition, seem to be motionless and static; a listener might be tempted to say of them, "Nothing happens."

Of our fifteen listening examples, the work that seems most static is the African drumming selection. The polyrhythmic drum ostinato and vocal chant are continually repeated, "freezing" our time sense. The Western lis-

Merle Freund, ***Musical Instrument.*** Musical ideas have influenced the creation of this stone and brass sculpture; not only the directional drive of music, but the curvilinear shapes of instruments themselves. Courtesy of artist.

tener may perceive the music as an object fixed in space, and can study its details as though it were a painting on the wall. (An African participant would most likely be caught up in the complete social and ceremonial experience, and would hardly study the music in isolation.) Even though the material appears fixed in time, it would be a mistake to believe that "nothing happens" in this music. On the contrary, repeated gestures acquire a unique power, gathering strength and intensity over ***cumulative*** time. The total effect may be quite hypnotic. There is a similar use of cumulative time in Riley's ***In C.*** Although the moment-by-moment responses indicate "nothing happening," each instant is contributing to an arc of great kaleidoscopic changes. There may be a goal to which these changes point, but it is so far in the future that it cannot be perceived; moreover, the listener is never sure when, or how soon, or how often, new changes will occur.

Forms that Stress Symmetry

Within the mainstream of Western music, most forms are concerned with goal-directed motion, activity, and variety. On hearing typical examples of Western music, listeners would assert that "something happens." A sense of ***beginning, middle,*** and ***end*** can often be felt in such music: growth to dramatic climax and then release, or motion away from a key center followed by eventual return. "Active" Western forms can be grouped in two general categories. There are those in which the end is like the beginning, and those which move away from a starting point without turning back. The first of these can be considered "symmetrical," and the second "narrative."

part forms

Symmetrical pieces have familiar material at both ends of the time span and contrasting music in the middle. They may give the impression of being patterned like flower arrangements in a formal garden: in fact, symmetry may seem more decorative than dramatic. That stereotype is not entirely accurate, since repetition has its own evocative power and contrasting "middles" may be quite expressive as well. In the Gregorian chant, for example, a certain serenity attaches to the return of the original motive, after the rhythmic activity and density of the middle. Musicians often refer to forms like this as ***part forms,*** since there are contrasting sections (parts) occurring one after the other. They may label the various parts with letters of the alphabet. The Gregorian chant selection, a ***three-part form,*** would be labeled *ABA*.

Rondo

Mozart's movement for horn and orchestra presents a more elaborate part form, alternating one catchy main theme with a series of contrasting tunes. The specific form used here is a ***Rondo,*** in five parts (*ABACA*), which was quite popular during the late eighteenth century. Its brisk, cheery nature is ideally suited for the closing movement of an entertainment piece. Mozart uses various devices to underline the different sections of the part form. There are not only new tunes, but changes in key center, subtle changes in register, dynamics, and instrumental timbre. Mozart does ***not*** alter the rhythmic flow, however, or upset the steady tempo and meter.

The part forms, with their use of repetition and contrast in successive time spans, stress the element of ***balance.*** The composer builds a musical arch: a column on the left and one on the right. There is the stability of familiar material and repetition, enclosing a multitude of inner contrasts.

strophic form

Another symmetrical approach, often found in songs, is the ***strophic form.*** In this form, different stanzas of a poem are set to identical music. "Yankee Doodle" displays this form; so does the Bessie Smith blues selection, and countless patriotic songs and hymn tunes.

What shape does Schubert's "Gretchen am Spinnrade" assume? The very last phrase is certainly like the beginning, and there are many contrasts along the way. Schubert is also working along the general lines of a ***strophic*** form, but with important differences. Each stanza begins with the same words (***"Meine Ruh ist hin . . . "***) and musical contour, but then leads us on a new journey in an unexpected direction. The overall form can be thought of as *AB . . . AC . . . AD . . . A*.

The entire song is unified by the constant reappearance of *A*, and the tonic key associated with *A*. It is also dominated by the persistent rhythmic figure of the piano accompaniment, symbolizing the endlessly turning wheel and Gretchen's obsessive state of mind. However, Gretchen's thoughts are not always on her spinning: as the second stanza (*AC*) moves to its climax, the left hand piano pattern ♪ 𝄾 ♩ ♪ 𝄾 ♩ is replaced by insistent chords, and just before the crucial phrase "his kiss" the accompaniment is entirely

Giovanni del Biondo, ***Madonna and Child Enthroned with Angels.*** 14th century. Tempera on wood panel. Symmetry dominates the composition of this painting, although in many subtle ways—such as the placement of the figures—it is far from absolute. The Fine Arts Museums of San Francisco, Gift of Mrs. Herbert Fleishhacker.

chordal and highly dissonant. The spinning wheel has stopped, and the musical motion as well. When they both reluctantly begin again, everything has subtly changed: psychologically, the "return" is not a return at all.

Forms that Stress Narrative

Many pieces are constructed so that ends are *not* like beginnings. The music appears to be concerned more with "narrative," a forward thrust to an unforeseen conclusion, than with symmetry or decoration. Perhaps the composer is creating the equivalent of a novel, introducing ideas and characters and then engaging them in dramatic situations. Or there may be a narrative with only one main "character," a single musical motive that undergoes constant change. The Bach Fugue presents one strong idea, extended in such a way that a literal return to the opening measures never takes place. There is an ever-changing context, rather than repetition. Purcell's lament, on the other hand, offers two strong ideas: the repeated ostinato melody in the low register, and the elaborate vocal line woven above it. One is continually altering the context of the other.

*In C** can be heard as a study in gradual change, with the repeated high Cs of the piano functioning as an over-powering ostinato, a tonal and rhythmic center against which all changes are measured. The Riley piece is also surprisingly "symmetrical," in that its chord changes eventually lead the ear back to C (and to the rhythmic piano ostinato sounding alone).

The Berlioz "March to the Gallows" has the contrasting sections of a part form, but their succession is oddly unbalanced. The *A* section begins immediately after the opening crescendo. It is characterized by a leap upwards in the violins and then a descending line. The vigorous and brassy *B* which follows is stated in a major key, contrasting with the minor of the *A* section. *B* then repeats, and is followed by a very noisy, rousing repeat of A; the second *A* is just different enough from the original that it could be called *A′*. There is a sudden shift to totally new material, *C*, which is in turn rudely interrupted by the solo woodwind melody and the surprising end. Should that last bit of material be called *D*? If so, the total form is an asymmetrical *ABBA′CD* that follows its own dramatic logic rather than any preconceived notion of balance.

through-composed

The sections of a part form may look forward rather than back. The term ***through-composed*** refers to a formal arrangement of parts in a straight line *ABCDEF*. . . . Listen once again to the African excerpt; the repetitive, hypnotic pattern of the opening is suddenly replaced by other patterns. In the complete performance* a second, third and fourth ostinato eventually appear in their turn. The shape of the total piece is a through-composed *ABCD*. Each part is, in fact, a self-contained piece, combined in a "med-

* Our recorded selection provides only an excerpt; the complete work may be heard on Columbia MS-7178.

* Recorded for Nonesuch II-72073.

ley'' for performance at a Nigerian ceremonial; in this respect it resembles the collection of well-known favorites played by a marching band at football half time.

The Indian Raga selection is through-composed as well, but in another sense. It is heard not as a series of different sections, but as a seemingly endless melody without breaks or seams or, apparently, cadences. Because of the persistent drone, Western listeners may hear the total fabric as motionless, whereas it actually teems with variety and activity. (In this regard it resembles the ostinato effect of ***In C.***)

On a different level, the Raga does subdivide into parts: two large parts, in fact, suggested by the performance ritual itself. The first part of a typical raga performance is played without drumming, and functions as a prelude; it establishes the general mood, and fixes the sound of the particular raga (melody type) in the listener's ear. When the players feel that this introduction has lasted a sufficient time, the drummer enters with his characteristic rhythmic pattern, or ***tala.*** At this point the main body of the performance begins.

Similar two-part divisions exist within the Western tradition. Even though Bach's preludes and fugues are not necessarily related, except by key, we almost always hear them as complementary members of a two-part unit, performed in succession. The C-Minor Prelude, for example, projects a relatively free, rhapsodic through-composed quality; its impulsiveness is answered by the security and discipline of the Fugue. On the operatic stage, the formal vocal solo known as the ***aria*** may be preceded by a statement in conversational prose rhythms supported by simple chords, known as ***recitative.*** In Purcell's opera ***Dido and Aeneas,*** a recitative of this nature is sung by Dido just before she begins her well-known ''lament.'' (See Chapter 10, for further examples of recitative and aria by Bach and Handel.)

The Principle of Variation

Every form contains the elements of ***unity*** and ***variety.*** It is held together by reference to an area of stability, a fixed ''norm.'' Yet it also offers deviations from the norm, subtle excursions or obvious contrasts. When unity and variety are presented successively in time, we think of these as ***repetition*** and ***contrast,*** the alternating building blocks of part forms. When the familiar and unfamiliar are heard simultaneously, the closest label might appear as $AA^1A^2A^3A^4A^5$; a recognizable body of material may be heard throughout, but in ever-changing contexts and situations. This is the essence of the principle called ***variation.***

variation

Consider it a ''principle'' at this point, rather than a specific formal model. The principle is broader than any stylized model, and occurs in widely contrasted situations. For example, Purcell's aria is a continuous elaboration upon a repeated ground melody, a stream of polyphonic interplay that juxtaposes "familiar" against "new." Similarly, the Bessie Smith blues selection superimposes a vocal line on a fixed ***harmonic*** "ground": this chord progression which dominates a majority of all the blues ever sung or played, remains constant from one stanza to the next.

The Bach C-Minor Fugue is also concerned with variation in the broad sense. So is the Indian Raga, spun from a fixed body of melodic and scalar material. In fact, the principle can be found in any musical fabric built upon a single idea presented in subtly changing contexts.

Theme and Variations

The Haydn string quartet example presents a more explicit kind of variation procedure: here the form is actually called ***Theme and Variations.*** The variations do not continuously unfold without a break, as over Purcell's repeated ground; rather, each statement of the complete tune reaches a brief pause before going on to the next version.

Haydn's variations adhere closely to the contours of the original tune. The tempo, meter, key melodic profile, and general harmony remain the same throughout; there is little attempt to disguise or obscure the important line. The changes introduced by Hayden are especially fascinating because they are so understated and unobtrusive. The first three variations explore differences in density: only two of the four instruments play in Variation I, and only three in Variation III. There are also rhythmic alterations, such as the rapid sixteenth-note patterns of Variation I and the syncopated cross-accents of Variation II. (During the first three variations there is also the opportunity for each "unsung" member of the quartet* to play a solo!) Variation IV is heavier than the rest, and uses all four instruments; the degree of chromaticism, and consequently the dissonance level, is also increased.

Compare the Haydn to Anton Webern's twentieth century ***Variations for Orchestra.*** The listener who expects a neatly laid out set of decorative pieces, in the manner of Haydn, will be sadly disappointed. Webern uses brief motivic fragments, not the expansive phrase groups of Haydn. Moreover, Webern handles them contrapuntally, in a distinctly atonal context. Whereas Haydn clearly delineates the beginnings and ends of individual variations, Webern allows his to merge into one continuous narrative. Furthermore he varies precisely those elements that Haydn leaves untouched: symmetry, phrase relationships, register, accent, and pace.

Finally, the listener may wonder where Webern's ***theme*** is. Does the piece have a distinctly audible motive, comparable to the tune of the Haydn quartet movement or the subject of a fugue or ground? In fact, Webern uses a number of motives rather than one single theme; these motives are drawn from a twelve-tone row. We will discuss the ***Variations for Orchestra*** in greater detail during Chapter 17. For now, note the orderly change of densities, as solo lines and duets give way to chords and repeated patterns. Such relationships become more apparent on repeated hearings, and the internal

*These would be second violin, viola and cello. See Chapter 6.

consistency, the sense of logic that pervades the whole, is certainly audible. The principle of variation underlies the entire work, providing great surface variety as well as a taut, integral unity that grows more amazing the more we listen.

Form and Tonality

There is another level, perhaps less conscious, at which Western listeners hear music composed in the major-minor tonal tradition. It is linked to the way in which the ear perceives movement ***away*** from a key center and then ***back*** to that center. Listeners who have heard many thousands of tonal pieces come to anticipate forward motion in music—a journey in time that eventually leads to the goal of tonic key.

Complete and Incomplete Forms

We can differentiate between two approaches to tonal motion in terms of what happens to the *first part* of a work. For example, when the first phrase of "America" ends (". . . of thee I *Sing*"), the original key center is confirmed. If the entire song ended right there, it would sound relatively complete; it does not ***need*** to go on. By contrast, consider "Home on the Range." The end of the first phrase (". . . the antelope play") lands on a pitch that is not the tonic, and which must be harmonized with V chord. A second phrase, returning to the tonic, is necessary to complete the first. In this song, the first phrase is tonally incomplete. Similarly, the opening three phrases of the Haydn quartet theme are incomplete, each coming to rest on the dominant (V). The rest of the tune is absolutely necessary to confirm the feeling of key center.

There are many differences between the Chopin Preludes of our listening, in meter, rhythm, register and general density. The heavy block chords of the C-Minor Prelude are far removed from the light, transparent effect of the A-major, with its lyric voice and discreet oom-pah accompaniment. But there is one more important distinction: the C-Minor Prelude has a tonally "incomplete" form, and the A-major a "complete" form.

Listen first to the A-Major Prelude, and note that the first half of the piece is harmonized simply with tonic and dominant chords, in the succession V-I-V-I. There is an underlying dissonant quality to the music, especially as the dominant chords receive an extra "bite" from added pitches. The dotted rhythmic pattern of the melody, and the fact that the pitch marked with an asterisk (Figure 5.4) is always the "wrong" note, create further tension. The first half of the Prelude comes to rest on the tonic, and is therefore complete. But it does not feel absolutely final: Chopin's melody note is not the tonic of the scale. So there is a slightly restless quality, which does not fully resolve until the ending.

Figure 5.4

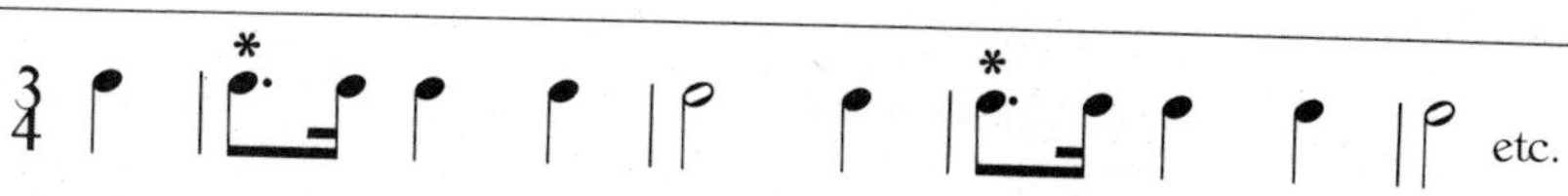

There is no such ambiguity with the C-Minor Prelude. The lengthy opening phrase leads directly to the dominant (V) chord. The answering phrase is essential, therefore, in order to return to the tonic. Like Haydn, Chopin decides to repeat his final phrase. It is worth hearing twice, if only because it is shaped in one continuous line; this makes an ingenious contrast to the four-beat "blocks" that were treated sequentially in the opening part.

Key Contrasts

When tonal composers work with large time spans, they can employ contrast among different keys to provide tension and release. The Mozart *ABACA* Rondo movement for horn and orchestra assigns specific tonalities to its various themes. Melodies ***B*** and ***C*** are heard in "foreign" keys, while ***A*** is always associated with the "home" key of E♭ major. The opening statement of ***A*** ends in the tonic, making the form tonally complete. The key of E♭ is gradually altered after this opening statement, so that theme ***B*** is introduced in the dominant key. The ***A*** theme returns in the tonic, and then ***C*** appears in the key of the subdominant.

modulation

The process of switching tonalities in midstream is called ***modulation;*** the composer introduces new pitches, the aural perspective shifts, and the listener's ear temporarily accepts a new key center. During the eighteenth and nineteenth centuries musicians assumed that such excursions into "foreign" territory were temporary. It was felt that the ear would demand the return of the original tonic; otherwise the piece would sound incomplete.

As we have observed in the Rondo, many tonal works utilize ***modulation*** and ***key contrast.*** For another example, listen to Bach's C-Minor Fugue. There is a modulation to E♭ major after all the lines have entered the texture (making the overall form tonally "incomplete"). The fugue later passes through other tonalities as well. The return to the tonic is an important goal: once it is reached Bach emphasizes the home-key feeling with a sustained C in the lowest part. One could hear this fugue in three sections, corresponding to the movement away from the tonic, excursions into other keys, and a solid grounding in the tonic once more. That interpretation may seem to conflict with the idea of the fugue as an example of "variation principle." But both approaches are valid: the ambiguity is built into the music.

Form, Tonality and Time

The relationship between many Western forms and the major-minor scale system is clear. Is it possible that both "form" and "tonality" reflect a Western way of viewing the world in general? The perception of ***time*** as forward-driving, pushing ahead to goals, dominates the culture of industrialized peoples; consider our notion of "progress," our reliance upon clocks, our calendars and ways of measuring recorded time as "history." A goal-directed series of musical chords is called a "progression." Tonality might be considered the epitome of this world view: all events work together, evolving towards a unified end.

Perhaps some comparisons can be made between the music of preliterate (so-called "primitive") people and literate cultures. In preliterate society, time is not perceived or measured in terms of linear progress, but by recurring cycles: births, deaths, seasons. Memory may also be less crucial; when communication is basically face-to-face, the immediate present is all-important, which may partly explain the significance of repetition in preliterate music. Some musicians have theorized, too, that preliterate music offers instant tonal satisfaction: repeated patterns constantly stressing the focal center. According to this theory, cultivated Western music is analogous to other civilized practices that delay gratification. The problem with both theories is their failure to explain the vast musical differences among equally literate, cultivated societies—those of India, China, Africa, the Near East, Western Europe and so on.

For whatever reasons, Western music has evolved in a way that stresses goal-directed time and "progress." Other systems offer alternate views; the African, Indian, and Gregorian chant examples each convey a more spacious, less hurried world picture. Terry Riley's music, based in part upon non-Western models, shares some of that "directionless" cyclic quality. A systematically ***atonal*** style, like Babbitt's or Webern's may be concerned with different goals and the use of other elements for contrast and climax. Or it may provide another unfamiliar, static time sense. Webern's concerns for imitative relationships of inversion and retrograde have led some musicians to ask: "Would a Webern composition sound as logically convincing backwards as forwards?" That sort of question will not be answered to everyone's satisfaction, but it is significant that it could be asked at all. We might consider whether terms like "backwards" and "forwards" have any meaning in the context of nontonal style, or if the time sense is suspended.

The key to the listener's comprehension of form is ***memory:*** relating the past to the present, so that "time" acquires a "shape." This involves not only simple hearing, but the ability to relate, compare, and look ahead. There are, after all, only a few simple facts to keep in mind. Human beings continually cope with them, whether listening to music or just going about the business of living. Composer Barney Childs has listed them as the "inescapable peculiarities of time:"

> It's always now.
> Something is always happening.
> One thing irrevocably succeeds another.
> Something just became "past."

6

Musical Instruments

> Shakespeare, dispensing with the customary exordium, announces his subject at once in the infinitive, in which mood it is presently repeated after a short connective passage in which, brief as it is, we recognize the alternative and negative forms on which so much of the significance of repetition depends. Here we reach a colon . . .
>
> *George Bernard Shaw*

Timbre: The Color of Sound

George Bernard Shaw, who was a leading music critic before he turned his hand to playwriting, constructed the above pseudo-analysis of "To be, or not to be" from Shakespeare's *Hamlet* to symbolize the absurdity of musical commentary in which "grammar" becomes the sole consideration. To concentrate entirely upon structure to the exclusion of actual sonic experience is to miss the primary dimension of music. *Sound* is the medium through which musical ideas and grammatical relationships are communicated, a "vessel" carrying shapes, patterns and colors from one location to another.

"Sound" is an abstraction: in reality, there is a bewildering variety of individual sounds, each different from the other. These differences are not always related to frequency: the pitch A-440 has one "color" when played on the oboe, but quite another when heard on a violin, or piano, or muted trumpet, or xylophone. This quality of tone color is called *timbre.* Every musical instrument has its own unique timbre, a special "voice" of its own. A few general principles underlie this great variety of colors:

timbre

Dog Orchestra. English porcelain. Courtesy Wadsworth Atheneum, Hartford.

1. Sounds are the result of vibrations in the air waves.

2. The larger the vibrating body, the slower the vibration rate, or the lower the frequency: larger vibrating bodies produce sounds of lower pitch. (Larger can mean longer, or wider, or thicker. The thick G string of the violin may be the same length as the thin E string, but it vibrates more slowly.)

3. Every ***material*** vibrates, or responds to vibrations, in a unique way. Violin strings made from gut do not sound like strings made from steel; flutes built to identical specifications but from different materials—plastic, bone, or silver—each have distinct timbral qualities.

4. The way in which an object is set into vibration adds another important factor to its timbre. The buzz of an oboe reed, or the striking of a piano string with a hammer influence the dynamic life of the sounds they produce. When a note is played on the piano, we first hear a brittle "pop," followed by a sustained tone that very rapidly fades away. A clarinet note cuts the silence more gently, seems to increase in volume after a split second, and can be sustained for a much longer duration. Those subtle differences in volume level are often referred to in the terminology of electronics as the "attack" and "decay" of a sound; they may be summed up with the single word ***envelope***.

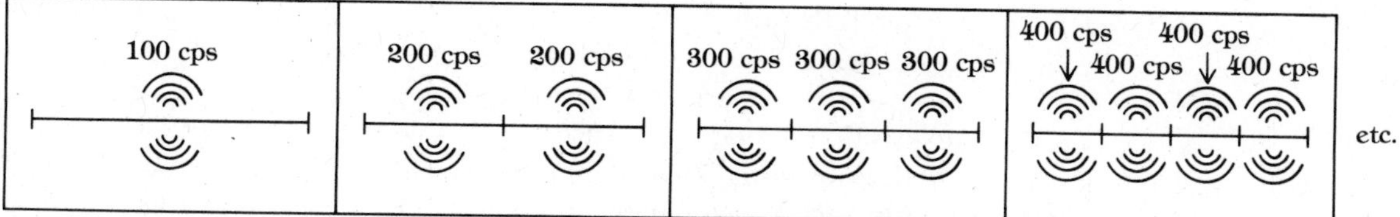

Figure 6.1

5. The acoustical phenomenon called the *overtone series* also affects timbre. When a body vibrates, it does so not only as a whole—in its entirety, at a particular frequency—but in fractions, or "partials." As shown in Figure 6.1, a violin string vibrates along its full length, and *simultaneously* vibrates in halves, thirds, fourths, and so on. Each of the partials, or "overtones," has its own particular frequency, related to the "fundamental" frequency of the entire vibrating body. (See the Appendix for a more detailed explanation.)

Certain instruments stress some overtones and not others in their vibrations; this is another factor in determining timbre. For example, the flute's timbre consists almost entirely of fundamentals, while a great many partials contribute to the sound of the violin. The clarinet timbre stresses every other overtone: only the even-numbered partials. Many instruments are constructed so that players can make their overtones audible; a particular pitch emerging from a flute, violin, trumpet, or trombone may be a partial rather than a fundamental.

Classification of Instruments

Music-making objects can be grouped together in any number of ways. We can classify instruments by historical periods, comparing those of the Middle ages, Renaissance and Baroque with the more modern ones constructed after 1750. On a socio-economic scale, we could compare the aristocratic instruments of court and church with those of serfs, farmers, and factory laborers. The instrumental traditions of Europe, Asia, and Africa might be compared as well. But as timbre is the chief concern of this chapter, instruments will be classified here according to their *sound.*

Classification by Register

Although the tonal range of human hearing extends over many thousands of cycles per second, most instruments concentrate upon a rather narrow register within that total. The human voice is no exception; since some people have larger larynxes and longer vocal chords than others, vocal registers differ. Humanity is therefore divided vocally into groups, called (from highest to lowest) soprano, mezzo-soprano, alto, tenor, baritone, and bass. Instruments can also be divided along these lines.

In general, the full size of the instrument—its greatest length of tubing, for example, or its thickest full-length string—determines its lowest tones. By pressing keys on a clarinet, or moving a trombone slide or placing a finger on a cello string, the player may artificially shorten the vibrating body, and thus raise the sounding pitch. Each instrument can produce a broad ***range*** of notes within the particular ***register*** decreed by its size and construction. Nevertheless, the flute is still generally considered a "soprano" instrument, the viola a "tenor" and the bassoon a "bass."

Instruments are often built in a variety of sizes, creating a family with similar timbral qualities. The violin, viola, and cello make up such a family; another such grouping would be the saxophones (soprano, alto, tenor, and

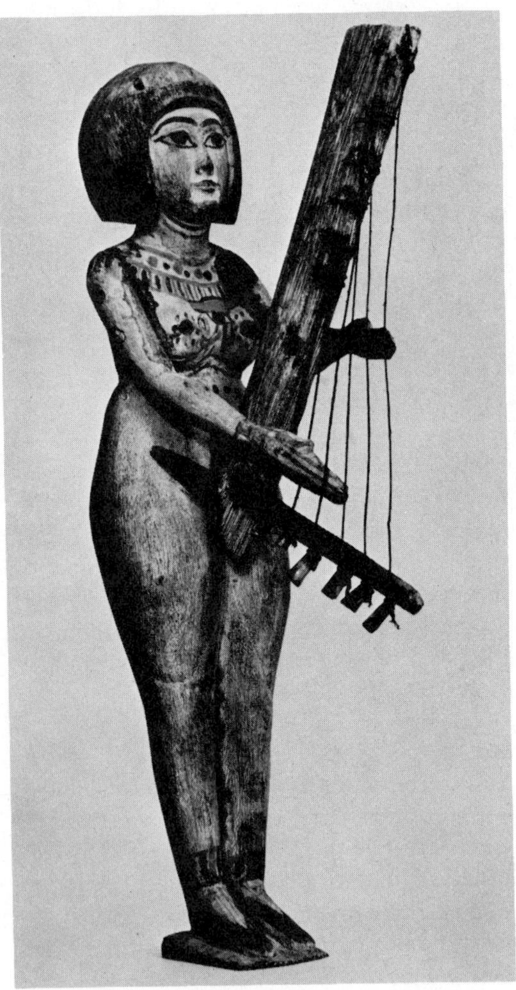

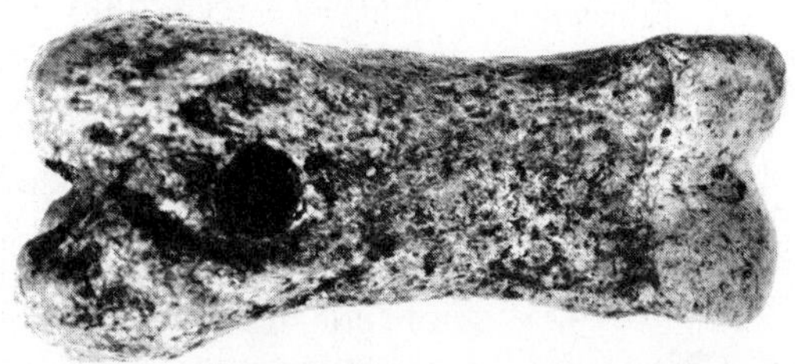

baritone). Still another "family" arrangement houses a large number of similar instruments of different sizes in a single box, with an attached keyboard mechanism to activate the sounds: the pipe organ, for example, or the piano with its many strings and hammers.

Classification by Material

Modern scholars who study the world's instruments have classified them in four large subdivisions, determined by the material being set in vibration. There are instruments whose sound is produced by the vibration of ***air,*** and those whose sounds are made by the vibration of ***strings.*** Other instruments produce sound by the vibration of tautly stretched ***membranes*** (in primitive

The four basic categories of the world's instruments are seen here; Whistle (top left) made from the phalanx bone of a reindeer, France, Paleolithic-Magdalenian (aerophone); Egyptian Harpist (far left), 19th dynasty (chordphone); American Indian tom-tom (bottom left), (membranophone); Gong Ageng (right) from Raffles Gamelan (idiophone).

societies, dried skin). A fourth group of instruments are themselves vibrating in their *entirety,* since they are made of especially sonorous material.* This last group, as well as those which rely upon the vibration of air, appeared very early in human history and still play an important role in the ceremonies of preliterate peoples. To have the player's own breath transformed, or to discover a "voice" within a rattle or gong, must seem almost magical in many societies.

Classification by Function

The traditional Western terminology also groups instruments in four subdivisions, roughly corresponding to the four sections of the symphony orchestra. This classification expresses *function,* since the four groups of instruments have traditionally occupied certain roles in the orchestral texture. (But as a comparison of the Mozart, Berlioz, and Webern excerpts illustrates, these roles have been altered considerably during the past two centuries.) The traditional classification also reflects the *activity* that sets vibrations in motion. Brasses and woodwinds use different means to activate a column of air. Percussion instruments are activated by striking or shaking.

In this chapter, we will examine instruments from the four traditional Western categories—***strings, woodwinds, brass*** and ***percussion***—with particular emphasis upon those found in the symphony orchestra. Once more, we must stress the importance of active ***listening.*** Verbal descriptions of tone color without the aural experience of actual sound are merely abstractions, like Shaw's parody analysis of Hamlet's speech. Words cannot convey the unique quality of a musical sound. Imagine trying to describe the taste of asparagus, or the "look" of the color blue: the phenomenon has to make its effect directly upon the senses. Similarly, each listener must discover the timbral difference between oboe and English horn, or violin and viola.

Before concentrating upon individual instruments, some may wish to hear the entire orchestra in all its sonic power and variety. Works that emphasize the four instrumental sections include the opening of Benjamin Britten's ***Young Person's Guide to the Orchestra*** (in which the sections are introduced in turn), and movement III of Tchaikovsky's Symphony no. 4, in which the stringed instruments are plucked throughout. We could also focus upon timbre by listening to arrangements and transcriptions. The famous suite ***Pictures at an Exhibition*** by Modeste Mussorgsky was originally composed for piano (see Chapter 12), and later transcribed for orchestra by Maurice Ravel: listen to identical passages in both versions. A Bach piece for "clavier," such as our familiar Prelude and Fugue in C Minor, may be performed on the harpsichord, clavichord, or modern grand piano, and it will be strikingly different in each of these realizations. There are also re-

*These are termed, respectively, ***aerophones, chordophones, membranophones,*** and ***idiophones.***

cordings of the C-Minor Fugue in Walter Carlos' famous "Switched-on Bach" version created on the Moog Synthesizer, and the "scat-singing" jazz rendition of the Swingle Singers.

Instruments of the Western Orchestra

The Strings

All stringed instruments have three simple features in common: (1) The player activates the instrument's strings by plucking, striking, or drawing a bow across them. (2) The frequency or pitch is determined not only by the length of the string, but by its thickness and tautness as well. (3) The tone is made richer, fuller, and louder if the string can resonate against a board or within a hollow box.

violin

The ***violin*** is the most familiar of Western orchestral stringed instruments. (See Figure 6.2.) It consists of four ***strings*** of different thicknesses, drawn tautly across a ***bridge*** from a ***tailpiece*** at one end to ***pegs*** at the other. A player, holding a ***bow*** in the right hand, draws the bow across one or more

Tobias Stimmer, *Woman Playing the Psaltery* (left) and *Woman Playing Viol* (right). As these sixteenth century woodcuts demonstrate, stringed instruments can be plucked or bowed.

Figure 6.2

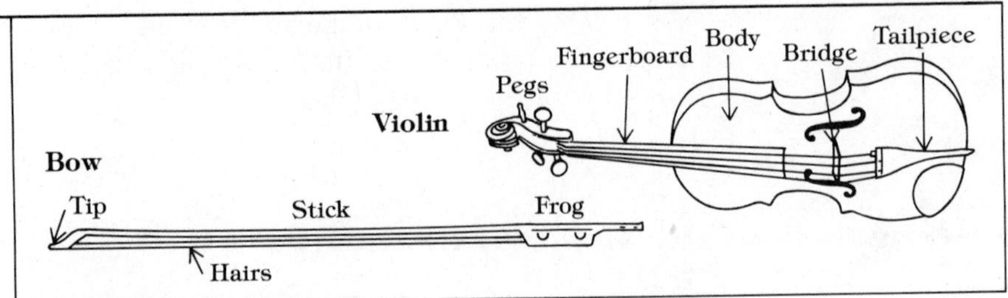

strings. The sounds are resonated and amplified within the hollow ***body*** of the instrument. Each of the four strings produces a different fundamental pitch at its complete length; when sounding at its complete length it is called an ***open string.*** The ***viola*** (a slightly larger violin) and the ***violoncello*** or simply ***cello*** (larger still) are constructed along identical lines; they have larger bodies, longer and thicker strings, and lower tunings of the open strings.

viola

cello

There is a fourth member of the orchestra string section, known by a variety of names: ***doublebass, contrabass,*** or ***string bass.*** It is even larger than the cello. Whereas the cello is rested between the knees of a seated player, the contrabass stands about as tall as the average person; the bassist must stand, or sit on a high stool, when performing. The contrabass shape is slightly different from that of the other three instruments, revealing a link to features of the Renaissance "viol" family. It, too, has four strings,* and plays in the lowest register of all.

doublebass

In playing any of the four instruments, the performer uses certain ***bowing*** skills, created by the motion and angle of the right arm, as bow makes contact with string. The left hand controls the pitch: the fingers press down upon a string at different locations, ***stopping*** the string and thus creating a temporarily shorter length and higher pitch. When a player bows two strings at once, creating two simultaneous sounds, the term ***double-stop*** is used. Rocking the left hand back and forth on a stopped string produces a slightly quivering sound called ***vibrato,*** considered highly expressive for certain styles. The singing tone often associated with romantic violin playing is due in part to vibrato; the flat sound of a country fiddler or student violinist has little or no vibrato.

vibrato

The strings may also be plucked rather than bowed. This technique is known as ***pizzicato.*** Jazz bassists pluck their instruments nearly all the time; their pizzicato playing in a low register is quite rich and resonant.

pizzicato

One more stringed instrument is often heard in the orchestra: the harp, a modern descendant of the ancient Greek and Egyptian harps and lyres. The modern instrument's forty-seven strings, covering a range of more than six octaves, are always plucked.

*Some contrabasses have five strings.

Richard Harshorne, double bass and Beth Pearson, cello (Apple Hill Chamber Players). Notice the difference in size between the bass (left) and cello (right).

The Woodwinds

These instruments are not necessarily made of wood, although they once were, and they are not all constructed on the same principles. They are all similar, however, in that they make sounds by causing a column of air to vibrate through a cylindrical pipe. There are three basic types of woodwind:

1. instruments in which the player's *breath* directly activates the sound;
2. those in which a very thin, flexible piece of cane called a *reed* vibrates against a *mouthpiece*;
3. instruments that use two reeds—a *double reed*—in vibration, activating the surrounding column of air.

flute

The first type is represented by the *flute,* and its smaller family member the *piccolo.* The instrument is a simple closed pipe, with one large opening at the player's mouth (and none at either end). Sound is produced by blowing across the top of this opening, very much as one might create pitch by blowing across the top of a soda bottle.

Figure 6.3

clarinet
oboe/bassoon
english horn

As seen in Figure 6.3, the *clarinet* uses a single reed and mouthpiece; the ***oboe*** and ***bassoon*** require that the player blow between two parts of a double reed. Both oboe and bassoon belong to the double-reed family, which consists of—from highest to lowest register—the ***oboe,*** the ***english horn,*** the larger ***bassoon,*** and still larger ***contrabassoon.*** (The English horn is a disaster of nomenclature: it is neither "English" nor a "horn," but simply an alto oboe.) Similarly, there is a single-reed clarinet family, including the ***bass clarinet*** and very large ***contrabass clarinet.*** In all cases the biggest instruments use such great lengths of pipe that the tubing is doubled back upon itself.

There is a characteristic timbre within each family, difficult to describe in words but easily audible. Closed-pipe sounds might be described as "pure" or "breathy" or "ethereal;" double-reed instruments have a penetrating quality; single reeds can be quite "mellow." Tone colors vary from one instrument to another within a family: for example, the English horn sound is fuller than that of the oboe. Note, too, that the timbre changes markedly within the different registers of one instrument. In this sense, the clarinet is practically three instruments in one, so different are its low, high and middle colors from each other. All are instantly recognizable, however, as "clarinet."

The usage of the woodwinds in the orchestra has varied over the past few hundred years. In the early nineteenth century, an orchestra composition might call for two flutes, two oboes, two clarinets and two bassoons—what musicians sometimes refer to as "winds in twos." By the later nineteenth century "winds in threes" were more frequently employed, as piccolo, bass clarinet, English horn and contrabassoon were added to the various family textures at the composer's discretion. Other wind instruments, such as the bass flute, contrabass clarinet, or saxophones are rarely used in the symphony orchestra, although they are frequently found in contemporary American concert bands.

All woodwind performers produce different pitches by covering and uncovering holes that run along the lengths of pipe, thus artificially shortening the pipe length. In addition, they control the placement of lips, jaw, tongue, teeth, and breath, so that vibrations are activated accurately. This controlled facial placement is called ***embouchure.***

Clarinetist Benny Goodman, whose career has spanned the worlds of jazz and concert music.

The Brasses

In the brass instruments a column of air is set into vibration by the buzzing of the player's lips—a kind of "double-reed" effect—against a cup mouthpiece. The sounds are resonated and amplified along the length of a tube, and the timbre is modified by a bell-shaped configuration at the end of the tube. Although modern tubing is made of brass, early and non-Western "brass" instruments have been made of ivory, shell, bamboo, gourd, and many other materials. Brass players can make music on the mouthpiece alone, just as wind players can create a variety of sounds from unattached reeds. In fact, when brass players demonstrate their instruments for school children they may play familiar tunes using no more than a mouthpiece, a length of common garden hose, and an ordinary funnel for a "bell," as

Figure 6.4

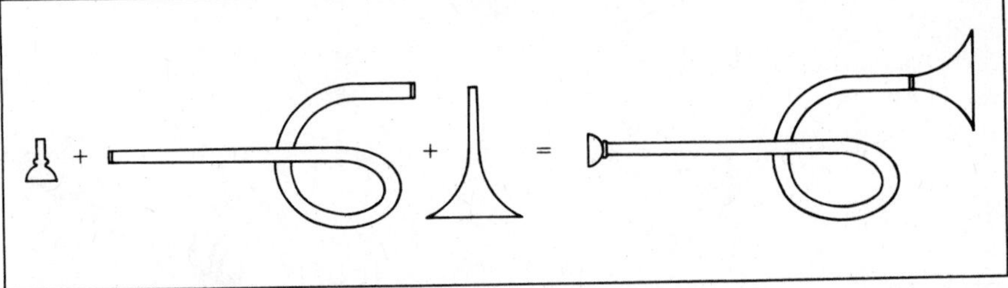

shown in Figure 6.4. One musician loves to refer to the trombone as an "adjustable-length garden hose."

One can play simple tunes on a garden hose by controlling the tension of the buzzing lips (an important element of brass ***embouchure***), thereby activating audible frequencies of the overtone series. The bugle is played this way as well; the pitches consist of upper partials. Pitches can be varied further by changing the length of tubing or the length of the air column passing through the tube. This is accomplished with a ***slide*** for the trombone, and keyed ***valves*** for other brasses.

trumpet / french horn
trombone / tuba

The important orchestral brasses are called the ***trumpet, french horn*** (or simply ***horn***), ***trombone,*** and ***tuba.*** The trumpet and trombone both use cup-shaped mouthpieces and cylindrical tubes that suddenly flare out at the bells. The warmer, more mellow tones of the horn and tuba are partly due to their wide conical tubes. In addition, the horn uses a longer, funnel-shaped mouthpiece. These are all shown in Figure 6.5. Various sizes of trumpet, trombone and tuba are occasionally used in the orchestral literature. A piece may call for tenor and bass trombone, for example, or the very small high-pitched trumpet associated with eighteenth century baroque music. The ***cornet,*** a slightly smaller variety of trumpet with a conical tube, is frequently found in concert bands, but only rarely in the orchestra.

The late eighteenth century orchestra of Mozart and Haydn might contain two horns or two trumpets, particularly if the mood was overtly military or triumphal. Although trombones were used in seventeenth and eighteenth century opera and liturgical music, they did not generally appear in the

Figure 6.5

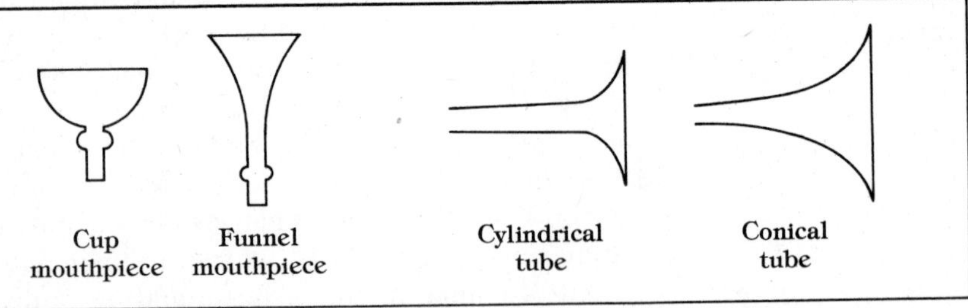

symphony orchestra until the early nineteenth century. By the year 1900, however, composers might write for an orchestral brass section of three trumpets, four horns, three trombones, and possibly a tuba as well. This increase in usage reflects a shift in esthetic priorities, but a very practical advance in technology as well: the development of ***valves,*** making it possible for trumpets and horns to play many pitches without inserting and removing different lengths of tubing.

Brass timbre can be brilliant, or smooth and warm. Its dynamic range is staggering: although the brasses can be quiet and gentle, at their very loudest they can totally overwhelm the rest of the orchestra. ***Mutes*** control volume, and also vary the timbre. They are a very important part of a brass player's equipment; basically cone-shaped, they are inserted into the bell of the instrument when needed. Since mutes come in a variety of shapes and materials—many originally derived from jazz playing—the possibilities of altering timbre with them are virtually inexhaustible.

Percussion Instruments

Literally anything can be a percussion instrument: a skull, the bones of one's enemies, or (in a more modern context) a milk bottle, anvil, automobile brake drum, the sharp rapping flute keys, and so on. Percussion instruments are defined by their *use;* they create sound by being struck or shaken. The Western tradition subdivides percussion into two categories: instruments which produce a definite musical pitch, and those which make complex sounds ("noises") of indefinite frequency. The first group is known as

tuned percussion/tympani

tuned percussion. It includes the ***tympani*** or ***kettledrums,*** which have a distinctive kettle shape to match their name. Altering the tension of the stretched membrane or drum head enables a drum to be tuned to a specific pitch. At least two drums are needed for melodic patterns, since a single drum cannot play more than one note without retuning. There are also tuned sets of ***bells,*** tubular ***chimes,*** and a variety of keyboard-like instruments consisting of many plates or bars struck with mallets. The latter include the ***xylophone*** and it larger family member the ***marimba;*** these use bars of sonorous wood. The ***glockenspiel*** and ***vibraphone*** have metal plates. The ***celesta*** produces a delicate, bell-like timbre. It looks like a small piano, has a traditional piano keyboard, and is played with the fingers.

untuned percussion

The ***untuned percussion*** include the ***triangle, snare drum, bass drum, wood block, cymbal, tambourine, castanets,*** and many others. Some of these are struck, while others are shaken or rubbed. They exist in various sizes: composers may call for five different wood blocks, or three cymbals, because rough "melodic" contours of high-medium-low can be achieved with such groups in graduated sizes.

Two facts about percussion should be remembered: first, they are capable of quiet, sensitive ***pianissimo*** shadings. Everyone knows that these instruments can be thunderously loud. It would be well to consider the other side of percussion playing—the murmurs and whispers, and exquisitely

A percussion ensemble, with tympani in the immediate foreground.

lovely timbres of percussion just at the threshold of audibility. Secondly, it takes *two* "instruments" to make a percussive sound, not only the instrument being struck but another object that does the striking. Players use metal rods, wooden sticks, sticks covered with various materials (such as rubber or plastic), brushes, and fingertips. Each will produce a distinctive timbre.

Western Keyboard Instruments

Not all the instruments we hear are members of the traditional Western orchestra. Other familiar Western instruments were designed for the parlor, salon, church, or recording studio, but not the concert hall or opera house; the best known examples are the piano, organ, and guitar.

piano

The *piano* has eighty-eight keys, covering a range of more than seven octaves. When a key is depressed, a small hammer strikes a string or group

Three keyboard instruments of different eras: a virginal of Elizabethan England (Wenceslaus Hollar, ***Lady Playing the Virginals.*** Etching, 1635); an Elaborate Victorian piano decorated with silver and gilt gesso by William Morris (1883); and a modern pipe organ. Notice the organ's multiple keyboards.

of strings. (For this reason we may consider the piano a percussion instrument.) The way a performer strikes the key determines the volume and articulation of the sound. The piano's dynamic range is extensive, so much so that its earliest inventor called it ***"cembal col piano e forte"*** (harpsichord with soft and loud), or ***pianoforte.***

The invention of the piano in the early 1700s marked a turning point in the history of Western music. (Few realized it at the time; J. S. Bach, for one, heard the new instrument and was apparently unimpressed.) By the nineteenth century, the piano had become the great status symbol of every American and European middle-class home: essential for song accompaniments, a commanding solo vehicle for great concert performers, the perfect outlet for "proper young ladies" of modest skills who aspired to "culture," and an indispensable tool for the study of music theory and literature at conservatories.

organ

The ***organ*** is basically a wind instrument, although one plays it at a keyboard; in fact, the performer usually controls a number of keyboards. Larger organs have at least two ***manuals,*** or keyboards for the hands and fingers (certain harpsichords will also have multiple keyboards); large organs also include a separate keyboard for the feet, a group of ***pedals.*** By operating manuals and pedals, the organist causes air to be blown into various pipes. These pipes are grouped in families, some even containing single-reed or double-reed characteristics.

Organ building reached its high point between the fifteenth and eighteenth centuries, mostly in the great cathedrals and churches of Europe. The electronic theatre organ of the early twentieth century, built for another species of "cathedral" or "palace," marked a new development in the life of the instrument.

Western Plucked Strings

Although pizzicato is available to all stringed instruments, the harp is the only member of the orchestra whose strings are ***consistently*** plucked. Many plucked instruments can be found outside the orchestral tradition, however: the ***guitar, mandolin,*** and ***lute,*** to name but a few. These are played by stopping the strings with one hand and plucking with the other. Many of these instruments have ***frets,*** or cross-bars running across the fingerboard, to indicate the location of specific stops.

guitar/lute

These instruments may be ***strummed*** as well as plucked; that is, all the available strings can be sounded at once. Thus the banjo or guitar frequently play chords and harmonic progression.

The ***lute*** was a tremendously popular instrument during the Renaissance, the same sort of all-purpose favorite that the piano was to become later. In the later twentieth century the guitar, riding a new crest of popularity, meets similar needs for many people.

The Voice

To conclude our survey of instruments, then, consider the one which is often regarded as the simplest and most natural of all: the human voice.

Is the voice really "simple?" As any physiologist could demonstrate, the interactions of larynx, vocal cords, and muscular contractions that produce speech are quite sophisticated. And as for "natural," there are no universally "natural" singing styles. Different cultures have drastically dif-

Lorenzo Costa, *A Concert.* 16th century. Courtesy of the National Gallery, London.

ferent preferences, from the nasal quality of Peking opera to the tight-throat quiver of the American Plains Indian or the Western concert tradition of open throat and vowel sounds. In addition, a unique twentieth century vocal tradition has grown up around the ***microphone.*** Whereas a "classical" soprano needs resonant timbre to project through an operatic orchestra, her counterpart in the folk, jazz, or rock world can whisper, hum or croon if she wishes. Musical styles reflect these differences.

The voice is not always referred to as an "instrument." That is, we may read about some composer's "instrumental works" as opposed to his "vocal works," or a piece for "instruments and voices." That convention will be retained in this book. On the other hand, the voice ***is*** undeniably an instrument: a wind instrument. The four most common voice classifications are (from highest to lowest) soprano, alto, tenor, and bass. In the worlds of opera and oratorio, further distinctions are often made on the basis of timbre and expressive convention; a singer's voice is therefore not only soprano or tenor, but "lyric," "dramatic," "buffo" (humorous), and so on.

As we end this examination of instruments, we must note that there are many instruments ***not*** mentioned here, that deserve serious attention. These include instruments of various non-Western cultures, instruments which date from the flourishing musical life of Europe before 1750, and mechanical or electrical instruments. A number of these are discussed in the Appendix.

Chamber Ensembles

The term *chamber music* refers to a group of eight to ten performers or less, who can play and be heard comfortably in a "chamber"—a drawing room, salon, or small banqueting hall. *Chamber music* is the general term for the literature that such small groups play. Historically, a number of specific chamber ensembles have developed a fixed instrumentation. Not all ensembles are this specific, of course. In all societies, there are random "pick-up" groups of any and all available instruments, performing familiar favorites: the average small-town elementary school band, or groups of noblemen playing for their own amusement during the Middle Ages and Renaissance. On the other hand, traditional Indian Raga performance offers a standardized grouping of three players that has remained the same for centuries: sitar, tamboura (drone) and drumming tabla.

The String Quartet

string quartet

The best known Western example of a fixed chamber grouping is the *string quartet.* This ensemble invariably consists of first violin, second violin, viola, and cello. We have already listened to some string quartet music: the theme-and-variations movement by Haydn. It will be revealing to contrast the Haydn work's clear texture with the richer, fuller sonority of the Schubert Quartet no. 13 in A Minor (a movement of which will be discussed in Chapter 13).

The designations "first violin" and "second violin" do ***not*** refer to differences in instrument design. Both parties play exactly the same kind of instrument; the difference is one of function and role (something like "center fielder" and "right fielder"), nothing more.

The Woodwind Quintet

wind quintet

The name for this ensemble is misleading: there are really four woodwinds (flute, oboe, clarinet, bassoon) plus the French horn. Perhaps the group should simply be called ***wind quintet,*** as it already is informally. Its timbre is ideally suited for contrapuntal, linear texture. (Because all five instruments are actually members of different families, their massed sound does not offer the homogeneous strength of strings or brasses.) We might compare Beethoven's Quintet for Piano and Winds (which instruments have been omitted?) and the ***Kleine Kammermusik*** by Paul Hindemith, discussed in Chapter 17. Note the role of the horn in helping to blend and unify these disparate timbres, and the sense of "breathing" that underlies the phrases of wind and brass music. After all, these instruments cannot play continuously, as violin or piano or pipe organ might; breathing is a natural part of their musical personality.

The Brass Quintet

brass quintet

Brass quintet instrumentation is not as standardized as that of other basic chamber groups. Four of the five members—two trumpets, horn and trombone—are constant; the fifth, however, may be a bass trombone or tuba. Compositions usually specify one grouping or the other. There are also larger brass ensembles that are more suited for outdoor performances or vast ceremonial spaces than intimate "chambers." For an example of this robust ceremonial style, listen to a later sixteenth century canzona by Gabrieli (see Chapter 9). This piece, composed for the enormous spaces of a great cathedral, exploits the idea of contrast—sudden changes in dynamics or register—which the brasses handle so effectively.

Mixed Ensembles

There are many compositions that call for unique chamber groupings, such as Mozart's trio for clarinet, viola and piano, or the Brahms trio for violin, horn and piano. Chamber groupings of woodwind and brass have become more familiar in the twentieth century; a well-known Octet by Igor Stravinsky calls for flute, clarinet, two bassoons, two trumpets, and two trombones. Mixed ensembles of all kinds have flourished during the twentieth century. These may often emphasize instruments that rarely appeared in chamber settings of the past: trombone, guitar, contrabass, or percussion.

The Orchestra and the Conductor

An ensemble of more than ten players has exceeded the limits of intimate chamber music. A group of twenty or more may be considered an ***orchestra.*** Historically, orchestras have been associated with royalty and the courts, since only a monarch could afford to engage many musicians at one time. Ancient Middle Eastern kings were buried with their orchestras—instruments *and* players!—to entertain them in the next world. The Chinese court of the T'ang dynasty (c. 600–900 A.D.) could boast of 500 resident musicians, and an orchestra including harps, lutes, flutes, bells, and drums. The Japanese later based their classical ***gagaku ensemble*** on the Chinese model. The Indonesian ***gamelan*** is another large "orchestra," consisting almost entirely of tuned percussion: bells, chimes, gongs, xylophones. This group plays a fixed body of traditional music, committed to memory and carefully rehearsed; its timbral subtlety and rhythmic synchronization continually amaze Western observers.

In non-Western orchestras, instruments are often assigned certain textural functions which are unchanging. For example, the woodwind players of the ***gagaku*** always have the melodic line, elaborated heterophonically; the plucked strings and percussion always play background patterns. By

A wind quintet, made up of (left to right) clarinet, flute, bassoon, oboe, horn (below); a brass quintet of horn, trumpet, tuba, another trumpet, and trombone (bottom left); a mixed ensemble of violin, viola, cello and oboe (top left). The brass quintet is not shown in its usual western setting!

Lyre. Sumerian, 3rd millenium B.C. This instrument (and, presumably, its performer) had been buried in the mass tomb of a Mesopotamian queen many thousands of years ago. Courtesy of the British Museum.

contrast, a clarinet player of a Western symphony orchestra might be given a lyric, prominent solo melody one moment and tiny background accompaniment (or twenty measures' worth of rests) the next.

The Western orchestra is dominated by the strings, in five distinct groups: first violins, second violins, violas, cellos, and contrabasses. As with chamber ensembles, there is no physical difference between "first" and "second" violins. Woodwinds "in threes" may be called for, and the brass section may be counted on to have four horns, three trumpets, and three trombones. Timpani are almost always present, and individual pieces may call for harp, piano, tuba, saxophone, various percussion intruments and the like.

The number of players in the string section has been growing steadily. When Haydn and Mozart wrote their string parts around 1790 or so, there were approximately fourteen violins (seven first and seven seconds), six violas, four cellos, and two basses. A century later, Gustav Mahler (see Chapter 16) was composing for a string section of at least thirty violins, twelve violas, ten cellos, and eight basses—at least sixty players in the string section. The difference in sheer density between these two ensembles is enormous. Trying to play Mahler with a Mozart-sized orchestra, or Mozart with the Mahler-sixed string body, would be silly (and unfair to the spirit of either work).

Today's orchestra may include woodwinds "in fours," so that individual players never have to switch instruments. There are between sixty and seventy players in the string section, and a number of percussionists to handle the needs of particular pieces. (Traditionally, the timpanist is concerned only with the kettledrums.) The strings sit nearest the edge of the stage, with the woodwinds directly behind them at center stage. Brasses, percussion, string basses, and auxiliary instruments such as piano or harp line the rear and side walls. A typical seating arrangement, subject to modifications by individual conductors, is shown in Figure 6.6.

Each composer uses the resources of the orchestra in a unique, personal way. Compare the way Haydn treats the orchestral sections as levels

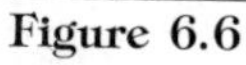
Figure 6.6

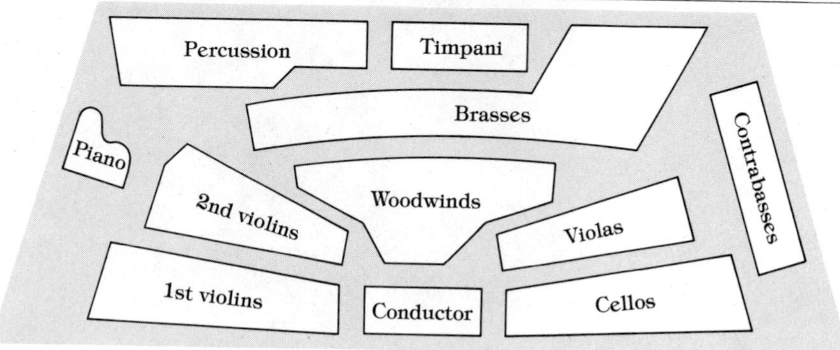

of contrast, in the opening of his ***Surprise*** Symphony (no. 94), to the freer mixture of timbres in Debussy's ***Prelude to the Afternoon of a Faun.*** The Debussy provides splashes of solo color, within a near-chamber-music texture. (Both works are discussed in Part 2.)

The Conductor

Orchestras, bands or large choral ensembles are directed by a ***conductor*** who coordinates tempo, gives cues for entrances, and controls the total balance of all the sounding forces. In these and other ways the conductor shapes various aspects of performance. Although synchronizing the group's beat is essential to the conductor's craft, there is much more to conducting than just beating time. A conductor may work with the players on phrasing and articulation, or subtle nuances of balance, or technical problems: the bowing or fingering of a tricky passage.

Most important, perhaps, the conductor is the only person on stage who really knows what everyone is doing, and who is directly concerned with the total effect. The conductor is responsible for the study of the complete ***score*** (see the next chapter), whereas the orchestral players are reading from ***parts.*** Only the conductor, standing on a podium at the direct center of the action, can grasp the total balance of the sound made by many individual players. Furthermore, one person has to make the ultimate decisions about tempo (how fast is "allegro con brio?") and phrasing; otherwise,

Rudolf Kempe conducting the BBC Symphony Orchestra.

The BBC Symphony Orchestra conducted by Pierre Boulez.

every player in the orchestra might be making a different decision, with some rather unfocused results.

For all these reasons, conducting is a somewhat autocratic profession. Certain conductors are indeed tyrannical, while others work wonders with genial prodding or a protective parental image. Some enjoy being "one of the guys," and others prefer to keep their distance. They must all possess a dazzling assortment of musical skills, a sure sense of their musical wishes, and the ability to transmit those wishes to 100 other musicians (half of whom probably wish that they were conducting instead). They must shape these 100 "voices" into a single musical personality. Much like their closest counterparts in other areas of group performance—theatrical directors and athletic coaches—conductors have demanding jobs and extraordinary responsibilities. To use one last analogy, they are masterly "performers" on that most difficult of Western "instruments," the orchestra.

Some "fantasy-instruments," that exist in the imagination of a musically inventive artist. (Don't look for these in a concert!)

7

Performance and Notation

Blessed are the arts that do not need interpreters.

Arturo Toscanini

Performance Ritual

Music is unlike many of the other arts, in that certain physical activities—those which set sound waves vibrating—must take place each and every time we want to hear it. A painter or sculptor engages in physical activity during the creation of a work, but once completed it is *there,* tangible and permanently fixed in space. It is the "original," from which reproductions in books, catalogs and films are made. In looking at copies, the viewer is aware of the existence of a solid, physically substantial original in a specific place: the Venus de Milo is in the Louvre in Paris, Rembrandt's "Night Watch" is at the Rijksmuseum in Amsterdam, the Empire State Building is on 34th Street in New York City.

On the other hand, where is Beethoven's Fifth Symphony? That question can be answered in many ways. There is Beethoven's own handwritten manuscript, the published editions of his time, and the modern editions of our own century. There are many orchestras performing the work every day, and a vast assortment of recorded versions as well. In fact, the symphony is not defined by a single printed manuscript, or one set of physical gestures that activate the sounds; it is, rather, the sum total of all of them. Each time musicians get together to read the written symbols, or each time a listener performance

puts a record on a turntable and causes loudspeakers to vibrate, the symphony takes shape. *Performance* is necessary to bring it to life.

In this sense, a musical composition depends upon "reproduction" for its continued existence. Any performance of a composition is an original, unique realization, not a copy.

In every society and historical period, the performance of music is associated with important events and rituals: birth, death, marriage, the cycle of the seasons, battles, street parades, sporting events, and so on. During the last few centuries, especially in the West, people have come to regard the performance of music as a "ritual" in its self. They gather in groups just to listen to music, and behave in culturally approved "ceremonial" ways when they do. Audience behavior varies widely, as we might guess: a group of Americans hearing music at a jazz club will behave and listen very differently from the way they would at a symphony concert, or performance of Italian opera. An Italian audience would respond to the opera in a manner that might surprise Americans: cheering, hissing, urging the characters on vocally, as the theatregoers of Shakespeare's time are said to have done.

The people assembled to hear raga performances in India are more than passive spectators. They respond by clapping, moving their heads and bodies rhythmically, crying out their approval, and applauding while the performance is in progress. Western listeners are equally uninhibited at pop concerts or rock events; on the other hand, they try to assume an attitude of absolute silence during the performance of a string quartet, concerto, or similarly "classical" music. The desired silence is only approximated, of course: invariably, sounds of rustled paper, coughs, squeaky seats, or jet planes overhead interact with the sounds of the music. Our radios produce hiss and static, and records have scratchy surfaces. If these all remain within tolerable limits we ignore them, just as other societies admit surrounding sounds into their performance rituals.

Performance Space

A musical performance takes places not in the abstract, but in a setting of some sort: a small room, an outdoor garden, a cathedral, a restaurant, the interior of an automobile (through loudspeakers), and so on. Traditional rituals which include music, such as parades, offer a wider variety of spaces than the more recent ritual of music-making in the concert hall. In the latter arrangement, the audience is usually seated in rows, all facing in one direction towards a raised stage on which musicians stand or sit. Furthermore, neither audience nor players move or speak during the performance. Compare this setting with: Main Street, U.S.A., the spectators line up on both sides of the street while a marching band parades down between them; or a medieval banquet in which music, juggling, conversation, food, and laughter intermingle at random; or an aristocratic nineteenth century salon in Paris, at which Chopin or Liszt plays his piano compositions amidst the

Abraham Bosse, ***Family Concert,*** 1636 (above). Two informal settings for music-making: a choral rehearsal (below) and a seventeenth century gathering. Note the singers, lute, viol, and the conductor with his back to us.

tinkle of glasses and cups, whispered gossip, guests arriving late or leaving early.

Of the fifteen selections in the preceding chapters, only one piece, the Babbitt ***Composition for Synthesizer,*** was heard in the performance ritual and space for which it was intended. This work was designed to be heard on a record or tape, and projected through loudspeakers or headphones. Note that our excerpt is not a "recorded performance" of a piece; it ***is*** the piece, as permanent and fixed as a work of sculpture. But in listening to the Berlioz March, we are responding to one particular performance that has been frozen by recording engineers. A live performance of the ***Symphonic Fantastique*** will sound very different from any recording—because the presence of 1,000 or more spectators makes it a communally shared experience, because the interpretation of tempo, phrasing, and the like will be altered, and because the sheer physical sound of 100 musicians will hit the ears in a way that the reproduction by two loudspeakers (or four or ten) can never begin to match.

In listening to the Gregorian chant example, consider the resonances and echoes of the cathedral or monastery in which the chant was traditionally performed, the placement of the singers, and possibly the movement of singers during a religious ceremony. Note that the Haydn string quartet excerpt was meant for performance in a rather large living room, a more intimate setting than the average concert hall. Purcell's opera ***Dido and Aeneas*** was composed for a school production; costumes and stagecraft are essential to its total effect. Chopin's works were most often heard in the private salons of Paris; Schubert's songs were performed in private homes before small groups of friends, with the composer himself at the piano. Even the blues began at the turn of the century as an intimate vehicle for the expression of very personal, and often painful, experiences of American blacks. The medium gradually evolved from fairly "private" music sung to oneself, or before a few others in small clubs, to an extroverted, "popular" form of entertainment.

The orchestral works of Penderecki and Webern assume the ritual traditions and acoustic space of the modern concert hall. Mozart's horn concerto was designed for concert performance, too, but of the eighteenth century variety: perhaps a large room of an aristocratic estate, for an invited audience. Terry Riley's ***In C*** might be considered an orchestral piece, since it is composed for any number of players on any instruments, but it does not necessarily assume the traditional concert ritual, or concert-hall seating. Since the work's duration is variable, and can last an hour or more, the audience may be invited to move about informally. In some performances of ***In C*** the total space becomes a kind of concourse, gallery, or waiting-room: some people stand and others walk about, still others sleep or read or converse with friends. The boundary between performer-and-audience "space" may be eradicated; players may be situated throughout the total area, with spectators looking at the music over the performers' shoulders.

Public Music and Private Music

In considering Bach's Prelude and Fugue from the *Well-Tempered Clavier* from the point of view of performance space, we might compare the various keyboard instruments (*clavier* means keyboard) on which the preludes and fugues have been played. During the late nineteenth and twentieth centuries they were most often performed by pianists in large concert halls. Bach meant them to be played either on the harpsichord, an instrument of fairly limited volume and thus more suitable for a chamber setting, or on the clavichord, which has an even more intimate dynamic range. Its sounds cannot be heard unless one is virtually on top of it. An audience for a clavichord performance can consist of no more than a handful—or perhaps just one, the performer.

Even though "performance" is usually associated with public ritual, there is also a tradition of ***private*** music. Bach's clavier works, the delicate plucked-string music of ancient China, the sung madrigals of the Renais-

Pieter Bruegel the Elder, ***The Wedding Dance*** (detail), 16th century (left). Chou Fang, ***Tuning the Lute and Drinking Tea*** (top), Vincent M. Langlois, ***Music Party with Guitar and Mandolins,*** 18th century.

sance that were often heard only by the performers, or teaching literature for master and pupil are just a few examples. Such music is often played for a wider public, of course, and modern ***recordings*** make any kind of music available for any situation. The very private world of the clavichord can be entered into by 200 students in a lecture hall; a mighty Mahler symphony for hundreds of performers can be summoned up for one private listener, walking the beach with a transistor radio, or driving a car, or taking a bath. Such situations are no longer rare. More music is being heard, and by more people, in an electro-acoustic state than in its natural form. As composer Murray Schafer has noted, perhaps recorded or amplified music should now be considered the "natural" state!

Listeners should be aware of the inherent ambiguity of recorded performance, the illusion of the very public (or very private) setting being altered to the dimensions of a table-model radio or stereo system. We should also realize that the recorded performance is usually not a single, continuous realization, but a collection of edited "takes" spliced together by a studio engineer: in this respect, akin to a tape composition! Finally, our surroundings create a unique "performance frame" for the recording. Loudspeakers or headphones can be located anywhere, in a rowboat or 30,000 feet up in the sky. When we wear a copy of the Mona Lisa on a T-shirt, or see a Rembrandt on a television screen, the visual image is surrounded by our furniture and the pictures on the walls: so, too, with the Berlioz ***Symphonie Fantastique*** heard during lunch-table conversation.

Performance and "Style"

Performance rituals and spaces influence the creation of music. For example, the qualities that make up Gregorian chant—melodic profile, rhythm, dynamic level and so forth—are linked to the solemn occasion and resonant space of its performance. With any piece of music, these individual qualities and their mutual interaction add up to a special profile often called ***style.*** Terms like "baroque style" or "romantic style" are a shorthand way of indicating the characteristic musical features of certain historical periods. One might also speak of the Italian style as contrasted with French style, or the style of clarinet writing as opposed to piano writing. These individual differences frequently arise from specific needs of performance. German musicians of the nineteenth century, for instance, worked with rituals and spaces different from those of seventeenth century Italy.

style

Composers also work within the limits of instruments, and the relation of these instruments to designated spaces. The clavichord which can create a subtle, distinctive timbre for a small audience a few feet away is not suitable for a larger group. Organ music often exploits the staying power of that instrument, the ability to sustain full tone so long as a key is depressed. But the envelope of harpsichord sound stresses a sharp, percussive plucked attack and almost immediate decay. This is one reason why Bach sustains the sound "wall" of the C-Minor Prelude with broken-chord ostinato configurations, and why so many baroque clavier melodies are embellished with ornaments and trills. Such devices help create the illusion of sustained line on an instrument that is really incapable of prolonging a single tone.

Piano timbre is also percussive, with a sharp attack and relatively long decay. Its ability to vary volume through key pressure led composers to attempt "singing" lines and lyric phrases, even though these are produced by the action of individual keys and hammers (going thud-thud, clunk-clunk, if one listens carefully). Although nothing can be done to disguise the sharp attack, the "meat" of the piano tone can be sustained through the use of the *pedal,* which prevents a damper from cutting off the string's vibrations. Listen to the two Chopin preludes, and note the way in which the pedal has enhanced the overall resonance and lyric quality of the instrument.

Considering the popularity of the piano, organ, and harpsichord, we could argue that the keyboard is the most familiar sight in Western music. What a typically Western object it is, too, summing up all the attributes that uniquely characterize our musical style. The keyboard makes it easy to produce simultaneous sounds (chords), and is ideal for homophonic texture. Secondly, it creates individual pitches in neat, precise steps: it is impossible to glide or slide or swoop from pitch to pitch, or to inflect by way of vibrato or tremolo, all techniques which are practiced in other cultures. Finally, the keyboard symbolizes the Western division of the octave into twelve equal steps. This intonation system has successfully unified the various national styles of European music, whatever their individual differences, under an international performance tradition. As musicologist Mantle Hood remarks, the development of twelve-note equal temperament throughout the West has made it possible for an Italian tenor to sing with a Dutch orchestra under the baton of a Brazilian conductor (perhaps performing the music of a German or French composer).

Tradition and Performance Practice

On the other hand, musicians would not switch from the performance of a French piece to an Italian one, or from eighteenth century music to contemporary music, playing them all the same way. Instead, the present-day musician tries to duplicate those aspects of performance that are associated with a national tradition or historical period: the *performance practice* which characterizes its style. A pianist might be discouraged from playing J. S. Bach's keyboard works on the grounds that a very different instrument is called for. But if the pianist does attempt Bach, he or she may be reminded to: avoid the use of pedal, maintain dynamics in "levels," and keep the tempo absolutely steady. A number of other scholars, with different theories about Bach's performance practice, might dispute some of these suggestions. Almost everyone would agree that none of the above suggestions

performance practice

would apply to the performance of Chopin; on the contrary, expressive dynamic shading, flexible tempo, and the use of the pedal are all important in the performance of romantic piano music.

It is reasonable to ask, "Why don't the players simply follow the printed instructions on the sheet music?" The problem is that many performance details are not included in the notation. Bach left little or no tempo markings or dynamic indications; phrasing was not specified until the late eighteenth century. Performers relied upon the nature of the music itself (and the customs of the time) in choosing details. During the baroque and classic periods it was customary to ***improvise*** certain areas of performance. Since these changed from one occasion to another, they were not fully notated. Furthermore, there was apparently no need to write out every detail if the composer was in charge of his own performance, as when Bach played his own music at the keyboard, or Mozart conducted his own operas.

The written symbols may even be at odds with the actual performance practice. The notated sheet music for a show tune, or the "Mean Old Bedbug Blues" of our listening list, would bear little resemblance to the actual pitch inflections, syncopations, and swinging rhythms that exist in performance. Similarly, scholars have evidence that the great orchestra of the seventeenth century French court played "equal" eighth notes (written) ♫ ♫ as "dotted" rhythms ♪.♬ ♪.♬. During the eighteenth century, melodic lines were embellished by many ornaments. Some of these were written out and others left to the discretion of the player.

There has also been a tendency in the opposite direction: for composers to specify ***all*** the instructions they possibly can, and for performers to adhere to these faithfully. With the invention of the metronome in the early nineteenth century, musicians had an exact index of tempo. Beethoven was one of the first composers to use the new device. Wagner, on the other hand, felt uncomfortable with the rigidity of the metronome, but his scores abound in detailed dynamic specifications. By the early twentieth century, one composer was telling brass players where to point their instruments; another calculated the number of seconds it must take for the curtain to fall in an operatic scene. Stravinsky and Webern scores are so detailed that, in theory, the music could simply "play itself" if each performer followed directions.

Even so, the printed page does not tell us all. It may convey the material elements of a style, but the performance practice for that style may remain elusive. As conductor Eugene Ormandy has stated:

> How are we to understand and follow out the wishes of the composer? The instruments of the orchestra are not what they were in Bach's day. . . . what was an emphatic dissonance for Mozart has become a commonplace harmony for us . . . our social background is not that of Beethoven.

Notation and the Performer

What sort of information ***does*** musical notation convey? A good deal: the written symbols not only tell us about a specific piece, but about broader musical values that are often taken for granted. All languages, spoken or written, are selective; meaning and value are attached to certain sounds or written symbols rather than others. Composers, performers, and listeners operate within a similar musical hierarchy, reflected by notation.

One major function of notation is that of instructing the performer. In telling the player what to do, the composer gives special instructions for musical features that he considers important. Consider, in Figure 7.1, a fairly typical example of Western notation: the opening of the Haydn movement for string quartet. Some of these symbols stand for actual musical events—sounds and silences of specific durational value—while others offer added information to the performer. For example, the Roman numeral II is not "played" by anyone; nor does a musician "play" a clef (such as 𝄞, 𝄡 or 𝄢) although the information conveyed by the clef determines which notes are to sound, and in what register.

There is a single sharp standing directly to the right of each clef. It is an F♯, and indicates that for every F in the printed score F♯ exists instead. This is a simple way of indicating the key of the piece—in the case of Haydn, G major. Composers of tonal music list the ***accidentals*** (sharps or flats) needed for a particular key directly to the right of the clef. it is called the ***key signature.***

Haydn does not indicate a specific tempo, but gives general instructions instead: "rather slowly, with a singing quality." Since this piece was composed before the invention of the metronome, there is no way of knowing whether he would have preferred an objective metronome speed or not. The meter is written as $\frac{2}{2}$, a shorthand symbol indicating two beats to the bar.

All of this general information has to be understood and agreed upon before a sound is made! But let us now assume that the four musicians have begun to play, reading simultaneously from left to right, at a predetermined speed and in tight synchronization. They are given detailed information about pitches, rhythms, and the order in which to play them. Haydn has also been careful to indicate differences in phrasing, connecting certain tones by a slur ♩♩♩. The fermata 𝄐 and the sudden ***sforzando fz*** at measure 12 are also important enough for Haydn to specify.

Now consider those areas that require interpretation, based on knowledge of eighteenth century performance practice. There are various ways of playing embellishments such as the turn 𝆗, and the musicians must agree on these. Haydn indicates virtually no change of dynamics but the players will very likely add subtle shadings of 𝆒 and 𝆓, according to the contour of the line and movement of the harmony. One might also ask: how long is the sforzando to be? How long is the fermata to be held? How sharp

Figure 7.1

Note that each player reads from a separate staff; each staff has its own clef, key signature, and (on the first line only) meter. Bar lines separate the music into measures. All synchronized beats "line up" vertically with each other. Players read from left to right, at an agreed upon speed (tempo).
tempo and mood indication
counting the measures
key signature
indicates 2nd movement of a mult-movement work
II
a "turn" (melodic ornament)
clef
Poco adagio; cantabile
bar line
violin 1
meter
violin 2
viola
dynamic marking
cello
p dolce
mood suggestion
"Accidentals" not already accounted for in the key signature (chromatic notes in this key)
fermata, sustaining the note beyond its rhythmic value
suddenly loud dynamic
fz
slurs
a very short "grace note," has no rhythmic value
slurs indicate phrasing and articulation

or "brittle" are the detached staccato notes? If those symbols were to appear in a nineteenth or twentieth century score, the unwritten codes of "performance practice" would indicate different realizations.

The performing musician responds to all of these signals, while reading at the agreed upon speed. This is in itself a distinctive feature of Western music, as opposed to that of India or China. In those cultures, notation provides an elemental framework upon which one improvises, or a detailed series of performance instructions that may be studied at leisure in advance (and which do not refer to specific sounds). The performer might read such notations as one reads a poem or philosophical treatise. The Western musician cannot read the notes "at leisure," except when practicing alone. During rehearsals or performances, the symbols are read ***as the music passes by***.

The English critic Hugo Cole has likened the Western musician to the driver at the wheel of a car moving along the highway. Driver and performing musician both need signs that are clear and easily readable (at high speed). There is no time to digest a sign reading ***"Left Turns at This Junction Strictly Prohibited."*** The simple **NO LEFT TURN** is much more effective, and is better still. In the same way, Western musical notation has evolved in the direction of greater efficiency. (Our notes, by their shapes and their staff location, combine two crucial items of information, pitch and rhythm, in a single symbol.) Both driver and musician learn to respect some symbols more than others, especially when our response is made on the run. Thus the driver interprets "55 m.p.h." as any speed between 50 and 55, or perhaps even 57, and the performer will give a broad interpretation to ***poco adagio*** or *mp*>. But the Western musician has learned that pitches and rhythms cannot be tampered with, just as the driver knows that STOP demands instant obedience.

Some musical possibilities are ***not*** dealt with in the Haydn score because they are not relevant to the Western tradition.

1. Players are not told which intonation system to use, because the octave division into twelve equal steps is assumed from the outset. Any subtle inflections beyond this, such as a C♯ being played slightly higher than a D♭, are simply considered part of the unwritten performance practice of stringed instruments.

2. Players are not told how to get from one pitch to another: it is assumed that they will jump from level to level ("like a bird hopping from one tree branch to another," as a Japanese listener once described Western melody). Non-Western notations may indicate slides between pitchs and bent inflections. Western performers may attempt such effects, too, but they are considered aspects of "expressive playing."

3. Timbral alterations within a sustained pitch—changes of color, or vibrato and tremolo rates—are not considered, although they are quite important in other musical cultures.

4. Varieties of attack are not given in detail. Haydn's players create sound either by drawing the bow across the strings (known as *arco*) or plucking with their fingers (*pizzicato*). But there are many techniques of bowing and a number of distinctive pizzicato timbres, which did not become important to Western composers until the nineteenth and twentieth centuries. By contrast, Chinese notation dictates the plucking of a string in a variety of ways: which finger to use, which part of the finger, what degree of vibrato or pitch glissando follows the plucking, and so on.

Figure 7.2

Figure 7.3

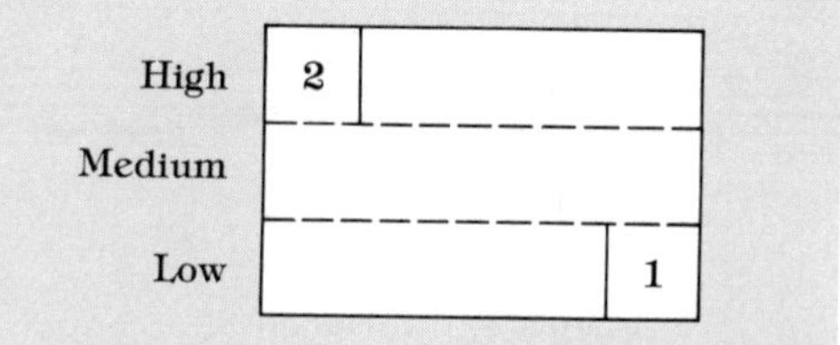

Thus languages reveal value systems. The Eskimo has a number of words that all stand for subtle states of "snow"; the modern American uses many words—convertible, station wagon—that mean "automobile." The Chinese may be concerned about the properties of pizzicato, but not with the elaborate system for synchronizing parts which evolved in the West. Even within Western styles, musical priorities have led to specific written symbols. The earliest examples of Gregorian chant notation show the rise and fall of melodic lines, but no specific pitches. We are given gestures (up or down) without exact levels or interval widths. The absence of specific pitches does not imply that pitch was unimportant; it is more likely that everyone performing the music knew the melody anyway. The notation simply functioned as a memory aid. In later centuries an entirely different tradition of chant notation developed to cope with the demands of an increased liturgical repertoire and the beginnings of polyphony. Note in Figure 7.2 that pitches *are* specified, on a staff of four lines and three spaces. The C at the far left of each staff (top line) is a clef, indicating the note C at that line.

Twentieth century composers also express their musical priorities through notation. In many of his chamber works Morton Feldman wants to create unsynchronized group textures. In scores for these pieces he indicates pitches, articulation and timbre, but does ***not*** specify synchronization. Each player within the ensemble moves at an individual pace without concern for a group "beat." Bar lines, rhythmic symbols and meter signatures are, therefore, all absent from the notation. In other pieces, however, the same composer is concerned with different priorities. Here Feldman carefully specifies all the coordinated relationships between players, but indicates ***no pitches.*** An instrument's total range is subdivided into high, middle and low areas with each large square lasting for four beats, at a set metronome tempo. The smaller boxes within the large squares represent sounds; numbers within the small boxes are the number of notes to be sounded. (See Figure 7.3.)

Types of Notation

Every notation example discussed so far is symbolic, in that a special code must be mastered before the written markings are translated into sounds. This is as true for the Haydn as for the other excerpts: the 𝅗𝅥 of Haydn's "code" does not necessarily ***look*** longer in relative duration than 𝅘𝅥𝅮. Musicians have to learn the rhythmic significance of the symbols.

Figure 7.4

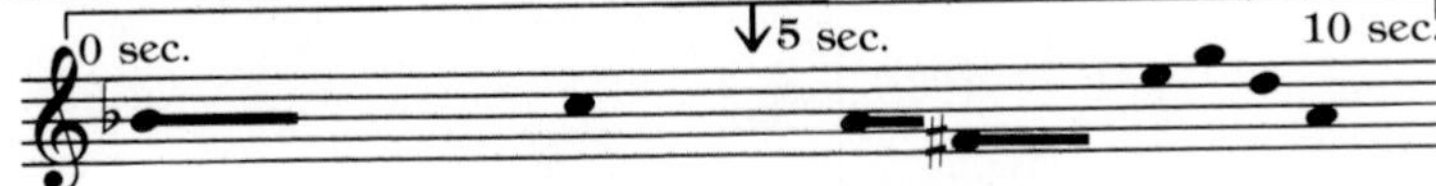

symbolic notations

Symbolic notations can refer to single events, or they may stand for a collection of events. The turn used in Haydn's quartet excerpt converts a single note into a melodic contour of five pitches. Similarly, in ancient Near Eastern music one symbol can represent a whole formula of notes. In a piece of Western tonal music a Roman numeral (IV) or shorthand symbol (Cm7) can tell a performer which chord to play.

graphic notations

Graphic notations, on the other hand, are more visually related to the sound of the music. The hooks and flourishes of ancient notation mentioned earlier indicate the general contours of melody quite graphically . Duration can be visualized, too: assuming that a horizontal line or musical staff takes up *x* number of seconds, some twentieth century composers show the duration of pitches in proportion to that time line, as shown in Figure 7.4. By extending the note head as long as it lasts (proportionally), they attempt to have the written music look the way it "sounds": The graphic approach may be combined with symbolic writing to produce unique, individual hybrid systems. (To read even the example above, we would still need to understand the special meaning of the staff, 𝄞, ♭ and ♯.

Dynamics may be "visualized" as well. It would be easy to estimate which of these two groups (and) is louder. In improvisatory situations, the composer might use a visual "picture" to show complex gestures and densities. Members of a chamber group could all read from the general "score" of Figure 7.5, choosing and interpreting pitches, rhythms, registers and dynamic levels.

A third type of notation is directly addressed to the performer, in terms of the physical activity to be carried out on his or her instrument—the *action* that will produce desired sounds. A familiar example of this type is the *tablature* writing for plucked string instruments. Modern tablature, such as Figure 7.6, indicates finger position for today's guitarist, using a diagram of strings, frets, and areas to be stopped. Other tablatures, similar in their intent, were used for the lutes of Renaissance.

tablature

Figure 7.5

Figure 7.6

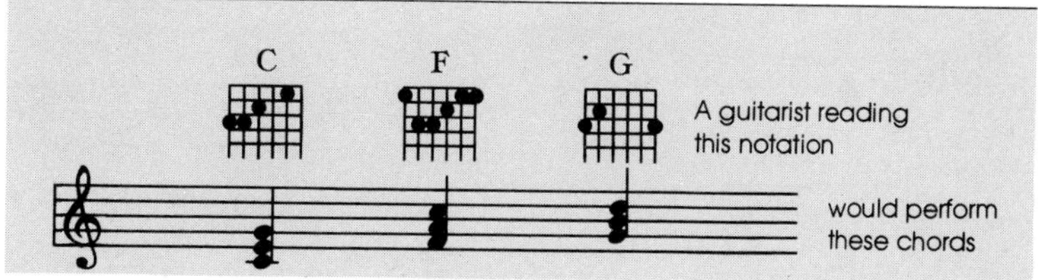

This "action notation" is so specialized that a nonstring-playing musician would have trouble reading it. It could be of great value to the string performer, but it cannot provide a visual record of the sounds to a very wide cross-section of musicians, now or in the future. And that is a legitimate function of written musical symbols in many societies.

The Functions of Notation

There are, in fact, a number of functions of musical notation. At least four can be listed here:

1. The *preservation of the culture,* ensuring that a traditional body of literature is recorded and passed on from one generation to the next. In Asian societies, where much music is either improvised or learned by rote memorization, the notation may consist of "action" tablature for performance, or an essay on the materials appropriate to certain ritual occasions, rather than a description of actual sounds.

2. Another function is that of *stimulating improvisation.* There are written ground plans and lists of suggested materials for the ritual improvisations of India and China. In contemporary Western music, improvisation takes many forms: certain aspects can be predetermined, others freely chosen at the moment of performance, still others flexible but planned in advance. In the excerpt from Barney Childs' *Nine Choral Fragments* (Figure 7.7), the form is flexible, since the fragments may be sung in any order.

3. Notation also communicates *specific instructions to performers.* In the Western tradition, this assumes a very high priority.

4. Notation is essential to *the composer;* it enables him or her to imagine sounds that do not yet exist, to calculate effects in advance, to compare, revise, and ultimately confirm the details of a work.

Notation and the Listener

It would seem that notation is of value to everyone involved in the musical experience—except the listener. But listeners use more than just their ears. They "listen" with their memories, experience, intelligence, and awareness of what's going on around them. They also "listen" with their *eyes,* looking at musicians in performance and looking at the printed score that activates this performance.

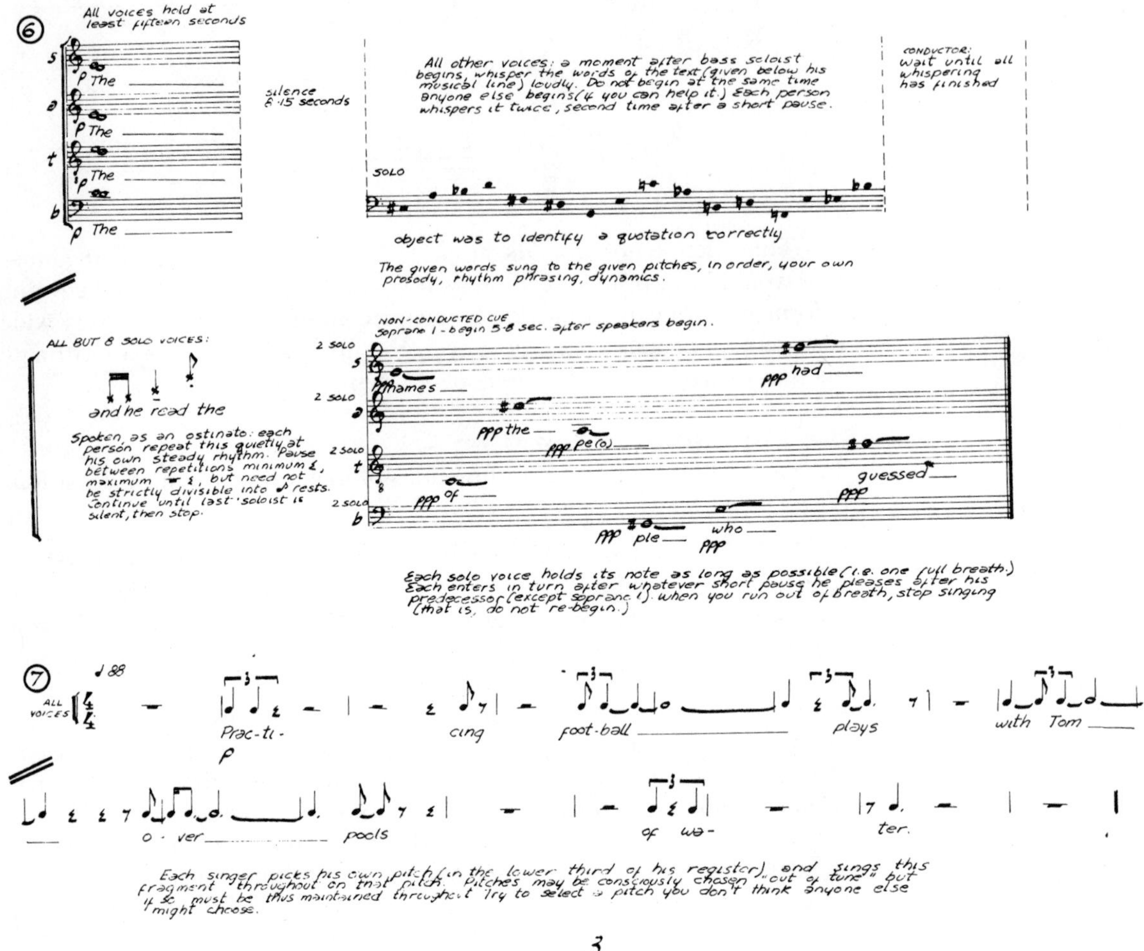

Figure 7.7

By following a performance with the score, the listener can more easily grasp the composer's intentions—what the composer's task was, so to speak. The score also shows what the performer's task *is,* at that very moment, in realizing and interpreting the composer's symbols. The listener does ***not*** have to read music well enough to perform it! That very demanding skill would involve coordination of eye and ear and hand, immediate responses to complex symbols, and many long years of intense training. The listener is not under any of the pressure felt by performers. By following the music and not having to "produce" it on demand, the listener can experience the pleasures of music reading without the tension.

It is not even necessary to become really fluent with pitches and rhythmic symbols on the staff. It will be enough, at first, to observe contours, tempo and meter, bar lines, the way in which different instruments contribute to the overall density and texture. The hardest aspect of reading-while-listening is that of adjusting reading speed (eye movement) to the pace of the music, while simultaneously scanning up and down to observe relationships between lines. Remember that someone else—the performer—has the heavy responsibility of identifying the individual pitches and rhythmic markings. That is not the listener's job.

A number of Western musical symbols have been introduced during earlier sections of this book; for those who wish to pursue the subject further, a more detailed explanation of Western notation will be found in the Appendix. At any level, though, music reading can enhance the activity of listening—making the music more meaningful, and ultimately more pleasurable. Let us now look at the printed music for some familiar pieces: the two Chopin Preludes of our listening list. (See Figure 7.8)

Following Piano Scores

Most piano music is written so that two staves are read simultaneously: the upper and lower staves usually represent the right and left hands, respectively. For listeners following the music, it may be easier to keep track of two lines than it was to follow the four simultaneous staves of the Haydn string quartet excerpt!

The numbers at the beginning of each piece refer to the fact that these are Preludes no. 7 and no. 20 from Chopin's complete set of twenty-four. Interestingly, there are also twenty-four preludes and fugues in Book I of Bach's ***Well-Tempered Clavier.*** Like Bach, Chopin was interested in writing a brief piece in each major and each minor key. One important difference is that Bach proceeded chromatically from key to key: first a Prelude and Fugue in C major, then C minor, then C♯ (or D♭) major, and so on. Chopin chooses to move by key signatures: first C major and then A minor (no sharps or flats), then the keys with signatures of one sharp, and then two sharps . . . all of these related to each other by what is called the ***circle of 5ths.*** This important feature of the tonal system will be discussed further in Part 2.

Prelude no. 7 is in the key of A major (with a signature of three sharps); the large number of accidentals, apart from the signature, reveal the chromatic nature of the music. Some notational features are related to the "tablature" of piano performance: the small numbers above the notes in measures 12 to 15, which indicate fingering, and the ***pedal*** markings below the bass staff. Many pianists would prefer ***not*** to pedal on the first beat of measures 1, 3, 5, 7 and so on, since they are afraid of "blurring" the chromatic dissonances into the rest of the fabric at those moments. But Chopin specifically requests pedalling at those points: perhaps the slightly blurry, unfocused effect at a delicate dynamic level was what he had in

Figure 7.8

The three repeated notes in the melody are always accompanied by a single repeated chord, until measures 11, 12, 13, and 14. What happens there?

* Andantino

7.

p dolce

The accompanying oom-pah is getting thicker.

Pedal indication
Foot engages at *Ped.*, and comes off at ✱.

Ped. ✱ *Ped.* ✱ *Ped.* ✱ *Ped.*

oom-pah is thicker still. Measure 12 begins with the weightiest sonority of all.

✱ *Ped.* ✱ *Ped.* ✱ *Ped.*✱ *Ped.* ✱ *Ped.* ✱ *Ped.*

Grace Note

Crescendo, leading to climax at measure 12

Note different phrase lengths indicated by slurs

Largo

20.

ff

ritenuto — slowing down a bit

p

Suddenly p, after crescendo

The first time that the tonic C occurs in both melody and bass.

Chromatically descending bass line

ritenuto

The repeat is even quieter, but grows to a <.

pp

cresc.

Ped.

* Note: measures are numbered, beginning with the first *complete* measure.

These two chords do not receive separate pedal articulations.

mind. The little grace note on the second beat of measure 15 is a lovely touch, forcing the player to break the chord ever so slightly. Although a pianist may be tempted to arpeggiate the big dissonant chord of measure 12, Chopin clearly indicates a simple break in two, rather than a harp-like sweeping upward.

In looking at the music, our eyes confirm what our ears may have already known—that measure 12 is the high point of the Prelude. It has the thickest chord, and the most dissonant chord of all; the chromaticism which had formerly been confined to melody is now extended to the harmonic progression. The melodic contour has also reached its highest pitch at measure 12. The effect is a strong one precisely because so many factors have converged to make it so.

The C-Minor Prelude, no. 20, apparently has no pedal markings. One might assume that the pianist should use no pedal at all. On the contrary, nineteenth century performance practice would indicate that *every* chord and beat be pedalled separately. However, at one spot in the Prelude Chopin *has* taken pains to specify a particular pedal effect: the final chord of the next-to-last measure. Chopin wants the chord of measure 13 to sound as an extension, or "resonance," of the chord that has preceded it, and not a new statement.

The phrase groupings of the C-Minor Prelude are fascinating in their variety. By following the slurs, note that these groupings are continually doubling: two four-beat phrases, followed by one of eight beats (marked off by a crescendo as well), and then a mysterious final phrase of sixteen beats. That last phrase holds our attention with its chromatically descending bass line, and its suddenly hushed dynamic level. The repeat of the entire final phrase begins as a pianissimo echo, but gains in volume near the end. What dynamic does the player aim for, at the peak of this last crescendo? Chopin has given no indication. He has noted, though, that the tempo is to grow slower at the very end— and he has *not* noted a similar relaxation of tempo at the end of the A-Major Prelude, even though many pianists insist upon one anyway.

Orchestral Score Reading: Some Examples

In following orchestral excerpts with the score, consider the layout of the score itself: the woodwinds (in order of descending register) are placed on the upper-most staves, followed by the brasses, then percussion, and finally the string section at the very bottom of the system. (Perhaps this confirms the strings' traditional role as the foundation of the total fabric.) The staves are placed one above the other, and bar lines often run through entire sections, grouping these staves together more clearly. Remember not only the order of sections from top to bottom, but the ordering of high to low instruments within each section.

The score is the composer's total "blueprint," the entire creation at a glance, and it functions as the conductor's guide in executing the compos-

The conductor (Edo de Waart, shown here in rehearsal) reads from the full orchestral score. But individual players have their own parts; such a part is seen in this photo, as we look over a musician's shoulder.

er's instructions. The orchestral player, on the other hand, typically reads from a part containing ***only*** the music for a particular instrument. Experimental contemporary pieces, particularly those that call for improvisation, may require all players to read from copies of the full score. For traditional styles, though, parts are still the rule.

Figure 7.9 shows the opening of Haydn's ***Surprise Symphony,*** no. 94, which will be studied in detail in Chapter 11. Haydn's orchestra consists of

Figure 7.9

in Nomine Domini
SINFONIA NO. 94
"Paukenschlag"/"Surprise"
London, 1791

Joseph Haydn

Figure 7.10 Marche au supplice
Der Gang zum Richtplatz/March to the Gallows

two flutes, two oboes, and two bassoons; two horns and two trumpets; timpani; a small string section. Note that the cello and contrabass parts are written on the same staff. It was customary for the two parts to duplicate one another in the eighteenth century, with the bass parts sounding an octave lower than the cello's identically written notes. (Later on in the movement, cello and bass will have independent roles to play on occasion.)

Observe Haydn's alternation of woodwind and string passages at the very opening, and the use of horns for added weight and resonance. Note that trumpets (*clarini*) and timpani are not being used; they will enter after a change to a faster, more vigorous tempo later in the movement.

Even in its opening pages, the Berlioz "March to the Gallows" (Figure 7.10) looks as remarkable as it sounds! The list of instruments alone reveals an outrageously inventive orchestral imagination: four bassoons among the woodwinds; a full brass section including two tubas; and a percussion force of four kettledrums (!), bass drum, and cymbals. The opening timbre of the "March" is no less amazing. Note the five-part pizzicato chord of cellos and contrabasses, the muted horns, and the timpani duet of low Gs and B$^\flat$s struck simultaneously. (Berlioz is also careful to specify the kind of drumsticks he wants.)

The Penderecki ***De Natura Sonoris I*** offers a very different visual picture, as seen in Figure 7.11. It is notated along a quasi-graphic time line, rather than with traditional note values. However, there are bar lines to aid synchronization, and a suggestion that the conductor beat in two—the parenthetical $\frac{2}{4}$—within those lines. The spacious appearance of Penderecki's score is partly due to the recent practice of leaving entire lines open (rather

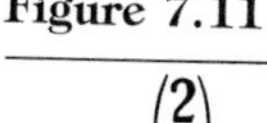

Figure 7.11

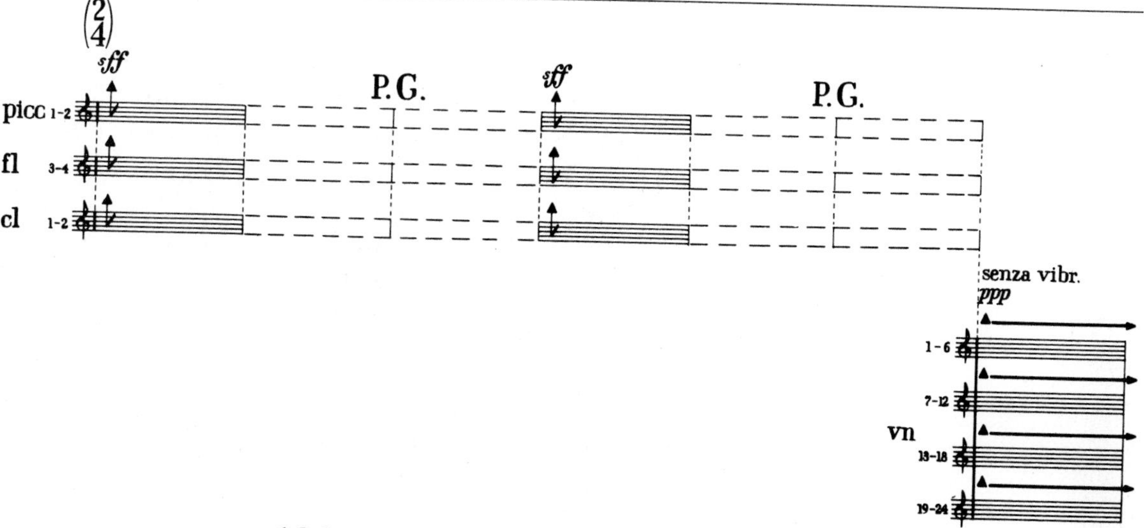

Figure 7.12

than filled with rests) if there is no activity. (A "grand pause" near the beginning is, similarly, indicated by P.G.) Just as there are no traditional rhythmic symbols at the outset, there are no conventional symbols for pitch, either: the opening woodwind and violin notes are indicated by ▲, standing for the highest sound one can produce on an instrument. The violins' ▲ result in a sustained cluster of unusually high sonority, and shortly after rehearsal marking **1** the violas create a lower cluster of specifically notated pitches. By the next page, lower woodwind pitches appear too, some of them altered with unorthodox vibrato effects (~~~~, ∼∼).

Terry Riley's ***In C*** has no score at all, only "parts" that are distributed among the players. The parts are all alike: it is on this premise that the work's entire logic is based. Each player performs a succession of fifty-three fragments, in order (starting with no. 1) and in strict tempo and precise rhythm. The repeated ♫ . . . of the piano ostinato acts as the rhythmic standard, against which all players coordinate their efforts. The first eight fragments of ***In C*** are shown in Figure 7.12. Not only does each musician play all the fragments 1 through 53, in turn, but he or she plays each one ***a number of times,*** the number decided upon individually. In our recorded excerpt, fragments are performed for about a minute or so apiece, on the average; therefore it would be some eight to ten minutes before all players had reached phrase no. 8. (And some might have advanced to no. 9 or beyond.) All players, then, are running the same course, but each at a private speed. A fabric of overwhelming canonic density emerges from this process, at once simple and complex.

Interlude 2
An Introduction To Style

We can now begin listening to music in context, relating different elements to a single impression: a "style." The *style* of a work is the sum total of its distinctive characteristics, such as rhythm or timbre, as they complement and reinforce each other.

Each composition has its own style, insofar as it offers a unique experience. But pieces are also grouped together according to commonly shared features, and we can speak of the style of a large body of literature. A Brahms symphony shares a number of characteristics with other *German* pieces; as a *symphony* it possesses qualities that would be absent in a chamber work or song. The Brahms symphony also reveals certain *nineteenth century* features, typical of a work composed during that period. Similarly, it could be discussed as an example of *"art" music* (as opposed to *"folk" music*), or a representative work of that particular composer. All of these would be stylistic considerations.

This book concentrates upon a *historical* approach to style, organized chronologically from Gregorian chant to the most recent developments of this century. We will draw upon the listening experience and terminology acquired during Part 1, in observing the stylistic traits of historical periods: the distinction between the Renaissance style of a sixteenth century work and an eighteenth century baroque piece, or a Haydn symphony of 1800 and one by Mahler composed a century later. Other style considerations, such as French versus German, will not be ignored, only because the very concept of "history" includes a bit of everything: the history of ideas and the history of great nations, the lives of individual composers, and even the history of style itself.

The very fact that we *have* a history worth exploring is a "stylistic" feature of its own, associated with Western music. During the last 1,000 years it is primarily in the West that striking changes in musical thought and practice have occurred. By comparison, traditions of other cultures have remained much more stable. In studying Japanese or Indian music, "history" would be a secondary rather than primary area of concern.

In Part 2 we will focus on the Western "art" music of the churches, courts, concert halls, and opera houses, rather than folk music, non-Western styles or commercial "popular" styles. This limited scope is not meant to foster a snobbish, elitist attitude: it simply reflects the great historical and geographical continuity of art music. (In earlier times, only a privileged few could travel extensively, and only the clergy and aristocracy had their music written down.) In the twentieth century "concert" and "pop" styles interact frequently. This productive cross-fertilization will be discussed in the final chapters.

Different styles call for different listening skills. A concentrated, focused ear will be essential, even when hearing some works composed before 1600 or after 1900, that were not intended for intense concert-hall listening. We may also observe that certain musical factors have evolved historically in a linear direction. Other aspects of style seem to alternate in great swings of taste, moving between the "abstract" and the "emotional," "rational" and the "mystical"—or what we often label classical and romantic.

Finally, remember that each composition has special features of its own. Textbooks invariably dwell upon similarities, comparisons and stylistic family resemblances among works, but very often it is the *unique* quality of a piece, an individual stroke of brilliance, that offers the greatest pleasure. Once we recognize and comprehend the common language of a style, we can take fuller delight in the unique things a musician may "express" within it. Music is, after all, not only sounds and durations but ideas, concepts and statements.

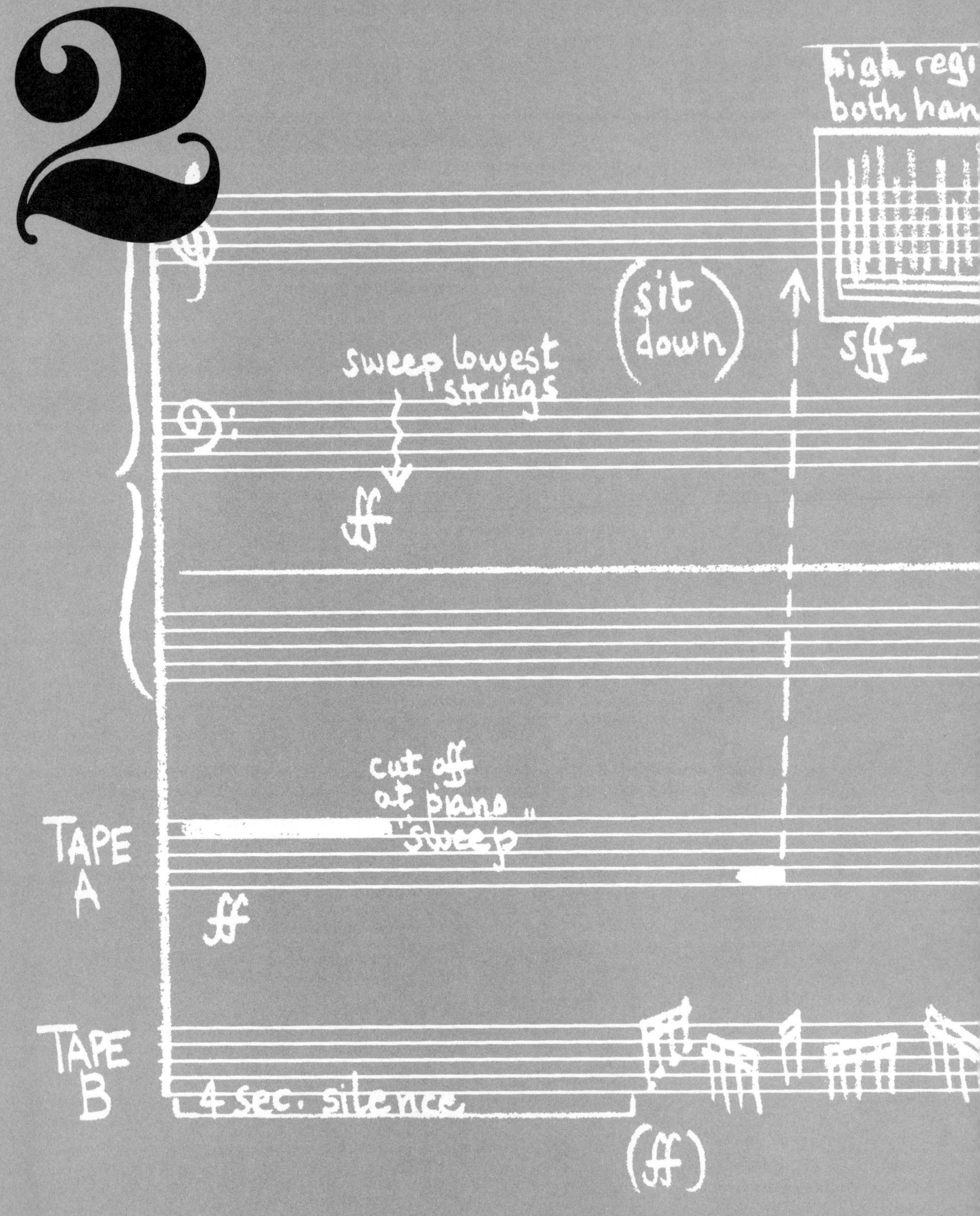

2
high regi
both han
(sit down)
sffz
sweep lowest strings
ff
cut off at piano "sweep"
TAPE A
ff
TAPE B
4 sec. silence
(ff)

Musical Styles

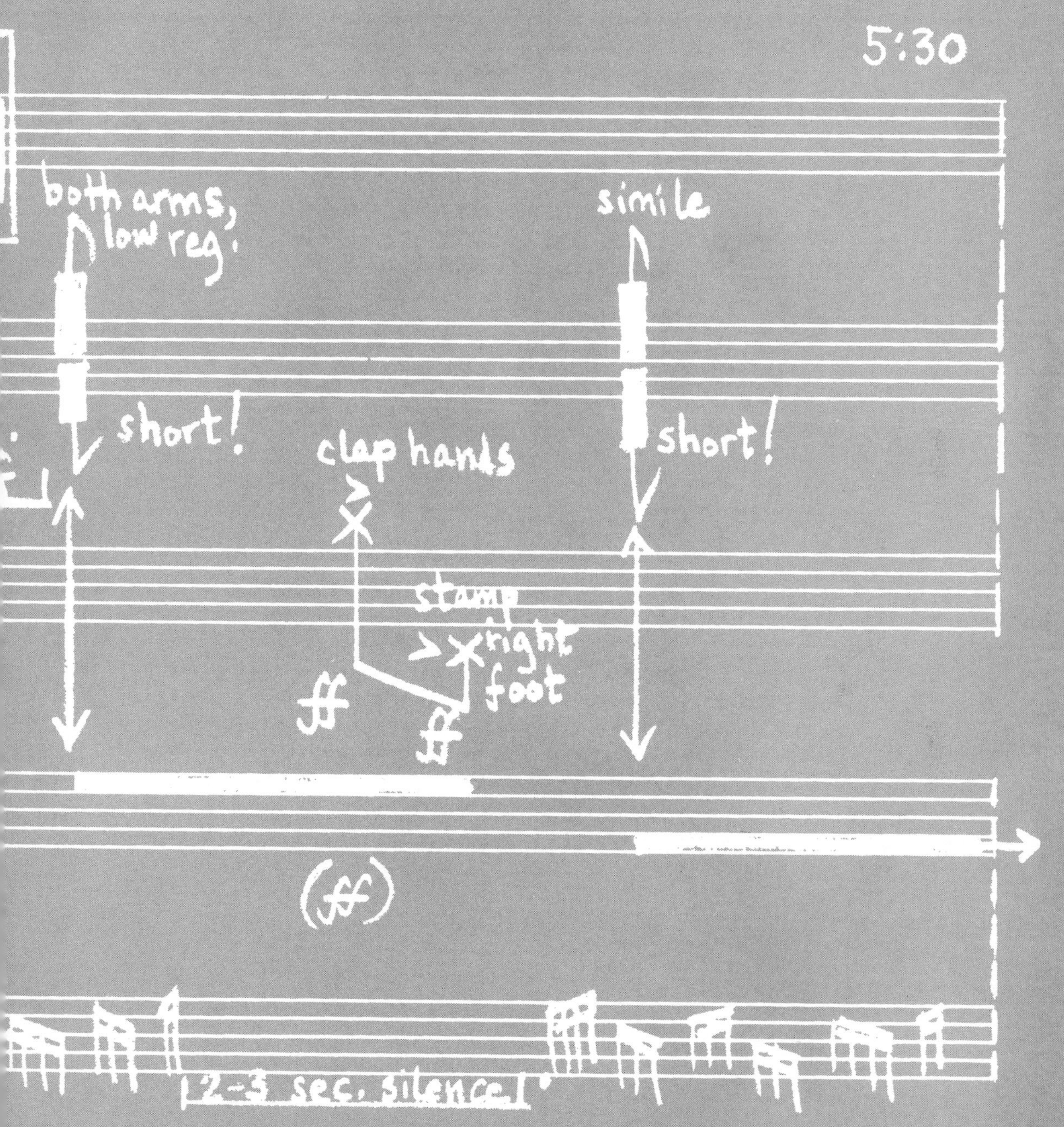

8

Music Before 1600

We need but one instrument: the peaceful word of adoration, not harps or drums or pipes or trumpets.

Saint Clement of Alexandria, c. 200 A.D.

Music in the Ancient World

Our knowledge of ancient music is basically knowledge *about* music. The Bible refers to the trumpets bringing down the walls of Jericho, or David singing his psalms. The Greek philosophers also wrote about music and dance; Plato is particularly eloquent on the subject of music's moral and political implications. Furthermore, much of Greek poetry and drama, from the epic tales of Homer to the plays of Sophocles, was probably sung or chanted, accompanied by plucked stringed instruments such as the lyre. We know what the lyre and other ancient instruments looked like, because Egyptian wall paintings and Greek sculpture and decorated vases show musicians and dancers in considerable detail.

Unfortunately, we do not know the actual *sounds* of ancient music. There are only a very few Greek fragments that seem to be notations for music making, and not enough information about the symbols to reconstruct their meaning. In all likelihood, notation was not a very important aspect of ancient music. Musical patterns were probably prescribed by oral tradition, passed from master to student, and improvised within traditionally fixed limits.

One could guess about certain features of ancient music by studying present-day Asian, Indian, Arabian and African ceremonial and court musics. These styles still resemble ancestral models to a remarkable degree, and their characteristics may have been common to early Western music as well:

1. Textures are mainly ***monophonic*** or ***heterophonic,*** with greater complexity resulting from the addition of percussion or a sustained drone. Such textures are not likely to require a sophisticated notational system for their perpetuation; the very fact that we have so little evidence of early notation may offer a clue about the texture of ancient music.

2. Music is conceived in many cultures as part of a total ritual, not as a separate phenomenon. Folksong researchers often discover that people in so-called primitive communities cannot separate music into "words" and "tune"; our modern Western distinctions may be literally meaningless. Some of Plato's baffling comments on music, morals, and citizenship may have to do with much more than music: perhaps poetry, dance, and ceremony were included in his definition. Musicians may have been less concerned with the manipulation of "form" and "material" than with the ritual usefulness of their work. To paraphrase musicologist Bruno Nettl's observation about modern preliterate culture, the ancient musicians were more concerned that music be "good" than "beautiful."

3. When any community abandons the nomadic way of life and settles on a particular piece of land, a separate class of "musician" emerges. There is also a distinction between vocal and instrumental music; from the written evidence of the ancient world, this may have even been a class distinction, with instruments accorded lower status. The Greeks felt that the words were crucial to music: Plato asks, "What can a melody and rhythm mean unless there is a text?" And Old Testament references to instruments alone, without voices, are practically nonexistent.

Blind Harpist (opposite,) Egyptian, and Etruscan Frieze, ***Women Playing Kithara, panpipes and aulos.*** In both of these examples we see several ancient instruments, including the double flute (aulos).

Saint Clement's statement, quoted at the head of this chapter, indicates that the early Christians also preferred the "word of adoration" to the sounds of instruments. Like the Hebrews and Greeks before them, they were concerned with total ritual; words, the bearers of literal meaning, had a prime role within that ritual. The early Christians also associated instruments with the more obvious excesses of the Roman Empire, from battles to drunken orgies to pagan festivals.

The Middle Ages

The number of Christians within the empire was growing all the time; by the year 311 A.D. the Roman government officially ceased persecuting members of the new sect, and the Emperor Constantine was baptized into the church a few decades later. A little more than a century later the Roman Empire fell, its political power dissolved and Europe was divided into a number of tribal kingdoms. The only centrally unifying force, the lone voice of cultural stability, was the church.

Between the fourth and sixth centuries the liturgical music of the church (music incorporated into actual services of worship) gradually evolved to a point where thousands of *chants* were in use. These melodies grew out of the meeting of Greco-Roman, Syrian, Egyptian, Jewish, and Oriental cultures in Constantinople (the wealthiest city in Europe after the fall of Rome). Late in the sixth century, Pope Gregory I supposedly organized and codified some 3,000 of these chants. Although there is very little evidence to support his involvement with such activity, this body of early Christian liturgical literature is called *Gregorian Chant.* (It is also called *plainsong* or *plain chant.*) Although Gregorian chants were gradually adopted throughout Europe, they were not yet written down; monks and priests taught the liturgy orally to succeeding generations. By 900 A.D. a technique had been devised for notating the chants, and for hundreds of years thereafter this was the only notated music. In music, as in other areas, the church held a virtual monopoly on learning and literacy.

Gregorian Chant

Gregorian Chant

Some important features of chant, particularly its *monophonic* texture and unaccompanied vocal timbre, have been discussed in earlier chapters. In the interpretation of our recorded example, the gentle, peaceful flow of melody, rhythm, and dynamics follows the natural inflections of speech. The entire effect is that of understatement, focusing our attention on the religious service. This music was not intended for concert performance before an "audience." The earliest audiences for chant were monks engaged in their daily devotions. Music was but one element in an elaborate service of worship. The movement of the robed participants, the candlelight, and the reverberation of the sounds in the great Romanesque or Gothic churches and monasteries, all contributed to the total effect.

Syllabic and Melismatic Styles

syllabic setting

melismatic setting

There are various ways in which the notes and words of chant fit together as shown in Figure 8.1. A *syllabic setting* of the text assigns one pitch to each syllable. A more impassioned, almost ecstatic setting occurs when a single syllable is given a whole series of notes, or *melisma.* The word "Alleluia," offers an ideal opportunity for an extended, joyous *melismatic setting.* There is also a middle ground, in which one syllable receives a few

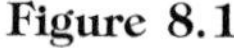
Figure 8.1

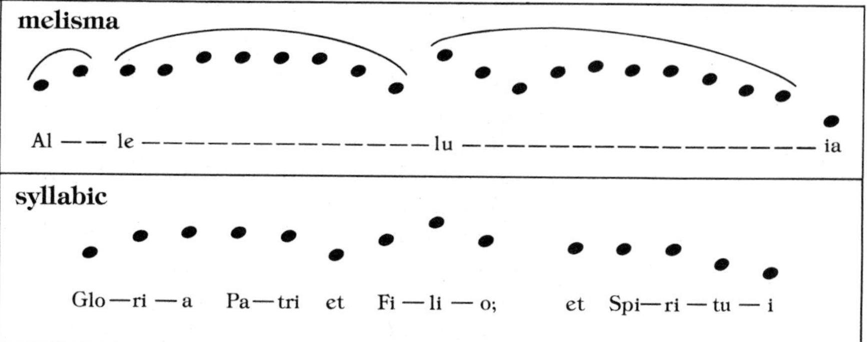

notes. Figure 8.2 presents a plainsong hymn that would have been quite familiar during the Middle Ages, called "Ave Maris Stella." It dates from the ninth century, and contains elements of different word-setting styles.

The Church Modes

A chant such as "Ave Maris Stella," or the example used in Part I in this book, may use a scale unlike the modern major or minor. The chant has a definite pitch center, and is called ***modal,*** because it is built upon one of the medieval ***church modes.*** As noted in Chapter 2, these modes can be found at the piano as successions of white keys. The mode of "Ave Maris Stella" extends from D to D (white keys only); it sounds almost like a D-minor scale, except for a half-step interval between notes 6 and 7. The intervallic arrangements within each mode give it a unique character, and account for the distant, archaic sense that some listeners associate with early music.

Chant and the Church Ritual

The texts of a plainsong were usually taken from a Bible, particularly from the Psalms (a carry over from Jewish liturgy). Chant was used in the celebration of the ***Mass,*** and for the various services that called the monks to prayer an additional eight times a day.

Mass

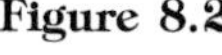
Figure 8.2

Ave maris stella,	*Hail, star of the sea,*
Dei Mater alma,	*Bountiful mother of God*
Atque semper Virgo,	*And ever Virgin,*
Felix caeli porta.	*Blessed gate of heaven.*

Ordinary
Proper

The ***Mass,*** the most important service of the Catholic Church, symbolizes and re-enacts the Last Supper of Jesus Christ. By the year 1000 it had developed a specific format, a series of prayers and acclamations in an unvarying sequence. There are two kinds of liturgy within the Mass: those texts that remain the same in every Mass (the ***Ordinary***) and those texts which vary according to the particular day of the Church year (the ***Proper***). The five sections comprising the Ordinary are the most familiar: (1) ***Kyrie eleison; Christe eleison.*** Lord, have mercy; Christ have mercy. (Note the Greek, rather than Latin, words here.) (2) ***Gloria in excelsis Deo*** . . . Glory to God in the highest . . . (3) ***Credo in unum Deum.*** I believe in one God. (4) ***Sanctus, Sanctus, Sanctus.*** Holy, Holy, Holy. (5) ***Agnus Dei, qui tollis peccata mundi*** . . . Lamb of God, who taketh away the sins of the world . . . These five fixed "movements" are interwoven with the variable sections of the Proper. The total ceremony, therefore, maintains great richness and variety within a familiar framework. The Mass provides the first large-scale multi-movement format in Western music. Its wide expressive range has fascinated composers of every century, including our own.

Secular Song and Dance

Outside the church and monastery walls a very different kind of musical life flourished. Wandering minstrels moved about the countryside entertaining people with songs, stories, jokes, acrobatics, juggling, dancing, and anything else that might get them a night's lodging and a meal. They were distinctly unpopular with civil and religious authorities, as their songs—and deeds—were often irreverent, satirical, and vulgar. They were the radio, television, newspapers, and magazines of the Middle Ages, bringing entertainment and information to town and castle. Their music was basically monophonic; although their songs were frequently accompanied by simple instruments, it is unlikely that they added truly independent parts. Most probably the music was modal as well, but it might have been more easily accented, boisterous, and timbrally varied than the music of the monastery.

Unfortunately, our hunches regarding this music cannot be verified. Secular music was not written down before the twelfth century; during the early Middle Ages, only the church musician had the comfort, motivation, and literacy to notate musical thoughts. But by the twelfth and thirteenth centuries a new class of secular musician had emerged. Many of the former street-musician class had found respectability by attaching themselves to the households of noblemen, acting as minstrels at court and accompanying battles or tournaments with their trumpets and drums. It was the nobles themselves who now composed music: songs of love, tall stories, obscene ditties, comments on politics or on the recently begun Crusades. It was very fashionable for a knight to be a musician and poet; the aristocratic creative artist was a far cry from the wandering minstrel turning somersaults, exhibiting trained animals and having coins tossed at him in the market square a few centuries earlier. The best-known example of the chivalrous noble-

troubadours
trouvères / Minnesinger

man-composer was Richard the Lion-Hearted (1157–1199), but there were many others. They were known as ***troubadours*** in southern France, ***trouvères*** in Northern France, and ***Minnesinger*** (who sang of ***Minne,*** or courtly love) in Germany. All of these poet-musicians used the vernacular language of their country or region.

More than 1,500 of their songs have been preserved in notated form. They may resemble folksongs with catchy, easily remembered melodies, and phrases or entire stanzas that repeat (often creating strophic forms). Their scales lean more to the major and minor than the church modes. We know that the songs were accompanied by instruments, even though the written music consists of monophonic single lines. Perhaps the instrument parts provided heterophonic embellishment, or a drone background. Different stanzas might have alternated singing and playing. The performers were most likely the noble's own court minstrels.

"Or la truix" (twelfth and thirteenth century trouvère song)*

Here is an example of a knightly love song of the Middle Ages, set to a French text of courtship. ("I find it hard to woo her, indeed, because she is so simple . . . I was too presumptuous . . . 'tis that which hurts me.") The melodic range of the song, like that of Gregorian chant, is relatively narrow—within an octave—although the song's contours are more angular. Note, too, the use of the major scale here, and formal structure that stresses the repeat of a catchy "refrain" both in words (at the very beginning and end) and music (three times during the song).

During this period, instruments were used in connection with vocal performances or dancing. The early minstrels and troubadours accompanied themselves with a wide variety of instruments, including lyres, fiddles, horns, bagpipes, and mechanical hurdy-gurdies. Very likely these songs were danced as well; the refrain of a trouvère song, for example, could be sung and danced by the onlookers. Dancing was enjoyed by all classes, except the clergy. They associated such revelry with the devil, and were most horrified when dancing took place in the churchyards, as it frequently did. Because of their link to dancing and carousing, medieval instrumentalists were considered socially inferior, even to minstrels.

*This can be heard on the "Masterpieces of Music Before 1750" Record Set, Haydn Society 79038E, Record 1, Side 1.

Medieval Dances

Instruments of the Middle Ages were often classified as either "indoor," with quiet, gentle voices, or raucously strident objects for "outdoor" use. The latter included extroverted, buzzing double-reed instruments such as the krummhorn and rauschpfieff, which were frequently used in the performance of dance music. Dances themselves, whether courtly or folk-based, were based upon sharply accented rhythmic patterns, grouped into melodic phrases which could be (and most likely were) repeated a great many times; the many repetitions allowed the music to go on as long as the dancers wished, and also encouraged melodic improvisation and switching of timbres among those playing instruments.

In such early dances as the ***Estampie*** or ***Ductia,*** or the very rapid Italian ***Saltarello,*** the strong metric feeling can be broken down into a "compound" grouping of triple patterns. The symmetrical, balanced phrases, repeating as often as the performers seem to wish, alternate two different phrase ***endings:*** these were known as "ouvert" (open) and "close." Examples of thirteenth century Ductia and slightly later Estampie can be heard in a performance by the Ricercare Ensemble of Zurich (Desto DC 7190). The instruments include recorder, krummhorn and tambourine. Note that the monophonic melodic contours are set against percussive beat patterns. A similar effect can be heard in the performance of a thirteenth century Saltarello, on rauschpfieff, tabor (drum) and tambourine (Vanguard VSD 71223).

Under certain circumstances, the melodic line and percussive part could be played by the ***same*** person—a "one-man band," so to speak, playing both ***pipe and tabor.*** The performer could hold, and finger, the woodwind instrument with one hand, while using the other hand to beat upon a drum slung over his arm or secured to his waist by a strap. A charming Medieval dance is performed in this manner on the Early Music Consort of London's record anthology ***Instruments of the Middle Ages and Renaissance*** (Angel SBZ-3810, Side 1, Band 9).

The Growth of Polyphony

The most important development in Western music, the movement away from monophonic texture, begins before 900 A.D. By this time there is evidence of chants being sung at simultaneous, parallel pitch levels: a treatise of the period, for example, instructs church musicians in the art of singing in parallel 4ths, 5ths, and octaves. (See Figure 8.3.) Singing in parallels is a common phenomenon among human beings, since high and low voice ranges are roughly an octave apart, with the middle range a 4th or 5th between these.

organum

The new church polyphony was called ***organum.*** Originally the voices were kept apart at a fixed interval, moving in parallel. This in turn led to a new development, in which the voices were ***melodically*** independent of

Figure 8.3

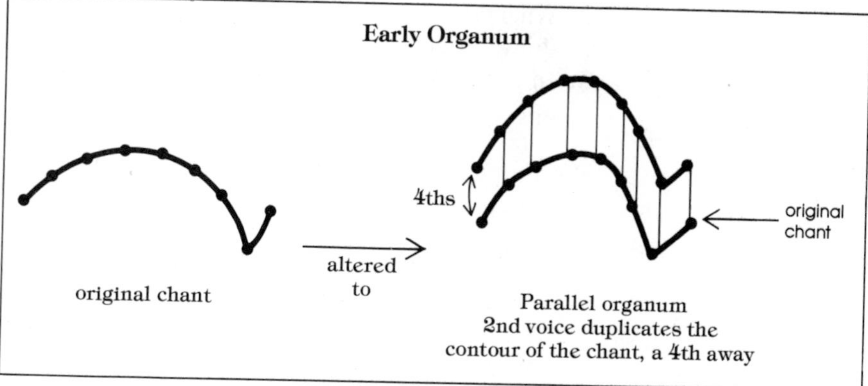

each other. By the twelfth century the voices had become ***rhythmically*** independent as well; these changes are suggested in Figure 8.4. The Gregorian chant, stated in long held tones, served as the lower voice of a two-part texture. Above it, the added voice sang many shorter notes, often melismatic, against each note of the chant. These developments established the 4th, 5th, and octave as the most important ***consonances*** of medieval polyphony. Such concepts as consonance or dissonance would be irrelevant to earlier monophonic music.

In comparing early polyphony, with Gregorian chant, the listener can detect some important changes in musical focus:

1. The smooth, measureless flow of monophonic plainsong is gone. By contrast, the earliest organum seems "bumpy," its two voices locked together in a series of cold, "hollow"-sounding (to our ears) 4ths and 5ths.

Figure 8.4

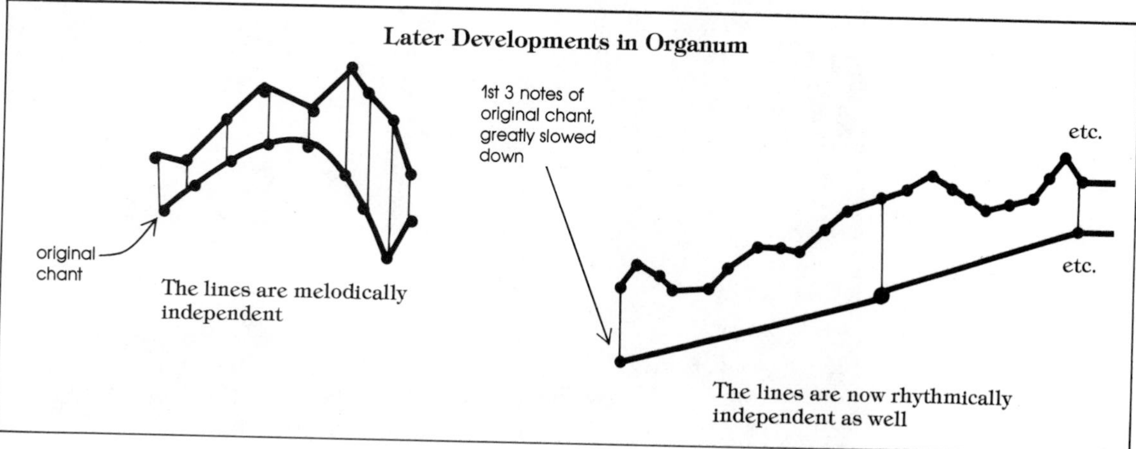

2. Whereas monophonic chant seems subservient to the text, organum draws attention *to itself* in a significant way.
3. In the later styles of organum, such as the melismatic, the added part appears more important than the liturgically sanctioned chant voice. It is certainly more *interesting:* a contradiction between the symbol of church, authority, and tradition, and the assertive, fanciful decoration which literally envelops that symbol.
4. The development of polyphony brought about important changes in musical *notation,* especially in rhythm; those singing different parts needed to know when to synchronize and coordinate their lines. Pitches and intervals had to be precisely indicated as well. The older oral and improvisatory traditions were gradually being replaced by a more tightly controlled practice.

The Gothic Style and the Motet

The mid-twelfth century marked important changes in the life of medieval Europe. After the first Crusade (in 1096), wealth from the East flowed back along the Crusade routes, to Italy and then northern Europe. Cities began to grow in size and power; one of them—Paris—had become Europe's cultural

Chartres Cathedral, Rose window, 14th century.

leader. A university (the Sorbonne) was founded there in 1140, and the first stones of Notre Dame Cathedral were laid in 1163. Significantly, the first important composers of Western history (at least the first whose names we know) were church musicians associated with Notre Dame. Their work took place not at a cloistered monastery, but in an urban cathedral setting, open to a broader public of townspeople, merchants, students, and nobility, as well as clergy. From this point on the large city was to assume the role of intellectual center.

The composer Leonin was active at Notre Dame during the 1160s and '70s; his successor Perotin flourished from the 1180s into the early years of the next century. The two men brought melismatic organum to a new stage of development, introducing measured, rhythmically patterned lines against the long notes of chant. Polyphony was extended to three and four voices, and new terms were used to describe the various voices. The lowest (chant) voice was known as the ***tenor,*** derived from the Latin "to hold" since that voice contained long held notes; the upper part were called duplum, triplum, and quadruplum. In a work such as Perotin's ***Viderunt Omnes,*** four voices create a grand, resonant sound. As the text refers to the Christmas season, we may assume a joyous, festive quality as well. "Viderunt omnes fines terrae salutare Dei Nostri: jubilate Deo . . . (All ends of the earth have seen the salvation of our God: sing joyfully . . .)"

Perotin

Viderunt Omnes (Gradual)*

Note the regularity of the "measured" polyphony; an unchanging triple beat underlies the entire texture. Our modern system of rhythmic notation had not yet developed; Perotin was limited to a few basic ***rhythmic modes*** or patterns of long and short which could be applied to any pitch contour. The rhythmic modes were all basically triple in their pulse, perhaps because the number 3 symbolized the Trinity and therefore the logic of the universe. (They can be written out in $\frac{3}{4}$ or $\frac{6}{8}$ time.) By combining "modal" repetitions of ♩ ♪, ♩♩♩, ♪ ♩ and other patterns into longer rhythms, Perotin creates complex structures.

The pitches often clash in a way that seems harsh and angular to modern Western ears: try to hear the total sound as a mixture of overlapping *lines,* rather than as "chords." The held tone of the lowest voice is quite prominent at first. This is one pitch of the original chant sung at greatly slowed tempo; after a while it moves on to the next note of the chant (but still sustained). Later on the tenor joins the other voices in rapidly moving triple-meter patterns.

*A performance by voices and instruments can be heard on Sine Qua Non album MS-5001 (Record 2).

Perotin enjoys tossing tiny figures back and forth from one voice to another, as each part echoes or anticipates the material of the next. With this technique, he approaches ***imitation*** (see Chapter 4), which became important some 300 years later. There are very strong cadences at points of arrival, but the pitch material is modal, rather than "tonal" in the modern sense.

Some scholars think that instruments may have been used in church services by the twelfth century. Large churches and cathedrals had organs: there are ninth-century descriptions of organs with as many as 400 pipes. And it is possible that other instruments, especially reeds and brasses, might have been added at special festive occasions—such as a Christmas performance of ***Viderunt Omnes.***

Hans Memling, ***Angels.*** An "angelic" concert of string, wind, and brass instruments, as shown in a Flemish Late Gothic painting.

Adjectives used to describe this new musical style ("spacious," "soaring," "fanciful") are often used to describe Gothic architecture as well. Ironically, the label ***Gothic*** was originally an insulting term, directed at a way of living thought only fit for barbarians (Goths)! In any case, the adventurous polyphony of Notre Dame, like the Gothic cathedral, spread from France to the rest of Europe. And like its counterpart in architecture, the Gothic musical style reflected a greater sense of security. The church was still the greatest force in Europe, and the church buildings themselves were the most imposing structures in towns and villages—often filling the role of school, community center, theater, and police station all in one. But Gothic cathedrals were less fortress-like than earlier churches: no longer refuges for those seeking protection from outside evil, but vast, joyous monuments to the glory of God.

The princely courts of Europe were gaining power, too; troubador and trouvère music of the thirteenth century reveals this secular confidence. In 1215 the nobles of England could force King John to sign the Magna Carta. Merchants were prospering, and Marco Polo was to leave for the Orient in the 1270s. The works of Aristotle, admired for their sense of "system," were being rediscovered; their principles were reconciled with Christian belief by Saint Thomas Acquinas. In many ways this was a highly "systematic" era, with or without Aristotle. People believed that a Divine Logic ruled the universe. Music was one of the subjects taught at the medieval universities, but from a viewpoint that we might consider closer to physics. It was the ***logic*** of music that was judged worthy of study: the overtone series and intonation systems, rather than literature.

The Gothic Motet

By the thirteenth century, words were added to the second (duplum) voice of measured organum. This voice was called the ***motetus*** ("mot" meaning "word"), and the entire composition was known as a ***motet.*** Strange as it may seem, the motet used several sets of words at once. The tenor retained the Latin text of the original chant; the motetus had an entirely different text, and eventually a third set of words was added for the triplum. The words for the upper parts could be in Latin or in the vernacular (French), and might be sacred or secular.

motet

The complete ***motet*** was named after the opening words of each of the lines. For example, a typical motet of the 1200s, ***Aimi! Las!/Doucement/ Omnes,*** sets the following texts:

Triplum:	Aimi! Las! vivrai je ainsi Que de mes dolours la bella n'avra merci? . . .	*Woe! Alas! Shall I so live, if my lovely will have no mercy? Her sweet figure, her little mouth . . .*
Motetus:	Doucement me tient amours Si que ne puis departir . . .	*Sweetly I am held by love, and I cannot leave her . . .*

Figure 8.5

The tenor has only the simple word Omnes at the very beginning. Its melody is based on a phrase from the Christmas gradual ***Viderunt Omnes*** (the same used by Perotin in our earlier example). The musical style is strongly rhythmic, in the characteristic manner of Notre Dame polyphony, and resembles the Perotin example in its sonorities—either clashing, or oddly hollow and open—as well. In Figure 8.5, observe the strong 4ths and 5ths on downbeats, and the harsh dissonances on weak beats.

The total effect is aggressively linear and "horizontal," each line strengthened by its alliance with an independent text. Moreover, sacred and secular concerns often mingled. The vernacular texts, like those of the troubador and trouvère songs, dealt with topics ranging from the delicate to the earthy and profane, although usually reflecting some aspects of the liturgical chant from which the tenor voice was taken.

Instruments may have been used to support the sustained tenor of the motets. Perhaps that part was simply played rather than sung. Some manuscripts have tenors without texts, or tenors drawn from dances of the time (which would be wordless). In other instances, fragments of secular song, even bawdy drinking tunes and cries of street vendors, were used as the source of the tenor part! The motet, an outgrowth of the church organum, served to link the worship ritual with the larger society outside the cathedral. It was performed in sacred ***and*** secular settings, enriching both.

We should also note a trend, increasing throughout the development of polyphony: the widening distance between the original chant (substance or spirit) and its ***use*** in complex musical texture. When a lengthy structure is based upon a single phrase of plainsong, or if a tenor is played on an instrument rather than sung, the original chant has become an abstraction, a springboard for the creative imagination. It was regarded as ***cantus firmus*** against which ornate textures could unfold. And if liturgical material could be so abstracted, why not also worldly songs? Apparently the greatest musical concern of Gothic composers was that of ***variation,*** not as a specific form or technique, but as a fundamental creative attitude. The basic principles of variation, that of unity and variety occurring simultaneously, lies at the essence of organum and Gothic motet.

The Fourteenth Century

Great changes took place in Europe during the fourteenth century. Most important were two tragic occurrences: the beginning in 1337 of the war between France and England that was to last until 1453 (aptly termed the 'Hundred Years' War), and the great bubonic plague known as the Black Death, which killed one-third of Europe's population around the year 1350. The authority of the church was severely tested by such events, and it was further weakened by corruption and dissension from within. During the late fourteenth century there were two rival Popes, one based in Avignon in southern France, the other in Rome. In contrast to the security and confidence of the thirteenth century, this was a period of great confusion, of beliefs shaken and traditions questioned.

There was an increased interest in the secular world: the depiction of individual personality and facial expression in the style of the Italian painter Giotto, or the sensual flavor of Boccaccio and Chaucer in their worldly, earthy tales. Similarly, the writings of Dante and Petrarch reconciled the "learned" and the "vernacular," the eternal and the immediate, not only as expressions of God's work, but for their own sakes. Composers of the time turned increasingly to secular employment at the courts of the aristocracy and to secular musical genres—songs and dances. With church and court competing for their services, composers developed facility in a variety of styles.

The Ars Nova

Ars Nova

In France, a system of rhythmic notation had evolved to the stage where *duple* patterns could be represented. The new notation was enthusiastically praised in a treatise entitled ***Ars Nova,*** contrasting the "new art" of the time with the old-fashioned ideas of the past (Ars Antiqua). The term ***Ars Nova*** eventually came to stand for the style itself. Its most distinguished adherent was Guillaume de Machaut (1300–1377), widely regarded as the outstanding composer of his time. (Note that musicians had begun to acquire individual reputations. By contrast, Leonin and Perotin might have been as anonymous as the men who built and designed Notre Dame Cathedral, had it not been for glowing reports written about their work by others.)

Machaut wrote music for court and church, and he knew both worlds very well. He was secretary to King John of Bohemia, and later a member of the court of Charles V of France; but he had also taken holy orders, and was a major cleric at Rheims Cathedral in the later years of his life. His secular songs include more than 100 works in the forms known to the trouvères: ***rondeaus, ballades,*** and the like. But Machaut is best known today for a single sacred composition: a polyphonic setting of the Ordinary of the Mass. To our knowledge he was the first composer to have treated the Mass as a unified multi-movement composition, one certainly meant for performance at a grand ceremonial occasion.

Guillaume de Machaut:
La Messe de Notre Dame (*Kyrie*) *R1 S1 B1*

The *Mass* is composed for four voices, rather than three; note that on this recording some lines are sung, while others are played by instruments. Notice as well that register has expanded outward, in both directions. Machaut's writing carries the melodic lines higher and lower than any of our previous examples, greatly enriching the overall sonority. The added (fourth) voice has been placed ***below*** the tenor, an approximation of our modern soprano-alto-tenor-bass layout. Furthermore, Machaut's sonorities include many modern ***consonances***: "chords" (that is, the momentary product of polyphonic motion) which stress the interval of the 3rd, and sound like major or minor triads.

The rhythms of Ars Nova style are highly complex. The ***Kyrie's*** inner rhythmic groupings are duple, even though the larger overall pulse is a slow, solemn three. In addition, rapid patterns and syncopated off-beat accents are frequent. Machaut and his contemporaries often used a texture in which alternating short notes and rests were exchanged between two or more parts: this was called ***hocket,*** or "hiccup," which the effect oddly resembles. Listen for hocketing between the two upper parts, near the end of the *Kyrie* (Figure 8.6).

Figure 8.6

Isorhythm was another widely used Ars Nova technique. It superimposes a repeated rhythmic pattern on the pitches of a pre-existing and perhaps familiar melody. In certain sections of this ***Mass,*** the tenor voice, a ***cantus firmus*** from a known chant, is handled in this way. For example, at the opening of the ***Kyrie*** the tenor repeats the rhythm 3/2 𝅝. | 𝅗𝅥 𝅝 | 𝅝. | 𝄺 | using the pitches of plainsong melody. The middle section (***Christe eleison***) uses a tenor line built on a different chant fragment, and a longer rhythmic pattern.

The *form* of the ***Kyrie*** is not only influenced by the variation principle, but also built in sections corresponding to the alternating phrases of the text. Although the text provides a literal ABA format ("Kyrie . . . Christe . . . Kyrie"), the music for the final section is not an exact repetition of the opening. The entire movement could be heard as ABC, bearing in mind that all sections are related through variation.

Italian Music of the Fourteenth Century

Although France was the musical capital of Europe, the cities of northern Italy were growing in power and wealth, and beginning to develop a musical style of their own. The secular Italian songs of the fourteenth century were more joyful, warmly sensuous and light-hearted than their French Gothic counterparts—closer to the worldly spirit of Dante, Boccaccio, and Petrarch than to the idealized chivalry north of the Alps. Italian style placed great emphasis upon ***melody:*** ornate, decorated, highly singable. In contrast to the linear texture of the French, the Italian ***madrigal*** provides a distinct hierarchy of voices: the upper parts florid and lyric, and the lowest voice often played rather than sung.

madrigal

The most important Italian composer of the century was the blind organist Francesco Landini (c. 1325–1397) of Florence, whose madrigals are wonderfully direct, open, and engaging. They are free of the structural abstractions that preoccupied the French; their melodic inventiveness adds another dimension to an age already renowned for great rhythmic discoveries.

Instrumental Music

During the Middle Ages, instrumentalists had sought to raise their station by forming guilds, acquiring the considerably higher status of civil servants. Eventually many large towns in Italy, Germany, and England employed groups of musicians as the equivalents of our municipal bands, to play at weddings, funerals, and civic functions.

By the early fifteenth century many dances were known throughout Europe under various national names. Each was characterized by tempo, meter, and rhythm-accent pattern; these were, in turn, related to social class, the dancers' garments, ceremonial function, and the like. Many dances had simple two-part binary forms. The ***instruments*** used for any given situation were simply those available; players read from, or elaborated upon, vocal parts, or improvised within an agreed-upon form and beat. (There was no music specifically written for instruments.) Diversity of timbre was encouraged, and performances often included vividly contrasted instruments set against the percussive colors of drums, bells, or cymbals.

Instruments were classified roughly as "loud" or "soft," "indoor" or "outdoor," but they could all adapt to different roles, with the possible exception of the church organ. New instruments were continually developed. These included the recorders (precursors of the modern flute), the double-reed shawms and krummhorns, and the family of bowed-string instruments known as the viols. The viols each had six strings, frets, and a relatively flat bridge that enabled the player to bow full chords. Keyboard instruments, such as the harpsichord and virginal, were becoming increasingly popular as well. The plucked-string, pear shaped lute was also gaining popularity. Like a number of the more recent instruments, the lute had resulted from the interaction between Europe and the Middle East during the Crusades.

The Renaissance, 1450–1600

The mid-1400s witnessed the fall of Constantinople, the end of the Hundred Years' War and the invention of the printing press. During the rest of the fifteenth and sixteenth centuries, there were equally dramatic changes, such as the great voyages of Columbus, Magellan, and Balboa, and the use of gunpowder (which, in effect, ended the age of chivalry). Scientific findings by such men as Copernicus made the physical universe more rationally comprehensible. The growth of secular interests, especially in Italy, was nurtured by a passion for the classical culture of ancient Greece and Rome. In their concern for the beauty of the worldly present, rather than the hereafter, people believed that they were reviving ancient values, buried for a thousand years since the fall of Rome. Thus they considered their attitudes a rebirth: a ***Renaissance.*** They were well aware of their historical role, and perhaps just a trifle smug about it: it was the writers of the Renaissance who invented the phrase "Dark Ages" to describe the thousand years that had preceded them!

Two geographic areas dominate the arts of the Renaissance: the Franco-Flemish region, consisting of Holland and Belgium plus parts of northern France, and the everblossoming cities of Italy. These two cultures interacted regularly, not only in the arts, but in banking and commerce as well. The Sforzas of Milan and the Medicis of Florence typified the wealthy Italian trading families that built magnificent palaces and encouraged the most lavish creations of art and sculpture. Raphael, Michelangelo, Leonardo da Vinci and Titian worked in the great Italian cities. They looked at the world in a way that emphasized its sensual qualities, and yet they observed its spatial-physical relationships, such as perspective, with the eyes of scientists: a concern for visual "truth" rather than divine symbolism. Facial expressions were made unique, personal, and intensely alive. The human body, after centuries of concealment, once more became a suitable artistic object.

Although artists still worked with church-related themes, they chose to represent these in spacious landscapes, realistic town settings, and vivid portraits of individuals: a cherub as a bouncy, fleshy infant, Jesus on the cross as a suffering young man in great agony, the Madonna as a beautiful woman. In this, as in other aspects of Renaissance life, the sacred and secular could be combined.

The wealth of northern Europe produced its own demand for art. Italians knew the Flemish works of Jan van Eyck and Hugo van der Goes among the earliest examples of oil painting. During the following sixteenth century such northern artists as Dürer and Breughel visited Italy.

The Burgundian School

When Henry V of England won the Battle of Agincourt in 1415, the Hundred Years' War was practically over. Henry styled himself "King of England and France," and sent the Duke of Bedford and his court to live in France as the King's Regent. It was the Duke who was instrumental in bringing Joan of Arc to trial; his presence in France, from 1422 to 1435, also influenced the history of music, for his court included the most important English composer of the time, John Dunstable (c. 1370–1453). Dunstable's style had a profound effect on the musicians at the court of Burgundy.

The Duchy of Burgundy, governed from a luxurious court at Dijon, comprised much of France, Holland, and Belgium. As the Duke of Burgundy had been an ally of Henry V, his court prospered with the English victories. The Burgundian court employed great numbers of musicians: minstrels for courtly entertainments and pageants, and a separate body of musicians for services at the court chapel. In both areas, Burgundy was justly famous. (One of the most spectacular banquets on record took place there in 1454: the "Banquet of the Oath of the Pheasant," at which twenty-eight musicians were hidden inside a gigantic pastry!)

What did the Burgundian composers learn from Dunstable and the English? The most obvious trait was a fondness for the intervals of the 3rd and 6th. In fact, during the preceding centuries when continental Europe was stressing 4ths and 5ths in organum and motet, the English had evolved a quasi-organum of their own, based on parallel 3rds and 6ths (see Figure 8.7). Dunstable's music, while learned in many respects (such as isorhythm and *cantus firmus* technique), shared the English preference for the warm, resonant sounds of 3rds, 6ths, and complete triads. The style of Dunstable and other English composers influenced the work of Burgundian composers, of whom the best known was Guillaume Dufay (1400–1474).

Equally at home in the words of secular and sacred music, Dufay was (like Dunstable) poised between two styles, and adept at handling either. True to the dying Gothic manner, he wrote intricate isorhythmic motets, but also used the more revolutionary English sonorities. Italian lyricism influenced his work as well, for Dufay traveled to Italy a number of times during his long career. He studied in Bologna, sang in the papal choir in Rome for a number of years, and composed music for the 1435 dedication of the great domed cathedral of Florence. That commission reveals the strong Italian interest in northern European music, and also the lack of interest in native Italian talent. Fifteenth century Italians (like the Victorian English and nineteenth century Americans of a later age) often imported their performers and composers from elsewhere.

Dufay wrote a number of complete Masses, setting all parts of the Ordinary; he was one of the first composers since Machaut to have done so. Significantly, Dufay based *all* sections (movements) of his Masses upon the

Figure 8.7

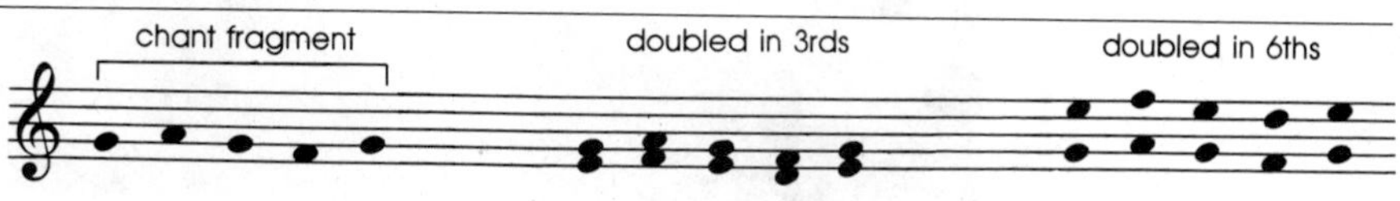

Hans V. de Vries,
Palace with Musicians.

149

same *cantus firmus.* This is actually liturgical nonsense: the five parts of the Ordinary have different ceremonial roots, and do not even succeed each other directly in an actual service. But Dufay's impulse was more humanistic than theological. He conceived of the Mass as an independent art work, apart from its ritual enactment. Dufay also used melodies other than plainsong as sources for a ***cantus firmus.*** One of his Masses is based upon a secular ***chanson*** called ***"Se la face ay pale"*** that was highly popular at the time. A typical ballad of courtly love, it proclaims: "If my face looks pale, the chief fault lies with love. I am so pained that I could drown myself in the sea . . ." (Such themes, by the way, were not necessarily tragic. Chivalric ritual simply placed high priority upon "grief," protestations, and worship from a distance.)

The composer of the song was none other than Dufay himself. He simply took one of his own tunes and reworked it into a solemn ritual of sacred worship. His chanson has a polyphonic three-part texture, an easygoing triple meter, and bouncy syncopations that "misplace" the internal accents. Although the voices retain their individuality in true Gothic style, they often create triadic sonorities as they move, so that modern-sounding "chords" begin to emerge with some frequency.

In listening to the chanson, concentrate upon the ***middle*** voice, the tenor, of the three-part texture. It is this voice which is used as ***cantus firmus*** in the ***Mass.***

Guillame Dufay

Missa "Se La Face Ay Pale" (Agnus Dei)*

This movement, even more than the chanson, demonstrates the enormous difference between Dufay's musical language and that of the medieval Ars Nova. Writing in four parts has now become the norm for sacred choral music. And the music is indeed ***choral,*** rather than soloistic. In earlier centuries, choirs had been used for monophonic or drone textures, with intricate polyphony reserved for soloists; by Dufay's time a number of voices were assigned to each contrapuntal part, resulting in greater resonance. The placement of a low bass part beneath the ***cantus firmus*** tenor (observed in the Machaut excerpt) has become a standard feature of fifteenth century choral style. The rhythmic flow is gentle, and strong accents are not crucial to the steady forward motion. Regular tempo and duple inner rhythms are more obvious than a sense of meter.

Most obvious of all is the sense of ***consonance*** dominating the flow: a succession of rich triads resulting from the polyphony. Dufay's four parts, although independent lines, seem to be working together in agreement. Whereas the medieval musician allowed the voices to clash on unstressed

*The chanson and Mass are available on Seraphim 5–60267.

*identical melodic line: originally drawn from chanson, now found in tenor voice of Mass passage (at half original rhythmic value)

Figure 8.8

beats, and preferred 4ths and 5ths as consonances because they were mathematically "pure," the Renaissance composer trusted his ears on both counts, responding to the logic of the sensual world. He favored a balance among lines, and the rich sonorities of the English influence.

Dufay creates a three-part formal structure for the ***Agnus Dei.*** The entire text is heard three times, allowing for three different settings. This could be considered an A-B-C outline, but the middle section is strikingly unlike the two outer ones: much lighter in texture, with many duos and trios. From a textural viewpoint, then, the overall form could be regarded as A-B-A'. The two outer parts use the chanson "Se la face ay pale" as a tenor ***cantus firmus.*** The beginning of A' is shown in Figure 8.8. Note that the tenor moves at a much slower pace than the other parts, and that is derived from a phrase of the chanson. The total effect is relaxed, spacious, and elegant in a new way. Dufay's concern for balance, proportion and sensual surface are all indicative of his times; so is the interaction of sacred and secular material. His use of triadic consonance, wide range and flexible rhythmic flow signals a new musical style—the beginnings of the Renaissance style.

Josquin des Prez

By the late fifteenth century Franco-Flemish composers occupied every important musical post in Europe. They built upon the traditions established at the Burgundian court, and added to these ingenious techniques of their own, primarily in the area of polyphonic *imitation.* Most medieval polyphony had stressed separate and distinct, even antagonistic lines, rather than imitative ones. Dufay's polyphony is more comfortably integrated and resonant, but his individual parts rarely borrow material from one another. The later generation of Flemish composers, however, made polyphony motivically unified as well as homogeneous in texture. They explored strict canon, and freer imitation of motivic fragments from voice to voice, using devices such as melodic inversion, "retrograde," and rhythmic transformation (noted in Chapter 4).

These techniques were used most often in sacred choral music; secular songs, on the contrary, could be quite chordal. Musicians of the time referred to "familiar style"—chains of triads, common in street music and courtly songs—as opposed to the "learned style" of imitative counterpoint.

The most distinguished composer of the late fifteenth century was a Frenchman called Josquin des Prez (c. 1440–1521), or simply Josquin; he was called the "prince of musicians," compared to Michelangelo, and greatly admired by such contemporaries as Martin Luther. Josquin's career brought him to Italy, where he served the Sforza court in Milan and the papal chapel in Rome. He may also have worked at the French court of Louis XII, and late in life he held a church position in Burgundy. In effect, Josquin was the first musician to win fame on a truly international scale. The fame was justified; his works are unsurpassed in scope, versatility and technical virtuosity, as well as immediate appeal.

Josquin
El Grillo (frottola)*

The *frottola* is a perfect example of the "familiar" style: a straightforward syllabic text setting, adhered to by all voices. This produces a series of chords rather than an interweaving of rhythmically different lines. The alternation of low and high registers is particularly charming. Note, too, the way in which the music gently comments on the words "tiene longo verso." Josquin's handling of the Italian style is quite convincing; apparently he could enter into the musical life of the great Italian courts with ease. (He was, of course, equally at home with the *chanson* of his native France.)

His chords appear to form "successions" rather than "progressions."

*Available on MCA 2503, or the "History of Music in Sound" series (Victor LM 6031), Volume III.

A. *El Grillo* (*frottola*)

El grillo, e buon cantore Che tiene longo verso. Dalle beve grillo canta. El grillo e buon cantore.	*The cricket is a good singer* *Who clings to a good verse.* *He sings when the wine is ripe* *The cricket is a mighty singer.*
Ma non fa come gl'atri uccelli Come li han canto un poco, van'de fatto in altro loco, Sempre el grillo sta pu saldo. Quando la maggior el caldo Alhor canta sol per amore. . . . etc. etc.	*But he doesn't do as birds do—* *When they have sung a little* *They go off someplace else.* *But the steadfast cricket stays put.* *When the heat is most intense* *Only then does he sing of love. . . .*

B. *Mille Regrets* (*chanson*)

Mille regrets de vous haban donner Et d'eslonger vostre fache amoureuse, J'ay si grand dueil et paine doulouereuse Qu'on me verra brief mes jours deffiner.	*A thousand regrets to leave you and your fair face. My grief is such that my days shall soon be at an end.*

That is, tonal relationships among the chords—driving towards a goal in the modern sense—do not exist. Josquin's pitch center is not always clear until the very last chord, and even then a certain sense of inevitability is missing. Although composers of this era were using chords frequently, and were intrigued by their expressive potential, they had not yet found an ordering which would make *one* of them central. Tonality had not yet evolved; the harmony of this period is still *modal* harmony.

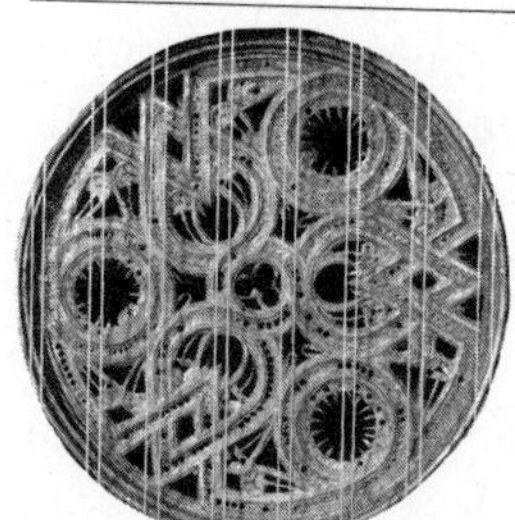

Josquin
Missa "Ave Maris Stella" (*Kyrie*)*

As the practice of composing complete five-part Masses based on one melody became common, an entire Mass was named after the single tune or chant from which it derived its material: for example the Dufay *Mass* noted earlier, or the present example by Josquin built on a ninth century Gregorian hymn (see Figure 8.2). Josquin abandons the earlier practice of assigning the source melody only to the tenor voice as a *cantus firmus,* using it instead in *all* parts in a truly balanced imitative texture.

In the opening of the *Kyrie,* seen in Figure 8.9, a melodic motive derived from the Gregorian hymn is heard in successive entries, each voice in turn imitating its neighbor. The lines overlap in such a way that the

*Available on MCA 2503, or Nonesuch 71216.

Figure 8.9

entrances are easily heard: first the altos, then the sopranos, basses and tenors. This overlap of phrases gives the music a gentle, flowing continuity, obscuring any strong metric sense. The consonant, freely floating modal harmony and spacious use of register add to the elegant effect, seemingly a far cry from the angular, jarring, exuberant or awesome sounds of medieval music. (On the other hand, note the archaic-sounding open 5ths at the end of the "Kyrie . . . Christe . . . Kyrie" sections.)

The three-part formal scheme is obviously related to the words: when the text changes, listen for a change in musical material (and *vice versa*). In each new section there will be a new series of imitative entries, growing from one line to four, on a fresh motive articulating the new words.

There was widespread regard for Josquin in his own lifetime. Significantly, the first volumes of printed music ever issued (in 1501 and 1507) contain a large number of his sacred and secular works. It is also interesting that the name by which he was known is, in fact, a nickname: the equivalent of our "Joe." When he died in 1521, a few months after the painter Raphael, Josquin was mourned as the greatest musical figure of his age.

Renaissance Sacred Music: Reformation and Counter-Reformation

By the sixteenth century liturgical music had evolved into a phenomenon quite unlike the austere, monophonic plainsong of Pope Gregory's time. Medieval Europe had seen the introduction of polyphony, bilingual Gothic motets, and dazzling rhythmic experiments. Sacred compositions borrowed material from the popular music of the day, and a good deal of sacred music was, in fact, "court" music, written for performances at private chapels of the aristocracy. These were more likely to be political or social occasions than true religious services.

a cappella

consort

To be sure, the striking sonorities of medieval polyphony had been transformed into a more subdued choral style. With the development of a true choral tradition—a number of singers to a part—musicians seemed to prefer the sound of the unaccompanied chorus: ***a cappella*** ("chapel") singing, as it was known. The instruments that were used to accompany singing were discreet rather than flamboyant. It was preferable to have a few instruments of similar timbre (a ***consort*** of recorders or viols), which would complement the balanced vocal ensemble, rather than the vividly contrasted colors favored during the Gothic age.

Despite these modifications, a number of people felt that the church had become too secular. Apart from music, there was concern over the church's unwillingness to deal with large issues, such as individual dignity, raised by the growing humanist movement. In 1517 Martin Luther posted a statement of principles on a door of the Wittenberg castle church, leading to a chain of events that we call the Reformation: the establishment of Protestant denominations, and the weakened power of the Roman Catholic Papacy.

Music of the Reformation

Luther was not the only leader of the Reformation. His position in Germany was echoed by that of Calvin and others in various parts of Europe. Each leader had his own notions of the best way to alter the existing liturgy. Calvin preferred simple music, such as the monophonic chanting of psalms by the congregation. Luther had more sophisticated tastes; he enjoyed complex choral polyphony, and revered Josquin. But he also believed that the church needed a flexible musical repertory, adaptable to small rural communities as well as cities. His ideal liturgical music would involve the entire congregation as singers, rather than a hand-picked trained choir, and it would use the vernacular language rather than Latin.

chorale

The Luthern church tune that emerged was, in effect, the Protestant equivalent of Gregorian chant. But it was strongly metric, with easily remembered rhythms and distinct melodic profiles, suited to the patterns of the German language. Folk songs, secular tunes and even revised versions of Gregorian chant were pressed into service, with new texts to take the place of the original ones. This church hymn, designed to be both simple and grand, was known as the ***chorale.*** We will return to it again in connection with J. S. Bach (see Chapter 10) and the late German Baroque.

Music of the Counter-Reformation

The reaction of the Roman church to Protestantism is known as the Counter-Reformation. This reaction took many forms: for example, the Inquisition, to suppress heresy forcibly, and the founding of the Jesuit Order to rally an enthusiastic counteroffensive. Another strategy was the gathering of Catholic leaders in a series of meetings known as the Council of Trent. During the Council's meetings, from 1545 until 1563, church music was among the topics discussed. Some prelates wished to eliminate polyphony, since it obscured texts. Others wanted to ban all melismatic melody for the same reason; this would have placed many Gregorian chants in a forbidden category. Many agreed that secular, worldly elements should not intrude upon the liturgy. Instruments were frowned upon; ***a cappella*** choral singing was the ideal. The words of the great Dutch scholar Erasmus must have expressed the dissatisfaction of many:

> We have introduced an artificial and theatrical music into the church . . . horns, trumpets, pipes vie and sound along constantly . . . amorous and lascivious melodies are heard such as elsewhere accompany only the dances of courtesans and clowns.

In general, it was felt that Catholic liturgical music should not be a distraction that drew the worshipper's attention away from the service.

Palestrina

Fortunately, some of the Council's recommendations were either defeated, or ignored by composers. Polyphony remained important, and Gregorian melody was retained. But an unobtrusive, restrained manner was encouraged, and could be heard in the music of those composers closest to the papacy. Chief among these was Giovanni Pierluigi da Palestrina (1526–1594). Palestrina, a town near Rome, was not only his birthplace but the name by which he is remembered. He lived and worked in Rome for most of his life, and held positions as choirmaster and organist in many of Rome's most distinguished churches, including the papal chapel itself. He was dismissed from the latter position, for being married in violation of the rules, but returned to papal service later in life. Palestrina composed a large body of music, almost all of it sacred: over 250 motets, and more than 100 masses.

Giovanni Pierluigi da Palestrina: Missa Papae Marcelli (*Agnus Dei*)

R1 S1 B2

The Mass is composed for an unaccompanied choir in six voices: soprano, alto, tenor I and II, and bass I and II. Notice that Flemish imitative technique is used here as unobtrusively as possible: rhythms, melodic lines, and chord successions flow into each other smoothly and effortlessly. As seen in Figure 8.10, strong metric "beat" is nonexistent, and the individual lines are intentionally lacking in rhythmic profile as well. In its deliberate attempt to avoid any connotations of the vulgar, "catchy" world of secular music, Palestrina's style is an ideal reflection of the Counter-Reformation. It is a return to the spirit, if not the letter, of the Gregorian era.

Consonance dominates the choral fabric; it is hard to believe that there are any dissonances at all. Actually, Palestrina uses the "modern" ten-

Figure 8.10

sion-release pull of dissonance more consistently than his fourteenth and fifteenth century predecessors. There are very few harsh "discords," but a great many sounds that, within the hierarchy of tonality, need to resolve to other sounds. This music is indeed verging on major-minor tonality.

Like every other facet of Palestrina's style, the dissonances are unobtrusive. The moments which lead to dissonances, and their resolution, have been carefully calculated in advance. The *dramatic* role of dissonance—angry, bold, assertive, the sort we will discover in Monteverdi, Bach, and Beethoven—does not interest Palestrina at all. He is only concerned with its *functional* role, that of keeping the music moving forward. The relaxed, seemingly effortless flow results from a subtle use of tension and release.

Renaissance Secular Music: The Madrigal

Sacred and secular vocal music of the Renaissance shared many features; just as a painter might have the same model pose one day as a saint and the next as a shepherdess, a composer could adapt similar techniques to Mass or chanson. On the other hand, there were some distinct differences between sacred and secular genres. Two important aspects of secular song should be noted:

1. The texts were not suitable for church! Renaissance courts delighted in naughty poems, satire, cries of love (noble or erotic), and political commentary. They also used vernacular languages, strong rhythmic profiles, and extremes of dynamics and tempo that might not be thought proper for church. And since the words themselves had to be heard clearly, simpler textures were often found. A complex web could be woven about the words ***"Agnus Dei"*** because listeners already knew the text. Dealing with unfamiliar words, perhaps outrageous puns or soulful, weeping metaphors, presented an entirely different problem.

2. The words themselves were often reflected directly in the music, especially if strong, violent emotions were conveyed: a sharp dissonance on the word ***moro*** (I die), for instance, or the word for "two" sung by only two voices. "I hurry to your side" could be expressed in a rapid flurry of notes, and the image of "rising" (to heaven, for example) linked with an ascending melodic line. Such attempts to represent a text literally through music are called ***word-painting.*** The more exaggerated effects are really far-fetched, especially if they are solely for the eyes: to represent "black gloom" by black

word-painting

notes ♬♬♬♬ ♫♫ might actually contradict the implied solemnity, since these notes will be very rapid in sound.

But the technique should not be judged by its extreme instances. The sixteenth century fascination for word-painting expressed deeper concerns: a profound love of literature, and admiration for the legendary union of words and music that had typified classical Greece (the Renaissance ideal). There was also the growing discovery that music could be made to appear joyous or tender or mournful to a degree untapped in previous centuries. Musicians still needed words to turn on the "tap": the drama-without-words of instrumental music was still off in the future.

Word-painting can also be regarded as a private game between composer and performers, another dimension to enliven their music making. Much of this music was intended for performance by amateurs at court or at meetings of artistic and literary societies. All courtly people were expected to read music, sing in a passable voice, and play a few instruments. They purchased the first printed music in the early 1500s, and supported the music publishing houses that began to dot the map of Europe shortly afterwards. Early printed works included solo songs, music for vocal ensembles, and arrangements of songs for the more popular solo instruments (lute and keyboard), all meant to be performed in the home. Of course, "home" might mean a stately palace, spacious French chateau, drawing room, or meeting hall: any place where people could gather for leisure and entertainment. Men ***and*** women could enjoy this music, as the church restrictions on female performance did not apply here. (Due to such restrictions the upper parts of Catholic sacred music was sung by boys.) People performed for themselves; in the secular as well as the sacred world, there were no "audiences."

The Italian Madrigal

Although the French chanson and the German lied were popular, they were overshadowed by the Renaissance ***madrigal,*** a much more elaborate and polyphonic genre than its earlier fourteenth century namesake. The madrigal was intended for a small group of voices, either ***a cappella*** or with simple instrumental reinforcement. It was set to a short poem, perhaps a Petrarch sonnet, and often used vivid word-painting to intensify the poem's message. ***Chromatic*** passages (see Chapter 2) frequently placed unrelated chords in surprising, wrenching juxtaposition to emphasize heightened emotion. The daring, hyper-expressive chord successions of many Italian madrigals astound listeners even now.

The English Madrigal

Under Henry VIII and then Elizabeth I, sixteenth century England emerged as a great political and commercial power; this period witnessed the careers of Shakespeare, Sir Francis Bacon, Sir Walter Raleigh, and the defeat of the supposedly invincible Spanish Armada. Henry VIII had declared his own Reformation of a sort, breaking with the church of Rome in 1509, but more for political than theological or liturgical reasons. Anglican church music retained many Roman features, preserving Latin for some functions and substituting English for others.

English madrigals

In 1588, the year the Armada was destroyed, Italian madrigals were first published in England; they immediately caught favor with the amateur music-making public. Many ***English*** composers produced ***madrigals*** of their own: part-songs for vocal groups, solo songs with accompaniment, polyphonic works and chordal ones. Many Italian features were transplanted, although the English preferred the more whimsical, light-hearted moods to the overwrought melodrama of the Italian madrigal style. Gently chiding love poetry, pastoral settings, and lilting nonsense syllables (''fa-la-la'' and ''hey-nonny-nonny,'' for example) were more suited to the English taste.

Thomas Morley
Two Madrigals*

R1 S1 B3

Thomas Morley (1557–1602) was one of the most distinguished madrigalists. His first song is ***through-composed*** in form, each phrase of text receiving slightly different musical treatment. There are many features of Renaissance polyphony: imitative entrances at phrase openings, and register contrasts between upper and lower voice pairs. These might be part of a sacred motet; the strong meter and expressive variance in tempo are typical of secular style, however. The succession of chords indicates a tonal center,

*Both songs can be heard on Vanguard HM-4.

but a weakly defined one: the free-floating quality of modal harmony still lingers. Appropriately, there is greater harmonic security in the cheery "April" phrase, and a complex, diffuse quality (note the descending sequences) as we approach "December."

For the second madrigal, three stanzas have been set ***strophically,*** with a repeated fa-la-la refrain. The fa-la-la provides an opportunity for some rapid-fire imitative counterpoint which offsets the otherwise chordal texture. As with the first song, the chord series are ***almost,*** but not quite, tonal, in the modern sense. The major and minor scales, and the chord progressions to articulate them, have gradually emerged by the sixteenth century, but they are not yet firmly established. This is why the music feels "almost tonal."

A. ***April is in My Mistress' Face***
April is in my mistress' face,
And July in her eyes hath place,
Within her bosom is September,
But in her heart a cold December.

B. *Now is the Month of Maying*

(1) Now is the month of maying,
When merry lads are playing
Each with his bonny lass,
Upon the greeny grass.

(2) The Spring, clad all in gladness,
Doth laugh at Winter's sadness,
And to the bagpipe's sound
The nymphs tread out their ground.

(3) Fie then! Why sit we musing,
Youth's sweet delight refusing?
Say, dainty nymphs, and speak,
Shall we play barley-break?

Scale forms evolve over the centuries very much as spoken and written languages evolve: by usage. The major and minor did not suddenly appear full-blown. On the contrary, they sneaked into prominence during the 500-odd years of the medieval and Renaissance eras, as performers acquired the habit of altering certain pitches of the church modes. Musicians would inflect pitches either higher or lower than written, either to avoid unpleasant intervals or to create a stronger sense of arrival at a resting point. In the Palestrina ***Mass*** example (Figure 8.10) there is a tiny sharp ***above,*** rather than to the left of, the note F on beat 1 of measure 6, Tenor I part. Even though the pitch was written as F, performers would raise the F to F$^{\#}$, thereby creating a half-step pull to the G that follows, and a D-major rather than a D-minor triad for the entire chorus on that beat. By this practice of ***musica ficta*** ("false" or "feigned" music), which was in evidence as early as the twelfth century, the various modes with their individual interval arrangements all came to sound ***alike*** in performance. Eventually they all resembled either the mode on A (forerunner of our minor scale) or the mode on C (the major). The entire process, as hinted above, was very gradual.

King Henry VIII of England was an accomplished musician. In this illustration, from an Elizabethan manuscript, he is shown playing a harp, perhaps accompanying one of his own compositions, such as the jolly "Pastime and Good Company" shown below.

Many English composers wrote in the madrigal style. One of the great periods of British music, oddly enough, was built upon a borrowed Italian model. The English also appropriated an Italian *literary* form: in their fervent embrace of the Italian Renaissance, they discovered the sonnet, a poetic genre that, in the hands of Shakespeare, Milton and Keats, would provide some of the finest moments in English literature.

Instrumental Music

By the late sixteenth century instrumental performance was entirely respectable among the nobility and ever-growing urban middle classes: in fact, it was a positive virtue. (It was still more respectable, though, to be an amateur instrumentalist than a professional one!) The lute and harpsichord had become popular as solo instruments, and the rage for playing these was fed by the printing of music, begun earlier in the century. Publishers turned out instruction manuals for beginners, simple pieces for rank amateurs, and florid, virtuosic music that could be played only by people with real facility. The earliest such works were based on popular vocal pieces, and by the late sixteenth century original works were issued as well. The simpler music was economically and culturally important, since it helped convert the middle classes to music making. But it was in the more advanced work that composers discovered a truly idiomatic style for instrumental writing: exploiting the capacities for runs, trills, and embellishments that make instruments uniquely different from voices and from each other. The polyphonic choral style of the Renaissance was translated into instrumental terms as composers wrote music for ***consorts*** of similar instruments—viols, or recorders—that simulated a balanced choral timbre. Lutes and keyboard instruments could also translate polyphonic texture into a vehicle for one soloist, and pieces in imitative style were written for them too.

The popular dances of the day were often played in paired groupings, with contrasting tempo (fast and slow) or meter (duple, triple). There were the ***Passamezzo*** and ***Saltarello*** of Italy, the ***Pavane*** and ***Galliard*** of France, the ***Jig*** and ***Hornpipe*** (both of these fast) in England. These groups of dances later developed into the ***suite.*** The early dance pieces are interesting on two counts: first, because they bring the dance medium itself—traditionally an improvisor's music—into the domain of written, fixed notes. Secondly, many of the dance pieces for lute or keyboard were never intended to be danced. They were too idiomatic in their decoration, and too heavily embellished for that; rather, they provided a background for polite gatherings, or technical display for the entertainment of one's guests. They could evoke the memory and the social togetherness of dance, without the physical bodily movements themselves.

Instruments builders were constantly making improvements in construction, and this also accounts for the spread of instrumental music during the Renaissance. The actual objects are remarkable; lutes, viols, and harpsichords were sensitively crafted in wood, often elaborately painted and

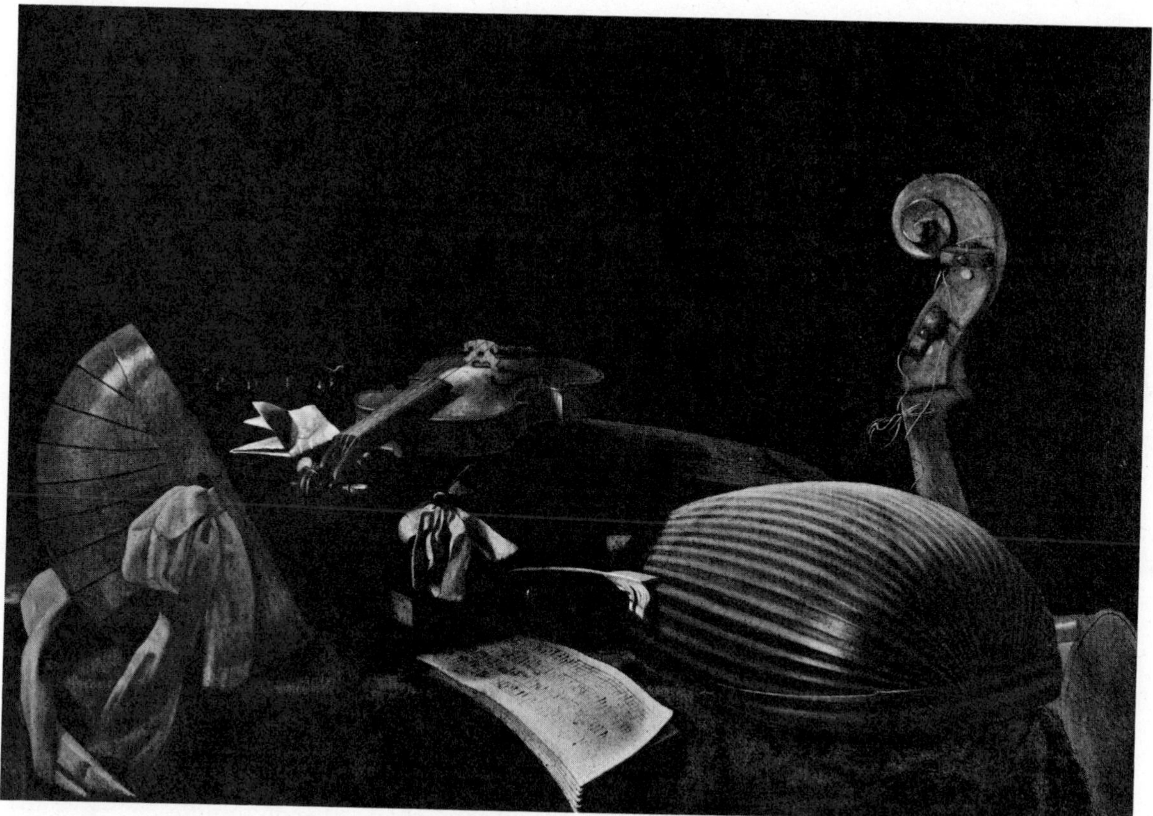

Evaristo Baschensis, ***Musical Instruments,*** 17th century.

decoratively trimmed. Perhaps Renaissance painters depicted instruments on their canvasses so frequently because they are so stunning. Many of these instruments are rather delicate looking—it is not advisable to drop one—and also delicate ***sounding.*** They could have become important only in an age of relative leisure, affluence, and comfort, in a society that took its relaxation indoors, and that assumed "indoors" to include amenities not found in a drafty medieval hut or feudal castle. The lute and harpsichord were ideally suited to the European middle classes, who could not afford an entire household of musicians but had the means to buy an instrument and some published books of music. It was their rapid growth as a class that made the development of independent instrumental music possible.

9

The Development of Baroque Style (1600–1700)

Wherefore, seeing that I had to do with Dramatic Poetry and must accordingly seek, in my music, to imitate one who speaks . . . it seemed to me that the ancient Greeks and Romans (who in the opinion of many sang the whole of their tragedies on the stage) must have made use of a sort of music which, while surpassing the sounds of ordinary speech, fell so far short of the melody of singing as to assume the shape of something intermediate between the two. . . .

Jacopo Peri, in published Preface to Eurydice, *1600*

An Introduction to the Baroque

"History" can be viewed as a gradually unfolding continuum, which is, of course, how its participants lived it day by day; it can also be regarded as a succession of periods. The Middle Ages and the Renaissance are chunks of time, bounded by important world events or artistic milestones, that symbolize (for later generations) commonly held attitudes and lifestyles. In music history, major developments seem to have occurred every 150 years or so, with really crucial ones at 300 year intervals. Beginning with the notation of organum around 1000 A.D., we observe that great changes in Western musical thinking have taken place around the years 1300, 1600 and 1900. Other important changes, perhaps less influential, characterize the midpoints between these milestones (1150, 1450, 1750).

A.D. 1000	polyphony, organum
1150	the Notre Dame School; Gothic style
1300	rhythmic/notational changes, Ars Nova
1450	Burgundian School; Renaissance begins
1600	still to be discussed. Homophony and major-minor tonality.
1750	1600–1900; new changes after 1900.
1900	

Most of these dates are loose approximations, of course. Notre Dame Cathedral was actually begun in the 1160s, and the year 1450 is not as significant for the Renaissance as 1453 (the fall of Constantinople) or 1455 (printing from moveable type). On the other hand, the years 1600 and 1750 mark events of real significance. 1600 witnessed the production of the earliest surviving opera, and 1750 the death of Johann Sebastian Bach. These two dates mark the boundaries of a formidable era in music history.

During this 150 year span, almost every major genre of Western music began: opera, oratorio, cantata, sonata, and concerto. Major and minor scales and goal-directed tonality replaced the church modes; chord progressions and homophonic texture dominated musical thinking. Important formal models were first explored and developed. The first public concerts, as opposed to private court functions or church services, were held. As a result, musical experience became fragmented in a new way: the roles of composer and performer, audience and patron, amateur and professional took on special significance. This vital 150 year period is known as the ***Baroque.***

The word baroque may have come from the Portugese "barroco," an irregularly shaped pearl, and was used to describe a style that abounded in eccentricity, exaggeration, and overwhelming decoration. The word was originally applied to painting and sculpture, and was appropriated for musical description much later in history. In any case, it was ***not*** intended as a compliment! It was meant to disparage a style that seemed bizarre, perversely convoluted, tasteless, and ugly. (Remember that the "Middle Ages" and the "Dark Ages" were so named by the Renaissance; similarly, the term "Gothic" was coined by Italians to describe the barbaric lifestyle of northern Europe). Admittedly, the most striking characteristics of baroque art could have provoked such a reaction. If one believed fervently in the Renaissance ideal of beauty—restraint, balance, nothing too extreme—the seventeenth century appeared utterly mad: in fact, "century of excess" would not be an unfair designation.

Distortion, stress, and shock value had become positive virtues in the visual arts as early as the mid-sixteenth century. The new flamboyance is expressed in "mannerist" paintings of El Greco, and in the late works of Michelangelo, particularly the "Last Judgment" painted on a wall of the

Saint Peter's Square, Rome, Italy is typically baroque in its grandiose organization of space.

Sistine Chapel. In architecture a similar boldness typified the colossal piazza of Saint Peter's in Rome, and reached its apotheosis in the extravagant sweep of Versailles, which was copied in countless other palaces in Europe. All of the arts had become ***theatrical,*** "grand," and monumental, employing striking contrasts and vivid color. Compared with the repose of the Renaissance, baroque attitudes appear overly effusive, undisciplined—more concerned with ***action*** than with proportion.

But in other areas of activity the period from the 1600–1750 was one of rationality and systematic discipline. Our knowledge of the physical universe was greatly expanded by the painstaking research of Sir Isaac Newton. Kepler calculated the paths of the planets, and Harvey discovered the circulation of the blood; Galileo's telescope and Leeuwenhoek's microscope both revealed new worlds, as did the great voyages to America. Calculus was invented; systematic quasi-scientific world views were developed by the philosophers Locke and Hume, and the French Encyclopedists subsequently attempted to organize all knowledge with similar sweeping dedication. Perhaps this reveals the same mania for action and "grand design" noted in the arts.

In fact, all this newly acquired information only contributed to a growing atmosphere of confusion, doubt, and unrest. The religious split between Catholics and Protestants led to actual violence: the Thirty Years' War in Germany, and the Civil War in England which saw the beheading of Charles I. Although religion was an area of impassioned feeling, no church carried the weight of ultimate authority. Many of the newer scientific findings questioned religious teachings. Ironically, they also cast doubts upon a major belief of Renaissance humanism: trust and faith in one's senses, rather than in an authoritarian "word." If observation and sense impressions were unreliable, then where could one turn?

As church authority weakened, many secular powers gained strength and wealth: the cities of Italy, a host of minor German courts, and above all the strongly centralized, absolute monarchy of France's Louis XIV. The courts demanded ceremonial art, architecture, and entertainment on a vast scale. At the height of the Counter-Reformation, the Catholic Church commissioned works of an equally spectacular nature. The splendor, pomp, and muscle of all this display was not lost on the emerging middle classes; from Venice to Amsterdam to London they too celebrated their growing power in an appropriately baroque way.

Musically, three important stylistic traits developed during the Baroque: (1) the notion of ***contrast;*** (2) ***homophonic*** texture; and (3) a fondness for the ***angular, ornate,*** and aggressively ***extroverted.*** Compare the gentle undulations of a typical Palestrina melodic line as represented in Figure 9.1, with that of Bach Prelude and Fugue composed more than a century later and studied during Part 1. There are similar contrasts in the area of rhythm. The constant tempo, regular rhythms and understated meter of the Renaissance a cappella choral style have been drastically altered. In their place we may hear the stop-and-go prose rhythms of speech, or a relentlessly driving, sharply accented motor rhythm.

In these ways, Baroque composers attempted to grab the attention of their listeners. That in itself indicates a striking change from previous attitudes. Music had been subtly integrated into the earliest Christian liturgy. (When Saint Augustine was more moved by the music than by words, as he confessed in a fifth-century essay, he felt "guilty of a grave sin.") Extroverted musical styles that had gradually developed over the centuries were censured by the Council of Trent, leading to the "backlash" of Palestrina style. And the Protestant chorale was, in its own way, as austere as the Gregorian chant.

The secular music of earlier periods had cultivated a more distinct stylistic profile, and that may have pointed the way to the baroque. In this sense, one can say that baroque music was overwhelmingly "secular" in its expansive, outward-looking quality, despite its wealth of religious pieces. It

Figure 9.1

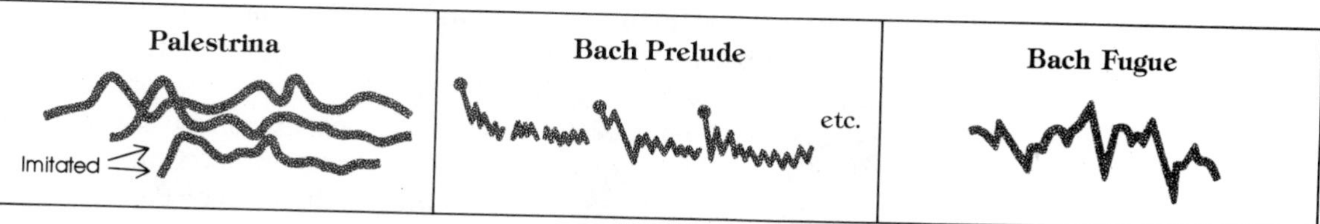

Jean Garnier, ***Louis XIV in an Oval with Musical Instruments, Flowers and Fruits.*** Louis XIV of France considered music an important element in the life of his court.

was also highly "theatrical," whether composed for theatre, palace, concert hall, opera house, or church.

We usually identify baroque music with the great figures who dominate the end of the period: J. S. Bach, Handel, and others who worked during the early-to-mid-1700s. This chapter will be concerned with their predecessors of the early Baroque. Bach, Handel and their contemporaries will be the subject of the following chapter.

The Transition between Renaissance and Baroque

One unfortunate drawback to studying history by periods is the danger of taking the boundaries literally, as though, by some drastic change in musical thinking, the Baroque suddenly began on January 1, 1600. Artistic movements usually take many years to gather momentum, and just as long a time to fade into obscurity. At any given moment in history there are conservative tendencies, radical experiments, and a variety of approaches in between. It is not surprising, then, to learn that some composers were writing in High Renaissance style well into the seventeenth century, or that others were exploring experimental ideas during the time of Palestrina.

During the later Renaissance, a number of musical factors began to assume importance, gradually changing the prevailing style. Two of these should be mentioned:

1. Interest in timbre led to a preference for contrasting colors within a texture, rather than the equal balance of similar lines. Some colors were perceived as "foreground," others as "background." This, plus the increased use of instruments, concern for clear settings of words, and a growing sensitivity to the expressive power of ***chords,*** were leading composers in the direction of ***homophonic*** texture: solo and accompaniment.
2. Italy had become the great musical power of the later Renaissance, and a number of her composers rejected the Franco-Flemish style with all its complexities: the obscure northern polyphony which had dominated the landscape for more than 150 years was no longer suitable. Bright colors and distinctive rhythmic profiles became more fashionable in Italian music.

Two Transitional Figures: John Dowland and Giovanni Gabrieli

Two composers working at the very turn of the century are often placed in the Renaissance, even though they show some very baroque traits in their music. One of these is John Dowland (1563–1626), who was widely regarded as one of Europe's great lute players. He left his native England for extended stays abroad: residence in Paris, travels through Italy and Germany, and eight years as lutenist to the King of Denmark. Dowland's ***First Booke of Songs or Ayres*** was published in 1597. In that collection he explored the ***solo song*** texture of single vocal line and lute accompaniment. Three more collections were published within the next fifteen years; *"In Darkness Let Mee Dwell"* (our example for study) first appeared in 1610.

solo song

John Dowland
"In Darkness Let Mee Dwell"

R1 S1 B4

The tempo is rather slow and steady, but there is no clear sense of meter or constant rhythmic pattern. We hear, rather, a changing and often syncopated series of stresses that mirror the words: there are surprising ***syncopations*** at "the ground shall sorrow be," and shocking ones for "jarring sounds." ***Suspensions*** are moments that confuse both rhythmic and harmonic sense. For example, the chord changes under the word "mee" in line 1, while the voice, now apparently dissonant against the accompanying chord, is sustained, only to resolve at "dwell" a moment later. The effect places chord and melodic line out of phase, and creates a harmonically wrenching dissonance. Another example of suspension occurs at the words "cheerful light from mee."

The emotional impact of *chord* successions is also quite striking; note the word "weep," which boldly rises chromatically into an unexpected region, and then sinks back again. But although chords are used with great effect, the texture is not entirely homophonic. Much of the time, in fact, this "ayre" is just as polyphonic as a Renaissance madrigal. The important departure is that of timbral imbalance: the upper voice is sung, and all the others incorporated into the lute fabric. That single change creates dimensions of "foreground" and "background," which are further substantiated by the more chordal passages.

The six lines of text are loosely grouped into three units, creating a through-composed ABC form. Note that the overall harmonic motion corresponds to the three-part structure. A reaches a cadence on the home chord at the end of line 2, and B veers off to a foreign area on the words "shall weep." The concluding C takes a while to return to the home area, and employs the most conservative means to achieve that return, almost as though the grinding dissonance of "weep" needed resolution in a more comfortable idiom. Note the sequences of line 5, and the almost lilting rhythm of "till death do come."

The final resolution to the home chord should occur at the word "come." But, in one last surprise, that chord is strangely incomplete (it contains one unexpected tone) and needs further resolution by the lute. As the opening phrase of the ayre repeats, it fades away on the chord that would be called the "dominant." Is that the wrong chord? Remember that major-minor tonality was not yet firmly established in 1610; the concept of "key" does not always apply to music of this era.

> In darkness let mee dwell, the ground shall sorrow be,
> The roofe dispaire to barre all cheerful light from mee.
> The wals of marble blacke that moistned still shall weepe,
> My musicke hellish jarring sounds to banish friendly sleepe.
> Thus wedded to my woes, and bedded to my Tombe,
> O let me living die, till death doe come.

Our second composer is Italian, more specifically a Venetian. This distinction is important, because there was no single nation called Italy in the seventeenth century. There were many independent city-states, Naples and the south under Spanish rule, Milan and much of the north controlled by Austria, and the papal states under the Vatican in Rome. Customs and artistic taste differed from one part of Italy to another: Milan built one of the great Gothic cathedrals of Europe, while Venice created the Byzantine splendors of Saint Mark's.

Services within Saint Mark's, as well as the colorful pageants on the vast piazza outside, featured instrumental music, particularly brass groups. The Venetian composers took advantage of the fact that Saint Mark's was built on the ground plan of a Greek cross rather than the Latin cross of Gothic cathedrals, and that it housed two organs at opposite arms of the

Canaletto, Venice: ***The Basin of S. Marco on Ascension Day*** (above) and ***Musician's Gallery, St. Marks Cathedral*** (left). A sweeping panorama of Venice where Giovanni Gabrieli created antiphonal works for the spacious interior of Saint Mark's Cathedral. Notice the musician's gallery at the right of the drawing.

antiphonal music

cross. They wrote ***antiphonal music,*** that is, music for widely separated performing forces, in this case choirs and instrumental ensembles in opposing lofts or galleries. Giovanni Gabrieli (1557–1612), who had succeeded his uncle Andrea Gabrieli as music director of the cathedral, carried the antiphonal technique even further. He would occasionally divide his performers into four separate groups. Choirs and instrumentalists would answer one another across the entire width of the great interior; sometimes they would play together, sometimes separately, often in question-answer dialogue. The younger Gabrieli grasped the essence of antiphony as a form of ***contrast:*** "here" versus "there," "near" and "far." He found it only natural to explore other kinds of contrast as well. He wanted high parts to answer low ones, loud passages alternating with quiet ones, instruments set against voices. He was one of the first composers to have specified ***dynamic*** levels, in an antiphonal piece called ***Sonata Pian e Forte*** ("Piece to be sounded soft and loud"). He was also one of the first to designate certain parts as instrumental, sometimes even specifying the instruments, and others as vocal.

Giovanni Gabrieli: **Canzona à 4, no. 2**

R1 S1 B5

The ***canzona*** was an instrumental piece derived from the French ***chanson.*** Gabrieli composed many canzonas for festive religious and municipal occasions. With Venice the richest city in Europe, and Saint Mark's its civic showplace, "municipal" and "sacred" were often fused into one. This particular canzona is scored for a single ensemble of four lines and does not call for an antiphonal spatial disposition of the instruments, but the way in which ***color*** and ***contrast*** are exploited creates an antiphonal effect nevertheless.

canzona

Basically imitative in texture, canzonas often interject simple chord series at unexpected moments: another kind of contrast. Conzonas almost always begin with a repeated note phrase and the rhythm ♩ ♩ ♩ our example is no exception. The form is sectional, with a series of brief motives introduced in turn. Each new section begins imitatively and leads to a cadence. In fact, the form is not unlike that of the Renaissance motet or chanson. Figure 9.2 presents the motivic contours in order.

The harmonic sense is strong throughout. We feel the presence of a major key and the drive toward cadences; also note the many sequences along the way. The driving quality is reinforced by the steady tempo and rhythmic vitality of the style. Most of all, the ensemble is used for maximum opposition and contrast; even those moments of homogeneous blending together become another kind of contrast. The performing bodies, as conceived by Gabrieli, could be antagonists as well as partners. We call this approach the ***stile concertato***—the "competing" style.

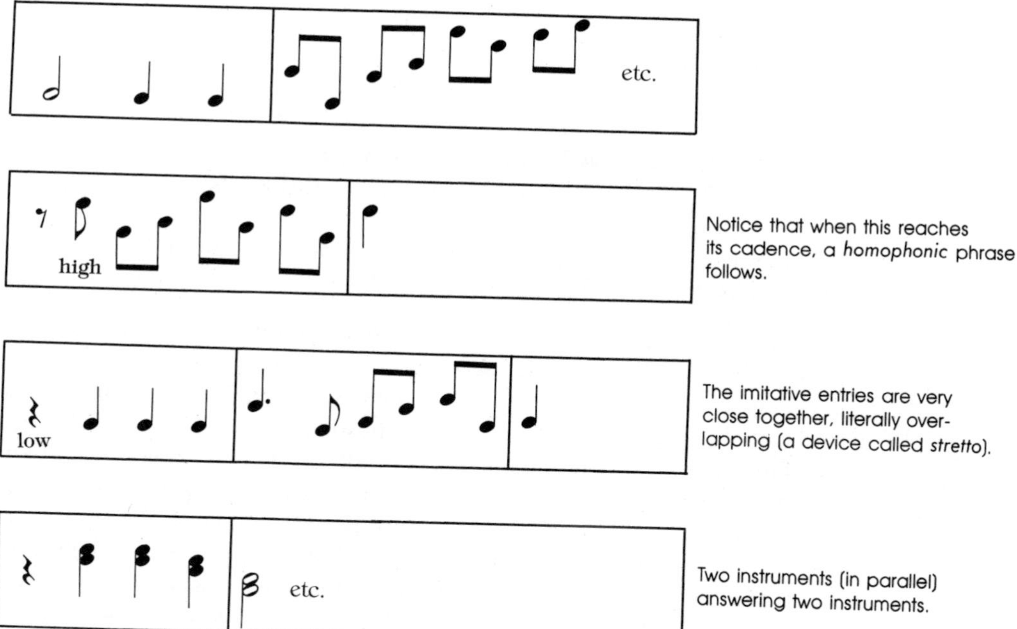

Figure 9.2

Monteverdi, Lully, and the Growth of Opera

In late sixteenth century Florence a group of noblemen formed a literary society or "academy,"—one of many in Renaissance Italy—to discuss the nature of ancient Greek drama. They knew that music had figured heavily in Greek theatre, and that words and music together had exerted legendary powers over the emotions. They could not reconstruct the actual sounds of ancient music, any more than we can today, but they were determined to capture its mythic expressive force. The Florentine group was called the *Camerata*. It included a number of amateur musicians and poets, such as Vincenzo Galilei (father of the great scientist Galileo), who had published a treatise on the relation of music to words, Giulio Caccini, who brought out a revolutionary edition of songs in 1602 prophetically entitled *Le Nuove Musiche* ("New Music"), and Jacopo Peri, whose musical drama *Euridice* (1600) is the earliest surviving opera.

Camerata

The Camerata believed, simply, that elaborate polyphony could not express the true meaning of words. Their "nuove musiche" stressed a solo vocal line that would imitate the rise and fall of speech inflections and rhythms, midway between song and rhetorical oratory, in the manner of an actor's impassioned delivery. Accompaniment for this solo line was restricted to a succession of chords, played by keyboard or lute: a truly homophonic texture. The new approach was meant to eliminate all distractions—tunes, sequential motives, refrains—that would draw attention away from the heightened ***declamation of words.***

Basso Continuo and the Figured Bass

By adding a chordal background to a solo line, two levels of listening were created: not only foreground and background, but ***melody*** and ***bass.*** The chord's lowest note, the bass, was regarded as the foundation for the sound built above it. As the triad was considered the chordal norm, an early seventeenth century composer could write a bass note (such as this C) as a shorthand indication of a complete triad, in this instance a C-major triad. Unless instructed otherwise, the player accompanying a song could assume that a given bass note implied the intervals of 3rd and 5th performed above it: that is, a complete triad built on the bass note. Any ***other*** intervals or chords required special instructions, in the form of numbers placed below the staff under the bass notes. Since a composer would write a bass line rather than actual chords, the bass part acquired a uniquely important function in baroque style. It was called the ***basso continuo*** part (often shortened to ***continuo***); the added numbers or figures below some of the notes also gave rise to the term ***figured bass.***

continuo
figured bass

The continuo part was invariably performed by ***two*** players: one low instrument, perhaps a cello or bassoon, playing the bass line itself, and a second party, usually keyboard, elaborating upon the line by adding the proper harmony. This is called the ***realization*** of the figured bass. When adding chords to the continuo part, a performer was free to choose the actual voicing (density) of the chords, or elaborate upon them in an improvisatory way. The continuo part remained a staple feature of baroque style from its very beginnings. The practice of continuo "shorthand" enabled composers to think in a ***linear*** way, melody against bass, even as they developed the language of ***chord*** progressions that eventually led to the dominance of major-minor tonality. Continuo parts will be heard in many of the works discussed in the next two chapters. Listen for the polarization of the outermost parts, with the inner chordal material realized by the continuo performers.

Claudio Monteverdi

Peri's ***Euridice*** was performed at the wedding celebration of Maria de' Medici and Henry IV of France. It was witnessed by many invited nobles, not only Florentines but representatives of neighboring powers. As court composer to the Duke of Mantua, Claudio Monteverdi (1567–1643) attended the performance and shortly thereafter composed a dramatic, staged work of his own using elements of the new style. It was entitled ***Orfeo,*** premiered at the Mantua court in 1607, and has come down to us as the first really great ***opera.*** In a single work, Monteverdi established many of the conventions of opera which held sway into the nineteenth century. Instead of following the principles of the "new music" dogmatically, he alternated passages in the declamatory style, known as *recitative,* with graceful rhythms and catchy melodies more akin to the Renaissance madrigal. (By this point in his career he had himself composed many madrigals.) Monteverdi wrote lyric *arias* for the important characters, and *choral* numbers that are virtually self-contained madrigals. *Instrumental* music also plays a crucial role in *Orfeo,* adding timbral variety and an expressive voice in the drama. Although Monteverdi called *Orfeo* a "favola" (fable), the term *opera* (for "opera in musica," a "work in music") became the accepted term by the mid-seventeenth century.

recitative

arias

Claudio Monteverdi:
***Orfeo* (excerpts from Acts I and II)** *R1 S1 B6*

The opening *toccata,* or overture, employs the brilliant colors of brasses, strings, winds and drums. Like Gabrieli, Monteverdi was among the first to specify instrumental timbres. Note the abrupt contrast in tempo, dynamic level, and instrumentation, between the overture and the *Prologue* that follows. In this Prologue the Spirit of Music introduces the legend of Orpheus, who attempted to calm the spirits of Hades with his ravishing singing, so that he could bring his dead wife back to the world. The music alternates between a heightened *recitative* and a repeated orchestral interlude (called a *ritornello*) between the stanzas.

ritornello

A more strophic song form can be heard when Orfeo proclaims his joy at marrying Eurydice; the same music is heard for each stanza of the poem. This solo song is called an *aria.* Note that it is immediately followed by the prose rhythms and speech inflections of *recitative;* contrast between aria and recitative has been an important component of opera ever since. When we add choral numbers, and the duets between Orfeo and Eurydice as he attempts to bring her back from Hades (much further along in the plot, and not included in this excerpt), we have a musical drama of great richness. The richness is even greater on stage, with the addition of lighting, costumes, scenery, action, and possibly dancing as well.

At the conclusion of the aria, a shepherd comments on everyone's happiness. At this moment a messenger appears to announce the news of Eurydice's sudden, cruelly unexpected death. The intense, dramatic style of the ensuing recitative dialogue is especially gripping because of Monteverdi's choice of chords. The G-minor triad, at Orfeo's "Ohime, che odo," (Figure 9.3), is as chilling today as it was when first heard in 1607. Our notated example presents a fully "realized" version of the continuo part; a seventeenth century keyboard performer would more likely have read from a figured bass line, without any notated chords.

Figure 9.3

Aria	*Orfeo:* Vi ricorda, o boschi ombrosi, Dei miei lunghi aspri tormenti, Quando i sassi ai miei lamenti Rispondean fatti pietosi? etc. . . .	Orfeo (from Act II) *Shady groves, do you remember* *my long, bitter torments* *when the cliffs, made pityful by my laments,* *responded to them?* *(Rejoice now, then, in my gladness. . . .)*

Recitatives

Shepherd: Mira, deh mira, Orfeo, che d'ogni intorno Ride il bosco e ride il prato . . . etc. . . .	*Admire, Orpheus, how all around* *the woodlands laugh, the meadow laughs* *etc. . . .*
Messenger: Ahi, caso acerbo! Ahi, fato empio e crudele! Ahi, stelle ingiuriose! Ahi, cielo avaro!	*Messenger:* *Ah bitter accident!* *Ah impious and cruel fate!* *Ah harmful stars!* *Ah miserly heaven!*
Shepherd: Qual suon dolente il lieto di perturba? etc. . . . etc. . . . etc. . . .	*Shepherd:* *What doleful sound disturbs the glad day? etc . . .*
Messenger: Pastor, lasciate il canto, Ch'ogni nostr'allegrezza in doglia è volta.	*Messenger:* *Shepherds, leave off singing* *for all our happiness has turned to sorrow.*

Orfeo:
Donde vien? Ove vai?
Ninfa, che porti?

Messenger:
A te ne vengo, Orfeo,
Messaggiera infelice,
Di caso più infelice e più funesto,
La tua bella Euridice. . . .

Orfeo:
Ohimé, che odo?

Messenger:
. . . la tua diletta sposa è morta.

Orfeo:
Ohimé!

Orpheus:
Where do you come from?
Where are you going?
Nymph, what news do you bring?

Messenger:
I come to you, Orpheus
as an unlucky messenger
of most unhappy and most distressing news,
your beautiful Eurydice . . .

Orpheus:
Oh, what do I hear?

Messenger:
. . . your beloved one is dead . . .

Orpheus:
Woe is me!

Monteverdi's ability to suggest intense emotional states by chord arrangement may remind one of Dowland or the Italian madrigalists. Adapting it to the declamatory style of "Le Nuove Musiche," and then joining this to melodic aria, was a brilliant stroke. The new art form, wedding poetry to music and stagecraft, was rapidly acclaimed throughout Italy.

Italian Opera until 1700

The operatic medium became instantly popular, an Italian obsession. All the ingredients were perfect: poetry, dramatic music, pomp, and spectacle. In addition, stagecraft of the time had become very sophisticated, and could depict fires, earthquakes, and gods descending from the clouds. The first *public* opera house was opened in Venice in 1637. Thus an art form originally devised for the aristocracy was now made available to other classes as well, in fact, to anyone who could afford the price of admission. (The elderly Monteverdi, now in his seventies, composed two major operas for the Venice public theatre.) The fashion for opera spread throughout Europe, and everywhere, except in France, the style was Italian. From Madrid to Copenhagen, London to Saint Petersburg, Italian-style opera houses were built and opera companies staffed with Italian personnel. It was equally fashionable during this century to hire Italian craftsmen and builders to create palaces and churches.

By the end of the 1600s Naples had become the major Italian operatic center. (Not that interest has slackened in other cities: in 1700 Venice had sixteen opera theatres!) The Neapolitan style was drastically different from the earlier generation of the Florentine Camerata. The relationship between music and drama had shifted in favor of vocal melody. Audiences were delighted by expansive, heavily embellished melodies, sung by star performers famed for their ravishing voices. Drama and characterization were sacrificed at the expense of *bel canto* ("beautiful singing"). Just as the audience demands had created vocal superstars, the stars in turn demanded showy *arias* to display their talents. In the arias of this period, a three-part ABA form emerged, known as the *aria da capo.*

bel canto

aria da capo

The typical aria would be preceded by a recitative, often a "dry" (*secco*) recitative accompanied only by the simple continuo chords. Most of the story line or dramatic action was advanced through the recitative. The aria presented a "response" to the action: an emotional out-pouring of grief, anger, joy or triumph. Its opening A section was followed by a contrasting B, and then by instructions to start again "from the beginning" (*da capo*). The return to section A, then, was so literal that composers did not bother writing it out again.

An actual performance, though, might be anything ***but*** literal. The vocal soloist would seize the opportunity to embellish the written notes, improvising upon a melody which had already been heard, and displaying some vocal virtuosity along the way. (We will be discussing a recitative and aria from Handel's ***Giulio Cesare*** in the next chapter.)

overture

The ***overture*** for Neapolitan opera developed into an expanded three-part form as well, not with repeated material—as in the aria—but in sections of contrasting tempo (fast, slow, fast) to represent conflicting dramatic states. The Italian overture was now called the ***sinfonia.*** We will return to that term again, because it was to serve as a model for the eighteenth century "symphony."

The vogue for opera was thus firmly established, originally in Italy and then throughout Europe. This mid-seventeenth century account, by an Englishman visiting Venice, is typical:

> We went to the opera, where comedies and other plays are represented in recitative music . . . with variety of scenes painted and contrived with no less art of perspective, and machines for flying in the air and other wonderful notions; taken together, it is one of the most magnificent and expensive diversions the wit of man can invent.

Opera in France

Although a form of opera developed in France, it did not follow Italian models. Festive entertainment at the French court had always stressed dance, rather than poetry or drama. In fact, France was to dominate the world of ballet until the late nineteenth century: the terminology of ballet is basically French, just as that of opera is Italian. Louis XIV was an enthusiastic dancer himself; he and his courtiers often joined in the ballet spectacle. Secondly, the operatic genre that emerged at Louis' court stressed the rhythms and inflections of the French language. It was, in fact, closer to the original spirit of the Camerata than to the Neapolitan ***bel canto.***

Ironically, the music of Louis XIV's Versailles court was dominated by a composer who had emigrated from Italy. Born in Florence as Giovanni Battista Lulli, he is known today by the French form of his name, Jean Baptiste Lully (1632–1687). Under Lully, the French opera was particularly majestic and stately. This befitted the court of an absolute monarch, and a great era of French theatre shaped by the work of Moliere and Racine. Spectacle, processional, and especially dance were essential.

Jean Le Pautre, Versailles Palace during a Performance of Lully's *Alceste.*

Unlike the Italians, Lully did not have to please an audience; his sole "public" was his kingly employer, the strongest monarch in Europe. Appropriately, the court orchestra was also the strongest in Europe, with an expanded string section, known as "the king's twenty-four violins," and outstanding woodwind playing. (France excelled in woodwind construction, contributing greatly to the development of the modern flute and oboe.) Lully conducted this great orchestra and used it to full advantage. For example, he was among the first to move the ensemble to a position in *front* of the operatic stage; by contrast Monteverdi's *Orfeo* orchestra was offstage, invisible to the audience.

Two of Lully's orchestral innovations should be mentioned. He enjoyed using a trio of wind instruments for textural contrast during passages of dance music. This will be noted again in a later chapter when we examine the evolution of the symphony. He preferred a two-part form for the operatic overture. The ***"French Overture,"*** as it is known today, consisted of a slow introduction (often a bit pompous, with stately dotted rhythms), followed by a rapid section in imitative style. This slow-fast format was common to many overtures of the eighteenth century: we will note examples in Handel's *Royal Fireworks Music* and *Messiah* (see Chapter 10).

French Overture

Sonata and Suite

Instrumental music continued to grow in importance throughout the seventeenth century. Although the word "orchestra" has already been mentioned, the standard instrumentation of the modern orchestra did not yet

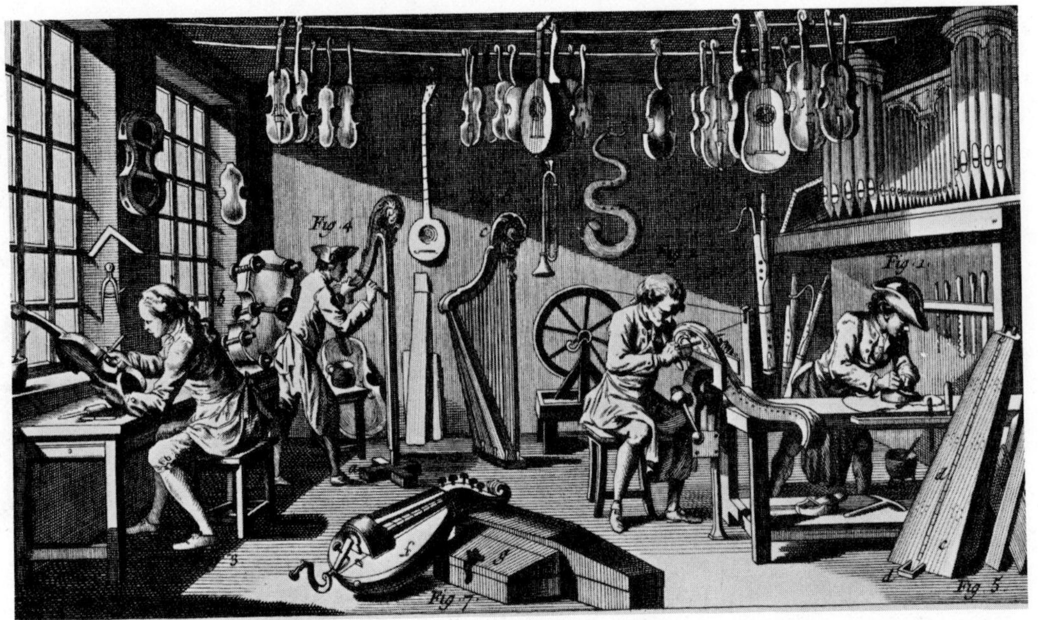

An instrument-makers' workshop, as shown (a bit fancifully) in an engraving from Diderot's Encyclopedia. There is a hurdy-gurdy in the foreground; note, too, the serpent hanging on the rear wall.

exist. Instead there was a flexible pool of instruments, mostly strings, from which a given ensemble could be drawn, plus the continuo. As composers specified the instruments they wished, they also gave more attention to the idiomatic styles of instrumental writing: busy runs, trills, arpeggiated figures, swirls of melodic decoration. The term "baroque" was indeed justified for this music.

Instruments themselves were developed to suit more robust, theatrical requirements. Whereas the viols, shawms, krumhorns, and lutes of earlier centuries had either private, intimate voices or raucously buzzing ones, the newer instruments were built for stength *and* sweetness. France led in the design of wind instruments, and Italy perfected the modern violin, an instrument with a soaring "operatic" quality lacking in the Renaissance viol. The great violin-making families of northern Italy flourished during the seventeenth century: Amati, Guarneri, and especially Stradivari. Germany excelled in organ building (to be discussed in the next chapter).

By the century's close *tonality* had been firmly established, strengthened by the use of the continuo and by chord series acquiring the directional logic of "progressions." Instrumental music made use of the grammar of tonality, particularly the relationship between tonic (I) and dominant (V) to hold the music together and sustain audience attention. These are always concerns of special importance if the music has no words.

The Sonata

sonata/Baroque

The term *"sonata"* had a very flexible meaning in the early *Baroque.* It was a "sounded" piece, played on instruments, as opposed to a "sung" piece (cantata) or a rapid, virtuosic "touch" piece (toccata). A sonata consisted of individual *movements,* short pieces to be played in succession, that would provide contrasts of tempo and mood. Many sonatas were composed for a solo instrument, usually violin, and continuo. Another popular format was the *trio sonata,* scored for two solo instruments and continuo.

trio sonata

Actually there are *four* players performing in a trio sonata, not three, since the continuo role involves a keyboard player and a low instrument reinforcing the bass line. The typical trio sonata will have four movements, in the order slow-fast-slow-fast; imitative textures may occur during the fast movements.

Listen for the *driving rhythmic quality* of baroque instrumental style. There is an obvious regularity of meter, rhythm, and tempo; at a driving fast pace, the effect can be overwhelming. The urgent, insistent rhythm and meter are undoubtedly related to the robust, out-going quality of all baroque art, but they also derive from the implication of tonality itself. As chord progressions push steadily towards goals, creating tension-release states, they generate energy easily translated into rhythmic stresses and accents.

Arcangelo Corelli (1653–1713), a native of Rome, was one of the great violinists in the early days of that instrument: he helped develop new bows and bowing techniques, and was among the most sought-after teachers in Europe. Corelli's compositions were primarily instrumental rather than vocal (unusual for that era), and included many trio sonatas in the four-movement format.

Arcangelo Corelli
Sonata Da Chiesa in F Minor, opus 3 no. 9*

The term *sonata da chiesa* ("church sonata") was given to works a bit more serious in mood, and imitative in texture, than other dance-like sonatas of the period. On the basis of instrumentation, we may consider this work a *trio sonata,* with four movements greatly contrasted in tempo and mood. There is a serious opening movement, a briskly running one, a lyric third movement, and then another rapid movement to end the work.

On the other hand, there is very little contrast *within* the individual movements. Each one presents a single idea, doggedly and systematically extended—perhaps with the same thoroughness that characterizes baroque science and philosophy. The trait also reveals an important esthetic belief of the time: that art must represent the "passions" or "affections," and evoke these in the observer. Ideally, each "affection" should be offered in its

*Available in the "History of Music in Sound" series (RCA Victor), Volume VI.

the unity of the affections

purest, most concentrated state. This theory was known as ***the unity of the affections.***

To properly convey grief, joy, or love, then, nothing less than a single unified presentation would do. Recall our *Orfeo* excerpt: the chorus is either solemn or gay, but not both in the same number. The grim dialogue with the messenger does not intrude upon the lilting quality of Orfeo's aria. In Lully's slow-fast French overtures, the contrasting moods are compartmentalized; they do not spill over into each other's territory. So, too, with the sonata. Each movement maintains one tempo, one characteristic rhythm, one overall texture, one strong melodic idea.

terraced dynamics

On another level, though, contrasts are frequent. Listen for changes in dynamics as loud and soft passages echo one another. Volume, as a factor to command attention, was more important to the Baroque than to earlier styles. In the Corelli sonata, different dynamic levels are sharply alternated and contrasted. This practice, which we also encountered in the Bach harpsichord selections of Part 1, is known as ***terraced dynamics.*** Baroque in-

Figure 9.4

Note the imitation among all three parts, and the figured bass markings for "realization" of the continuo. (The continuo would have been performed by two players.)

strumental style features terraced dynamics until the mid-eighteenth century.

Trio sonata ***texture*** stresses the polarity between the upper lines and the bass, with improvised chordal elaboration in the middle register. But there are subtle distinctions within that texture. Even though the two solo parts of movement I are highly imitative, the presence of the chordal continuo makes the total effect homophonic as in an accompanied duet. In movement II, however, the polyphonic texture is more pronounced as the continuo line joins in the imitation, creating a three-voice "fugue." (See Figure 9.4.) Even though the Baroque was the first great homophonic age, ***polyphony*** (as in this fugal example) never really went out of fashion: it was transformed by the new contexts of tonality and harmonic logic. Corelli's polyphonic lines, when heard together, form chords that succeed each other with the peculiar "intelligence" and harmonic drive of tonality. (This is equally true of the Bach fugue heard during Part 1.) Just as the Renaissance textures could be called ***modal harmony*** and ***modal counterpoint,*** the Baroque witnessed the rise of ***tonal counterpoint*** and ***tonal harmony.***

Movement III resembles movement I in its slower tempo, triple meter, and chordal texture. Movement IV gives the basso continuo a nicely angular melodic contour of its own. Listen to the upper parts imitating each other; note, too, the melodic sequences that maintain the sense of steady forward motion. The movement has a two-part (AB) form, with each part repeated. The cadence at the end of A occurs on the dominant (V) chord, thus making the entire form tonally "incomplete;" the second section completes it.

The Suite of Dances

Keyboard instruments continued to grow in popularity, and for good reason: they could cope with many polyphonic parts at once, and were also ideal for the performance of chordal accompaniments. Although the lute was gradually replaced by the more full-bodied guitar, the harpsichord and its English variant, the virginal, survived the transition from Renaissance to Baroque. In fact, harpsichord building reached a peak in the seventeenth and early eighteenth centuries which was not seen again until its revival in the twentieth century. Elaborate organs, the best of them designed in Germany, were also installed in churches and courtly chapels being built across Europe.

Keyboard instruments were not only essential in continuo roles, but they were also valued as ***solo*** instruments—particularly since amateurs could easily make music with them. An extensive solo literature emerged, including music for church, home, and court: flashy ***toccatas*** and ***fantasias; preludes*** that often elaborated upon chord progressions; highly contrapuntal ***ricercars*** that led the way to the fugues of the following generation; and ***suites of dances.***

suite

The ***suite*** originated in the late Renaissance practice of performing dances in pairs. By the mid-seventeenth century, soloists would often perform suites of four or more dance-derived movements. There were four basic movements, in the following order: (1) the ***Allemande,*** a moderately slow dance in duple meter; (2) the ***Courante,*** in triple meter and a bit livelier; (3) the ***Sarabande,*** in a stately, dignified triple meter; and (4) the ***Gigue,*** derived from the British "jig," in a rapid, spritely compound meter such as $\frac{6}{8}$. These movements are nicely contrasted, not only in the obvious areas of meter and tempo, but in rhythmic details unique to each dance: dotted rhythms in one, syncopation in another, and so on. There is also an attractive balance of national influences, since the four dances are derived respectively from German, French, Spanish, and British models.

Most individual dance movements were composed in two-part (AB) binary form: the opening section moving to a closely related key (usually the dominant), and the second part returning to the tonic. The movements of a suite were further unified by a common tonality. The slower dances often provided an excuse for extensive ornamentation, almost to the point of obscuring the basic dance rhythm. Of course, this music was not meant for actual dancing; the only physical activity would have been the performer's intricate fingerwork.

Purcell and English Music

Musical developments in seventeenth century England were complicated by severe internal troubles. Political and religious conflicts led to the beheading of Charles I in 1649 and the establishment of a Commonwealth under Puritan control. The Commonwealth years were very difficult for the performing arts: the Puritans banned organs from their churches and ordered theatres closed. When the monarchy was restored in 1660, it was with a French, rather than Italian or native English, musical emphasis. Charles II, the new king, had spent his exile in France, and organized his own court in the image of Versailles. The English public was uninterested in any kind of drama (musical or otherwise) presented in a foreign language. The ***masque,*** an entertainment built about simple tunes, dances, and spoken dialogue rather than recitative, flourished; opera did not.

There had also been a prior tradition of English music of the theatre. During the Restoration, a few composers began using their experience with masque and incidental music for plays to attempt an English style of opera. The most gifted of these composers was Henry Purcell (1659–1695), and his ***Dido and Aeneas*** is now acknowledged as the only great English opera of that century. In his short lifetime Purcell wrote a great deal of music: court masques, works for harpsichord, "catches" or rounds, often with ribald texts, anthems for the Anglican church, and music for the theatre. He served as organist at Westminster Abbey, and his burial place is beneath the Abbey's great organ.

Dido and Aeneas was composed in 1669 for performance at a girls' school in London. Very likely its brief length and chamber instrumentation of strings and continuo are related to the practical considerations of the school performance. The story, taken from Vergil's *Aeneid,* concerns the legendary Aeneas, who is said to have escaped the fall of Troy and later founded Rome, and his ill-fated love for Dido, Queen of Carthage. Purcell had to convert this story to a script suitable for operatic treatment: arias, recitative dialogue, perhaps opportunities for duos or trios, choral numbers or dances. All opera composers work with such a script; even if their dramatic material is a play to begin with, it still needs to be restructured into an operatic play. The script for an opera is called the ***libretto,*** and the person who writes it is known as the ***librettist.*** (On occasion, composer and librettist are the same person.) The word "libretto" means "little book," and compared with spoken drama, an operatic script is indeed little: it contains surprisingly few words. This may seem puzzling until we recall that words often take longer to sing than to speak. Furthermore, in certain operatic styles whole phrases may be repeated.

libretto

librettist

Purcell's librettist was Nahum Tate, who later became Poet Laureate of England. He added a number of scenes to the *Aeneid's* original story to allow for choral singing and some dancing. The chorus of witches (more Shakespeare than Vergil!) is a notable example.

Henry Purcell
Dido and Aeneas (excerpt from Act III)

The opera's most famous aria, known as "Dido's Lament," was discussed during Part 1. To be fully understood, this eloquent soliloquy should be perceived as the culmination of a total dramatic *scene* (complete with recitative and choral elements). Our excerpt provides the narrative immediately preceding the aria.

In forging an operatic style, Purcell used English madrigal technique, especially in the choral passages, and drew also on his knowledge of French and Italian developments. The French influence, for example, shows in the slow-fast overture format, and the great emphasis on choral singing and dancing.

The opening statement, by Dido's lady-in-waiting, Belinda, is set as recitative, but with great regard for the expressive import of the lines. It is heard against an accompaniment of full, sustained orchestral chords (a French-influenced departure from the *secco* recitative of Neapolitan opera). The heated dialogue between Dido and Aeneas retains the inflection and syllabic stress of recitative, but it also offers strong melodic shape and tonal direction: at times it seems on the verge of breaking out into full-blown aria. Short phrases, rapid chord changes, and the rhythms of impassioned speech heighten the pace of the scene.

Certain musical gestures enhance the drama of the confrontation: Dido's mocking repetition of Aeneas' phrase, "by all that's good" (parodying the melody as well), and her striking melodic inflection over a dissonant accompaniment at the word "weeps." Note, too, the furious exchange of imitating leaping octaves as Aeneas exclaims: "I'll stay . . ." and Dido answers "No! away!" A brief choral statement, in the imitative style reminiscent of Renaissance madrigal, leads to Dido's last brief recitative and then her great aria.

Purcell was neither the first, nor the last, composer to create variations upon a "ground," but like all first-rate artists, he had the knack of taking commonly known formulas and transforming them in a very special, personal way. For any number of reasons—the chromatic bass line, its asymmetrical five-measure length, the unexpected, haunting high G of the final "Remember me."—the aria known as "Dido's Lament" is strangely unsettling and genuinely moving.

Belinda
See, Madam, where the Prince appears!
Such sorrow in his looks he bears
As would convince you still he's true.

Aeneas
What shall lost Aeneas do?
How, Royal fair, shall I impart
The Gods' decree, and tell you we must part?

Dido
Thus on the fatal banks of Nile,
Weeps the deceitful crocodile!
Thus hypocrites that murder act,
Make Heaven and gods the authors of the fact!

Aeneas
By all that's good!

Dido
By all that's good, no more!
All that's good you have foreswore.
To your promised empire fly,
And let foresaken Dido die.

Aeneas
In spite of Jove's command I'll stay,
Offend the Gods, and love obey!

Dido
No, faithless man! Thy course pursue,
I'm now resolved as well as you . . . etc.

Aeneas
Let Jove say what he will, I'll stay—

Dido
No, no! away. away!

Aeneas
I'll stay, and love obey.

Dido
No, no! To death I'll fly if longer you delay!
Away, away!
(*Exit Aeneas*)

But death, alas, I cannot shun,
Death must come when he is gone.

Chorus
Great minds against themselves conspire,
And shun the cure they most desire.

Dido
Thy hand, Belinda—darkness shades me,
On thy bosom let me rest.
More I would, but death invades me,
Death is now a welcome guest.
When I am laid in earth, may my wrongs create ⎤
No trouble in thy breast. ⎥ Aria
Remember me!—But ah! forget my fate. ⎦

("Dido's Lament" indicated by bracket)

Purcell once remarked about English music, "Being farther from the Sun, we are of later growth than our neighbor countries, and must be content to shake off our barbarity by degrees." His own synthesis of English and European models marked the real beginning of a mature English Baroque style; his death at the age of thirty-six cut short that beginning. For the next two centuries English musical life would be dominated by foreign influences. As we shall note in Chapter 10, her greatest eighteenth century composer was a German immigrant named Handel.

Aside from Purcell and Handel, England's major contribution to baroque music is probably the invention of the public ***concert.*** In 1672 a violinist named John Banister, formerly of Charles II's royal orchestra, arranged public performances of music for the entrance fee of one shilling. This innovation led to a weekly series in London, organized in 1678 and paid for by subscriptions, that lasted thirty-six years. The public concert, like the public opera, added a new dimension and a new location for music making.

Baroque Style Characteristics

Before moving on to the late baroque era of Bach and Handel, let us pause to summarize those features of baroque style observed thus far. The most prominent is probably the ***continuo,*** a word that can refer either to the part or to the instruments playing that part. In either case, listen for a bass line and a series of chords, the bass line performed by a low-register instrument and chords by a keyboard instrument realizing a written ***figured bass.*** The importance of the continuo gives baroque music a characteristic ***polarity of textures:*** the topmost melodic lines and the bass usually assuming greatest priority, and the inner parts simply filling out the continuo's harmonic scaffolding. The most obvious exceptions to this general rule are strictly imitative pieces—fugues or sonata movements—that treat all polyphonic lines equally.

Baroque ***rhythm*** and ***tempo*** (except for the speech patterns of recitative) are steady, hard-driving, and aggressive, with an invariable sense of regular "beat." ***Melodic contours*** can be extroverted and forward-driving, often mirroring the bold, surging quality of the rhythm. Extensive, ornate embellishment may be found in some melodies while others are jagged and angular.

The dynamic limitations of the keyboard lead to ***terraced dynamic*** effects, with various levels juxtaposed for contrast. ***Timbre*** is explored more systematically than in earlier periods, as composers specify particular instruments for given passages. The instruments themselves are more flexible and full-voiced, more "theatrical" or "operatic," than their predecessors.

Major-minor ***tonality*** is an overwhelming force by the late seventeenth century. Tonality is related to the ***homophonic*** nature of baroque texture, both as cause and as effect: harmony now consists of convincing progressions, not just chords in series. The driving force of tonality influences the directional thrust of melody and rhythm, as in the frequent use of extended melodic sequences, and the use of *forms* that exploit this thrust. Both the three-part ABA and two-part binary (AB) depend upon the logic of tonal goals.

All of the above features are audible: they can be heard and recognized by the listener. There are other equally important baroque features that are *not* so immediately audible. Perhaps the details noted so far should be regarded as the "surface" manifestations of more fundamental, deep-rooted concepts:

1. *The Idea of Contrast.* Striking contrasts are frequently used within the same musical statement: perhaps terraced dynamic levels, or widely polarized upper voices and low bass line. Contrast is also expressed in the alternation of slow and fast in the operatic overture, or the dichotomy between recitative and aria. The confrontation of "heavy" and "light" density, or greater and fewer numbers of players, will be discussed in the next chapter.

2. *The Idea of the Chord.* Composers have come to view the triad as more than a pleasant sound arrived at polyphonically: it is a vertical "thing" in itself. Before the late Renaissance, open 5ths were considered the consonant norm and triads a more resonant option. By the mid-seventeenth century, however, open 5ths seem empty and somehow incomplete. Even baroque counterpoint is "chordal"; polyphony creates, or implies, harmony along the way. The ideal baroque texture, as suggested in Figure 9.5, is a merger of homophony and polyphony, with linear elements dominating homophony and chordal considerations underlying counterpoint.

3. *The Doctrine of the "Affections."* This concerns the belief in music's power to represent strong emotions, and its obligation to evoke these in the listener. It was felt that a work or movement should express a *single* emotion. This accounts for the cohesive quality of baroque music (each individual statement offering but one tempo, one prevailing texture, one characteristic rhythm, and so on), and counteracts an opposing tendency towards vivid surface contrasts. The mood being expressed is often larger-

Figure 9.5

than-life, appropriate to the theatrical nature of the period; emotions may be conceived as prototypes—components of a highly stylized ritual art.

4. ***The Existence of an Audience.*** As opera, dance suite, and sonata evolve, the act of making music gradually becomes less dependent upon a larger ceremony; it has become self-sufficient. A class of listeners, or ***audience,*** has also come into being: those who participate in the musical "ritual" without actually performing themselves. This change inevitably leads to others. The composer may write for an audience he does not know personally; composer and performer(s) find themselves in the foreground, without the traditional camouflage of pageantry or liturgy; listeners, who have ***not*** assembled to express their own feelings of grief or triumph, are nevertheless asked to ***respond*** in a sympathetic way to the emotions represented in the music. These changes, begun during the late Renaissance, became quite important during the Baroque and succeeding eras.

10

The Late Baroque

It is only when we know how to arrange a series of harmonies appropriately that we can derive from them a melody suitable to the subject . . .

Jean-Phillipe Rameau, from Treatise on Harmony, *1727*

Introduction: The Era of Bach and Handel

Many listeners associate the baroque period with the figures who dominated its closing decades, the great composers of the early eighteenth century. Obviously, there is much to be said for exploring the *entire* 150 years of baroque style: the pleasures of listening to Monteverdi and Purcell are self-evident. Still, there is no denying the power and grandeur of late baroque music. A convenient beginning date for this period-within-a-period would be the year 1685, in which two of its greatest composers, Handel and J. S. Bach, were born. 1685 is also the birthdate of Domenico Scarlatti, whose music foreshadows important trends of a style to come, just as Bach and Handel sum up the best features of the older esthetic. The French composer Rameau, whose ideas about harmony influenced the entire era, was born in 1683; the Italian Antonio Vivaldi was born in 1675, ten years before his great German colleagues. Rarely has such an impressive cast of characters appeared on the world's musical stage within a single decade.

Bach and Handel are the major figures of this generation. Although surprisingly different in many respects, as we will see, they also shared important characteristics. Both men wrote music for aristocratic patrons, but many works for a middle-class bourgeois public as well. Both were *German* by birth, although Handel became a British citizen in 1725, and both are perhaps best known today for *religious* compositions.

Religious Music during the Baroque

Let us turn the clock back, and return to the early 1600s. The craze for opera made a great impression on the Roman Catholic Church. A form of sung religious drama, derived from opera, developed in Rome, specifically at a prayer-hall and popular meeting place called the "oratorio." The new dramatic genre was called ***oratorio*** as well. It was seized upon by Counter-Reformation leaders as a way of making religion attractive and understandable to the masses. In fact, the first major composer of oratorio, Giacomo Carrissimi (1605–1674), was the director of a Jesuit school. The oratorio used Biblical passages, either in Latin or in the vernacular, set in recitative-and-aria format. Vocal soloists portrayed the characters, and a chorus and instrumental ensemble were used as well. By mid-century a singing narrator was also needed to hold the story together, since a tradition for ***not*** staging these works had developed.

oratorio

cantata

The ***cantata*** was, in its own way, an operatic offshoot, too. Originally meaning "sung piece," as opposed to "sonata" or "played piece," it consisted of a collection of arias, recitatives, and instrumental interludes. Cantatas, like oratorios, were unstaged. The early Italian examples were often written for small chamber groups, including no more than a few solo voices, rather than the large forces of oratorio and opera. Texts were drawn from sacred or secular sources. By the late seventeenth century, German composers had adapted the cantata to the needs of the Protestant service, added a chorus, and wedded the format to the Lutheran hymn tune known as the ***chorale*** (see Chapter 8). A Protestant cantata will be examined later, when we discuss Bach's music. German composers also set the ***Passion,*** the story of the Crucifixion according to one of the Gospels, in a style similar to that of oratorio and cantata.

All of these genres used the dramatic gestures and musical devices of opera for religious purposes. But they were not necessarily liturgical: although the German cantatas were used in Protestant church services, Italian cantata and oratorio did not fall within the Catholic liturgy. Handel's English oratorios, as we will see, were meant to be performed in theatres rather than churches.

The Rise of German Music

Germany had gradually become an important musical center during the seventeenth century, due largely to the efforts of German composers who had traveled to Italy. A number studied with Giovanni Gabrieli, and returned home armed with the latest developments in Venetian antiphonal style. Germany had become the world's great center of organ design, with special emphasis on the contrasting timbres and dynamic levels essential for large-scale terraced effects. The organ symbolized German craftsmanship and musical values, as the Stradivarius violin represented the musical art of Italy.

Politically, Germany was recovering from decades of religious warfare. Although a unified central government, on the French or English model, did

Martin Engelbrecht, ***The Organist.*** An eighteenth-century German engraving of a choirmaster and pupil, rehearsing at a small church organ of the period.

not exist, there were many states, minor courts, and cities displaying as much pomp and dignity as each could muster. Churches were objects of great civic pride, and religious observations were taken seriously by largely middle-class congregations. Frederick the Great of Prussia was as absolute a monarch as France's Louis XIV had been a century earlier. He was quite knowledgeable about music, an excellent amateur flutist and composer, and the founder of the Berlin opera. Frederick began his rule in 1740, as the Baroque was coming to an end, but his passionate support for the arts speaks for a tradition that had been growing for more than a century.

Tonality

One important difference between the late Baroque and Monteverdi's generation can be stated in a single word: *tonality.* The weakening of the church modes could already be observed during the Renaissance (see Chapter 8), and the modes declined even further during the seventeenth century. Concepts of chord progression, strongly directional bass line, and driving forward motion led musicians to favor *two* modes, called "major" and "minor," over the others.

The triad was the basis of baroque tonal harmony, as it had been for Renaissance model harmony. Baroque composers, however, used triads in a way that related each to the other, and all of them to one *central* focal triad. The relationship between dominant (V) and tonic (I) is especially strong. The subdominant (IV) is considered the mirror image of the dominant, lying a 5th below (rather than a 5th above) the tonic, and it, too, plays an important role in the logic of tonality. (See Figure 10.1.) Other triads, such as the ones built on pitches II, III and VI of the major scale, can act as way-stations between I, IV and V, and also create interesting sub-relationships among themselves.

Rameau's *Treatise on Harmony,* quoted at the opening of this chapter, attempted to gather this knowledge into a system: a typically baroque "encyclopedic" gesture in itself. Interestingly, scholars of the time often used the word "harmony" to mean natural law. (A number of cosmic theories, dating back to the early 1600s, had titles such as *Universal Harmony* or *The Harmonies of the World.*) Rameau saw that melodies were now being derived from, or constructed upon, their harmonies; as opposed to the tendencies of earlier ages. He was also the first to state that chords with identical pitches but different bass notes had a very special family relationship. They are, in fact, different *inversions* of the same basic triad: each variant in Figure 10.2, for example, possesses the same *root* (the note C) which identifies it and its tonal function.

The relationships between chords and keys generate long-range *forms* that can hold the interest for extended lengths of time. Just as pitches and

Figure 10.1

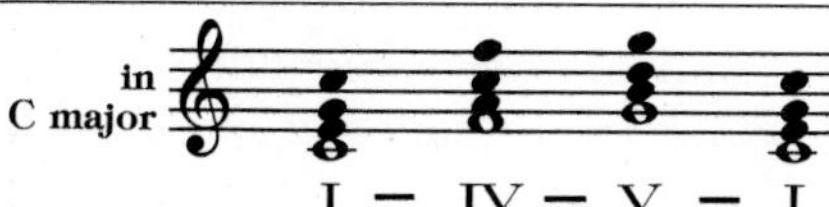

Figure 10.2

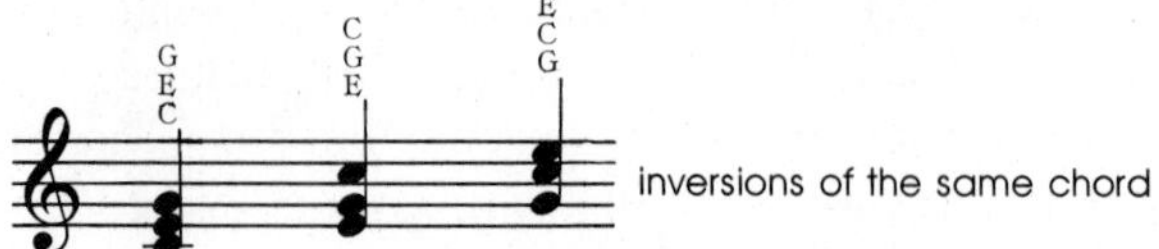

chords are related hierarchically about a center, various tonalities are related to the central tonality of a piece. ***Modulation*** from one key to another, changing the listener's focus so that a new key center is accepted, is vitally important; thus different sections of a movement, or different movements of an extended work, might be stated in contrasting ***keys.*** The total work remains tonal so long as the ending returns to, and confirms, the original key. Melodies could be transposed from one key to another, and the many ***sequences*** of late baroque melody, moving from level to level, testify to the fascination composers must have felt for this procedure. Sequences often follow a strict harmonic logic, in the service of long-range tonality.

The most ***closely related keys*** were assumed to be those with the most notes or chords in common. Strongest relationships are those of tonic-dominant, and tonic-subdominant, tonalities that lie only a 5th apart (such as C major and G major). ***Minor*** tonalities have a slightly different orbit of related keys. The closest is the "relative major," a major key built a 3rd above the minor tonic (such as D minor and F major), with the dominant key also very closely related.

Tonality assigns priorities not only to the pitches in a scale (the moons orbiting a planet, in our Chapter 2 illustration), but to all scales and keys in relation to the central one (an entire solar system). If these relationships seem puzzling, rest assured that they will appear again and again in the chapters on classic and romantic music.

Vivaldi and the Concerto

Baroque instrumental music evolved with incredible rapidity. It is difficult to believe that a single century could have produced such changes: from the oddly assorted band of Monteverdi's *Orfeo* of 1607, to the idiomatic orchestral writing of the 1700s. This phenomenal growth was aided by the new homophonic style and the basso continuo, which freed the upper parts for florid virtuosic display. Other factors included developments in instrument construction, and the festive entertainments, including opera, for which instruments were increasingly important.

concerto grosso

Arcangelo Corelli also did much to develop the early ***concerto grosso,*** the most brilliant orchestral genre of the Baroque. The format of the early concerto grosso exploited the fact that an orchestra of strings and continuo contained within itself the instrumentation of a trio sonata. Corelli composed pieces in which trio sonata textures emerged from the weightier orchestral mass. (To reverse the image, we could imagine early concertos as

Gabriel Metsu, *Reverie.*

trio sonatas with orchestral reinforcement in selected passages.) The smaller body of players was also a member of the larger ensemble, and continued to play during the orchestral sections as well.

concertino
ripieno

The basic idea of the concerto grosso was contrast: the *stile concertato* observed earlier in the music of Garbrieli. The contrast was mainly one of weight and volume between the smaller group, the ***concertino,*** and the full ensemble, the ***ripieno,*** or ***tutti*** (''all'').

In the generation following Corelli, the Venetian Antonio Vivaldi (1675–1741) carried the concerto idea even further. Like Corelli, Vivaldi was an outstanding violinist; he trained for the priesthood, but shortly after being ordained in 1703 was forced to retire due to ill health. (Because of his calling and the color of his hair, he was known as the "red priest.") He became a teacher at the Ospedale della Pieta, a music academy for foundling girls in Venice, and conducted their orchestra. This ensemble, which included performers of great skill on just about every known instrument, acquired widespread fame during Vivaldi's tenure, partly because it was composed entirely of women. This reaction of a visiting Englishman is typical:

> The sight of the orchestra still makes me smile . . . it is entirely of the feminine gender . . . nothing is more common than to see a delicate white hand journeying across an enormous double-bass, or a pair of rosy cheeks puffing with all their efforts at a French horn.

But, from all reports, in most instances the smiles turned to admiration and applause: the performances were outstanding. We can guess at the level of Vivaldi's students, since he wrote most of his concertos for them. There are more than 450 Vivaldi concertos. Many of them are ***solo concertos*** for one player and orchestra: solo violin, flute, piccolo, horn, bassoon, or mandolin, plus the standard orchestra of strings and continuo. The *solo concerto* exploits the difference in timbre between the single instrument and ensemble, as well as the density contrasts of the concerto grosso.

solo concerto

Earlier concertos had favored the four-movement (slow-fast-slow-fast) format of the trio sonata. In contrast, Vivaldi concertos often consisted of *three* movements, in *fast-slow-fast* sequence. This is reminiscent of the Italian operatic overture, except that there are now separate movements rather than connected sections. Vivaldi's use of the *ritornello* in the faster movements was also derived from the opera. The alternation of an unchanging orchestral motive (the ritornello) with a succession of different solo passages can be traced back to Monteverdi; it has already been noted in the Act I Prologue of his *Orfeo*. Vivaldi treated the solo instrument as a "voice" in the operatic sense; this voice was allowed a certain idiomatic, rhapsodic freedom, while the overall structure was anchored to familiar, regularly recurring orchestral passages.

Antonio Vivaldi

Concerto in G Major for flute and orchestra opus 10, no. 4*

Movement I: Allegro. The movement's main *ritornello* theme is stated briskly by the orchestra, in the home key of G major. The compound $\frac{6}{8}$ meter contains many syncopations and forceful accents. The solo flute is *not* heard during the ritornello, in direct opposition to the concerto grosso style.

When the soloist enters, the basic ritornello tune is altered, and then

*Recorded by Jean-Pierre Rampal on CBS Records D3S-770.

very quickly abandoned in favor of new material. During this extended flute passage there is a modulation to the dominant, and a restatement of the ritornello in that key. The soloist enters again with fresh material, and another modulation carries the music to the key of the relative minor; there is hardly time to adjust to this, when another modulation leads to the return of the orchestral ritornello in a fairly "distant" minor key. An extended passage for flute and orchestra, more lyric and certainly less syncopated, leads back to the tonic key and a vigorous repeat of the opening orchestral ritornello.

The unity of the "affections" has been maintained: there is but one mood, tempo, and overall texture to the movement. But within that unity Vivaldi has juggled great contrasts: density and timbre, terraced dynamics, high and low registers. Tonalities are also contrasted, as the music moves from one key level to another, often by melodic sequences, eventually returning to the tonic.

The slow movement, not illustrated here, is in a contrasting key, a practice begun in the late works of Corelli. Many of Vivaldi's slow movements are lyric and expressive, reminding one of operatic arias. Instead of an alternation between two contending forces, the slow movements often feature a solo melody of great eloquence and a subdued orchestral accompaniment.

Vivaldi's concertos were widely known throughout Europe. Bach and Handel were among his admirers and imitators. But he was virtually forgotten, like most of his baroque colleagues, during the nineteenth and early twentieth centuries. The great early-music revival after World War II brought his music back to public attention. Vivaldi was in fact, one of the composers most seized upon by orchestras, conductors, and producers during the early days of the long-playing record: those 450-plus concertos (all under public domain, rather than held by copyright) were too rich a resource to be ignored! Thanks to the recording industry he is as well-known now as he was during his lifetime.

Handel: Opera, Oratorio, and Pageantry

The career of George Frideric Handel (1685–1759) illustrates the cosmopolitan, theatrical, flamboyant aspects of baroque music at their best. Handel's musical life was spent amidst the pomp, glamour, and intrigue of opera house, theatre, and royal court. From his boyhood in a small German town, he was led to the great European cities, where he met smashing success and some resounding failures. Although born a German, he made his early reputation as a composer of Italian opera, and found London so congenial that he spent more than half his life there. Indeed, he is often considered one of the great figures of ***English*** music: in every respect a citizen of the world.

Born to a prosperous middle-class family in the town of Halle (Saxony), Handel showed great musical talent as a child. His father wanted him to study law rather than enter the disreputable profession of music. Handel enrolled in the university for a year, but then firmly decided upon a musical career, and journeyed to the great north-German city of Hamburg; he was now eighteen years old. In Hamburg he first heard Italian opera, played the violin in the opera orchestra, and then advanced to the post of conductor. Shortly after his first opera was staged in Hamburg in 1705 he set out for Italy, and spent four years there perfecting his craft. He heard all the latest operas, oratorios, and concertos, and produced works of his own.

His operas met with great acclaim in Italy; he was known affectionately as "the Saxon," and honored by cardinals and princes. An appointment as court conductor at Hanover brought him back to Germany in 1710. Almost immediately, Handel obtained a leave of absence to visit London, which was just beginning to develop a passion for Italian opera. His ***Rinaldo*** (1711) made him the idol of London society. Although he returned to Hanover for a year, Handel obtained a second leave and set out for London in 1712; he remained in England virtually the rest of his life.

Handel and Italian Opera

It must be remembered that Italian opera of the early eighteenth century was quite different from the declamatory theatre of Monteverdi. In fact, the opera had departed from the ideals of the Florentine Camerata in just about every respect. Dramatic story line had been sacrificed in the interests of vocal virtuosity, lush arias decorated with trills and runs, and all the egocentric excesses of the "star system." The Neapolitan ***bel canto*** was the European rage. People flocked to the opera houses to hear spectacular voices; composers and impresarios were kept busy turning out a steady stream of works that would make the stars and their audiences happy. It was all vaguely reminiscent of Hollywood during the Golden Age of the movies.

The singers most idolized for their glorious voices were the ***castrati:*** castrated males who retained their high boyish range, but with breath and lung power that no female could match. Boys who showed particularly lovely voices might be likely candidates for castration. Parents would consent to the operation, dreaming of glamorous, lucrative careers for their sons; indeed, the public did bestow riches and celebrity status upon the greatest ***castrato*** voices. We may marvel at the cost! But perhaps we injure our own entertainment-media-sports superstars in a different way.

Dramatic "realism" was practically nonexistent: audiences paid their money for monumental sets, spectacular special effects in staging, and the privilege of hearing thirty arias in an evening. The flimsy stories depicted gods and goddesses, mythological heroes and monsters, kings and queens, all objects of identification or wish-fulfillment for the audience. These characters would be shown in situations that could exploit a wide range of passions or "affections," displayed in florid arias.

The dramatic narrative would be advanced during recitative passages. There were two kinds of recitative: the *secco* (dry) syllabic speech setting, and the more elaborate recitative of sustained harmony and melismatic singing. Arias, duets, trios, and possibly choral numbers or dances, would be featured as well. Extended orchestral passages, especially one or more overtures in either French or Italian style, completed the fairly predictable formula.

Handel worked within this routine, and apparently delighted in it. His best operatic moments, though, are truly dramatic as well as decorative.

George Frideric Handel
Arias from *Giulio Cesare*.

Giulio Cesare (Julius Caesar) of 1724 is a fine example of Handel's operatic art. Act III features a number of dramatically convincing recitatives, dialogues and arias. Early in the act, Cleopatra is shown in a particularly unhappy state; she has been captured by her rivals, and believes her lover Caesar to be dead. After an intense, agitated recitative, she sings a *da capo* aria, "Piangero la sorte mia" ("I bemoan my own cruel and unjust fate"), whose mood is basically that of quiet resignation. This mood is altered suddenly by the faster, churning middle section ("after death, my ghost will wander restlessly"), but then resumes at the aria's *da capo* end.

Cleopatra then bids farewell to her handmaidens, in a style midway between recitative and aria. Caesar suddenly enters—obviously very much alive—and the style abruptly shifts to an urgent *secco* recitative dialogue, accompanied only by continuo. Caesar rushes off again, leaving Cleopatra to sing another elaborate aria: "Da tempeste il legno infranto" ("out of the storm the vessel makes safe to port"). Its joyous opening mood is tempered by a more pensive, contrasting B section; the *da capo* return of the opening allows the soprano to display her improvisational skill and vocal virtuosity in a spendid way.

The entire opera has been recorded, with Beverly Sills as Cleopatra, for RCA Victor (RCA LSC-6182). One may also hear the "Piangero la sorta mia" aria, plus its preceding recitative, in a performance by Elly Ameling for Phillips (6570–113).

Music For the Royal Court

Although Handel had requested a short leave to visit England in 1712, he did not return to Hanover; he had, in fact, become a great favorite with Queen Anne. But in 1714 Queen Anne died. England's new King George I was none other than Handel's ex-employer, the former Elector of Hanover. George I may have been upset at Handel's previous defection, but he increased the composer's annual subsidy and made him music master of the palace. Handel's standing was probably enhanced by his long-standing friendship with the king's son (the future George II), whom he had known

William Daniel, ***London.*** 1804. A view of London, as Handel might have seen it. The Tower of London is in the foreground, and the River Thames at the left.

in Hanover; George I, as a none-too-popular German ruler of the English, also needed the support of his musical countryman who was the darling of London society.

And so Handel divided his activities between the commercial world of the public opera house—"show business" in every sense of the term—and the security of the court. When George II succeeded to the throne in 1726, Handel's stipend increased further. His court duties included the composition of anthems, ceremonial music, and incidental music for various kinds of entertainment. Two of his best-known works fall in the last category: the ***Water Music,*** originally performed at a boating pageant on the river Thames, and the ***Royal Fireworks Music,*** meant to accompany a grand public fireworks display in the royal park. Both works can be regarded as grand examples of the late Baroque suite.

George Frideric Handel
Royal Fireworks Music: Overture; Bourrée *R1 S2 B1*

By the eighteenth century, suites were being composed for chamber ensemble and orchestra as well as solo instruments. The format of the suite had expanded to include an "overture" in the slow-fast French manner, and a variety of dance patterns—the ***Minuet, Gavotte*** or ***Bourrée,*** to name a few—which might be added to or substituted for the standard Allemande, Courante, Sarabande, and Gigue. Handel's music for the fireworks entertainment follows this general format: an expansive, festive overture, followed by a number of dance-derived movements, including a Bourrée and two Minuets. None of it was meant to be listened to attentively, as it would have been played amidst processionals, refreshments, constant talking and walking about, and a generally festive carnival air. Thousands of people attended the park celebration in April 1749, and reports indicate that the orchestra numbered over 100 players: dozens of oboes and bassoons, nine each of horns and trumpets, and three pairs of tympani! (Modern performances are usually given in standard orchestral instrumentation.)

Listen first to the overture, in the traditional French sequence of slow and fast sections. The characteristic dotted rhythms of the slow opening are truly majestic. Most likely the royal processional across the park took place when this music was heard. The faster section, beginning with a rapid fanfare for trumpets and drums, is in itself an ABA part form. Part A consists of the fanfare, an answering motive of descending scales, and another highly syncopated tune for full orchestra. A relaxed, contemplative B is followed by A again; another stately passage, reminiscent of the opening mood, is added just before the final climax.

Handel's ***key*** contrasts are worth mentioning. For any late Baroque composer, the form of a piece lay in its tonal scheme as well as its succession of motives. The slow opening of the overture begins in D major, and moves to the dominant, subdominant, and back to D again. The fast section is also based in D major, with the gentle B section in the relative minor.

The dance-derived Bourrée which follows is in binary form: an opening section leads away from the tonic, and the answering section returns to it. Observe how ingeniously Handel adds unique twists, turns and subtleties to that straightforward ground plan. The Bourrée is in the key of D minor. Its opening A section has two phrases of unequal length, a phrase of four measures answered by one of six, reaching a cadence in the key of the relative major. Section B is both simpler and more complex: although its phrases all seem equal in length, there are more than two of them. In fact, the final cadence is delayed, not once but twice, by a cleverly deceptive chord progression. The Bourrée is in a swinging, spritely duple meter, beginning on an upbeat; its overall shape is outlined in Figure 10.3. ***Repeats*** of each section were customary in performing baroque dances. These provided an even more complex shape.

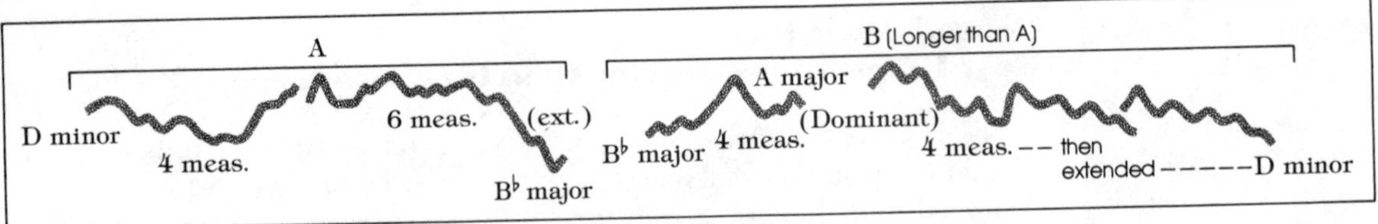

Figure 10.3

The English Oratorio

Although Handel continued to compose Italian operas for the London public, he gradually discovered that English enthusiasm for entertainment in a foreign language had run its course. An impresario and manager himself, he was made painfully aware of this change when, in the early 1730s, his own opera companies went bankrupt. As his operatic enterprises collapsed, he suffered a complete breakdown and returned to Germany for a period of rest.

Rivalries, political intrigue and bad management had all contributed to the failure of Handel's opera companies. Beyond this lay the general decline of Italian opera in London. Although the aristocracy doted on opera, England's powerful middle class had little interest in the medium. Blessed with one of the world's grandest traditions of ***spoken*** drama, the English public

Rowlandson, ***John Bull at the Italian Opera.*** 18th century (right) and ***Handel Conducting an Oratorio Rehearsal*** (left), 18th century. A contemporary caricature gives a clear view of the English response to Italian opera, which eventually was felt by Handel. At a later stage in his career, Handel is shown conducting an oratorio rehearsal; he is seen on the right.

had little patience with sung drama, and none at all for stage works in a foreign language. One writer of the time, bemused by opera's linguistic difficulties, observed:

> . . . our great-grandchildren will be very curious to know the reason why their forefathers used to sit together like an audience of foreigners in their own country, to hear whole plays acted in a language which they did not understand.

It was said that Sir Isaac Newton attended only one opera. According to a contemporary account, "The first Act he heard with pleasure, the 2nd stretch'd his patience, at the 3rd he ran away." In 1728 the poet, John Gay produced a ribald parody of Italian opera, called ***The Beggar's Opera,*** basing his work on popular tunes, even a snatch of Handel's music. It was the perfect vehicle for poking fun at a dying institution.

Handel's many enemies thought his collapse had marked the end of his career. On the contrary, it signaled a new beginning. The middle-aged composer returned from his self-imposed exile to conquer the English public once more. This time he set English texts and not Italian ones, and dealt with subjects that a middle-class audience could comprehend. Handel turned to the ***oratorio,*** a well-known medium in Italy but relatively unfamiliar to the British. Since sets and costumes were unnecessary, oratorios were much easier to produce than operas; most of the stories were taken from the Old Testament, which the English middle class knew well. Furthermore, audiences could easily identify with the ***chorus,*** which Handel made the real protagonist of his oratorios. His choral passages comment upon the narrative, respond to it, and participate in it, all in a manner that symbolized the responses of ordinary people attending the performances.

Handel's oratorios were aimed directly at the broad base of the English public. They were operatic in scope and length, with recitatives and arias but with none of opera's upper-class affectation. Frequently based on religious subjects, although ***not*** liturgical (produced in theatres and not churches), oratorios drew upon the rich choral tradition of the English, and, of course, their own language. Such oratorios as ***Israel in Egypt, Saul,*** and ***Judas Maccabaeus*** created a new force in English music.

George Frideric Handel

Messiah: excerpts from Part I

R1 S2 B2

The most famous of Handel's oratorios is called ***Messiah.*** It was composed in the space of three weeks, premiered at a 1742 benefit concert in Dublin, and then performed in London a year later. ***Messiah*** differs from the bulk of Handel's oratorios in many respects: it uses a New Testament theme, has no external story line, and treats its solo voices as commentators rather than characters. In dealing with the life of Christ, Handel decided to attempt a nondramatic, symbolic representation, drawn from prophecies, mystical allusions, and meditative prayers which, taken together, would create the image of a life.

The work is vast in scope, lasting between two and three hours, and subdivided into three parts roughly corresponding to the acts of a stage work. The parts subdivide further into fifty-three individual movements: choruses, recitatives and arias for four soloists, and movements for orchestra alone. It is impossible to do justice to the entire ***Messiah*** here. Many listeners know the "Hallelujah Chorus," which ends Part II. This so impressed George II at the London premiere that he stood up, thereby causing the entire audience to stand as well—a practice that has continued to the present day. Part III contains two memorable arias, "I Know That My Redeemer Liveth" (soprano) and "The Trumpet Shall Sound" (bass). Our discussion, however, will be restricted to selected movements from Part I.

The orchestral overture, in E minor, is based on the French slow-fast model. Note the sequence of movements after the overture: a ***recitative,*** an ***aria,*** and a ***chorus.*** This is a three-part arrangement that Handel often enjoys using. The accompanied ***recitative*** for tenor, "Comfort Ye My People," has the melodic line of an aria, and an orchestral ritornello as well. This style, midway between aria and recitative, is called ***arioso.*** The present example differs from aria mainly in its lack of formal direction: it breaks off at a cadence in the dominant, where an aria might just be at the halfway point, and ends unexpectedly with a dry, syllabic setting. In this sense, the recitative is not a complete piece; its function is to introduce the aria which follows. We sense this as soon as the ***aria*** begins, because the tenor remains the featured soloist, and because the original key of the recitative is resumed.

The formal plan of the aria ("Every Valley Shall be Exalted") stresses key contrast. The opening E-major phrase moves through a succession of rising sequences, to the dominant. The modulation takes place during the passage (Figure 10.4) shown here. Note the addition of the accidental A♯, which pushes the tonal direction to another center. And observe Handel's marvelous word-painting: the ecstatic melisma at the word "exalted," and the rise and fall of "mountain" and "low."

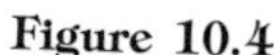
Figure 10.4

The first statement of "the crooked straight," (using new material which also depicts the words literally) appears in the dominant. With the repeat of "every valley," there is a sudden detour to the subdominant, but then a return to the home key for the rest of the aria; even the "crooked straight" passage, formerly in a foreign key, appears in the tonic.

The ***chorus*** which follows ("And the Glory of the Lord") acts as a summation of the recitative and aria that preceded it. Certainly the three textual messages are related. Furthermore, the A-major tonality of the chorus is related to the E-focus of the preceding numbers. In retrospect, the recitative-aria may appear to be in a kind of extended "dominant": a prelude to the overwhelming chorus.

The next three vocal movements form a similar set of recitative, aria, and chorus. Cast in the minor mode, they reflect the severity of the texts dealing with the awesome power, rather than the "comfort," of the Lord's coming. The two solo movements are written for bass voice, a traditional symbol of the Lord's pronouncements. In the recitative passage "I will shake the heavens," the extended melisma on "shake" is another fine instance of word-painting. Like the earlier recitative, this one leads to an aria in the same tonality. The aria "But Who May Abide" contains two strikingly contrasted sections: a meditative first part in slow triple meter, and a fierce, rapid whirlwind of sound at "For He is like a refiner's fire." Both sections are repeated, creating an overall form of ABAB. But the repeat of B is ***not*** literal; what was formerly a tonal no man's land is now placed squarely in the tonic key. The chorus that follows is in a closely related key, and textually allied to the two bass movements.

In many instances the ***chorus*** functions as a focal point for a group of movements: a verbal summing-up, the greatest density and sound mass, and the tonality of "resolution." To conclude this brief study of ***Messiah,*** listen to the powerful chorus "For unto Us a Child Is Born." This movement has been preceded by an unusually sombre bass recitative and aria. These are set in the minor mode, depicting the "darkness that shall cover the earth" and the "people that walked in darkness." Although there are references to a great "light" to come, the music only dimly reflects that light. The chorus, then, comes as a joyous fulfillment. It is brisk, in a cheerful major key, overflowing with optimism and hope. Three motives appear throughout the movement. The first two (see Figure 10.5) stress linear texture: voices imitating each other in turn, with no more than a few heard at any single time.

The greater accumulation of voices during B drives to a strong cadence, and a sudden change of texture at the words "Wonderful, Counselor." Motive C beginning with these words is rich, chordal and brilliantly spectacular in the best baroque manner. The total effect—A and B gathering energy, driving to C—is so stunning that Handel repeats it three more times. But in each statement of "Wonderful, Counselor," only the second and last are stated in the tonic G major of the movement.

Figure 10.5

Handel delighted in a highly theatrical brand of music. His oratorios are at least as dramatic as religious in inspiration. Significantly, he appreciated the value of contrasts: in texture, density, register and volume, and in tonal areas. Note, for example, the unexpected silences and tempo changes, often just before the endings of movements. (It would be convenient to point to Handel's brilliant timbral contrasts as well, but unfortunately, the orchestration of ***Messiah*** we usually hear is not the original.) Finally, Handel was adept at handling language for maximum dramatic effect. Although he spoke English with a thick German accent, we would hardly know that from his fluent English settings. He was a musical citizen of the world.

J. S. Bach: Cantata, Concerto, Fugue and Suite

Unlike Handel, Johann Sebastian Bach spent his entire life in a provincial corner of Germany, rarely venturing more than a hundred miles from his birthplace. His career and work are quite different from Handel's; it would be a mistake to think them synonymous, or to believe that either of them singlehandedly symbolizes the Baroque. Of course, there is no such monolithic creature as *the* baroque (or Renaissance, or romantic) period. Each age embodies contradictions within itself. To acquire a reasonable picture of the late sixteenth and early seventeenth centuries, we must consider Palestrina, Monteverdi, Dowland, and Gabrieli. Other eras, too, are grasped best by examining the works of a few composers rather than one.

Contrasts between Bach and Handel aptly illustrate the point: Bach devoted most of his life to the church, whereas Handel knew the glamorous secular worlds of theatre, court, and opera house. Handel was acclaimed in the great international centers of Europe, while Bach stayed tied to posts at provincial minor-league German churches and courts. Handel's middle-class father opposed his musical inclinations, but Bach's family tree was predominantly musical. The Bach family of east-central Germany had been identified with music for generations, so much so that all musicians in the area were known simply as "Bachs"! Handel, a bachelor, with virtually no domestic life, devoted all his energies to grandiose, ambitious ventures. Bach was very much of a family man; he was married twice and fathered a total of twenty children, four of whom became famous musicians, thus carrying on the family tradition. Many of his keyboard pieces were composed for the instruction and entertainment of his family. Most surprisingly, Handel's fame and influence far exceeded that of Bach. During his lifetime, Bach was not considered the best composer in Germany, and probably not the second best, either. He was appointed Cantor at Saint Thomas' Church, Leipzig, in 1723 only after Georg Philipp Telemann (1681–1767) had turned the offer down. Upon hiring Bach, one of the city fathers publicly apologized for having to "settle for second best."

Bach is thus the first composer discussed here, although certainly not the last, who was judged differently by his own contemporaries than by posterity. Music historians studying eighteenth-century Germany are faced with a dilemma. Should they concentrate attention upon J. S. Bach who was, by *our* standards, the greatest musical figure of the period? To do so would misrepresent the dominant mood of the time, which was much more excited by "modern" developments than by fusty, old-fashioned Bach. German contemporaries considered Telemann a dazzling genius, and Bach a great organist and teacher who wrote hopelessly out-of-date music. By the end of his life Bach was also known as the *father* of some of Europe's most fashionable composers; a psychologist might regard that as the ultimate indignity.

To understand this fully, we should know that the popularity of baroque style had begun to fade by the 1730s and '40s: new musical attitudes, to be discussed in the next chapter, were aleady taking their place. Even more than Handel, Bach was a traditionalist; today this is regarded as his great strength. Coming as he did at the end of a long era, he had an uncanny ability to assimilate and synthesize many diverse influences. He effectively combined aspects of German organ style and the Lutheran chorale, the Italian sonata and concerto, and French keyboard writing; he knew the work of Gabrieli, greatly admired the music of Vivaldi, and transcribed some of Vivaldi's violin concertos for keyboard. Bach was a master of polarized figured-bass technique and of tonal harmony, and possessed an unsurpassed gift for tonal counterpoint. It was Bach's counterpoint, in fact, that made many regard his music as stuffy and old-fashioned. Even though Bach's life was rather provincial, his musical style was as international in its own way as Handel's. He was, simply, the last great baroque composer.

Concerto and Suite

Bach's early reputation was based upon his virtuoso organ playing, and he held minor positions as church organist while in his teens. In 1708 he became court organist to the Duke of Weimar, a position he held for nine years before moving on to the directorship of music at the court of Cöthen. The Prince of Cöthen made Bach conductor of his small orchestra and encouraged him to compose instrumental works in the style of Vivaldi. Bach stayed at Cöthen from 1717 until 1723. It was during this period that he composed the set of six concertos dedicated to the Margrave of Brandenburg and known collectively as the ***Brandenburg Concertos.***

The Margrave had heard Bach perform, and was sufficiently impressed to request some new music for his own court orchestra. A few years later, in 1721, the Margrave received a set of six concertos, with an inscription in Bach's handwriting. Bach's statement, including such phrases as

> . . . I now take the liberty of presenting my very humble respects to Your Royal Highness with the present concertos . . . (do not) judge their imperfection by the severity of that fine and delicate taste which everyone knows you have for music . . .

may seem overly servile by modern standards, but eighteenth-century musicians and aristocrats occupied different worlds. The court musician was a high-class servant, subject to the whims of his employer. (At Weimar, Bach had been imprisoned for requesting permission to resign!) Humility towards one's betters was an accepted fact of life; flattery was necessary in requesting, or hinting at, possible gifts or favors—a very likely motive on Bach's part.

Each of these works is an example of the ***concerto grosso,*** and each is scored for a different combination of instruments. Numbers 3 and 6 of the set do not differentiate between ***concertino*** and ***ripieno,*** but the other four pieces do make this distinction. Two of the Brandenburg Concertos seem to have a special appeal for modern audience. No. 5, scored for orchestra and a smaller group of flute, violin and harpsichord, is remarkable for the soloistic prominence given the harpsichord; at one point, it actually becomes a virtuoso keyboard piece. No. 2, with a concertino of oboe, recorder (or modern flute), violin and trumpet, dazzles present-day listeners with its brilliantly high solo trumpet part.

Johann Sebastian Bach

Brandenburg Concerto no. 2: movement I

R1 S2 B3

This concerto follows the three-movement format made popular by Vivaldi: two lively outer movements, with a lyric, contemplative, middle movement for contrast. Movement I makes a strong use of the *ritornello* plan used by Vivaldi. Bach's ritornello is a brisk, strongly rhythmic tune. It is played first by the full ensemble, and then varied so that the orchestral statement of the melody is answered by one or more soloists. Figure 10.6 shows the opening figure of ritornello, and its answer by the solo oboe.

Bach planned the opening of the movement so that each of the four soloists would be introduced in turn, alternating with the ritornello. Some ritornello passages are longer than others: the longish one at the very begin-

Figure 10.6

ning is balanced by an extended ritornello after the trumpet solo, ending on a strong cadence in the dominant. The entire first part of the movement, then, might be diagrammed as in Figure 10.7.

The rest of the movement can be subdivided into three more sections. The divisions are of course arbitrary; the music actually surges forward in an unbroken pattern most of the time. Nevertheless, there are three landmarks that one can listen for:

1. a series of sequences with terraced dynamic contrasts for the full ensemble, which move in a succession of foreign key areas and land on the subdominant;
2. solo entrances by *flute, violin, oboe,* and *trumpet* plus continuo, piling up in a gradually growing imitative texture. This leads to a full *tutti* and another extended series of sequences for full ensemble, coming to a cadence and a full stop in a minor key;
3. after a half-beat's worth of silence, the orchestral ritornello enters with a *tutti* melodic line, back in the home key of F major. The driving patterns continue, now with harmonic accompaniment, and the movement ends with a full orchestral statement of the complete ritornello tune.

The high register of Bach's trumpet part must baffle many listeners. Rest assured that eighteenth-century players did *not* suffer strokes or apoplectic attacks when they performed this music. They were playing on different instruments than the ones we are accustomed to; since these early trumpets were valve-less, the pitches were realized by varying the position of the *embouchoure* (see Chapter 6) to get natural harmonics high on the overtone series. Modern players can easily duplicate these conditions, and they have the advantages of valves as well.

Figure 10.7

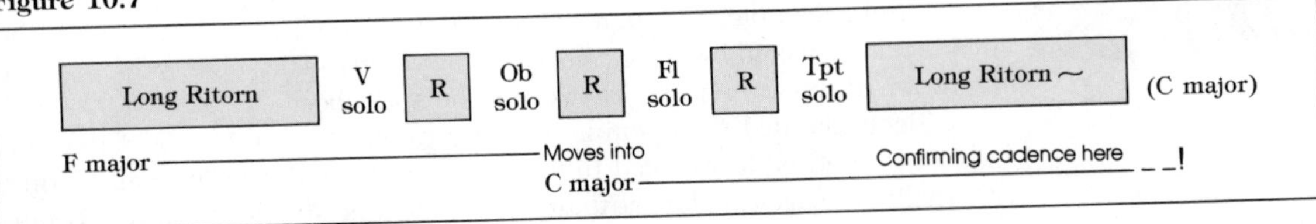

The slow movement of this concerto, in the relative key of D minor, dispenses with orchestra and solo trumpet. Violin, flute, oboe, and continuo expound upon a lyric, slow-moving line in a way that suggests the imitative slow movement of a Corelli trio sonata. The movement unfolds steadily and gracefully in triple meter: the baroque passion for regular beat was just as evident in slow works as faster ones. For movement III Bach brings the trumpet back to the ensemble. It was considered more suitable for an outgoing, festive affection than for the pensive slow movement. (Perhaps Bach was giving the trumpeter time off to rest his "lip" as well!) The trumpet plays a dominating role in this jaunty, high-spirited fugue. The movement is based on the home key of F, with the side excursions to related keys that are customary in eighteenth-century style.

Bach wrote a number of solo concertos as well as concerti grossi. In fact, he composed in every one of the baroque genres except for opera. (Considering the circumstances of his employment, it is unlikely that he would have had the opportunity to write an opera.) Like Handel, Bach wrote a number of ***suites.*** There are a number of keyboard suites, and a famous set of six suites for unaccompanied cello. He also composed four ***orchestral suites,*** each consisting of an overture and various movements, most of them based upon fashionable dances. All the movements are stated in the same key, as opposed to the sonata or concerto format.

Johann Sebastian Bach

Suite No. 3 in D major

Bach's Third Suite is scored for a festive-sounding ensemble of two oboes, three trumpets, timpani, strings and continuo. It begins with a stirring ***overture*** in the slow-fast French style, which is followed by a graceful, lyric ***air:*** closer in spirit to an operatic aria than any dance. The remaining movements of the suite, however, have strong associations with dance. We hear two ***Gavottes*** in succession (performed, in fact, with a repeat of Gavotte I at the end, so that Gavottes I-II-I create an ABA format); these are followed by a ***Bourrée,*** slightly quicker than the Gavotte, and a very rapid, spritely ***Gigue,*** with a triple swing to its compound meter.

Each of the movements, except the overture, is cast in a binary AB form, with repeats taken after A and B. In performance, therefore, the form is AABB. Part A moves away from the tonic to a cadence on a related chord of key; B returns to the starting point. Although listeners unconsciously feel that arc of tension and release, not everyone hears it readily. It might help to concentrate upon the cadence points and starting points—the very ***first*** and ***last*** chords of part A and B. If the end of A differs from its beginning, a new key or chord has been established. The ***repeats*** allow the listener to compare just those two points, (see Figure 10.8). It is not unusual for part B to be longer and more complex than A. The modulation from tonic to related area

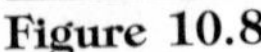

Figure 10.8

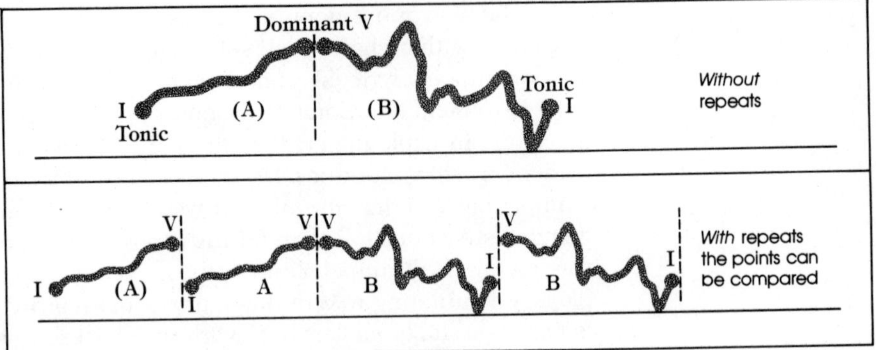

always seems fairly easy, about as natural as rolling downhill. The return to the tonic, though, apparently requires more effort and ingenuity. Perhaps it should, if only for the sake of adventure; during part B a number of key areas and cadences may be touched on, before the final release. The binary form offers a tonal journey of sorts: more often than not, the first leg of the trip seems to be taken on the freeway, with the return via the winding back roads.

The Lutheran Chorale and the Cantata

When Bach's years at Cöthen had become unpleasant, he searched for another post and found one as Cantor (music director) of Saint Thomas' Church in Leipzig. The position entailed providing music for the city's four main churches, and instructing students, in Latin as well as music, at the St. Thomas' School. The Bach family moved to Leipzig in 1723; they were to remain there for the rest of his life. As Bach was employed by the Leipzig town council, his duties were civic as well as religious. He composed music for municipal occasions; a funeral motet written for the postmaster's widow has come down to us as one of his best known choral works, ***Jesu Meine Freude.*** The musical resources of Leipzig included a small orchestra and a chorus of about thirty voices. Bach had to rehearse and conduct these groups, and play the organ as well; in addition, he was expected to provide compositions for each Sunday's church service.

Much of his church music was based upon Lutheran ***chorales:*** those simple, strong hymn tunes mentioned in Chapter 8. To a Protestant musician the chorale functioned very much as the Gregorian chant did within Catholicism. It was a body of literature known to the faithful, rich in symbolism, and capable of musical expansion and elaboration. Bach worked chorale tunes into organ compositions called ***chorale preludes;*** such pieces were understood implicitly by the congregation without a word of text being sung.

He also used chorale melodies in his many ***cantatas*** composed for the Leipzig services. The cantata had changed from its original Italian format to become one of Protestant Germany's richest musical genres. It made use of recitatives and arias, ensemble numbers and powerful choruses, concerto and sonata textures, overtures and instrumental interludes. A different cantata was needed for each Sunday and holiday of the church year, and was thus analogous to the Proper of the Catholic Mass. Bach composed about 300 of these works, relating each to the Gospel reading for that day. For example, Cantata no. 140 (*Wachet auf, ruft uns die Stimme*) is based upon the chorale of the same name, whose text refers to the parable of the wise and foolish virgins. The cantata must have been composed for the twenty-seventh Sunday after Trinity (November, 1731), when that parable would have been the Bible reading for the service.

> The kingdom of heaven shall be likened unto ten virgins, who took their lamps and went forth to meet the bridegroom. Five of them were wise, and five foolish; the foolish ones took no oil with their lamps . . . at midnight the cry was heard: "The bridegroom is coming! Go out to meet him." All the virgins arose, and trimmed their lamps. The foolish said to the wise, "give us some of your oil, for our lamps are going out." "No," said the wise ones, "there will not be enough for all of us; you must go and buy some for yourselves." And while the foolish ones were away, the bridgeroom arrived. Those who were ready went in with him to the wedding, and the door was shut . . . Keep awake, then, for you never know on what day or hour your Lord is to come. (Matthew, 25)

The congregation members believed that the virgins symbolically represented the faithful, and Christ the bridegroom. As serious churchgoers, they knew the text from Matthew, and they certainly knew the chorale *Wachet auf* as well. The cantata then, effectively dramatized and commented upon a familiar parable, by way of an equally familiar hymn tune that they would all join in singing at the end.

Johann Sebastian Bach
Cantata no. 140: *Wachet Auf*

R1 S2 B4

This cantata consists of seven movements, with the outer and central movements—that is, numbers 1, 4, and 7—based directly upon the chorale tune. Each of these movements uses as its text a stanza of the original *Wachet auf.* These three movements are also the only ones written for chorus; the others are grouped as two recitative-aria pairs. As suggested by Figure 10.9, the entire work outlines a symmetrical "arch," with the central fourth movement assuming a particularly prominent spot.

Movements 3 and 6 are not really arias but in fact *duets* for soprano and bass voices. Their texts, by an unknown author, deal with the imagery of wedding and bridegroom in a literal, but equally symbolic, way: the union of Christ and the believer's soul. They are, in a sense, *love* duets,

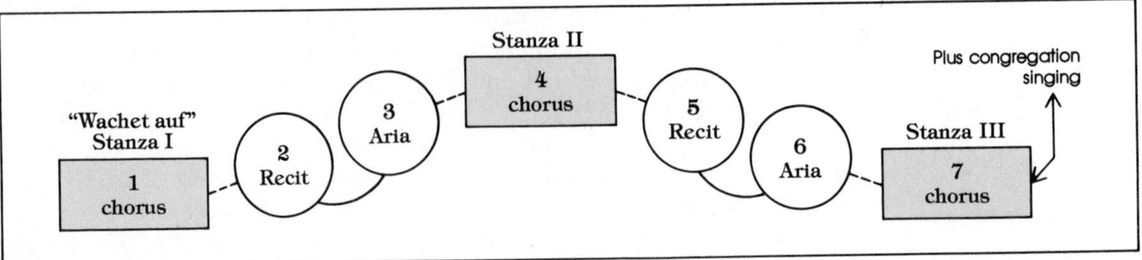

Figure 10.9

expressing yearning, tenderness and joy: a direct relationship between the individual soul and the Saviour.

The original chorale is a glorious tune in itself. It might be helpful to hear it before listening to the cantata, either by having it played at the piano or by listening to the ***last*** movement. As the final statement of the cantata, it appears in it simplest form as notated in Figure 10.10. Note the triadic, fanfare quality of the two opening phrases, and the high G of the second phrase as the peak of the tune; the third phrase, striding downward, reaches the initial note of the hymn again. After the double bar, every phrase but the last employs smooth stepwise motion, as if to compensate for the great energy of the opening. The phrases grow shorter as they reach the end with a repeat of phrase 3 rounding off the whole. Since the first section of the chorale is repeated, the overall form is AAB. Interestingly enough, this form has strong roots in the German courtly love songs of the Middle Ages.

Movement 1 This is the longest and most elaborate movement of the cantata, scored for chorus and orchestra. Stanza I of ***Wachet auf*** is used. "'Awake!' the watchmen call from high on the tower . . . it is midnight, the bridegroom is coming." Bach offers a steady, march-like orchestral ritornello at the beginning (Figure 10.11), perhaps intended to represent a wed-

Figure 10.10

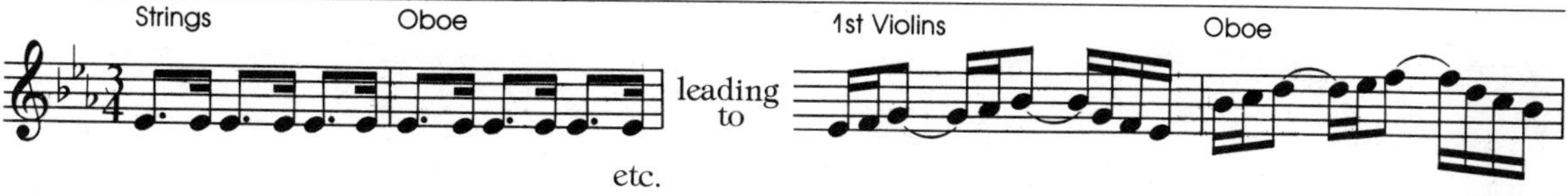

Figure 10.11

ding procession. This ritornello acts as a constant underpinning throughout the movement, as two distinctly different choral levels are built above it: sopranos singing the choral tune in slow, long notes, and the three lower voices weaving an imitative web in a spirited rhythm. There are breaks between the chorale phrases, and when the sopranos are silent during these breaks the other levels become even more prominent; as a result, foreground and background are frequently shifting position. The middle level of activity—the chorus minus the sopranos—assumes a supporting role much of the time, but also breaks into an ecstatic imitative "Allelujah" of cascading melismas that dominates the texture most brilliantly.

Movements 2 and 3 The key shifts from E♭ major (movement 1) to the relative minor. A *secco* recitative for tenor announces that the bridegroom is coming. That was the message of the opening movement, to be sure, but now the tone is more urgent: "He comes! Daughters of Zion, come forth . . . wake up, bestir yourselves to receive him."

The duet which follows is touching, tender and positively operatic. Christ and the Soul engage in an exchange of questions and answers, partly devotional and partly courtship ritual. *Soul:* When will you come, my salvation? *Jesus:* I am coming, your own. *Soul:* I am waiting with burning oil . . . *Jesus:* I will open the banquet hall . . .

This dialogue is set for soprano, bass, violin, and continuo. The resulting texture can be heard on distinct levels (as with movement 1), in that the solo violin, weaving an ornate melodic arabesque, offsets and complements the singers' lines.

Movement 4 Once more Bach asks us to listen "contrapuntally" to different levels of activity. An orchestral ritornello of only two lines (melody and continuo) gently wends its way through the movement, while stanza II of the chorale is sung by the tenors against it (see Figure 10.12). The chorale is stated with breaks between the phrases, as in the first movement, allowing the warm string melody to command attention. Bach obviously wanted a rich, full-bodied sound for the ritornello: its single line is played by first violins, second violins *and* violas. He liked the total effect so much that he later arranged this movement as a chorale prelude for organ, with the three lines of the cantata setting transferred to two keyboards plus foot pedals. The text indicates the beginning of the symbolic wedding: "Zion hears the watchmen calling . . . she wakes and rises hastily. From heaven comes her

Figure 10.12

friend, resplendent . . . Hosanna! We all follow to the joyfull hall, and share the Lord's Supper." This movement is in E♭ major, the cantata's opening key.

Movements 5 and 6 An accompanied recitative for bass voice depicts Jesus pledging his love for the Soul: in essence, he is declaring a wedding vow. The use of a bass for the Saviour, soprano for the Soul and the tenor for the third-party narrator was a convention of the time. The sensual, earthly longing of the text derived in part from Solomon's *Song of Songs,* was not unusual in Bach's day, either, although it caused some embarrassment among later nineteenth-century generations.

The recitative moves from the tonic E♭ to the dominant key of B♭ major, and it is in the latter tonality that Bach presents the second of the love duets. It resembles the first duet in its lighter texture and use of a solo instrument, in this instance the oboe. There are important differences, however. Whereas earlier the Soul and Saviour were tentatively exploring a relationship, they are now comfortable, blissful newlyweds. Earlier, the voices had engaged in question-and-answer dialogue, rarely singing together; now they are musically united. The first duet is characterized by a restless alternation of phrases moving from one key to another. This movement assumes the most static and self-assured of operatic forms, the *da capo* aria. *Soul:* My friend is mine! *Jesus:* And I am his! *Both:* Love shall separate nothing! *Soul:* I will feed with you among heaven's roses . . .

Movement 7 The original chorale returns again in its simplest form, a four-part harmonization for chorus and orchestra in which it was assumed that the congregation would join. (Remember, they all knew the tune and the words.) Note that this movement is in the tonic E♭. Thus every statement of the chorale—movements 1, 4 and 7—has confirmed the tonic, and balanced the digressions of the other movements. The decision, gradually evolved over the years, to place the straightforward hymn ***last*** in the cantata ground plan was a masterstroke. It allows for great dramatic impact, the resolution of all ambiguity, both musical and textural, and the transition from allegory back to the real-life church service. This summing-up was accomplished by the entire congregation, affirming their own belief and unshakeable faith. "Gloria be sung to you, with men's and angels' tongues . . . of this we rejoice . . . forever in sweet joy."

Bach's choral music is not restricted to the sacred cantata. He wrote secular cantatas as well: one famous example is the ***Coffee Cantata,*** a satire on the craze for coffee-drinking and coffee houses that had become the vogue in Leipzig. Two grand sacred works that are not cantatas must also be mentioned: his setting of the ***Passion*** according to Saint Matthew, and the monumental Mass in B Minor. It may seem odd that the devoutly Protestant Bach should have composed a Catholic Mass. In fact, the work's great length alone would make a liturgical performance impossible. He wrote the Mass for practical, not liturgical reasons, hoping to secure a position at the Court of the Catholic prince of Saxony, who later became king of Poland. His tactic failed: in this venture, as in so many of his dealings with real or prospective employers, he was frustrated.

Bach's Fugues: *The Well-Tempered Clavier*

Apart from the genres aleady noted, Bach wrote many works for solo keyboard. His most impressive keyboard collection is the ***Well-Tempered Clavier,*** a series of twenty-four preludes and fugues composed in 1722. The title page carried an inscription in Bach's most ornate handwriting, in which he stated that the pieces were "composed and written down for the profit and use of musical young people eager to learn, as well as for a special pastime for those already proficient . . ."

The phrase "special pastime" has proven to be quite an understatement. Generations of performers, composers and scholars have found this collection, and second book composed some twenty years later, a source of infinite fascination and delight. The entire collection was related to the practice of ***equal temperament,*** the then-new system of tuning the octave into twelve equal half steps. This system had become important by the early eighteenth century, mainly because major-minor tonality had supplanted the church modes. The earlier practice of tuning to the natural partials of the overtone series created gorgeous-sounding 5ths and triads, ideal for the performance of modal music. But ***tonal*** music had other needs—especially an increased facility for modulating to many keys within a piece, or playing a collection of pieces in different keys on the same instrument without having to re-tune before each change. By observing the practice of equal temperament (in effect, making all the intervals except the octave slightly "out-of-tune"), a performer could play all the individual pieces of the ***Well-Tempered Clavier,*** which cover all twelve major and minor keys, at one sitting without re-tuning.

fugue

It was a typically baroque gesture to collect and organize a systematic body of information in this encyclopedic way; Bach, as a teacher, may have been even more systematic than most. One aspect of the ***fugue*** that he treated very flexibly, however, was its form. Bach regarded the fugue as a particular approach to texture—a ***procedure***—that could assume a number of forms. On the other hand, his fugues all stem from the variation principle, in that they cover considerable territory with a minimum of material. And they are all ***tonal:*** not only in the harmonic implications of counterpoint, but in the use of key contrasts as an essential aspect of their unfolding.

A fugue usually begins by introducing the ***subject**** in each of its lines, one by one, until all parts have entered the texture. During this opening section, called the ***exposition,*** a modulation usually takes place as well, ending on a closely related key or chord. Although the remainder of the fugue is not as predictable in form, it is virtually certain that there will be a return to the tonic. A continuously moving texture, in which the subject can appear in various guises, is more common than distinct sections. There may be modulations to closely related areas, or perhaps a chain of sequences: the same tonal devices, in fact, found in most music of the period. A few further aspects of fugal texture should be mentioned:

1. The ***subject*** must be so distinctive that it can be heard at any level of the texture. It is usually fairly short, irregular in some facet of its contour, and "incomplete" in that it does not come to a full cadence. We hear it first as a single line, and then in imitation as the second line appears. The appearance of the subject in the second line is known as the ***answer;*** it usually states the pitches of the subject in a transposed form, a 5th away from the original. Subsequent entrances may appear in the tonic, or at other pitch levels.

2. When the ***answer*** enters in the second voice the opening voice continues, but with new material. This new material, called the ***countersubject,*** is designed to provide an effective counterpoint for the main subject. In many fugues subject and countersubject invariably appear together.

3. The subject is varied by techniques suggested earlier in Chapter 4 (in connection with Babbitt and Webern examples). We may hear it in ***inversion*** (the rise-and-fall of its contours "mirrored") or in melodic ***retrograde*** (the succession of pitches reversed), or a combination of the two. It may be presented with rhythmic values lengthened so that it sounds twice as slow

* Note two terms used in connection with fugues: the "subject" (or main motive), and "voice" (a polyphonic *line,* whether instrumental or vocal).

Figure 10.13

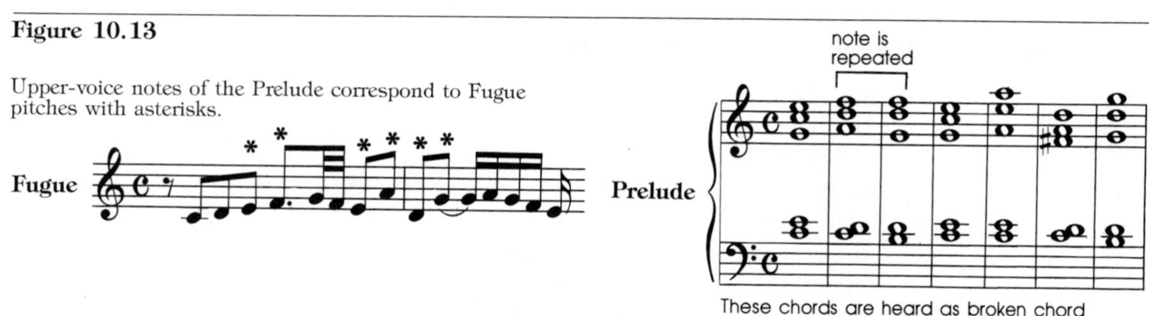

(in ***rhythmic augmentation***) or twice as fast (***rhythmic diminution***). There may also be a ***stretto:*** the subject is stated in imitation, but at closely spaced time-intervals; one voice has barely begun when another voice starts. As this is a sure device for building tension, composers often save it for the final moments of a fugue. Near a fugue's end, the sense of tonal return may also be reinforced by a sustained or repeated note (tonic or dominant) known as a ***pedal point*** or ***organ point.*** As one might guess, the device is common in organ music, the sustained pitch being played on the pedal-board. But pedal points can appear in works for other instruments: The C-Minor Fugue for "clavier" has one, for example, at the very close.

From Book I of the *Well-Tempered Clavier,* listen to the Prelude and Fugue in C Major. The Prelude, with its smooth arpeggios, makes an interesting foil for the aggressive Fugue which follows. (The pairing of two contrasting *affections* can also be noted in the French overture, or the *da capo* aria.) With this particular Prelude and Fugue, there is also a direct motivic relationship. If the Prelude's figurations are reduced to simple chords, as in Figure 10.13, this becomes apparent. The C-Major Fugue, in four voices, uses *stretto* frequently, not just as the ending but throughout the texture.

Listen to the Prelude and Fugue in G Major as well. The Prelude is a brilliant, spirited movement, built (like its C-major counterpart) on arpeggiated chord patterns. The three-voice Fugue offers a subject that stresses directionality: up, down, and up again. It is not surprising, then, that it becomes *inverted* shortly after the exposition (see Figure 10.14). The lively mood of the Prelude is maintained for the Fugue. The two seem almost to be halves of the same pieces.

Figure 10.14

Domenico Scarlatti: Changes in Texture and Form

Bach and Handel both represented a style that had begun to lose its popularity. Their music might be characterized as "heroic": noble, often densely polyphonic, controlled by the doctrine of the *affections* and an operatic sensibility. But a new esthetic had begun to develop in the 1720s and '30s. One side of it is evident in Vivaldi's concertos, with their simple, catchy tunes and generally homophonic textures. The same approach to musical material was found in the comic opera (*opera buffa*), which became popular in Italy, and then swept through Europe. Originally produced as an "intermezzo" between the acts of serious Neapolitan opera, the opera buffa became a separate genre in its own right; it poked fun at the absurdities of opera and the pomp of the class system that supported it.

The newer developments stressed simple harmony, folk-like melodic clarity, neatly balanced phrases and surface brilliance. These traits were to lead directly to the classic period (to be discussed in the next chapter): in this sense, the beginnings of "classic" style were already present while Bach and Handel were alive. A number of younger composers were active in the newer idiom: Carl Philipp Emanual Bach, for example, who was thirty-six years old (and already a famous composer) at his father's death. It is especially interesting, though, to hear "radical" music composed by a man born in 1685, someone of exactly the *same* age as Handel and J. S. Bach! This was Domenico Scarlatti (1685–1787), son of the opera composer Alessandro Scarlatti, and famous in his own right as a brilliant harpsichord virtuoso. Scarlatti's early career was spent at the Vatican and the royal chapel at Lisbon. It was only after he had moved to the Spanish court at Madrid, in 1729, that he began composing the keyboard music for which he is known today.

Scarlatti composed more than 500 sonatas for solo harpsichord. Exuberant and wildly virtuosic, they were composed for that most brilliant of baroque instruments, one which he played supremely well. They are nearly all single movement pieces, although probably performed in pairs, each cast in a two-part *binary form* which goes beyond that of the baroque dance movement. Like a bourrée or gavotte movement, a typical Scarlatti sonata is divided into two sections: a digression from the tonic key, and return to it. In the Bach and Handel dance examples; the point of arrival at the end of each section had been a simple dance leading to a final chord. (See Figure 10.15).

Scarlatti's scheme was much more elaborate. The point of arrival in each section now became the excuse for the introduction of *new material,* almost as though reaching one's goal justified a little celebration. The *same* "celebration" music used at the end of part A is also used at the end of B. A general diagram for Scarlatti's formal plan might look like Figure 10.16. Note that an important motive, stated midway through the piece in a *foreign key,* appears at the end of the piece in the *tonic key.* This principle states the

Figure 10.15

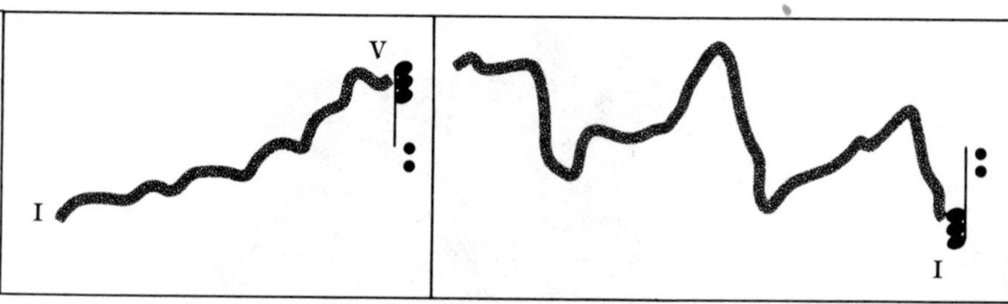

essential kernel of ***Sonata-form,*** which was to develop later in the century (and which will be discussed at length during the next few chapters). But the Scarlatti sonatas are important not only for their ingenious formal plan, but for ***other*** attributes that depart from baroque tradition. Listen for the short balanced phrases, the overwhelmingly homophonic writing, the striking contrasts within sections (which would destroy any unity of ***affections***), and the lilting folk-like tunes, many of them influenced by the composer's years in Spain and Portugal. Scarlatti's sonorities, his virtuoso effects, and his surprising harmonies, often sensual or brutal, are remarkable even today.

Changing Fashions—Then, Now and Yesterday

Interest in the music of the Baroque, in fact in all music composed before 1750, is as high now as it has ever been in history. Many people purchase harpsichords or lutes for their homes; some even assemble instruments from kits. Amateur recorder groups abound in communities throughout the United States and Europe. For many, there is a special delight in a musical language that is just different enough from our own to be fascinating: the modal scales, surprising chord changes and unfamiliar instrumental timbres weave a unique spell. Modern listeners enjoy the great range and variety of early music, from the intimate to the spectacular, devout to bawdy. They also delight in the places where this music may be performed: outdoor gar-

Figure 10.16

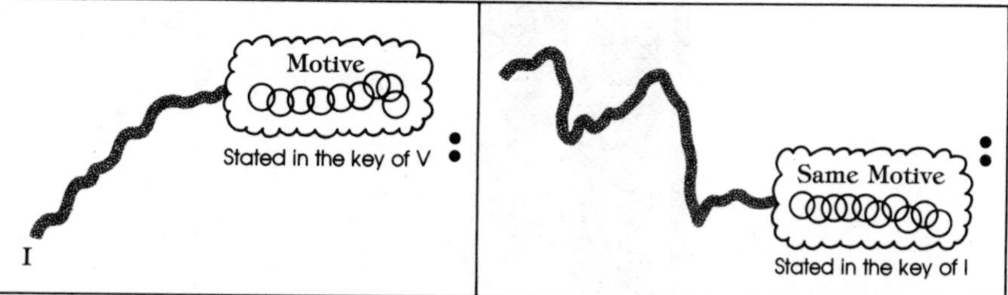

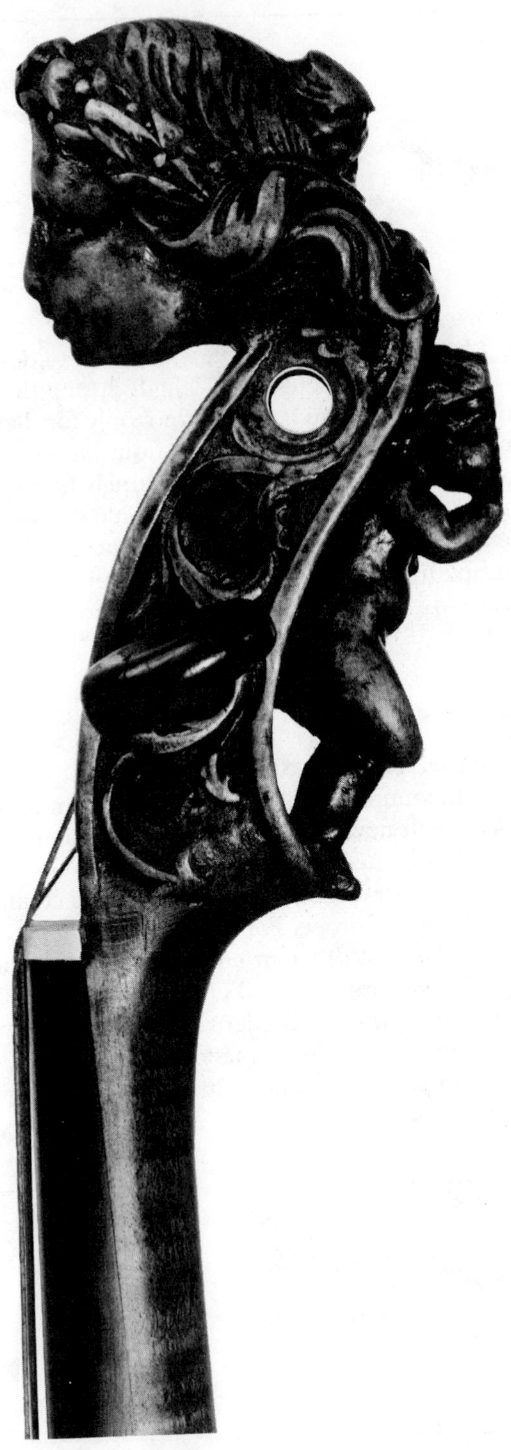

English Violin, carved tuners and finial, c. 1675.

dens, dining halls, chapels, all refreshing alternatives to the monotony of concert halls.

But only fifty years ago, early music aroused very little enthusiasm. Handel, Palestrina and J. S. Bach were considered the only composers worth listening to. Even their works were performed rarely, and hardly ever in their original instrumentation. Going back in time still another century or so to the year 1800, we would find a decided bias ***against*** certain types of early music. Many musicians believed that the High Renaissance, which they equated with Palestrina, represented a "Golden Age," and that the styles of Machaut, Dufay, and Josquin could be discounted as primitive ancestral experiments by comparison. Similarly, the Baroque was generally considered a perverse, bizarre distortion of Renaissance ideals. Of all the Baroque composers, only Handel maintained his reputation. J. S. Bach's music was forgotten, and did not attract widespread attention until the late 1820s, more than seventy-five years after his death.

One reason for the lack of interest in early music was the association, until very recently, of the concert hall with the experience of "serious" music. Much of the literature composed before 1750 is unsuited to the concert hall; it belongs in a chapel, cathedral, town square, around the fireside, in a banquet hall, or drawing room. The invention of the long-playing record changed many perspectives and priorities. It became possible to hear a great deal of music at home—private "chamber music" on discs—at little expense. Touring groups of performers, dedicated to the realization of early music as authentically as possible, have become increasingly popular. Amateur musicians, too, have discovered that chamber music intended for the middle-class household of seventeenth-century Amsterdam or London can be equally delightful when played in the living rooms of Chicago or Seattle.

Finally, listeners and amateur performers have become conscious of ***style,*** savoring the distinctions between Gothic and Renaissance motet, or French and Italian opera. In the same sense, the composers of the early 1600s were also acutely aware of style, perhaps more than any other generation before them. They knew that certain situations called for the conservative polyphony of Palestrina's school, and that other needs might call for the newer Florentine ***stile rappresentativo***; they recognized the existence of a ***choice*** between legitimate and potentially useful alternatives. Modern listeners are privileged to recognize the similar choices every time they hear music. Fortunately, we can approach the great range of available styles with more knowledge and genuine delight than any other generation in history.

11

The Classic Period: Haydn and Mozart

He alone has the secret of making me smile and touching me to the bottom of my soul.

Mozart, referring to Haydn

He was truly a great musician. My friends often flatter me about my talent; but he was far above me.

Haydn, referring to Mozart

The Viennese Style

Names given to great musical periods may be misleading and ambiguous, often unrelated to their original meanings. For example, "baroque" was originally a derogatory term; or we often call Thomas Jefferson a "Renaissance" man, even though he lived centuries after the Renaissance.

The term "classic" may be the most confusing of all. Used originally to denote the culture of ancient Greece and Rome, it has come to mean restraint, balance, and grace, as opposed to the "romantic" stereotypes of freedom and passion. In slang terms, "classical" music seems to be any music that is not "popular," even though certain jazz styles may be more complex and "elitist" than Bach chorales or Verdi operas. To confuse the issue further, we may refer to *anything* of historical importance as "classic." An antique automobile is called a "classic" car; *Citizen Kane* is a "classic movie;" the World Series is known as baseball's "Fall Classic."

The *classic era* in music refers to a particular set of stylistic traits which dominated European taste in the late eighteenth century: a concern for balance, proportion, grace, and symmetry.* The period's chronology is almost as ambiguous as its name. It would be tempting to mark it off as 1750 to 1800, from the death of Bach to the dawn of the new "Romantic" century. But the classic period really should be extended into the early nineteenth century, if only to cover the career of Beethoven who, with one foot in each of the two periods, was just as "classic" in his outlook as "romantic." Furthermore, the mature works of Haydn and Mozart did not appear until the 1770s. Perhaps we could assume that the period begins in 1760 (the year of Haydn's appointment to the Esterházy Court) and ends with the death of Beethoven in 1827 or that of Schubert a year later.

Some historians choose to abandon the term "classic" altogether, referring to the style of Haydn, Mozart, and Beethoven (and perhaps Schubert as well) as the "Viennese style." All four chose to live in Vienna, that cosmopolitan, elegant, capital city and musical center of the Western world. Vienna was the seat of the Hapsburg Empire, which included not only Austria but also parts of Italy, Hungary and Czechoslovakia. Vienna's geographic location with Italy to the south, Hungary to the east, Germany to the northwest and Bohemia to the northeast, brought about a unique melting pot of cultural influences. The city was a center for theatre and opera, concerts at the palaces of wealthy aristocrats, informal music in coffee-houses and gardens, and amateur music making everywhere.

Historical and Musical Background

The late eighteenth century was the last truly aristocratic era in Europe. The great rulers—Frederick the Great (Prussia), Louis XV and XVI (France), Maria Theresa (Austrian Empire), and Catherine the Great (Russia)—held absolute power, and a rigidly stratified class system dictated every citizen's "place" in society. The arts flourished under the patronage of the courts—centers of entertainment and luxury with an insatiable need for new music. Interest in ancient Greece and Rome, partly stimulated by the excavations at Pompeii and Herculaneum, prompted artists and architects to pattern their works upon what they considered "classic" ideals of proportion, symmetry, and balance. There were major scientific advances, such as the discoveries of nitrogen, hydrogen and oxygen, well-documented in the greatest storehouse of knowledge ever compiled, the French *Encyclopedia.* All these developments contributed to that surge of intellectual confidence known as the Enlightenment.

Other aspects of the period were more dynamic, restless—and prophetic. Scientific experiments led to the invention of the electric battery, the steam engine, improved iron foundries, and textile machines—in short, to

*But it was not unexpressive or overly delicate. In fact, the music of Haydn and Mozart was criticized on occasion for being too dramatic and irrationally "romantic."

The classic "ideal" was revealed in many arts of the eighteenth century. This french example (the Pantheon) is "classic" in two respects: its sense of balance and restraint, and its reliance upon ancient Greco-Roman models.

the beginning of the factory system and the Industrial Revolution. Many writers and philosophers were inspired by the "classic" ideals of the ancients, but not for love of balance and reason. They saw the Greeks and Romans primarily as libertarian statesmen who had thrown off tyrants and constructed "just" governments. The French writer Jean-Jacques Rousseau (1712–1778) passionately advocated freedom as the natural state of mankind: not only political freedom, but a more sweeping rejection of all civilized institutions. His belief that the natural state of human beings was basically good contradicted the basic assumptions of aristocracy and clergy, but gradually gained acceptance within the intellectual community. Remember, for example, Jefferson's "We hold these truths to be self-evident" at the beginning of the Declaration of Independence.

Music and literature were infused with a growing need for intense, impassioned expression of moods: not the stereotyped cardboard "affections" of earlier generations, but unique, individual statements. The title of a mid-1770s German play, ***Sturm und Drang*** ("Storm and Stress") came to symbolize this entire movement; it already expressed aspects of the esthetic we now call "romantic." It may seem a contradiction to think of ***Sturm und Drang*** as an aspect of "classic" style. On the other hand, great historical periods are perpetually fascinating just because of such contradictions. At one level, the late eighteenth century produced such Enlightened figures as Benjamin Franklin and Thomas Jefferson, fine amateur musicians, inventors, concerned with social reform and human rights, widely read in the classics. But we have only to recall Dicken's opening paragraph for *A Tale of Two Cities* (''It was the best of times, it was the worst of times . . .''), and remember that, at least in France, the Enlightenment was to lead to the Reign of Terror.

Musical Influences

As we noted at the end of Chapter 10, a new style based on simple chordal textures and folk-like tunes had begun to emerge even before Bach's death in 1750. In its more lyric, graceful aspects it was referred to as the ''gallant'' style. Delicate and playful, with ornately decorated melodic lines, it is related to ***Rococo*** art and architecture of the ill-fated French court: fanciful interior decoration, vividly embellished with curved scrolls and a profusion of mirrors, or the elegant paintings by Watteau and Fragonard.

Antoine Jean Duclos. This engraving depicts a concert of chamber music, in a princely french drawing room decorated in the elegant, airy Rococo style. The imposing figure in the center may even be Louis XV himself.

In Germany, a more dramatic approach, known as the "sensitive" style, featured striking contrasts and unusual juxtapositions of mood. One of J. S. Bach's sons, Carl Philipp Emanuel Bach (1714–1788), excelled in this style, and composed a number of instrumental works in which sudden, violent contrasts command attention. This tendency hastened the final breakdown of the baroque "unity of affections."

The "gallant" and "sensitive" approaches were related in several respects. Both attempted to bridge the gap between the courtly "heroic" music of the Baroque and the tastes of an increasingly influential middle-class audience. Middle-class people were invited to concerts held in courtly salons or palaces, and also sponsored subscription concerts of their own. Accordingly, composers drew their materials from popular music, street music, folk song, and comic opera. Secondly, the newer experiments were centered about instrumental, rather than vocal, music. Some composers may have felt that the unique, personal quality of their music (a crucial departure from the universal "affections") could not be stated in words. Moreover, the best European orchestras had acquired near-virtuoso status. Their skills stimulated many a creative imagination.

Thirdly, mid-eighteenth-century styles were solidly ***homophonic.*** By the 1740s and '50s almost every composer had accepted the international dominance of light, chordal textures. And finally, the new texture relied less and less upon the supportive continuo part; in many instances the practice of figured bass was dropped. The new stress on melodic foreground and simple chord figuration had replaced the old soprano-bass polarity. Furthermore, composers who were concerned with unique personal expression specified more details, trusting less to the discretion of improvising players. Then, too, the newer idiom was partly based upon outdoor music, such as garden-party and street serenades, which rarely used keyboard instruments. For whatever reasons, the continuo ceased to be a potent force. It was still heard in vocal recitatives of the mature classic period, but not in symphonies or chamber music.

Mannheim and the Symphony

One of the great orchestras of the 1750s could be found at the court of Mannheim. Led by court composer Johann Stamitz (1717–1757) and later by his two sons, the ensemble was famed for its virtuoso performances. Stamitz's music featured vivid contrasts, in the manner of C. P. E. Bach, but also special effects that displayed the orchestra's brilliance to fullest advantage. These effects were even given pet names: the "Mannheim rocket" (a rapidly rising arpeggiated melody); the "Mannheim steamroller" (a gradual crescendo over a persistently repeated bass tone); the "Mannheim bird" (a twittering trill). Many of these gestures were derived from ***operatic*** music, where they signified love, vengeance, fires, earthquakes, and the like. The Mannheim orchestra's crescendo effect, a very un-baroque way of dealing with dynamics, was so overwhelming that it literally brought

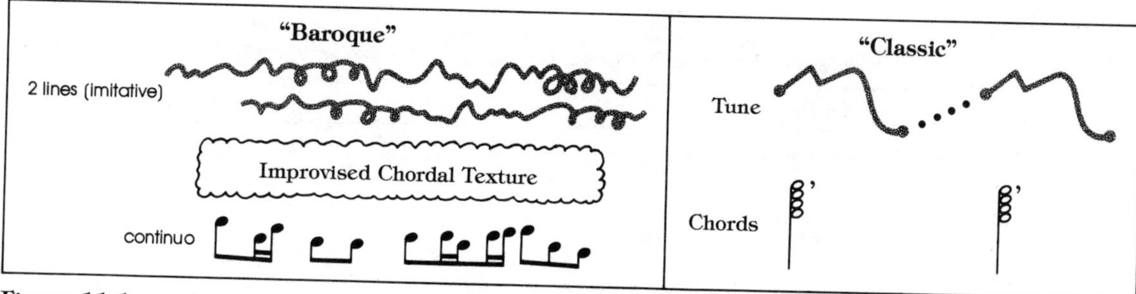

Figure 11.1

audiences out of their seats and on their feet. Stamitz's consistent use of the crescendo became a trademark of sorts, and made his orchestra the most talked-about in Europe.

Stamitz's orchestral works, and those of other mid-century courtly composers, adhered to a three-movement format modelled on the Italian *sinfonia* or operatic overture. Like the overture, this format alternated fast, slow and fast sections; but these had now become separate movements, separated by pauses. The new extended nonoperatic *sinfonia* (or *symphony*) became a popular genre; we will return to it soon.

Style Traits of Classic Music

One music historian has summed up the esthetics of the 1750s in three words: "nature, simplicity, passion." Of the three, "simplicity" may seem most obvious. On closer hearing, though, it turns out to be deceptive. Classic music may *sound* simpler than baroque music, just because it is *less dense.* If we compare a typical baroque fragment of two measures with a similar fragment of Viennese classic writing, as in Figure 11.1, we notice a vast difference: The classic fragment seems "simpler." It is light and transparent, articulated in brief symmetrical phrase groups. By contrast, the baroque fragment is quite complex.

But what happens when the two hypothetical examples are extended (See Figure 11.2) to eight measures (or fifty measures) each? The complex pattern heard at the outset of the baroque movement would probably be retained throughout. Density and a single affection remain constant. But the classic style presents constant *change:* dramatic action rather than dramatic "states." Over an extended time span, then, the baroque example may well turn out to be "simpler," if only because it allows the listener ample time to absorb the details of its single gesture.

The Viennese classic composer was not content to deal with a single gesture. Instead, he provided many changing textures, rhythms, and tunes in rapid succession. Figure 11.3 shows the opening pages of a piano work composed by Mozart in 1778. Note that the phrases are mostly arranged in four-measure groups. Aside from some brief imitation in measure 7 and 8, the entire excerpt is homophonic. But see how many different accompani-

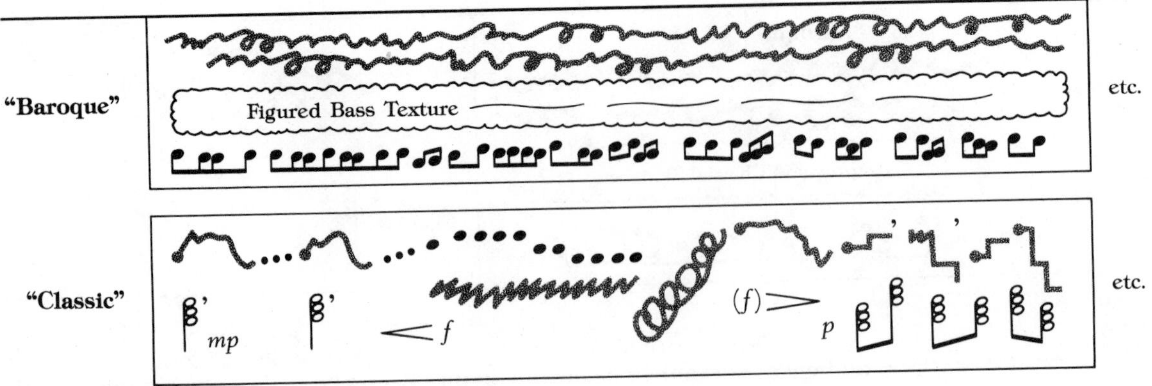

Figure 11.2

ment patterns, rhythmic stresses, melodic contours, and moods are crowded into these few measures! In fact, it is hard to find two phrases that are alike.

Why does this passage sound so unified? One reason is its regular, steadily maintained ***tempo;*** this was one baroque "affection" that was adhered to throughout the eighteenth century. Then, too, the short motives are heard as the components of larger phrases, each one answering its predecessor. The phrases are neatly arranged so that they often overlap: note how measures 4 and 5 are joined, so that the overall motion surges forward.

Eighteenth-century listeners could associate Mozart's musical vocabulary with familiar genres of the time: dances, opera clichés, martial fanfares, exotic Turkish or gypsy music, and so on. For example, phrase 2 has a learned contrapuntal air, while phrases 4 and 5 evoke images of hunting horns. The surprising D-minor entry at measures 22–23 begins with nothing less than a "Mannheim rocket" figure. Through such combinations, composers could weave various strands together—middle-class music and aristocratic music, opera and dance—into a purely instrumental fabric.

Concentrate as well upon the accompaniment. There is one pattern that classic composers found very useful: the broken-chord ***Alberti bass.*** It is not restricted to any single mood; note that Mozart employs it here in a lyric passage (measures 1–4), and in a dramatic one starting at measure 23.

The strongest force organizing this disparate material is ***tonality.*** A long-range key scheme enabled the classic composer to work with gradually unfolding goals ***and*** sharp internal contrasts at the same time. In this instance Mozart moves from the key of F major first to the relative of D minor (the sudden *f* at measures 22–23) and, after a number of sequences, to the dominant C major (measure 41). The logic of chord progressions was not only perfect for organizing long time spans, but also ideal for highlighting expressive nuances. In other words, harmony had become the essence of form ***and*** content. A chord's tonal function and its expressive power were one and the same.

phrase 1
phrase 2
Allegro
5
p
10
phrase 3
phrase 4
phrase 5—a variant of phr. 4
p
15
20
surprise!
phrase 6
25
cadence
in F major
repeated
again
f
to D minor!
V–I
V–I
V–I
phrase 7
smaller phrase groups
begins like phr. 6 - - - - - - - - - - - but modulates - - - - -
30
- - - - - - - - - - This can be thought of as an
35
(C minor)
extended phrase - - - - to the cadence figure in C minor - - - - - - - - - - - - - - -
V
I
V
I
(C minor scale)
40
V
New Tune
p
C major!

Figure 11.3

Genres of Classical Music

Composers of the late eighteenth century worked primarily in three important media: symphony, chamber music, and opera. For the time being, we are grouping the concerto under the general heading of symphony. In addition, music for solo instruments is included under chamber music.

Although Haydn and Mozart composed a number of Masses, interest in church music was not so strong in this period as in preceding eras. Haydn wrote two impressive oratorios late in his career, one of which will be discussed in this chapter. Mozart's ***Requiem*** Mass was left unfinished—under peculiar circumstances, as we will note later. Both men were raised as Catholics, and both joined the Freemasonry movement during their maturity.

Opera continued to flourish at courts and in public opera houses. Haydn composed many operas for the Esterházy court; at Mannheim, too, operas were performed regularly, although the orchestral concerts over-

A performance by Haydn's orchestra at Esterházy Palace, where Haydn spent much of his career. Haydn can be seen at the lower left, conducting from a position at the harpsichord.

shadowed them. The Neapolitan conventions of *opera seria* had been weakened by the dynamic competition of *opera buffa,* and by new French and German national styles, sung in the vernacular rather than in Italian.

Apart from opera, the important genres were instrumental. Most of these instrumental works consisted of a number of movements in a certain sequence, employing forms that had proven to be useful and popular. This overall ground plan was generally the same whether the piece was a sonata, string quartet, or symphony. We will refer to it here as the *sonata cycle.*

sonata cycle

The Sonata Cycle

sonata form

concerto

symphony

string quartet

The word "sonata" had been used, with varying meanings, since the early baroque. By the late eighteenth century, a specific format emerged; the Viennese classic *sonata* was a piece for solo piano, or for piano plus a solo instrument, such as the violin. It consisted of three movements in the order fast-slow-fast. (To complicate our terminology, however, the *form* usually associated with the opening fast movement is known as *sonata form.*) This is the basic skeleton of the *sonata cycle.* A "sonata cycle" for solo instrument and orchestra was called a *concerto.* Similarly, a "sonata" for orchestra was called a *symphony.* Sonata cycle works for string quartet, woodwind quintent, or piano-violin-cello trio were called simply *string quartet, trio,* and so on. While the sonata and concerto maintained the three-movement format, the symphony and string quartet had four movements; the extra movement was a *minuet,* inserted between the slow movement and rapid finale. Whereas the basic three-movement sonata cycle can be related to the early sinfonia or concerto grosso, the minuet is something of an interloper, a refuge from the baroque dance suite.

As used by Haydn and Mozart, the minuet provided a refreshing contrast to the slow movement: a slow tempo answered by a faster one, and "song" answered by "dance." It also offered tonal balance (see Figure 11.4), with the slow movement stated in a foreign key and the minuet usually in the home key. In fact, the chief concern and driving force of the sonata cycle was *tonality* itself. Key conflicts and contrasts, modulations and resolutions provided the material for this dramatic, though nonverbal, medium. Nowhere is this more evident than in the form frequently associated with first movements; sonata (or "sonata-allegro") form.

Figure 11.4

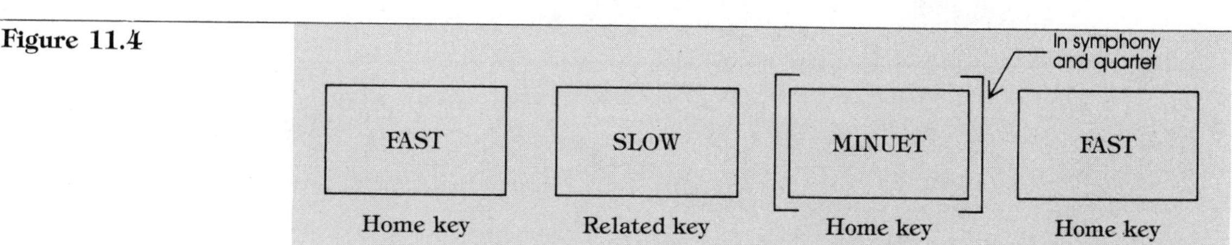

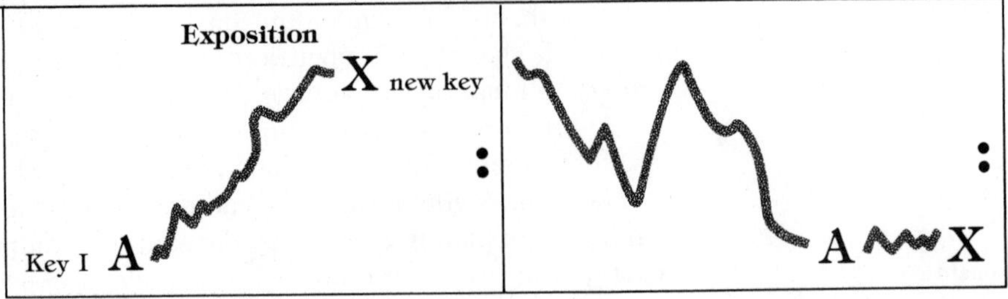

Figure 11.5

Sonata Form

The term "sonata-allegro" is often used to refer to the form of most opening movements. But this hyphenated term can be misleading, since the form can be found in slow movements as well as fast "allegro" tempos. For this reason, we will use the simpler—if equally confusing—term "sonata form."

The sonata procedure of Haydn and Mozart gradually evolved from the binary two-part scheme of Scarlatti's harpsichord pieces. This was expanded to include two motives or themes in the opening section. One is heard in the home key, and the other celebrates the arrival to the related key. *Both* themes are stated in the *tonic* key when, during the second section, there is a return to that home-key area. If the two themes are called A and X, the expanded binary form might be diagrammed as in Figure 11.5. Note that the entire opening section is called the ***exposition.*** The musical realities of the late eighteenth century, were, in fact, much more detailed than this. In a typical Haydn or Mozart sonata form, the music associated with the foreign-key area of the exposition may consist of two, three, or more motives in rapid succession (see Figure 11.6). This wealth of material was presumably aimed at confirming the new tonality in the listener's ears, making it seem "right." Since all of these themes had appeared in the exposition, it was highly likely that they would be heard again—all in the tonic—during the final home-key return.

The modulating passages, represented by in our outline, became crucially important in the classical sonata. The second in particular, leading from the foreign key back to the tonic, acquired a special function of its own: that of exploring and recombining fragments of A, X, Y, Z, and all the other motives stated initially in the exposition. It

Figure 11.6

therefore takes on the weight and status of a separate section within the overall form, known as the *development* section. The return of the tonic key (and themes A, X, Y, Z) is considered a third section, called the *restatement* or *recapitulation.*

Note (Figure 11.7) how the sonata form, with roots in the *binary* dance format of the Baroque, has taken on the proportion and characteristics of *ternary* form: a kind of extended ABA. It is precisely this ambiguity that makes the form so fascinating for many composers and listeners. The sonata has the symmetry and balance of the *da capo* aria in its melodic curve, but the restless drive of a tonally "incomplete" binary form in its key scheme.

Return to the Mozart piano excerpt examined earlier (Figure 11.3). It is the very beginning of a sonata-form first movement.* The *exposition* begins immediately at measure 1; with the sudden *f* and swing into the area of D minor, at measures, 22–23, the bridge (or first ~~~ of our outline) begins. At measure 41, the dominant key of C major is introduced with a new, distinctive theme . . . at which point our written example ends. Mozart adds further tunes, all in C major, to the "second theme group." *Development* of this material, and a *recapitulation* restating all the events of the exposition in the home key, make up the rest of the movement.

The Slow Movement

theme and variations

Slow movements often function as a lyric contrast, more introspective, decorative, or simply sedate than the dramatic openings that had preceded them. A typical slow movement might take the form of *theme and variations;* the Haydn string quartet movement featured during Part 1 is, in fact, the second movement of a larger work. Or it may be a simple part form, such as an *aria* with a contrasting middle section (ABA). In some pieces, the slow movement is even in sonata form.

Figure 11.7

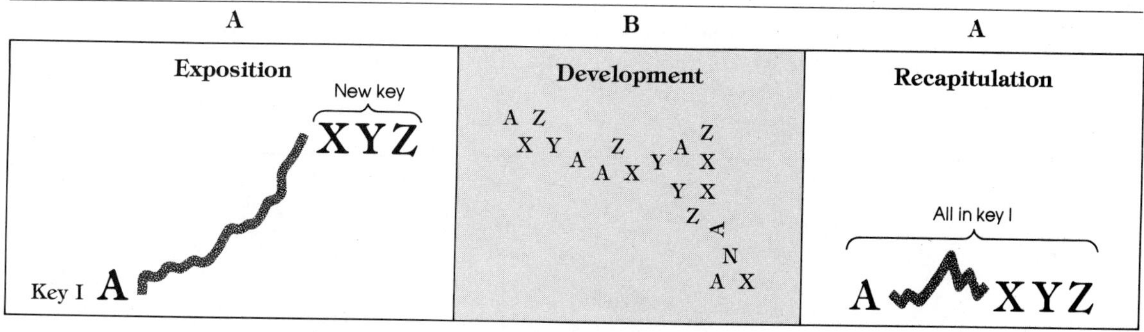

*The complete work is Mozart's piano Sonata in F Major, K. 332. It can be heard on a London recording, LON 7085, performed by Alicia De Larrocha.

Square Piano by Christopher Gainer.

The Final Movement

In a three-movement scheme, the slow movement is followed directly by the *finale,* a movement designed to bring the entire work to a satisfying close. The last movement may return to the dramatic mood of the opening, with violent eruptions and extreme contrasts. Or, as frequently found in Haydn's music, the final movement may be the most relaxed and easygoing of all: jolly and cheerful, a comfortable way of ringing down the curtain on an evening's entertainment.

rondo

There could very well be another sonata-form moment, or a set of variations upon a theme. If one wished for a spritely good-humored finale, this would be the ideal situation for a *rondo,* an extended part form with recurring refrain, such as ABABA, ABACABA, and so on. The selection by Mozart for horn and orchestra studied during Part 1 is a typical example of the Viennese classic rondo; the movement is the finale of a horn concerto.

Rondo form differs from sonata form in a number of respects: (1) it is usually "complete" tonally, with the first statement of A ending in the home key; (2) each excursion into new tonal and thematic territory is answered by a return to the security of the main tune and the tonic key; (3) the A tune is a miniature aria or dance in itself, and not likely to be fragment or "developed." Compared to the average sonata-form, a rondo may appear lightweight. It is certainly a more decorative than dramatic procedure; any tension that arises is always defused by predictable returns. The sonata movement, on the other hand, thrives upon tension.

Figure 11.8

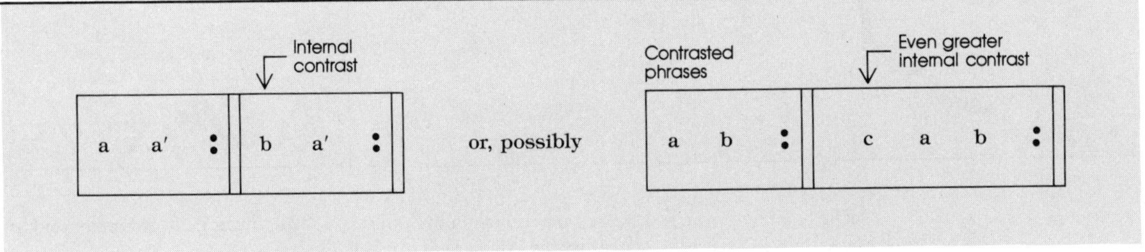

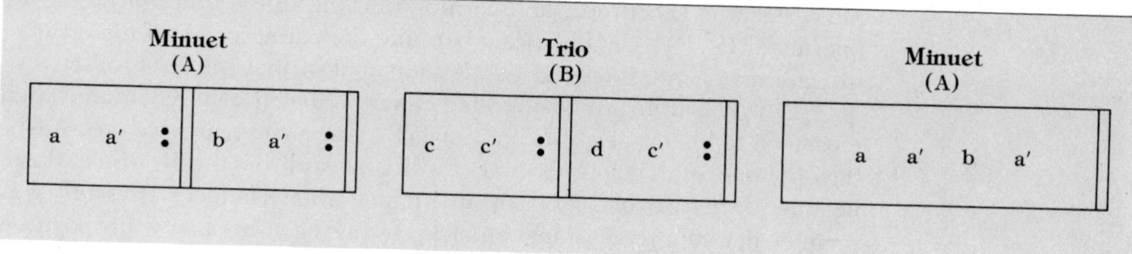

Figure 11.9

Minuet and Trio

The classic symphony or string quartet had one additional movement, dance-derived and usually placed third in the four-movement sequence. The choice of the *minuet* as a model was fortunate. Its tempo was brisk, but not dynamic enough to compete with the outer movements; its triple meter provided another pleasant contrast. The dance itself had associations with both the middle classes and a long courtly tradition.

Following the baroque practice of pairing dances, the classic composers presented two minuets: Minuet A, Minuet B, and the repeat of Minuet A. The middle minuet (B) was known as the *trio,* another throwback to the baroque: the name refers to the early practice of using an ensemble of three players in the light, contrasting sections of dance movements. During the classical period the trio may have had a lighter texture than the minuet, but it was usually scored for more than three instruments. The entire ABA form is known as *minuet and trio.* Each of the large sections is a miniature part form in its own right (see Figure 11.8), usually organized in a group of balanced phrases. In the tradition of the early dance suite, these internal sections are repeated. However, the return of the original minuet after the trio is performed *without* any repeats, as shown in Figure 11.9.

minuet and trio

Be prepared for unique twists and variants in pieces. Although all the forms noted in the sonata cycle appear clear-cut, *every* example of sonata form, rondo, or minuet and trio will provide its own surprises. In some sonata movements, "first" and "second" themes will be the *same,* differentiated only by key levels. Some sonata movements begin with a slow introduction, possibly one final link within slow-fast (stately-lively) format of the French overture. Minuets may have two trios, or asymmetrical phrase groupings within the large sections. The sonata-cycle format, then, is infinitely flexible. Two symphonies or sonatas, or string quartets resemble each other about as closely as two sonnets, two Gothic cathedrals, or two human faces.

Haydn: The Court Composer

The man who, perhaps more than any other individual, helped develop and perfect the sonata cycle was Joseph Haydn (1732–1809). Haydn wrote 83 string quartets, making that ensemble the most popular vehicle for amateur music making in Europe, and earning him the title "father of the string quartet." His 104 symphonies, spanning the entire length of his creative life, are major milestones in the development of that genre as well.

Haydn had an unusually long career, situated at a remarkably rich crossroad in history. He was born in 1732 (the same year as George Washington), one year before J. S. Bach began work on the B-Minor Mass; he was a ten-year-old choirboy in Vienna when Handel's ***Messiah*** was premiered, and a professional musician, working at his first court position and composing his first symphony, in the year of Handel's death. Haydn was a close friend of Mozart, and also taught the young Beethoven. By 1809, the year of Haydn's death, Beethoven had already composed six of his nine symphonies; Franz Schubert was twelve years old, and like Haydn some sixty years previously, a choirboy at Saint Stephen's in Vienna. Born during the last decades of the baroque era, Haydn lived to witness the start of the romantic movement.

In addition, he was the last important composer to work within the courtly patronage system, devoting the greater part of his life to the service of an aristocratic employer. For thiry years (1761–1791) Haydn worked for the Princes of Esterházy, Hungarian nobility who maintained a lavish estate modelled after Versailles in the Hungarian countryside some fifty miles from Vienna, and a town residence in Vienna itself. As part of the Esterházy entourage, Haydn shuttled back and forth between the Austrian capital, where he became friendly with Mozart, and the rural isolation of the family estate. He was required to wear the uniform and powdered wig of the court staff. As music director, he was a high-ranking servant, but a servant nevertheless, living in the servants' quarters and taking his meals at their table. His duties were considerable: not only composing and conducting for every sort of occasion, but taking responsiblity for the discipline and behavior of the musicians, and the neatness of their uniforms. He was required to keep track of the library of scores and the condition of the instruments; he even tuned the keyboard instruments himself.

He did not rebel. This was, after all, the only life a musician had known, other than the service of the church (another brand of patronage), the hand-to-mouth existence of a street performer, or the intrigues of the opera house. Moreover, it was a musically challenging life. The vast quantity of new work he had to produce, the existence of a first-rate orchestra at his disposal, the very fact of his isolation: all of these stimulated his creative thinking. In his own words:

> My Prince was always satisfied with my works . . . as conductor of an orchestra I could make experiments . . . be as bold as I pleased. I was cut off from the world, there was no one to confuse or torment me, and I was forced to become original.

Haydn, like generations of composers before him, composed music to fit the needs and tastes of society and of his patrons, ***not*** from an obsessive

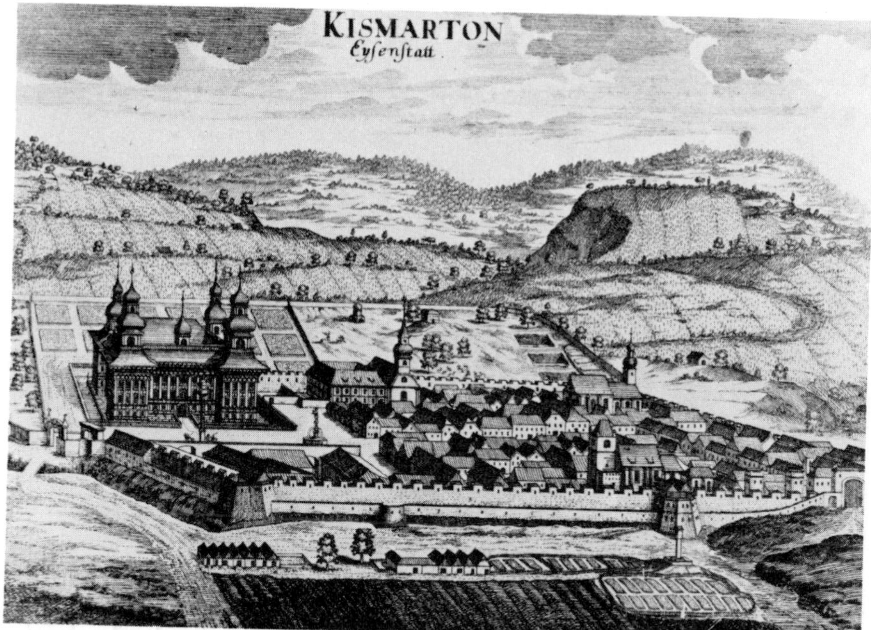

Matthias Greischer, View of Esterházy Palace, Engraving, 1697. The building on the left is the palace.

urge for "self-expression," a characteristic of nineteenth-century romanticism. Listeners of today may be shocked to learn that Handel borrowed chunks of his early operas and reworked them into oratorios, or that some Bach concertos are really transcriptions of Vivaldi. But this simply reveals the practical, craftsmanlike attitude of composers working within a clearly defined network of supply and demand, specific purposes and performances. Haydn, the last great exponent of this attitude, was perfectly content to create music on demand. When asked once when he had written no quintets, he replied, "Nobody has ordered any." He occasionally complained about the claustrophobic isolation of the Esterházy estate, claiming it was like being "buried alive," but never about its musical atmosphere.

A Late Symphony

Haydn's reputation gradually spread far beyond the environs of Vienna. In 1786 he was commissioned to write symphonies for a well-known subscription series in Paris. When he was retired from court service, upon the death of his Prince in 1791, a much more elaborate invitation came from London. The famous concert promoter Johann Peter Salomon brought Haydn to England, engaged him to compose six new symphonies for his London series, and offered him a handsome fee. The journey must have been exciting for a composer approaching age sixty, who spoke no English and who had never been more than fifty miles away from Vienna in his life! He was greeted warmly by royalty, wined and dined by ambassadors and princes, even awarded an honorary Doctorate of Music by Oxford University. He wrote after the Oxford ceremony, "I wish my Viennese friends could have seen me."

Joseph Haydn
Symphony no. 94: *Surprise*

R2 S1 B1

This symphony was one of the set of six composed for Haydn's 1791–1792 London tour. Today it is probably the best-known of his symphonies. Its fame and its familiar nickname derive from one chord heard in the slow movement. Even without that chord, though, the work offers a multitude of delights.

Movement I: Adagio cantabile; Vivace assai. A slow, lyric introduction precedes the main body of the movement. The G-major introduction moves in a graceful triple meter, as winds and strings answer and counterbalance one another. Then the motion stops, poised, questioningly on the dominant chord.

At this point the ***Vivace assai*** in sonata form begins (see Figure 11.10), still in G major, with a perky tune played by the first violins, suddenly answered (note the *f* at the very end of our example) by a rousing passage for full orchestra. The first five notes have been bracketed, because they form a motive that Haydn explores and develops throughout the movement. In our example, the bracketed motive is immediately repeated in sequence; furthermore, its rhythm pervades the entire passage.

The bridge is directly related to the theme, and grows naturally from it. When the dominant key of D major is reached, a new theme begins. It is frothy and busy; its simple oom-pah bass also makes it easy to recognize. For the classic composer, first and second themes do not have to present contrasting moods: both tunes are gay and cheerful. A closing theme, still in the dominant, rounds off the exposition. Listen for its wide skips, repeated pitches, and rhythmic contours reminiscent of the opening theme.

The development section begins with a variant of the first theme, noted in Figure 11.11. The wide interval at the opening has been changed, and the harmonic implications are totally different. The ♪♪♪ scale figure is extended in a sequential passage, with sudden changes from *f* to *p* impart-

Figure 11.10

Figure 11.11

ing a dynamic thrust to the overall motion. Haydn manipulates the large-scale modulation so that the note B becomes insistent; a teasing little passage, using the ♩ ♫ ♩ and the B, gently eases into the recapitulation. During this final section, the basic material returns, all of it in the tonic, before a brief coda and strong G-major cadence bring the movement to an end.

Movement II: Andante. This takes the form of a theme and variations, based upon a simple, folk-like tune; the tonality is C major (the subdominant). Haydn presents the theme (Figure 11.12) at a stately tempo, in an atmosphere of hushed quiet and transparently light texture. Its eight measures alternate gently between tonic and dominant. They are repeated, and at the very end of the repeat (measure 16) the famous "surprise" chord appears—just at the asterisk in Figure 11.12. The chord is full, loud, and punctuated by a sharp timpani stroke. Haydn is said to have remarked, "This is where all the ladies will scream." The tune continues gently onward, as though the surprise had never taken place; there are eight more measures, also repeated, reaching a firm cadence in the tonic C. The entire melody is heard as four phrases (see Figure 11.13).

The rest of the movement consists of four variations and a brief coda. As with the variations of the *Emperor* Quartet movement (Chapters 1–7), the initial theme is always recognizable even though its contours are continually altered. This is because tempo, meter, tonality, and the basic melodic shape are *not* changed. For the most part, Haydn even retains the measure-by-measure proportions (including repeats) of the original. Variation 1 places the theme at the lower level of a graceful two-part dialogue between first and second violins. In variation 2 the theme is shifted abruptly and loudly to C *minor,* allowing Haydn to explore keys and chords that would be considered "remote" in the context of C major. Variation 3 moves back to C major; the theme is presented in rhythmically altered form, stressing double-time repeated notes. As it progresses, a slow, lyric woodwind countermelody appears above it. Variation 4 is forceful, bright in color, and rhythmically complex. It propels the listener's interest forward, by its use of running triplet patterns and, later on, dotted rhythms.

Figure 11.12

Figure 11.13

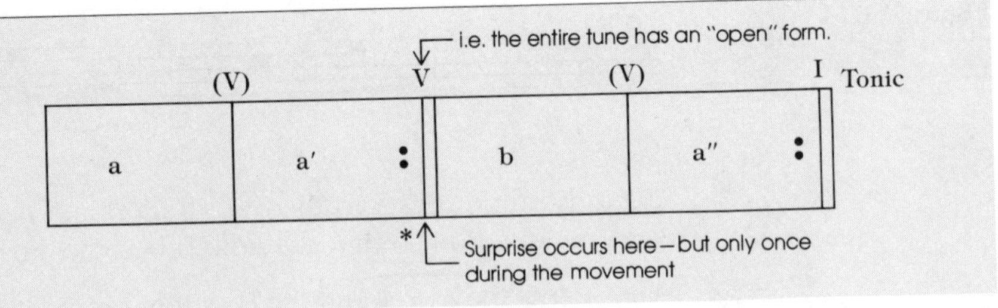

The coda offers another quiet, subdued variant of the theme, featuring a C pedal point and an unexpectedly chromatic chord progression. In fact, some musicians regard this closing chromatic harmony as the *real* "surprise" of the movement! We don't usually associate Haydn's name, as we might Mozart's, with intense, expressive chromaticism. This lovely passage and the slow introduction to movement I are the only strikingly chromatic moments in the symphony.

Movement III: Allegro molto. This movement moves at an unusually fast tempo. In its forceful, pounding beat and the off-centered stress on measures 4 and 8, it resembles a robust peasant dance—the entertainment of country folk—much more than refined courtly diversion. Figure 11.14 shows the first two phrases; in listening further, be prepared for odd turns of phrase and asymmetrical phrase lengths, as the two four-measure phrases shown here are followed by another four-measure phrase and then one of six measures. After the repeat of this opening, a rather elaborate passage appears: it sounds for all the world like a "development," complete with sudden modulations, quasi-fugal imitation, and abrupt shifts to the minor mode. This is a "surprise" of a different sort, as Haydn inserts a weighty, learned style in the middle of a rustic farm dance. The minuet tune returns, but now altered and securely tied to the tonic key. The Trio is quiet and lighter in texture, featuring bassoons and violins. As one might expect, both Minuet and Trio sections contain internal repeats, while the return of the Minuet does not. The tonality is G major.

Movement IV: Allegro molto. This movement contains elements of both *sonata* and *rondo*. The material is brisk, bouncy and jovial, and quite rapid,

Figure 11.14

Figure 11.15

with a main tune (Figure 11.15) that is hard to forget: it combines a distinctive rhythm, catchy repeated-note contour, and neat internal sequences and symmetries. In Rondo-like fashion, this tune is always stated in the tonic, and alternates with other materials. A contrasting theme, originally stated in the dominant key, balances the irrepressible opening tune, but it is that opening theme which remains in the memory, and which Haydn enjoys toying with. He develops fragments in modulating sequences, suddenly switches to the more dramatic minor mode, and eventually returns to the tonic major. There the recapitulation stresses both main themes, and a startling coda—one last "surprise," ushered in by a drum beat—brings the entire symphony to a close.

A Late Oratorio

The symphonies composed for Haydn's two London tours (1791–92 and 1794–95) were his last works in this medium. On his return from England he took an apartment in Vienna, where he gave lessons to the young Beethoven. He also turned his creative attention to choral music.

Haydn's achievements in instrumental music are so immense that we may not think of him as a vocal composer. But he was trained as a choirboy, and composed a number of operas for the entertainment of his Prince; Empress Maria Theresa herself once commented, 'When I want to hear good opera I go to Esterházy." Haydn composed more than a dozen Masses as well, some of them at the twilight of his career. But the great passion of his later years was acquired during his London stays. He had witnessed a great Handel festival at Westminster Abbey in 1791, and became acquainted with a number of Handel oratorios. Two of Haydn's last major works are oratorios based upon Handelian models: *The Creation* (1798) and *The Seasons* (1801). The latter is a secular oratorio, depicting the changing landscape during a year in the countryside, while *The Creation* deals with a religious subject loosely based upon passages from Milton's *Paradise Lost.*

The entire *Creation* is divided into three large parts, possibly following the model of Handel. Listen to the opening numbers of Part 1, beginning with the wonderfully imaginative orchestral prelude, "Representation of Chaos." Note the flashes of color, solo writing for the woodwinds, and the chromatic "chaos" that dominates the movement, even though it begins and ends in C minor. The recitative which follows ("In the beginning . . .") continues the hushed, tentative sense of the opening: it stresses low registers, dark instrumental colors, and quiet dynamics, all hovering about C minor. But at the words:

Gainsborough, ***Music Party.*** Chalk drawing. 18th century.

And God said: Let there be light,
And there was ***Light*** . . .

the entire texture comes alive, brilliantly, with a C-***major*** chord at the word "light." Contemporary audiences were stunned by the effect. Evidently Haydn's love for surprise had not diminished, even in a serious, sincerely religious context.

In the Handelian tradition, the recitative is followed immediately by an aria, and then by a choral number. Haydn links these in a single ex-

Figure 11.16

tended section; he also signals a change of mood with a new key, A major. Positive, joyous words are set in broad, diatonic phrases of Figure 11.16. But the dark spirits of hell ("despairing, cursing rage . . . black in throngs") receive a distorted chromatic treatment, further intensified by the tight imitation within the chorus. At the words "A new created world springs up at God's command," the music becomes secure, relaxed, and comfortable; the texture is chordal, and the key once more solidly A major. This is the most important choral statement of the opening, and in the Handelian tradition it effectively sums up everything that has gone before.

Mozart: The Free-Lance Composer

When Haydn composed ***The Creation,*** as an elderly man in his mid-sixties, his friend and colleague Wolfgang Amadeus Mozart (1756–1791) had already been dead for a number of years. As Haydn's life was long and rich, Mozart's was tragically short; in fact, Mozart's total span of years falls roughly within Haydn's middle age, as shown in Figure 11.17. The two composers first met in 1781 during one of Haydn's stays at the Esterházy Vienna quarters. Mozart had recently come to Vienna to make a career as a free-lance artist. Haydn was forty-nine years old, Mozart twenty-five (and with only ten more years to live). Haydn had gradually established a reputation as one of Europe's most distinguished composers; Mozart, having already been one of the most famous musicians in history as a ***child,*** was attempting what show-business people now call a "comeback."

Obviously the two men were of different generations. In fact, Mozart was among the first to bestow the nickname "Papa" on Haydn, as an affectionate gesture of love and respect for his older colleague. But they differed in much more than age. While Haydn had an unspectacular working-class boyhood and a traditional career as court musician, Mozart was one of the most publicized child prodigies of all time. His father was a violinist in the

Figure 11.17

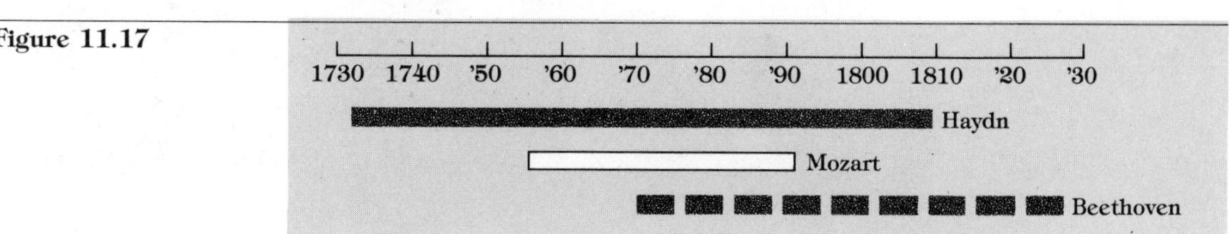

Carmontelle, ***Mozart with his Father and Sister*** (left) and Autograph by Composer, ***God is our Refuge.*** Mozart's career as a child prodigy took him to the major centers of Europe. We see him performing at the keyboard in a painting that dates from his visit to England in 1765. At that time the 9 year old wonder presented a manuscript to the King. (His childish signature is at the upper right.)

service of the Archbishop of Salzburg (Austria) and the author of a respected book on violin playing; he was Wolfgang's first teacher, and became his agent and impresario as well. Mozart showed extraordinary musical gifts as early as age three, and by the age of ten he had been hailed as a sensation in Vienna, Brussels, Paris, London, and at Versailles. He had charmed Madame de Pompadour, and flirted with the young Marie-Antoinette. By the age of fourteen he had toured Italy and had been decorated by the Pope. His skills as pianist and violinist, his compositions, improvisations, and incredible memory had been the talk of musical Europe.

Mozart, having known urban luxury, was a confirmed city-dweller, relatively uninterested in nature or the outdoors. He hardly ever made use of folk music in his work, except for humor or parody. In contrast, Haydn did not leave the environs of Vienna and Esterházy until his maturity. His love of folk music was genuine, and its influence upon his work profound. He was a truly pious, reasonably modest man who never forgot his humble roots, who loved to hunt and fish, and who felt comfortable in the role of servant.

Because Mozart was widely traveled, and possessed such superhuman facility, his own style contained a unique synthesis of varied influences. He had heard many operas in Italy, but he had also visited Mannheim, where he marveled at the new orchestral style. A major influence upon his development was Johann Christian Bach (1735–1782), the youngest son of Johann Sebastian, and a bit of a renegade among the Bachs. J. C. Bach had gone to Italy, converted to Catholicism, composed operas, and settled in London. His work emphasized the "gallant" style, in contrast to the more violent, dramatic experiments of his older brother Carl Phillip Emanuel. The eight-year-old Mozart first met J. C. Bach in London in 1764, and later sought his advice on many matters; the lyric, arioso quality of Mozart's melody owes much to the guidance of the youngest Bach. Haydn was another strong influence, especially in subtleties of sonata-cycle structure and dramatic contrast. But the benefit was mutual: Haydn's work acquired a new expressive dimension after his contact with Mozart.

Mozart knew the Haydn quartets well—he felt that only Haydn really understood the medium—and in 1785 he gave a performance with friends of a new set of string quartets dedicated to Haydn. The older composer attended the private performance, and afterwards said to Mozart's father, "I tell you before God and as an honest man, your son is the greatest composer I know, either personally or by name."

Mozart's Free-Lance Career

Perhaps Mozart was spoiled by the adulation of his youth; perhaps concertgoers expected him to remain an adorable prodigy the rest of his life. In either case, both were disappointed. All that the elder Mozart had wanted for Wolfgang was a prestigious church or court appointment: success within the patronage system. But the brilliant son was unable to land the best positions, and felt confined by the atmosphere of a small court establishment. Mozart clashed with his father, left the service of the Archbishop of Salzburg after a stormy confrontation, and came to Vienna to begin a career on his own, composing, performing, and conducting. He was the first important composer to renounce the established patronage system. It is not difficult to see why he rebelled against the drudgery and indignity of serving the nobility and the sleepy small-town atmosphere of Salzburg itself. Mozart must have found Salzburg's musical life incredibly boring. The tone set by the Archbishop and his court was frivolous and lightweight. (Haydn was

extremely fortunate to have a Prince who encouraged strong, daring music. Other patrons were not so adventurous.)

Mozart hoped to support himself as a composer of opera, which he would also conduct, and as a virtuoso pianist performing his own works. Accordingly, much of his creative energy during the last decade of his life was devoted to opera and piano concertos. His early ventures were successful; he launched a subscription concert series in Vienna, and elsewhere triumphed with the operas *Don Giovanni* and *Le Nozze di Figaro* ("The Marriage of Figaro"). Then everything began to go sour. He struggled to pay the rent, and as his financial situation became more precarious, his strained health grew worse. One major commission came his way in 1791: a request, made by a stranger dressed in black, to write a Requiem Mass for the dead. Mozart, already extremely ill, became obsessed with the notion that the mysterious man was the messenger of death, and that he was composing the Requiem for himself. In fact, the man represented a nobleman who wished to pass the work off as his own. Mozart died in December of 1791, his Requiem unfinished.

Why did Mozart fail? To begin with, public concerts were a recent innovation in Vienna when Mozart attempted to organize them for a profit. Support of the aristocracy was essential, and many wealthy subscribers who had originally helped Mozart abandoned him at the end; they may have been suspicious of his political or moral beliefs (his operas were occasionally daring in their libretti), or biased against his newfound religious belief in Freemasonry, or just annoyed at the complexity of his music. (The Emperor Joseph II had once dismissed his work as having "too many notes.") Furthermore, Mozart had no talent for business organization, and his wife was equally hopeless: together they squandered every bit of money as fast as it was earned. To succeed as a free-lance composer or performer, one apparently needed more than sheer talent. One also needed administrative ability, important friends, and the charismatic personality that would electrify an audience. Beethoven had all of these, as we shall see; Mozart had none.

Wolfgang Amadeus Mozart

Symphony no. 40 in G Minor, K. 550*

R1 S2 B5/6

During the summer of 1788, when his fortunes had already taken a turn for the worse, Mozart composed his last three symphonies. It is an amazing feat to have written such a substantial body of music, at a consistently high level of quality, in so short a time. It is even more remarkable that the three symphonies are totally contrasted in mood. The Symphony no. 39 (E♭ major) is lyric, no. 40 (G minor) tragic, and no. 41 (in C major, dubbed the

*The "K" number refers to the work's place in the complete Mozart catalogue compiled by the musicologist Ludwig Von Köchel.

Jupiter) extroverted and triumphal. Most remarkable of all, considering the social history of music, is the fact that no one had asked for them. They were, to our knowledge, ***not*** composed on commission, or to please a prospective patron. Mozart, the first truly free-lance composer, was also among the first to create music independent of specific social needs—an act of self-expression usually associated with "romanticism" and not with "classicism."

There is a "romantic" quality about the music, too. Mozart's style, with strong roots in Italian opera, was always dramatic, whether intended for the stage or not. His brand of drama was highly convincing, capable of moving listeners beyond the level of entertainment. In the G-Minor Symphony, no. 40, he sustains a ***single*** mood (call it tragic or solemn) throughout the four movements. In all probability, Haydn would have been equally capable of composing a dramatically unified symphony if he had wished to. But the esthetic attitude of Haydn's generation favored balance and objectivity above all. Mozart's mature works are more intensely single-minded; they seem to tip the "classic" balance, just a bit, in favor of expression.

Movement I: Molto Allegro. There is an impassioned *Sturm und Drang* quality to the sonata-form conflict, and great urgency about the opening G-minor theme (Figure 11.18). Note that there are three distinct theme fragments, which will all be used for development. The first motive, marked A, acts as the prime generating force of the movement; the upward skip of a 6th at B commands our attention as well. These two are combined into one phrase that rises and falls, answered by a sequential repetition a step lower, always using the same insistent rhythmic pattern. As noted in Figure 11.19, there is also a provocative ambiguity, as to where the phrases "breathe." Since the theme (and the movement) begin with a measure's worth of ***accompaniment*** one could feel the subtle stresses at measure 3, 5, and 7, rather than at 2, 4, and 6. That tension contributes to the restlessness of the passage. (Note, too, that the rising 6ths of motive B are already present in the accompaniment before the melody is ever sounded.)

Figure 11.18

Should the phrasing place stress on measures 1 and 3, or 2 and 4?

Figure 11.19

A thematic bridge leads to the relative major key area and a new group of themes. The falling lines of Figure 11.20 are exceptionally chromatic by prevailing eighteenth century standards; Mozart loved to explore the expressive, even "romantic," implications of chromaticism. (Similarly, J. S. Bach's music is highly chromatic when compared with that of his late baroque contemporaries.) Just before the end of the exposition, a fleeting reminder of motive A comes as a jolt, upsetting the equilibrium usually expected of "closing material."

The development is taut, aggressive, and concerned with the rearrangement of A, B, and C, cut loose from their original sequences and harmonic underpinning. As the music modulates through distant key areas we hear oddly chromatic inflections of the first theme's descending phrase, and then the whole of theme I in the bass against an angular counter-melody. A recombination of motives B and C creates an extended sequence; eventually A, now just an isolated fragment, is stated, restated in sequence, inverted, and hammered home (see Figure 11.21). It has become the sole focus of the music, Mozart's way of revealing the prime atomic unit of the movement.

The recapitulation features a restatement of the second theme group in the tonic *minor,* rather than in the major mode of the exposition. Mozart had

Figure 11.20

Figure 11.21

a conscious choice to make here, as either mode could be regarded as legitimate for restatement. His choice of a minor ending only deepens the sense of drama, and even carries it forward into succeeding movements.

Movement II: Andante. The slow movement is also cast in sonata form. Although the stormy outbursts have been subdued, the tension is still greater than expected in a slow movement, and the many chromatic dissonances (gentle "sighs") transform the courtly surface elegance into something much more poignant. The key of E$^\flat$ major is also unusual, perhaps just remote enough to be subconsciously unsettling.

Movement III: Allegretto. An aggressive, driving nature returns in this Minuet and Trio. Mozart has set up a series of cross-rhythms and syncopations. The asymmetrical phrase structure of the main theme is worth noting: three measures, then three, four, and four. Observe, too, that the opening three notes (Figure 11.22) span the D-B$^\flat$ 6th of motive B (movement I). Furious imitative counterpoint and striking dissonant suspensions maintain this mood. The Trio, by contrast, is rather delicate and mannerly (in G major), with marvelous scoring for flute and horns.

Movement IV: Allegro assai. A weighty movement is needed to balance the intensity of the preceding three, and this angry "storm and stress" movement provides great power and sweep. Note that Mozart has used the sonata design for three of the four movements, surely a sign of serious dramatic intent. The opening theme (Figure 11.23) begins with a "Mann-

Figure 11.22

Figure 11.23

heim rocket'' figure, and exploits sudden contrasts between loud and soft. Motives A and B from the first movement are hinted at here: the rising D-B♭ 6th of B, and the falling half step and repeated patterning of A. One may also be reminded of A's half-step motion, and the chromaticism of the second theme from movement I, in the Finale's second subject. It is stated in the relative major of B♭; note, in Figure 11.24, that the 6th of motive B is hinted at as well.

In addition, an angry, forceful succession of 6ths ushers in the development section (Figure 11.25). The idea of ''development,'' formerly confined to a single movement, now appears to run through an entire sonata cycle, unifying all its movements structurally and expressively. Finally, note that in the recapitulation, the second theme is brought back in G *minor,* confirming the melancholy sense of the whole.

The Classic Concerto

Of all the Viennese classic genres, opera and concerto had the most direct ties to the past. Both could claim a rich tradition, representing the height of baroque vocal and instrumental styles. During the classic period, the *con-*

Figure 11.24

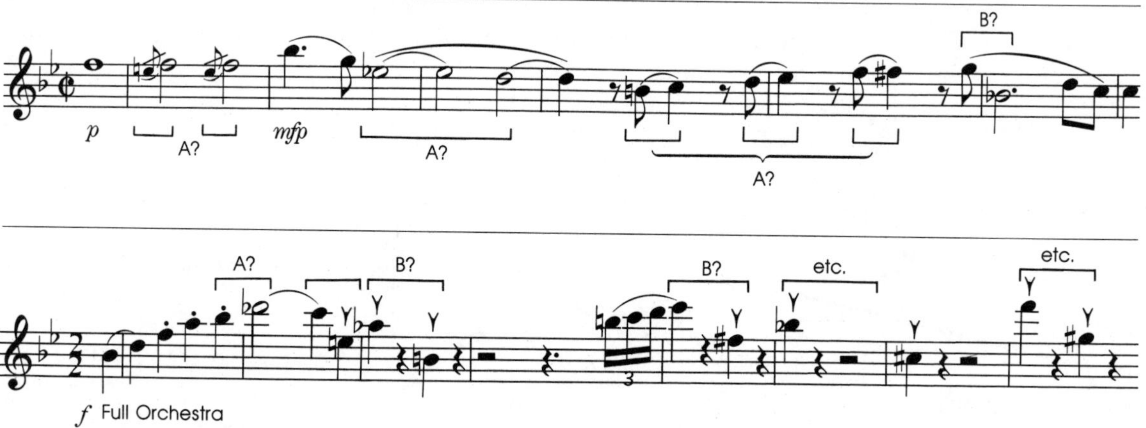

Figure 11.25

certo was transformed by the dramatic format of the sonata cycle, and by the institution of the public concert, into an effective showpiece for a virtuoso instrumental soloist.

Two traditions of the earlier baroque concerto were retained: the three-movement format (as opposed to the four movements of a symphony), and the *ritornello* concept of alternation between familiar orchestral material and fresh commentary by the soloist. The solo concerto had become more popular than the concerto grosso; audiences enjoyed observing a single performer and an orchestra engaged in the joint presentation of a sonata cycle. In adapting ritornello procedure to sonata form, a unique hybrid resulted: an exposition that unfolds first *without* the soloist (the equivalent of a baroque opening ritornello), and then becomes more elaborate once the soloist enters. In other words, there are *two* expositions. We refer to them both with the phrase *double exposition.* The typical classic concerto employs the double exposition during its sonata-form first movements.

double exposition

During this movement, there is also a special section in which the soloist plays without accompaniment, a virtuosic display of technique and interpretive skill lasting for several minutes while the orchestra waits silently. This section is called the *cadenza,* because it occurred near the very end of the movement, just where one would expect a final "cadence." In fact, it was meant to suspend that cadence momentarily. When the cadenza ended—usually, in eighteenth century practice, on a trill by the soloist—the actual "cadence" would be completed as well, with the orchestra joining in once more. Most eighteenth-century cadenzas were improvised by the soloist, using the material previously heard during the movement (and displaying "virtuosity" on yet another level). The Classic concerto first-movement format is shown in Figure 11.26.

cadenza

Slow movements and finales usually followed the general models of the sonata cycle. A spirited rondo was a favorite way of bringing the concerto to an entertaining close. The Rondo finale of Mozart's Horn Concerto no. 3 is a fine example (see Part 1). Notice how the soloist and *tutti* engage in a continual dialogue, imitating and exchanging lines, asserting individuality and relinquishing it.

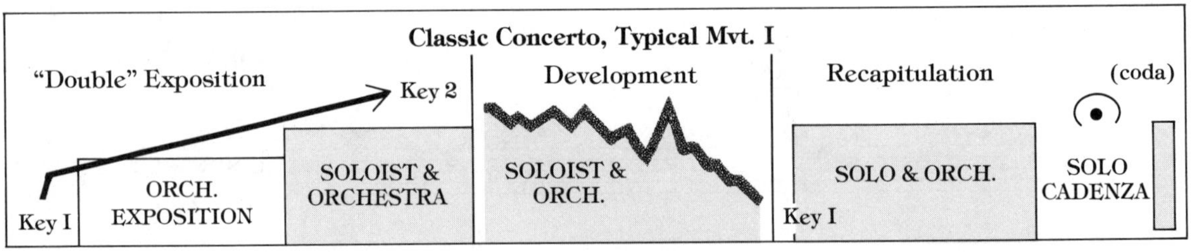

Figure 11.26

Haydn wrote only one really well-known concerto, a brilliant work for trumpet and orchestra composed late in his life. It was Mozart who excelled in the medium, composing more than forty concertos for such solo instruments as horn, violin, flute, and clarinet. There are more than twenty Mozart piano concertos, written for his own concert appearances as soloist. For these works, of course, he felt no need to write out his cadenzas: he simply improvised them, in the tradition of the time. Modern pianists usually prefer ***not*** to improvise cadenzas for Mozart. They may play versions that Mozart did write out, or those composed and written down by Beethoven and other great nineteenth-century pianists. (Or, of course, they may compose their own.)

Mozart's Operas

Opera, more than most musical genres, seems to reflect the ***political*** life of its times, whether conservative or revolutionary, pro-establishment or anti-establishment. Significantly, opera buffa became an important force during the decades before the French Revolution, and anticipated certain revolutionary feelings. Audiences who had begun to question the heroic posturing and lifeless plots of ***opera seria*** enjoyed seeing servants outwit their masters on stage, and noble pomposities deflated. National vernacular opera, influenced by the buffo style, also made great strides. The German ***Singspiel*** and French ***Opéra Comique*** had acquired partisan champions by the late eighteenth century, although many aristocrats considered such ventures uncouth.

The buffo style had also introduced ***musical*** changes: a more flexible kind of rapid, conversational recitative, and the rousing, often slapstick, ensemble "finale"—in which all members of the cast, in a rapid succession of arias and ensemble combinations, would bring an act to smashing conclusion. Greater emphasis was placed upon dramatic narrative and a convincing theatrical text, in serious as well as comic opera.

Mozart loved the opera. We know that from his many letters to his father on the subject, and examples of operas he composed as early as age eleven. He wrote operas in each of the three important types he knew, ***opera seria, opera buffa,*** and the German-language ***Singspiel,*** and excelled at all three, as he did at everything musical he put his hand to. He was perpetually fascinated by human character. It is revealing that in his many letters he rarely refers to landscape, or the architecture of the places he visits (Haydn would have delighted in both), or to such political matters as the French Revolution. But his writings are filled with descriptions of ***people*** he has met—nobles, tradesmen, strangers—and their intriguing foibles. That sensitivity to subtle shades of character, plus the ability to depict character musically, make Mozart one of the great opera composers.

Two of his finest stage works are considered examples of ***opera buffa: Le Nozze di Figaro*** (1786) and ***Don Giovanni*** (1787). In both, Mozart used elements of the ***buffo*** style, especially the ensemble Finale with many characters on stage and rapid-fire action. On the other hand, it is difficult to call either work a comedy. Mozart, like Shakespeare, had a facility for exploring the tragic and serious sides of the same subject simultaneously. For these two operas he was also blessed with an exceptional librettist, Lorenzo da Ponte. Da Ponte had been born an Italian Jew, converted in childhood and trained for the Catholic priesthood; he was also Viennese court poet, friend, and confidant of Casanova, and something of a rake in his own right. Later an emigrant to the United States, da Ponte taught at Columbia University, where he became first professor of Italian Studies in this country. He and Mozart were ideal collaborators, since they shared similar assumptions about operatic pacing, character, and language. Operatic history has known few teams as distinguished as this.

Don Giovanni

Le Nozze di Figaro had strong political overtones, with a libertarian script drawn from the most inflammatory play of the period, and in certain respects *Don Giovanni* was even more revolutionary. Audiences were familiar with the "Don Juan" legend, which had been the subject of folk-dramas, puppet shows, and a famous Spanish play; they regarded the character as a vulgar, lecherous figure of fun. But in Mozart's opera, he is portrayed as more than that: a demonic figure, superhumanly energetic and attractive, beyond the social restrictions of lesser mortals; in short an existential "hero." He is also an evil hero, a ruthless, shameless villian whose obsessions bring about violence and death. For Mozart and da Ponte, such contradictions made for exciting theatre—opera buffa expanded beyond the limits of comic farce to an intensely dramatic level. *Don Giovanni* had political implications as well, since the amoral hero who disrupts and scandalizes the social fabric is, after all, an aristocrat.

In addition, the Don Juan story provided an ideal vehicle for varied stage action: comic scenes, slapstick, mistaken identity, peasant revelry, courtly dances, seduction, a duel to the death, a horrifying cemetery scene, and the ghostly supernatural. To briefly summarize the plot: Don Giovanni, and his all-purpose servant and accomplice Leporello, are surprised by the father of a woman who has been fighting off Don Giovanni's advances. The father, known as the Commandant, exchanges harsh words with Don Giovanni. The two engage in a duel, resulting in the Commandant's death. Donna Anna, his daughter, vows vengeance, but the spirit of the dead Commandant exacts its own vengeance. When Don Giovanni comes upon a large statue of the Commandant in a cemetery, it speaks to him, warning of impending doom. Don Giovanni ignores the threats, and in a show of bravado invites the statue to dinner.

The statue accepts the invitation, appears at the banquet hall (in one of the most terrifying moments in opera), and orders Don Giovanni to repent. He proudly and courageously refuses, and is dragged down to hell. This is not the complete plot of the opera, but merely a summary of its

A scene from a performance, by the New York City Opera, of *Don Giovanni,* including the menacing statue of the slain Commandant.

opening and closing moments. The remainder of the story shows us a few of Don Giovanni's adventures and escapes, as fate closes in on him; in these intervening scenes of flirtatious escapade, the comic aspects of the ***buffo*** style are uppermost.

Mozart gave each of his main characters a distinct psychological profile, and a unique singing style drawn from diverse operative models. Leporello, for example, resembles the ***buffo*** lower-class comic buffoon, while Donna Anna's music is more characteristically aristocratic, proud and ***seria.*** Don Giovanni himself is capable of adopting many styles, perhaps symbolic of his larger-than-life universality. Moreover, Mozart exploited the stereotypes that had become attached to various vocal ranges and timbres, the varieties of soprano, bass, and tenor characterizations.

Finally, he presented his drama on the nonverbal level of key relationships, expressing conflict and resolution ***tonally.*** It has often been remarked that Mozart's concertos are highly "operatic" in their dramatic interplay of soloist and ensemble. In the same vein, his operas are highly "symphonic" in their sonata-cycle gestures and key schemes. *Don Giovanni* can be heard as a large-scale work in the key of D (major and minor), the tonality that dominates the overture, the descent into hell, and the final curtain.

Wolfgang Amadeus Mozart

Don Giovanni: excerpts from Acts I & II *R3 S1 B1*

The overture opens forcefully and rather frighteningly in D minor. Notice the chromatic chord progressions, syncopations, and unsettling dynamics. (This material will be heard later in the opera, in connection with the Commandant's statue.) The tension revolves upon a brisk D-major tune at a much livelier tempo, and a subsequent sonata structure which constitutes the rest of the overture. At the very end of the movement, the music veers away from D to a new tonal area, providing a sense of anticipation, rather than resolution, as the curtain rises.

We see Leporello keeping watch outside the Commandant's residence, grumbling about his work, the long hours and bad food, the ingratitude of his master. The sudden *f*s of the music (Figure 11.27) suggest various details of staging: pacing back and forth, sudden turns, perhaps kicking at the ground or a tree. Leporello hears a sudden noise and hides, as Don Giovanni and Donna Anna emerge from the palace locked in a struggle. He is trying to hide his face; she is hanging on to him and calling for help. All the while, Leporello comments upon the scene from his hiding place: "My master in trouble again . . . what an uproar." The ***ensemble*** convention of opera enables these various moods to be expressed simultaneously. Another ensemble passage occurs after the Commandant has been struck down in the duel. The fiercely dissonant chords of the duel are suddenly silenced, and replaced by a *pp* figure against plucked strings. Against this hushed

Figure 11.27

Lep:	
Notte e giorno faticar	*To toil night and day*
per chi nulla sà gradir;	*for someone whom nothing can please,*
pioggia e vento sopportar,	*to put up with wind and rain,*
mangiar male e mal dormir!	*to eat poorly and sleep badly!*
Voglio far il gentiluomo,	*I want to play the gentleman;*
e non voglio più servir,	*I don't want to serve anymore,*
no, no, no, no, ... etc.	*no, no. . . . . .*

background, the dying Commandant gasps for help; Don Giovanni observes the scene cynically and dispassionately; Leporello (as usual) fears for his own skin and further "trouble." The tragedy of the Commandant's death is thrown into greater relief by the shockingly casual recitative that follows: "Who's dead, you or the old man?" "What a dumb question—the old man." "Bravo!! Raping the daughter and killing the father." "He asked for it."

The last scene of *Don Giovanni* (Act II) is the supper to which the Commandant's statue has been invited. True to the tradition of the opera buffa, this *Finale* (of the act and of the entire opera) is a complex interweaving of many arias and ensembles in rapid succession. Mozart has also composed the entire scene in D, the most important key of the opera, offsetting the central key with arias and other numbers in related tonalities.

The opening minutes are comic and scatterbrained in a slapstick way, as the table is set and Leporello tries to filch food behind Don Giovanni's back. In the background a band of musicians plays popular tunes of the day, including a fragment from Mozart's own *Figaro.* (Leporello's wry aside at that point: "This one I know only too well.") Donna Elvira, another old love who has appeared in previous scenes, rushes in, begging Don Giovanni to change his way of life. When he refuses in a hearty toast to women and wine, she rushes offstage; then, with a shriek, she rushes back again and out the other side. Leporello runs out to investigate, and cries out as well: by this time, we can guess that the statue has come to dinner. The mood has suddenly become stark and chilling. The key is now D minor, and the grim chords, with trombones added, have brought us back to the slow, syncopated beginning of the overture. As seen in Figure 11.28, the material and mood of the opera have come full circle.

What follows is more tortuously intense than anything heard so far. Don Giovanni, his hand caught in the icy grip of the Commandant's, still refuses to change his ways. Amidst chromatic swirls of flutes, the warnings

Figure 11.28

of an offstage chorus, and awesome trombones and drums, he vanishes into a flaming eternity of damnation.

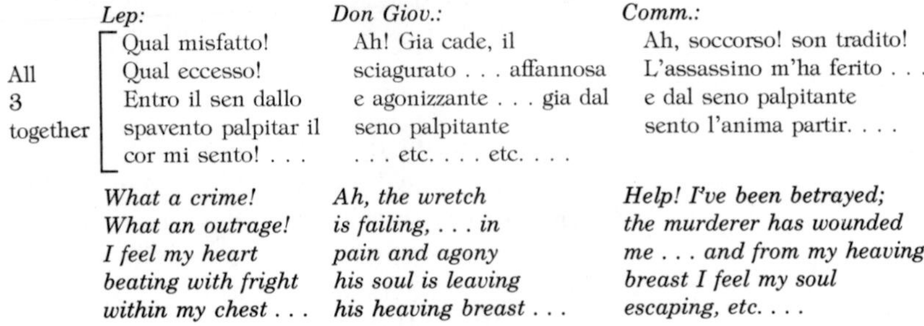

	Lep:	*Don Giov.:*	*Comm.:*
All 3 together	Qual misfatto! Qual eccesso! Entro il sen dallo spavento palpitar il cor mi sento! . . .	Ah! Gia cade, il sciagurato . . . affannosa e agonizzante . . . gia dal seno palpitante . . . etc. . . . etc. . . .	Ah, soccorso! son tradito! L'assassino m'ha ferito . . . e dal seno palpitante sento l'anima partir. . . .
	What a crime! What an outrage! I feel my heart beating with fright within my chest . . .	*Ah, the wretch is failing, . . . in pain and agony his soul is leaving his heaving breast . . .*	*Help! I've been betrayed; the murderer has wounded me . . . and from my heaving breast I feel my soul escaping, etc. . . .*

Then, suddenly, the comedy resumes. The remaining characters enter, at a jolly tempo, and engage in a brisk resolution of all the plot strands: Donna Elvira will enter a convent; Donna Anna pledges her hand in marriage; others remember that their supper is growing cold; all comment on the justness of Don Giovanni's punishment. It is a marvelously ambiguous *buffo* ending to a uniquely tragic-comic work. At the height of nineteenth-century romanticism, this last number was often omitted in performance, since it detracted from the splendor of the monumental, tragic hero meeting his grisly end. But Mozart's contemporaries would have been puzzled if that last summing up hadn't taken place. It was the perfect stroke to bring all the dramatic levels—comic, demonic, supernatural and moral—into "classic" balance.

To consider a different sort of balance: Mozart creates detailed psychological portraits of his characters, and then allows them to be caught in a confused whirlwind of action. Physical on-stage activity has become an important component of opera. In earlier styles "action" had been conceived of as intensified speech, or grand pageantry. Almost all the important events of Monteverdi's *Orfeo* take place off-stage; Neapolitan opera had stressed static tableau rather than physical movement. Mozart's stage, though, is alive with real people running, shouting, hiding, dueling, eating, seducing and betraying one another. The operas, like his instrumental works, demonstrate the intensity that could be summoned up within the balanced context of the classic ideal.

Interlude 3
Music and Words

Before leaving the eighteenth century, we might pause to reflect upon its most impressive musical achievement: the creation of a style that could convey "meaning" and hold interest for long stretches of time *without words.* Earlier instrumental music had either been danced, associated with pageantry, or copied directly from vocal models. The newer instrumental genres of the baroque and classic periods created a stylistic "language" of tones: by the late eighteenth century, composers could convey arguments and dramatic narratives through the medium of pitch, color, duration, and texture alone. In this sense, a Bach fugue or Mozart symphony provides statements and "meanings" just as specific as those associated with words.

The term *absolute music* refers to nonverbal compositions that attempt the expression of ideas or arguments. Very likely the meanings inherent in musical relationships are those that cannot be expressed in words. Musical language is usually not as specific as verbal language in referring to concrete physical objects of the real world. In other situations—where inflection, emphasis, and expressive gesture are crucial—musical language is more specific than verbal. And as Jacques Barzun has pointed out, words are not necessarily that "specific." The word "chair" might refer to someone who convenes a parliamentary meeting. If it means an object of furniture on which we sit, that still doesn't provide a clear picture of the object—wooden or metal, green or red. In certain areas, music can be more detailed than any words.

In absolute music, meaning resides almost exclusively in the material itself and the logic of its organization. With most Western music from 1600 to 1900, that logic is directly related to tonality; after 1750, the logic of the sonata cycle is important, too. Even non-tonal twentieth century music states its premises and priorities, and then acts upon them along a time path that we can follow with varying degrees of difficulty.

Music *with* words is, paradoxically, both easier and more difficult to listen to. It is easier, in the sense that we latch on to the words and allow *their* meanings to hold our attention. Perhaps we feel more certain of the exact "mood" of a piece if it comes with a ready-made set of concrete references. It may also be easier to follow music form when it corresponds to the poetic logic of stanzas and strophic repetitions. On the other hand, listening to vocal music in this way misses half the significance of the music. To grasp the experience of vocal music fully we should note how the musical setting enhances, comments upon, or even contradicts the verbal message. In any music with text, these two levels of meaning interact in a unique kind of tension. Words themselves are also musical: phonetic sounds arranged in rhythmic successions.

Words, in fact, have three different functions in a musical setting. (1) They convey specific symbols relating to reality: the meaning of the messenger's phrase to Orfeo, "Thy well-beloved bride is dead." (2) They articulate a series of consonant-and-vowel sounds, making perfectly lovely music in themselves, whether one understands the symbolic references or not. (3) They provide the singer with raw material for timbral exploration, with different symbols producing unique vocal embouchures and colors. For the last two reasons, Italian is traditionally the favored language of opera: its open vowels and rhythmic stresses make for exquisitely liquid sounds, and also allow the singing voice to "open up." Compare, for example, the Italian line (". . . la tua diletta sposa e morta") to the English translation above.

Monteverdi created *Orfeo* with Italian in

mind. Dowland's songs are specifically English, and Schubert's thoroughly German. What happens when any of these is heard in translation? If the translation converts the words from an unfamiliar language to one we know, we will understand the meaning of the text, at least at the level of basic information. But on a subtler level, another "meaning" has been lost, and not only because meanings and associations are always lost in translations. The interactions between music and speech, which the composer may have planned with great care, has been weakened; finally, the actual "music" of the original word-patterns is destroyed.

For these reasons, "to translate, or not to translate" becomes a controversial problem in the production of opera. Some people argue that opera should be offered in the language of the audience, so that dramatic action, dialogue and plot details are immediately comprehensible. Thus, *Orfeo* should be sung in English when presented in Chicago, in Swedish in Stockholm, in French in Paris. If the main concern is *theatre*—the immediacy of spoken drama—there is great logic to this argument. In practice, though, it would depend upon the existence of trained local singers in each country, who could really handle the operatic repertory in their native Danish or Russian, *and* high-quality translations which conveyed the "music" of words as well as their sense. Actually, most major roles are sung by a group of international "stars" who jet-hop from San Francisco to Berlin to Helsinki and cannot be expected to learn their parts in more than one or two languages. Moreover, many translations leave a good deal to be desired, and reduce meanings to their most absurd equivalents. It was probably an awful translation that led H. L. Mencken to remark, "Opera in English makes as much sense as baseball in Italian."

It can be argued, too, that opera is not just theatre. It is a very special kind of "ritual theatre," and the ritual itself entails a concern for the sounds (rather than the sense) of language. As part of the ritual, a listener may very well study the libretto and know the plot before ever witnessing the production. That would be unthinkable for the average theatregoer, but perfectly understandable to the opera-lover. To advocate translated opera on the grounds of immediate "understanding" raises other questions: no one really "understands" an opera without some prior knowledge of its conventions, traditional roots, social, political, and religious meanings. The witches of *Dido and Aeneas* were very real in an age when witches were being burned; the heroic stature of the gods and kings of *opera seria* was meant to flatter the live kings and courtiers sitting in the audience boxes; the most shocking aspect of Don Giovanni's behavior may have been his betrayal of nobility and the chivalric code that accompanied rank. "Understanding," then, is a highly relative affair; perhaps we should not destroy the special quality of operatic language in pursuit of it.

"Nonsense!" comes the cry from another quarter. English-speaking peoples have enjoyed the works of Goethe, Moliére, Chekhov, Lorca, Dante, Tolstoy, and Strindberg in translation for centuries. When New York audiences go to see performances of Ibsen or Pirandello, they hear them in English. The Shakespeare who was so highly revered by Berlioz, Beethoven, and Verdi was a Shakespeare translated into French, German and Italian.

On the other hand, operatic language—intimately allied with syllables, timbres, and musical references—is not spoken language, even less the language of silent reading . . . and so the debate goes on forever. It is a critically important one, and one in which everybody concerned about music can take part. The relationship between music and words is a duality as old as art itself.

12

Beethoven

> Beethoven will in time fill the position of one of Europe's greatest composers, and I shall be proud to be able to speak of myself as his teacher.
>
> *Haydn*

> Watch out for him. He will have something to tell you.
>
> *Mozart, after a performance by the young Beethoven*

The Classic Beethoven

Ludwig van Beethoven (1770–1827) is the only composer to occupy a chapter of his own in this book. To make one single individual the focus of a chapter affords us greater depth—an examination of style, biography, and social context—and a different perspective for the study of music. Of course, any major composer might have served as the subject for this sort of focus: Bach, or Mozart, or Wagner. Beethoven was certainly such a major composer, and also a very special figure in the history of Western music. He was not necessarily the "greatest" of composers—that would be a matter of opinion—but he was very possibly the most influential. His life and work altered the perceptions and assumptions of every succeeding generation, including our own. One of these assumptions is the very concept of the "great" composer, a role that Beethoven created almost singlehandedly.

His career and work are poised between two different styles, each reflecting particular social and political values. Born during the last years of the aristocratic patronage system, and trained in the classic idiom, he bent that system to suit his own purposes. He succeeded (where Mozart had failed) as a free-lance musician, sided with the forces of social revolution, and by his death was regarded as the symbol and champion of the romantic movement. Clearly there are "classic" and "romantic" sides to his nature.

The "classic" aspects of Beethoven are revealed in his use of the basic forms and genres of the Viennese style. He may have altered and expanded upon these, but he saw no need to abandon them. Beethoven's innovations were those of sonority and gesture; his materials and forms were hardly different from Haydn's or Mozart's. His careful, painstaking attention to form is another "classic" trait. Beethoven worked with longer durations and more violent surface contrasts than Haydn, but he still fused these into balanced structures of exquisitely calculated ***proportions.*** Even though Beethoven's musical statements are highly personal and expressive—that is, "romantic"—they are also integral parts of an imposing structural logic.

Tonality as Structural and Expressive Force

In the Viennese classic style, key relationships often generate not only the "form" but the dramatic "content" of much music. Beethoven, like Haydn and Mozart, was concerned with the expressive implications of key contrasts: the tensions, conflicts, and eventual resolutions of the sonata cycle.

The importance of ***tonality*** in Viennese musical thinking must be stressed, if only because it is so tempting to emphasize themes or motives instead. Obviously, melodies and thematic development were significant. But this was also an age when the major-minor tonal system was reaching its full potential. For composers of this period, the most important aspect of music was its key scheme: the relationship of all pitches, chords and rival tonal areas to a single central tonality. As suggested by Figure 12.1, this tonal "point" has often been compared to the vanishing-point that characterizes ***perspective*** in the visual arts. Comparisons between the arts are notoriously misleading, but perspective and tonality occupy similar positions within the histories of their respective arts. (1) Both techniques distinguish post-Renaissance "humanistic" styles from earlier Church-dominated ones. (2) They are more closely associated with Western-European

Figure 12.1

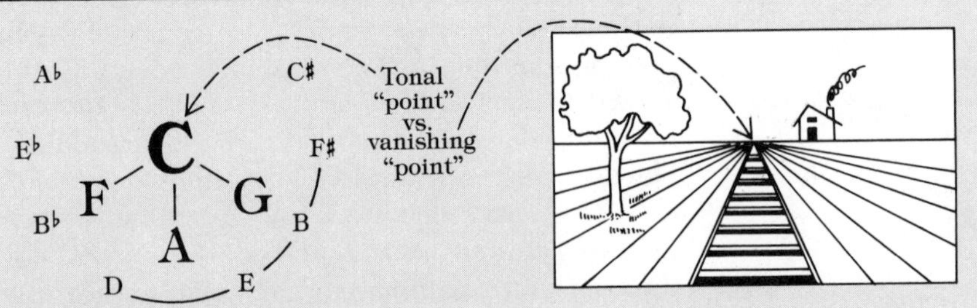

esthetics than with those of other world cultures. (3) They impose a sense of *direction* upon space or time. (4) They equate the ***"point"*** with an individual ***point of view:*** with regard to perspective, a slice of visual "reality" as witnessed or imagined by one person, standing at one spot on earth at a particular time (rather than by God, who is everywhere). Tonality allowed the eighteenth-century composer to express his individuality, too, using the passage of time and the stresses and pulls of tonality to create drama.* The sonata cycle became the ideal vehicle for that drama.

Instrumental Resources

The eighteenth century had witnessed the growth and standardization of the orchestra, from Bach's typical Leipzig ensemble of about twenty players to the instrumentation, a half-century later, of a Haydn or Mozart symphony: winds in twos, two horns, two trumpets, timpani, and about twenty-five string players. Continuo parts were no longer provided for keyboard instruments, as they would have been in Bach's time, although the practice of conducting from the keyboard lingered on into the early nineteenth century.

Beethoven's early orchestral works stayed well within this framework: only gradually did he expand his orchestral palette. He also composed chamber works for the popular Viennese combinations. The Classic period had seen an increasing distinction between orchestral and chamber styles. The former assumed a large body of players, with more than one on a part, and formal presentation at public concerts; the latter was intended for a small private group of soloists, usually amateurs. This distinction became even more pronounced with Beethoven.

The Piano

During the classic period the piano replaced the harpsichord as Europe's most popular keyboard instrument. Its broad dynamic range, lyric potential for sustaining pitches, and dramatic power lent themselves well to the new, homophonic styles of the mid-eighteenth century. The elderly J. S. Bach had seen a piano during his visit to the court of Frederick the Great; it was still something of a curiosity then. Bach's sons composed music for the new fortepiano, but also wrote for the more traditional harpsichord. Mozart played both instruments as a boy. His later performing career, however, was centered about the piano. Beethoven was a pianist from the start, and made his initial mark upon the Viennese musical establishment as a piano virtuoso.

The instrument itself was changing—acquiring a stronger, more resonant body, expanding its dynamic and pitch range, increasing its timbral flexibility. Beethoven's piano works coincided with these technological advances in instrument design, and took full advantage of the changes. It is

* One more point of similarity: both techniques have been seriously questioned in the twentieth century.

A silhouette of Beethoven at his piano, contrasted with a photo of the actual instrument he used (now on exhibit at the Beethoven House in Bonn). By Beethoven's lifetime the piano had acquired greater strength and dynamic flexibility. His music stimulated even further improvements.

important to realize that Beethoven's early fame as a *pianist* contributed to his growing importance as a composer. He capitalized upon that fame by emphasizing the piano in much of his early music: recital pieces, sonatas, piano-violin-cello trios, and piano concertos, rather than the string quartets and symphonies that would place him in direct competition with his idols. He explored the latter two genres only after he had built a secure reputation and an eager audience for his music.

Beethoven and the Viennese Tradition

Like Haydn and Mozart, Beethoven came to reside in Vienna. He first visited in 1786–87, and was taken to play for Mozart (whose reaction is quoted at the beginning of this chapter). Beethoven returned to Vienna in 1792; Mozart had died, and Haydn—just returned from his first London tour—accepted the young Beethoven as a pupil. The two did not get along very well: apparently Haydn was not a disciplined teacher, and Beethoven secretly studied counterpoint with others. For his part, Haydn must have found his pupil's abrasive personality and radical social views a bit difficult. In any case, Beethoven's music shows a strong affinity for Haydn and Mozart. He respected, and learned from, the work of both. The critic who characterized the entire classic period as ''two friends and their disciple'' was not exaggerating.

Beethoven's music also reflects the influence of Vienna itself: the growing traditions of amateur music making and public concerts, street tunes and outdoor serenades. Like Mozart and Haydn before him, Beethoven tried to combine elements of ''high'' and ''popular'' art in his work, another way in which he revealed his affinity for the Viennese classic style.

The Composer as Revolutionary

Beethoven also departed from the Viennese style in radical ways. His musical language was brasher and more outspoken than anything previously heard. His social demeanor—his view of the artist's role in the world of aristocratic patronage—was equally outrageous. It is appropriate that someone with the forceful personality of a Beethoven was ready to upset the musical establishment at precisely the moment when the French Revolution destroyed Europe's political establishment. The two phenomena, Beethoven and the Revolution, were whirlwinds within their respective spheres of influence, and the two have been inseparably linked ever since.

Actually Haydn, Mozart, and Beethoven all came from middle-class, provincial backgrounds. Whereas Haydn retained the outlook of a servant, although a highly respected one, and Mozart acquired urbane, cosmopolitan ways, Beethoven presented a curious contradiction: a gruff, rude unpolished figure of a man, he refused to conform to society's expectations, insisting instead that society change to meet *him.* When performing in aristocratic

The Beethoven House—in which the composer was born, now a museum devoted to his personal artifacts, and a major landmark of the city of Bonn.

homes, he would leave the piano and refuse to play if he overheard any conversation; he might abuse and insult the offending nobleman as well. Goethe also recalls Beethoven's refusal to bow his head as the Emperor's party passed by. In utter disregard of the prevailing class system, he reacted to a calling card flourished by his brother ("Johann Beethoven, land-owner") by proclaiming himself "Ludwig van Beethoven, ***brain***-owner." And he wrote these strong words in a letter to Prince Lichnowsky: "What you are, you are by circumstances and by birth. What I am, I am through myself. Of princes there have been and will be thousands. Of Beethovens there is only one.''

Ironically, Beethoven was as fervently devoted to a class system as any aristocrat, but he believed in the superiority of an *intellectual* and artistic class; he was, on his own terms, as great a snob as any prince. Perhaps for that reason, or for some undefinable magnetism in his explosive, overpowering personality, princes and countesses accepted him. They welcomed him into their homes, subsidized his public concerts, and engaged him to teach their families. In fact, Beethoven's career was greatly aided by his noble friends: Prince Lichnowsky (in whose home Beethoven lived for a few years), Archduke Rudolf and many others. His piano pupils included countesses with whom he fell in love; in some instances, the strong attachments were mutual. He succeeded in making his public concerts major events in Vienna. He enjoyed mingling with wealthy patrons and teaching aristocratic ladies. By writing hack pieces and arrangements of his own music, he capitalized on the growing amateur market and music publishing business. Mozart had been offended by such activities, and reluctant to engage in them. This may partially explain why it was Beethoven, not Mozart, who survived as a successful free-lance musician.

At the height of Beethoven's fame, tragedy struck, in a form that any musician would regard as profoundly cruel and unjust: he began to lose his hearing. The loss began about 1796, and reached a point in 1800–1801 where he could no longer keep it a secret. His friends had noticed his ''absent-mindedness'' in following conversations, and puzzling slips in his piano playing. In 1802 his physician sent him to spend the summer at Heiligenstadt, a quiet village where he could rest. During that summer Beethoven's mental anguish reached its crisis point. He contemplated suicide, and wrote a letter to his brothers with the instructions ''to be read only after my death.'' The letter was, in fact, discovered after Beethoven's death, and has since become known as the Heiligenstadt Testament. In it the composer wrote:

> Fellow men, who believe or say that I am ill-tempered and your enemy, you do me a great wrong. You do not know the secret reason . . . I could not say to men, speak louder, shout, for I am deaf! How could I confess to the weakness of a sense that in myself ought to have been more perfect than in others? . . . I almost took my own life. Only music could hold me back. I felt it impossible to leave this world before having fulfilled my calling . . .

The Testament reveals enormous humiliation and torment—understandable in a man of great pride, and a practicing musician who needs to perform, teach, and conduct in order to earn a living. But the Heiligenstadt Testament also reveals the colossal courage and moral conviction that enabled Beethoven to face the world again. He believed not only in the superi-

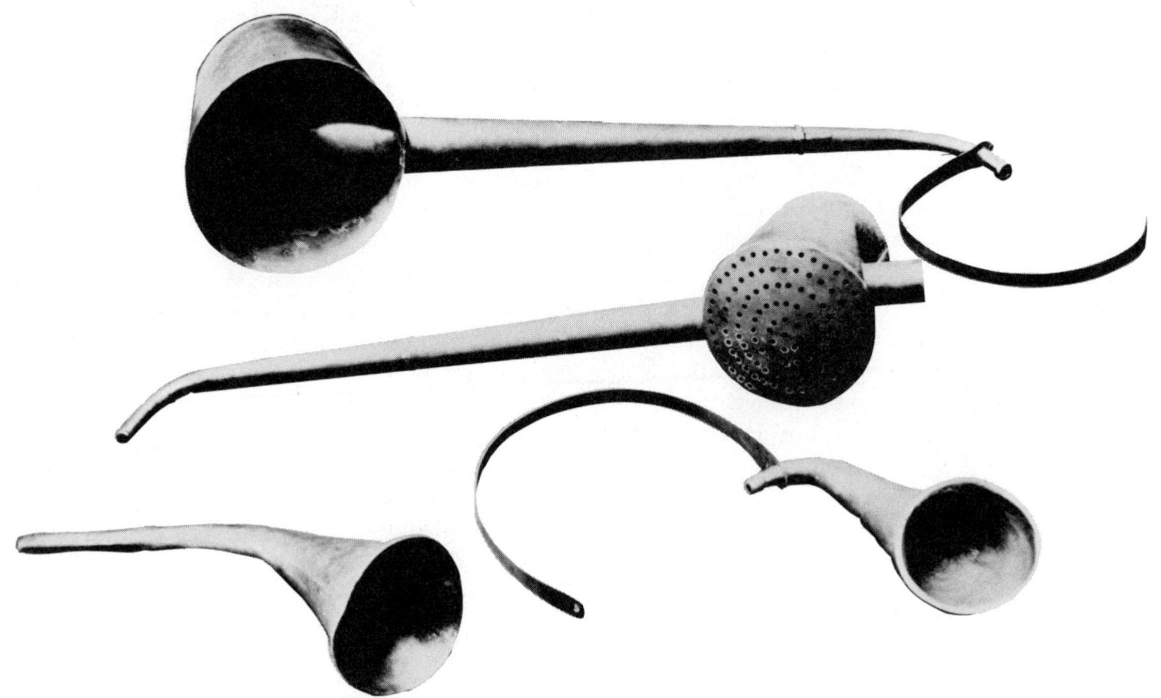

A collection of hearing aids used by Beethoven. None of these was entirely successful in helping him to overcome his affliction.

ority of artists over the "princely rabble," as he called them, but in the *moral* obligation of artists to make their message known. He regarded music as a mission, or calling; thus he forced himself to overcome his obstacle and defeat the forces of despair, if only so that he could continue making music.

In doing so, he fostered a "revolution" of another sort, a musical, rather than political, revolution. It had two unique aspects. First of all, Beethoven found traditional avenues of music making—performance, conducting, teaching—closed to him. He became, in effect, a full-time composer, continuing to earn a living from publishers' fees, commissions, and the support of his wealthy friends. Secondly, his life inevitably became more private and withdrawn; he turned to music as his chief means of communication with the world. His music increasingly became a vehicle for self-expression, almost as though he regarded the drama of the sonata cycle as a moral, personal, autobiographical drama. We may suspect the composer's own struggles and lofty ideals became the subject matter for his work. The relatively objective, socially useful music of earlier, patronage-dominated eras had given way to a new viewpoint: the creator drawing upon his own life as material for an intensely personal art.

Stylistic Features

Beethoven's compositions range over a great variety of media: symphonies; five piano concertos, plus concertos for other instruments; thirty-two piano sonatas and sixteen string quartets that are major landmarks of their genres; one opera (***Fidelio***), and two large-scale settings of the Mass; a host of overtures, chamber works, songs, recital pieces, and choral works. Historians often divide his creative life into three distinct periods:

1. the years before 1802, when Beethoven is most strongly related to the Viennese tradition, although this work is bold and aggressive even at this stage;
2. the period 1802–1815, when his deafness and torment had become obsessive, and the need to reconcile his infirmity with his creative energy most urgent. During those years Beethoven withdrew from public performance, and composed many of the works most associated with "heroism" and "struggle," such as the Fifth Symphony and the ***Appassionata*** Sonata;
3. the last dozen years of his life, spent in nearly total silence, resulting in profoundly moving, complex music: the last piano sonatas, the later quartets and the Ninth Symphony. Much of this music baffled his contemporaries, but impressed later generations deeply.

Certain traits characterize Beethoven's style in ***all*** of these periods, observable even in the early works. Here are a few of these traits:

Heavy Sonorities, Violent Contrasts. Beethoven's fondness for extremes, of register or dynamics, reflects his assertive, strong-willed personality, a desire to make the listeners sit up and take notice. We may find his unexpected or syncopated off-beats, surprising; think how fiercely unsettling, or even terrifying, the audiences of his own day must have found those gestures! The heavy, aggressive sonorities also reflect his experience as a virtuoso pianist. The instruments he played were stronger and more resonant than any known to Mozart; their heavier construction allowed for greater tension, sonority, and volume. (Even so, Beethoven's tendency to snap strings and break hammers with the force of playing were legendary.)

More Extensive Markings. Beethoven's specifications for details of tempo, dynamic subtlety (for example, a swelling that suddenly becomes quiet $<$ *p*) and articulation are precise and painstaking. They indicate the great importance he attached to aspects of performance that go beyond pitches and rhythms, which in earlier times might have been left to the collective wisdom of "common practice." Since many of Beethoven's passages were intended to ***disrupt*** traditional expectations, he needed to specify as many details as possible, if only to ensure that performers would not lapse into comfortable habits.

Great Concern for Tempo. When friends would report to Beethoven on performances of his music, his first question was invariably said to be,

"How was the tempo?" Beethoven was so particular about finding the right tempo for each passage that he added metronome markings to many of his scores (see Chapter 3).

Beethoven's concern for tempo extended to the level of large-scale musical structure. Within much of his sonata-cycle movements, ***tempo contrasts*** occur at important structural or dramatic points; significantly, this marks the end of the last bastion of the baroque "unity of affections," one which had still been observed by Haydn and Mozart.

Expansion of the Classic Forms. Beethoven's sonata cycles are much longer than the classic examples of Mozart and Haydn, not because his forms contain more parts, but because the parts themselves are larger in scope. In many instances Beethoven provides brief motives rather than balances, phrases or themes; these motives often begin to develop as soon as they are stated, taking on shape and substances as they relate to one another. Even introduction, bridge and coda may be ***developmental:*** the basic material is continually unfolding and revealing new aspects of itself. The result is a strong sense of growth and a tight unity.

That sense of development and growth may pervade the ***entire*** sonata cycle. (We will discuss this tendency further under "Cyclic Form.") Development does not need to cease at the end of the movement. On the contrary, each movement may present the same basic material in a fresh light; in certain works, the total picture might not be perceived until the finale.

character variation

The Character Variation. The strength of Beethoven's technique depends upon the ability to extract as much surface "variety" as possible from a minimum of material. It is only natural, then, that his approach to the theme-and-variations format would be different from the models of Haydn and Mozart. A typically classic set of variations is a study in embellishment, ornamentation and decorative filigree. There is no wish to disguise the theme. In fact, the opposite is true: the basic tune is easily recognizable in each of its varied presentations, because its critical defining characteristics (melodic contour, harmony, tempo, meter, phrase structure, tonality) have been left intact. Consider that the basic thematic skeleton was retained for the variations in both the slow movement of Haydn's ***Emperor*** Quartet (Chapters 1–7), and the slow variations of his ***Surprise*** Symphony (no. 94).

On the other hand, a set of variations by Beethoven might deliberately alter the basic mood and surface shape from one variation to the next. A graceful ***arioso*** theme might appear in the guise of a hearty, robust allegro, or a courtly minuet, or a slow, mock-solemn funeral march. The variations might appear in different keys as well.

Beethoven's aim is not surface decoration of a static "object," in the classic manner, but a dynamic process—perhaps even a "developmental" one—by which a given body of material undergoes striking transformations. This style is referred to by the term ***character variations,*** as opposed to the more refined ***ornamental variations*** of the eighteenth century.

Key Relationships. Just as Beethoven has expanded the dimensions of the classic forms, he expands the sense of tonal hierarchy by admitting more keys and chords into the select circle of "closely related" members. This will be discussed further as we examine individual works.

Cyclic Forms

Beethoven's major contribution to the sonata cycle was the practice of integrating and unifying all the movements, making the entire work a ***single organic statement*** rather than a classic succession of balanced parts. This was accomplished by using a small body of musical material to generate all the themes and motives. As noted earlier, Mozart's Symphony no. 40 owes some of its strength to the extraordinary resemblances its themes have to each other. We do not know whether Mozart consciously planned these resemblances; it is certain, though, that many of Beethoven's motivic cross-references ***were*** conscious. The technique of generating an entire multi-movement work from a few ideas is called ***cyclic.*** The sonata or symphony that is built cyclically is therefore an example of ***cyclic form,*** no matter what other forms its individual movements might take.

cyclic form

Cyclic form can be approached on the twin levels of "structure" and "expression." In either case, we sense Beethoven's unique power as a composer. Structurally, the movements are welded together by painstaking logic; this tightening of form is a stunning feat of musical architecture. The dramatic impact is equally impressive: the listener senses an emotional narrative running throughout the movements. Each movement offers fresh insights—relationships revealed and ambiguities unraveled—so that the totality is only fully perceived at the very end of the process. In many instances the last movement is crucial: the remainder of the puzzle, the bottom line of the ledger. As suggested in Figure 12.2, it is a true ***finale***—not a relaxation of the drama (as with Haydn), but its greatest intensification.

Listen now to an entire composition, so that Beethoven's stylistic traits can be heard in context. The work to be examined is one of his best known sonatas for piano, the C-Minor Sonata (opus 13) known as the ***Pathétique.***

Figure 12.2

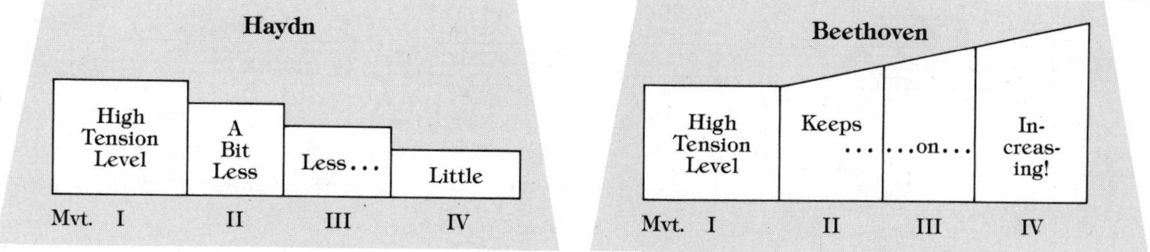

Ludwig van Beethoven
Sonata in C Minor (*Pathétique*) R2 S1 B2

This is a relatively early piece, published in 1798—the year Haydn was finishing *The Creation*—but it is brash and striking nevertheless. The subtitle *Pathétique,* like so many of the names attached to Beethoven's works, is probably not attributable to the composer. Many of these titles were the inspiration of publishers, friends and patrons. Nevertheless, the fact that subtitles seemed appropriate says a great deal about the emotional significance Beethoven's contemporaries attached to the experience of listening.

Movement I: Grave; Allegro di molto con brio. The intensity and massive textural weight of Beethoven's keyboard style is apparent in the very first chords of the slow introduction (see Figure 12.3). Note the sudden alternations between loud and soft chords. As the entire pattern is heard in ascending sequence, each alternation takes on increased urgency. Contrary motion between the hands contributes to the growing intensity as well; after a dissonant peak, the passage finally settles in the relative major. Beethoven begins to "develop" his material almost immediately, magnifying the contrasts with the added dimension of register as high statements alternate with low ones. Other aspects of the initial chord progression, such as its dotted rhythms and contrary motion, are extended and varied. The overall effect is that of tremendous unleashed energy, just barely kept under control.

A rapidly falling chromatic scale and cadence to C minor lead directly to the sonata form proper (Figure 12.4), at a surprisingly low *p* whisper: Further, contrary motion between the hands and sudden dynamic shifts propel the rapid passage onward, in a series of sequences. As the second key of the movement ordinarily should be the relative major of E♭, the appear-

Figure 12.3

Figure 12.4

ance of a new theme in E$^{\flat}$ minor (Figure 12.5) may come as a surprise. Like the first theme, it begins quietly but erupts in sudden *sfz* outbursts. The interval of a minor 3rd, so important to the introduction, is also prominent here. A new figuration in the "proper" key of E$^{\flat}$ major begins calmly, but then becomes intensified by rising sequences and still more contrary motion between the hands. Its climax leads to an unexpected statement of the first theme, still in the secondary key. At this point, the music plunges into a new key: a return to the clangorous chords and slow ***grave*** tempo of the introduction applies a squealing brake to all the energy accumulated so far. Beethoven uses ***tempo*** for dramatic effect; his reference to the opening, in this unforeseen context and foreign key, is gripping. It also provides structural articulation at a critical way-station between exposition and development. (Figure 12.6 depicts the use of tempo throughout the movement.) The development section is fairly brief, combining contours of introduction and first theme at a single brisk tempo, and plunging directly into the recapitulation. Here Beethoven brings the second theme back in the unexpected key of F minor; the "closing theme," with its dramatic contrary motion effects, follows in C minor. Just when the final cadence seems certain, another wrenching harmonic shift and sudden tempo change signal the return of the slow introduction—a brief fragment of it—and, equally sudden, a crashing end to the movement.

Movement II: Adagio contabile. The lyric, singing melody of this movement has great sweep and contemplative strength. It is heard first against a

Figure 12.5

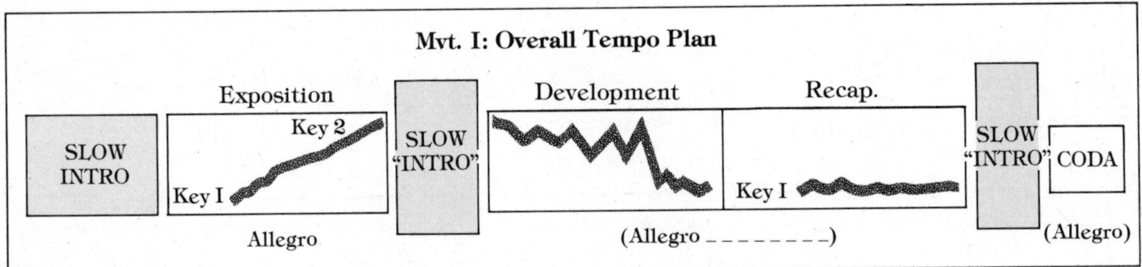

Figure 12.6

simple accompaniment (Figure 12.7); note that contrary motion between melody and bass is still present, and that the C-E$^{\flat}$ interval of a 3rd generates the rising arc of the opening phrase: The entire movement takes the form of a slow A-B-A-C-A: a *da capo* aria with two contrasting middle sections rather than one. The C section is especially dramatic, with its sudden shift to the tonic minor, triplet rhythms, and unsettling chromatic harmonies. The final return of A retains the triplet rhythms of C, and the movement ends quietly and peacefully.

The tonality of the movement is A$^{\flat}$ major, a key that is neither dominant (G) nor relative major (E$^{\flat}$). The choice reveals Beethoven's fondness for unusual key relationships separated by a 3rd, since the sonata's principal tonality (C minor) and A$^{\flat}$ are linked by that interval.

Movement III: Allegro. Here is a rondo, at a brisk tempo, built around an elaborate tune (see Figure 12.8) in which the minor 3rd C-E$^{\flat}$ is prominent. The first four notes of the tune bear close examination: they are identical to the beginning of the second theme of movement I (Figure 12.5) transposed to C minor—the key where Beethoven refused to take it in that early move-

Figure 12.7

Figure 12.8

ment. (Was he saving the C-minor version for its appearance in this final guise? That sort of question makes for enjoyable musical arguments.)

Listen for the striking dissonances and dynamic contrasts in the bridge between A and B, and the comparative hymn-like simplicity of themes B and C. Note, too, the subtle use of contrary motion in the accompaniments of B and C, and the slight tempo changes—pauses, alterations from lyric to agitated passages—that break up any sense of predictable regularity. As noted in Figure 12.9, the tonal ground-plan of the movement has a sonata-like "binary" cast, and might be considered a hybrid of sonata and rondo. In addition, the entire sonata is an example of ***cyclic form.*** Its complex multi-movement structure is the outgrowth of a few basic ideas.

Figure 12.9

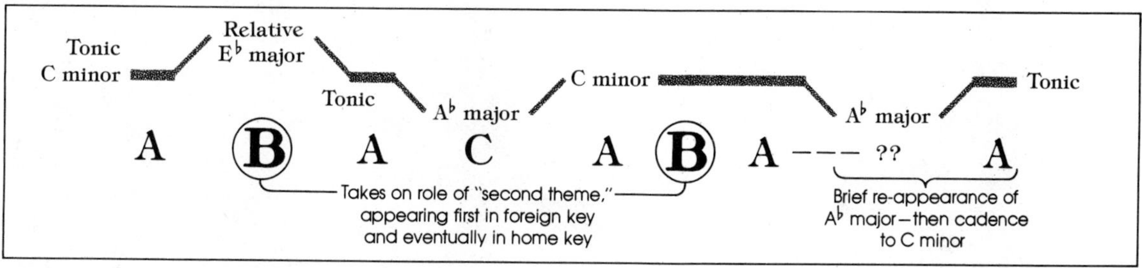

Symphonies and Concertos

It is safe to say that Beethoven, although an important composer in many genres, is best known for his nine symphonies. Even if he had written nothing else, those symphonies would guarantee him a preeminent place in the history of music.

Why only nine of them? Mozart composed forty-one, and there are over one hundred to Haydn's credit. But Beethoven's symphonies are more complicated stylistically and longer in duration, often twice as long as a typical Haydn symphony; they were, therefore, much more time-consuming in their creation. Economic and social factors account for other differences. Beethoven's early career was centered about the piano. It was only after his performing had won him a reputation that he attempted to write symphonies; he never turned out orchestral music on a regular basis, as he was not

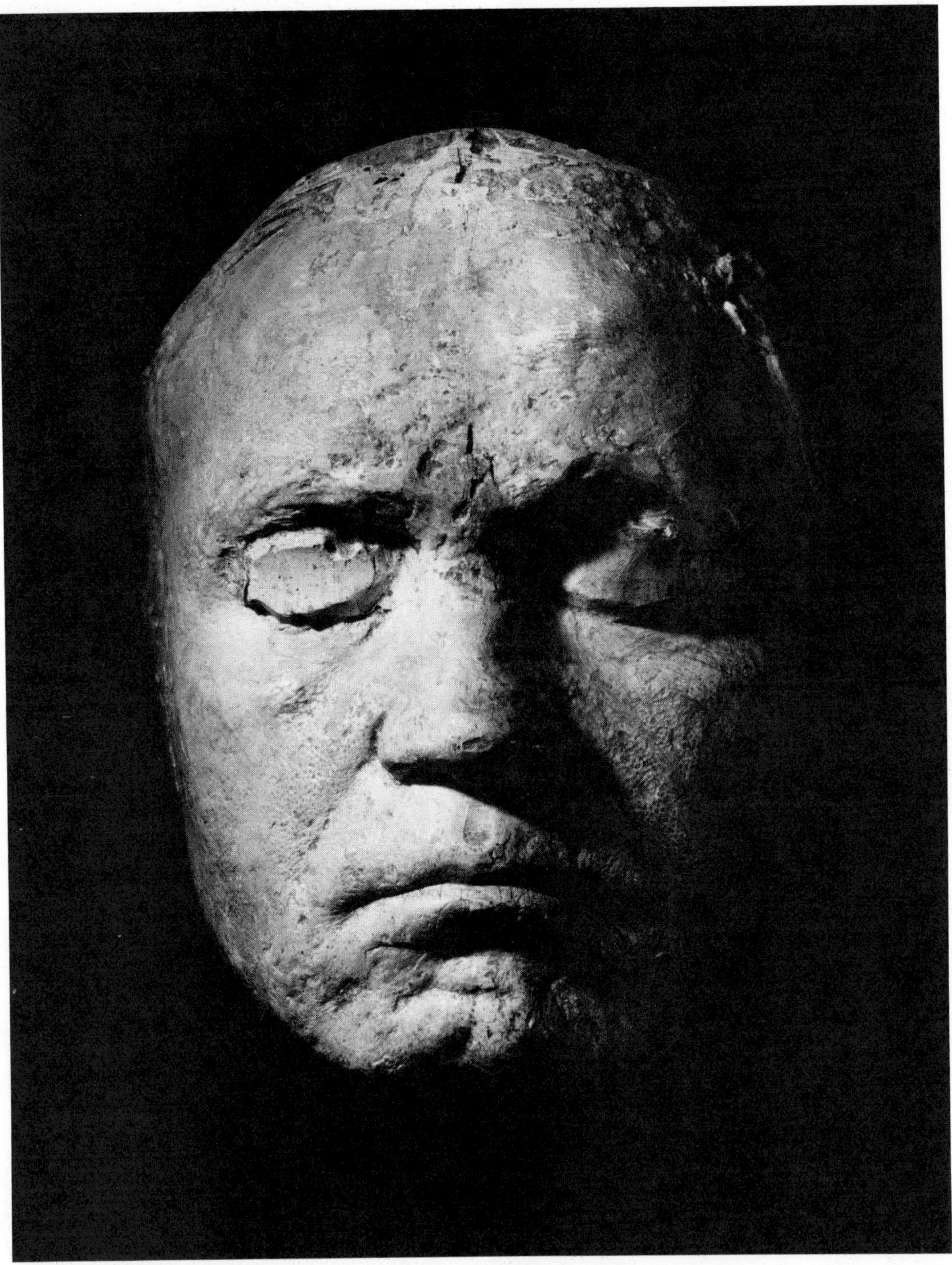

Klein, *Life Mask of Beethoven.*

directly employed by any court. Europe's new political structure altered the patronage system after 1800, and by that time the composer's growing deafness had also altered his career. He was changed (unwillingly) from free-lance entrepreneur and public personality to private, profound musical philosopher. He was driven to compose not only for practical reasons, but for deep-seated expressive needs which often took years to crystallize. Beethoven was a painstaking worker: when shaping his deepest, most private musical statements, he took his time.

The first two Beethoven symphonies, although highly adventurous, are still approachable within the context of the late Haydn or Mozart. But with the Symphony no. 3 (***Eroica***) of 1804, Beethoven altered the dimensions and character of the genre. The ***Eroica*** is unprecedented in its size, scope, cyclic unity and dramatic breadth; Ernest Bloch, in commenting upon the work, once wrote, "The step between the Second Symphony and this one is the greatest a composer has ever taken." It was twice as long as any previous symphony, much of the increase due to weighty developments and codas. The instrumentation attracted immediate notice as well, not always flattering. As Beethoven had increased the number of horns and made woodwind sonorities relatively prominent, contemporary critics thought his new symphony more suitable for wind band than for orchestra!

As a digression, we should mention the political factors involved in the creation and naming of the Third Symphony. Beethoven had originally called it the ***Bonaparte*** Symphony in honor of Napoleon, who appeared to be a libertarian saviour of the French people. When informed that Napoleon had declared himself Emperor, Beethoven is said to have torn up his title page in anger, renaming the work "'Heroic Symphony,' to celebrate the memory of a great man." As one might gather, Beethoven's social ideals were lofty and grand. He based a number of works upon Goethe's ***Egmont*** and the Prometheus legend, both heroic subjects, and made Schiller's poetic "Ode to Joy," which might be translated "Ode to Freedom," the capstone of his Ninth Symphony. His only opera, ***Fidelio,*** extols loyalty and courage in the face of political oppression. His commitment to the ideals of "liberty, equality, fraternity" was sincere, and a major force throughout his life.

Beginning with the ***Eroica,*** Beethoven's symphonies took on an interesting pattern. The odd-numbered symphonies are weighty, intense and monumental, while the even-numbered ones are genial, good-natured and even downright humorous at times. The overpowering Fifth Symphony, joyous Sixth (the ***Pastorale***) and deeply philosophical Ninth are particularly striking examples of Beethoven's symphonic art. In taking a broad view of all his symphonies, note that the classic format has been altered in quite a few respects:

scherzo

The Scherzo. Beethoven often substitutes a fast movement called a *scherzo* in place of the minuet. The scherzo has little to do with dancing; instead, it evokes an emphatic, boisterous, perhaps even violent humor.

The word "scherzo" means "joke." (Very few of Beethoven's scherzos would make you laugh: they are usually too rough, bold and disquieting for that.)

The typical scherzo is presented in three-part ABA form, with the middle referred to as the Trio. The scherzo resembles the minuet in this respect, and in its triple meter. But the scherzo's greater speed and jarring effects make it more suitable, in Beethoven's terms, for the continuity of symphonic drama. It can sustain the mood of a work, carrying it from slow movement through to the finale.

Changes in the Number and Order of Movements. The *Pastorale* Symphony (no. 6) contains five movements, the "extra" one being an added scherzo. In the Ninth Symphony, the scherzo is placed *after* the opening sonata movement, thus positioning the slow movement third in the sequence. There are also instances of links *between* movements: as we will observe in the Fifth Symphony, the scherzo and finale are joined together by a musical "bridge." Similarly, the last three movements of the *Pastorale* are connected.

"Program" Symphony. It often becomes difficult to regard Beethoven's mature symphonies as absolute music. The title page of the Eroica, for example, may lead one to consider what "heroic" concepts went into its creation. Note, too, Beethoven's own remarks about the main motive of his Fifth Symphony: "thus fate knocks at the door." With the *Pastorale,* Beethoven added subtitles to each of the movements (I. Cheerful Impressions on Arriving in the Country, II. By the Brook, and so on). He wrote an inscription for the entire work: "Recollections of Life in the Country—more expression of feeling than tone-painting." That is, the general sense is one of the atmosphere or mood, rather than specific extra-musical references. But there are also exceptional instances that are literally "programmatic": the twittering of birds, and the violent thunderstorm leading to the last movement.

In the Ninth Symphony, Beethoven made his extra-musical meanings as specific as possible, by adding voices and words to the finale. To a later generation of nineteenth-century composers, that gesture signaled the breakdown of barriers between instrumental and vocal—or "absolute" and "programmatic"—music. For Beethoven the innovation was logically related to his general view of symphony, as a platform for important statements. Significantly, the words he chose to round off his last symphony, taken from Schiller's "Ode to Joy," deal with the concerns he valued most: human freedom and brotherhood.

Expansion of Orchestral Effects. The symphonies provide many examples of bold scoring and sonorities that must have astounded contemporary audiences. There is a general fondness for rich woodwind timbres, and an increased number of horns; the timpani are given prominent roles, and even used as solo instruments on occasion. Listen now to the Fifth Symphony, the most famous of the nine, and note that it is remarkable for its *orchestration* as well as other, better-known features: the use of piccolo and contrabassoon to give extra "edge" to the winds, the prominent passagework for string basses, and the entrance of trombones in the final movement.

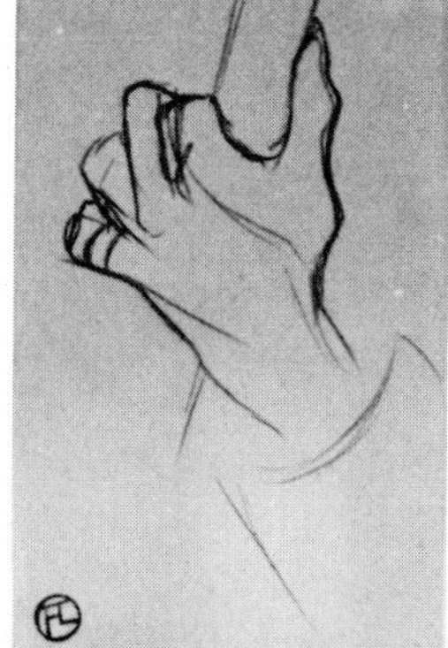

Ludwig van Beethoven

Symphony no. 5 in C Minor, opus 67

R2 S2 B1

This work, first performed in Vienna in 1808, has always held the public interest and excited the imagination, usually because of the four-note motto with which the piece begins. Its striking ♪♪♪ 𝅗𝅥 rhythm and descending 3rd are indelibly etched upon our consciousness. Some listeners are fascinated by the persistence and creative energy Beethoven reveals in exploring every facet of that motive throughout the symphony: in other words, how the motto is *used.* Others are more stimulated by what Beethoven supposedly *said* about the motto: "Thus fate knocks at the door." Although there is little evidence to suggest that he actually said that, the musical motto does suggest an ominous summons. "Fate" is a gripping word, and one that we associate with the composer who managed to harness and defeat his own cruel fate. Audiences of the nineteenth and early twentieth centuries were greatly moved by this association. In the 1940s the symphony became a rallying cry for the World War II Allies, because the rhythm of that same motto (short-short-short-*long,* or - - - ——) stood for the letter V in Morse Code. And, as a famous photograph of Winston Churchill indicated to the world, "V" stood for "Victory." In more recent years, Rock groups have discovered the Fifth of Beethoven and used its insistent rhythms to convey a different message. The appeal of the symphony is as strong as ever.

Movement I: Allegro con brio. The strongest overall impression of this movement is one of taut intensity; there is apparently not a wasted, extraneous or relaxed note in it. The music begins immediately (Figure 12.10) on a point of tension, and relentlessly drives forward from there. The basic motto generates sequences, overlapping and imitating, to create one sweeping phrase. The motion is temporarily halted by an extended variant of the motto, hammered at by full orchestra, and then a sustained high note (the dominant G) on the violins. The surge of energy begins again, with a further

Figure 12.10

Note the interval of a 3rd (bracketed).

Figure 12.11

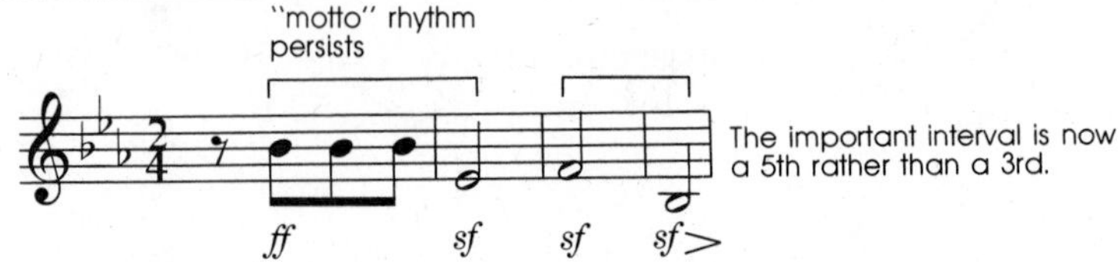

extension of the basic rhythm. This passage suddenly reaches a strong dissonance and, with two abruptly detached chords, modulates to the relative major of E♭. A bold horn call functions as a concise bridge, forcefully confirming the new tonality (see Figure 12.11). The horn call is also developmental in its own right, propelling the original motto into new terrain by expanding the intervals of its outer boundaries. (The interlocked 3rds of the opening have now become interlocked 5ths, with the same pitches in the middle.)

Following the horn call, a graceful second theme provides lyric contrast. But note that the contours of the new theme fill in the skips of the preceding horn call: everything seems to grow organically out of everything else! And throughout this lyric passage, the rhythm of the initial motto doggedly persists (Figure 12.12). The motto-rhythm finally comes to dominate the entire texture, bringing the exposition to a vigorous close in the relative major. At this point, Beethoven specifically indicated a repeat: even at his most intensely "romantic," he still retained the classic concern for formal proportion. (In modern performances, some conductors may decide not to observe the repeat.)

The development section is concentrated in its impact. An inverted form of the motto generates a long sequential passage, and the horn-call motive is broken up into smaller and smaller fragments, as noted in Figure 12.13. The music becomes hushed, and then explodes in a sudden *ff* burst of passagework. Hushed once more, the passage erupts again, and its extended repetitions lead directly to the original motto in the original key—louder and more impassioned than ever before.

The recapitulation does not allow the tension to subside. There is only one moment of calm, just after the recapitulation has started: a slow, highly

Figure 12.12

Figure 12.13

expressive meterless "recitative" for solo oboe. Here Beethoven uses *tempo contrast* with brilliant effect, creating a momentary stillness—a single, sad voice—that is swept away by the renewed drive of the first theme. For some listeners, this oboe solo is one of the most poignant moments of the symphony.

The rest of the recapitulation proceeds predictably, with the second theme stated in C major, retaining the major mode heard in the exposition. But just when a strong cadence is expected, the music takes a sudden turn in the direction of C *minor,* and explores a new variant of the original motto. The coda is, in fact, one more "development," another round of struggle with the great obsessive idea of the movement. This elaborate ending balances the tonal ambiguity of the earlier development section with the stability of an extended tonic passage: Beethoven's way of proclaiming that the dramatic struggle is resolved, at least temporarily.

Movement II: Andante con moto. Beethoven chose the "distant" key of A♭ major for this movement: a 3rd away from the tonic, but in the opposite direction from the relative major. (This relationship also characterized the slow movement of the *Pathétique* Sonata.) The music is dominated by a broad, sweeping theme of great lyric strength, elaborated in a series of variations. A gentle triple meter prevails throughout the movement, as the initial theme alternates with a bolder, more aggressive tune; these are shown in Figures 12.14 and 12.15. This second theme is reminiscent of the symphony's "motto," with its rhythm. It alternates with the first theme, and at times seems to intrude upon it; at its loudest and most striking, the second

Figure 12.14

Figure 12.15

tune affects a brassy, military quality. It is with that quality that the movement ends, although using the melodic contours of the main theme.

Movement III: Allegro. The key of C minor is resumed, and triple meter is retained, but now at a much faster tempo; this is one of Beethoven's scherzo movements. The first motive is stated by low strings, and then answered by higher instruments. The entire mood is mysteriously quiet (see Figure 12.16); then the stillness is broken by a repeated-note horn call, using the rhythm of the initial "motto." These two musical ideas alternate combining in a strong crescendo to create a single dense fabric. Suddenly everything grows quiet, and we hear a whispered cadence in C minor.

Just as suddenly, a curious running passage in C major begins in low cellos and doublebasses: the beginning of the trio section. This is the closest Beethoven comes to the notion of a "joke." The texture is highly imitative, at a dynamic level between *f* and *ff*, and gradually takes shape as a thunderously jovial tune for full orchestra. Unexpectedly all becomes still again. The trio, still scurrying, retreats at a *pp* level, and the scherzo resumes, even more hushed than in its original statement. Although the scherzo-and-trio format corresponds to an ABA, this repeat is anything but literal.

Plucked strings and whispers of solo woodwind sound are just barely audible; we finally reach a point where a very quiet cadence would be expected. Instead of a resolution to C minor, there is an inconclusive C-A♭ 3rd quietly sustained by strings, and a repeated-note pattern softly articulated by timpani. (As we can observe in Figure 12.17, it is related to the motto rhythm.) Against this constant ostinato, violins enlarge upon the scherzo theme. They stretch and expand its rising shape, leading to a sudden crescendo. The finale begins on a blazing *ff* C-*major* chord; the extended ostinato and questing violin line have "bridged" the last two movements of the symphony together.

Figure 12.16

Figure 12.17

Movement IV: Allegro. This is a sonata form in the key of C major. The major mode is enormously significant, for in Beethoven's terms it represents *victory*—the conquest of "fate." The movement radiates optimism and enthusiasm. It is also more brilliant in sonority, due to the addition of piccolo, contrabassoon and trombones. The new *sound* is one obvious way to say, "This movement is something special." And it is just that: the culmination and resolution of everything that has gone before.

The exposition begins (at the very climax of the ostinato "bridge") with a brilliant, brassy theme, immediately followed by a bold fanfare for horns which functions as a bridge, modulating to the dominant key of G major. A second theme-group in that key offers two new tunes, both vigorous and energetic. They each delight in abrupt alternations of loud and soft dynamics. Note, too, that each has qualities reminiscent of the ♪ ♪ ♪ 𝅗𝅥 motto: rhythm in the first case, repeated-note patterns in the second (see Figure 12.18).

The triplet rhythms become central to the development section. As a massive climax is reached on repeated thrusts of the dominant chord, we are suddenly transported to the eerie, hushed triple meter (and – – – —— rhythm) of the scherzo. The effect of one movement unexpectedly "remembered" in the midst of another is disturbing. But the relationships between

Figure 12.18

the two are surprisingly clarified, with the reaffirmation of "victory" (the recapitulation) all the more satisfying after the momentary flashback. The quote also permits a gradual build-up to the recapitulation, analogous to the ostinato "bridge" which had begun the movement.

The coda at the very end functions as coda to the entire symphony as well. Beethoven draws upon fragments of earlier themes, now speeded up to a frenzied, almost ecstatic *presto* tempo. Finally, he confirms the triumph of C major with a series of driving chords, each chord a celebration in itself.

The symphony's taut ***cyclic*** organization is noteworthy. All movements work together, contributing to a single statement; Beethoven ensures that effect by fusing the last two movements together, and quoting material from one in the other. The pervasive influence of the basic motto is clear in every movement.

There is another, less obvious, cyclic unity within the symphony. The entire first theme of the opening movement creates a characteristic melodic shape, shown in Figure 12.19, stressing the outlines of two broken chords. That shape is found in many of the symphony's themes—most obviously in the finale (Figure 12.20), where it has been inverted and transformed to the major mode. Cyclic procedures of this sort abound in Beethoven's music. Although they operate below the surface texture of listening, they still contribute substantially to our sense of unity and the "rightness" of the whole.

Concertos

Beethoven composed five piano concertos, the first three of them during the height of his success as a performer. The Piano Concerto no. 4 (ca. 1806) was written during his growing deafness; the composer's appearance as the soloist for the 1808 premiere was virtually his last public performance. The Concerto no. 5, known as the ***Emperor,*** was composed for a super-pianist of the imagination, but not for a specific performer.

In both concertos, Beethoven explores a slightly different alternative to the classic practice of double exposition. The Fourth Concerto begins with a piano *solo,* stating the opening phrase of the first movement's main theme. That phrase is answered by the orchestra, and from that point on the orchestra retains a hold on the material in the traditional manner. With the *Emperor* Concerto, both orchestra and soloist participate in a highly stylized, majestic introduction. But when the sonata form proper begins, the

Figure 12.19

Figure 12.20

orchestra presents the material first in the customary way. Note, too, that Beethoven wrote out the entire cadenza for the *Emperor* Concerto, rather than entrusting it to improvising performers. His practice in that respect was followed by virtually every composer after him.

Beethoven wrote only one concerto for violin and orchestra, but it is regarded as one of the monuments of that genre. Composed in 1806, it is quite faithful to the classic ideals of balance and proportion. On the other hand, many of the novel effects and expanded horizons associated with Beethoven are present: sudden contrasts of dynamics and register, formal subtleties, and novel instrumental timbres. (For example, the concerto begins with a timpani solo!)

Ludwig van Beethoven

Violin Concerto in D Major, opus 61

Movement I: Allegro ma non troppo. The first theme (Figure 12.21) is stated by winds and timpani; strings are silent. This is a lyric, expansive melody, sweeping up and down scale steps. True to the Viennese tradition, the opening material is introduced by the orchestra and only later presented by the soloist; at this stage in his career, Beethoven had not yet reworked the double exposition format. Curiously, the second important theme of the movement (Figure 12.22) is just as gentle and lyric as the first. In fact, its contours suggest a close family resemblance to the first motive. The insistent repeated-note figures punctuating the second theme also recall the timpani strokes of the very opening.

Beethoven's materials seem to grow organically from a single gesture, with formal cohesiveness and expressive "content" both intensified as a result. In Figures 12.21 and 12.22, both themes appear in the key of D

Figure 12.21

Figure 12.22

major, which is how they are presented in the *orchestral* part of the double exposition. After the entrance of the violin, the key scheme features a modulation to the dominant, where the second theme is heard. The two themes, and a more dramatically violent motive, interact with each other in a sonata-form scenario of key conflict and resolution.

The slow movement, in G major, begins with a simple hymn-like melody. This is repeated with increasingly fanciful, delicate ornamentation, in the spirit of an operatic aria for the soloist. Surprisingly, the slow movement culminates in a lyric ***cadenza,*** which in turn leads directly to the opening of the last movement. The Violin Concerto ends with a spirited rondo, built about a cheerful, genial tune that reflects the radiant atmosphere of the entire work.

The Romantic Beethoven: Composer as Hero

Although Beethoven's genres and forms were thoroughly "classic," he nonetheless emerges as the first "romantic" composer in history. This is due partly to the innovations of his music, and also to his own *personal* impact and the new image he created for the word "composer." It is not enough to speak of Beethoven as a great composer, or a genius. We must realize that his life and work have given terms like "genius" and "great" their very meaning. The "great" composer of popular imagination is, in fact, based upon the Beethoven prototype: a serious, intense, possibly eccentric individualist, singlemindedly and passionately devoted to the creation of monumental art works. This heroic figure struggles with his material, disregarding convention and practicality, attempting to solve Great Universal Problems through the medium of his art.

Obviously, none of the composers studied earlier—not Dufay, not Josquin, nor Monteverdi, Bach or Mozart—fit that awe-inspiring Promethean prototype. In fact, neither did Beethoven. He knew what it was to be a practical, socially functioning performer, and he respected the formal conventions of art more than any of his contemporaries realized. But his unique personality and life made a special impact upon the musical world, an ideal to which later nineteenth-century generations aspired. Most obviously, his deafness marked him as a tragic, but inspirational, figure. By middle age, Beethoven could hardly hear anything, and used ear trumpets in attempts to hear simple conservation. In later years visitors "spoke" to him by writing their halves of conversations into notebooks. His eccentricity was legendary

Lyser, ***Beethoven in the Streets of Vienna.*** In this contemporary caricature, Beethoven is shown walking the streets of Vienna, absorbed in his creative thoughts and apparently oblivious to his surroundings.

Stober, ***Beethoven's Funeral.*** This depiction of Beethoven's funeral procession, shows that it was an event of solemn magnitude in Vienna, and one worthy of the "hero" this artist had become.

as well. Goethe wrote of him, "I have never seen a more comprehensive, energetic or intense artist. I understand very well how strange he must appear to the outside world." Descriptions of the disarray and squalor of his lodgings—according to one account by a visitor, "clothing on the floor, the bed unmade, broken coffee cups on the table, the open pianoforte without any strings left and thickly covered with dust"—reinforce the image of an individual beyond conventional niceties.

Furthermore, he did indeed wrestle with his material, struggling for the exact shapes and relationships to articulate his ideas. Apart from his conversation tablets, Beethoven kept a different sort of notebook: sketchbooks in which he recorded his musical ideas and their pain-staking revisions. These books reveal a working procedure of careful labor and infinite patience. Beethoven's major works were intended to be "great," noble and profound in a way that earlier generations would have found inconceivable. As a uniquely distinguished figure, not bound to any patronage system, he could afford to be deliberate and totally devoted to each of his works.

His most mature music was not meant for court ritual or the middle-class parlor. Nor was it always meant for average performers; Beethoven's remark to a violinist having trouble with a passage ("Do you think I have your wretched fiddle in mind when genius speaks to me?") indicates his notorious disregard for performance problems. He was the first composer to deliberately write ***difficult*** music—difficult to play and to hear, stretching the capacities of performers and listeners all the while. The nineteenth century, looking back at Beethoven, approved; Mozart, who also had a bit of the "romantic" in him, would have understood. But the generations of Palestrina and Haydn would have been baffled at such impracticality.

Finally, Beethoven was the first composer to impose his own ***personality*** upon his material, making his own struggles, insights and triumphs the subject matter of his art. He was also the first to consider music in terms that go beyond "service" or social function, to the level of ***ethical*** and ***moral*** force. He honestly believed that art could make mankind better, and that some specially gifted individuals called "artists" were morally obliged to bring their message to the world. In each of these respects he became the Hero of the Romantic movement, as we will see in the following chapters.

13

Introduction to Romanticism

Music is the most romantic of all the Arts.

E. T. A. Hoffman

No color is as romantic as a tone.

Jean Paul

The Romantic Image

Our historical survey of style has arrived at the nineteenth century and the romantic movement, a period familiar to many listeners. Whereas much of the music previously discussed may have seemed strange and genuinely new, the romantic style is well-traveled territory: it is the most frequently represented on concert and opera programs, and the image it projects—of heightened "expressive" feeling—is often mistakenly assumed as typical of all concert music.

As with other periods, it is difficult to determine specific boundary dates for romanticism. The entire nineteenth century could be used as a convenient yardstick; some historians, however, prefer 1815 or 1820 as a starting point. Beethoven's final period dates from 1815, and Schubert's "Gretchen am Spinnrade" was composed in 1814; that decade also witnessed important "romantic" writings by Keats, Shelley and Sir Walter Scott, to name only a few. For other historians, the first great "romantic" gesture was the French Revolution of 1789, and some stretch the boundary forward as well, to the start of World War I in 1914.

It is also difficult to state exactly what the romantic style is, and who best represents it. There is no single romantic idiom, because nineteenth-century composers were a remarkably diverse collection of rugged individualists. In earlier periods, style had been a matter of collective taste and social function: one can speak of baroque style, without referring to the personal touches that distinguish Bach from Vivaldi or Handel. In contrast, the quest for ***originality*** was an essential aspect of romanticism. In listening to nineteenth-century music we respond to the individual composer's unique language: to the style of Brahms or Chopin or Wagner, rather than to "romantic style" in general.

Partly because their historical age is still close to the present, and partly because they ***were*** so successful in cultivating unique profiles, a great many important composers of the romantic era clamor for our attention. Only a few of them can be discussed in this book, even though three chapters are devoted to Romanticism. The period seems characterized by a vast range of positions and contradictions, and a succession of "personalities"—oddballs, mavericks, rebels—rather than a smoothly integrated musical development. The many personal styles of the movement, however, spring from a few common sources. Let us discuss these now.

The Influence of Beethoven

The obsession with "greatness" and "originality" was partly inspired by the image attached to Beethoven, often based on misconceptions. The romanticists were most impressed by Beethoven's rebellious spirit, his flouting of society, and his apparent liberation from the restrictions of classic form. They seized upon the programmatic implications of the ***Pastorale*** and the Ninth Symphony, or the eruptive surface violence of his textures, without considering his painstaking control of structure. Subconsciously they also assumed certain aspects of Beethoven's career to be universal truths:

1. that composers created music on a full-time basis, and a free-lance basis, if they could afford to;
2. that their music was an autobiographical statement of personality;
3. that music possessed a ***moral*** force, the power to encourage serious, lofty ideals; and
4. the composer placed higher priority on these ideals and personal statements than on balance, utilitarian social needs, or the expectations of his audience.

Edvard Grieg was undoubtedly referring to this uncompromising attitude when he wrote of Beethoven: "With him began the new era, the motto of which might be expressed in the words, 'Truth first, then Beauty.'" It is doubtful whether any pre-romantic composer would have thought of music in terms of either "truth" ***or*** "beauty"; such concepts flowered during the nineteenth century.

Social Factors

The romantic movement was not confined to music. Literature and visual arts developed similar outpourings of individual feeling. In all the arts, romanticism flourished as a ***reaction*** to the stylized formality that had delighted the previous century, expressing great changes in the social fabric. The orderly universe of the Enlightenment had been replaced by a seemingly chaotic world gone out of control: the roles of church, class, and nation had all been dislocated. A series of revolutions had weakened aristocratic privilege and brought more power than ever to the middle class. These revolutions had also led to a fierce brand of nationalism, especially among the many exiles and political refugees who settled in Paris and Vienna.

Changes in patronage exaggerated musical distinctions to the point where they became real schisms. It is in the nineteenth century that "serious" music began to part company with "popular" music, and difficult virtuoso music with middle-class amateur music. Opera and symphony each developed its own audience, social base, and musical style. Earlier composers, including Beethoven, had generally written music in many genres. By contrast, romantic composers often specialized in just a few.

Nationalism became an important musical factor as well. The Viennese classic style had been truly international: a fusion of Italian opera and German symphony, practiced in European capitals. By the mid-nineteenth century, Germany and Austria were still centers of the symphony. But Paris had become the base for such expatriates as the Pole Chopin and the Hungarian Liszt and, along with Milan and Venice, the hub of new developments in opera. Czech, Bohemian, Russian, and Scandinavian composers were to make their voices heard by the end of the century.

A rising middle class, interested in music as a mark of social distinction and culture, had been recognized for at least a century before the romantic era; it had been the first audience for Handel's oratorios. By the nineteenth century, the middle class had become even more powerful, particularly in spurring the sales of published music for amateur home performance. The ***middle-class composer*** was another romantic phenomenon. For centuries, musicians had regarded their work as an honorable craft, often as a family calling. By comparison, many romantic composers were sons of the middle class and rebels against the wishes of their respectable families: Berlioz, son of a physician and trained in medicine; Schumann, son of a book-seller, trained in the law (as was Tchaikovsky); Borodin the analytical chemist, and so on.

Love of the Past

Romantic poets and painters found certain kinds of subject matter most congenial to their expressions of drama, fantasy, and passion. Nature was one such subject: mystical, primitive, untamed, dangerous. The forests and the sea were favorite springboards for the nineteenth-century imagination.

This nineteenth-century "palace," built in the seaside resort of Brighton, England, shows the great fascination for exotic influences—Turkish, Indian and Moorish, in particular.

The *past* was another source of inspiration. This included the literal past of history, such as the Middle Ages, long scorned by other generations, and the worlds of mythology and folklore. All were viewed with a peculiarly romantic bias, bordering on reverence, for the ancient, exotic, and irrational. Knighthood, the Orient, ghosts, gods, and heroes were crucial to an art of fantasy and escapism.

Composers were captivated by such subjects. They also had to contend with "ghosts" of another sort: the memories of past composers. For the first time, the notion of ***history*** and "immortal masterworks" had become important. Beethoven's influence was extraordinary, and J. S. Bach's music became increasingly well known; the revival of the ***Saint Matthew Passion*** in 1829, conducted by Mendelssohn, brought Bach popular acclaim nearly a century after his lifetime. Significantly, the memorial held for Haydn on his death in 1809 featured a performance of the Mozart ***Requiem,*** a work composed eighteen years earlier, rather than a piece newly written for the occasion. By this time, of course, Mozart had become something of a historical legend himself.

When nineteenth-century artists idolized anything—knighthood, the forest, Beethoven, or epic mythology—they romanticized it. Their hero-worship produced fascinating distortions: the innocent, childlike Mozart, kindly old "Papa" Haydn, or Gounod's perception of Palestrina's music as "a translation in song of the vast poem of Michelangelo." Concern for the past also led to the practice of performing old, rather than current, music. This put living composers in a peculiar position. Cut off from traditional sources of patronage and forced to compete with each other for the attention of the middle-class public, they were also forced to compete with the historical masterworks. As a result, they became increasingly self-conscious, defensive, and strengthened in their quest for novelty and originality.

Music Among the Arts

As children of the middle class, romantic artists were well-versed in many creative areas. Composers were moved by the great fiction and poetry of the age; Schumann and Berlioz were excellent writers themselves. Mendelssohn was a gifted artist and writer, while Wagner, brought up in a theatrical atmosphere, wrote plays as a youth. Chopin was a close friend of the painter Delacroix, and lover of the distinguished woman novelist George Sand. A good deal of nineteenth-century music carried literary, pictorial, philosophical, or political associations. There are so many romantic references to "tone painting," "tone poems," "symphonic poems," and "music drama" that one might imagine nineteenth-century composers as frustrated artists or novelists in disguise.

Surprisingly, the reverse is closer to the truth: the great majority of romantic writers and painters would have given anything to be composers. They believed that music was the highest of the arts, since it was freed from the necessity of dealing with "real" words or pictorial images and could therefore strike directly at the heart of emotional experience. Many felt that purely instrumental music occupied a more universal expressive plane than music with words; orchestral music, with its sensuous color and density, was considered by some to be the highest art form of all.

Musical Factors

Romantic music is characterized by a number of specific factors, most of which cut across individual stylistic lines, and are just as applicable to Liszt as to Brahms. These include:

1. *Color.* Instrumental timbre became a primary factor in romantic composition, far more than in previous styles. Although instruments are used skillfully in a Beethoven symphony or Bach concerto, such pieces would sound quite impressive if transcribed for piano solo: their most important ideas deal with pitch, duration, and formal design. But an orchestral piece by Berlioz played at the piano might sound dull and a bit silly. Many of Berlioz's ideas ***are*** "colors," to which specific notes and rhythms are attached. When musicians talk about Berlioz they often recall the spectacular, ravishing ***sounds*** of particular passages, and fiendishly inventive orchestral effects. (Very likely they won't remember what the notes of those passages were.) Similarly, the brilliant harmonies of Wagner and Liszt, the clarity of Mendelssohn, or the mellow sonority of Brahms are inconceivable without their own specific timbres.

2. *Tonality and Chromaticism.* During the nineteenth century the organizing power of the tonal system became weaker. Compositions were still tonal, in that they assumed the existence of a central key and the traditional grammar of chord progressions. But increased ***chromaticism***—the consistent use of all twelve chromatic pitches—blurred the identity of individual scales. Chord progessions might seem perfectly logical, and yet be so ambiguous that they could resolve in any number of directions. The resulting tension, or high ***dissonance*** level, appealed to many romantic composers. They equated it with the more concrete varieties of "tension"—anger, yearning, passion—that they were trying to express in their music.

Similarly, contrasts ***between*** keys were much more difficult to follow by ear. Viennese classic forms depend upon the listener intuitively recognizing a change in tonal center and responding to that contrast. In a basically diatonic framework, the contrast is clearcut: C major really ***is*** different from G major, because there are some specific pitches found in each scale but not in the other. In a highly chromatic style, with the possibility of all twelve pitches weaving in and out of both scales, how can the listener tell them apart? Composers, recognizing this problem, turned to other kinds of contrasts to articulate their large sonata-cycle forms.

3. *Texture.* The homophonic emphasis of the classic style was retained, but now with stress on expansive, sweeping melody and intense chromatic harmony. Chords were often explored for their own sake as expressive "colors," similar to the color of instrumental timbre. In many instances, motives would be associated with specific harmonies, chord color being their most memorable feature.

There was also a tendency to linger over spacious, lyric passages. These might appear in situations that would have been unlikely in the Viennese classic style. Romantic composers often conceived of structure in melodic terms: they viewed sonata form as based on a series of contrasting "themes," rather than tonal areas or developmental motives.

4. ***Rhythm and Tempo.*** Consistency of tempo, the last stronghold of the baroque "unity of affections," had been broken by Beethoven. Romantic composers enjoyed the alternation of slow and rapid sections within a single movement. These were important in sonata-form movement, providing the contrast and conflict that had been formerly articulated by key change. To make sure that the listener grasped the start of the second theme group, a romantic composer would not only modulate to the proper related key, but might also slow the music down. It was in the nineteenth century that a popular image of the sonata movement's two theme areas became widespread: the rapid, aggressive dramatic first theme and the slow, lyric, contemplative second.

Tempo, like color, was assumed to have expressive power. Composers not only used tempo contrast, but explored the areas between one tempo and another: speeding up (marked *accelerando*) or slowing down (*ritardando*) for dramatic situations. Performers were also encouraged to treat tempo flexibly. A subtle yielding and stretching of beats within a supposedly regular meter was considered the hallmark of expressive playing. This technique is known as ***rubato,*** literally meaning "robbed" time in Italian. Rubato did not originate in the nineteenth century, but it came into its own during the romantic era.

rubato

Another important factor concerns the relationship between rhythmic motion and harmony. Our ears apparently need time to comprehend chord changes. If the opening of "Mary Had a Little Lamb" is harmonized with just one chord, it can be played at a furiously fast tempo (see Figure 13.1). Notice that the note D is not harmonized during its two appearances. If it is

Figure 13.1

harmonized with a dominant chord, the tempo has to be slowed down to allow that change to sink in. And if *every* note of "Mary" is harmonized with a different chord, including some chromatic ones, the pace needs to be even slower.

A good deal of romantic music, especially the sort that explores harmonic color, moves fairly slowly. In a sense, the nineteenth-century passion for harmony finally laid the driving motor-rhythms of the baroque to rest. There is great forward drive in romantic music, but it is often generated by the dissonant pull of pitches rather than by motor activity.

5. ***Surface Contrasts.*** Sudden, dramatic surprises could be heard in music of earlier periods, but most often as a way of stepping outside a stable norm. With Beethoven, contrasted moods and abrupt changes *were* the norm, and a regular feature of his style. Nineteenth-century composers carried the idea of extreme contrasts even further. They juxtaposed strikingly different moods, melodic styles, and instrumental sonorities, and also asked performers to play more loudly and more quietly than ever before. Some scores are marked with levels of *fffff* and *ppppp*, virtually impossible to perform, although they may stimulate the imagination wonderfully.

6. ***Large and Small Forms.*** Many nineteenth-century compositions are either very short or very long; there are brief vignettes, highly expressive miniatures that reach the emotions directly and immediately, and colossal, monumental works on the grandest of possible scales. Both extremes were motivated by the romantic urge to express deep feelings. The smaller pieces seem impulsive, almost improvisatory at times, and intimate in a very private way. Many of these, especially brief songs and piano pieces, were intended for private performance. They were played by amateur middle-class music lovers who frequented the music shops for new publications and then enjoyed them at home.

By contrast, gigantic symphonies and operas were conceived as major public utterances, scored for large orchestras, choruses and soloists, and occupying vast time scales. The model for many of these grand works was Beethoven's Ninth Symphony, which had established the precedent for a new durational span of more spacious proportions.

7. ***Musical Specialists.*** As we noted previously, schisms in musical society emerged and began to grow during this period. Composers were now less likely to encounter patrons who encouraged versatility, or social situations that required it. Economic pressure, a desire for novelty, or sheer impulsiveness also directed composers' energies to a few genres rather than to all of them. The romantic period was an age of great specialization: for example, Chopin's music for solo piano, Verdi's operas, Berlioz's programmatic works for large forces. Schumann, who composed for a variety of media, systematically specialized in another way, devoting one year of his life to practically nothing but songs, another year to piano solos, and so on. Berlioz was uninterested in the piano; Wagner cared little for chamber music; Brahms composed no operas.

Felix Vallotton, ***La Symphonie*** (above) and Thomas Eakins, ***The Violinist*** (right). The great middle class interest in music was most clearly revealed in two contrasted settings: amateur performance in the home (note the woman at the parlor piano), and the virtuoso on public display.

virtuoso

8. *The Virtuoso.* The romantic era was an age of modest amateur music making at home. It also included spectacular professional performances of unmatched technical wizardry and showmanship. Pianists such as Liszt and Chopin, and the legendary violinist Paganini, made a staggering impact upon European audiences. The subtle interaction of virtuosity, celebrity-stardom, and sheer sex appeal was exploited by many artists. Liszt swept dozens of women off their feet (literally and figuratively), arousing passionate ardor among his listeners. He was supposedly the first pianist to

turn the instrument around so that audiences could see his profile, and his preliminary ritual of slowly removing gloves and cape before a performance caused many a countess to swoon. Paganini was no less a showman, breaking his violin strings in mid-performance but continuing anyway; he did little to discourage the rumor that he had sold his soul to the devil in exchange for superhuman skill. This was an age that still believed in devils, magic, and heroes.

An entire body of romantic music was designed to display such awesome levels of virtuosity. Much of it is ferociously difficult, and otherwise rather trivial: simpleminded variations on popular arias or patriotic tunes, for example. But some of the finest examples of virtuoso writing by Chopin or Liszt can be wonderfully evocative and sensitive. The romantic ***orchestra*** was a virtuoso body as well, especially in the hands of composers who best understood its resources. The nineteenth century also saw the emergence of the virtuoso conductor, a new breed of performer, specializing in the most complex of all "instruments." Berlioz and Mendelssohn were two of the earliest great orchestral conductors; the end of the century saw the imposing figure of Gustav Mahler, who until recently was more widely acclaimed as a legendary conductor than as a composer.

9. ***Program Music.*** Because all the arts became so closely allied, the romantic urge to be expressive led music in literary or pictorial directions. Pieces set to words already carried explicit meanings. In the domain of instrumental music, so-called "absolute" forms were increasingly allied with extra-musical ideas. Often these were expressed only in the titles of short pieces—***The Happy Farmer, Butterflies*** and the like—that were otherwise abstract. More detailed musical references could be made, too, so that specific passages would evoke nonmusical images. If the composer wanted to be highly specific, he could provide a full literary "program" detailing the "meaning" of the sounds.

The program for a musical work could be a story, a philosophical essay, a depiction of emotional states or visual images: anything that would bring the music out of the realm of pure sound, and into the larger world of explicit feeling and drama. Pieces which appeal to the pictorial or literary sense in this way are considered examples of ***program music;*** such works were among the most important of the romantic period.

program music

Berlioz and the Programmatic Symphony

Hector Berlioz (1803–1869) was one of the most imaginative composers of program music who ever lived, and a particularly brilliant orchestrator. We have already heard the "March to the Gallows" from his ***Symphonie Fantastique*** (Part 1), which is typical of his spectacular orchestral effects. Berlioz, the man, was as romantic a figure as one could wish: a highly sensitive individual, capable of intense passions. His ***Symphonie Fantastique*** amounted to a public declaration of his desire for the Irish Shakespearian actress Harriet Smithson, a love so great that he was said to have taken poison in her presence. He survived, and they were eventually wed. Unfortunately, they did not live happily ever after; Berlioz's personal life remained turbulent to the end.

The ***Symphonie Fantastique*** was first performed in Paris in 1830. The composer issued a printed program which he expected his audience to read while following the music. His work was subtitled "Episode in the Life of an Artist," an autobiographical dream (or, literally, ***fantasy***) of dizzying proportions. The program went on to indicate narrative details for each movement. Berlioz regarded his program as the "spoken text of an opera"; in fact, one could regard this symphony as an ingenious fusion of sonata-cycle form and dramatic, operatic gesture.

> A young musician of morbid sensibility and ardent imagination, in despair due to hopeless love, has poisoned himself with opium. As the drug was too weak to kill him, he falls into a deep sleep accompanied by strange dreams and visions. His sensations and memories are transformed by his drugged mind into musical ideas and images. The beloved one herself has become a melody, which haunts him everywhere. . . .

The most brilliant idea of the symphony was probably the simplest: constructing a theme which would represent the beloved throughout all the movements. Berlioz's own literary program states the basic principle: ". . . the beloved one herself has become a melody." This melody recurs in various transformations throughout the symphony; it is known as the ***idée fixe*** ("fixed idea," or obsession).

idée fixe

Hector Berlioz

Symphonie Fantastique

The symphony contains five, rather than the usual four, movements. This departure from the norm was not unprecedented, as Beethoven had created five movements for the ***Pastorale*** Symphony (also a programmatic work). Berlioz worshipped Beethoven, and composed the ***Symphonie Fantastique*** only three years after his idol's death. As revolutionary as the ***Symphonie Fantastique*** is, it follows Beethoven in its autobiographical implications of personal struggle, and (on a more technical level) in it use of cyclic form and character variation. The traditional succession of movements has been retained as well; the fifth movement is an extra scherzo.

Movement I: Reveries, Passions. "He remembers first the uneasiness, the emotional emptiness and elations he felt before seeing his beloved. Then the volcanic love she suddenly aroused in him, his delirious torments, his raging jealousy, his tenderness, and his religious consolation."

This manic-depressive swing of moods may seem too much to encompass in a single movement; but Berlioz uses color, dynamics and tempo to create a surprisingly faithful expression of his literary idea. The whole is laid out in a loose sonata design, with a *very* long slow introduction, longer than any in a Haydn, or even Beethoven symphony. Everything preceding the entrance of the *idée fixe,* in fact, can be thought of as introductory.

The *idée fixe* (Figure 13.2) functions as the first theme for this sonata-form movement, as well as being the motto for the entire work. It is, by classic standards, a highly unsymphonic idea: broad, expansive and self-contained, closer to an operatic aria than to a classic sonata-cycle theme.

Note the descending half step (bracketed); this becomes a "cyclic" motive of its own during the symphony

Figure 13.2

The motion from the notes F to E (bracketed in our example) is particularly poignant. Note how the tune keeps returning to that descending half step in an arc of intensity and then relaxation. This broad theme, representing the beloved, dominates the Allegro. It is heard, in fact, at both first and second key levels, and is particularly brilliant in its final *ff* appearance before the "tenderness" and "religious consolations" evoke a quiet close.

The outrageous ingenuity of Berlioz's orchestration deserves special mention. There is coloristic daring not only in the loud bombastic passages for which he was notorious, but also in the many exquisite, delicate sonorities involving a few instruments in combination: horn, pizzicato strings, distant percussion. The orchestra itself has been enlarged well beyond the eighteenth century norm, adding piccolo, English horn, E♭ clarinet and two more bassoons to the winds; three trombones and two tubas to the brasses; two harps; and a percussion section swelled by the addition of two more tympani, bass drum, cymbals, and bells.

Movement II: A Ball. "At a ball, in the midst of a noisy, brilliant celebration, he finds his beloved again."

This is a festive, swirling waltz in triple meter. Its gaiety verges on the nightmarish; as the tempo and sonority continually relax and intensify, the scene appears to move in and out of focus. This imaginary dance is a "scherzo" within the symphonic cycle, not one that might have occurred to Beethoven, but brilliantly suited to the nature of Berlioz's literary program. At an unexpected moment in the festivities, the *idée fixe* appears against a quiet string background (see Figure 13.3). It has assumed the rhythmic shape of a waltz fragment, and is stated in a distant tonality. This glimpse of *idée fixe* occupies the position of a trio within the overall scherzo design.

Figure 13.3

Very soon Berlioz returns to the home key and the initial waltz material. Just before the very last cadential passage, another reference to the beloved takes place, distantly sounded by solo clarinet. It is rudely cut off as the dance rushes to a furious conclusion.

Movement III: Scenes in the Country. "Summer evening in the country: he hears two shepherds piping . . . the gentle rustle of the trees, newfound hope. . . . But his beloved appears anew: he feels dark premonitions. What if she has been faithless? Only one of the shepherds resumes playing; the sun sets. There is rumbling thunder in the distance—then silence."

There is great lyric breadth here, and the use of quiet instrumental sonorities for "nature-painting." Oboe and English horn represent the two herders. Their opening folk-like tune fragment expands to an elaborate duet. Another theme, more complex in contour, dominates thereafter, interrupted only by reference to the *idée fixe* (and a heated response). At the end the shepherd-pipe tune is heard in the distance, stated by the English horn, against the faint "thunder" of four timpani.

Movement IV: March to the Gallows. "He dreams that he has killed her; he is condemned and led to his execution . . . finally, like a thought of love, the *idée fixe* appears for an instant, only to be cut off by the fall of the axe."

This movement has been discussed at length before (Chapters 1–7), but can be reviewed now in the context of the entire symphony. The return of the beloved theme, suddenly cut off by the "execution," now sounds totally different in view of all that has gone before. Most likely it has become as great an obsession for the listener as it was for the composer.

The "March" and the "Ball" are both scherzo-like, surrounding a central slow movement. In none of these three movements have we returned to the tonality of the opening Allegro (C major), which by classic standards would be regarded as the key of the symphony.

Movement V: Dream of a Witches' Sabbath. ". . . He is surrounded by sorcerers and monsters of every kind, united for his burial. Unearthly groans, shrieks of laughter . . . the melody of his beloved is heard, but it has lost its gentleness and timidity. It is *She* who comes to the Sabbath! The funeral knell . . . burlesque of the *Dies Irae* . . . round dance of the witches . . ."

This is the most sensational movement of all, and must have shocked the Parisian audience of 1830 to its foundations. Berlioz unleashes some

Figure 13.4

marvelously grotesque, frightening orchestral effects—cackling high strings, raucous outbursts of brass and drums—leading to the final entry of the *idée fixe* (Figure 13.4). But the beloved has been transformed into something evil and repellent: the tune is witch-like, heard in the piercing register of the little E♭ clarinet, with grace notes and a rollicking rhythm added for further distortion. "Her" arrival is greeted by frenzied orchestral howls, subsiding quietly to the lowest register and the tolling of deep bells. Against the repeated bells, we hear the ***Dies Irae,*** the most solemn and terrifying of Gregorian chants (sung only during the Mass for the Dead). What a blasphemous stroke, to place a profound liturgical melody (Figure 13.5) in the graveyard amidst the witches' revelry! It is also a brilliant musical stroke at the level of "absolute" symphony. In the tradition of Beethoven, Berlioz draws the threads of all movements together, making his finale the focal point. And, at the tolling of the bells, he has returned to the key of C, the tonality of the symphony. It is a grisly C minor at first, but C nonetheless. Berlioz uses the finale for a last tonal confirmation, once more in the tradition of his hero Beethoven.

The witches' round dance, in C major, follows the "Dies Irae." A new time is set imitatively against itself and then in counterpoint with the chant fragment. The ***idée fixe*** never returns: all thoughts of the beloved are swallowed up in the diabolical dance. The orchestral effects must have been mind-boggling in 1830. Listen to the entire string section playing ***col legno*** (with the wooden part of their bows) near the end of the movement, or to the sputtering woodwind pattern blotted out by a wall of brass shortly thereafter. Such sonorities convey the macabre, obscene images of the program perfectly.

Berlioz went on to write other programmatic—or should we say operatic—symphonies during his long career, as well as substantial operas that verge on the symphonic. The two genres were never far from his mind, whether he was writing for instruments or voices, concert hall or theatre. In all his music he was motivated by a flair for the spectacular, great literary sensibility, and an incomparable ear for timbre. We can enjoy the ***Sympho-***

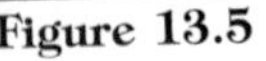
Figure 13.5

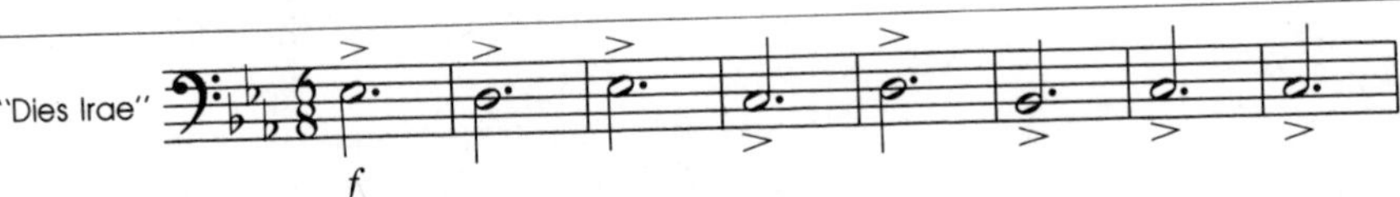

nie Fantastique for its sheer sonority alone or, on strictly formal grounds, we might even find it a convincing symphony in the tradition of conflict, resolution, tonal adventure, and cyclic technique. But to hear it exclusively in either of those ways would be to miss the point. Berlioz wanted listeners to be moved, overwhelmed, scandalized, and just a bit terrified by the ***total*** effect: the literary program, ***and*** diffuse feelings, ***and*** dazzling colors—all of it. It is the mixture of all these elements that makes the ***Symphonie Fantastique*** programmatic and romantic.

Schubert

A romanticist of a very different sort was Franz Schubert (1797–1828). Whereas Berlioz was extroverted, flamboyant and celebrated throughout Europe, Schubert was a shy, unassuming man, little known musically beyond a close circle of friends. His lack of recognition is hardly surprising in view of the pitifully brief length of his career: he died at the age of thirty-one, when he was just beginning to develop his gifts in a new direction. In his few years, Schubert wrote a staggering amount of music: symphonies, string quartets, middle-class dance pieces, and more than 600 songs.

The grand monumentality of Berlioz may be traced to his French heritage: not only to the tradition of Lully, but to the supercharged tempestuous atmosphere of post-revolutionary Paris. Schubert, on the other hand, was Austrian, the only one of the "Viennese" composers who was actually a native of Vienna. The folk dances and street serenades of the region are echoed in his style. Like Haydn before him, Schubert had been an imperial choirboy at Saint Stephen's Cathedral. He lived and worked in Vienna when the figure of Beethoven dominated the city, and he was profoundly influenced by Beethoven's music, although apparently too shy to introduce himself to the older man. Like Beethoven, Schubert was a free-lance composer, but he had none of his idol's ability to dominate patrons and publishers. During the last decade of his life he rarely held a steady job, preferring a lifestyle that later generations might call "bohemian": a financially meagre existence among a close-knit group of artistic friends.

Schubert's career reveals the more private face of romanticism: young artists and poets meeting in cafes and sharing what little they had of money, food, and lodging. Much of Schubert's music was composed for his own small circle, and was performed at private parties, known as "Schubertiads," where his comrades would gather. When listening to his songs, imagine the composer himself accompanying them at the piano at an informal gathering in someone's living room. Those pieces of Schubert's that were published during his lifetime (songs, dances, short piano pieces, and chamber music) found their way into similarly intimate home surroundings. It is no wonder that Schubert's output has been called "the music of friendship."

Mortiz von Schwind. ***A Schubert Evening at Josef von Sapun's House.*** Here is a "Schubertiad" in full swing—an evening's gathering at a private home, where friends would listen to Schubert's performance with rapt attention. The composer is shown here at the piano (in profile, head slightly bent).

Lieder (songs)

Schubert, like Berlioz and other romantic artists, was passionately devoted to literature and drama. He began setting verses to music as a teenager; "Gretchen am Spinnrade" (see Part 1), on a poem by Goethe, was composed when he was seventeen. Even at this age Schubert had a remarkable gift for capturing the musical essence of a poem. During his short life he composed hundreds of songs—sentimental, dramatic, humorous. He virtually invented the "art-song" genre singlehandedly, and made it one of the nineteenth century's most cherished vehicles for intimate expression. The German word for song is ***Lied*** (plural ***Lieder***); Schubert's Lieder, and later examples by Schumann and Brahms, became popular throughout Europe.

Lied

Schubert explored a variety of forms in his songs. One of his most famous songs is entitled "Erlkonig" ("The Erlking"); it was written not long after "Gretchen am Spinnrade," and is also set to a poem by Goethe. As with "Gretchen," this song took about a day to write. Many of Schubert's works were created in similar bursts of fiercely channelled energy—quite unlike the careful sketches, drafts, and revisions of Beethoven.

Franz Schubert
"The Erlking"

Goethe's well-known poem tells of a father and his desperately sick child, riding furiously on horseback through the night. The child hears the voice of the Erlking (or "Elf-king") whose presence, according to legend, signals impending death. The evil king tries to entice the boy to come away with him and then threatens the child; the father can hear none of this. The dialogue becomes increasingly frantic, and the child more hysterical. By the time father and son reach home, the boy is dead. (The complete poem is given below.)

Goethe's narrative is a masterpiece of early romantic writing, containing many ingredients that fascinated the nineteenth century: death, child-like innocence, the savage beauty of nature (night, hoofbeats), and the supernatural. We probably rationalize the Erlking's voice as the figment of a delirious child's imagination. But nineteenth-century readers might have interpreted the king's presence in more literal, spine-tingling ways.

Erlkönig—Franz Schubert	*The Erl-King—Franz Schubert*
Wer reitet so spät durch Nacht und Wind? Es ist der Vater mit seinem Kind; Er hat den Knaben wohl in dem Arm, Er fasst ihn sicher, er hält ihn warm.	*Who is riding so late through the night and wind? It is a father with his child; He grasps the lad in his arm, He holds him securely and keeps him warm.*
"Mein Sohn, was birgst du so bang dein Gesicht?" "Siehst, Vater, du den Erlkönig nicht? Den Erlenkönig mit Kron und Schweif?" "Mein Sohn, es ist ein Nebelstreif."	*"My son, why do you hide your face so fearfully?" "Father, don't you see the Erl-King? The Erl-King with crown and long robe?" "My son, it is but a streak of mist."*
"Du liebes Kind, komm, geh mit mir! Gar schöne Spiele spiel ich mit dir; Manch bunte Blumen sind an dem Strand, Meine Mutter hat manch gülden Gewand."	*"You dear child, come go with me! Truly lovely games, I will play with you; Many a beautiful flower is on the water's edge, My mother has many golden garments."*
"Mein Vater, mein Vater, und hörest du nicht, Was Erlenkönig mir leise verspricht?" "Sei ruhig, bleibe ruhig, mein Kind: In dürren Blättern säuselt der Wind."	*"My father, my father, don't you hear, What the Erl-King is softly promising me?" "Be calm, remain calm, my child: It is the wind rustling in the dry leaves."*
"Willst, feiner Knabe, du mit mir gehn? Meine Töchter sollen dich warten schön; Meine Töchter führen den nächtlichen Reihn Und wiegen und tanzen und singen dich ein."	*"Beautiful lad, do you wish to go with me? My daughters will wait on you dutifully; My daughters dance their nightly round And will cradle you, dance to you and sing you to sleep."*
"Mein Vater, mein Vater, und siehst du nicht dort Erlkönigs Töchter am düstern Ort?" "Mein Sohn, mein Sohn, ich seh es genau: Es scheinen die alten Weiden so grau."	*"My father, my father don't you see over there The Erl-King's daughters in that dark place?" "My son, my son I see it clearly: It is the grey light of the old willow-trees."*
"Ich liebe dich, mich reizt deine schöne Gestalt; Und bist du nicht willig, so brauch ich Gewalt." "Mein Vater, mein Vater, jetzt fasst er mich an! Erlkönig hat mir ein Leid's getan!"—	*"I love you, your beautiful form provokes me; And if you do not come willingly, I will use force." "My father, my father, now he is seizing me! The Erl-King has hurt me!"*
Dem Vater grauset's, er reitet geschwind Er hält in den Armen das ächzende Kind, Erreicht den Hof mit Müh und Not; In seinen Armen das Kind war tot.	*The father, gripped by fear, rides quickly, He holds the moaning child in his arms, He reaches the house with effort and difficulty, In his arms the child lay dead.*

The Song opens with an agitated, rapid piano figuration, shown in Figure 13.6. It suggests the furious tempo of the wild ride, the relentless tension building up, and the dramatic backdrop (a galloping horse), all in one concentrated gesture. Although Schubert's vocal writing is ingeniously

Figure 13.6

effective, it was his use of the ***piano,*** the favored household instrument of the middle classes and the collaborative partnership between piano and voice, that brought the Lied to prominence. Recall the accompaniment for "Gretchen am Spinnrade" which also evokes mood and physical setting.

When the singer enters, it is apparent that each character in the drama has a special kind of music: a lower register for the father than for the child, and a persuasive, cajoling melody stressing the major mode for Erlking. The entire song is ***through-composed*** in form, its changing line unified mainly by the insistent, galloping piano pattern. The child's cries ("Oh father, my father") are repeated throughout the song at successively higher pitch levels, creating greater tension each time (see Figure 13.7). Uniting all this is the incessant piano motive, gently distant when the Erlking murmurs sweet invitations, but threatening when he grows violent. The hoofbeats cease just before the final words of text: the ride has ended, and the piano's silence allows the last grim line—"The child was dead"—to register more vividly.

Figure 13.7

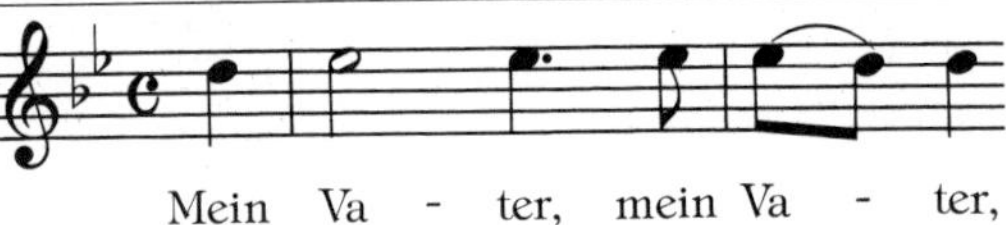

The Song Cycle

song cycle

A group of songs combined in a collection is known as a ***song cycle:*** perhaps a continuing narrative, or different approaches to a single idea. There may be continuing musical threads as well: common melodic motives, tempo contrasts, or key relationships among the songs. Although one may hear individual numbers sung in recital, it is more rewarding to experience an entire cycle in a complete performance. In this way the expressive and musical whole emerges from the interaction of its parts. Schubert wrote two song cycles near the end of his life: ***Die schöne Müllerin*** ("The Lovely Maid of the Mill") and ***Die Wintererreise*** ("The Winter Journey"), both set to poetry by Wilhelm Miller.

Franz Schubert
"Das Wandern" ("Wandering")

This is the opening song of Schubert's first song cycle, *Die shöne Müllerin.* It is composed in strophic form (see Chapter 5); one graceful, lilting tune is repeated for five stanzas. We learn from the song that the narrator is a traveler pausing by a stream; he is innocent, curious, restless—like the stream itself, he reminds us—and delighted to wander through the countryside. Typically of Schubert, the piano accompaniment suggests virtually all of this within a few measures: the optimism of the singer, the splashing of the water. (The musical depiction of rushing water creates a backdrop for many songs of the cycle.) The setting is a mill, and the narrator is a miller's young apprentice. But those details only acquire significance over the course of the cycle; for this one song, the important message is an expression of delight and wonder.

During the strophic repetitions, the text provides most of the variety. Aside from a *pp* echo effect at the end of each stanza, and a swelling of the accompaniment between stanzas, there are no indications of dynamic contrast. But many performers will add dynamics of their own: a light airy quality when the stream is mentioned, and more robust dynamics when referring to the churning wheels and heavy stones.

What we do not know, and cannot guess from this one song, is that the young miller will meet a girl and fall hopelessly in love with her. During the next few songs of the cycle he is ecstatic, and sings of his joy to his most faithful companion, the stream. As the songs continue, a rival appears on the scene: a dashing hunter in a green jacket. Musical references to hunting horns, and textual ones upon the color green, begin to haunt many of the later songs. The lovely maid is lost, and the young boy's heart is broken. He comes once more to the stream and ends his life in it. The last song of this lengthy cycle, which comprises twenty songs in all, is narrated not by the boy, but by the brook: a lullaby sung to the boy sleeping in its bed.

With many references linking the songs together, the entire cycle has a unified sweep that is almost symphonic in scope. Aside from obvious connections of character and place, there is a further unity of concentrated time; the joys and sorrows of *Die schöne Müllerin* all take place during a single spring and summer. Similarly, the bleak narrative of *Die Winterreise* conjures up the still, lifeless quality of winter. Schubert composed the latter cycle during the winter of his own life—his final year, 1827–1828, plagued by continual ill-health and depression. Perhaps these cycles are as autobiographical, in their own literary symbolic way, as the *Symphonie Fantastique.* We will never know.

Symphony and String Quartet

In his large-scale instrumental works Schubert preferred the genres of "absolute" music. There are no literary or pictorial references, except for the few chamber works which contain variations on some of his own song themes. But the melodic lyricism of his songs pervades his sonata-cycle works. Just as Schubert's song cycles might be considered quasi-symphonic, his sonatas, symphonies, and quartets are never far from a lyric, singing impulse.

Like Berlioz, Schubert often used a broad sweeping melody where a more classic approach would have suggested a concentrated motive. His ***Unfinished*** Symphony (no. 8 in B Minor) is best known for a graceful, lyric G-major tune that might be found in a book of Lieder. Similarly, the Symphony no. 9 in C Major (known as the ***Great***) contains proportions as vast as those of Beethoven, but in a context of unhurried spaciousness rather than firm dramatic thrust. That spaciousness proved an obstacle to early performances: a London premiere of the C-Major symphony, more than a decade after Schubert's death, was destroyed by the orchestra players' breaking into laughter! Apparently a lyric approach to the instrumental sonata cycle, and the expansive view of musical time this implied, were as novel in the early nineteenth century as the bizarre sonorities of Berlioz, and just as difficult for traditionalists to accept.

Franz Schubert

String Quartet no. 13: movement I

R3 S1 B2

The opening movement of the String Quartet in A Minor, no. 13 is a fine example of soaring melody within the sonata context, and provides an opportunity to examine other aspects of Schubert's instrumental style. As we might expect from his songs, Schubert's ***accompaniments*** are remarkable. The manner in which he creates an infinite variety of musical surfaces from a basically chordal format is just as impressive as his ability to write distinctive, singable tunes. (Schubert was reluctant to write polyphonically, and seriously considered studying counterpoint during the last year of his life. Although the massive fugal passages in Beethoven's music had impressed him greatly, he felt inadequate in this area himself.)

The string quartet movement begins with a characteristically evocative accompaniment figure. Only after two measures does a melodic line appear above this texture (see Figure 13.8). Stating the accompaniment first and then superimposing a broad tune upon it was associated in Schubert's day with operatic aria or Lieder rather than sonata form. Here again classic approaches were giving way to romantic ones.

Some critics have noticed a similarity between Figure 13.8 and the opening bars of "Gretchen am Spinnrade." Allowing for differences in rhythm, the two examples are surprisingly alike. There is no concrete evidence that Schubert used his song as a springboard for this quartet movement. On the other hand, we do know that during the early months of 1824, when the quartet was composed, he felt especially depressed. In a despairing letter to a friend, Schubert quoted the opening ***text***—Gretchen's

Figure 13.8

thoughts, sitting at her spinning wheel—that he had set to music ten years earlier:

> 'Meine Ruh ist hin, mein Ilerz ist schwer, ich finde sie nimmer und nimmer mehr!' That could be my daily song now, for every night when I go to sleep I hope never to wake again . . .

Is there a connection between the two pieces? It is tempting to consider this possibility, so long as we realize that we have entered the realm of possibility and not hard fact.

Returning to the written score, note the persistent bass rhythm of the opening passage. The 𝅗𝅥. ♬♬ rhythmic figure becomes a motive of sorts in its own right. It also provides a secure ostinato framework for adventurous harmonic shifts. Schubert's style, in fact, abounds in daring harmonic progressions, just about straining the logic of the tonal system to its limit. Although traditional key centers and large-scale key contrasts exist, they are expanded by subtle chromatic means. It is typically Schubertian, for instance, to move easily between major and minor modes of the same key. The A-minor theme of this movement acquires a new expressivity when it appears in A major. The music abruptly shifts back to minor, however, with a sudden *ff* and a vigorous statement of the opening melodic figure. It is much more agitated, with an angry trill and triplet rhythms contributing to the increased urgency.

This intense passage is actually the beginning of the bridge, modulating between the two main keys of the movement. It gradually subsides on a rising violin figure; after a breath of silence, the second theme (Figure 13.9) is heard in the relative major. It is just as lyric as the movement's opening

Figure 13.9

theme and, like that opening theme, it is suddenly restated boldly against agitated triplet rhythms. The theme's opening gesture is repeated sequentially with sharp dynamic contrasts. In a particularly bold stroke, the music suddenly veers to a totally foreign key, and then gently slides back to C major once more just before the end of the exposition.

The development may seem uneventful by the highly dramatic standards of Beethoven. Schubert's themes are not pulled apart, recombined or superimposed in the classic manner; they are too lyric, and too complete in themselves to warrant such treatment. On the other hand, the exposition has ***already*** been "developmental," with the introduction of triplet rhythms and the intense, angry transformation of the themes. Moreover, the ***tonal*** scheme of this section is anything but uneventful: Schubert's melodies may not tolerate much motivic fragmentation, but they certainly travel to unexpected key areas. A series of urgent sequential repetitions, leading to a dissonant *ff* chord, gradually subsides upon the 𝅗𝅥. ♫♫ rhythm of the opening and resolves to the tonic A minor.

Schubert's recapitulation is particularly moving after this tonal instability. The key of A (major and minor) forms a secure base, and the restless material appears to be subdued. A brief coda at the very close brings back the throbbing main theme, and then, for one last surprising instant, its fierce, agitated "twin." The intense face of the motive has prevailed.

Franz Schubert's death at the age of thirty-one, only a year after his idol Beethoven, was one of music's great tragedies. If Schubert had been granted even four more years he would have lived as long as Mozart did. If we consider what music Mozart would not have composed if ***he*** had died at thirty-one rather than thirty-five—the list is formidable, including the last three symphonies and ***Don Giovanni!***—we may sense Schubert's true stature, and the profound wonder expressed by musicians whenever his name is mentioned.

Chopin and the Piano

The unique personality of Fryderyk Chopin (1810–1849) provides another synthesis of romantic elements. Like Schubert, Chopin possessed a striking melodic gift and an ear for adventurous chromatic harmony, and like Schubert he died young. At this point the resemblances cease. Chopin was hardly a shy, unassuming, penniless "bohemian." During his brief career he was the darling of aristocratic salons, a brilliant virtuoso, a widely respected composer, and an elegant figure of fashion. The social, intellectual, and literary elite of Europe were numbered among his friends.

Chopin was reputed to be one of the finest pianists of his time, blessed with a superb technique and a delicate, lyric touch as well. He gave highly successful public concerts as a young man in such major centers as Vienna,

Warsaw, and Paris. But he withdrew from active concert life after settling in Paris in 1830; he preferred the small-scaled intimacy of salon life. Much of his own music was directed at a cultivated private audience of aristocratic admirers, and an acoustical setting where his naturally light, graceful playing style would be most effective.

His frail health and slight build may have contributed to that exquisitely sensitive style. Chopin could never physically overpower a mass audience with sheer volume of sound, as his friend and rival Liszt could. On the other hand, his delicate *ppp* whispers were unmatched by anyone. In later years, his tubercular condition only enhanced the glamour of his romantic image; and even as a young man his sickly appearance, like his Polish nationalism, was a fashionable social asset.

As a composer, Chopin was a specialist of the first rank, devoting almost all his creative energy to piano music. The great bulk of his work consists of nocturnes, etudes, preludes and waltzes, most of these relatively short, composed for the instrument he knew and loved best. To a certain degree, Chopin also specialized in the smaller genres. Although he created two substantial concertos and three sonatas, he is best known for his many single-movement works. They range from intense miniatures, and sectional dance forms to more extended developmental shapes such as the scherzos and ballades. These pieces are not programmatic: very few contain extra-musical allusions or literary-pictorial nicknames. But no one who has ever heard them can doubt their passionate, ultra-romantic expressivity.

The titles of Chopin's compositions, although not specifically programmatic, may provide a general reference to the character of his music. The ***preludes*** are usually quite brief, poetic miniatures, and self-sufficient rather than preliminary to anything else. Some of them are little more than momentary fragments, however, and may in fact seem introductory; Chopin must have anticipated this ambiguous situation when he used the title. (Two preludes were discussed at length in Part 1). His ***etudes*** were conceived as "studies to help solve such pianistic problems as rapid finger-work, wide skips, or difficult hand positions." But they are certainly not dry or mechanical; most listeners respond to them as intense, evocative musical or mechanical; musical statements. The ***nocturne,*** or "night piece," suggests a lyric, warmly moving work of generally quiet dynamics and slowish tempo. The name is ideally suited to some of Chopin's most intimate, expressive pieces.

Chopin wrote four elaborate single-movement works entitled ***Scherzo.*** Here again, as with the preludes, we need to revise our previous associations with a name. These scherzos are not movements within a large sonata cycle, nor are they necessarily rapid; what Chopin mainly derived from Beethoven's model was the furious intensity and demonic sense of cosmic joke. In this sense Chopin used the title in a highly personal way. Similarly, Chopin, Schubert, and Brahms all wrote "waltzes," quite different in spirit from one another (and from those of Johann Strauss).

Georges Sand, *Frederick Chopin.*

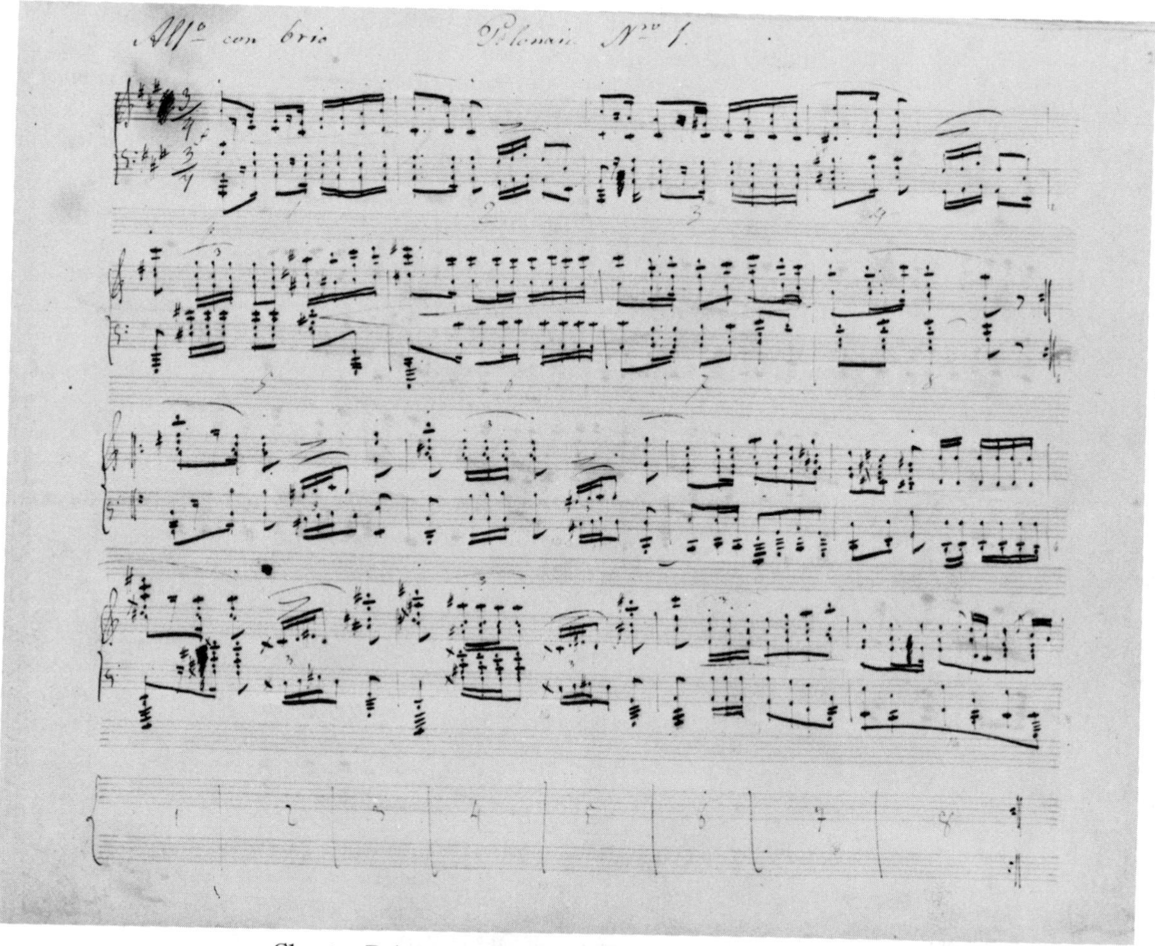

Chopin, Polonaise no. 1, Autograph of the composer. Chopin's manuscript was as fastidious as his personal lifestyle. Here is the original score for one of his best-known Polonaises.

Finally, Chopin wrote in two strongly nationalistic genres, both derived from the dance: the vigorous ***mazurka*** and the heroic, courtly ***polonaise.*** To fully understand Chopin's art we must remember that his homeland, Poland, was his greatest love. Although he made Paris his home from the age of twenty until his death at thirty-nine, Chopin was deeply involved in the cause of Polish freedom. He protested the suffering of his countrymen under Russian domination, and aided Polish refugees. He carried a fistful of Polish soil with him, a parting gift from friends when he left in 1830, and on his deathbed requested that his heart be buried in Poland. It is appropriate that his first composition, written at the age of eight, was a polonaise, and the last a mazurka. Chopin's nationalistic yearning was coupled with dejection at the fate of his country and a fierce pride in its glories. His loneliness and homesickness was just one aspect of a life that had grown increasingly sour: his love affair with George Sand collapsed after a decade, and his physical decline during the final struggle with tuberculosis was marked. On hearing of Chopin's death, Berlioz commented, "He had been slowly dying all of his life."

Fryderyk Chopin
Nocturne, opus 9 no. 2 (E♭ major) and Polonaise, opus 53 (A♭ major)

These two pieces, both single-movement miniatures, represent very different sides of Chopin's personality. The Nocturne establishes a slow tempo at the outset; its flexible rhythmic pulse can be heard either as a moderately flowing "triple" or a slower "duple" (see Figure 13.10). The sense of pulse may be further weakened by the degree of *rubato* taken during the performance. It is unlikely, for example, that measure 1 would be played as twelve metronomically even beats. Note the expressive rise and fall of the melody, with an octave skip in measure 2 and an even greater skip up to high D in

Figure 13.10

measure 4. Even as early as measure 2 the melodic line has acquired a decorative embellishment: the ∾ on the 3rd beat. Chopin was a great admirer of Italian opera, and the exquisite embroidery of his melodic lines has much in common with virtuoso coloratura aria.

Concentrate now on Chopin's artful use of ***dissonance*** in these same four measures. If the $\frac{12}{8}$ meter is regarded as a compound pattern of four beats per measure, we can say that there are only three consonant beats in the entire example, those designated by an asterisk. All others convey various states of tension, propelling the passage forward. On some beats, chromatic pitches have been added to the harmony (when accidentals appear in the score), and in other cases melody and harmony are at odds. Another beat has been labelled with a ?; it appears to be stable, until the pitch G (beat 12 of the $\frac{12}{8}$ measure) intrudes at the last moment, again propelling the music forward. This consistent use of chromaticism and dissonance typifies the romantic approach to harmony.

The complete melody is immediately repeated (Figure 13.11), with more complex ornamentation, against the basic broken-chord accompaniment. Listen for the added trills, grace notes, and syncopated accents in this variant. A contrasting phrase group appears at this point, beginning and ending on the dominant chord (B♭ major). It returns to the main melody by a highly chromatic progression, destroying the tonal sense, and then recapturing it at the last moment. As the main theme is repeated, it is varied again with new embellishments and decorations, noted in Figure 13.12.

The lyric theme and its contrasting phrase group alternate twice more; each time the time is restated in a new decorative filigree setting. With each repetition the final melodic figure of the theme (bracketed in the opening example) becomes increasingly dazzling and virtuosic—although, curiously, it remains delicate and lyric as well. At this point, Chopin introduces new material, still against the simple broken-chord left hand pattern. It rises to a forceful climax, and then subsides quietly.

The ***Polonaise*** presents a more complex formal structure than the Nocturne, but it, too, subdivides into contrasting phrase units that alternate with each other. Chopin's concept of the stately, aristocratic dance has been

Figure 13.11

Figure 13.12

stylized (or romanticized) so that the heroic aspects are stressed. Note the stately tempo, triple meter, and striking dotted rhythms, all derived from the original dance model. As with the Nocturne, the practice of ***rubato*** in performance may stretch or contract individual beats.

After a brilliant, stirring, and highly chromatic introduction that blurs the tonal sense and then finally confirms the proper key, the actual Polonaise begins, noted in Figure 13.13. This is the A section of a three-part ABA form, dominated by a distinctive, bold tune.

Figure 13.13

Figure 13.14

A, B, A, Coda.
aba cc aa

The music grows and recedes in tension, reaching a strong cadence at the tonic. Contrasting material is introduced, and then resolved to a restatement of the main tune.

Just when another strong A-major cadence has been confirmed, there is a sudden move to the key of E major. (This is not a gradual modulation, just the abrupt juxtaposition of two chords.) Over a running bass pattern of octaves, a stately new theme emerges. This signals the start of a new large section, the B of the ABA form. The passage veers chromatically to another unexpected key, then repeats, eventually leading back to the original tonic. Section A returns in abbreviated form, without its lyric internal contrast; a brilliant coda brings the Polonaise to a fiery, proud conclusion. The sectional form of the work could be diagrammed as A in Figure 13.14.

We have used music by Berlioz, Schubert and Chopin to introduce the romantic movement, because all three were active during the early decades of that movement; Schubert, in fact, worked virtually in the shadow of Beethoven. Furthermore, the differences among the three are sharp enough to indicate the great variety in the nineteenth-century musical scene. We will continue to explore that variety during the next few chapters.

14

Romanticism: The Early Nineteenth Century

The most beautiful music is where the Faust-mantle of fantasy envelops powerful forms . . .

Robert Schumann

Strangeness will always be the sublime, envious misfortune of every musical genius. Innovation goes beyond what is familiar, and so must appear strange . . .

Franz Liszt

Some General Considerations

As noted in the previous chapter, a few basic features common to many individual, unique styles dominated nineteenth century music. The following concerns were shared by virtually all romantic composers.

1. *Music's expressive role.* Western European music had developed traits that were unique among the world's music. Western listeners came to accept the idea that music was created by a special class of people who often claimed special privileges, although their music was not necessarily "useful" to society. Such music was often listened to as a ceremonial ritual of its own, in a performance space set aside for that activity. It was intended to express the emotions of the composer and arouse the emotions of the listener; these were not always emotions provoked directly by outside events at the time of creating or listening, as they might very well be in non-Western or pre-Renaissance cultures.

The prevailing romantic philosophy could be summed up in the belief that music was the "language of the emotions"—not raw, direct emotional outbursts, but emotions channeled and organized: abstracted, stylized and transformed into a symbolic "code," so that they could be evoked by the composer and recollected by the hearer.

2. ***Chromaticism and the decline of tonality.*** Europe's symbolic code for musical expressivity was the tonal system. This musical language had, over the centuries, acquired important associations with tension, release, the forward thrust of time, and emotional states. ***Chromaticism*** had a special function within this language. It brought out heightened feelings, ambiguity, a sense of unresolved yearning and searching. Therefore, it was most important to the vocabulary of romantic composers. But extreme chromaticism weakens the tonal system itself. Without a clear-cut diatonic frame of reference, the two most important aspects of form were in danger: ***unity*** (automatically provided for with a strong tonal center) and ***variety*** (the classic polarization of distinct keys).

3. ***Form.*** It might appear contradictory for romantic composers to worry at all about form. After all, they were fond of proclaiming their freedom from classic restrictions, and delighted in programmatic subjects that were often irrational or dreamlike. But their concern with form was genuine. They displayed their romanticism not in any avoidance of the problem, but in the nature of their solutions. For example, they could practically guarantee unity by writing very short pieces: concise epigrams or momentary fragments requiring no further elaboration. With longer works, striking contrasts could bounce off one another, providing the equivalent of classic balance. And in pieces of any duration, the notion of cyclic unity, or "character variation," could provide unity and contrast at the same time.

4. ***Personal styles, and controversial responses.*** In this age of revolution, creative artists were preoccupied with "liberty" in every sense of the word. They did not regard themselves as servants composing music for masters; rather, they composed for middle-class audiences, for each other, for virtuoso performers, and perhaps for posterity. Romantic music, then, does not reflect a single social or divine order. Instead, it offers a diversity of private responses to an increased *dis*order.

Since romantic composers cultivated such markedly individual, even controversial, styles, it is only natural that listeners will find some more to their liking than others. Those who dislike Berlioz or Liszt find them cheap, bombastic, and vulgar. Mendelssohn may strike some as trivial and sentimental, Wagner as unbearably pretentious, Brahms as dull and boring, and so on.

John Singleton Copley, ***Watson and the Shark***. Courtesy of The Detroit Institute of Arts, The Dexter M. Ferry, Jr. Fund.

In this context, it may be worth noting that the famous romantic composers didn't always like each others' work, either! Witness some typical comments: "It irritates me that this self-conscious mediocrity should be recognized as a genius . . . so chaotic, so dry and meaningless" (Tchaikovsky, about Brahms), or: "As a creator, he is an ass . . . a clever craftsman without a vestige of talent" (Chopin, about Liszt). On the other hand, many composers—Liszt, Schumann, and Mendelssohn, in particular—supported and encouraged their colleagues.

5. ***Some groupings of composers.*** Obviously, nineteenth-century music can be studied as a succession of striking personalities. On the other hand, romantic composers can also be grouped together, and in a number of ways. On strictly national grounds, one could consider the German-Austrian composers, such as Schumann, Mendelssohn, Brahms and Wagner, as one group, with others such as Chopin, Berlioz, Mussorgsky, Dvorak, Verdi, Grieg, and Tchaikovsky loosely gathered together under the general heading of "nationalism." A grouping of ***vocal*** versus ***instrumental*** concerns would reveal two figures who emphasized instrumental timbre (Chopin and Liszt) and two who devoted almost all their energy to the operatic stage (Wagner and Verdi).

Romantic composers are often grouped according to their positions along a "conservative" to "radical" continuum. Although no-one has ever defined either category to everybody's satisfaction, musicians would probably agree about most of the names in these groups:

radical	**conservative**
Berlioz	Schubert
Liszt	Schumann
Wagner	Mendelssohn
Chopin	Brahms
Mussorgsky	Dvořák

"Radical" composers were concerned with brilliant sonority, experiments in form and harmony, and programmatic or nationalistic references. "Conservatives," on the other hand, were supposedly more interested in chamber music, symphonies, and other absolute works using the time-honored forms. But these distinctions do not account for the many occasions in which composers cross categories, or the many figures, such as Verdi, whose works are both conservative and radical in special ways.

The "Vintage Generation"

In this and the following chapter, romantic composers will be discussed chronologically; this chapter will be concerned with the developments up to and including the 1850s. Specifically, we will study five composers born during the 1809—1813 span that has been called the "vintage generation:" (see table) Mendelssohn, Schumann, Liszt, Wagner, and Verdi. A sixth member of this generation, Chopin, has already been discussed.

1809 Lincoln, Darwin, Poe, Tennyson, Mendelssohn
1810 Cavour, Chopin, Schumann
1811 Thackeray, Greeley, Liszt
1812 Dickens, Browning
1813 Verdi, Wagner

The last three composers on our list had rich, full lives, Verdi's extended until the age of 88. Even so, the stereotype of the romantic artist is often that of an early, untimely death: the youthful voice suddenly stilled. The tragic pattern is followed in the careers of Mendelssohn, Chopin and Schubert; among the romantic poets, Keats, Byron, and Shelley also died young. Although Schumann lived into his mid-forties, he, too, is best remembered for the impassioned music of his youth. In all these lives, we may sense the dashing, impulsive, fragile quality of the early romantic movement. Verdi and Wagner, who matured slowly to produce their best work after middle age, were the exception rather than the rule.

Note, too, that during the early romantic era Vienna lost its major role as the center of Europe's musical life. The new centers were now Paris, especially for opera, and a number of German cities, such as Dresden, Leipzig, and Weimar, with flourishing orchestras and opera houses. It was not until the second half of the century that Vienna, dominated by Brahms and Johann Strauss, would again play an important musical role.

Mendelssohn

Felix Mendelssohn (1809–1847) was born about a week before Abraham Lincoln, to a banker's family in Hamburg; his boyhood was spent not in a log cabin, but amidst great wealth, culture, and social refinement. His grandfather was the famous Jewish philosopher Moses Mendelssohn, and in his youth he was introduced to such notable men as Hegel and Goethe. He traveled widely, and was trained in languages, literature, and painting as well as music. Mendelssohn's musical gifts were revealed early: he was performing publicly as a pianist at age nine, and became a prolific composer in his teens. In fact, one of his best-known works, the Overture to ***A Midsummer Night's Dream,*** dates from his seventeenth year. He conducted the first performance before an invited audience of family friends and guests at his parents' Berlin residence.

concert overture

Mendelssohn's Overture is a fine example of an orchestral genre that captured the attention of many romantic composers: the ***concert overture.*** Like a Chopin "prelude," a concert "overture" is not meant to be the introduction to anything else. The format is entirely self-sufficient, although it could be used as curtain-raiser for a theatrical production if one wished. It is a single orchestral movement, usually set in one of the symphonic forms such as sonata form or rondo, and inspired by a dramatic or literary subject. Mendelssohn's overture was drawn from the well-known play by Shakespeare, whose supernatural plays fascinated the romantic imagination. Berlioz also composed a number of concert overtures, and the genre can be traced back to Beethoven, who left some outstanding examples.

Felix Mendelssohn

A Midsummer Night's Dream: Overture and Incidental Music

The Overture to *A Midsummer Night's Dream* is in sonata form, preceded by the briefest of introductions—four woodwind chords. The Allegro proper captures the spirit of Shakespeare's fairyland in its opening material, and then becomes bold and aggressive in tone, with an imposing theme of regal stature. The second theme group contains a lyric, flowing melody, depicting the intense feelings of the human lovers, and a brash bumbling tune that suggests the slapstick comedy of clowns. The huge skip of the comic tune (bracketed in Figure 14.1), very much like the braying of a donkey, reminds us of the magic spell that has given Bottom the Weaver an ass's head. At the Overture's end, a hushed coda recalls the opening four chords and a more relaxed variant of the forceful "regal" material. The music fades off, as though the performers were stealing away into the distance.

Mendelssohn has channeled his literary, programmatic references into a traditional classic form that would make "absolute" sense even if we knew nothing of Shakespeare. The freshness and agility of the writing, admirable for a composer of any age, are miraculous for a boy of seventeen. As George Bernard Shaw wrote many years later, the Overture is "the most striking example I know of a very young composer astonishing the world."

Mendelssohn's Overture was written in 1826, when the composer was a university student. Sixteen years later, the King of Prussia commissioned him to compose more music on the same Shakespearian subject, this time for a production of the play. Music which is intended for functional use in a staged production as background or between-the-acts interludes, is known as ***incidental music.***

incidental music

In modern performances, the Overture may be followed by three of the numbers composed for the *Midsummer Night's Dream* production years later. These are, in order: a Scherzo; a Nocturne which in this context functions as a slow movement; and the "Wedding March," composed for the

Figure 14.1

multiple weddings of Shakespeare's play. (This march is often heard today at wedding ceremonies throughout the Western world.) In connection with the Scherzo, we should note that Mendelssohn wrote many scherzo movements during his career. They are invariably light and airy, with a playful spirit far removed from the highly charged drama of a Beethoven or Chopin scherzo. Combining the Overture of 1826 with the incidental music of 1842 produces a four-movement programmatic suite of great charm.

The ease with which Mendelssohn could expand upon an Overture composed sixteen years earlier, without creating an awkward contrast of styles, is amazing. Of course, he had been an unbelievably sophisticated adolescent, blessed with great talent and prodigious technique. Sadly, the mature, adult Mendelssohn never really grew or developed beyond the first, triumphal skills of his youth. He never felt the need to and, even more sadly, he was granted very little time.

Even as an adolescent, Mendelssohn revealed an unfailing ear for classic balance, and a dramatic sensibility that was refined rather than vulgar. His sense of good taste never deserted him; it was the very opposite of Victor Hugo's call for "pure artistic freedom," or the bombast of Berlioz. (He considered one Berlioz score so "dirty" that he wanted to wash his hands after touching the pages!) The impulsiveness of much romantic music, the exhilarating sense of going "out of bounds," did not appeal to Mendelssohn: temperamentally, he was a classicist at heart.

Mendelssohn was a classicist in many ways. He had a consuming interest in music of the past, and was active in bringing Bach, Mozart, and Beethoven to public attention. In 1829, at the age of twenty, he organized and conducted the first performance in a century of Bach's Saint Matthew Passion. By his thirties, Mendelssohn had made several tours to England, conducting the London Philharmonic and visiting with Queen Victoria, and had directed musical activities in Leipzig and Berlin. His charm, talent, social poise, and administrative skill brought him great fame, as well as positions in which he was heavily overworked. The constant strain on his health brought on apoplexy and a sudden end at the age of thirty-eight.

The "classic" aspects of Mendelssohn's music are revealed in his sonata-cycle works, built upon the traditional models of the past; his belief in the classic concepts of balance and restraint tempered his programmatic instances. Mendelssohn's "romantic" side appears in his short lyric pieces and in his descriptive music: the brief ***Songs without Words*** for piano, and the incidental music with its sensitive landscape-painting. Certain thoroughly romantic stylistic features—his sustained lyricism, or concern for instrumental timbre—are found in all his music.

One of his best-known compositions is the Violin Concerto in E Minor, composed in 1844. In listening to this work, consider not only the composer's style, but the way in which the concerto format itself was being altered and adapted—"romanticized"—during the nineteenth century.

Felix Mendelssohn
Violin Concerto in E Minor

R4 S2 B1

The three movements of the concerto are played without pause. Mendelssohn's desire to link the movements was a characteristic gesture of the century, derived from the precedent set by Beethoven in his Fifth Symphony.

Movement I: Allegro molto appassionato. There is no double exposition in this sonata-concerto form. Instead, soloist and orchestra immediately present the material together, each taking turns in occupying the spotlight for a brief passage or phrase. This sense of partnership between performing forces is remarkably strong and reveals the exquisite feeling for balance that we associate with Mendelssohn. The opening theme (Figure 14.2) first heard in the violin's high register, is followed by a particularly attractive bridge that soars over a wide range. This bridge passage eventually modulates to the relative major, and becomes more relaxed and leisurely in tempo by the time the new key is confirmed. The second theme (Figure 14.3) is quite gentle, emphasizing a narrow range and many repeated notes. Its instrumentation when first stated—soft woodwinds, against a low G pedal point held by the soloist—is wonderfully imaginative.

During the development, the first theme and bridge material are stressed; note the full orchestral *tutti* as the first theme appears *ff* in the major mode. As far as volume is concerned, this is the high point of the movement. It recedes to a gentle level, and, where we might least expect it, the solo *cadenza* begins; this is shown in the graphic design of Figure 14.4.

Figure 14.2

Figure 14.3

Figure 14.4

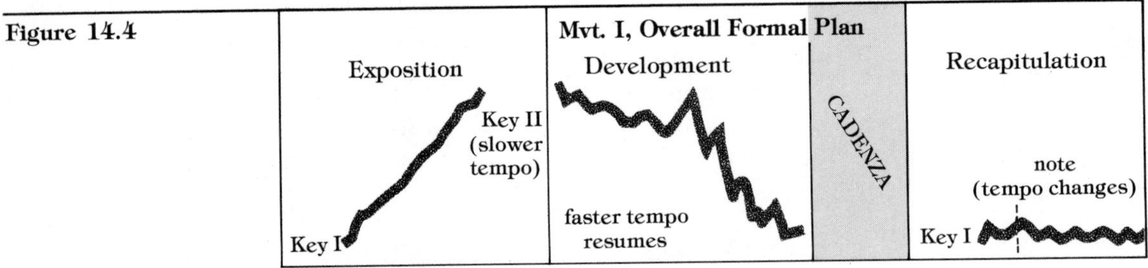

No double exposition

Mendelssohn's cadenza is notable for two reasons. First, it occurs at the end of the development section, making it structurally and psychologically important, rather than appearing as throw-away virtuoso frosting at the end. Second, every note has been written by the composer: the improvised cadenza has become a relic of the past. The nineteenth-century composer took the cadenza very seriously, as a developmental part of the total form and as a critical soliloquy in the on-stage drama. It was unthinkable to leave that up to a performer.

The cadenza fades away quietly in a rapid figuration of broken chords, and the recapitulation begins with this solo figuration as accompaniment. A strong coda at the very close leads to a forceful E-minor cadence. The movement is apparently over, but out of that final chord a sustained bassoon note is held: this note grows to a chord, and gently leads into the slow movement.

Movement II: Andante . . . connected to Movement III: Allegro molto vivace. The middle movement is slow and lyric, built about a warm, intimate C-major theme in meter: the six beats can be heard in the context of a slowly flowing "2." The form is ABA′ (with the repeat a modified return of A), apparently dying away to silence. But, once more, a thread is maintained between movements: this time, an impassioned dialogue between soloist and orchestra, related to theme B. At the return of the tonic key of the concerto (E), a flourish of trumpets proclaims a breezy new tempo, and the confirmation of the major mode.

Figure 14.5

Figure 14.6

The E-major finale, beginning with the theme of Figure 14.5, is a rapid, playful sonata-form allegro. In its delicate texture and high spirits, it resembles a typical Mendelssohn "scherzo." The second theme, in the dominant key, is bold and martial at first (see Figure 14.6) but then retreats to the running passagework of the opening motive.

There appears to be no lyric theme at all, but Mendelssohn introduces one, surprisingly, during the development; he emphasizes it further during recapitulation and coda. Notice how easily the lyric tune fits in counterpoint with the scherzo-like passagework of the opening theme. In subtle ways—the dotted rhythm, the insistence upon a repeated note B— the lyric theme recalls the soaring melody that begins the entire concerto. Mendelssohn knew all the cyclic devices of romantic variation, as well as traditional polyphonic technique. It was characteristic of him to employ both at once in an understated, amiable manner.

Schumann

Robert Schumann (1810–1856) was as literary and intellectual as his friend, colleague, and (for a time) Leipzig neighbor Mendelssohn. He was the son of a writer and bookseller, and grew up surrounded by literature and love for the printed word. Schumann was trained to be a lawyer, but decided during his university years that music was his true love and vocation. An injury to his finger forced him to abandon a pianistic career; instead, he quickly acquired a reputation as a composer. Throughout his career he was also a writer; he was one of Europe's first modern critics, reviewing performance and printed music for various journals. Even if he had never composed a note himself, Schumann would be famous today as the critic who first discovered Chopin and championed him in print, and who years later launched the young Brahms with a glowing review. He also wrote perceptive, supportive comments on the work of Mendelssohn, Liszt, and Berlioz. (Chopin and Mendelssohn did not return the compliment: they were frequently cool to Schumann's music.)

Schumann's reviews give a fascinating picture of the cultural scene in central Europe. Middle-class interest in the arts had created a growing demand for musical journalism. On the other hand, middle-class taste had moved in a different direction from the interests of composers. Schumann was constantly trying to educate the public away from empty-headed "philistinism" (as he called it); his efforts led him to found a journal of his

Robert and Clara Schumann, husband and wife, and two of the nineteenth century's most influential musicians.

own, ***Die neu Zeitschrift für Musik*** ("The New Music Magazine"), which became highly influential.

As a young piano student, Schumann worked with the well-known teacher Friedrich Wieck, and lived in Wieck's Leipzig home for a number of years. He also fell in love with Wieck's daughter Clara, her father's prize pupil and one of Europe's most sensational young pianists. When Schumann first met her she was only eight years old (a decade younger than he), and already an accomplished performer. They were married a dozen years later, after an intense courtship and stern opposition on the part of Clara's father. The elder Wieck objected not only to Robert's slender economic prospects, but to growing evidence that the composer was emotionally unstable. As early as the 1830's Schumann had shown manic-depressive personality

Figure 14.7

swings, and had attempted suicide in 1833. Significantly, his journal reviews often featured commentary by three fictitious characters: Florestan (active, impulsive), Eusebius (reflective, the dreamer), and Mister Raro (a thoughtful mediator between the other two). According to modern psychologists these may have symbolized the sharp divisions within Schumann's own personality. (The title page of his first piano sonata reads, "Dedicated to Clara, by Florestan and Eusebius.")

During his first decade as a composer, Schumann wrote nothing but piano music: wildly passionate, delicate, filled with literary and programmatic references. Many of these early works were brief pieces with suggestive titles, called ***character pieces,*** grouped together under a general programmatic heading: the nonverbal equivalent of song cycles. The many short pieces in a single collection might be related musically, in the cyclic manner of "character variations."

character pieces

One such collection familiar to pianists is called ***Kinderszenen*** ("Scenes from Childhood"). It consists of thirteen short pieces, with evocative titles such as "Playing Tag" or "Falling Asleep." The first of the series "About Strange Lands and People" (Figure 14.7) is a simple ABA form, gentle and musing; it could be contrasted with the mock-seriousness of "Important Event" (Figure 14.8), another ABA form.

The most famous of the ***Kinderszenen*** is the poetic gem called "Träumerei" ("Dreaming"); a long, arching melodic line that gently rises and falls (Figure 14.9), undergoes a brief imitative "development" and then subsides most poignantly. The final piece of the collection (Figure 14.10) is

Figure 14.8

Figure 14.9

even more meditative. In this work, called "The Poet Speaks," Schumann makes use of single lines, pauses, and breaths, to create an evocative stillness.

Note that a simple melodic figure , unifies the various pieces within the set. (It has been bracketed in each of our examples.) Although Schumann didn't call the collection "variations," a cyclic thread runs throughout. Romantic composers, then, could extend ideas of cyclic character variation to brief genres as well as large ones.

After the Schumanns were married in 1840, Robert suddenly turned to the composition of songs, combining his great interest in literature with a celebration of his love. A period of intense work on chamber music followed, and by the end of his career he had explored many other media as well. Although Clara assumed the role of wife and mother (to eight children), she remained active as a pianist, premiering many of her husband's works, and was a successful composer in her own right as well. She also became Robert's quasi-ambassador (or interpreter) to the outside world, as he became increasingly withdrawn, shy, and in his last years, virtually inarticulate. His quiet voice, long silences, near-illegible handwriting and impulsive manners had become legendary in musical circles.

He had been through a period of deep depression in 1845, but apparently recovered from it. By the mid-1850s, he began to hear imaginary

Figure 14.10

musical tones; thoughts of approaching mental illness terrified him. In 1854 he attempted suicide by throwing himself into the Rhine River, was rescued, and voluntarily committed himself to an asylum. He died there, two years later.

Schumann made some novel experiments within the large sonata-cycle genres. Like Mendelssohn, he gave programmatic titles to a number of his symphonies; his Symphony no. 4 (untitled) is noteworthy for its linking of movements and cyclic treatment of themes. The A-Minor Piano Concerto is another interesting large work, and another fine example of the romantic concerto.

Robert Schumann

Piano Concerto in A Minor

R3 S2 B1

Movement I: Allegro affetuoso. A bold, dynamic figure, briefly surging to a cadence, immediately introduces soloist and orchestra; it also leads directly to the body of the sonata allegro movement. A broad, lyric theme (Figure 14.11), is stated first by the orchestra, and then answered by the pianist. This is not only the first theme of the movement, but a cyclic "motto" for the entire concerto. The falling-rising contour C-A-E, and the octave skip a few measures later, are both integral to the concerto's overall plan. After an expansive bridge that builds to a strong climax, the music subsides to the relative C major, and a second theme in that key. Note that this "new" theme (Figure 14.12) is really a variant of the opening. It is stated in the woodwinds, accompanied by rushing cascades of piano arpeggios. Surprisingly, it returns to the bridge material, and reaches a furious climax. An unexpected modulation and slower tempo usher in the development section. Here Schumann presents an alternation of moods, tempos, and tonal centers, using the main theme and brief introduction as springboards; we are eventually brought full circle to the A-minor opening.

Figure 14.11

Figure 14.12

The recapitulation is memorable for a brilliant shift of key (too abrupt to be called a modulation) during the bridge passage, enabling the music to retain the tonality of A when the "second" (major-mode) theme reappears. There is also a deeply moving cadenza, fully written out by Schumann, followed by a coda built on a rapid (faster) variant of the main motto theme.

The cadenza illustrates an important feature of the entire concerto: its anti-virtuosic quality of understatement, a reluctance to indulge in any flashy display. As a critic, Schumann waged a one-man campaign against mindless instrumental gymnastics, writing: "Music does not exist for the fingers, but the reverse," and at greater length:

> The public has lately begun to weary of virtuosos, and, as we have frequently remarked, we have too. The virtuosos themselves seem to feel this, if we may judge from a recent awakened fancy among them for emigrating to America. Many of their enemies secretly hope they will remain there. . ."

And so his own concerto is introspective and poetic, rather than brilliantly glittering. Significantly, its cadenza, the traditional vehicle for technical fireworks, contains the most intimate passages of the movement.

Figure 14.13

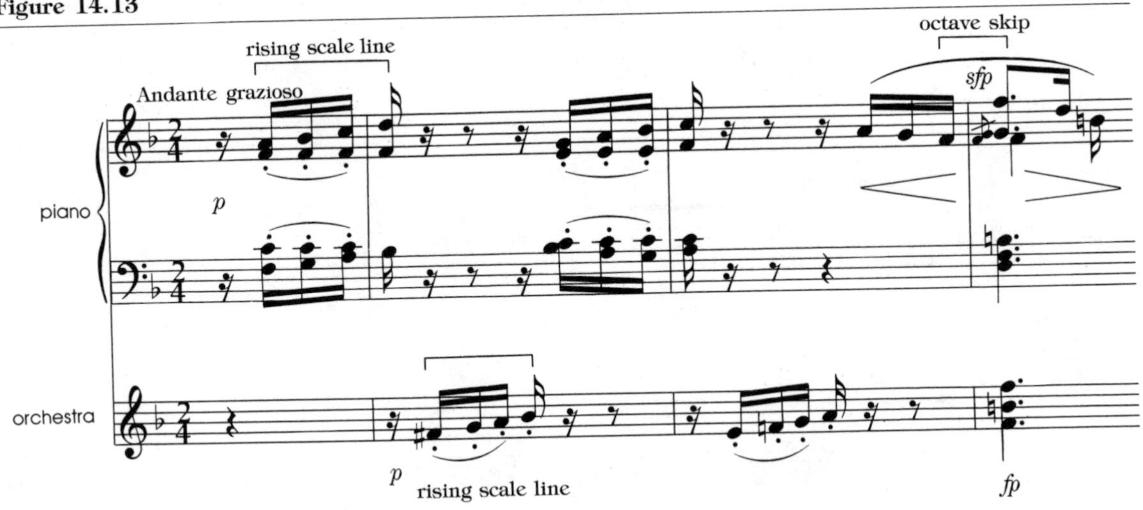

Figure 14.14

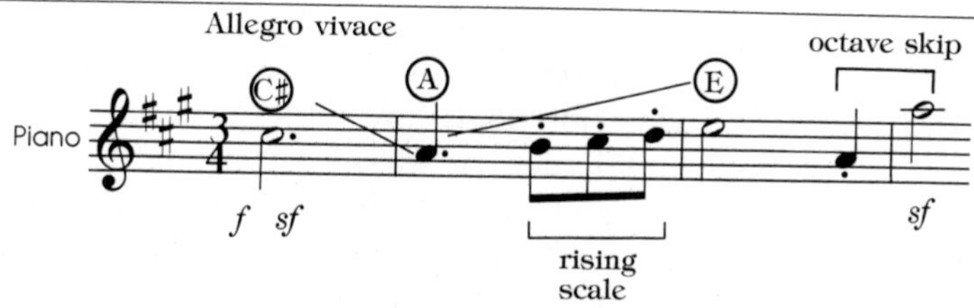

Movement II: Andante grazioso . . . leading to Movement III: Allegro vivace. Schumann called the middle movement an Intermezzo, and it is light in spirit, midway between an *arioso* slow movement and a really spritely scherzo. Its principal theme (see Figure 14.13) is tossed back and forth between soloist and ensemble. (Note the prominent octave skip in the melody, related to the "motto.") A more sweeping melody appears later, elaborated by strings, and then the perky main tune returns. The ending of the movement is whispered and tentative; it leads us unexpectedly to a literal restatement of the motto—that is, the opening figure of the first movement, in A major and then in A minor. The tempo quickens, the volume increases, and the major mode returns once more. The finale, linked directly to the preceding passage, begins with an aggressive, lively theme, shown in Figure 14.14. It is related cyclically to the rest of the concerto by its contour and its octave skip, and is therefore an ideal vehicle for a final, "summing-up." The movement is in sonata form, with a rhythmically unsettling second theme of great charm. But it is the first theme that continually commands attention: Schumann develops it polyphonically, and hammers it home one last time during the coda.

The Schumann Piano concerto, with its cyclic unity and linking of movements, is a large work with a typically romantic "grand" design. Paradoxically, its warmth and tenderness afford a glimpse of romanticism's other, more intimate, side as well.

Liszt

The piano had universal appeal during the nineteenth century, because of its stronger case and improved pedal and keyboard action, it was a more versatile instrument than Mozart or Beethoven had ever known, capable of lyricism, harmonic richness, and great dynamic contrasts. It served equally well for the introspective fantasies of Schumann, Chopin's aristocratic salon music, and the ultra-brilliant spectacle of the virtuoso Franz Liszt (1811–1886).

Liszt practically invented the piano concert as we know it, and dazzled audiences for decades. His fame equalled that of a modern film or rock star: he collected countesses the way other people collect stamps. If that were the whole story, we might dismiss Liszt as shallow and insensitive. But he was also one of the era's most original composers, an unselfish colleague and teacher. He championed the work of others including Chopin, Schumann, Wagner, and Berlioz. He was also a devout Catholic who spent much time in prayer and fasting, eventually receiving Holy Orders in Rome. He embodied such striking contradictions that his own contemporaries referred to him as "half saint, half charlatan," or "a mixture of priest and circus rider."

Liszt was born in Hungary, about thirty miles from Vienna. His father worked on the estate of the same Esterházy family that had employed Haydn. His early triumphs took place in Vienna where, as an eleven year old, he met Beethoven, but he soon began performing throughout Europe. Paris was his home for many years, and his later interests spread to Weimar, Rome, and Budapest. The only language he felt comfortable with was French; he spoke German with an accent and—one more contradiction—never really learned Hungarian.

There were three great influences on Liszt's early career, all formed in Paris: Berlioz, Chopin, and the legendary violin virtuoso Nicolo Paganini. Liszt's charismatic appeal soon matched Paganini's. His fantasias on popular favorites, dazzling transcriptions of Beethoven symphonies, and other display pieces astounded, delighted, and terrified the public. His personal magnetism must have been overwhelming; accounts of people swooning in his presence, or fighting over the half-smoked stub of his cigar, indicate the extent of his power.

In 1848 Liszt abandoned public concert-giving, and took a position as music director to the court of Weimar. He stayed there for a dozen years, and during that period established it as a major musical center, organizing and conducting premieres of works by Berlioz, Schumann, and Wagner. His other serious activity during these years was composition, particularly large-scale programmatic works.

The Symphonic Poem

Liszt was interested in ways of combining the balances and contrasts of the old sonata cycle with the format of an extended programmatic movement: a middle ground between "concert overture" and "symphony." The genre that he developed was known as the ***symphonic poem.*** (Later in the century similar pieces were called ***tone poems.***) Liszt's symphonic poems all had programmatic titles, and a strong extra-musical stimulus. A typical symphonic poem consisted of a single movement with striking internal contrasts, the equivalent of separate movements joined together. But the contrasting sections were also related to each other, by reference to the program and by the cyclic thread of common musical material.

symphonic poem
tone poem

Other examples of cyclic technique have already been discussed: Beethoven's Fifth Symphony, the ***Symphonie Fantastique*** of Berlioz, with its ***idée fixe,*** and Schumann's use of character variation in his ***Kinderszenen.*** Liszt and his followers called the technique ***thematic transformation.*** By altering surface characteristics, such as register and tempo, Liszt could use the same basic material to suggest pastoral calm one moment and a raging storm the next.

The best known of the symphonic poems is called *Les Preludes* ("The Preludes"), drawn from a philosophical essay in which life is depicted as a series of "preludes" to the unknown adventure of the afterlife. The program evokes a number of these "preludes" in detail: "The enchanted dawn of every life is love . . . When the storm subsides, the soul rests its memories in a pastoral calm . . . When the trumpet sounds we hasten to the struggle," and so on. This is not a narrative that could be translated easily into music, and Liszt does not even make the attempt. Rather, he aims for a general impression corresponding to the sequence of moods—mysterious, searching, romantic, stormy, peaceful, warlike—presented in the philosophical poem.

Franz Liszt

Les Préludes

R4 S1 B1

The predominance of a three-note motive (Figure 14.15), heard near the very beginning, holds the entire work together. At the outset its rising interval of a 4th appears hesitant and questing. But the motive is soon embedded in a strong, heroic passage (Figure 14.16) which will reappear at the very end of the work. As this subsides, a lyric mood prevails; two themes appear (Figure 14.17) both related to the basic motive. The second of the two leads from the original C-major tonality to the "distant" key of E major. The momentum of Liszt's chromatic harmony now drifts from one tonality to another, gently at first and then with an increasingly ominous quality. Finally we are left at a silence, with no discernible key center at all.

At this point, the "storm" begins, hushed and distant but intensifying rapidly. Note how Liszt begins each mysterious rushing passage with a murmured reference to the basic motive; this is suggested in Figure 14.18. Our sense of the music being in "no key" is quite accurate. Liszt deliberately bases the storm music on a highly dissonant chord which could belong to many possible keys, depending upon its resolution, and then *avoids* the resolution entirely. By working with a series of such chords strung together,

Figure 14.15 **Les Préludes**

Figure 14.16

he creates a supercharged intensity and tonal chaos. The calm "pastoral" scene which follows, with triads and key centers once more secure, is all the more effective because of the preceding turbulence.

Tension gradually grows stronger during the pastoral section as the harmonies become more intense and the overall register moves higher. As the "trumpet sounds," the original key of C is resumed. Two vaguely familiar tunes boom forth in the brasses and full orchestra. They are the two melodies originally associated with the lyric "love" passages, now transformed into a martial call to battle. The music increases in force, culminating in a restatement of the heroic, broad theme of the opening.

Les Préludes can be heard in many contexts: as a musical commentary upon a literary essay, or as an expanded concert piece for orchestra with its own musical shape. One could associate the various sections with the movements of a quasi-symphony, as suggested in Figure 14.19. Or, if the cyclic transformations are recognized, the entire work could be regarded as a set of variations. Finally, considering thematic successions and key relationships, we could hear the work as a sonata-form movement in C major

Figure 14.17

Notes with asterisks create ✓ contour of motive.

Figure 14.18

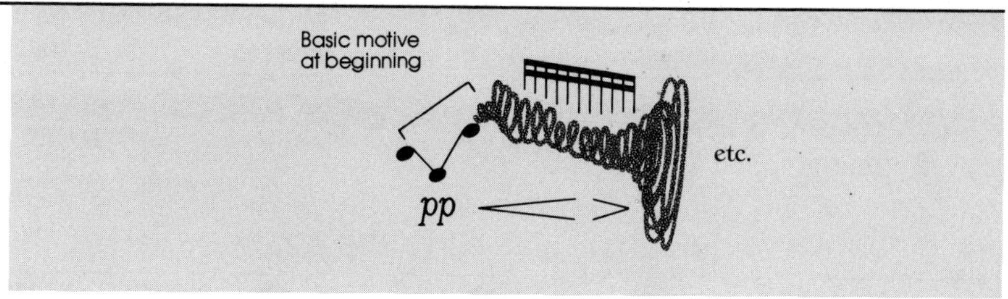

(Figure 14.20). The fascination here lies in the ambiguity: the fact that ***all*** of these interpretations are possible, and simultaneously valid.

Liszt used the same principles of thematic transformation and large single-movement structure in pieces without programs, most notably his Piano Sonata in B Minor and his two piano concertos. As with ***Les Préludes***, ambiguity makes the design all the more fascinating. The concertos also provide another aspect of the romantic concerto format, especially if compared to the Mendelssohn or Schumann concertos heard previously. The genial partnership of those examples has given way to a spirit of fierce competition. Liszt's soloist is a ''hero''—isolated, courageous, outnumbered by his antagonists (the orchestra) but able to stand up to them. Accordingly, Liszt writes a stunning virtuoso part for the soloist—big, bold, and aggressive, designed to stagger the sensibilities of a large audience. Liszt's piano writing is remarkable for its leaps, rapid scales, flying octaves, and a vast range of dynamics from whispers to booming thunderclaps. In a sense, anyone who has mastered such a part is already a ''superhuman'' being of sorts, and equipped to confront a symphony orchestra.

During Liszt's later years, religion became increasingly important to him. After a stay in Rome devoted to theological study, he took orders and became the Abbé Liszt. Those who could recall the diabolical, hedonistic image of the young virtuoso were either shocked or amused; Liszt, as always, embraced his own contradictions with good humor. He returned to Weimar to direct an institute for pianists, and found time to support the work of younger composers such as Grieg and Rimsky-Korsakov. And he continued to compose, in a much more experimental style than ever before, looking ahead to the new harmonic language of the twentieth century.

Figure 14.19

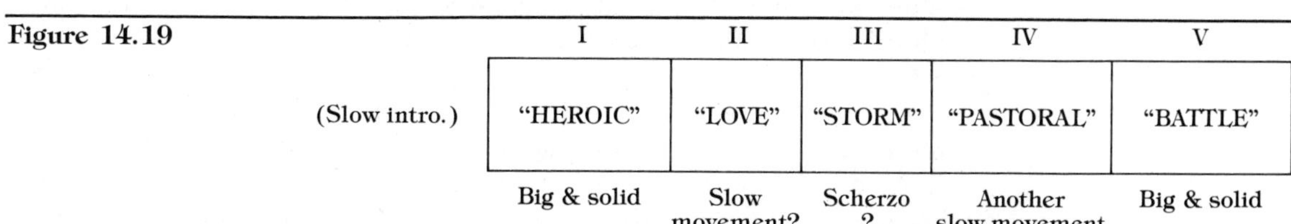

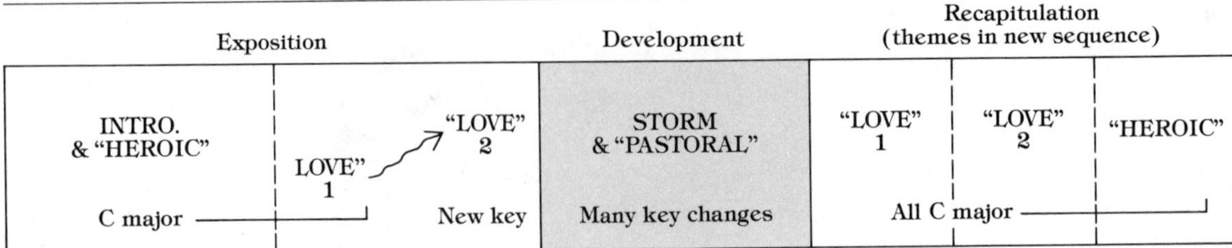

Figure 14.20

Wagner

The composer who did most to synthesize all the strands of romanticism was Richard Wagner (1813–1883). Wagner was the most important musician of his era, and in his last decades he had become the most important and the most controversial ***artist*** of the Western world. His ideas influenced the course of painting, poetry, philosophy, drama, and music. But that overpowering influence was felt much later in the century; this chapter will only trace his career through the late 1850s, by which time his major theories had been published and two of his most important works composed.

Significantly, although both works were created during the 1850s, ***Tristan und Isolde*** had to wait until 1865 and ***Die Walküre*** until 1870 for a public hearing. Wagner composed both without any specific commission or prospective performance. In this regard he typified the romantic composer's unique position of being a creator without an immediate audience. Although many works of this era were popular successes, other compositions were written with little hope of performance. They were created out of an inner urge, the composer's conviction that he had something important to say. Wagner, like Schumann, had great difficulty in coping with official music positions; he preferred to be a lone maverick, struggling to impress his unusual ideas upon the public. He succeeded only by virtue of his enormous energy and the strength of his convictions. (This may sound like a description of Beethoven! Indeed, Beethoven's unshakeable faith in himself was one of the qualities that endeared him to the romantics.)

Wagner's difficulties in securing performances for his music were compounded by the fact that he wrote elaborate ***stage*** works, radical approaches to the medium of opera. With very few exceptions, all of his music was composed for the stage. He grew up with a passion for the theater, perhaps influenced by his stepfather who was an actor and a dramatist. A boyhood love for Beethoven drew him to music as well, but to a kind of music that was intimately connected with poetry and drama. Wagner was convinced that "absolute" music had died with the choral Finale to Beethoven's Ninth Symphony, and that music's future lay in its alliance with words, gestures, and ritual, strengthening art's inherent moral power (another highly romantic assumption). Wagner gradually discovered that he could fuse the moral fervor and structural sophistication of the Beethoven symphony with theatrical needs and traditions. The result was a radically transformed kind of opera.

Operatic Tradition in Wagner's Time

As a nationalistic German, Wagner knew the history of German opera dating back to the early ***Singspiel*** (see Chapter 11). He certainly knew of the early romantic German operas based on myth and fairy tale; these appealed to German nationalism, not only by the use of the German language, but through reference to folk heroes and the medieval past.

Wagner realized that such isolated German landmarks did not add up to a glorious operatic tradition, although they constituted the beginning of one. The great tradition was still that of Italian opera, now transplanted to Paris in a luxurious French format known as ***grand opera.*** Paris was the great operatic center, and even Italian composers needed a successful production in Paris to prove that they had "arrived." Grand opera was characterized by spectacular staging and melodramatic plots. The traditional set "numbers" were still important; operatic structure was still centered about recitatives, arias, ensemble pieces, and choruses.

grand opera

Both grand opera and German romantic opera influenced Wagner's early work. His opera ***Rienzi*** was conceived in the grand opera tradition; in fact, it was completed during the composer's stay in Paris (1839–1842). Wagner moved on to a conducting position at Dresden, and there produced more of his own works. During the Dresden years, his harmonic style became increasingly chromatic, and his subject matter more reliant upon myth and legend. Robert Schumann wrote of him at this time: "Wagner is certainly a clever fellow, full of crazy ideas and audacious to a degree." Wagner's "crazy ideas" were often political, and he spoke freely on the subject of social reform. In the wake of the 1848 Dresden revolution, he realized that he had backed the wrong side. To escape imprisonment, he and his family fled Germany to settle in Zurich (Switzerland). This was not the first or last time that Wagner would be forced to change residence, or become deeply involved in controversy. His political views, amazing egotism, scandalous personal life, and colossal ingratitude to those who befriended him became well known in artistic circles.

Wagner's Theories of Music Drama

Wagner's ideas on the union of music and drama had crystallized and were set forth in two books, *Art and Revolution* (1849), and *Opera and Drama* (1852). The main premise of his esthetic was that opera should not be mere entertainment, but should be lofty and moral in tone. In the spirit of early Greek drama, it should use myth and folklore to raise the spirit of the national character. The theater was a place for edification, not trivial amusement. It followed that the ideal opera composer was not just a mere musician, but a dramatist and philosopher as well. The composer's job was to use the power of music for ethical purposes, appealing to his public as a minister does to his congregation; he should draw upon a variety of resources—instruments, voices, structural complexity, folklike simplicity—to influence the masses. (Here the ideal was Beethoven's Ninth Symphony.)

Wagner wanted audiences to experience a work in totality, as a unified ritual with magical, religious overtones. To this end he was concerned about the integration of music, poetry, drama, and stagecraft. He coined the term

Gesamtkunstwerk
music drama

Gesamtkunstwerk ("Total Art Work") for his operatic ideal, and referred to his own compositions as ***music drama*** rather than "opera." Wagner attempted to create a ***Gesamtkunstwerk*** with each of his own music dramas by controlling set design, stage effects, the choice of singers and conductors, and eventually the design of the opera house itself. He was also his own librettist, practicing his strong beliefs about poetry and text setting.

Wagner believed that myths and legends were ideal as subject matter: not Greek myths, but northern-European ones which would better represent the German spirit. The set numbers of traditional opera were abandoned in favor of "continuous melody" (as he called it) that could accommodate declamation, lyricism, prose, or poetry. His word settings tended to be heroic and a bit archaic, stressing alliteration rather than rhymed verse endings. Furthermore, he wanted the words clearly understood: a syllabic, rather than melismatic, setting (see Chapter 8), and realistic alternation of voices in dialogue rather than ensemble writing. Since people don't speak at the same time in real life, why should they sing simultaneously on stage? Of course many of these beliefs, including the inspiration of ancient Greek drama, echo the words of the Florentine Camerata and Monteverdi some 250 years earlier! Wagner did not know the early Florentine operas, but his instincts led him in similar directions.

Wagner's Musical Style

By "continuous melody" Wagner meant more than elimination of recitative-aria boundaries. He also desired a musical fabric with few strong cadences or tonal resting places: music continually in motion. Accordingly, his harmonic language became more ***chromatic.*** Individual chords or series of ***harmonies*** might be highly dissonant; entire chord progressions, tonally ambiguous in themselves, would become even more so if extended in sequences.

Wagner unified his chromatically fluid texture by using a series of distinctive motives, such as melodic fragments or chords, to stand for important elements in the drama: characters, objects, ideas, or emotions. These motives gave listeners something familiar to hang on to as the "continuous melody" unfolded. Wagner called these strong reference points ***leitmotifs*** ("leading motives"); a typical example is shown in Figure 14.21. They were crucial to the dramatic narrative: not only actions and words on stage, but the "inner" drama of psychological tensions, thoughts and motives.

leitmotif

Since a ***leitmotif*** is linked to some aspect of the drama, its musical appear-

Figure 14.21

ance later on refers back to that character, object or emotion. It provides access to inner thoughts and feelings not expressed in words, perhaps not even known to the characters themselves.

Leitmotifs are not long enough to make complete "statements" by themselves; because of their brevity they can be strung together in an extended fabric. They helped Wagner create his "continuous melody," steer away from cadences, and underscore the psychological drama—all at the same time. He could also create new leitmotifs by varying old ones, usually to stress dramatic relationships. He was simply employing the techniques of thematic transformation, character variation and idée fixe already known to many composers; it was the adaption to the context of opera that was startlingly original and highly effective.

Wagner's concern for the inner drama also led him to emphasize the orchestra, far beyond any operatic precedent of the past. Much of the emotional and psychological narrative is expressed in the orchestra pit, rather than on stage; most leitmotifs, in fact, are stated by the orchestra and not sung. And Wagner was one of the century's most brilliant orchestrators, able to coax undreamed-of sonorities out of the vast ensemble at his disposal. He required large orchestras for his music dramas. It was not unusual to have winds "in fours," a brass section of about twenty players, often including eight horns and special "Wagner tubas" that he devised himself, timpani, cymbals, drums, harps, and sixty to sixty-five strings.

Tristan und Isolde was composed during the period 1856–1859. It was drawn from a Celtic legend about a knight who, under the spell of magic (or is it the eternal spell of romance?), falls in love with the woman promised in marriage to his own king. The faithful knight Tristan and his beloved Isolde find that honor, willpower, and pride are no match for the consuming force of their mutual attraction. Their love eventually results in their death, but an ecstatic, joyous death that unites them in ultimate consummation of their passion. (Wagner called it ***Liebestod,*** "love-death.") The music drama transforms the myth, so that it is both a love story and an allegory glorifying passion and sacrifice. It is a study of intense emotion, but also a philosophical commentary on love, reason, guilt, responsibility, and justice.

Richard Wagner
Tristan Und Isolde: Prelude

R3 S2 B2

The orchestral introduction to Act I, which Wagner called a "prelude" rather than "overture," begins with a significant leitmotif (Figure 14.22) that dominates the entire music drama to come. In the later context of stage action, it will conjure up heated passions, yearning and tenderness. Even here one can sense that it is a remarkable passage, conveying a very special frame of mind. This opening phrase is highly dissonant and chromatic; as it repeats in sequences, it grows more achingly unresolved all the time. Al-

Figure 14.22

though each momentary fragment may appear to be tonal, the kaleidoscopic effect of constantly changing sequence renders the entire passage tonally meaningless. On the other hand, it has great *expressive* "meaning."

Wagner uses harmony, register (note the rising contour of the sequences), timbre, and dynamics to create an emotional crescendo of great power. At each peak, a climax occurs, but not a true release of tension. Wagner continues to build levels of intensity through sequences and unexpected modulations; cadences are continually being delayed or interrupted.

Listeners may feel that this orchestral Prelude could be a symphonic poem (á la Liszt) in its own right. There is some justification for this interpretation, if only because the actual music drama, once the curtain rises, is dominated by the orchestra. Although the two title roles are vocally overwhelming in their emotional and technical range, Wagner emphasizes the orchestral atmosphere of night, sea, and love's intoxication rather than the external plot. To quote Wagner's own advice, partly tongue-in-cheek, to someone about to attend a performance of ***Tristan***: "Take your glasses off, and hear nothing but the orchestra."

The Prelude has often been performed in concert, as though it were a tone poem. Because it was devised to maintain its tension directly into the opening curtain, the Prelude never reaches a point of tonal stability. In concert performance it is combined with ***Liebestod,*** the great "love-death" final scene, minus its vocal line. This combination creates a large symphonic poem of sorts. The ***Liebestod*** is built around a different melodic contour and churning chord sequence; as in the Prelude, continual expansion builds to a climax, this time an enraptured one. As the music fades away, the initial leitmotif of the Prelude reappears, now fully resolved in a serene cadence.

Tristan und Isolde was one of the great landmarks in the history of art and ideas. On musical grounds alone, it is fair to say that harmony and tonality were never the same again. Berlioz confessed that he was baffled by the harmony of the work; musicians have argued about, and marvelled at, the Prelude's opening chords for over a century. Of course, not everyone was equally impressed. Clara Schumann wrote, "It is the most repulsive thing I ever saw or heard in my life.'' As always, Wagner had the ability to excite controversy.

The composition of ***Tristan*** was actually a diversion of sorts, a change of pace for Wagner. During this period he was also engaged in a much more ambitious project, a cycle of four related music dramas based on Nordic myths. The entire cycle, written over a period of twenty-two years (1852–1874) was called ***Der Ring des Nibelungen*** (''The Ring of the Nibelung''), and its four component music dramas are: ***Das Rheingold*** (''The Rhine Gold''), ***Die Walküre*** (''The Valkyrie''), ***Siegfried,*** and ***Die Gotterdammerung*** (''The Twilight of the Gods'').

The detailed plot of the cycle is too complex to be recounted here. It involves gods, humans, giants, objects with magical properties, a dragon, elves, and so on, engaged in pursuit of a ring made from gold that originally lay at the bottom of the river Rhine. The ring has been cursed, so that those who choose to possess it must deny love. Wagner used this ancient tale as the springboard for a psychological drama; he understood the elemental power of myth to speak of human fears and hopes, even the ''unconscious.'' On that level, his vast cycle is not about gods or rings at all. It is, rather, an epic drama about materialism, the pursuit of power, the nature of human heroism, and the redeeming quality of love.

Die Walküre, second drama of the cycle, was composed between 1854 and 1856. The plot concerns a goddess named Brünnhilde, one of a race of warriors known as Valkyries who were given the task of carrying dead heros up to Valhalla, home of the gods. By Act III of the drama, Brünnhilde has become the focus of attention: she has betrayed and disobeyed her father, Wotan and must be punished. But at the ***beginning*** we are concerned only with humans. (They are, in fact, the first humans encountered in the ***Ring*** cycle, since all the characters of ***Das Rheingold*** were dwarfs or gods.) One of the humans, a young man named Siegmund, takes refuge in a simple dwelling amidst a furious thunderstorm. He has been fleeing his enemies, and is practically faint from exhaustion. The young wife of the household aids and revives him; we later learn that her name is Sieglinde. When her husband Hunding arrives on the scene, he discovers that Siegfried has killed one of his kinsmen. Although the stranger is permitted to spend the night, it is agreed that he and Hunding will fight to the death the next day.

The plot becomes complex with the expressive power conveyed by the orchestra. There is a ''continuous melody'' winding through the narrative, and much of it consists of orchestral leitmotifs. When Siegmund recalls that his father—who, we will discover, is Wotan, king of the Gods—had promised him a sword in time of need, a ''sword motif'' resounds. Later, as Sieglinde recalls a mysterious old man who appeared at her wedding feast and thrust a magic sword into a tree trunk a new motive (Figure 14.23) appears quietly; those who have seen the first drama of the cycle will recognize that as the motive of Valhalla. The audience may realize that the old man was Wotan, although this is still unknown to the characters.

Figure 14.23

Actually, Siegmund's promised sword and the old man's sword are one and the same. The young couple on stage realize that they are brother and sister, children of Wotan and a human mother, and deeply in love. Significantly, Wagner portrayed taboo love relationships in both *Tristan* and *Die Walküre.* Perhaps he wanted to nudge the repressed, middle-class morality of his listeners; he was also involved in a scandalous love affair of his own during the 1850s with the wife of a wealthy benefactor.

Since Siegmund and Sieglinde are guilty of a sinful, incestuous love, Wotan is obliged to bring about Sigmund's death in the fight with Hunding. He instructs Brünnhilde, who will be present, to see that Siegmund falls. Out of compassion, she disobeys; it is this willful disobedience that brings about Wotan's wrath in Act III.

Richard Wagner
Die Walküre: Act III, excerpts

Act III begins with the famous "Ride of the Valkyries" (see Figure 14.24), a brilliant orchestral prologue evoking the wild ride to the mountaintop where the Valkyries have gathered. The warrior goddesses have their own leitmotif which dominates the instrumental texture. The Valkyries' cries ("Hojoto! Heiha!") are one more element in the swirling, rushing fabric. Brünnhilde joins her comrades, bearing Sieglinde, who is not dead. Siegmund has been killed after all, Wotan having intervened to have his orders carried out, but Sieglinde will live to bear Siegmund's son; we will meet him in the next two music dramas as the hero Siegfried.

Moving closer to the end of the act, Wotan's wrath bends considerably in the presence of his beloved daughter: Wagner now turns his attention to a

Figure 14.24

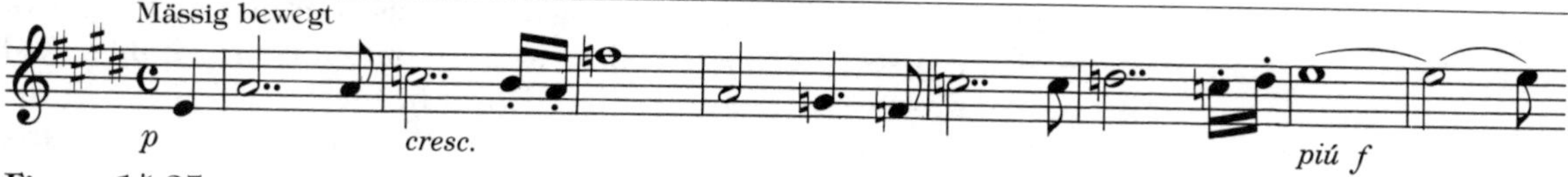

Figure 14.25

different kind of love, that of parent and child. The inner drama now revolves about justice, responsibility, and mercy. Wotan's punishment, then, is relatively mild. Brünnhilde loses her immortal powers and is put into a deep sleep, surrounded by a ring of magic fire that can only be broken by a true hero who knows no fear. The man who will rescue Brünnhilde is the yet unborn Siegfried; the audience realizes this, because Siegfried's leitmotif (Figure 14.25) becomes increasingly important. Wotan and his daughter embrace deeply (Figure 14.26), and as he sings to her she falls into a deep sleep. From this point on Wotan sings a soliloquy, close to an aria of traditional opera. The motive of "fate" appears just before Wotan points his spear towards the area he wishes surrounded by fire. Note, in Figure 14.27, the combination of leitmotifs: the "spear" merges with the beginnings of the "magic fire." As Brünnhilde sleeps among the flames, three motives can be heard at once: the bold motive of Siegfried, a reference to the slumbering Brünnhilde, and the ostinato figurations of the "magic fire music." As the curtain falls, the music dies away on the "fate motive."

Figure 14.26

Figure 14.27

Wagner's style is ideal for depicting human passions or the elements of nature—night, mists, fire, and so on. His orchestration is brilliantly suited to his subjects, as violent or as voluptuous as he chooses. His use of the voice is more controversial: Tchaikovsky felt that Wagnerian vocal parts were no more important to the total texture than the third horn of the orchestra! The harmonic language may be unsettling, as it was intended to be, but it is often basically tonal. The melodic and chordal structure of ***Die Walküre*** is much more diatonic and triadic than that of ***Tristan und Isolde.***

Parent-child relationships of great intensity as seen in two very different operas: a nineteenth-century artist's depiction of Wotan's farewell to Brunnhilde amidst the rising flames of the magic fire (below left), and a fierce dialogue between Gilda and Rigoletto (below right). Two more scenes from a staged production of ***Rigoletto*** opposite: the invocation of the curse (above), and the famous "quartet" in which two duets occur simultaneously on either side of a wall.

In fact, the entire Act III of *Die Walküre* is built on a dominant-tonic relationship, moving from an opening built on B to a vast E-major conclusion. Wagner's tonal narratives, like his dramatic ones, require a vast time span in which to assert themselves.

Verdi

Giuseppe Verdi (1813–1901), like Wagner, wrote music for the stage, but he did not have to reform his national traditions in order to do so. Opera *was* the national art of Italy, dominating the music scene to the virtual exclusion of other genres. (The instrumental sonata cycle held little interest for Italians.) In the tradition of Neapolitan opera and ***bel canto,*** Italian composers placed the singer first, emphasizing prominent, sweeping vocal lines and lyric melodies. The operas of Vincenzo Bellini (1801–1835), Gaetano Donizetti (1797–1848), and Gioacchino Rossini (1792–1868) typify the tradition that Verdi knew well: lyric, melodramatic in plot, vivid in emotional portrayal, and geared to the requirements of virtuoso singers (whom Robert Schumann, in a review, called "the canaries.")

Above all, Italian opera provided direct, immediate entertainment of the sort that Wagner despised, not a vehicle for profound philosophy. Many Italians found the esthetic weightiness of their northern neighbors rather silly. Rossini commented that ". . . When I read big, ugly words such as Progress, Decadence, Future, my stomach heaves." Similarly, Verdi dealt with stage action and emotion, not as the ceremonial enactment of ritual myth, but as a frankly realistic slice of life and a high level of melodrama.

With opera houses in every city and audiences eager for new works, Italian composers regarded their work as a practical craft. Unlike the uncompromising, revolutionary Wagner, Verdi tailored his music to meet the needs of production. During his early career he worked with whatever libretto he was given. He might have to write an opera in a few weeks to meet a deadline, or perhaps design it around a singer's vocal range, or a theater's closing hour. It was only *after* he became famous that Verdi exercised the sort of control over production that Wagner always assumed from the start.

Both composers, born in the same year, had equally slow beginnings to their careers. Verdi's first major opera, *Nabucco,* was produced in 1842, two years after Wagner's *Rienzi. Nabucco* was a huge success, not only because of its music, but because Italian audiences responded to the political implications of the Jews struggling against Nebuchadnezzar's Babylonians. During this period, most of northern Italy was still controlled by Austria, and revolutionary feelings were high. Listeners were quick to see the overtones in the many Verdi plots which dealt with oppressed peoples overthrowing their masters. The details of the plots were frequently altered in subtle ways to pass Austrian censors, but their meaning fooled no one.

Verdi was also blessed with a name that lent itself to a secret meaning.

When audiences cried *"Viva Verdi,"* or wrote those words as wall graffiti, they were not only referring to the composer but to **V**ittorio **E**mmanuele ***R**e* ***D'I****talia* (Victor Emmanuel, King of Italy), the symbol of a united nation. Verdi became such a genuine folk hero that he served as a member of the first Italian parliament. In his own way he was as great a nationalist as Wagner, an ardent patriot in his country's fight for unification.

By the 1850s, Verdi's musical style had become more subtle and complex. He was now in a position to choose subjects and librettists, and work directly on text and staging. His literary taste was outstanding, and he drew his plots from Schiller, Dumas, Hugo, and Shakespeare. Moreover, his use of the orchestra had become an integral part of the dramatic fabric, going beyond that of mere support for the voices. Most surprising of all, Verdi was also experimenting with the traditional format of set "numbers." He did not totally overthrow recitative and aria, in the Wagnerian manner, but he explored the idea of an entire act as an artistic entity, relating the succession of material to the large-scale drama. He wrote hardly any recitative for Act I of ***La Traviata,*** and very few solo arias in all of ***Rigoletto,*** conceiving this opera as "one long series of duets." It is not surprising, given these features and the stronger role of his orchestra, that Italian critics should have accused Verdi of drowning out the voice, and betraying the ***bel canto*** tradition!

Verdi composed three major operas during the 1850s: ***Rigoletto*** (1851), ***Il Trovatore*** (1853), and ***La Traviata*** (1853). Each of these reveals a fresh side of his musical personality. The first two are violent tragedies, filled with intrigue, horror, and supernatural references that delighted audiences. Both are inherently political, too, dealing with corruption in a courtly setting and with ghastly consequences.

Rigoletto was adapted from a play by Victor Hugo called ***Le Roi s/Amuse*** ("The King Amuses Himself"). The plot was so offensive to the Austrian censors that Verdi and his librettist were forced to change it. The despicable, lecherous monarch, originally the King of France, was converted to the Duke of an Italian state, and the period of the drama was moved back to the remote past. Rigoletto, the hunchbacked court jester who plays a crucial role, also worried the censors because of his physical deformity. But here Verdi defended his dramatic instincts, writing:

> In my view, the idea of this character, outwardly ridiculous and deformed, inwardly filled with passion and love, is superb. It was precisely because of these original traits that I chose the subject. . .

Briefly, the plot revolves around the Duke's insatiable passion for women, among them Rigoletto's daughter Gilda, who is abducted and raped by the monarch, and a curse placed upon Rigoletto and the Duke by an old man being led off to prison. Rigoletto conspires to have the Duke murdered, and eventually a hired assassin brings him a sack containing a body. But the body is that of his daughter Gilda instead. Rigoletto, horrified, cries "la maledizione" ("the curse") as the final curtain falls.

Giuseppe Verdi
Rigoletto: excerpts from Act III

R3 S1 B3

The final act of ***Rigoletto*** is famous for its "quartet," an ensemble number of four characters, each with a separate melody, text, and expressive mood, and for the Duke's great aria "La donna e mobile."

The aria appears early in the act, as the Duke enters a roadside inn (see Figure 14.28). The music captures his cynical, swaggering air, as he orders some wine and a room for the night. Rigoletto and Gilda watch him from another room through a chink in the wall: the opera stage is divided so that the audience can see both rooms.

As Rigoletto and Gilda secretly watch, the Duke begins to flirt with a young woman named Maddalena (who is, in fact, an accomplice of the assassin hired by the jester.) Rigoletto has wanted his child to see for herself that the Duke is a scoundrel, and he derives a certain grim satisfaction from the scene; Gilda, on the other hand, is heartbroken. The quartet, involving Rigoletto, Gilda, the Duke, and Maddalena, takes place on both sides of the wall. The lordly rake and his new lady friend are engaged in flirtatious by-play, while father and daughter express their own ambivalent feelings.

Verdi is careful to introduce each of the four lines separately before putting them together. Note, in Figure 14.29, that the lines retain their individual characters. The Duke's melody, a mock "love" song, is a *da capo* aria in itself; the others, responding and reacting to his presence, are more fitful in their outbursts of cynicism, grief or anger.

Listen to the very end of the opera if possible: here, in the midst of a raging storm, Rigoletto has the sack before him. He believes it contains the body of the Duke, until the impudent tune of "La donna e mobile," and the Duke's voice, sound in the distance. Verdi's decision to bring that tune back at the climax of the opera was a masterstroke.

Figure 14.28

La donna è mobile	*Woman is fickle*
Qual piuma al vento	*Like a feather in the wind,*
Muta d'accento	*She changes her words*
E di pensiero.	*And her thoughts.*

Duke:

Bella figlia dell'amore	*Beautiful daughter of love,*
Schiavo son de' vezzi tuoi;	*I am the slave of your charms;*
Von un detto sol tu puoi	*With a single word you can*
Le mie pene consolar. etc.	*Console my sufferings. etc. . .*

Maddalena:

Ah! Ah! rido ben di core,	*Ha, ha! I laugh heartily, for*
Chè tai baie costan poco.	*such flattery costs very little.*
Quanto valga il vostro gioco	*Believe me, I can judge how*
Mel credete, so apprezzar.	*much your game is worth. . .*

Gilda:

Ah! cosi parlar d'amore. . .	*Ah! To speak that way of love. . .*
a me pur l'infame ho udito!	*now I too have heard the villain!*
Infelice cor tradito,	*Unhappy, betrayed heart,*
Per angoscia non scoppiar.	*Do not burst with anguish, no! etc. . .*
Ah, no! etc. . . .	

Rigoletto:

Taci, il piangere non vale.	*Be quiet, weeping has no value.*
Ch'ei mentiva sei sincura.	*You know that he was lying;*
Taci, e mia sarà la cura	*Be quiet, and I will take care*
La vendetta d'affrettar. etc. . . .	*to hasten vengeance. etc. . . . .*

Figure 14.29

As noted earlier, Verdi planned ***Rigoletto*** as a series of duets. Apart from a few arias and the celebrated ensembles, two-part vocal texture pervades the work; even the famous quartet can be viewed as two simultaneous duets, sung on either side of the wall. The duets between Rigoletto and Gilda are especially touching; they reveal a warm, human side to this monstrous-looking figure of a jester. Throughout his long career, Verdi depicted parent-child relationships most sensitively, and often made them critical to his plots. Armchair psychologists have often speculated on the fact that Verdi never had mature relationships with his own children. The unexpected deaths of his first wife and small infants constituted the great tragedy of his life.

The third Verdi opera of the early 1850s was called ***La Traviata,*** based on the well-known novel and play by Dumas, "La Dame aux Camelias" ("The Lady of the Camelias"). ***La Traviata*** can be translated as "The Strayed One." Its plot concerns a beautiful, seemingly heartless courtesan who comes to know genuine love, only to die of consumption. The swashbuckling, epic quality of other Verdi works is missing here; in its place we have a bourgeois tragedy of manners and morals, staged in the present, in contemporary dress. The novelty of the staging and the scandalous subject matter—a "loose woman" as sympathetic heroine—puzzled audiences at the 1853 premiere. To make matters worse, the star soprano who played the frail Violetta that evening was a stout, un-consumptive looking lady; some viewers laughed out loud. But a new production of ***La Traviata*** the following year was successful, and the opera has been a favorite ever since.

The work abounds in lovely melodies, undoubtedly a major reason for its huge popularity. But other aspects of Verdi's art are equally impressive. His use of the ***orchestra*** had become just as sensitive and dramatically important, in its own way, as Wagner's. Themes associated with Violetta's love or tragic illness are heard at times as orchestral "leitmotifs" while other action takes place on stage. Note, too, how ***chromatic harmony*** underlies the more impassioned, anguished moments of the drama. Finally, the separate numbers succeed each other in an organic way, making an entire act one artistic whole. This is especially so in Act I, with almost all of the action taking place against a background of festive, frivolous partying and military band music. (Audiences might have wondered where to applaud!)

Giuseppe Verdi

La Traviata: excerpts from Acts I and III

The opening Prelude is brief but poignant, concentrating upon two dramatic elements: the illness and death of Violetta, and her heartfelt love for Alfredo Germont. The music then plunges into the gay social whirl of a soirée. Alfred and Violetta notice each other amid the crowd of noisy, fashionable guests. He raises his glass in a drinking toast (Figure 14.30), and she adds a toast of her own.

Alfredo:

Libiamo, libiamo ne'lieti calici,	*Let us drink, let us drink from the cheerful cups*
Che la bellezza infiora;	*which are wreathed with beauty,*
e la fugge vol ora s'inebrii a voluttà	*and may the fleeting hour*
	be intoxicating with voluptuousness.

Figure 14.30

Later, the two of them have a chance to speak undisturbed. Alfredo confesses his love: Violetta hands him a flower, and asks him to return "when it has faded." She then embarks on an elaborate closing scene of her own, beginning with a recitative: "How strange! How strange! His words are burned upon my heart. Would a real love be a tragedy for me?" The recitative leads to a slow, melting aria (known as a "cavatina") featuring the alternation of one major and one minor-key theme, both in triple meter. The section in F minor appears to be tentative and hesitant, whereas the more expansive F-major passage reveals Violetta's need for real love (see Figure 14.31). A new recitative, dramatic and angry, intrudes upon this mood. Violetta cries out, "Follie! Follie! Delirio vano. . ." ("All is folly! This is mad delirium!"), and plunges headlong into a new aria (Figure 14.32) at a much faster tempo.

In a spirit of forced gaiety, Violetta declares her vow to continue pursuing an independent life of pleasure. Her vocal line traces an ornate, vituosic arc of rapid scales, trills, and high notes: the climax of her extended monologue of recitative-aria-times-two. The brilliant fireworks are not only exciting for an audience, but dramatically justified by the plot and the flighty characterization Verdi has given her.

By the final act of *La Traviata,* that characterization has undergone severe changes. The two lovers have already consummated their affair, but she has broken off the relationship at the urging of Alfredo's father. She is now a deeply saddened woman, and in dangerously ill health, in fact, near death. Verdi created a difficult role here in more ways than one. The technical facility demanded of Violetta is matched by the *acting* skill necessary to create convincing changes of personality. Violetta has been transformed

Ah, fors'è lui che l'anima
Solinga ne tumulti
Godea sovente pingere
De'suoi colori occulti! . . .

Ah, perhaps it is he who my soul,
lonely in the midst of tumult,
often secretly depicted with pleasure!

- -A quell amor ch'è palpito
Dell'universo intero. etc. . . . .

Ah, this love which is the heartbeat
of the entire universe.

Figure 14.31

from the shallow, brittle worldliness of Act I, through the radiancy and pain of sincere love (Act II), to the state at which we now find her.

One of Act III's memorable moments occurs as Violetta, in her weakened condition, quietly reads a letter to herself. Against the spoken reading, there is a shimmering orchestral background drawn from one of the great loves themes of the opera, the F-major passage heard in Violetta'a Act I monologue and later used for a tender love duet. The reappearance of this melodic fragment here is especially moving. At the end of the act, when Alfredo and his father are at the dying woman's bedside, the same thematic fragment returns. It is extended chromatically as Violetta feels a final, sud-

Figure 14.32

Sempre libera degg'io
Folleggiare di gioia etc.

Always free, I must flutter
from one enjoyment to the next.

den rush of vitality: "E strano! Cessarono gli spasmi del dolore. . ." ("How strange! The deadly pains and faintness are gone . . . I feel my life returning! What rapture!") At this, she falls back, dead.

Verdi was no less romantic a figure, given the tradition he served, than his German colleagues. He understood the expressive power of chromaticism, the wider relationships of tonality and the principles of the "leitmotif" in building musical narrative. His orchestra went beyond the level of simple accompaniment to moments of real brilliance. And as an ardent Italian patriot, he infused his art with a profound sense of national spirit, a subject to be examined more fully in the next chapter.

15

Late Romanticism and Nationalism

Our (Italian) composers are not good patriots. If the Germans, stemming from Bach, arrive at Wagner, they are doing as good Germans should. . . . But for us, descendants of Palestrina, to imitate Wagner is to commit a musical crime . . .

Verdi

The Music of the Future

Verdi's words, quoted above, indicate two predominant features of late nineteenth-century music: intense nationalism, and the powerful influence of Richard Wagner. Wagner's dominance extended far beyond the borders of Germany; composers of all countries were excited by his controversial innovations. Although quite a few composers disputed his ideas and works, nobody could ignore them.

By the time of Wagner's death in 1883, he had realized virtually all of his early, seemingly impossible ambitions, and was the most commanding artistic figure in Europe. He had found an enthusiastic patron in Ludwig II (the "Mad King") of Bavaria. Ludwig supported the construction of a festival theater, designed to meet Wagner's own specification, in the little town of Bayreuth. This theater was remarkable for its mechanical innovations, including a covering for the orchestra pit. Wagner wanted his orchestra almost completely under the stage, to eliminate distractions that might counteract the ***Gesamtkunstwerk*** spell, and to create acoustical balance between

The elderly Liszt, in his clerical garb, is shown seated at the piano. His listeners include his daughter Cosima (at the left, holding a fan) and Richard Wagner (to Cosima's left, with an open book on his lap).

vocal and instrumental timbre. (Coincidentally, Monteverdi's *Orfeo* orchestra of 1607 had been placed behind the stage area, perhaps for some of the same reasons.) The first major Bayreuth event was a presentation of the entire *Ring* cycle in 1876, and the Bayreuth festivals rapidly became known as a place of pilgrimage for all those attracted to the Wagnerian movement.

Franz Liszt remained a staunch champion of Wagner's music. By one of the more improbable twists of history, he had become Wagner's father-in-law as well: Liszt's daughter Cosima, who had been romantically involved with Wagner for years, eventually left her husband, the conductor Hans von Bülow, for Wagner. The music of Liszt and Wagner shared many stylistic traits as well, and it was inevitable that critics and followers should link the two composers to a "school." The philosophy of Liszt and Wagner became associated with a convenient catch-phrase: "The Music of the Future." This slogan was used with equal passion by those who adored the music and those who despised it.

The slogan had an oddly political ring to it. That was not surprising, in view of Wagner's talent for polarizing the world about him, creating either worshipful converts or deadly antagonists. He had created not just a body of art works, but an entire esthetic known as Wagnerianism, midway between a religion and a radical political party. The phrase was also strangely accurate as prophecy: it underlined the sense of an age coming to an end. In many respects Liszt and Wagner went beyond romanticism, much as Beethoven had expanded the limits of classicism for an earlier generation. Their highly programmatic, ultra-chromatic music had developed beyond all expectations, with tonality pushed almost to its breaking point, and the older forms dissolved into a fluid, through-composed continuum.

In many ways, of course, the Wagner-Liszt style looked backward, rather than to the future, summing up many musical tendencies that had existed throughout the nineteenth century. Thus the "music of the future" could also be interpreted as a synthesis of the past. Whether "past" or "future," a composer's response might very well be the same: after Wagner, what more can be done? Where do we go from here? Those were difficult questions to answer. Wagner's influence was as overpowering, for the end of the nineteenth century, as Beethoven's had been at the century's beginning.

Some Wagnerian ideas reflect nonmusical concerns of the time. One might interpret the concept of ***Gesamtkunstwerk,*** all the arts contributing to a unified goal, in the light of Marxist socialism; similarly, the notions of "continuous melody" and "thematic transformation" can be related to Darwinian evolution. For musicians, there were more specific issues raised by Wagner: chromaticism, tonality, the expanded orchestra, form, music as an instrument of national myth, and the like. The most devoted Wagnerian composers explored genres other than opera, perhaps not wishing to compete with their idol on his own ground. A number of composers concentrated upon songs or symphonies. In the area of the symphony, the shadow of Beethoven still loomed very large; moreover, the late nineteenth century fondness for folk material (which we will note shortly) provided the symphonic composer with fresh problems and challenges.

Brahms

Johannes Brahms (1833–1897) was most definitely not a Wagnerian, and found his name used with increasing fervor (if not always with his permission) as the symbol of opposition to the "music of the future." In truth, he was not unimpressed with Wagner's work, although he found Liszt's music a bore; Wagner in turn had some kind words to say about Brahms. The seemingly intense "feud" between the two composers was really created by their partisan supporters on both sides. Brahm's standing among the Wagnerians was hurt by the fact that, early in his career, he had signed a manifesto opposed to the ideals of Wagner and Liszt. Two other journalistic comments, both intended as compliments, aroused further controversy. One of these was the famous linking together of the names Bach, Beethoven, and Brahms: the "three Bs." Secondly, Brahms's First Symphony was labeled "the Tenth" by one writer—the first new work deemed fit to stand beside the Beethoven Ninth, or at least interpreted that way by many music lovers.

Brahms and Wagner became figureheads in a heated rivalry between those who believed in classic forms and genres and those who spoke for revolutionary Wagnerian ideals. It was assumed that if you liked the music of one composer, you would therefore find the other totally unacceptable. This may seem puzzling from a late twentieth century vantage point; today it is possible to enjoy the work of both composers (or dislike both) equally! After a century or so, their similarities have become more significant than their differences.

Influences on Brahms

The music of Brahms is "romantic" in its harmony and emotional expressiveness, but "classic" in its restraint and concern for formal balance. Structural clarity was important to Brahms, and he was deeply drawn to the music of Beethoven, not the "radical" liberating myth of Beethoven, but the painstaking craftsman building complex forms. In the area of symphony, Brahms found the figure of Beethoven so intimidating that he waited until the age of forty-three, after many false starts and rejected plans, to bring out his own First Symphony. He was also interested in J. S. Bach, and studied Bach's scores intently. (By Brahms's lifetime, the complete works of Bach and Handel were being collected, edited, and published. Brahms actively supported both projects, and subscribed to both series.) Significantly, he was one of the few romantic composers to use counterpoint as a natural, comfortable aspect of his texture.

Brahms also loved the music of Schubert (ironically, neither a patient craftsman nor a polyphonist) and composed Viennese waltzes and Lieder with Schubertian spirit. He confided in friends that he envied Schubert, not only for his unbelievable facility but for the times he had lived in, when the romantic age was just flowering, when great musical schisms of "form" versus "expression," or serious versus popular, had not yet developed, when Vienna was the center of the musical universe and Beethoven walked its streets. It was in Vienna that Brahms, a native of northern Germany, chose to live.

The influence of Robert and Clara Schumann was perhaps strongest of all. Brahms was a young man of twenty, just beginning to make a musical name, when he first met the Schumanns. Clara was thirty-three, and married to an increasingly withdrawn father-figure ten years older than she. Robert became a "father" to Brahms as well: he praised Brahms in print, helped promote his career, encouraged his classic instincts and steered him away from the Wagner-Liszt camp. Schumann's tragic end came as a great shock to Brahms, and must have complicated what was already a terribly complicated relationship with Clara. It has been claimed that Brahms and Clara Schumann were lovers; one could also argue that their love was more "platonic," on the level of deepest friendship. It's entirely possible, of course, that both statements are true: their relationship may have gone through changes over the years. Clara was undeniably the most important woman in Brahms's life. He never married, a fact that amateur psychologists explain in a variety of ways: his double standard towards women (hav-

Johann Strauss (left) and Brahms were important figures in the revival of Vienna as a major musical capital. "Vienna" (right top) became synonymous, for many listeners, with the splendor of opera [its elegant Opera House (right below) is seen here in a contemporary print] and the gayety of the waltz.

ing practically grown up playing the piano in Hamburg's sleazier brothels), his mother fixation, his abiding love for Clara Schumann. In any event, he remained a bachelor; his eccentric, gruff ways and ironic wit became legendary—in the tradition of that earlier unmarried Viennese, Beethoven. His presence in Vienna, and that of the "waltz king" Johann Strauss, brought the city back to musical prominence. The close relationship with Clara Schumann lasted 43 years, from their first meeting in 1853 until her death, one year before Brahms's own, in 1896.

Brahms's Style and Works

Dense textures and a fondness for warm, low registers can be heard in much of Brahms's music. He often seems determined *not* to provide the brilliant sonorities of the Berlioz-Wagner-Tchaikovsky orchestra, or the piano of Chopin and Liszt, favoring mellow timbres instead. His harmony is chromatic and romantically expressive, but within a tonal context of clear key relationships. Brahm's melodic lines are broad and expansive, often stated in great sweeping phrases. But they are rarely extroverted or sentimental; the composer had little use for the self-indulgent, theatrical aspects of romanticism. Textures are frequently contrapuntal in subtle ways that may not reach the ear on first hearing: canonic imitation embedded within seemingly simple lyric passages, for example. Rhythms are equally complex, including syncopation and a special fondness for the interaction of duple and triple patterns.

Brahms enjoyed the challenge of adapting romantic chromaticism to the classic formal structures of sonata, rondo, variations and the like. Accordingly, he wrote music in such traditional genres as the symphony, concerto and string quartet. In these, he explored large-scale formal schemes and cyclic relationships. Whereas Schumann, Mendelssohn, and Liszt wrote symphonies with extra-musical subtitles such as "Spring," "Italian" or "Dante," the four Brahms symphonies are simply listed by number. Moreover, there are no symphonic poems in his catalog.

Although he wrote many intense, expressive piano pieces, here, too, he kept to simple titles such as "Rhapsody" or "Intermezzo." Programmatic music was obviously ***not*** an interest of his. He reserved literal meaning for those compositions that contained words: his many songs and impressive choral works. (Brahms was first known in Vienna as a choral conductor.) Lighter works for amateur performers—waltzes, choral numbers, and mildly ethnic "Hungarian" dances—were immensely popular as well.

Variations: A Classic Approach

Nowhere did Brahms reveal his synthesis of classic and romantic tendencies more readily than in his approach to the variation form. The fact that he wrote variations at all, rather than "fantasias" or tone poems, is itself the mark of a traditionalist. But beyond that, Brahms shows a fascinating hybrid attitude towards variation technique: a cross between the classic desire to ornament a theme while retaining its formal contours, and the romantic urge to "disguise" the theme within a series of character pieces. Remarkably, Brahms often manages to do both at the same time.

One of his best known works in this genre is the ***Variations on a Theme by Haydn,*** written in 1873. In listening to the opening theme (which scholars now suspect was not actually written by Haydn), we are struck by its solid diatonic harmony in the key of B♭ major and its asymmetrical balancing of phrase groups. There are two phrases, each five measures long (rather than the usual four), and then a repeat of these two phrases. The second section of the theme has two phrases of four measures each, then a return to part of the opening tune, resolving on an extended pedal point over the note B♭.

Brahms takes care to retain many of these features in the first eight variations following the theme. All of the variations maintain the peculiar phrase structure of 5 (bars)–5: 4–4–4–7. The key of B♭ and the general harmonic scheme of the theme are adhered to as well. Brahms's romantic sensibility, however, led him to make the eight variations remarkably dissimilar in mood and color. Variations number 2, 4, and 8 are all cast in the minor mode but present striking contrasts in tempo. The graceful, lyric qualities of Variations 1, 3, and 7 differ sharply from the scherzo-like brilliance of no. 5, or the vigorous, athletic nature of no. 6. After these eight variations, Brahms adds an elaborate finale (basically an extended ninth variation), in itself a series of connected variations built on a melodic "ground" bass line* derived from the theme. Like the theme's opening phrase, the ground-bass line is five measures long. Of course, the "ground" and its contrapuntal elaboration are more associated with the Baroque than with the late nineteenth century. Brahms's attachment to the past enabled him to adapt traditional techniques to his own needs. (The grand finale itself, even one built on a repeated ground, is actually a highly romantic gesture!)

A German Requiem

Brahms was a fine choral conductor; indeed, the only official position he ever held was the directorship of the Vienna Singakedemie. He also composed a number of outstanding choral works. One well-known example is ***Ein Deutsches Requiem*** ("A German Requiem") for chorus, soprano and baritone soloists, and large orchestra. This piece was composed over a period of eleven years, originally conceived as a memorial to Robert Schumann, and then spurred on by the death of Brahms's mother in 1865. It was completed in 1868, and was his first large-scale work to capture public attention. (It was also his first attempt at a major work without a virtuoso piano part for himself.)

In studying medieval and Renaissance music (Chapter 8), we discussed the structure and significance of the Catholic Mass. The ***Requiem*** Mass, or Mass for the Dead, has always occupied a very special place—for many people, a terrifying one—within the liturgy. It has its own traditional Latin texts and Gregorian melodies; one such melody, the ***Dies Irae,*** was noted earlier with reference to the Berlioz ***Symphonie Fantastique*** (Chapter 13).

Brahms was not composing a setting of the Catholic Requiem Mass at all. His title—"A German Requiem"—might just as easily have been "A Protestant Requiem." He chose texts from the German translations of the Bible (Old and New Testaments), rather than the customary Latin liturgy. His aim was not to pray for the souls of the dead, but to offer hope, consolation, and faith to the living.

Johannes Brahms
Eine Deutsches Requiem

R4 S1 B2

Movement I Brahms's highly personal Requiem begins with the following text. The first two lines derive from Matthew, while the rest come from Psalm 126. Throughout the composition, Brahms continues this practice of combining phrases from different sources, relating them solely to his expressive purposes.

*In this it resembles the genre of "Dido's Lament" by Purcell, studied during Part 1.

Johannes Brahms

Ein Deutsches Requiem (Erster Teil)	*A German Requiem* *(Opening Portion)*
Selig sind, die da Leid tragen, denn sie sollen getröstet werden. Die mit Tränen säen, werden mit Freuden ernten. Sie gehen hin und weinen und tragen edlen Samen, und kommen mit Freuden und bringen ihre Garben.	*Blessed are they who mourn,* *for they will be comforted.* *They who sow in tears* *will reap in joy.* *They will go forth weeping,* *bearing precious seed,* *and will return rejoicing,* *bringing their sheaves with them.*

The music begins with instruments alone. Against a repeated pedal note (see Figure 15.1), a rich strong texture grows from a series of imitative entrances. Brahms has intentionally omitted violins from this movement, using only violas, cellos, and contrabasses. In this way he achieves dark, warm timbres throughout. The chorus enters in simple chordal style, at first maintaining the same pedal point and then expanding to a smooth harmonic progression. Choral and orchestral sonorities alternate for a while, as though the two forces are hesitant about combining. When the two joint (at "Denn sie sollen geströstet werden") the passage grows in intensity, and then subsides.

Just when a relaxed cadence is expected, a new section begins at the words "Die mit Tranen." It is more impassioned and chromatically driving, and then gains rhythmic vitality and a brisk, rising inflection as the concept of "joy" ("werden mit Freuden") becomes paramount. As the phrase concludes, it comes to rest in an unexpected key, only to descend back to the original tonic pedal point. The music of the opening now returns, with a different text (at the line "Sie gehen") and changes in texture. Note that the chorus has now been integrated into the unfolding imitative fabric over the pedal bass. The more intense chromatic material is heard as well, and the rising "joyous" lines (on the words "dommen mit Freuden") once more subside in the secondary key.

Figure 15.1

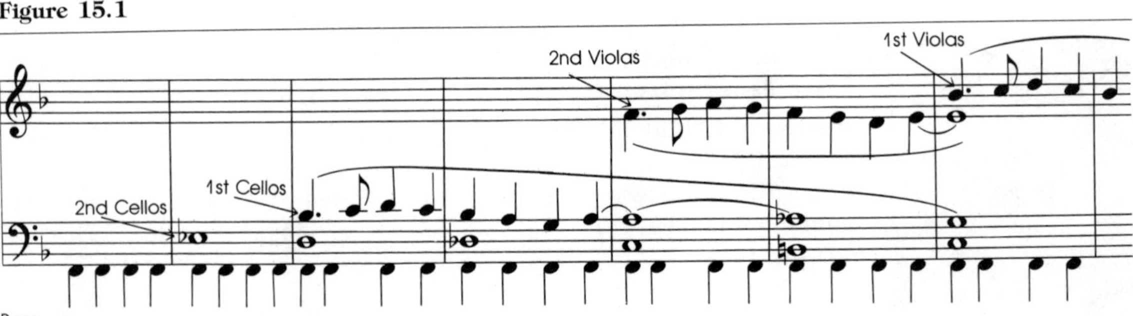

The new tonality stresses a pedal-point repetition of its own. Through a subtle chromatic shift of focus, it miraculously returns to the original tonic again. The opening material is stated a third time, against the original lines of text. A series of falling imitative lines, peacefully fading away, provides a brief coda for the movement. (That coda recurs at the very end of the final movement as well, thus rounding off the entire work.) The form of the opening movement can be interpreted as an extended part form: A B A′ B′ A″, with B containing two distinctly contrasted motives, followed by a coda.

Brahms was not a religious man in the conventional sense, and critics have noted that the name Christ never appears in the Requiem text. However, he knew the Bible and the Psalms well, and was deeply concerned about the great problems of existence—enough to attempt a personal statement of his own. As he described it to a friend, the ***Requiem*** was "not a theological argument, but a human document."

Brahms and the Sonata Cycle

During the late nineteenth century Brahms dominated the world of "absolute" music just as Verdi and Wagner ruled the musical stage. He had strong feelings about structural proportion, the articulation of key relationships, and cyclic unity. Taking his cue from Beethoven, Brahms was adept at treating successive movements as though they were acts in a play: gradually increasing and relaxing tension, saving his strongest statements for the end. These traits can be observed in all his sonata-cycle works.

They are especially striking in his concertos, since in dealing with this genre Brahms, like Schumann and Mendelssohn, was working against the tradition of virtuoso showmanship that had come to dominate his century. His concertos are, in essence, tightly integrated symphonies for solo and orchestra, rather than shallow, dazzling display pieces. Brahms composed one violin concerto, a double concerto for violin and cello, and two weighty piano concertos intended for his own appearances as soloist. The Piano Concerto no. 2, composed in 1881, is a gigantic work, with four large movements rather than the usual three. The extra movement, a powerful Scherzo placed as Movement II, is especially bold and aggressive—stronger, in fact, than many inner movements of Brahms's symphonies. Contemporary critics, disappointed at its lack of flashiness, tried to damn the work by calling it a piece of "chamber music." From Brahms's viewpoint, of course, that remark could be taken as a compliment.

Johannes Brahms

Piano Concerto no. 2 in B♭ Major, opus 83

R4 S2 B2

Movement I: Allegro non troppo The concerto begins with the piano in the understated role of quasi-accompanist, echoing a lyric horn motive (Figure 15.2). Note that the motive actually consists of two brief figures, one

Figure 15.2

beginning with a rising arc and the other a falling one. The second part of each figure (with the rhythm [triplet eighths, quarter, dotted half], bracketed above) seems to be stressed: it is this fragment which is heard in the pianist's "echoes." One might assume that the opening scale line B♭ C D will not figure prominently during the movement, since it is not emphasized at the outset. In fact, Brahms's concern for organic development will lead him to find important uses for that rising scale figure later on.

The relaxed gesture of the opening is suddenly cut short by an angular phrase for piano, stressing abrupt dotted rhythms. The orchestra has dropped out as the soloist moves incessantly forward, driving to a strong cadence in the tonic B♭ major. At this point the orchestra seizes the opening motive, and restates it vigorously. New material is introduced by the orchestra as well, in the manner of an old-fashioned double exposition; the motives of the second theme group are now presented without the soloist. Most prominent among these are a broad, lyrically flowing line (Figure 15.3), and an angry, jagged passage centered about another related key, with dotted rhythms reminiscent of the earlier piano solo. At a sudden harmonic shift, the soloist returns again, reminding us of the opening motive and pushing the focus back to the tonic key. This section reaches its peak at a *ff* state-

Figure 15.3

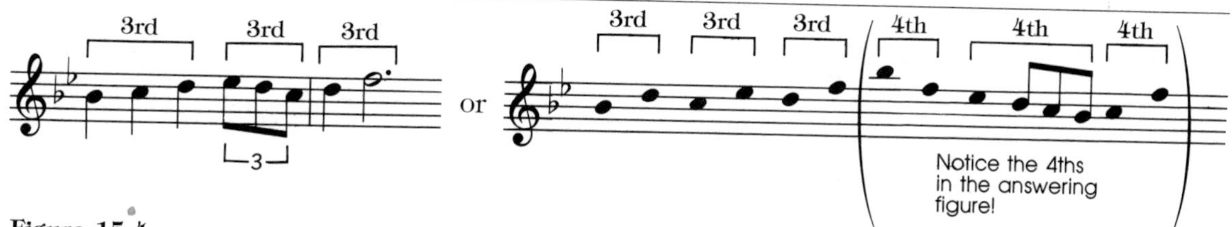

Figure 15.4

ment of the opening three notes (B♭ C D) by the full orchestra, solidly in B♭ major. The three notes are hammered out again with different harmonization and then repeated in faster rhythms and higher pitches, leading to the second descending figure of the opening motive. As far as the movement's key scheme is concerned, Brahms is only *now* prepared to leave the tonic. (Remember, the second theme group has not yet been played by the soloist!)

Obviously Brahms has stretched the dimensions of sonata form, very much as Beethoven did in his larger works. And, like Beethoven, Brahms enjoys making every gesture "developmental." Although the exposition is not yet complete, fascinating relationships among the motivic fragments are being explored: the use of angular dotted rhythms, and the prominence of 3rds and 4th. These are indicated in Figure 15.4.

The rest of the exposition brings back the second-group motives, introduced by a new bridge idea in the orchestra (see Figure 15.5) and expanded at length by the pianist. The dominant of F major is reached, leading to a stormy climax, and gradually subsiding to a plaintive minor variant of the opening horn-call motive, complete with its piano "echo." By this point, the development section has begun. It is difficult to state where one section begins and the other ends, because Brahms is not working with self-contained sections. Instead, he approaches sonata form as a continuous process, and unfolding of thematic and tonal relationships.

The development moves to a number of distantly related keys, and reveals new aspects of familiar material: for example, a light, rippling passage (Figure 15.6) that stresses dotted rhythms, and a consistent use of 3rds and 4ths. There is a gradual crescendo, and an extended sequence built on a variant of the horn call's descending figure. This passage finally leads to a bold *ff* statement of three chords, the rising scale line ♩ ♩ ♩ of

Figure 15.5

Figure 15.6

the horn call, in a very unlikely key. The intensity lessens a bit, but then comes rushing back; the three-note motto repeats, and then continues sequentially to a stunning climax on F major (see Figure 15.7). F major is, of course, the dominant of B♭: precisely the tonal goal that an eighteenth-century composer would have aimed for at this stage of a sonata-form movement in B♭. Brahms has maintained the traditional hierarchy of arrival points within the key scheme. His *means* of arrival reveal his romantic leanings.

The passage gently eases back into the tonic key and the recapitulation with amazing smoothness. Against a quiet piano ostinato pattern, the horn-call figure, now played by strings and oboes, emerges from the texture; it only reaches a fully relaxed B♭ cadence as the piano "echo" begins. Note the great calm achieved by omitting the angry dotted-rhythm passage as the recapitulation proceeds. On the other hand, the turbulent motives of the second group grow in a great crescendo. Another rising sequence leads away from the tonic. But there is a sudden shift back to B♭ for a strong coda based on the horn call.

How does Brahms follow such a complex, dramatic movement as this? Surprisingly, by not letting up on the tension: the Scherzo is powerful and

Figure 15.7

rhythmically unsettling. The slow movement, placed third in the sequence, has a long *arioso* line and highly expressive writing for solo cello and oboe. But the final movement is gentle and light: a sparkling rondo, with a Hungarian "gypsy" flavor to one of the tunes. Brahms loved dance music, and in the context of this concerto the lilting phrases and gentle scoring, with trumpets and drums notably absent, are joyous as well as ingratiating.

Italian Opera: Late Verdi, Puccini, and "Verismo"

Italian opera of this period was dominated by the figure of Giuseppe Verdi, whose longevity was matched only by his continued ability to grow creatively. In 1871 he composed *Aïda,* commissioned by the Cairo Opera to celebrate the opening of the Suez Canal. Set in ancient Egypt, *Aïda* is filled with pageantry and spectacle along the lines of grand opera, but it is also a personal, human drama of great expressive impact. By this time Verdi was a revered national hero. After Wagner's death in 1883, Verdi was the sole "grand old man" of musical theater; he was now in his seventies, and it was assumed that he would not compose again. With surprising creative energy, he went on to create two more operas, *Otello* (1887) and *Falstaff* (1893), both based upon plays by Shakespeare.

Did Wagner's influence, so powerful throughout Europe, exert itself over Verdi's three late operas? Although the increased importance of his orchestra or the use of "motto" themes might indicate such a connection, Verdi always denied it. He had great respect for Wagner's work: indeed, on Wagner's death he wrote, "A great personality has gone from us, a name which will leave the most powerful imprint upon the history of art." However, Verdi was a "great personality" in his own right. Many of the "Wagnerian" features of *Otello,* for example, can be traced back to Verdi's own precedents in *Rigoletto* or *La Traviata.*

verismo

By the last decade of Verdi's life, a passion for realism began to dominate the Italian operatic stage. The 1890s and early 1900s witnessed a turn towards an extreme form of realism known as *verismo.* The strongest quality of *verismo* was its supposed faithfulness to real-life situations: ordinary people caught in webs of great crisis, or violent confrontations, or sordid poverty. The mood of *verismo* was not exclusively Italian or turn-of-the-century. We may find it in fiction and drama by Ibsen, Chekhov, and Zola. Nevertheless, the movement became closely allied with Italian opera, especially two shocking, violent, one-act works: Ruggerio Leoncavallo's *I Pagliacci* ("The Clowns") of 1892, and the 1890 *Cavalleria Rusticana* ("Rustic Chivalry") by Pietro Mascagni.

The most important successor to Verdi was Giacomo Puccini (1858–1924), who combined the Italian long singing line, an uncanny *verismo* sense of theater, and a flair for brilliant orchestration and chromatic harmony that was almost Wagnerian. Puccini's first great success was *La*

Bohème (1896), which made him an international celebrity. The opera was based upon a well-known novel, depicting the lives of struggling young artists ("Bohemians") in the Latin Quarter of Paris. One of these is Rodolfo, a poet; the plot focuses upon the love between Rodolfo and a young woman named Mimi. Mimi is seriously ill, and the love ends tragically with her death. *La Bohème* is not as starkly realistic as some of Puccini's later operas; for example, the more painful aspects of Bohemian poverty and Mimi's tuberculosis are withheld in favor of a romantic, fanciful gaiety. On the other hand, Puccini's characters are convincing as real people, not stereotypes. Their stage actions—fumbling, forgetful, touchingly prosaic—are as intentionally realistic as possible.

Giacomo Puccini
La Bohème

Act I, Scene 1 A sense of Puccini's style can be gathered from Act I of *La Bohème*, in the scene where the two lovers meet for the first time. Mimi's candle has gone out, and she feels faint from climbing the many stairs to Rodolfo's rooms. She also loses her key; as a breeze has blown out Rodolfo's candle as well, the two become acquainted as they grope about on the floor in the dark searching for the key. The action takes place amidst a continuous recitative, bordering on ***arioso,*** supported by the orchestra. As their hands meet, Rodolfo's patter begins to coalesce into a moving aria.

Che gelida manina,	***What a cold little hand***
Se la lasci riscaldar.	***Let me warm it.***
Cercar che giova? Al buio	***What's the use of searching?***
Non si trova. Ma per fortuna	***We'll never find it in the dark.***
È una notte di luna, etc. . . .	***But fortunately, the moon is out. . .***

The aria begins on a repeated vocal note, a favorite device of Puccini's, letting his most lyric moments evolve from seemingly casual monotone "conversation." In such passages, the melody may be carried by the orchestra. Rodolfo tells Mimi something about himself, his writing, and his optimism in the face of poverty. But then his words become more intensely ardent. The broad, sweeping theme that emerges here (Figure 15.8) will become one of the most important motives of the opera.

Rodolfo wonders if his lovely neighbor might say a few words about herself. She begins hesitantly, but goes on to describe her work as a seamstress, her love of the spring, flowers, and sunshine. By the time Rodolfo's friends call up from below, breaking the spell, the two have become deeply attached to each other. Puccini depicts their growing love in a continuously flowing dialogue. It alternates between recitative and aria, just as trivial conversation in real life may become revealing or touching. The semi-darkness, and asides about keys and candles, only add to the expressive imme-

Figure 15.8

Talor dal mio forziere	*My treasure is robbed*
Ruban tutti i gioielli	*By two thieves:*
Due ladri: gli occhi belli.	*A pair of beautiful eyes,*
V'entrar con voi or ora, etc.	*That came in just now with you, etc. . . .*

diacy on stage. Listen, too, for Puccini's harmonic inventiveness, and his coloristic use of the orchestra, all signs of a late nineteenth-century composer at work.

At the opera's end, the dying Mimi's last moments of recollection will bring back much of this love music from Act I, as though remembered by the orchestra. This is a poignant reminder of their first innocent encounter, and a convincing way of unifying *La Bohème* musically and dramatically.

Nationalistic Styles

Revolutions and political alignments had created a strong nationalistic atmosphere throughout Europe. Germany and Italy were evolving from collections of city-states to unified nations, and smaller countries were acquiring political consciousness: both Hungarians and Czechs were trying to assert an identity to set them apart from neighboring Austria, while Poles wished to break free of Russian domination. Russians and Scandinavians, feeling cut off from the rest of Europe, attempted to articulate their culture and relate it to the international mainstream. All of these urges and ideals are grouped together under the single heading of ***nationalism.***

nationalism

Certain musical periods and personalities might be considered "international." For example, Handel and Mozart felt comfortable in many countries and spoke a number of languages. Until the nineteenth century, Italian had been the international tongue for musical terminology, and the language of opera everywhere. (Queen Victoria reputedly once asked Wagner to translate a music drama into Italian, so that it could be performed in England!)

Honore Daumier, *The Orchestra During the Performance of a Tragedy*

The fusion of Flemish and Italian styles during the Renaissance, and the diverse influences which united Viennese classicism, also go beyond national boundaries.

This situation changed in the nineteenth century, beginning with the strong political consciousness of Beethoven. Opera in the German language, based on Germanic subjects, became more frequent; Beethoven and Schumann used German for the printed instructions in their scores as well. We have already mentioned Wagner's convictions about national myth and

Aubrey Beardsley, ***The Wagnerites.*** The seriousness of romantic opera was characterized in various ways by graphic artists of the time. Daumier's print shows members of the orchestra, during a weighty performance, less than totally captivated. By contrast, Aubrey Beardsley's audience seems solemn, almost worshipful—perhaps a bit oppressive as well.

Verdi's attachment to the Italian revolutionary movement. Chopin's concern for the Polish cause, and the renewed love for Hungary shown by Liszt late in his life, also illustrate the nationalistic nature of romanticism. During this century it was important, then, for many composers to make "political" statements through their art. There was also a new approach to musical *materials,* as composers drew upon the patterns and traditions of their native styles to make their work *sound* more typically Hungarian, French, Russian, or Norwegian.

French and German Styles

National style characteristics often color our general assumptions in thinking or talking about music. For example, the popular image of opera is frequently based on an Italian stereotype: the rhythms and speech-sounds of the Italian language, *bel canto* singing style, and melodramatically violent narratives. Similarly, the strongest qualities of instrumental music are assumed to be those of the sonata cycle; although we may think of them as "universal," they are really German or Austrian traits.

Because listeners have been taught to revere the works of Haydn, Mozart, the three Bs, and Wagner, they may conclude that all good composers "develop" their material, or that dissonance is always used to drive forward towards a tonal goal, or that complex textures are more meaningful than simple ones. On the contrary, these qualities are national and not universal; we associate them with an overwhelming amount of concert music, because German and Austrian composers contributed so heavily to the evolution of the sonata cycle. By the nineteenth century, Germany had come to dominate the entire musical scene, and young composers from Denmark, Hungary, Britain, or the United States would often travel to Germany for their studies.

A number of French composers, in a nationalistic spirit of their own, resisted the Germanic influence and attempted instead to write a uniquely "French" music stressing clarity, elegant outlines and transparent textures. The French, like the Italians and Russians, often relied upon clear sectional divisions and contrasts to generate forward motion and form. Their harmony tended to be more diatonic than German counterparts might be. Complex, profound development was never a major concern; in fact, the most crucial moments in a work might be the simplest and most direct. In this vein, recall the Berlioz *Symphonie Fantástique,* an achievement of international importance, but also in many ways a very "French" piece of music.

Perhaps the most gifted French composer after Berlioz, Georges Bizet (1838–1875) died tragically young. His major work, the opera *Carmen,* was premiered a few months before his death, and was a total failure. The composer never knew it would become one of the world's most popular operas. *Carmen* concerns the obsessive—and eventually destructive—love of Don José, a Spanish soldier, for a flirtatious gypsy girl. It was originally conceived as an *opera comíque,* with spoken dialogue rather than recitative. This was one reason for its lack of success in 1875; it was difficult for audiences and theatrical directors to comprehend a "comedy" that ended with the heroine's murder on stage or, for that matter, with a heroine so obviously unsavory and immoral. We may be reminded of Verdi's problems with *La Traviata* twenty years earlier; at this point *verismo,* in any language, was not yet popular.

Bizet's style is direct, immediate, and always clear-cut in its tonality. Crisp rhythms, clear textures and relatively diatonic harmony typify the French musical style. For those critics who questioned Wagnerianism or the overall influence of Germanic style (Tchaikovsky and the philosopher Nietzsche were two such critics), ***Carmen*** was a revelation, and a model alternative.

Exoticism in Music

Significantly, ***Carmen*** was set in the Spanish city of Seville, a locale far from Bizet's Paris. Europe's fascination with national identity was so strong that it reached outward to distant foreign cultures. In fact, ***Carmen*** was composed during a French craze for all things Spanish, aided perhaps by the fact that Napoleon III had taken a Spanish bride. Verdi's ***Aïda*** owed part of its success to a similar mania for Egyptian culture. The Japanese locale of Puccini's ***Madame Butterfly,*** the Arabian-Nights flavor of Rimsky-Korsakov's ***Scheherezade,*** even the ***Italian Symphony*** of Mendelssohn, all illustrate a tendency called ***exoticism,*** as distinguished from concern for one's homeland (nationalism). Traditionally, northern Europeans have been obsessed with the warm, sunny south, specifically Spain and Italy. On a larger scale, Europeans everywhere were fascinated by the remote, fairy-tale charm of the eastern Mediterranean and the Orient.

exoticism

To some degree, national and exotic styles may be indistinguishable when political and cultural differences spill over boundaries. The Austro-German use of Hungarian color, or the Russian link to Asia, simply reflect the ethnic diversity of large empires. Furthermore, we should remember that exoticism reinforces other romantic traits: love of the mysterious, the eccentrically individual, the picturesque.

Two Bohemian Composers: Smetana and Dvořák

The emergence of Czech nationalistic art took place against the background of strong Austrian rule and Bohemian struggles for independence. Bedřich Smetana (1824–1884) took part in the revolution of 1848, and was deeply committed to the radical cause. But in the face of Austrian oppression, Smetana found little encouragement for his fiercely nationalistic creative energy. He lived in Sweden for a number of years, and returned to Prague in 1862 only when the political atmosphere had become more relaxed. By the 1860s a Czech national theater had been formed, and the Czech language was being used in political and cultural writing. Smetana composed a number of operas in Czech; one of these, ***The Bartered Bride,*** became immediately successful. In its strong identification with peasantry, village folklore, and the native language, ***The Bartered Bride*** marked the beginning of Czech national music, with Smetana as its unofficial leader.

Bohemia and Hungary, because of their proximity to Austria, were in touch with the mainstream of European tradition. Unlike the Russian composer, working in comparative isolation from the mainstream, the Bohemian had to tear himself away from it consciously. So it is not surprising that Smetana's musical technique was polished and secure in the Germanic manner. He was deeply attached to the programmatic music of Liszt, and channeled his patriotic feeling not only into opera but the Lisztian symphonic poem as well.

A cycle of six symphonic poems entitled ***Má Vlast*** ("My Country") was composed during the 1870s; ***Vltava*** ("The Moldau") being the best known. In the manner of a travelogue, Smetana depicts Bohemia's great River Moldau as it flows through valley and woods, alongside castles, near pastures where a peasant feast is being celebrated, to the grand city of Prague and beyond. The work is unified by a broad, memorable theme representing the sweep of the River Moldau, and by frequent use of running figurations to evoke the sense of moving water, sometimes gently rippling sometimes massive and majestic. ***The Moldau*** is a splendid example of nineteenth-century program music; it is stirring to listeners of any nationality, and we can only imagine the effect it must have upon the Czechs.

Antonin Dvořák (1841–1904) succeeded Smetana as the leading Bohemian ambassador to the musical world. Of a younger generation (he played the viola in Smetana's theater orchestra while still a struggling artist), Dvořák was more influenced than Smetana by the conservative aspects of the Germanic mainstream. He found his greatest support in the music, and personage, of Johannes Brahms. It was Brahms who brought Dvořák's ***Slavonic Dances*** to public attention, encouraged him to tour Europe, and helped him find publishers. Like Brahms, Dvořák was attracted to traditional forms and genres such as the symphony and the string quartet.

At the height of his international fame, Dvořák was invited to become director of the National Conservatory of Music in New York. He arrived in the United States in 1892, and rapidly became influential on the American scene. He encouraged young American composers to tap their own national resources more fully; influenced by his black student Burleigh, he himself made every effort to become acquainted with Negro spirituals and Indian music. Dvořák also spent some time at the Czech colony in Spillville, Iowa. After three years, homesickness made him give up his American position and return to Prague. His stay in the United States had been brief but highly productive: while in America Dvořák wrote a number of major works, including his best-known composition, the Symphony in E Minor, ***From the New World.***

The ***New World*** Symphony, as it is often called, was composed in 1893. For years it was designated as Dvořák's Symphony no. 5. Only recently have four more symphonies been discovered and authenticated by scholars; the ***New World*** is now listed as no. 9. It is a highly ***cyclic*** work, not in the sense of thematic transformation or a single ***idée fixe,*** but in its literal quoting of themes from one movement to the next, the familiar material helping to draw the movements together.

Antonin Dvořák

Symphony no. 9 in E Minor, op. 95 from the New World

Movement I: Adagio; Allegro molto. This symphony is doubly nationalistic. It is charged with the composer's impressions of America, but in many ways it also evokes a homesick memory of Czechoslovakia. Dvořák's choice of musical material can be related to both locales. An American listener, hearing the profusion of syncopated rhythms, pentatonic scales (spirituals?), and flatted melodic inflections (Indian?), might well think of the New World. But it turns out that these traits are found just as frequently in Czech folk music. It is best to disregard the "nationality" of the work, and approach it simply as a romantic synthesis of folklike material and sonata-cycle formal structure.

The first movement opens with a slow introduction (Adagio), in which cellos are prominently featured. A sudden outburst of horns and timpani breaks this meditative calm, but the earlier mood returns. A melodic figure in the low strings begins to gain strength through sequential repetition; a crescendo leads to a forceful timpani roll on the dominant note B, fading away to a high tremolo for *pp* violins.

At this point, the tempo becomes a robust ***allegro molto,*** and the exposition proper begins with a strongly syncopated theme which is related to the low string figure heard earlier in the introduction. Note the off-beat accents in the opening horn figure, and the dotted rhythms in the answering figure for winds (Figure 15.9). The dotted rhythm is explored in a series of sequences, leading to a plaintive, folklike "bridge" tune with a lowered-7th scale degree adding to its rustic quality. Note, too, that the tempo has become relaxed. As the bridge tune slows down, it leads directly to the second subject in the relative major. This is a broad, pentatonically conceived melody, strongly reminiscent of "Swing Low, Sweet Chariot." (See Figure 15.10).

Syncopations and dotted rhythms are both prominent here. "Swing Low" is never quoted fully, but the first two measures of Dvořák's tune and the song's phrase "cha-ri-ot" are identical. "Swing Low" was one of Dvořák's favorite Black spirituals, and it is entirely possible that he would use it in a symphony. Notice, as well, how slow the tempo has become. Dvořák, like many romantic composers, is using vivid tempo contrasts to differentiate first and second sonata-movement subjects.

Figure 15.9

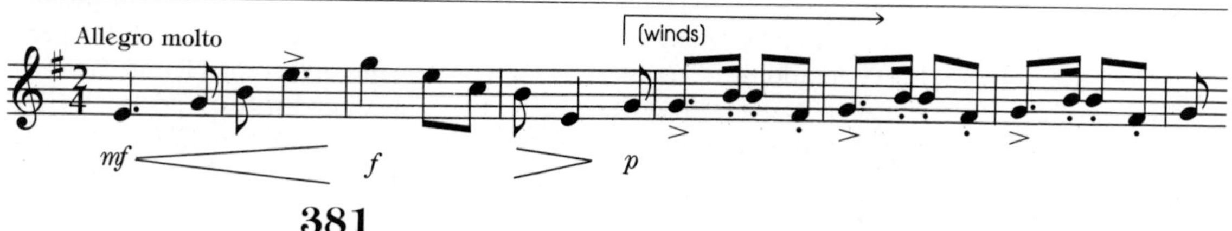

Figure 15.10

Not surprisingly, the tempo increases as we enter the development section. Beginning with a quiet variant of the "Swing Low" tune, fragments of both themes, especially the dotted rhythms of the opening, combine and build to a stormy climax. Dvořák's basic material is self-sufficient, laid out in neat phrases like folk dances or songs. In sonata-form context, such material seems to resist the organically evolving development processes of Brahms or Beethoven. Dvořák prefers to alternate and re-combine motivic fragments, within a complex key scheme that eventually returns to the tonic. The recapitulation in the home key follows the lines of the exposition, including the tempo adjustment for the "Swing Low" tune. The tempo picks up for a brilliant, dramatic coda, in which descending chromatic lines and brassy orchestration create great intensity.

The slow movement which follows is notable for its main theme, a broad melody for English horn that, like others in this symphony, stresses pentatonic contours and dotted rhythmic figures. Many people have believed this tune to be a spiritual, because it had words affixed to it ("Goin' Home") many years later. But like many nationalists, Dvořák preferred to compose his own folk-*like* melodies rather than use pre-existing material.

The Scherzo and Finale are fiery and dramatic, and obviously related to folk (Czech or American) influences. The last movement, like the first, is cast in sonata form. Themes from preceding movements return, during movements II, III, and IV, so that a growing body of "flashback" memories unifies the listening experience.

In contrast to this hybrid blend of folk material and sonata structure, listeners might prefer Dvořák's more direct, spontaneous re-creations of the Bohemian folk idiom, such as the inspired *Slavonic Dances* for piano duet. These, like the Brahms *Hungarian Dances,* provided hours of entertainment for any middle-class home with a piano. They also brought the spirit of the Czechs to many families in different countries, for whom Bohemia had been only a name on a map.

Some Scandinavian Composers

Scandinavia's isolation resulted in a musical style that was basically imported (from Germany), and which rarely drew upon native folk influences. For generations, Scandinavian composers wrote in acceptable international styles. The Dane Niels Gade (1817–1868) studied with Mendelssohn and Schumann; Franz Berwald of Sweden (1796–1868) studied in Vienna, Paris, and Berlin. In neither case did folk influences play a major role.

This situation changed drastically with the music of Edvard Grieg (1843–1907), a Norwegian with a passionate commitment to artistic nationalism. Norway, frequently a pawn in the struggles between Denmark and Sweden, had little political independence until the late nineteenth century. Apart from folk art, its cultural life had been severely limited as well. Grieg, who had studied the polished international style in Leipzig, was dissatisfied with his own work until he discovered the musical language of his country. Then, as he wrote, "I had found myself . . . My imagination was free, and I could write one work after another." Caught up in the wave of Norwegian national consciousness, Grieg gave concerts of native music, planned a national conservatory, and found inspiration in the writings of Ibsen and Holberg. Many of Grieg's most characteristic pieces are small-scaled, intimate songs, dances, and piano miniatures. In these he is often concerned with Norwegian tone-painting, the landscape, legends and customs of everyday life, and the melodic inflections, ostinato (drone) textures, and rhythms of his national art.

Two major symphonists appeared on the Scandinavian scene by the end of the century: Carl Nielsen of Denmark (1865–1931), and Finland's Jean Sibelius (1865–1937). Each adopted a distinctly personal style on the periphery of the mainstream. Many of Sibelius's early works, such as the tone poem ***Finlandia,*** are strongly nationalistic as well.

Two Russians: Mussorgsky and Tchaikovsky

In Russia the split between official court art and native folk art was extreme; the aristocracy spoke French, and supported French and Italian culture. Russian composers gradually began to explore folk elements in their work, and also allied themselves with the growing interest in national literature that brought Pushkin and Dostoyevsky to attention.

The second half of the century witnessed a virtual explosion of musical creativity in Russia, in effect, a national "school" created almost overnight. As might be expected, musicians differed in the intensity of their nationalism. Before long, two distinct camps of Russian music emerged: a fiercely independent group that worked directly with folk roots, avoiding any contact with Western models, and a more conservative faction that sought a synthesis of folk styles with the great international mainstream. We will discuss one composer from each camp, the "radical" Mussorgsky, and the more cosmopolitan Tchaikovsky.

Mussorgsky and the "Mighty Five"

The most strongly nationalistic music was centered in Saint Petersburg, where a group of five young composers met periodically to discuss artistic trends. Only one of the group, Mily Balakirev, generally acknowledged as their leader, was a professional musician. The rest were all amateurs: César Cui, a military engineer; Alexander Borodin, chemist and medical school professor; Modest Mussorgsky and Nikolai Rimsky-Korsakov, both military officers. (Borodin and Rimsky-Korsakov probably had the most polished "European" technique.) The five were united by their desire to create a Russian art that stemmed directly from native sources, including Asian influences. They wanted as little connection to the learned Western tradition as possible. Through propaganda and performances of their own works, the group acquired a collective nickname, ***"The Mighty Five."***

The Mighty Five

The "Five" examined every aspect of their national style: modal scales, asymmetrical phrases and meters (such as $\frac{5}{4}$), and the unusual harmonies of peasant music. In matters of form, Russian song and dance models suggested a sectional approach instead of the Germanic "developmental" one. Individual moments—an exciting chord, or a fleeting sonority—were as highly valued by the group as any complex formal process. Modest Mussorgsky (1839–1881), the most outstandingly inventive of the Five, would reputedly play sonata-form movements by Beethoven and Schumann at the piano for his colleagues, stop abruptly at the end of the expositions, with such comments as "That's where all the dull, dry stuff begins"—and then refuse to play the rest.

Victor Hartmann, *The Great Door of Kiev.*

Mussorgsky became a government clerk after his military service. He was, in fact, determined to remain an amateur, not only in his career, but in his total identification with the Russian people and his rejection of sophisticated Western art. In his highly original opera ***Boris Godunov,*** for example, he took great care to have his melodic lines imitate the rhythms and inflections of Russian speech. He wanted nothing to do with "effete" romanticism, and instead sought a direct realism, a Slavic ***verismo,*** that sprang from the spontaneous music of the peasants.

One of Mussorgsky's best known compositions, ***Pictures at an Exhibition,*** was intended as a memorial to a friend and colleague, the artist Victor Hartmann. Hartmann was also fond of integrating Russian influences into his work, and Mussorgsky was greatly moved by a posthumous show of his pictures. He created a musical representation of the exhibit, a succession of brief images for solo piano, that may remind one of Schumann's "character pieces." It can also be thought of as an extended suite, and an outstanding example of programmatic tone-painting. In the early twentieth century the suite was orchestrated by French composer Maurice Ravel; in this version it has become a brilliant showpiece of spectacular instrumental effects. Mussorgsky's original piano writing, on the other hand, has a unique force, a raw, awkward power, of its own. Listeners might enjoy comparing ***both*** versions, just to savor the difference.

Modest Mussorgsky
Pictures at an Exhibition, orchestrated by Maurice Ravel (excerpts) *R5 S1 B1, 2*

The cycle begins with a "Promenade" (Figure 15.11), depicting the viewer walking about the gallery. The easy alternation of $\frac{5}{4}$ and $\frac{6}{4}$ gives the passage an air of ambling; it also reflects rhythmic patterns of the Russian tradition. The "Promenade" pauses briefly, and then leads into the first picture, "Gnomus," which refers to the drawing of a nutcracker carved in the shape of a gnome. Mussorgsky's music is rhythmically angular and unstable, and delights in sudden shocking changes of volume and register. He obviously wanted to capture the frightening aspects of the gnome figure.

Figure 15.11

Figure 15.12

The Promenade material returns, a bit subdued and with some of its angular edges smoothed out. The use of the Promenade in this way occurs a number of times during the suite, unifying the collection. Note, too, that the Promenade undergoes changes of mood and texture, suggesting a corresponding change in the viewer's responses; it actually resembles a Wagnerian ***Leitmotif,*** although Mussorgsky would have despised that thought!

Let us skip to the last three pictures (nos. 8, 9, and 10 of the series). The music suggests an eerie view of the Paris catacombs and their ancient tombs. The chord progressions are unpredictable and strangely moving as they slowly unfold. (Ravel's orchestration uses no strings except contrabasses in this passage; wind and brass timbres prevail.) Unexpectedly, the Promenade melody is heard, quietly and very gently, against the ghostly catacombs music. The subtle intrusion of a human element, the gallery viewer, into this dead world is particularly touching. Mussorgsky, moved by the picture, is supposed to have thought of his friend Hartmann among the dead.

The music suddenly becomes loud and ferocious. Picture no. 9 is the "Hut on Fowl's Legs," a reference to the Russian witch Baba-Yaga who lives in that bizarre dwelling. This image of Figure 15.12 is absolutely grotesque: note the wide melodic skips, and the unsettling alternation of silence and brutal rhythm. The fragments assemble into a steady rhythm, from which a very nasty tune (Figure 15.13) arises. This passage then plunges into a lengthy contrasting section, in which the opening fragments are surrounded by an eerie, hushed ostinato. The return to Baba-Yaga's hard-driving motive creates an obvious ABA form.

The witch makes her exit in a flurry of rapidly rising notes—is she flying on her broom?—and we are immediately thrust into a grand processional at "The Great Gate of Kiev" (no. 10). Victor Hartmann had made architectural plans for this triumphal gate, but it was never built; it existed only in Mussorgsky's remarkable imagination. The processional consists of two themes, both strongly nationalistic. The first (Figure 15.14) is a melody of great weight and dignity, and the second a gentler, subdued line. Both lead to a majestic Finale in which the Promenade returns, perhaps suggesting that the viewer (composer) has joined the processional, at least in spirit.

Figure 15.13

Figure 15.14

Mussorgsky wrote ***Pictures at an Exhibition*** in 1874, shortly after his opera ***Boris Godunov***. The remaining years of his life were increasingly painful. Always emotionally unstable and given to heavy drinking, Mussorgsky died of acute alcoholism at the age of forty-two. After his death a number of his works were revised, edited and "improved" on by his well-meaning friend Rimsky-Korsakov. Only recently have we begun to hear Mussorgsky's music as he originally wrote it.

Tchaikovsky, the "International" Nationalist

Peter Ilyich Tchaikovsky (1840–1893) was as musically cosmopolitan as Mussorgsky was outspokenly provincial. Tchaikovsky could not comprehend Mussorgsky's barbarisms. He once wrote that Mussorgsky's "gifts are most remarkable," but also added "He likes what is coarse, unpolished and ugly." The "Mighty Five" in their turn were rather unkind to Tchaikovsky, scorning him for having apparently sold out to the West. Admittedly, Tchaikovsky was steeped in the European tradition. He was sufficiently interested in the Germanic approach to attend the first Wagner festival at Bayreuth; although he never fell under Wagner's spell, he adored Mozart, Verdi, and Bizet.

Nonetheless, he was a distinctly Russian composer, keenly aware of his national heritage. His melodic inflections and rhythmic traits are drawn from Russian folk music; the swooning melancholy and hyper-emotional expression can be found in the literature of Chekhov, Tolstoy, and Dostoyevsky. This quality in his music has certainly contributed to his great popularity. There is, in fact, a certain irony to Tchaikovsky's superstar status with the public, considering that the composer was really an elitist, writing a highly personal (and highly neurotic!) kind of music within the cultivated international tradition. Mussorgsky, who really ***wanted*** to reach "the people," has been all but ignored, while Tchaikovsky's soaring melodies and brilliant orchestral colors continue to appeal to larger numbers.

The personal intensity of his work exerts a strange fascination, too: the late romantic extension of the idea, first implied by Beethoven, that composing was a form of autobiography. For Beethoven's generation, at the start of a revolutionary century, the Artist was a Hero. Tchaikovsky offers us the Artist as Everyman: worried, hypochondriac, impulsive, repressed, neurotic. Perhaps this reveals as much about the changing times as it does about the two artists.

Tchaikovsky was a versatile composer, known for songs, ballet scores, symphonies, and operas. His opera ***Eugene Onegin*** is still performed regularly; of his six symphonies, the last three have become standard items of the orchestral repertoire. Symphonies no. 4 and 5 are highly cyclic, and use "motto" themes with great effectiveness. The Sixth (*Pathétique*) Symphony is unusual in that it ends with a slow movement, a particularly poignant Finale summing up the symphony's sense of resignation.

Tchaikovsky composed a good deal of program music as well. One of his best known works in the genre is ***Romeo and Juliet,*** a piece for orchestra that was subtitled an "overture-fantasy" rather than a tone poem. Tchaikovsky's designation is most apt: ***Romeo and Juliet*** can be considered a "concert overture," in that it needs no detailed literary explanation to be perfectly effective in the concert hall. Although certain motives can be associated with Shakespearian characters once the title is known, we can also respond to the music on an absolute level. In fact, Tchaikovsky has constructed the piece along the lines of a sonata movement.

Peter Ilyich Tchaikovsky: Romeo and Juliet: Overture-Fantasy

The music begins slowly, a characteristic of many Tchaikovsky sonata-form allegros (including the three symphonies noted earlier). The hymn-like motive of the opening (Figure 15.15) may remind us of kindly Friar Laurence, whose efforts to aid the lovers only hasten their death. To confirm the religious association, Tchaikovsky states the theme as a four-part chorale. It repeats with a new orchestral texture, and comes to rest on a series of quiet wind chords and harp arpeggios.

But then new stirrings begin. The passage begins to grow in volume and increase in tempo. With a new, rhythmically vigorous theme (and brisk *allegro giusto* tempo), the sonata-form proper begins, as noted in Figure 15.16. We might think of the feud between the two families when we hear this, or the violent workings of destiny, or even a particular quarrel or duel; Tchaikovsky wisely declined to be specific. At any rate, the theme builds to an explosive climax punctuated by cymbal crashes.

The second theme, in typically late romantic fashion, is much slower and obviously more lyric than the first (see Figure 15.17). Tchaikovsky creates a broad, sweeping line of operatic scope that we can identify with the young lovers. This slow theme is stated simply at first, and then in a more

Figure 15.15

Figure 15.16

Figure 15.17

impassioned orchestral setting of full strings against a prominent countersubject by the horns.

The development is immediately apparent because of the renewed rapid tempo. During this section, the violent "feud" theme and a fast variant of the "Friar" motive are alternated, fragmented, and super-imposed. Brass and percussion are used extensively for rhythmic punctuation and brilliant color; the effect is undeniably exciting. During the recapitulation all the motives are brought back, with special prominence given to the "love" melody. That expansive *arioso* line is also heard during the Epilogue (see the diagram of Figure 15.18); it appears in muted, sombre guise over distant drum beats, reminding us of the way Shakespeare's drama ends. But the music builds once more to a powerful close, perhaps Tchaikovsky's way of bringing down the curtain. There is a hint of the "chorale," a strong statement of the "love" motive, and then fierce, crashing, abrupt chords—the rhythm of the "feud" seems to flash by, or does it?—against a resonant roll of the timpani.

Figure 15.18

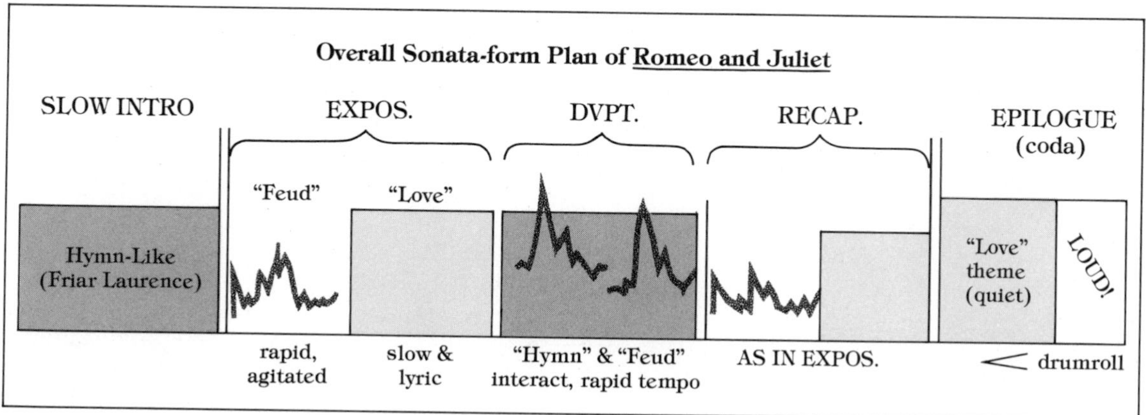

Tchaikovsky's style is about as "romantic," in the emotional sense, as music can get; its great surges carry the listener along. There are structural problems, to be sure. Extreme tempo contrasts alternate just a few times too many, and development sections often don't really "develop" anything. Tchaikovsky himself was aware of such problems; he complained that in his larger forms "the seams always show." But for many listeners, his passionate, volatile moods are sufficient cause for endless fascination.

Tchaikovsky, Mussorgsky, Dvořák, and Smetana present a great variety of approaches to nationalism. Tchaikovsky's national feelings were strong, but couched in a style that was thoroughly international. Dvořák's art may not have been as consistently patriotic as Smetana's but its Czech roots are just as genuine. We might, then, distinguish between composers—perhaps Mussorgsky was one—whose works are best appreciated by their own countrymen at home, and those who act as ambassadors for their native idiom to the rest of the musical world. Whose service is more "patriotic?" No one can say.

Similarly, "program music" is a flexible term with many individual directions. One could hear ***The Moldau*** as a quasi-travelog, or ***Pictures at an Exhibition*** as though in an art gallery. But Dvořák's ***New World Symphony*** has nothing to do with travelog: it contains no depictions of prairies or Indian campfires or plantations. Although ***Romeo and Juliet*** has programmatic references, their order cannot be related to a "story line." Tchaikovsky's choices were based on the logic of musical narrative and formal structure, not the logic of Shakespeare. Even this most shamelessly romantic of the romantics was acutely conscious of his compositional craft.

Interlude 4
Composer and Critic

It is difficult to consider romantic music without paying special attention to the individuals who created it. During the nineteenth century public attention became focused upon the composer as the noblest of musical "heroes;" for many present-day listeners the composer is still the most glamorous and mysterious of beings. The very word composer often conjures up an image of a "genius" who is likely to be a nineteenth century stereotype, modeled after Wagner or Tchaikovsky, rather than on unheroic, workmanlike musicians such as Bach or Haydn.

Perhaps this romantic image of the composer signifies the last step in the "westernization" of music. By the nineteenth century, Western society had come to rely upon a special class of highly trained, egocentric individuals for the creation of music, rather than on group expression, improvisation, and oral tradition as practiced elsewhere in the world. Compare the relatively anonymous communal music of the Middle Ages to the extroverted activities of individual specialists, each with a distinct role to play, in the late nineteenth century. In our own era the virtuoso performer has become the focus of similar attention. Here, too, listeners have created an image associated with a certain glamour and mystery; performers, conductors, and composers have become fascinating as "personalities."

A glance at some of the writing about music in earlier times is quite revealing. Prior to the nineteenth century, writing on music concentrated upon instrument building, esthetics, and acoustic theory, topics that might be classified today under physics or philosophy. But during the romantic period *biography* became a major subject. (Our own period's avalanche of "guides" for the listener—such as this book!—may reveal a great deal about the late twentieth century and its highly mobile, broadly based consumer-oriented society.)

Is our fascination with the personal lives of nineteenth-century composers justified? *Were* they really as passionate, melodramatic, or extravagant in their behavior as we are led to believe? Remember, it was quite fashionable then to cultivate eccentricities. Romantic composers were actively engaged in rebellion of one form or another—not only against their own middle-class origins, but against the stifling, oppressive influence of Beethoven or Wagner, and the shift in popular taste towards light entertainment music. During this era, popular music specially composed for the urban masses, as distinct from anonymous rural folk music, acquired a style and a sizeable audience. Many romantic composers were unable to span the gap between "serious" and "popular" audiences; in their work as in their lives, they had distanced themselves from a large segment of the public. Other composers, attempting to court or shock the public, flaunted their unconventional ways as visibly as possible.

Many romantic composers led exciting (or tragic, or wicked, or disturbed) lives. We are free to glamorize those lives, if we wish. But it would be a mistake to glamorize their day-to-day work as composers. Composition is a laborious, solitary, painstaking craft. Some composers sketch their work while sitting at the piano (true to the fictionalized biographies of Hollywood), while others simply need a large desk and manuscript paper in a quiet location. Much composing is done in one's head, imagining sonorities and densities, or directly on manuscript paper, allowing the visual symbols to suggest their own future directions. Beware, too, of the notion that a composer's personal triumphs or tragedies are "translated" into a specific piece of music. Perhaps one gains greater insight into a composer's total output from an examination of his life or certain personality traits: Beethoven's rage, Tchaikovsky's repressed sexuality, Schubert's shyness, Schumann's incipient insanity. But it is virtually impossible to link a particular crisis with a particular work. Although Schubert might have written a song in an afternoon, a symphony or opera entails many months of work for the composer—early sketches, revisions, orchestration and the like—during which time he or she has probably gone through as many moods as any other individual. When a composer is actually at work, the mood is usually that of being businesslike.

Finally, we might reconsider the romantic notion of inspiration. There may be *any* external stimulus to compose: a vivid painting or novel, the prospect of writing for a special performer or instrument; a lucrative fee or, in earlier times, the demand of a patron. Once a piece is under way, a composer cannot wait to be "inspired" to work on it. "Mood" is irrelevant; in order to do the job well, the composer's mood must be dispassionate. Beethoven wrote his cheerful Second Symphony and Tchaikovsky his sunniest ballet scores when suffering acute periods of depression. Some of the darkest, weightiest passages by Wagner or Brahms were written during pleasant summer holidays, including some mornings when the composer didn't feel "inspired" at all.

The nineteenth century witnessed not only the cult of the composer, but the rise of another familiar phenomenon: the music critic. The middle classes that supported musical events such as public concerts and commercial opera wanted to read about them in newspapers. Periodicals specializing in music, such as Schumann's *Neue Zeitschrift,* sprang up as well; these were directed to the professional or the devoted amateur, and were often quite partisan on heated issues of the day. Schumann's own axe to grind was the flimsy level of taste in bourgeois Germany, an indication that the schism between popular music and weighty "art" music had already begun by the 1830s.

Today, too, there are critics who write for the daily papers and those who comment in greater depth for specialized professional journals. Critics who write daily press reviews often have a strained relationship with composers. This is partly because they may concentrate more on performances of established "masterworks" than on new pieces being premiered. When critics do mention contemporary scores, they may not have enough time or newspaper space to comment at length, or enough experience with new musical concepts to respond beyond the level of the rest of the audience.

Should the critic, in fact, be anything other than a spokesman or representative for the average person in the audience? There are some who believe that a critic's job is to speak for a "constituency" and to articulate its collective response. (In the same sense, the performers on stage may represent the composer. While performers and audiences share the immediate experience of music-making, composer and critic often seem to stand on either side of the process.) Others feel that the critic should lead the readers, and shape public taste as a teacher might. If so, the critic should be broadly educated, not only in the standard repertoire but in contemporary developments as well. In either case, critics have a challenging job. No matter what they do, they will always infuriate someone! They are hardly encouraged by the realization that their daily column has little direct influence. (Since the average concert is a one-night occurrence, there are usually no future performances to be affected.) And they may find it sobering to consider the classic examples of critics who have had their opinions contradicted by the weight of history. The famous Viennese critic Hanslick, a strong supporter of Brahms, had very little good to say about Wagner and was positively vicious in writing about Tchaikovsky. Brahms was just as frequently attacked by other writers: a Boston reviewer suggested that Symphony Hall put a sign over one of its doors reading "this exit in case of Brahms."

Many composers have also *been* critics; Berlioz, Wagner, and Schumann are prominent nineteenth century examples. As we know, the romantics often showed a passion for literature and a flair for writing, and some of them found the idea of criticism irresistible. For others, the chief lure was economic; with the collapse of the patronage system, journalism, along with virtuoso performing, opera production, and "popular" music, became one of the few fairly reliable sources of income for composers. Of course, any composer who expresses strong musical opinions, even in a diary or letters, is an informal critic of sorts. Many of the romantics had firm, dogmatic opinions about their musical colleagues. Perhaps we can take heart in the fact that they have been proven wrong just as often as professional journalists. The very qualities that make a creative artist strong and commanding often make that artist a poor judge of others.

Besides, who can say what makes a critic "right" or "wrong?" And what is the judgment of "history?" Is it accurate, or fair? Let us consider these questions of history, judgment, and criticism as we begin studying music of our own century.

16

Beyond Romanticism: Music From 1890 to 1920

I came into the world very young at a very old time.

Erik Satie

Kill the Nineteenth Century Dead!

Gertrude Stein

The Cultural Background

We noted earlier that the years, 1300, 1600, and 1900 have been especially crucial in the evolution of Western music. Looking back at the early 1600s, we can understand the musical revolution brewing then and its implications for the future: the power of the chord, homophonic texture, dramatic expressiveness, new forms and genres. Tonality eventually became the cornerstone of that revolution: for the next 300 years major-minor tonality controlled Europe's musical thinking. By the end of the nineteenth century, though, the tonal system had reached a point of crisis. The esthetic and expressive assumptions of romanticism were being stretched to their limit as well. A new revolution was brewing.

Equally striking changes were taking place in other fields. They revealed many of the same tensions, explosive new insights and destruction of old values as their musical counterparts. Technology had opened up new avenues of communication and comfort: the telephone, telegraph, radio, phonograph, motion picture, the first flight of the Wright Brothers (1903), and the production of the Model T Ford (1908). Scientific advances also shattered our complacent view of the universe. Research into protons and electrons, the discovery of X-rays (1895), and Einstein's theory of relativity questioned our assumptions about the physical world; Freud's work in psychoanalysis and dreams also opened up internal worlds beyond consciousness. Freud's concern for inner levels of thought and feelings was reflected in the pioneering literature of James Joyce, Franz Kafka, and T. S. Eliot. They, too, explored dreams, stream-of-consciousness narrative, and the contrasts between internal and external reality.

In the visual arts, the ***impressionist*** painters Monet and Renoir, and their followers, renounced the monumental romantic ideal, in favor of a more immediate approach to light and color. They also avoided heroic subjects, preferring to capture a "moment" of the ever-changing visual universe around them. Other painters, notably the young Picasso, explored the possibilities of fragmentation. The ***cubist*** movement that developed from their work shocked Paris in the early 1900s. Radical approaches to texture characterized the paintings of Van Gogh, Cezanne and Seurat. In Germany and Switzerland, painters such as Klee and Kandinsky attempted to depict the Freudian world of dreams, fantasies, and emotional upheaval in an abstract style called ***expressionism.*** The shocking distortions and violent colors of painters Matisse and Rouault led their critics to dub them "Fauves," or primitive wild beasts.

In this context, most Westerners believed that the refinements of European civilization were infinitely superior to the "barbaric" cultures of other peoples. But at the same time artists and scholars were discovering the works of other cultures, such as African sculpture, and ***primitivism*** really became a force in European art. The science of anthropology was just beginning to make a strong impact, demonstrating that all human societies are equally "civilized" and undeniably linked in important ways.

The unsettled European political scene loomed over this entire panorama—seemingly peaceful, moralistic as only a romantic age could be, but headed for destruction. Intense nationalism prevailed; eventually the devastating First World War (1914–1918) and the Russian Revolution (1917) punctured European optimism with shocking force. The World War seriously affected the creative arts. Not only were composers forced to reexamine their romantic attitudes about art as an enobling "moral" force, but on a more practical level, the economy had collapsed. The sprawling, complex symphonies, oratorios, ballets, and music dramas of late romanticism assumed the existence of a lavish supply of money. Indeed, the economic health of nineteenth century music had always depended upon the interaction of many forces: wealthy patrons, middle-class consumers (audiences, buyers of sheet music), managers, virtuoso performers, composers, conductors, critics, and a vast army of musical "workers" who sat in orchestras, sang in choruses, built stage sets, and so on. This broad base was thoroughly undermined by the 1914–1918 War.

Post-Wagnerian Music and Expressionism

There was a great crisis implicit in Wagnerian romanticism. With its expanded chromatic vocabulary, the tensions of dissonance had become extreme; tonality itself was often unrecognizable. This created problems in matters of ***form***, since all the major formal models since the Baroque were based upon key relationships. It was also critical in areas of ***expression***. The great intensity of chromaticism can lose its power without the backdrop of a diatonic norm; if every moment in a piece sounds like the climactic high point, it is difficult to express levels of intensity. In coping with this crisis, composers were aware that they were moving beyond romanticism—that the era was, in fact, coming to an end. George Bernard Shaw, a devoted Wagnerian, sensed this when he commented that the "Music of the future" was really a summation of its past. Debussy expressed the same idea in referring to Wagner's music as "a beautiful sunset mistaken for a dawn."

Many composers who were ***not*** German or Austrian attacked the Wagnerian crisis by dismantling its basic assumptions. A significant number, however, mostly of Austro-German tradition, firmly believed in the Wagnerian esthetic. They decided to follow the esthetic as far as they could, extending the great romantic tradition in new directions. These composers are often called ***post-Wagnerian***. Three of the best known were Richard Strauss (1864–1949), Gustav Mahler (1860–1911), and Arnold Schoenberg (1874–1951)—at least the early Schoenberg, before his radical innovations of the 1920s.

post-Wagnerian

Strauss and the Tone Poem

Richard Strauss, son of a great Bavarian horn player, virtually grew up in the midst of a grand romantic symphony orchestra, and used that virtuoso ensemble brilliantly in his own works. Strauss carried chromatic dissonance beyond late romantic norms, and created jagged, convoluted melodic lines that span many octaves. His thematic motives, while memorable, are not always singable: they were designed specifically for instrumental players and not voices. Strauss first achieved fame through a series of spectacular ***tone poems*** (the term he preferred to "symphonic poem") modeled after Liszt and Berlioz. Many of these tone poems are quite literal in their extra-musical references and make fully coherent sense only if the listeners know the "program." Strauss and other late romantic composers were careful to build an "absolute" musical logic into their programmatic work. Even so, the sequence of ideas in such pieces may seem a bit arbitrary without knowledge of the extra-musical stimuli.

tone poems

For example, the 1888 tone poem ***Don Juan*** depicts the same legendary love that had inspired Mozart's opera (see Chapter 11), but now treated as a case study in sensual boredom. In this version Don Juan, disgusted with himself and the entire world, allows himself to be killed in a duel. The tone poem paints a portrait of its hero in athletic themes of great, bold leaps and chromatic inflections, and also presents material depicting two extended love scenes. These all combine as ***leitmotifs*** in a psychological-musical continuity reminiscent of Wagner. (Strauss's critics occasionally called him "Richard II.")

On another level, however, Strauss's tone poem can be heard as a loose sonata structure. The recapitulation occurs just ***after*** Don Juan has been run through; it provides a flashback of final, fleeting memories passing before him as he lies dying. The coda is hushed and still. Unless one knows the program, ***Don Juan's*** quiet, sad ending will always remain a mystery.

Strauss also composed a number of operas, including three of the most notable stage works of the early twentieth century. Two of these, ***Salome*** (1905) and ***Elektra*** (1909), were brutally shocking, violently chromatic, and even branded as obscene. They carried the romantic, Wagnerian ideal of intense emotional expression as far as Strauss would go. He retreated afterwards, in the lush, ingratiating ***Der Rosenkavalier*** (1911), into a world of humor, gaiety and light waltzes.

Mahler: Songs and Symphonies

Gustav Mahler's music is as chromatically tempestuous as Strauss's, and much more complex in its immense proportions. Mahler was one of the great conductors and opera directors of the era; like Strauss, he understood the workings of the large Wagnerian orchestra perfectly. But he used that enormous ensemble in a more adventurous way, extracting unusual sonorities and chamber textures from it. Mahler was high-strung, and given to emotional extremes. He believed that music should express a composer's individual world view, and his own works reflect his self-doubting, contradictory, tortured personality. Each of his nine symphonies* is a monumental, comprehensive universe of contrasts, quasi-programmatic references and gigantic time spans. Their sheer duration approaches that of miniature operas. In fact, it may be useful to approach them as operas of a sort, since they depend so greatly upon vivid contrast rather than organic development, and since four of them have significant vocal parts.

There are many passages in Mahler's music where the continuous level of chromatic dissonance leads to unbearably high tension. Paradoxically, there are also many folklike diatonic moments—rustic country tunes, military marches, simple lullabies. These innocent tunes often have grotesque, sinister implications: during the course of a work they may be distorted, wrenched, or virtually disintegrated. We have some inkling of the

*There are also fragments of a tenth.

A contemporary caricature demonstrating the impassioned nature of Mahler's conducting. Courtesy of Gesellschaft der Musikfreunde in Wien-Archiv, Vienna, Austria

ambivalence Mahler felt towards "harmless" triadic folk music. He was once interviewed by Freud and related a traumatic childhood experience, in which he rushed out of his house to escape a violent battle between his parents, literally into the arms of an organ-grinder playing "Ach, Du lieber Augustin." Mahler admitted that he had associated banal, trivial music with great personal anguish ever since.

In addition to symphonies, Mahler also composed a number of extended song cycles with orchestral accompaniment. These cycles are "symphonic" in their own right. In fact, melodies from the songs are occasionally quoted in the symphonies. The song cycle ***Kindertotenlieder*** ("Songs on the Death of Children") is particularly moving. The words are by Friedrich Ruckert, a minor early romantic poet who had lost his own children. Mahler was fascinated by the poems, and began setting them to music in 1901. The cycle was completed in 1904, and premiered the following year. As an ironic postscript, Mahler's eldest child, not even born when the cycle was begun, died tragically in 1907.

Gustav Mahler
Kindertotenlieder, nos. 1 and 2 *R4 S2 B3*

The first song sets the tone for the entire cycle: alternatively innocent, grief-stricken, and angry. (We gather from the text that the child has died during the night, and that the sun is now rising as though nothing had occurred.) Mahler's opening is simple and child-like, in a diatonic D minor. But a chromatic inflection soon pushes the context into D major. The line ends on a D-major cadence, but an orchestral ritornello allows the inflection to sink into the minor once more. Note the quiet strokes of glockenspiel as the ritornello comes to rest, and the evocative writing for solo woodwinds throughout.

This material is repeated, and the orchestral ritornello now extended, but without the glockenspiel. The music then changes characters; it is increasingly intense and chromatic, and eventually plunges into a furious, anguished orchestral passage just barely held together by a stable low pedal point. As the orchestral tension subsides, we return to the calm resignation of the opening. The final lines are set to the basic material, once more moving from minor to major and then back to minor again. Mahler's vocal line now extends into the ritornello passage; the song fades away on soft glockenspiel strokes and a sustained D-minor chord. The overall form, then is a straightforward AA'BA''.

The second song presents a stark contrast. It is much more fluid and less divisible into sections; it is also intensely chromatic. These two features are related, since the lack of tonal relaxation brings about the effect of a single continuous fabric. Note the strong dissonance level even in the very first seconds of the orchestral introduction. The chord on the downbeat of measure 2 is quite wrenching, and resolves to one only slightly less so. Mahler thus establishes a fever pitch of intensity before a word is sung (see Figure 16.1).

As in Wagner's ***Tristan*** Prelude, we are in a tonal no-man's-land, where each individual fragment may sound tonal by itself, but seems always to be "resolving" somewhere else, to some point that keeps receding into the distance. There are stretches of time where no single key is discernible.

Figure 16.1

Although the song ends in C major-minor (one mode gradually inflecting the other), there is no hint of this at the opening. The constant modulation ***almost*** reaches a firm C-major cadence at line 8 (beginning "Dorthin. . ."), only to shy away from it.

Nun seh ich wohl, warum so dunkle Flammen
Ihr sprühtet mir in manchem Augenblicke,
O Augen! Gleichsam um voll in einem Blicke
Zu drängen eure ganze Macht zusammen.

Doch ahnt ich nicht, weil Nebel mich umschwammen,
Gewoben vom verblendenden Geschicke,
Dass sich der Strahl bereits zur Heimat schicke,
Dorthin, von wannen alle Strahlen stammen.

Ihr wolltet mir mit eurem Leuchten sagen:
Wir möchten nah dir bleiben gerne,
Doch ist uns das vom Schicksal abgeschlagen.
Sieh uns nur an, denn bald sind wir dir ferne!
Was dir nur Augen sind in diesen Tagen,
In künft 'gen Nächten sind es dir nur Sterne.

Only now do I comprehend why your eyes flashed such dark flames
At me in many a moment.
Oh those eyes! As if a single glance was able
To capture all of your power.

However, I could not sense, because blinding fate,
Was shrouding me in its mist,
That your bright light was preparing to go homeward,
And return from whence all light comes.

You wanted to tell me with your shining light:
We would gladly stay close to you,
But fate has denied us our wish.
Look at us closely, soon we will be far from you!
What seems to you in these days to be only eyes
Will seem to be only stars in nights to come.

We may detect a sectional ordering of events, roughly analogous to ABCA'B'. B projects an extended lyric melody (at the words "Dor't ahnt' ich . . ." of line 5, and then at "Sieh'uns . . " of line 12.) The opening orchestral figure is used as a constantly recurring leitmotif, often against a vocal setting ("O Augen!" of line 3). Note, too, that the final cadence is drawn from the "thwarted" C-major material of line 8, now resolved at last.

The remaining songs of the cycle are similarly pensive, agitated, or worshipful in mood. The final song, which begins violently, comes to a close in the key of the opening song, D, with a folklike lullaby and a brief reminiscence of the early glockenspiel strokes.

Schoenberg: Atonality and Expressionism

Arnold Schoenberg was the youngest of the post-Wagnerians, and the one whose work led in new directions to a point where tonality was obliterated. He did not begin with this style: on the contrary, his 1899 tone poem *Verklarte Nacht* ("Transfigured Night") is accessible to anyone who enjoys Wagner, Strauss or Mahler. Schoenberg was deeply attracted to Wagner; he also loved the music of Brahms, and wrote an essay entitled "Brahms the Progressive." Perhaps he saw similar Germanic virtues, such as seriousness of purpose and organic developmental form, in both. Born in Vienna, Schoenberg was acutely conscious of the great Austro-German tradition. He is said to have remarked once, "Either what *we* do is music, or what the French do is music. Both cannot be music."

Gustav Mahler was one of Schoenberg's friends and early champions. The Viennese public was frequently hostile to both composers. Musically,

Vienna had become a very conservative city, devoted to the great masters and to light waltzes, but very little else. Then, too, there was strong anti-Semitic feeling in Vienna (which affected such prominent Jews as Mahler, Schoenberg and Freud). Mahler's battles with symphony and opera patrons were notorious, and he eventually accepted the conductorship of the New York Philharmonic to escape them. Schoenberg, like Mahler, came to regard the bourgeois Viennese audience as his adversary. In addition, he accepted the romantic notion of the artist as a special being with an important mission, and the uniquely Germanic view of art as "evolution"—certain tendencies inevitably emerging from the seeds of the past and growing in directions that could not be halted. In this connection Schoenberg believed that post-Wagnerianism could only lead to the end of tonality, and he developed the courage to follow that belief to its inescapable conclusion, making his music increasingly dissonant and freely chromatic.

Arnold Schoenberg, ***Self-Portrait*** (left) and ***Der Rote Blick*** (right). Schoenberg was a gifted painter, as we can see by these two self-portraits. One is a representative likeness, but the other is a far more nightmarish expressionistic inner view.

In the early years of the twentieth century, Schoenberg began to dispense with key signatures, triads and tonal centers. The results were often referred to as *atonal.* We will use the term *atonality,* meaning the absence of tonality, to describe Schoenberg's work before the 1920s. (The composer hated the term, though, because of its negative-sounding connotations.)

atonality

To get an idea of Schoenberg's atonal language, listen to his 1912 song cycle, *Pierrot Lunaire* ("Pierrot of the Moon.") The cycle is scored for voice, flute, clarinet, violin, cello, and piano, and set to a group of twenty-one poems by the Belgian symbolist poet Albert Giraud (in German translation). The poems abound in dreamlike frightening images, with a highly nervous intensity. For the vocal part of *Pierrot Lunaire,* Schoenberg devised a peculiar delivery which is half song, half speech; a technique in which the performer slides from one pitch to the next, creating an intensified, even nightmarish, effect. This technique is called *Sprechstimme.* For contemporary audiences, it was the most obviously baffling aspect of a profoundly disturbing experience.

Sprechstimme

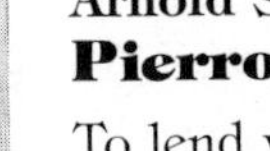

Arnold Schoenberg
Pierrot Lunaire, no. 1

R5 S1 B3

To lend variety to the cycle, Schoenberg decided not to use all the instruments together. Instead he grouped them in different combinations for each movement. The first song, "Mondestrunken" ("Moon Drunk"), is scored for voice, flute, violin, cello, and piano. The words alone are sufficiently giddy, elusive, and rich in imagery to convey an expressionistic atmosphere, and Schoenberg weaves a hypnotic fabric of his own around them. In Figure 16.2, note the piano's hushed ostinato figuration in the high register, and the equally static violin pizzicato: the instrumental texture only begins to "move" at the end of measure 5. *Sprechstimme* notation for the voice is indicated by a cross through the note stems (✗).

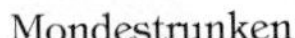

Mondestrunken

Den Wein, den man mit Augen trinkt,
Giesst Nachts der Mond in Wogen nieder,
Und eine Springflut überschwemmt
Den stillen Horizont.

Gelüste schauerlich und süss,
Durchschwimmen ohne Zahl die Fluten!
Den Wein, den man mit Augen trinkt,
Giesst Nachts der Mond in Wogen nieder.

Der Dichter, den die Andacht treibt,
Berauscht sich an dem heilgen Tranke,
Gen Himmel wendet er verzückt
Das Haupt und taumelnd saugt und schlürft er
Den Wein, den man mit Augen trinkt.

Moon-Drunk

The wine that one drinks with one's eyes
Is poured at night in waves by the moon,
And a spring tide inundates
The still horizon.

Countless longings, terrible and sweet,
Swim across the high tides!
The wine that one drinks with one's eyes
Is poured at night in waves by the moon.

The poet, driven by devotion,
Becomes enraptured with the holy drink;
In ecstasy he turns his head heavenward,
And reeling, swills and laps
The wine that one drinks with one's eyes.

Figure 16.2

Familiar triads and scales, the standard references to tonality, are missing. Schoenberg deals exclusively in highly unstable sonorities. His chief building blocks are intervals and motivic fragments, handled in relatively traditional ways: ostinato repetition, overlapping textures, fugal or canonic imitation. In fact, the language is "developmental" in its logic, as one might expect from an admirer of Brahms and Wagner.

Figure 16.3

Schoenberg creates his dissonant fabric out of all twelve tones in the octave. Note that nine of them have already been heard before the voice enters; eleven of them by measure 3. (See Figure 16.3). The remaining twelfth note (F) is not sounded until the very end of measure 5 and start of measure 6, at the word "Wogen." (Interestingly, the music begins to suggest cascading "waves" at this point, too.) Regular tempo and a fairly rigid beat, despite the notated changing meter, reinforce the song's hypnotic, "drunken" effect.

Note that great tension and activity have been compressed into a few moment's worth of time—as though the most emotionally charged phrases of Strauss or Mahler had been joined together. This sort of music evokes intense emotional associations in the minds of listeners. The post-Wagnerian composers cultivated these associations; they wanted their music to depict vivid psychological states and expressive extremes. Schoenberg was no exception: he was drawn to the most super-romantic movement of the time in literature and painting, known as ***expressionism.*** In its exploration of inner drives, dreams, and violent fantasies, expressionism owed much to the discoveries of Freud. It could be observed in the writings of Joyce and Kafka, the paintings of Munch and Kandinsky, and such early films as ***The Cabinet of Dr. Caligari.***

expressionism

The response to Schoenberg's atonal works was quite negative. Mahler was not convinced about this new direction, athough he remained supportive; Strauss commented that Schoenberg "would do better to shovel snow than scribble on music paper." But Schoenberg's reputation had grown, and he began to attract a number of gifted pupils. His most famous students were Alban Berg, whose music will be discussed in the next chapter, and Anton Webern (1883–1945), a composer already examined in Part 1 of this book.

Webern and "Klangfarbenmelodie"

Recalling Webern's orchestral *Variations* studied in Part 1, we may remember their terse, understated language: isolated points of pitch and color etched against a backdrop of silence. Many of these traits appeared early in Webern's career. His chromatically atonal ***Five Pieces for Orchestra*** (1913) are worth exploring; in contrast to the full-blown, sweeping style of his teacher Schoenberg, Webern's music is whispered, concentrated, and unbelievably brief. (All five pieces take a total of five minutes to perform.)

Webern's kaleidoscopic textures may seem thoroughly unique, but there are earlier precedents for them, even within the Viennese tradition.

Klangfarbenmelodie

Mahler was fond of drawing chamber combinations out of giant Wagnerian orchestras. Schoenberg had also introduced the idea of creating "melody" by sounding tones on different instruments in turn, leading the ear to follow a continuity of shifting timbre. This technique is known as ***Klangfarbenmelodie*** ("tone-color melody"). Webern, particularly fascinated by ***Klangfarbenmelodie,*** placed the stamp of his personality upon it, and transformed it into an entire esthetic attitude.

Webern's "orchestra" for the ***Five Pieces*** is actually a small body of seventeen players, including such exotic instruments as guitar, celesta, harp, and mandolin. Very few overlapping lines or chordal sonorities occur during the first piece; one can hear this as a single expressive, delicate melodic line, passing from one instant to the next at the very threshhold of audibility. The piece lasts all of twelve measures, plus up-beat: an entire epigrammatic experience in about thirty seconds.

Impressionism: Debussy

In France, the dilemma of Wagnerian chromaticism was viewed in an entirely different light. While French composers may have been schooled in the German romantic tradition, it was not their own personal heritage. They had no stake in extending that tradition for reasons of historical "necessity;" for the average French musician, art was a vehicle for pleasure and entertainment, not a platform for weighty thoughts or a stage in the history of ideas. Moreover, there were French composers who simply did not agree with the major premises of Wagnerianism—the grand themes, the sober moralistic tone, the suffocating density of texture. For them, there was no point in continuing down that road any longer.

The most influential member of this new French generation was Claude Debussy (1862–1918). As a student at the Paris Conservatory, Debussy quickly established a name for himself as a rebel. When a professor asked him what rules of composition he followed, Debussy replied, "My pleasure." His questioning of the Germanic style led him to explore other traditions, including premises that were uniquely French: form as a succession of sections, consonance (rather than chromatic dissonance) as the norm, sensual values having priority over intellectual ones. Debussy really did compose according to his "pleasure;" in fact, he may be the first major composer to make his ear the ultimate judge in matters of compositional choice. For Debussy the *sound* of a work was pre-eminent. He felt that if he found the perfect sonority—an aural "environment"—for a composition, lines, shapes, and form would flow naturally from it.

Ancient and Exotic Scales

Debussy found many ways of avoiding dissonant Wagnerian chromaticism. One such way was the use of unusual scale forms, which minimize chro-

Figure 16.4

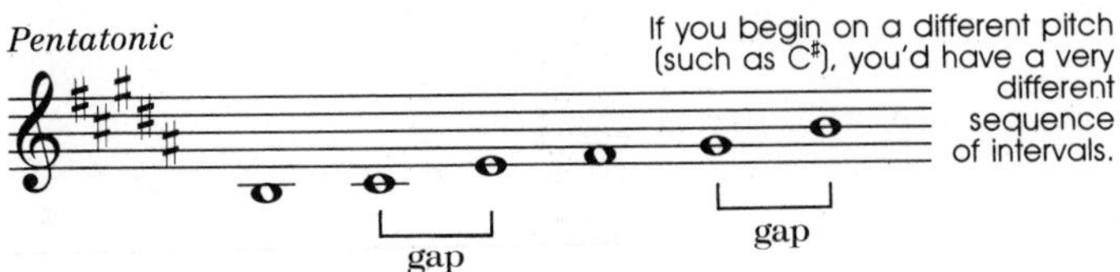

pentatonic scale
whole-tone scale

matic elements and have far less tonal "pull" than European scales. Debussy was especially fond of the ***pentatonic scale*** (five pitches, analogous to the black keys of the piano) and the ***whole-tone scale*** (six whole steps, located by playing every other note of a chromatic scale). As shown in Figure 16.4, both scales lack tonal direction, since there is no half step pulling the ear to the tonic; it may even be difficult to tell which pitch *is* the tonic. The use of either scale leads the musical fabric away from driving dissonance and towards a relatively relaxed, unhurried approach to sheer sound. Debussy associated these scales with the wind, air, sea, distant bells, horn calls, shepherds' pipes. In this he was still very much a romantic at heart.

Debussy shared the romantic passion for exotic subjects, but went one step further and actually experienced the music of other cultures. At the great international Paris Exposition of 1889 celebrating the centennial of the revolution, for which the Eiffel Tower was built, he first heard the Indonesian gamelan. The free-floating, consonant sonorities of the gamelan and other non-Western textures made a profound impact upon his work, certainly related to his love for pentatonic and whole-tone scales. He also used ancient Western modes, virtually ignored since the 1600s, for similar purposes, delighting in their symbolic connotations and musical properties. In all this, Debussy combated the crisis of chromaticism by looking outside the Western tonal tradition which had brought about that crisis.

Parallel Harmony

Debussy's revolutionary harmonic style also bypassed the Western tradition. From the very first chord progressions to the dissonances of Schoenberg, that tradition had assumed that chords were connected—that a chord had a function within a logical chain or chord events. Moreover, individual ***pitches within*** the chord were related to their neighbors in adjacent chords on either side as suggested in Figure 16.5. This may be because chords had evolved from linear, polyphonic styles. Even the simplest diatonic harmony

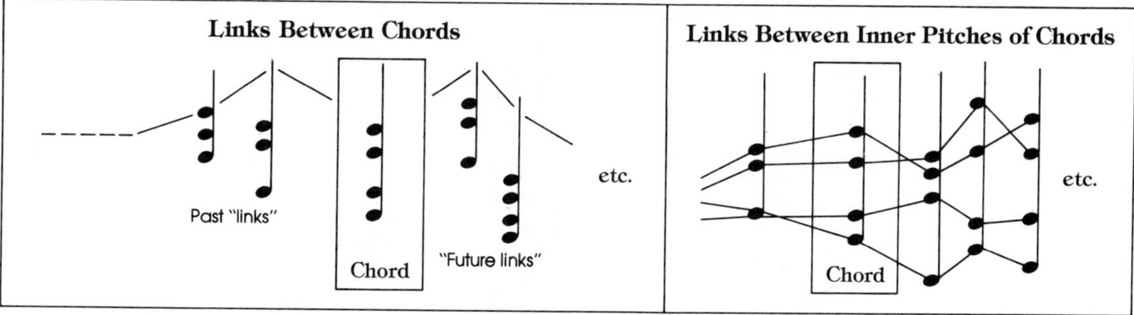

Figure 16.5

contains these relationships. In highly chromatic music, the relationships create a taut network, like that of coiled stretched springs, finding release, if ever, at a final cadence.

But many of Debussy's chords are used without regard to function. For him, a chord's chief virtue may simply be its *sonority,* its particular "color" as a sensuous object. We may become aware of that color if we hear the chord as an isolated thing in itself, or if we hear the *same* chord color moving up and down on successive pitch levels. This technique is called

parallel harmony

parallel harmony, or simply ***parallelism.*** It is usually forbidden in traditional Western harmony, because it severely weakens the sense of "progression" or tonal drive; that was precisely why Debussy was so fond of it.

The effects of parallelism can be demonstrated easily, with any familiar tune. Figure 16.6 presents the opening measures of "America," with the lovely "color" of a dominant 9th chord hanging from each note of the melody and following the tune's contours up and down. The music becomes tonally directionless and lacking in tension. Moreover, ten of the twelve chromatic tones have been used in this two-measure passage. However, in this context, they are not *functionally* chromatic at all. Ironically, Debussy's style, like Schoenberg's, could create a fabric of free atonality with the use of all twelve tones. Their sound worlds, however, were vastly different: Schoenberg spoke proudly of his "emancipation of the dissonance," whereas Debussy wanted consonance to be as prominent as possible.

Figure 16.6

Leon Bakst, ***Nijinsky in L'Après Midi d'un Faune.*** This design was developed for the Diaghilev Ballet production of Debussy's ***L'après midi d'un faune,*** in which Nijinsky danced as the faun.

Impressionism

impressionism

Debussy's music reflects a love of ambiguity and indistinct outlines, as well as an open, spacious sense of light and color. Not surprisingly, he found himself allied in the public mind with the French art movement called *impressionism.* He disliked that label, as much as Schoenberg hated the word "atonality;" even so, the label is useful in considering Debussy's music.

The basic assumptions of impressionism and German expressionism are quite different. With the latter, the inclination is to turn inward, and "express" the interior psychological landscape of personality: its dreams, fears, and hopes. On the other hand, we have "impressions" of the physical, external universe, the senses responding to the play of light, shade, wind, and rain upon the earth. The subject matter of Debussy's programmatic works bring to mind the everyday, understated visual world of the impressionist painters. He shared their fascination with fleeting, simple, elusive symbols and their rejection of the monumental, pretentious, or grandiose. The titles of his pieces are likely to reflect this outlook: "Clouds," "The Snow is Dancing," or "Dead Leaves," to name but a few.

Most of Debussy's music is programmatic, inspired by natural phenomena or by other art works. During most of his career he had little use for absolute music, and once wrote that composers would learn more from watching a sunset than from studying Beethoven symphonies. Accordingly, his own symphonic music consists of a few evocative tone poems, although he never used that term. The best known is entitled ***Prélude à l'après-midi d'un faune*** ("Prelude to the Afternoon of a Faun"), based upon a poem by his friend Stéphane Mallarmé, a major figure in the French "symbolist" movement. The faun of the poem is a mythic creature, half man and half goat. His afternoon is an idyllic one: lazy, sensuous, and balmy, with memories—or were they dreams?—of lovely nymphs and the drowsiness of wine.

Claude Debussy

Prélude à l'après-midi d'un Faune

R5 S1 B3

The composition begins with an undulating, rhythmically fluid line for solo flute (Figure 16.7). The tonality is obscure, perhaps because the whole-tone scale is so strongly emphasized in the line. Just when a central key begins to appear, the figure settles on some indecisive chords, and is then lost in the haze of a harp arpeggio. Instruments are used in a discreet, chamber-ensemble manner: two harps, horns, a quiet woodwind chord, muted strings.

This opening motive occurs many times during the piece, often emerging from a diffuse timbre and then dissolving once more. Debussy's handling of color is so memorable that the characteristic flute sound of the opening—the faun's panpipe, we suppose—becomes a "theme" in its own

Figure 16.7

right. Although there is a general ABA form for the entire work, the opening flute motive is the most prominent feature, heard about ten times during a nine-minute piece, and never far from the listener's memory. Note that it is never strictly developed; it merely appears in new contexts and settings.

Many musical elements contribute to the dreamy, sunlit atmosphere: the relaxed tempo and unobtrusive rhythm, with hardly any strong beat for long stretches of time; the use of instruments in their breathiest, or least focused, registers for elusive timbres; the indistinct tonality, that only asserts its E-major tendencies at the end. Scale forms vary throughout the work. The surging melodic line of the lyric B section (Figure 16.8) begins pentatonically; whole-tone, pentatonic, diatonic, and thoroughly chromatic passages mix freely within the gently flowing fabric. Like the impressionistic painters, Debussy favors pure colors (in this case, timbres), and leaves the "mixing" to the ear. Like them, too, he favors shimmering, muted suggestions of line, rather than bold, clear boundaries.

Listen, as well, to some of Debussy's music for solo piano. In its imaginative sonorities, extreme registers, and pedal effects, it marks the first major step in piano writing since Chopin and Liszt. Debussy wrote many piano preludes, miniature "character pieces" with programmatic subtitles. One well known Prelude, ***La Cathédrale engloutie*** ("The Sunken Cathedral") bases its program upon the myth of a lengendary cathedral,

Figure 16.8

notes of pentatonic scale (D♭, E♭, F, A♭, B♭)

Claude Monet, ***River Scene.***

submerged at the bottom of the ocean, which at times rises to the surface. Debussy uses sonority and stately tempo to suggest vast, watery depths. Highest and lowest registers sound simultaneously at the beginning, creating a spacious effect; the rising pentatonic line which follows is stated in the parallel 4ths and 5ths of medieval organum, creating an utterly ambiguous sense of tonality. We have the suggestion of chanting voices and tolling bells; in this style, of course, a "suggestion" is all that one desires. A gradual crescendo leads to a booming pedal point on low C. The cathedral is no longer blurred, but clearly etched against the sky, as it rises from the waters: the fragmentary opening motive is now a fully rounded melody, stated in parallel harmony (see Figure 16.9). Gradually the texture grows thinner and the sonority more blurred. As the cathedral sinks beneath the sea, the hymnlike melody is heard distantly against a rolling muffled bass ostinato.

Figure 16.9

In his alliance of music with expressive states and programmatic tone painting, Debussy was just as "romantic" as any post-Wagnerian. Even though he was scornful of Wagner and was especially nasty in writing about leitmotifs, comparing them to "those silly people who hand you their visiting cards," he was under the spell of Bayreuth for many years. Debussy's fragmentary motives, woven into a continuous musical fabric, could be compared to Wagner's and his concentration upon the enveloping, hypnotically seductive power of sound is strangely Wagnerian as well.

Despite this, he was a great revolutionary. He recognized that one had to look outside the Western tonal tradition for an alternative to chromaticism. In his approach to harmony, sonority, and form, he provided a new listening focus: the *moment,* rather than the extended line. And he demonstrated that an artist's creative thinking could be intuitive and eclectic, rather than systematically logical.

Beyond Impressionism: Satie, Les Six, Stravinsky and Jazz

Other Paris-based composers made an even cleaner break with the romantic past. One of these was the young Igor Stravinsky, Russian-born but living in France, whose work will be discussed shortly. Another was Erik Satie (1866–1925), a Parisian who knew Debussy well and counted him among his closest colleagues, but who believed that *all* romantic art, including the French impressionist variety, was affected and pretentious. Satie and Debussy were allies in their hatred of German music; Satie once commented that "We must have a music of our own, without sauerkraut." But Satie found Debussy's delicate approach somewhat precious. He preferred a cleaner, simpler, antiexpressive esthetic. Many of his own titles, meaningless and nonsensical, poke fun at the romantic passion for illustrative, evocative "meanings." Satie devised titles like ***Flabby Preludes,*** or ***Pieces to Make You Run Away,*** and then surprised listeners with music that was cool, distant, and even formal at times. His musical style seemed to alternate between a reserved detachment and bold wit, qualities that were both quite rare during the ultraserious twilight years of "expressive" romanticism.

Satie's textures are strikingly clear and transparent, without impressionistic haze. His harmony may seem very puzzling at times, often using simple triads moving in directions that are totally illogical by the standards of tonality. This use of chords is called ***non-functional harmony.*** For example, in the opening pages of his oddly-named (even for Satie!) ***Three Pieces in the Form of a Pear,*** we hear E minor, C♯ minor, E minor, B minor, D minor, A minor, E minor, B♭ major, and so on, all stated as simple oom-pah chord patterns against the innocent melodic line. Satie also wrote syncopated tunes in "popular" style, reminiscent of the French music hall or cabaret. This was his way of attacking romantic postures of dignity, high culture, and self-importance. He felt that the seriousness of "art" music was a balloon that needed to be punctured; he hated (to use his description of Wagner) the "sort of music you listen to with your head in your hands."

Satie even went so far as to write music that was not meant to be listened to at all: repetitive, nondirectional patterns of sound that were intended to blend into a social environment. One famous example was created for a 1920 opening at a Paris art gallery; Satie hoped it would attract no more attention than the furniture or wallpaper. (Our own society has devised recorded "Muzak" for elevators and supermarkets, with similar intent.) This was a far cry from the romantic view of music as intense personal expression, or Wagnerian demands upon the listener's total attention.

"Les Six" and Polytonality

By the time of the First World War, Satie had begun to influence younger composers, and important Parisian figures in the other arts, such as Picasso and Jean Cocteau, as well. The poet, playwright and filmmaker Cocteau wrote, "Satie teaches the greatest audacity of our age: simplicity;" he became literary spokesman for the movement growing up around Satie. Six young composers were the nucleus of this movement. A 1920 article comparing them to the legendary "Mighty Five" led to the use of a collective label, ***Les Six*** ("the Six"). Only three of ***Les Six*** achieved international fame: Arthur Honegger (1892–1956), Francis Poulenc (1899–1963), and Darius Milhaud (1892–1974). Poulenc and Milhaud in particular, emulated the clever wit, clarity and grace of their idol Satie. Their attitude to romanticism was summed up in Milhaud's cry, "Down with Wagner!"

Les Six

Poulenc's charm, pixie humor, and attachment to cafe and circus tunes were related to his background as a sophisticated Parisian. By contrast, Milhaud was a native of southern France whose musical ideas were also shaped by visits to the New World. During the First World War he spent a number of years in Brazil, as secretary to the French ambassador. South American popular music made a deep impression on Milhaud. He was also greatly attracted to North American jazz, and was a regular visitor to Harlem

Figure 16.10

night clubs and dance halls during frequent trips to New York. These diverse influences are felt in such pieces as his *Saundades do Brazil* for piano (1920–21), with obvious Latin-American rhythms, and the jazz-inspired ballet of 1923 *La Création du Monde,* which combined elements of Dixieland, blues, and a Broadway-like lyricism.

Both works also have a peculiar bite to their harmony: not an odd succession of familiar chords, as in Debussy or Satie, but an unusual quality to the chords themselves. This sound is created by combining two or more tonalities at the same time. The resulting effect is called ***polytonality.*** Polytonality is definitely not "atonal;" on the contrary, it is supertonal, an affirmation of tonality that spills over the boundaries of a single key center. And polytonality, tonal music conceived in multiple levels, is really no more dissonant than any other tonal music. It may sound more ***discordant,*** biting, exotic, or unusual—but not in urgent need of resolution. In listening to the fabric of Milhaud's *Saundades,* as in Figure 16.10, the sense of high discordance but average dissonance level should be apparent. Polytonality may add spice to the sound, but does not disturb the essential tonality of the music.

polytonality

The Influence of Jazz

Milhaud's jazz ballet typified a Parisian interest in American popular music that had been growing since the turn of the century. Debussy had been interested in post-Civil War minstrel-show music; both Satie and Stravinsky were fascinated by the ragtime style made popular by the compositions of Scott Joplin. French taste responded to the syncopated rhythms and percussive sonorities of jazz. Composers were also attracted to the vocal tradition of the blues (see Chapters 1–7): the repeated harmonic ***ground*** patterns, the subtle rhythmic flexibility of the vocal solo line, and the scales containing major and minor elements. The *improvisatory* aspects of blues and jazz (as opposed to the fully notated ragtime style) exerted a special influence as well.

At first the French were interested in jazz as an "exotic" element, part African and part American, in the same way that they enjoyed oriental or

Spanish "locales." By 1914 they had acquired a real taste for its style, and sympathy for its popular, "anti-art" base; these feelings were reinforced by close contact with Americans during the War. The Austro-German musical world, by contrast, was still too dedicated to the post-Wagnerian ideal, and too antagonistic to American culture, to pay much attention to jazz. This situation would change drastically under the Weimar regime during the twenties, with the emergence of Berlin as a great center for experimental art.

Ironically, jazz had no impact upon the serious musical establishment of the United States either. Before the twenties, American art music was as steeped in the grand European tradition as it could be. The most talented Americans were sent abroad to study, and they were more concerned with Wagner, Brahms, or Dvořák than with their native music. Even the broad-based musical theater took its cue from European popular music: the stage works of Victor Herbert, for example, reflect the influence of Viennese operetta. Significantly, the first major American attempt to bring jazz into the concert world of high culture came from a popular composer, George Gershwin, whose ***Rhapsody in Blue*** was premiered in 1924, one year after ***La Création du Monde.***

Stravinsky before 1920

The strongest attack upon romanticism came from a young Russian composer living in Paris, Igor Stravinsky (1882–1971). Like Schoenberg, Stravinsky has had enormous impact on this century's musical thinking; in the next chapter, we will discuss the work of both composers after 1920. In the first decades of this century, Stravinsky was just beginning his career, having recently come to Paris at the invitation of ballet impresario Serge Diaghilev. Diaghilev's "Ballets Russes" company drew upon an exciting collection of extraordinary talents, including Satie, Picasso, Nijinsky, and Pavlova. The presence of these innovative artists, along with others such as Cocteau and Gertrude Stein, made Paris the liveliest creative center of the Western world—a city remarkably open to experimental ideas, in contrast to Schoenberg's Vienna.

The young Stravinsky had no use for the Wagnerian mystique, or for its impassioned chromaticism: he often criticized the "Wagnerian tyranny." Although Stravinsky admired Debussy and learned much about harmony and timbre from him, he was equally uninterested in the romantic affectations and suggestive haze of impressionism. He preferred the direct, sharp outlines and bold colors of his own Russian heritage. That heritage is reflected in the three large ballet scores he wrote for the Diaghilev company. The ***Firebird*** of 1910, based on an exotic fairy tale, was followed by ***Petroushka*** (1911), based on the garish, earthy subject of a street carnival and puppet theatre. Stravinsky's style became increasingly sharp-edged, with more frequent use of folk tunes and a high degree of polytonality. (The simultaneous use of the C-major and F♯-major triads, in his second ballet, has often been called the "Petroushka chord.")

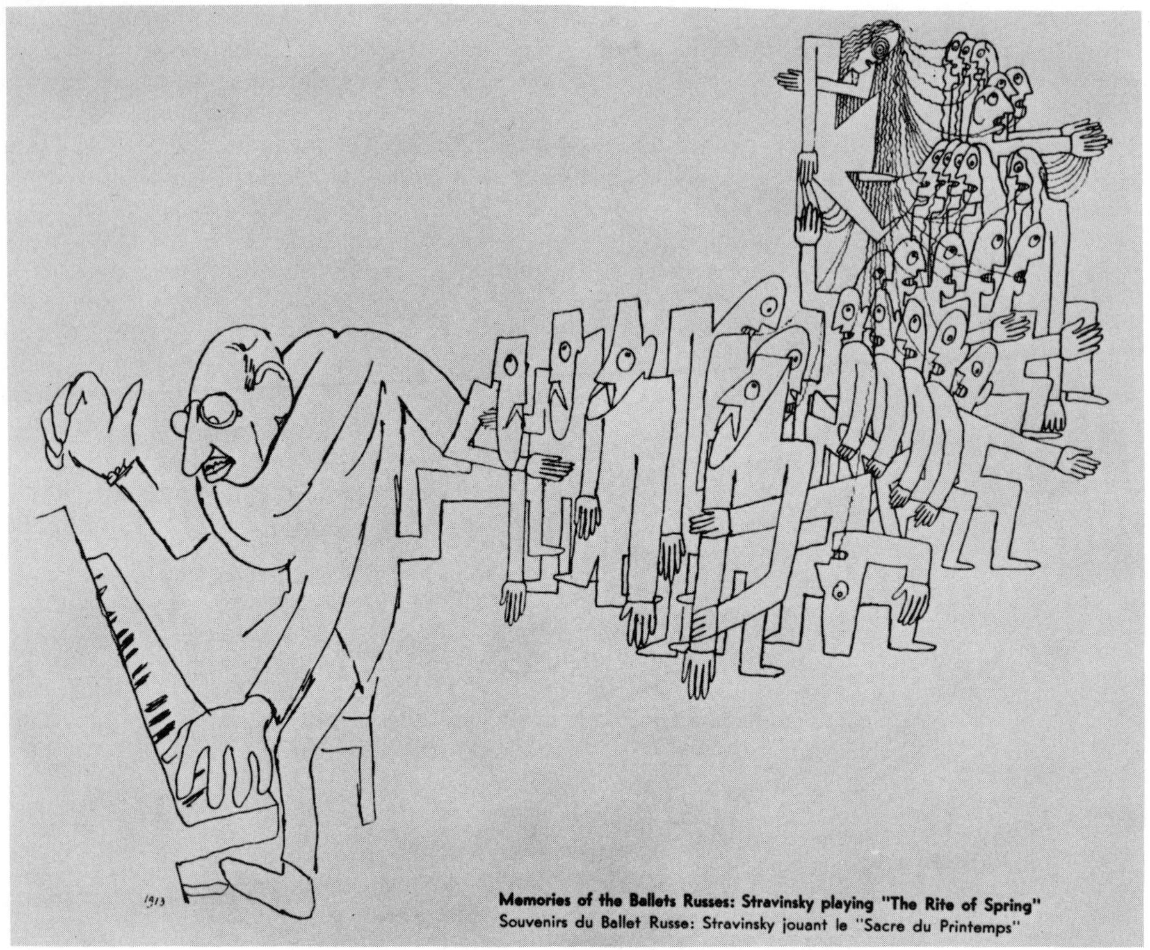

Jean Cocteau, ***Stravinsky playing the Rite of Spring.***

The third ballet for Diaghilev proved to be one of the most provocative works in the history of music: ***La Sacre du Printemps*** (''The Rite of Spring''), a depiction of prehistoric religious rites culminating in a human sacrifice. African sculpture and other discoveries about ancient culture and mythology had begun to influence European thinking. In this vein, Diaghilev's production was intended to be raw and powerful rather than ''pretty;'' the dancers wore rough, primitive-looking costumes, and moved with an angular, fierce strength suggestive of cave dwellers. The public response at the premiere was surprisingly violent. Members of the audience hooted, shrieked, insulted each other, and attacked their neighbors with canes, purses, and fists. Objects were thrown onto the stage; Debussy rose from his seat, urging people to let the performance go on, but to no avail. Gertrude Stein later commented that the crowd noise had completely obliterated the sound of the music. Stravinsky, embarrassed and humiliated, fled the theatre. The riot at the 1913 premiere of *Le Sacre du Printemps* has since become a legend, and the piece itself has become a twentieth-century classic.

Not everyone disliked the music. On the contrary, much of the violence was caused by fighting between Stravinsky-supporters and Stravinsky-haters. Nonetheless, it is easy to see why many people would have been shocked and offended at the performance. *Le Sacre du Printemps* was as far removed from romantic "beauty" as possible. Its rhythms and sonorities were jarring and brutal; the scenery, costumes and dance movements were equally harsh. There seemed to be no melody, no grace, nothing "lovely" or morally uplifting. Although modern audiences would hardly claim that *Le Sacre* lacks melody or harmony, Stravinsky's music still makes an extraordinary impact today.

Igor Stravinsky

Le Sacre du Printemps: Part I

R5 S2 B1

The music is divided in two large parts, corresponding to the acts of the ballet: we will discuss Part I here. In the orchestral introduction, Stravinsky wanted to depict the "awakening of nature." He begins with a single line that gradually blossoms into greater density and activity. The opening motive (Figure 16.11) is given to the highest register of the bassoon: Note the narrow range of the melody, and its repetition of a tiny figure again and again with different rhythmic stresses (here bracketed) each time; such traits can be found in Russian folk song. The bassoon is answered by other instruments, each adding a brief figure that remains static. The overall texture seems to evoke the sound world of a primeval forest: motionless, and yet vibrating with the life of bird calls and animal cries. The harmony is polytonal, giving a feeling of "discord" but not unusual dissonance. The activity fades to silence, and then we hear the opening bassoon motive again. Quiet polytonal sonorities are sustained against a regular rhythmic ostinato pulse; by this time, the dancers have appeared on stage.

Suddenly, the ostinato becomes loud and harsh, its accents staggered unpredictably. This section is called the "Dance of the Adolescents:" we

Figure 16.11

Figure 16.12

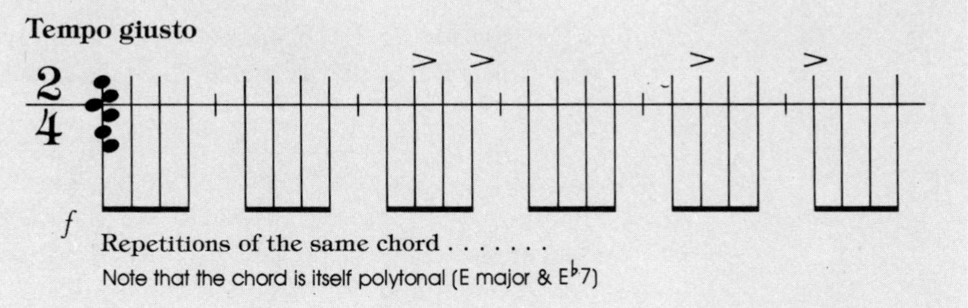

might imagine the opening-night audience growing restless here. The brutal offbeat accents on a single repeated chord (Figure 16.12) must have seemed utterly mad to them: The pounding rhythm suddenly becomes quiet, and functions as a background for a variety of melodic fragments. Like the opening bassoon solo, these snippets have the repetitive patterns of folk song. Stravinsky chooses not to "develop" any of these; he simply repeats them in a hypnotic "primitive" ostinato, and then discards them in favor of new ones.

The "Dance of Abduction" which follows is even more violent rhythmically. The meters are constantly changing, punctuated by brilliant drum strokes and flashing orchestral colors. A sense of regularity is provided only by the steady tempo and the limited melodic material. This frenetic activity subsides to a quiet passage featuring woodwind trills, and a new dance begins: "Round Dances of Spring." The pace is slow, regular, and stately. Against a slightly syncopated ostinato figure we hear another folklike melody, shown in Figure 16.13. This section grows louder and more dense, eventually reaching a ferocious level in which gongs and sliding trombones are prominent. Stravinsky's handling of sonority is brilliant throughout; he uses orchestral forces for rhythmic articulation, bursts of color, mass and density. Such extroverted scoring is essential in a style that depends upon ***contrast,*** rather than development, to hold the attention. There are three more dances before the first part of ***Le Sacre du Printemps*** is completed. The "Games of Rival Tribes" leads to the very formal, stately "Procession

Figure 16.13

of the Sage.'' (The Sage will preside over the ritual sacrifice at the ballet's end.) The ''Dance of the Earth'' is rapid and almost hysterically frenzied, built around a repeated ostinato of changing meter.

Note that Stravinsky has built the entire work as a series of contrasted sections. There are very few gradual transitions between one episode and the next; usually a section goes on to an abrupt stop. This nondevelopmental ''mosaic'' approach to form is typically Russian. We can detect it in the music of Mussorgsky or Tchaikovsky or, for that matter, Debussy (who idolized Mussorgsky). Stravinsky has simply taken an existing process to previously unheard-of limits, not unlike Schoenberg with regard to Wagnerian harmony.

The Russian influence also appears in Stravinsky's bold, coloristic orchestration, and bitingly discordant harmonic language. His folklike tunes are always focused around a central pitch, avoiding Germanic chromaticism and retaining tonality. But, like Milhaud, he uses ***polytonality*** to create an added sting to the fabric.

Ironically, ***Le Sacre du Printemps*** is really more ''Romantic'' than anyone in 1913 (including its composer) might have imagined. In particular, note its vast performing forces—an orchestra at least as large as Mahler's—and the use of those forces to express an overpowering ''idea,'' although not a very pretty one. These were features that reflected a dying age.

Nationalistic Influences

As we have noted, the early Stravinsky ballets were all nationalistic in their musical style and in their subject matter: ***Le Sacre*** was even subtitled ''Pictures of Pagan Russia.'' Perhaps the young Russian composer, living in Paris, felt a certain homesickness that he expressed through his art. On a more cynical level, he and Diaghilev knew that ''exotic'' works held tremendous box-office potential with the French public. Nationalism and its artistic effects were intensely felt throughout Europe. We have seen some of the patriotic urges behind the esthetics of Schoenberg, Satie, and Debussy. The great 1914–1918 war would grimly demonstrate how powerful European nationalism really was.

During the early twentieth century, nationalistic composers wanted to go beyond mere splashes of local color. Many of them delved deeply into the style features of their native music. In some cases, composers joined other musical scholars in the intensive study of folk culture. Armed with pen, manuscript paper and (in later decades) recording devices, researchers traveled about the countryside, taking down songs and dances as performed by local villagers. Ralph Vaughan Williams collected English folk songs in this way, and Béla Bartók (see Chapter 17) was a major figure in the scholarly study of Hungarian folk music.

The final moment of *Le Sacre du Printemps.*

Arthur Davies, *Dancers.*

The vast range of nationalistic styles includes the work of (1) Jean Sibelius (1865–1957), who drew upon the musical resources of his native Finland to formulate a unique, strongly tonal language and an organically cyclic approach to form; (2) Sergei Rachmaninov (1873–1943), one of the great pianists of the century, and a composer in the vein of sweeping melancholy made popular by his idol Tchaikovsky (revealing the super-emotional aspect of Russian art that Stravinsky had intentionally bypassed); and (3) Ernest Bloch (1880–1959), a citizen first of Switzerland and then of the United States, but one who regarded his Jewish heritage as his strongest cultural identification. In many works he tried to evoke the color and splendor of the Hebraic tradition, using melody and harmony derived from mid-Eastern scale forms. (4) Ralph Vaughan Williams (1872–1958) discovered his own style in the rich resources of English folk music, and strongly urged young composers everywhere to look to their own traditions before succumbing to the international concert style. His love of ancient modes, contrapuntally weaving lines and parallel harmonies grew from his study of early English song and dance, and he entitled one of his own works *A London Symphony.*

American Experiments

Nationalistic ideals were felt in the United States, too. At the turn of the century, most American composers drew upon European models, rather than native folk or popular material. The works of such outstanding Americans as Amy Beach and Edward MacDowell continue the traditions of Liszt and Brahms. "Good" music was equated with concert music and high culture, and it was assumed that foreigners possessed a special gift for this that Americans lacked. Indigenous art, on the other hand, was regarded as socially and intellectually inferior. This situation had existed in the United States since colonial times. But it was beginning to change, just as it was changing in Vaughan Williams's England, and had already changed in mid-nineteenth-century Russia.

The American developments of this century were uniquely different from anything in Europe, for two important reasons. First, the great distances separating the United States from Europe encouraged a certain freedom from tradition—a maverick, experimental streak, and an unprecedented flair for innovation, not bound to "history" or "culture." Moreover, Americans could draw upon a greater variety of ethnic, native styles, simply because America was a collection of communities drawn from the rest of the world. There really is no "typical American;" there are, rather, individuals with their own special roots and strong contacts with other subcultures. Similarly, there is no typical American composer. When asked how to write American music, composer-critic Virgil Thomson replied, "Just be an American, and then write any kind of music you want to."

Two grand old men of American music, and good friends, in conversation: Henry Cowell, at the left, and Charles Ives.

In the early twentieth century a few Americans began to explore their own traditions, and while doing so departed from many European norms. They became founders, unintentionally, of an "American tradition," an experimental tradition that has grown richer with each passing decade.

One such composer was Henry Cowell (1897–1965). His musical background typified America's "melting pot." Born into an Irish-American family and given traditional (Germanic) musical training, Cowell also drew upon his close contact with the Asian communities of the San Francisco Bay area. He pioneered in the development of new sound resources for everyday Western instruments, and by the 1920s was known for his unorthodox piano timbres. He frequently used ***tone clusters,*** sounds made by playing the keyboard with palms, fists, or arms. He also required pianists to strum, scrape, or depress the inner strings of the instrument. Cowell was one of the first composers to make a serious study of world folk music. His own work draws upon a staggering variety of sources, from Persian chant to Irish jigs to colonial New England tunes, all handled with unquenchable curiosity and great wit.

tone clusters

Charles Ives

Charles Ives (1874–1954) was a close friend of Cowell's and an equally adventurous spirit. Ives was a product of New England, and deeply believed in the qualities of fierce independence and philosophical inquiry that characterized the best of Yankee thought. In this respect, he felt a kinship to Emerson, Thoreau, the Alcotts, and other New Englanders who had created a climate of intellectual rigor and social concern. Charles's father, George Ives, was a former bandmaster in the Civil War and an insatiably experimental musician in his own right. The elder Ives explored microtonal intonation, mistuned pianos, ensembles of drinking glasses, the simultaneous sounding of unrelated rhythms. He would place several bands in different locations and have them all play at once to test their spatial effects, or have instruments played across a lake or on hilltops to catch the echoes. He encouraged his son Charles to be equally inventive and curious about musical experience. (Such phenomena ***are*** indeed part of everday experience! Spaces and audience locations make for unique resonances and echoes; performers miss beats and may play slightly out-of-tune; simultaneous musical events often tickle our ears at a country fair or city street corner, or in the halls of a music school. Charles Ives was taught to respond to these ***positively*** as exciting stimuli, not to ignore or "correct" them.)

Ives' musical language was shaped during his Connecticut boyhood, and reflects the musical culture of small-town America: town bands, country fiddlers, church hymns, college songs, and ragtime. Although he received a traditional "European" training at Yale, he decided that it was more important to recapture musical experience as he knew it than to be academically "correct." Significantly, he decided not to make music his profession; as he put it, he did not want his family to starve on his dissonances. He became, rather, one of the most successful insurance executives in America, the co-partner of a multimillion-dollar agency.

Ives never saw any distinction between his art and his business. In his view, ***both*** were truly creative; both required ingenuity and invention, and dedication to the ideals of human happiness and enlightenment. At the turn of the century the United States was the ideal place for such a daring, boldly imaginative person to be, *if* one's creative genius could be channeled into business or commerce. Ironically, the same qualities that made Charles Ives a rich man spelled oblivion for his artistic career. For many years his music was considered unplayable and just plain crazy. Although he had a number of isolated supporters, he was a little-known musical figure for much of his life. Fame came to him only in his last decade, nearly half a century after his best works had been composed.

Ives wrote very little music after a serious illness in 1918, and some of his most striking works are dated between 1895 and 1910. In these Ives explored atonality many years before Schoenberg, and polytonality decades before Stravinsky or Milhaud. He also wrote music concerned with spatial placement of players, quasi-improvisational performance instructions, and quarter-tone intonation. His use of such techniques was never systematic, or incorporated into a unified, consistent language in the European manner. He simply handled materials as he wished, for the purposes of a particular piece or passage. In fact, if we were to define an Ives "style" its strongest feature might be the juxtaposition of wildly incongruous elements—tonal melodies, quotations from familiar tunes, complex chromaticism, tone clusters—in succession, or even simultaneously. Listen to an excerpt from one of his large orchestra pieces, in which many "levels" are heard at the same time: different tunes, in different keys and rhythms.

Charles Ives

Three Places in New England

R5 S2 B2

Movement II This movement is entitled "Putnam's Camp: Redding, Connecticut." Here Ives wanted to evoke the memories of his boyhood, when his father would have two or three bands, each playing a different number, march from widely separated locations towards the town square. The music is festive and joyous, filled with the life and spirit of a Fourth of July picnic. It is set as a loose ABA′ form, alternately raucous and tender, with a distant, hazy, suspended quality to part B. In Ives's program, a child attending the festive picnic wanders into the woods, and dreams (part B) of the Revolutionary soldiers who once camped there long ago. Then he awakens (the return of A), hears the music and runs back to join the celebration.

In depicting the different bands at the picnic, Ives enjoys the juxtaposition of two or more tunes, each in a separate key. This produces not only a polytonal fabric, but a network of conflicting rhythms and meters called

polyrhythm

polyrhythm. (In other pieces by Ives, polyrhythmic levels can be so complex that two or more conductors may be used to coordinate passages.) Out of the opening, chaotic-sounding mass of early monuments, one particular march tune emerges, surrounded by conflicting rhythms and fragments of other melodies. We hear snatches of familiar Sousa marches; there is also a brief reminder of "Yankee Doodle" passing from one key to another and one instrumental timbre to another as well, so that we just barely make it out before it vanishes.

The music becomes quieter, with reference to lyric tunes of the day, and then dissolves in a dreamlike, slowly moving polytonal web. Gradually, the activity starts up again, a distant snare-drum rhythm becomes louder and louder, and then a new grand march begins, including Revolutionary period fragments. There is a quiet reference to the brief lyric phrase heard much earlier, and then all the important tunes of the movement return at the same time, with a bang. The concluding section, right up to the last crashing polytonal chord, is perfect tone painting of joyful, patriotic confusion.

In hearing Ives's reference to familiar American tunes, note that these motives are rarely quoted in their entirety. Usually they are tiny fragments, altered and distorted, that emerge from and recede back into complex textures. Even so, we may feel a shock of recognition, or a glow of pride or pleasant memories, when these references appear. (Imagine how intimately a Norwegian must respond to Grieg, or a German to Schumann or Brahms.) Apart from quotations, Ives's most striking feature is the creation of many simultaneous "levels" of texture. It almost seems as though the performers are playing different pieces! Ives frequently regarded his "parts" as individual "personalities," and even conceived complex ensemble passages as a conversation, (or collision) among these personalities, rather than as tightly integrated European counterpoint.

There is a wide expressive range in Ives's work: loud, boisterous music one moment, and then wonderfully evocative passages the next, as "impressionistic" as any French example. In many respects, Ives was a nineteenth-century romantic at heart, deeply concerned about the relations between art, life, morality, and expressive needs. Like so many of the composers studied in this chapter, he was caught between two centuries, with an adventurous attitude towards his ***materials*** and a grand romantic view of his creative ***purpose.*** Mahler, Schoenberg, Stravinsky, and Debussy faced similar dilemmas; they too are characteristic of the age.

Edgard Varèse

Our third American experimentalist was, like Ives, little known until the end of his long life. Edgard Varèse (1883–1965) was not a native American; he was born in France and trained in the grand romantic tradition. But he rejected all his early works in favor of a more radical approach to sound and timbre. He also decided to leave the tradition-bound environment of Europe, and emigrated to the United States in 1915; here he actively promoted, organized, and conducted concerts of radical new music.

Varèse was influenced by the ideas of Ferrucio Busoni (1866–1924), a composer who astounded the musical world with his theories and prophecies, virtually all of which have since come true: new intonation systems, artificial scales, the return to a new classicism, the use of electricity to make music. Varèse also read widely in science and philosophy. It was in one of his readings that he came across the definition of music as "the corporealization of the intelligence that it is in sounds." He made that definition the basis for his own esthetic. Varese was convinced of the strong ties between science and music, and found that scientific developments stimulated his musical thinking. For example, he tried to create musical shapes and processes which would reflect those of the physical-chemical universe (such as crystallization or gravitational fields), rather than the traditional forms borrowed from literature and drama. Sounds could thus be enjoyed for their own sake, not as "expressive" symbols in a language of affections. Varèse also believed that composers should explore acoustic properties, sonority, balance, instrument building: in short, the physics of their art.

Varèse wrote very few compositions after his radical change of style, and most of these during the 1920s. *Octandre* provides a fine example of his explosive musical energy. This 1924 octet is scored for flute, oboe, clarinet, bassoon, horn, trumpet, trombone, and string bass.

Edgard Varèse:
Octandre

R5 S2 B3

Movement I The stark solo quality of the opening oboe line, and its reliance upon the repetition of brief figures, may recall the start of *Le Sacre du Printemps.* Like Stravinsky, Varèse creates ostinato lines from tiny cells, and overlays them with other ostinatos. Also like Stravinsky, he consciously avoids European "development" of his material. But Varèse is not drawn to the simple contours of folklike tunes. Rather, his motivic fragments are jagged and irregular, (see Figure 16.14), often combining repeated tones in ways that articulate sonority and overall density.

The combination and interlocking of motives is also directed to sonority, rather than any traditional notion of harmony or counterpoint. Varèse seems to be sculpting planes, masses and densities of sound, using silence and time as his sculptural space. Timbre is often at its most brilliant, and instruments are placed in particularly piercing registers. Notice the changing meters, too, focusing the ear upon rhythmic energy for its own sake, rather than a beat. The music reaches a ferocious climax, and then gradually alters its mass, so that the weight eventually diminishes to the single oboe and its original motive once again.

The style of this music could hardly be called chromatic, let alone atonal: Varèse's use of pitch is nothing like Schoenberg's or Webern's. But to call it tonal or polytonal would be equally misleading, since that might imply a sense of direction or goal. On the contrary, Varèse uses entire mo-

Figure 16.14

tives as static blocks, sonic objects in a time-space continuum. (This is suggested in Figure 16.15). The blocks may shift and recombine to form larger crystals or (to alter the metaphor) they may blink on and off like a fixed bank of lights, but they do not move. Here we really do have an approximation of musical "space."

By the 1930s Varèse had given up composing, discouraged because his ideas demanded new instruments that did not yet exist. He wanted to work with engineers in designing such instruments, but was denied the opportunity. After some twenty years of retirement, Varèse began composing again in the late 1950s for the *electronic* media that had emerged during that time; his *Poème Électronique* of 1958 was hailed as a pioneering tape piece. Like Ives, Varèse discovered that he had become famous. His long-standing cry for electronic instruments had been met; he had become an idol for such pop stars as Frank Zappa and the Beatles; the avant-garde of the musical world had at last caught up with him. By that time, as we shall see in the next chapters, the American experimental tradition was thriving.

Figure 16.15

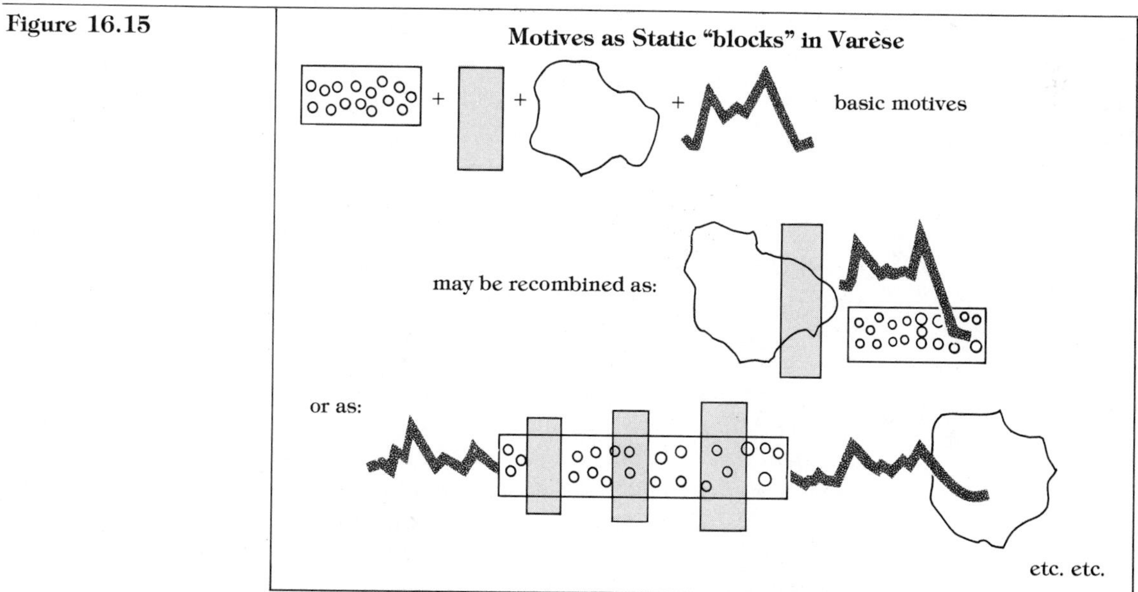

17

The Twentieth Century Mainstream

Once in Amsterdam, a Dutch musician said to me, "It must be difficult for you in America to write music, for you are so far away from the centers of tradition." I had to say, "It must be very difficult for you in Europe to write music, for you are so close to the centers of tradition."

John Cage

Music of Our Century

In the last chapter, we passed gradually from the world of late romanticism into a new musical world that can truly be called "contemporary." Perhaps we should pause and consider some of the important features already noted in the early twentieth-century music of Schoenberg, Stravinsky, Ives, and Varèse. This is especially important if, like many inexperienced listeners, we find such music odd, or even a bit mad. Judging from the riots, scandals, or neglect which greeted this music in its own era, most listeners *then* considered it strange indeed!

The outraged cries of the audiences hearing *Pierrot Lunaire* (1912) or *Le Sacre du Printemps* (1913) for the first time were genuine expressions of shock and revulsion at radically unfamiliar experiences. Other audiences at other times have had a similar response to drastic change. We read that during the premiere of Beethoven's ***Eroica*** Symphony someone from the gallery cried out, "I'll give a Kreutzer (coin) if they stop!" And in a famous contemporary attack on Monteverdi's *Orfeo* of 1607, a shocked colleague wrote, "One hears a medley of sounds, a harmonic rumour intolerable to the ears. How can the mind find itself amid such confusion?" It is tempting to assume, from those misguided audiences of the past, that *all* great art is unappreciated in its own time. Actually, this assumption is part of our romantic heritage, created in the nineteenth century. Many musical works, using the common language of shared experience, have been immediately enjoyed by listeners. Other pieces, obviously, have not; it is *these* compositions which provoked audiences to exclaim, "We can't understand strange modern music."

The fact that some composers deliberately address their audience in an unfamiliar language says something about the complex relationship between creator and listener, one which has certainly changed since the era of patronage died out with the classic period. However, listeners who accept the possibility of different musical languages have discovered that twentieth-century styles are not really hard to understand. We may not *like* all the varieties of twentieth-century music equally; different people may have a wide range of responses to the contemporary works discussed during the last chapter, or those studied earlier in Chapters 1–7. But these pieces can all be understood if we trust the experience of our ears, and deal with that experience in historical context. With this in mind, let us consider some features of the twentieth-century music we have already heard:

Melody is no longer bound to the range of the voice, or to the background, actual or implied, of tonal harmony. Contours may be angular and jagged over a wide range, or they may center about a limited set of repeated pitches. Key center may be absent, or highly ambiguous; brief motivic fragments may take the place of traditional phrases, especially in styles where tonal cadences are weakened. Motives may be fragmented even further by being tossed about among different instrumental timbres. Note, too, that melody is not necessarily a prime factor iin conveying *form.* Other elements—ostinato, a driving rhythm, an interval, a sonority—may be more "motivic" than melodic contour.

Rhythm has broken away from the regular, symmetrical patterns of earlier periods. Instead there may be an impulsive forward thrusting, or a still, motionless quality. Composers enjoy working with irregular meters, syncopated beats against the meter, or perhaps meter changes with each bar.

Harmony is freed from its dependence upon tonal function. Simple triads may move in unpredictable ways, or follow the melodic contour in a parallel stream. The practice of building chords in 3rds can lead far beyond triads, to create complex polytonal effects, as with Stravinsky and Milhaud. (The chord of C-E-G-B♭-D-F, for example, contains the triads of C major, G minor, and B major.) Chords can also be built on intervals other than 3rds; the *clusters* of Ives and Cowell can be thought of as groups of 2nds, and Stravinsky achieves a spacious quality by building chords in 4ths and 5ths.

Notions of consonance and dissonance are also expanded. In traditional tonal harmony, dissonance is the generative force and strongest feature, with resolution (consonance) the ultimate justification and rationale. But in a style such as Schoenberg's chromatic dissonance may be an end in itself. There may also be nonfunctional successions of free-floating consonance, or the brutal but static "discords" of Stravinsky and Varèse.

Texture has also undergone great changes. There is a renewed interest in counterpoint: for example, Schoenberg's complex strands of interweaving lines (a legacy from Brahms and Wagner), or the multiple levels—polytonal or polyrhythmic—of Ives, Stravinsky, and Milhaud. Densities may vary from the weighty mass of post-Wagnerian style to the anti-romantic clarity of the French. In the work of Varèse, density itself occupies the very forefront of our attention.

Many of these innovations can be traced to the wide variety of available ***scales,*** including medieval modes, blues, non-Western scales, microtonal divisions of the octave, and the authentic folk scales sought out by dedicated nationalists. By 1920 ***tonality*** was no longer the sole means for organizing pitch. Other options included freely chromatic ***atonality, polytonality,*** and a return to the key-centered procedures of early modal music, folk music and non-Western music.

Timbre has gone beyond mere "color," to become a major musical element in its own right; the unique sonorities of Debussy, Cowell, and Varese attest to this newfound interest. Composers discovered new instrumental resources, many of them borrowed from jazz: unusual uses of the string bow, flutter-tongue effects for winds and brasses, ***glissandi*** (slides), a novel use of brass mutes. Extremes of register and density as well as ***Klangfarbenmelodie*** also create unique sonorities.

Percussion instruments began to come into their own during the twentieth century, both for their qualities of sheer timbre (without the "intrusion" of focused pitch) and for their association with jazz and popular music. The increased rhythmic activity of much contemporary music seems to demand percussive force and bite. Not only are drums, cymbals, blocks, and mallet instruments prominently featured, but such instruments as the piano, clarinet or violin may be used ***percussively*** as well.

Twentieth century instrumentation also began to reflect the influence of modern technology and the machine age. By the 1920s various composers, including Strauss, Satie, Varèse, and Milhaud, had used such exotic sound sources as the airplane propeller, siren, typewriter, wind machine, police whistle, and phonograph record in their ensembles. The new age of steel, glass, and concrete had obviously made its impact upon the arts.

Finally, ***esthetic*** attitudes had become more flexible. The post-Wagnerians were led to an escalating spiral of ever-growing emotional intensity, depicting extreme states of heightened passion. Anti-romantic attitudes, centered about Paris, dictated an opposite course; this ranged from satiric humor, to a flirtation with jazz and pop, to a barbaric nihilistic "primitivism."

The great majority of composers working at the turn of the century, whether pro- or anti-romantic, still retained traditional assumptions about the "affections" and the expressive nature of music. If we say that a passage of Schoenberg's sounds "mysterious," or that Debussy is "gentle" or the Stravinsky of *Le Sacre* "brutal," our comments reflect a legitimate response to a time-honored relationship between sounds and emotional states, acknowledged by musicians and listeners alike. But as we will see shortly, Stravinsky was to alter his attitude regarding expression during the 1920s. And with some of the mystical works of Satie, and virtually all of Varèse, a powerfully abstract quality emerges: music that is strictly concerned with its own inner world of sound and time. A work such as ***Octandre*** has the organic integrity of a unique object in nature. To call Varèse's work "mysterious" or "brutal" is, in a sense, irrelevant; it would be like giving expressive labels to trees or rock crystals.

Three Traditions

The various features of early twentieth-century music may appear confusing and contradictory. But if we group them together as components of style, we discover three major viewpoints which had come to dominate Western musical thinking by 1920:

1. The ***German tradition,*** which includes Austro-Hungarian music as well, is familiar to concert listeners. It uses the tug of pitches to drive music forward, placing great stress upon the pulling power of chromatic dissonance. Textures may be quite linear, even in supposedly homophonic contexts: inner voices may become prominent as "foreground" and "background" exchange roles. Form is inclined to be developmental, the single-minded "working out" of a few motives. Rhythm and timbre clarify pitch relationships and formal structure but are usually cast in a secondary role.

Time appears to move unswervingly forward, pulled ahead by the force of dissonance-consonance tension, driving towards a goal. (In atonal styles, the goal is intentionally frustrated; the listener may sense that routes to resolution are blocked.) It was this tradition that fostered the evolution of symphony, sonata, and Lied, and it was ideally suited to these genres.

2. There is also a ***French-Italian-Russian*** tradition, in which more emphasis is placed on consonance than on dissonance. Diatonic materials are the norm, to which chromaticism adds a bit of expressive inflection. Rhythm, color, and sudden contrasts keep the music moving, and often generate the unfolding of form. Textures are either obviously homophonic *or* polyphonic, and rarely change in mid-stream. Harmonic tension and release are not all-pervasive factors; even harsh, unsettling sounds are treated more as colors than as dissonances requiring resolution. Forms are often sectional, moving from one block-like state to another: a projected slide-show as opposed to a motion picture. It is not surprising, therefore, that we associate this tradition with opera and ballet.

N. A. Udaltsova, ***At the Piano.*** The "cubist" painters pursued the analysis of visual reality, allowing planes to penetrate one another as though space were being perceived at different moments in time simultaneously. This example has a musical subject. (Perhaps the cubists felt a kinship with music as another "time"-art, and a ready-made source of familiar shapes for fragmentation.)

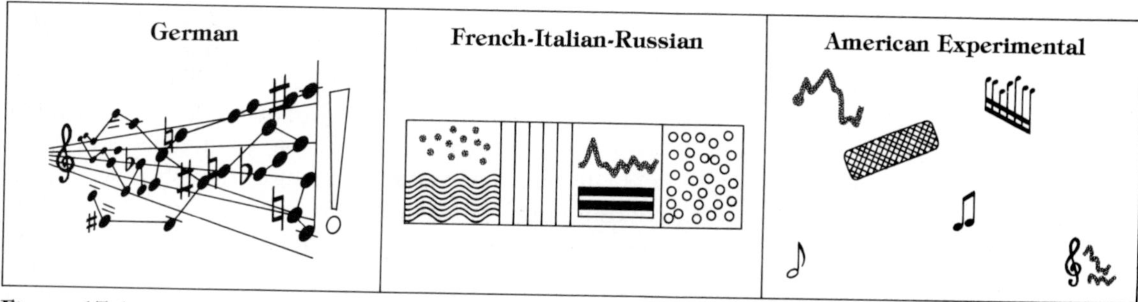

Figure 17.1

3. Thirdly, there is the ***American experimental tradition.*** It is not exclusively American, of course. Erik Satie was certainly one of the great early mavericks of this century; the Italian Luigi Russolo advocated a "music of noises"—thunderclaps, factory whistles, screams, electric motors, and so on—as early as 1913. But the greatest sense of freedom, beginning with the turn of the century, has been uniquely American. It takes nothing for granted, and challenges every assumption of Western European concert music: the physical space of performance; the ritual actions of players and listeners; the twelve-tone division of the octave; the kinds of sounds coaxed out of instruments; the relation between written notation and actual music making; the need for music to be "about" anything at all. In many works, time seems less directional and more spacious: a multi-dimensional "field" in which sonorities, durations, and relationships seem to float. (This distinction is suggested in Figure 17.1).

That sense of sounds being themselves, allowed to resonate in a floating non-directional time frame, can be related to the musical traditions of non-Western societies. European interest in Japanese and African art led to a new creative sensibility for music as well, beginning with Debussy and his fascination with the Balinese gamelan. As we will see, the influence of other cultures has remained a strong force,* affecting styles as diverse as those of Cowell, Satie, Ives, Mahler, and Varèse, and shaping the work of John Cage and others in succeeding decades.

A Widening Schism

Composers of serious concert music, of whatever tradition, had been directing their efforts to smaller and smaller audiences ever since the decline of the patronage system. By 1920 the audience for symphony, opera, or ballet was tiny indeed compared with the millions who enjoyed popular songs or music for social dancing. Before the nineteenth century, composers had

*The influence is mutual. There are Japanese and Korean concert pianists, violinists and conductors specializing in Western art music; American pop music has attracted listeners and stimulated performers throughout the world.

written "serious" ***and*** "light" music without considering one socially inferior to the other. But during the romantic period many middle-class listeners threw off the pretense of "high" aristocratic culture. They were interested in, and could afford to pay for, their own songs, dances, and light entertainment. Workers had also begun to demand a commercial equivalent of folk music, individually composed rather than anonymously homegrown.

Some romantic composers responded to middle-class frivolity (as they viewed it) by writing weighty, intense scores; others tried composing virtuoso display pieces or spectacular symphonic poems to attract mass attention. Furthermore, the performance of ***past*** music had become an integral aspect of cultural life. Many listeners preferred Beethoven or Handel to new compositions; the styles of the old masters were familiar and comfortable, and their status undeniably that of "high" art. It was economically unwise for a composer to attempt the radically unfamiliar, yet this was an era when creative artists were most caught up in the search for novel effects and individual voices, catching the ears of some listeners, but repelling others.

By the early twentieth century, then, a severe schism had developed between "serious" and "popular" music. There was a tendency for most listeners to think of music as a relaxing comfortable pillow: the predictable patterns of pop tunes, or familiar "serious" masterworks. Only a small percentage of listeners enjoyed the challenge of new ideas. That situation is unchanged today. Composers have adopted various defense mechanisms to cope with it: they may maintain the romantic notion that geniuses are destined to be unappreciated. They may revel in their isolation as a positive component of their working life. Or they may reach out for whatever fraction of the audience they feel close to. Experimental jazz artists—for jazz is hardly a "popular" medium—have felt a similar estrangement from the average listener. When they feel most neglected, they may often play for each other rather than for public acclaim.

At any rate, the twentieth century has produced a fiercely independent breed of creative musician. Today's artists have few illusions about being "popular." They use a musical language that is unfamiliar to most listeners, knowing from the outset that very few people will care about their activity. They are ***not*** being willfully uncommercial, and listeners are ***not*** being insensitive, because they are mean or stubborn or perverse. We are all simply what we are, products of history and habit. Fortunately, both history and habit can undergo changes. Perhaps the "widening schism" will close before the century is out.

The Twelve-Tone School

Arnold Schoenberg typifies the spirit of uncompromising independence. At the height of his creative activity, he was called to military service during World War I, and during that time he began to reconsider his position regarding atonality. From 1915 to 1923 he wrote no music; when he returned to composition, he had adopted a technique that astounded the musical world. This new method was referred to as "composition with twelve notes, related only to each other," more commonly known as ***twelve-tone technique.*** It provided Schoenberg with a systematic procedure for organizing atonal material, giving his music the same degree of structural support that tonality had supplied in the past, and tempered the impulsive freedom of atonality with a strong logical quality. For Schoenberg, this was a way of rescuing music from the brink of chromatic chaos: restoring organization and also confirming in his own mind that the older form of organization, tonality, was no longer necessary.

twelve-tone technique

The twelve-tone technique was based on the principle that all the tones within an octave were to be treated as equal, "related only to each other," ***not*** to a central tonic. Certain rules ensure that this principle is maintained. Schoenberg arranged the twelve pitches in a pattern, with each pitch appearing only once. This ordering of pitches is called a ***tone row,*** or ***series,*** or ***set.*** One such set is shown in Figure 17.2. There are no scale lines or arpeggiated triads outlined by these successive pitches, for the same reason that no tones are repeated; Schoenberg wanted to avoid any suggestion of a tonic.

tone row

series/set

A tone row provided Schoenberg with all the material needed for a complete piece. Its pitches could be used for a melodic line, and groups of successive pitches could be combined into chords. In any case, Schoenberg would use all the pitches of a row, in the given order, before repeating any of them. He could explore the prominent intervals of the row, and also consider other possible forms: ***inversion, retrograde,*** and ***retrograde inversion.*** (See our previous discussion of fugal technique.) Any of the four forms of the row could be transposed to any other starting pitch. In other words, forty-eight possible rows (4 × 12) could be derived from the original set. Rhythm, dynamics, phrasing, tempo, instrumentation, and register are at the composer's discretion; the organizational controls are strictly related to pitch, but to no other element.

Schoenberg's earliest twelve-tone pieces of 1923 were cast in brief forms, and scored for piano solo or other small groups. As he discovered the organizing force of the technique, he began to apply it to more extended works such as concertos and quartets. The tone row shown in Figure 17.2 is, in fact, the basis for his String Quartet no. 4 (1936). The first movement is a modified sonata structure, with every note of the music growing out of

Figure 17.2

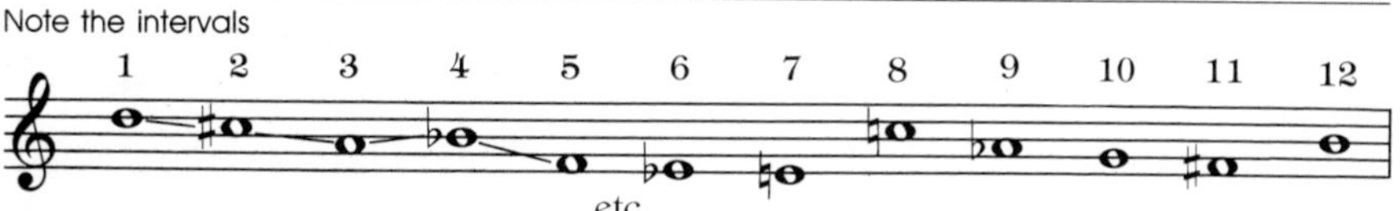

Figure 17.3

one of the row forms. Here are the opening measures (Figure 17.3). The original row is rhythmically converted into a vigorous melody for the first violin; the accompanying chords are also derived from the same row form. A more lyric phrase that occurs later on (see Figure 17.4) grows from the row inversion, transposed to begin on the pitch G.

One might expect a piece of music constructed in this way to sound stiff or mechanical, but Schoenberg's Quartet doesn't *sound* contrived or stilted at all. It retains the warmth and intense fervor of post-Wagnerian chromaticism. Despite the rigor of his method, Schoenberg was still a passionate romantic. He always composed in bursts of feverishly high speed, and had great difficulty finishing any works that were interrupted; his music often sounds urgent and instinctive. He regarded the twelve-tone technique as the product of sheer historical necessity. When asked once if he was the famous Arnold Schoenberg, he replied, "Somebody had to be, and no one else volunteered."

Schoenberg was appointed to the prestigious professorship of composition at the Berlin Academy in 1924. But when Hitler came to power in 1933, Schoenberg, born a Jew and converted to Catholicism, was dismissed. He left Germany, converted back to Judaism, and emigrated to the United States. Now in his sixties, Schoenberg settled in Los Angeles, and

Figure 17.4

taught composition at UCLA and the University of Southern California. He became something of a minor celebrity in Hollywood, the dinner guest of such luminaries as Harpo Marx and Fanny Brice, as well as the constant tennis partner of fellow-composer George Gershwin. But in many other respects America was far from kind. Because Schoenberg had taught for only a few years, his UCLA retirement pension was very small; his repeated efforts to secure foundation grants were unsuccessful. Performances of his music, even his later American works which almost approached tonality again, were far from frequent. To a degree, the controversy surrounding his innovative technique remained as intense as ever, even at the end of his long life.

The "Second Viennese School"

There is no doubt, though, that the twelve-tone method has greatly influenced twentieth century composition. Schoenberg's music and his writings made a strong impact; he was also an impressive teacher, and had two especially gifted pupils in Anton Webern and Alban Berg (1885–1935). Both began working with Schoenberg during his Viennese atonal period, and later employed the twelve-tone technique after Schoenberg had introduced it. They regarded their teacher as a close friend and musical mentor, and it is fitting that all three figures are often grouped together as the "Second Viennese School." The label is also something of an honor, since the "first" school was composed of Haydn, Mozart and Beethoven.

The three composers had strikingly different musical personalities. (It is a tribute to Schoenberg's teaching that he didn't stifle the individuality of his pupils.) We have already commented on Webern earlier, with regard to his fondness for delicate, whispered textures, and the distillation of his lyric impulse into brief flashes of line and color.

Alban Berg

Berg, on the other hand, was more of an old-school romanticist, delighting in the dynamic surges and sweeping melodic lines of the great Austro-German tradition. He was reluctant to abandon tonality completely, and used tone rows which implied triads or key references. He seemed to enjoy the psychological effect of tonality, its relation to dream and memory, rather than its traditional function as structural support. Like Schoenberg and Webern, Berg was profoundly influenced by the esthetic of German expressionism, probing the half-hidden world of inner emotions. His opera ***Wozzeck*** (1917–22) is a brilliant depiction of the unconscious rage, frustration, and potential violence of humans under stress—the concerns that fascinated Freud, Kafka, and Joyce as well. Although the play which inspired Berg's opera (***Woyzeck*** by George Büchner) was written in the 1830s, it foretold the dilemma of the twentieth century individual—crushed by an impersonal society, victimized at every turn, highly repressed, and finally lashing out, destroying himself as well as those he loves.

Alban Berg is shown next to his portrait painted by Schoenberg (left). Berg's greatest success was the opera ***Wozzeck.*** The title character, as portrayed in the premiere performance is shown above (right).

Wozzeck, the main character, is a soldier confronted by a taunting superior officer and exploited as a subject for demeaning medical experiments. He is also betrayed and humiliated by his mistress Marie, who is having an affair with a handsome drum major. Eventually he kills Marie and, returning later to the scene of the murder, drowns himself. Berg fashioned a libretto of three acts from the original drama, and built each act about the structural models of traditional forms and genres. For example, Act I consists of five scenes which introduce Wozzeck's hapless torment. These are organized along the lines of a ''suite'' with a lullaby, march, passacaglia, and the like. The confrontation with Marie and the drum major occurs during Act II, whose scenes approximate a ''symphony'' in five ''movements'' (including a sonata-form allegro, scherzo and rondo.) The operagoer doesn't need to know of these devices, but the knowledge does provide insight into Berg's working process, especially the need to channel the turbulent energy of post-Wagnerian chromaticism into cohesive formal units. ***Wozzeck*** was composed before the advent of the twelve-tone technique, when Berg, like his teacher, was trying to temper atonal freedom with logical structure.

Act III presents us with the actual murder and its subsequent horrors. Like the other acts, it is divided into five scenes—here conceived by Berg as five "inventions."

Alban Berg
Wozzeck: Act III (excerpts) *R6 S1 B1*

Scene 1: Marie's room. Wozzeck's mistress is there with her little child, reading from the Bible the story of Mary Magdalene, and then breaking off into a pathetic fairy tale. She is consumed by feelings of guilt, self-pity and love for the child. Berg conveys her emotional confusion by alternating tonal references (the key of F major for the fairy tale) with a generally atonal fabric. He also contrasts a ***Sprechstimme*** vocal approach for the Bible reading with Marie's more lyrical outbursts. A brief orchestral interlude connects this scene and the next.

Scene 2: a path by a pond. Wozzeck and Marie appear, and converse in a way which suggests a sort of delirium, distant and menacing. The rising moon, blood-red in color, obsesses Wozzeck; overcome by violent rage, he stabs Marie to death, still apparently in the same delirious state. Whereas Berg thought of Scene 1 as an "invention on a theme," this is an "invention on a ***tone***," focused on the note B which has been sustained through the orchestral interlude. It grows imperceptibly louder all the time, and eventually comes to symbolize Wozzeck's mental breakdown; as he murders Marie, the note is pounded out with repeated timpani beats. (The constant pitch also makes the scene curiously ***tonal***.) As Marie falls, Wozzeck cries out one word, "Tot!" (Dead!), and the B is heard again, now in a sustained orchestral crescendo (Figure 17.5) that leads to a brutal *fff* rhythm for drums. The crescendo on B appears once more, and dissolves immediately into the next scene.

Scene 3: a tavern. Wozzeck rushes in, still incoherent and half-crazed. A distorted honky-tonk piano sets the tone for the nightmarish quality of the scene. It also duplicates the ***rhythm*** of the vicious drum beats that ended Scene 2. In fact, the scene grows out of this single obsessive rhythm, another of Berg's "inventions," capturing the dramatic mood perfectly.

Figure 17.5

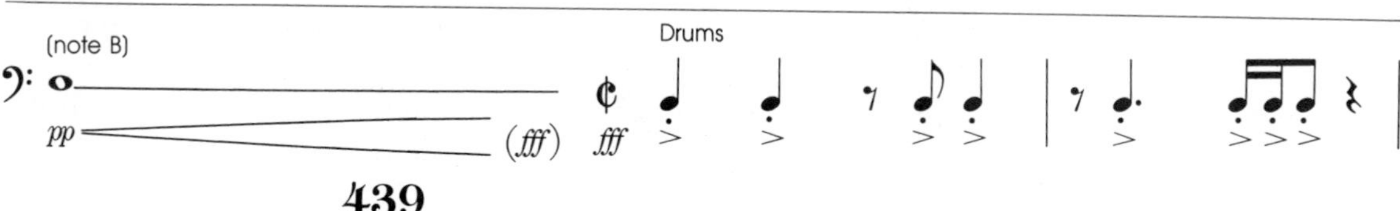

Wozzeck tries to dance, but is caught up short when blood is discovered on his hands. All the people begin to chant "Blut, Blut . . ."; they appear to be closing in on Wozzeck, and he rushes out wildly.

Scene 4. We are back at the path by the pond, where Wozzeck has returned to look for the murder weapon. He finds his knife, throws it into the pond, and then, as though in a trance, wades in after it. In both scenes at the pond, Berg uses the orchestra for suggestive tone painting: the stillness, night sounds, and in this case swirling waters. The evocative, shimmering textures would be almost impressionistic, were it not for the hysterical, half-crazed intensity of the nocturnal landscape. As Wozzeck descends into the waters, the orchestra envelops him in a series of rising figures—a surprisingly gentle whirlpool of sound. Two of Wozzeck's former tormentors happen to walk by at this moment; they hear the sounds of someone struggling in the water, but have no wish the "get involved." (Another prophecy of modern society, perhaps?)

Ich bin blutig. Da ein Fleck . . . und noch einer. Weh! Weh! Ich wasche mich mit Blut! Das Wasser ist Blut. . . .	*I'm bloody. Here's a spot . . .* *and here . . . Woe! I wash myself* *with blood! The water is blood . . .* *blood. . . .*

A somber orchestral interlude follows, in which Berg combines a number of earlier ***leitmotifs*** into a strong, unified statement. Note that the impassioned climax of this passage embraces tonality: a resounding cry in D minor. This gradually fades away, and we are suddenly transported to Marie's house.

Scene 5: the street beside Marie's house. A group of children are playing ring-around-the rosy; they sing an innocent tune which, like the honky-tonk piano of Scene 3, is twisted out of shape. The little child of Marie and Wozzeck is sitting on a hobby-horse, crying "Hop! Hop!" Some other children come running in; Marie's body has been found. One youngster turns to Marie's child and exclaims, "Hey you! Your mother is dead." The child doesn't seem to understand, and keeps riding his hobby-horse for a moment more. He then decides to follow the others. The orchestra subsides very gently, on a repeated bittersweet chord.

Wozzeck is indebted to the Wagnerian tradition in many ways: in the emphasis upon continuous narrative rather than set arias, in the relation of orchestra to voices, and in the use of motives for dramatic purposes. Nevertheless, it is unique. In this balance of structural complexity, brilliant theater, and moving social commentary, Berg achieved something rare and special.

Berg maintained his flexible approach to tonality even *after* he began using the twelve-tone technique. For example, he chose a row with relatively "tonal" properties for his Violin Concerto of 1935 (his last composition). This enables tonal and atonal languages to merge without abandoning the control afforded by the Schoenbergian technique.

Alban Berg
Violin Concerto

Berg's set for the Violin Concerto is surprisingly triadic, as shown in Figure 17.6. It consists entirely of 3rds, except for the four notes of a whole-tone pattern at the very end. The brackets indicate that certain triads—G minor, D major, A minor, E major—could easily emerge from the use of this set. In fact, the Andante movement of the concerto begins with these chords. Berg also explores the fact that pitches 1–3–5–7 of the row correspond to the opening strings of the violin. We hear that pattern played quietly at the very outset, as though the soloist were musing while tuning up, and then the same gentle arc played with pitches 2–4–6–8 of the row (Figure 17.7).

The concerto was composed as a memorial for a young girl who had died unexpectedly. Perhaps for this reason, Berg makes the finale a kind of prayer. He quotes a German chorale melody (see Figure 17.8) that begins with the whole-step motion, bounded by a tritone, of row pitches 9–10–11–12. The fourth note of the chorale melody is striking in its poignancy; when Bach set this tune in the eighteenth century, he harmonized the note with a particularly wrenching dissonance. Berg wisely retains the Bach harmonization in the initial statement, so that the listener's associations become somber, resigned to the existence of death. The chorale melody is then interwoven with other material, the entire fabric fading away peacefully.

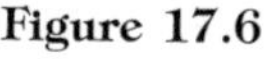
Figure 17.6

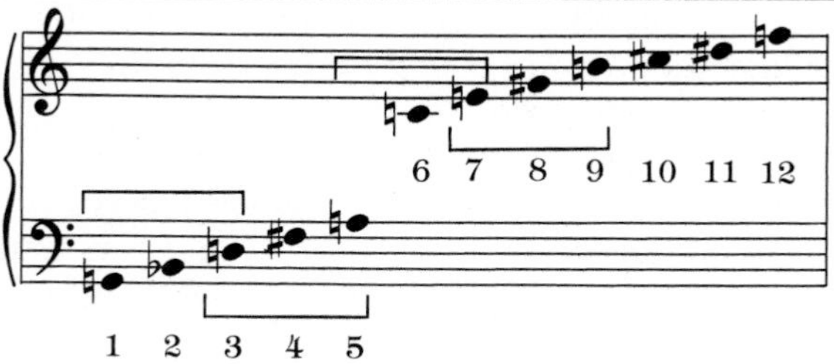

Figure 17.7

Figure 17.8

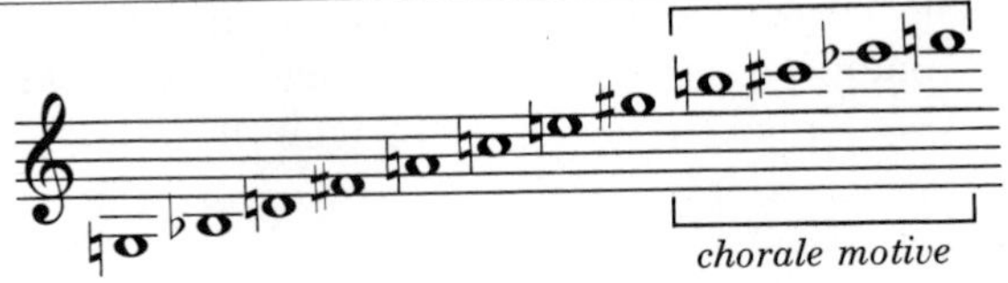

Webern and Twelve-Tone Technique

Anton Webern's use of tone rows is very different from Berg's. In fact, just as Berg explored the more triadic, "traditional" (even tonal) aspects of Schoenberg's innovative approach, Webern concentrated upon the abstract, internal logic of intervallic relations. Let us listen again to his *Variations for Orchestra* (1940), which was discussed during Chapters 1–7.

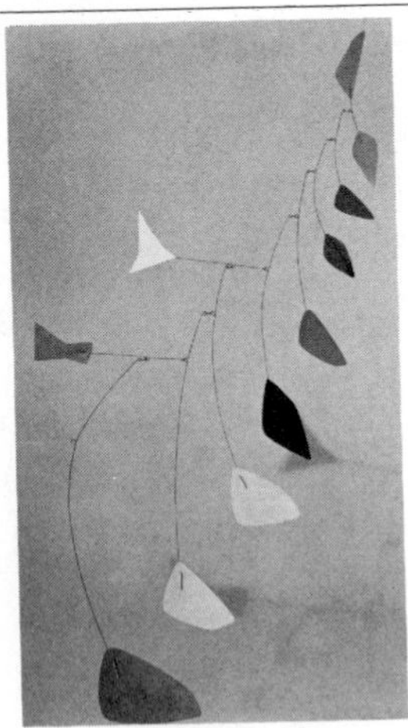

Anton Webern
Variations for Orchestra

There is no single "theme" for this set of variations. Webern uses a number of brief motives instead, all drawn from the tone row shown in Figure 17.9. Webern is fond of rows that subdivide into symmetrical fragments, often related to each other by ***inversion, retrograde,*** and other factors discussed earlier in connection with contrapuntal imitation. In this row, for example, the first six pitches (or more accurately, their intervals) are related to the next six by ***retrograde inversion:*** that is, the contour of one group is reflected, but backwards and upside down, in the other group. If the row is divided into four groups of three notes apiece, then groups 1 and 4, and 2 and 3, are related by retrograde inversion as well. In Figure 17.9 below,

Figure 17.9

(RI is the "retrograde inversion" of the "original" O.)

Figure 17.10

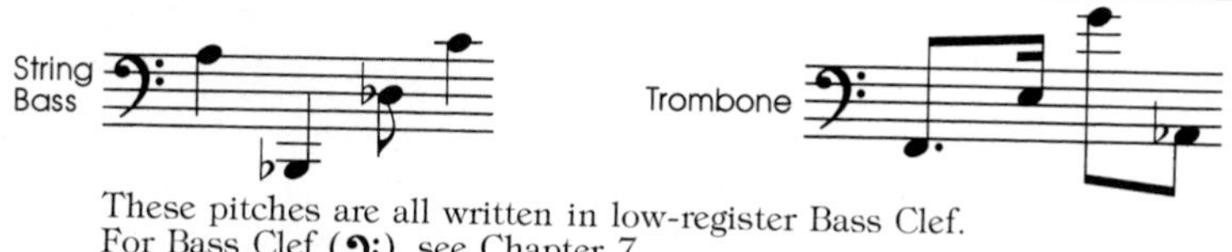

These pitches are all written in low-register Bass Clef. For Bass Clef (𝄢), see Chapter 7.

pitches 1–4 and 6–9 have been bracketed, to indicate that they have identical patterns (at transposed pitch levels). Pitches 4–7 are a transposition of 9–12; these have also been bracketed. And, as shown by the symbols "O" (original) and "RI," these two fragment pairs are related to each other by retrograde inversion.

Webern uses these features of his row to create a family resemblance among all the motivic fragments of the variations. They are, in fact, all portions of the row, related in the ways previously noted; as the piece progresses, their similarities become more apparent to the ear. Individual variations are marked off by subtle changes in density. The earliest moments consist of solo lines alternating with duets. We then begin to hear thicker lines played by a number of instruments, and chords (also drawn from the familiar interval collections of the row). Then longer lines emerge against chords stated in rhythmic repeated patterns, and so on. In this way we sense the passage of one variation to the next.

Be aware of ***rhythmic*** relationships as well. At the very beginning, for example, the opening quiet string bass line is answered soon afterwards by a startling trombone solo. The two are related melodically by retrograde inversion; they are, in fact, the first four notes of the row answered by the last four (see Figure 17.10). But they are also rhythmic retrogrades of each other: the string pattern of two long notes, one short and one long answered by the exact reverse. The trombone passage moves by twice as rapidly: it is the rhythmic ***diminution,*** as well as the rhythmic retrograde and pitch retrograde inversion, of the string bass passage. Later on, the slow lyric solo violin line (heard against repeated bass chords) plays the pitches of the original string bass pattern, but in the rhythm of the trombone in fourfold ***augmentation.*** This is shown in Figure 17.11.

Webern, then, carries the twelve-tone concern for pitch ordering into other areas than pitch—texture, for example, or rhythmic pattern. These relationships are not always immediately audible, but they become more so on repeated hearings. And the internal consistency, the sense of "logic"

Figure 17.11

Wassily Kandinsky, *Open Green No. 263* (right) and Piet Mondrian, *Composition with Blue and Yellow* (opposite). There are as many attitudes and techniques in twentieth century art as in music. Compare the impulsive, seemingly irrational flow of a Kandinsky work with the cool, measured elegance of Mondrian's abstraction. In neither painting is the canvas treated as a "window" through which the viewer perceives a continuation of the solid physical world.

that pervades the whole, certainly is audible. In this work the principle of variation underlies the entire style, providing great surface "variety" and a taut, integral unity that grows more amazing the more we listen.

Neoclassicism

neoclassicism

Although the twelve-tone school was undeniably important, it was overshadowed by a far more popular movement that dominated Western music between the two World Wars: ***neoclassicism.*** Igor Stravinsky was regarded by many as its chief proponent and spokesman, perhaps signaling a temporary victory of the French-Russian-Italian tradition over the hallowed Austro-German one. For whatever reasons, Stravinsky and Schoenberg came to think of each other as rivals. It is sad to note that, after Stravinsky settled in

the United States in 1939, the two most influential composers of the century lived within a few miles of each other in Los Angeles, and ignored each other's presence.

Although neoclassicism was a term used with varying meanings, there was one that all could agree upon: the return of ***tonality.*** Neoclassic composers enjoyed using diatonic scales, simple folk melodies, medieval modes with a minimum of chromatic "pull," and the bite of polytonality. They avoided the voluptuous textures and emotional outpourings of romanticism in favor of ***clarity.*** Elegance, detachment, wit, and a strong rhythmic impulse also typified neoclassic styles. There were parallels in the visual arts, such as the formalized, geometric distortions of cubism, or the sleek functional look of modern architecture. But there were strictly musical motivations as well.

Neoclassic composers decided to bypass the rhetoric of romanticism by jumping a century or more back in time; they were fascinated by aspects of the musical *past* which seemed refreshingly healthy and productive. Many composers used the *forms* and *genres* of eighteenth-century music: concerto grosso, fugue, dance suite. In fact, certain aspects of the movement could have easily been named "neo-baroque"! *Counterpoint* returned as a prime factor in musical texture: not dense and knotty, but a spacious layout of clean, crisp lines in homage to eighteenth-century models. *Texture* was lighter and more transparent. Small Haydn-sized orchestras began to flourish, and a chamber music intimacy prevailed even in works composed for larger forces.

The movement began to emerge in France around the time of World War I. The understated simplicity of Satie's work can be heard in neoclassic terms. Debussy once called Satie "a gentle medieval musician," and he does indeed seem to have come from another time and place. Another colleague of Debussy's, Maurice Ravel, moved from a generally impressionistic style to more clean-cut, sharply etched sonorities. Ravel's 1917 *Le Tombeau de Couperin* includes a prelude, fugue, and toccata based on baroque models. In the same year a young Russian composer named Sergei Prokofiev produced a work for small orchestra called the *Classical Symphony,* transporting the elegant style of Haydn and Mozart into a twentieth-century world of wide melodic skips, sudden changes of key, and abrupt discords—a witty fusion of two centuries. In a sense, the *Classical Symphony* lent its name to an entire movement.

Stravinsky and Neoclassicism

By 1918 the Stravinsky of *Le Sacre* had been forced to reconsider his style. He found Europe's musical life severely disrupted after the war. The grand moralistic tone of nineteenth-century art no longer seemed appropriate (if it ever had), and the lavish funds for spectacular ballets no longer existed. Stravinsky decided to work on a low-budget theatrical piece that would involve only a few players and that could easily be taken on tour. Absorbed in Russian folktales at the time (having been cut off from his homeland by the 1917 Russian Revolution), Stravinsky created a work out of a Russian legend about a soldier who sells his soul to the devil. The piece was called *l'Histoire du Soldat* ("The Soldier's Tale"), and scored for narrator, three actor-dancers, and seven musicians.

In *l'Histoire du Soldat* Stravinsky constructed a series of brief movements, in keeping with his anti-"developmental" bias, and derived many of them from traditional genres and popular dances: a tango, waltz, ragtime, four-part chorale setting, and so on. This approach marked the beginning of a new turn in Stravinsky's career. He became increasingly attracted to light textures, objective moods, and relationships to traditional models. His 1919 *Pulcinella* was based on music by the eighteenth-century composer Pergolesi, and he later used Tchaikovsky, Grieg, Rossini, and Gounod as springboards for other pieces. A number of works, from the 1918 ***Ragtime*** to the 1945 ***Ebony Concerto*** composed for Woody Herman, explored the idioms of jazz as well.

Was there a "real" Stravinsky behind this dizzying profusion of styles? Many listeners must have asked that, very much as viewers wondered at Picasso's equally frequent change of position. When Stravinsky replied, he left his questioners more puzzled than before—claiming that the "real" Stravinsky was nobody's business, that he did *not* need to reveal his personal feelings, or "express" anything, in his music. For him, neoclassicism was more than just a fondness for certain textures. It symbolized the composer's basic attitude towards his work: objective, detached, and totally unrelated to the expression of individual personality. In Stravinsky's view, composers solve problems, make choices, order their materials, and delight in the act of creation. This may explain why his individual pieces are so different from each other; as the problems change, so do the musical solutions.

The *Symphony of Psalms* (1930) gives us an idea of Stravinsky's workmanlike, anti-romantic creative processes. Commissioned by the Boston Symphony Orchestra to write a symphony, he decided upon a piece using a chorus because he felt the contrapuntal possibilities would be better, and chose a Latin text for its special syllabic clarity. He eliminated high strings, but added piano and harp sonorities; the choice of religious texts for the chorus was among the last of his calculations. (Compare that with the urgent desire of a romantic composer to "say" something religious, and only then consider a performing medium!) This is not to imply that the *Symphony of Psalms* lacks expressive character or "mood." Its textures, rhythms and Latin words all evoke images of ancient ceremonial ritual, intensified by Stravinsky's choice of narrow melodic range and ostinato. Obviously the Symphony *does* express a mood quite vividly. But, the composer might reply, that's due more to our listening habits than to his intentions. In any case, the mood itself is communal and formal, rather than personal and impulsive: the attitude is still anti-romantic.

Igor Stravinsky

Symphony of Psalms

R5 S2 B4

Exaudi orationem meam, Domine et deprecationem meam; auribus percipe lacrimas meas.
Ne sileas, quoniam advena ego sum apud te, et peregrinus, sicut omnes patres mei. Remitte mihi, ut refrigerer, prius quam abeam et amplius non ero.

Hear my prayer, O Lord, and my cry; Listen to my tears, for I am a stranger with Thee, a sojourner, as all my fathers were. Forgive me, that I may recover strength, before I go and return no more.

Figure 17.12

Movement I: Psalm 38 (Vulgate). The opening movement begins with a sharp, staccato, E-minor chord answered immediately by rushing woodwind figures. The two elements, chord and rhythmic pattern, alternate in an asymmetrical burst as twin poles of an irregular ostinato (see Figure 17.12). The text is first heard in the alto voices, sung to a melodic line of only two pitches. This might suggest the quality of Gregorian chant, but it is set against a polytonal ostinato background, as shown in Figure 17.13. The remainder of the chorus joins in, and then the opening staccato chord suddenly interrupts. Chord, woodwind figurations, chorus, and ostinato are treated as alternating blocks. A new ostinato has begun at the words "Ne sileas" (melodic line on a single pitch), but is abruptly cut off by the staccato chord. Just as unexpectedly, the texture of the music seems to change at this point. The entire chorus and orchestra join in a gradual crescendo to *fff* and then become quiet at the words "Remitte mihi." Another crescendo grows, and reaches a surprising climax on a *G-major* chord: a very strong tonal ending, but at an unanticipated location.

The second movement begins as a fugue for orchestra, based upon an angular line first stated by solo oboe. A fairly complex woodwind texture is built up, and then a totally different fugue subject is stated by the voices.

Figure 17.13

The text, from Psalm 39 (Vulgate), recounts that the Lord "heard my cry, set my feet upon a rock, and directed my steps. And He hath put a new song in my mouth, a song to God . . ." That "new song" is the elaborate praise put forth in the final movement, the longest movement of the Symphony. It begins with a quiet "Alleluia," settling on C major. The tempo suddenly shifts to ***allegro,*** and a repeated-note rhythmic figure appears in the horns; syncopated rhythms drive the music forward, and the repeated-note figure is now sung by the chorus. A series of triplet patterns creates even further rhythmic agitation. The words of Psalm 150 (Vulgate) are ecstatic in their thanksgiving and exultation: "Praise ye the Lord . . . Praise Him with strings and organs . . . Praise Him upon the high sounding cymbals . . . Let everyone praise the Lord." The music turns unexpectedly slow and hushed; a stately processional—a choral ostinato and an orchestral one heard simultaneously—grows and fades away. We are left with the "Alleluia" and a hushed cadence on C major.

Hindemith and "Gebrauchsmusik"

One might assume that neoclassicism, as an anti-romantic movement, was strongest outside the German tradition. Consider, however, Berg's use of traditional models for the structure of ***Wozzeck:*** that is certainly "classicism" of a sort. Even Schoenberg's early twelve-tone works have a "classic" restraint about them, a certain distance that he could put between himself and his material, as opposed to the intense involvement he had felt previously. Schoenberg's first work using the new technique, the 1923 ***Suite*** for piano, consists of movements entitled Gavotte, Gigue, and Minuet.

On the other hand, Berg and Schoenberg are clearly romantic in their deeply felt personal expression and their chromatic atonal language. To find a more thoroughly neoclassic German composer, we should examine the work of Paul Hindemith (1895–1963). Hindemith believed passionately in tonality; he felt that atonality contradicted the laws of acoustics and the psychology of listening. He also believed that a composer could best serve the needs of contemporary society by looking to the past for models.

His own greatest model was Johann Sebastian Bach. Even though Hindemith's music is definitely of this age—it contains strong dissonances, and striking chordal sonorities often built in 4ths—one can also feel the spirit of the eighteenth century. Contrapuntal textures and strongly metric pulses abound, and the feeling for tonal center is always present. Similar rhythmic figures and melodic contours pervade many of his works, causing critics to complain that Hindemith pieces "all sound alike." It is significant that Hindemith was one of the first composers since Beethoven who did ***not*** feel obliged to write a totally "new" piece each time out. The urge to constantly surpass oneself in a series of masterworks was a romantic legacy; Hindemith preferred the earlier traditions of honest craftsmanship.

His concern for the social purposes of art led him to a concept known as ***Gebrauchsmusik***—"workaday music" or "music for use." He felt that

Gebrauchsmusik

the great schism between composer and society might be erased if more works were written for specific occasions and needs. Accordingly, Hindemith composed music for schools and factories, music to celebrate state events, music to be performed by amateurs, or for neglected instruments. He composed operas and weighty concert-hall works as well, but never to the exclusion of "useful" pieces. He also believed that the composer needed to get into communities and make music with people, by performing, conducting, and coaching. He never forgot that his idol Bach was not considered a "great composer" at Leipzig. Bach was, rather an all-around musician, organist, choral director, concert administrator, and teacher; his creative work grew naturally from all these activities. This was Hindemith's ideal for a twentieth-century musician.

The ***Gebrauchsmusik*** ideal led him to write a variety of unpretentious chamber pieces, such as the charming 1922 woodwind quintet entitled ***Kleine Kammermusik*** ("Little Chamber Music"). Its opening movement is notable for polytonal harmonic levels, and the teasing way one key center seems to slip into another. The steady tempo, regular meter and pervasive rhythm are reminiscent of baroque texture: once a particular fabric, or "affection," is established, it is maintained for quite a while. There is a plaintive middle section, followed by a return to the opening, making for an overall ABA form.

One of Hindemith's best known works is ***Mathis der Maler*** ("Mathias the Painter"), an opera based on the life of the sixteenth-century German painter Mathias Grünewald. The music combines elements of medieval, Renaissance, and contemporary techniques; the operatic plot concerns the struggles of an artist in the face of political upheaval, a very touchy subject during the 1930s, when the work was composed. The Nazis banned the scheduled 1935 premiere of the opera, and also dismissed Hindemith from his Berlin professorship, accusing him of writing "dissonant Bolshevik music." Like so many artists of the time, Hindemith came to the United States, joining the faculty of Yale University.

Hindemith fashioned a ***Mathis der Maler*** Symphony from elements of the opera and the work is best known in this three-movement orchestral form. Each movement bears a subtitle related to a panel of Grünewald's famous Isenheim altarpiece. The first movement, "Angelic Concert," provides an expanded sonata-form of great contrapuntal clarity and triadic strength. The style mixes biting discords, chords built in 4ths, modes and textures of early music, including one tune built on an old German chorale, all of these focused upon key centers. It is a remarkable combination of "old" and "new."

Other Neoclassic Composers

The neoclassical attitude was easily adapted to individual creative tastes. A return to simpler textures and traditional forms appealed to composers of tonal or modal music; Stravinsky's view of the detached creative act expressed the feelings of many composers who wanted to be free of romantic personal involvement. Some composers with strong national or ethnic ties, such as Bloch or Vaughan Williams, balanced romantic leanings with a fondness for structural elegance or a ***Gebrauchsmusik*** sense of ethical obligation to their countrymen. There is a similar dichotomy in the highly eclectic style of the Englishman Benjamin Britten (1913–1976). Britten's music shows influences of Berg, Stravinsky, Purcell, jazz, Japanese drama, Handel, and Verdi; the wide range of his compositions includes many full-scale operas—in fact, some of the major operas of the twentieth century—and little pieces for children or amateurs.

In the Soviet Union, musical versatility of this sort was frequently dictated by the government, which during the Stalin years made "workaday music" into a national artistic policy. Sergei Prokofiev (1891–1953) and Dimitri Shostakovitch (1906–1975) were continually forced to temper their brash "modernistic" styles to meet the cultural rules laid down by government edicts. More than once they were reprimanded for writing music influenced by the decadent West. In such cases they would publicly apologize, and turn their musical thinking in more publicly accessible directions (for the time being). In fact, Shostakovitch's Fifth Symphony (1937), composed in the wake of a stinging confrontation with the government, was subtitled "a Soviet artist's reply to just criticism."

Finally, the neoclassic influence was felt strongly in the United States. Let us now examine the American scene at greater length.

American Developments

Musically speaking, we are living in what might be called the "American century." The European dominance of artistic direction has given way to the influence of the New World, not for one reason alone, but for a combination of many:

1. *The spread of jazz and American popular music throughout the world.* Jazz had made an impact upon European culture even before World War I. Ragtime, as a written-out genre, was already available in printed sheet music form; the early improvised group jazz, born in New Orleans and transplanted to other American cities, had been heard by many visitors from other countries. American groups toured Europe as well, carrying on a tradition that extended back to the post-Civil War minstrel shows. By the twenties people were referring to the "jazz age" as a symbol of the total culture; jazz influences could be heard in a wide range of European styles, from Satie to Hindemith to Ravel to Shostakovitch.

American composers were also attempting to combine indigenous New World idioms with the formal models of "concert" music. Scott Joplin and Charles Ives created unique hybrid styles at the turn of the century; a few decades later, George Gershwin used his experience with Tin Pan Alley and

Duke Ellington, a major composer and performer in the jazz idiom during the era when American ideas began to influence the European musical scene.

Broadway in his more "serious" ***Rhapsody in Blue.*** His ***Porgy and Bess*** (1935) successfully combines elements of popular musical, opera, black spiritual, and jazz. Popular music underwent changes during the thirties and forties, as the "Big Band" sound (and its danceable offshoot, "Swing") swept the country. A new style developed, basically composed and written out, in a quasi-symphonic ensemble texture; improvisation was limited to soloists. The most creative composer in that style, Duke Ellington (1899–1974), was known for his complex harmonies and a unique timbral blend of winds against muted brasses.

The 1950s and '60s witnessed a fascinating hybrid of abstract, "arty" jazz and dissonant contemporary concert music. Leonard Bernstein fused the languages of Stravinsky, jazz, pop, and Schoenberg in his 1949 piano concerto ***The Age of Anxiety*** and the operatic-balletic musical ***West Side Story*** (1957). Jazzman Dave Brubeck, who had studied with Milhaud, and the Juilliard-conservatory-trained Modern Jazz Quartet rose to prominence. Gunther Schuller's integration of modern jazz and the Second Viennese style, and twelve-tone jazz works such as Milton Babbitt's ***All Set,*** led to a vigorous movement known as "Third Stream Music." In more recent decades, experiments in electronics, improvisation and mixed media have linked popular and serious music (Stockhausen, Frank Zappa, Varèse, the Beatles, John Cage) inseparably.

2. ***"Serious" American composition after 1920.*** After World War I a new generation of American composers made an unprecedented impact upon the international scene. These young artists had gone to Europe to study, since this was still considered necessary; significantly, though, almost all of them went to France rather than Germany, and a surprising number of them studied with the same teacher, a young woman named Nadia Boulanger. Mlle. Boulanger was a devoted advocate of Stravinsky's music, and communicated the Stravinskian passion for clarity and extended tonality to her students.

Boulanger's first American pupil, in 1921, was Aaron Copland (who will be discussed later in this chapter). In the ensuing years many more Americans came to her classes: Walter Piston (1894–1976) from Maine and Harvard; Roy Harris (1898–1979) of rural Oklahoma stock; Virgil Thomson (1896–   ) fresh from Kansas City and Harvard. Each of these composers absorbed some of the linear austerity of Stravinsky's neoclassic style. Virgil Thomson added to this the simplicity, irreverence and outlandish humor of Satie. In many ways, then, the French influence upon twentieth-century American music was profound.

But there were other tendencies as well. The expressive chromaticism of Roger Sessions (1896–   ) was related to the Second Viennese school. A strongly "romantic" style also flourished, concerned with broad, lyric statements, and deriving more from Sibelius, Vaughan Williams or Puccini than from atonal models; we can hear its grand sweep in works by William Schuman (1910–   ) and Samuel Barber (1910–1981).

3. *The coming of European composers to America.* During the politically turbulent 1930s and '40s many European artists uprooted their homes and families and came to the United States to escape the censorship and potential violence of Nazi rule. The American melting pot had always been open to creative energy from abroad, as we know from the examples of Dvořák and Varèse. There are many earlier instances of immigrants enriching the culture of adopted countries: Handel in England and Lully in France, to name but two. But the American situation was unique in that an unprecedented number of artists, scientists, novelists, and scholars of all kinds settled here in the 1930s and '40s. Among composers, Stravinsky and Schoenberg came to Los Angeles, Hindemith taught at Yale, while Milhaud joined the faculty of Mills College in the San Francisco Bay area. Bartók spent the last five years of his life—very painfully, as we shall see—in New York. Bloch took a position in Cleveland, and then settled in Oregon. Rachmaninov came to southern California; an important figure of the chromatic Viennese tradition, Stefan Wolpe (1902–1972), came to New York and exerted considerable influence there as a teacher.

The presence of so many distinguished artists greatly enriched the American tradition. Ironically, their presence in the New World also preserved and transmitted the ***European*** tradition during a period when—first under Nazi pressure, and then because of the havoc of war—"advanced" music disappeared from the European scene. At the war's end in 1945, young European musicians found that Schoenberg, Bartók, Hindemith, Stravinsky, and Webern had become mere names in books. Students in the United States were, by contrast, the group most familiar with the twentieth-century mainstream of Europe.

4. *The strength of the American experimental tradition.* Charles Ives and Henry Cowell were not the only rugged individualists in American music. Early in this century we had the intense, expressionistic sound masses of their friend Carl Ruggles (1876–1971), the mystical patterns of the astrologically inclined Dane Rudhyar (1895–   ), and the mathematical logic of Ruth Crawford Seeger (1901–1953). This great variety reflected the wide-open curiosity and optimism of the American experience, independent of European precedent. For certain composers, the influence of the ***East*** was much more important than anything European. A number of composers explored unusual tuning systems and gamelan-like ensemble textures, as well as Indian-derived *raga* and *tala.*

Certain experimental figures began to acquire the status of legend. One such figure was the remarkable Harry Partch (1901–1974). An iconoclastic individualist who distrusted musical institutions and was largely self-taught, Partch lived for years as a hobo, handyman, dishwasher, and carpenter, avoiding the musical establishment and developing an esthetic outside the Western tradition. Believing that our tempered twelve-tone division of the octave was irrational, Partch devised a system based on interrelated natural overtones that gave him a forty-three-tone octave. This led him to construct special instruments: a veritable orchestra of unique plucked and bowed strings, reed organs, and sculpted percussion objects made of glass, metal, bamboo, and gourd. He also had to invent a notational system for writing his music down, and train many assistants to play his instruments. The Canadian-born Henry Brant (1913–) has also worked outside many assumptions of the Western tradition, especially those concerning the placement of performers and ideas of ensemble coordination. His antiphonal use of space and unsynchronized polyrhythms revealed an Ivesian streak years before the establishment came to "discover" Ives at all.

Many strands of the American "experimental" tradition met in the early work of John Cage (1912–): the interest in percussion ensemble, unusual intonation, non-Western esthetics, and unorthodox instruments (as in his ***Imaginary Landscape*** for twelve radios.) Cage had studied with Cowell and Schoenberg, the latter commenting once that his pupil was "not a composer, but an inventor—of genius." Like Cowell, Cage extended the sonorities of the piano. His ***prepared piano,*** with objects such as screws or rubber erasers between the inner strings, produced delicate gamelan-like timbres. Similarly, Cage's friend Lou Harrison (1917–) created music for "found objects" (flower pots, coffee cans, brake drums) which would exploit their unique sonorities.

In the 1940s Cage was among the first to use found ***electrical*** objects: buzzers, audio oscillators, phonograph records on variable speed turntables, sound-effects machines or radios. The sounds might be carefully ordered for some pieces, and randomly overlapped in others. Like Ives, Cage drew on the musical environment of everyday culture and multiple stimuli; in another sense, he followed Varèse in shaping the planes and densities of pure sound. And he was certainly moving towards "electronic music" long before most of his contemporaries. (As we will note in Chapter 18, Cage was also exploring aspects of improvisation during these years.) By the 1950s a most unusual situation had developed: young European composers were greatly stimulated by the music of John Cage, and heatedly debated the work and philosophy of this remarkable American. The iconoclastic American tradition had crossed the Atlantic to influence the hallowed European mainstream.

Two Representative Composers: Bartók and Copland

Obviously, there is no single twentieth-century style, and no one composer who epitomizes contemporary music. Let us consider two important figures of the twentieth-century mainstream who had had to deal with many alternatives: the great romantic tradition, neoclassicism, tonality, national roots.

Copland

For many Americans the name Aaron Copland (1900–) has symbolized a style of concert music to which they could relate as a nation. In its subject matter and materials, Copland's music draws strength from the American landscape: the Great Plains, the West, city skyscrapers, jazz and show tunes, rural village folk songs. Growing up in Brooklyn as the child of Russian-Jewish immigrants, Copland knew the culture of the city; he was to discover more of his country's heritage as his style developed. But his most important musical education took place in France during the 1920s under the supervision of Nadia Boulanger. His music of this period had a Stravinskian, anti-romantic thrust with a strong emphasis on jazz, and a taut, biting harmonic language, becoming even more austere and dispassionate during the thirties. An example of his abstract, "international," neoclassic approach is the ***Piano Variations*** (1930): harsh, percussive insonority, and compelling in logic.

In the late 1930s, however, Copland began to reconsider his position. Like Hindemith, he was distressed by the gulf between the composer and society, and excited by the possibilities of using stage, film, folk, and popular idioms to bridge that gulf. His sense of ***Gebrauchsmusik*** told him that the effort would be socially worthwhile and musically challenging. As he put it, "It made no sense to ignore them (traditional concertgoers) and to continue writing as if they did not exist. I felt that it was worth the effort to see if I couldn't say what I had to say in the simplest possible terms." Copland echoed the sentiments of many artists whose social consciousness was aroused by the great Depression; he was determined to leave the ivory tower.

A children's opera and a piece for high school orchestra were among his first works in a deliberately simplified style. His film music reached a broad audience, and he scored a great popular success with ***A Lincoln Portrait*** (1942) for narrator and orchestra. Copland also captured the idiomatic flavor of folk and popular music in a series of ballet scores based on Mexican sources and authentic cowboy tunes of the West. The last of these rural "frontier" ballets was ***Appalachian Spring,*** dealing with pioneer life in the Pennsylvania hills. It was commissioned for the famous Martha Graham company and premiered in 1944. Originally scored for a small chamber group of thirteen, the work was later revised as a suite for large orchestra.

Martha Graham, who choreographed the ballet and danced in its first production, described it as a "celebration in spring around a newly built farm house . . . in the early part of the last century." The main characters include a young bride and groom-to-be, a preacher, and farm neighbors. Copland's music emphasizes the rhythms and gestures of folk song and dance, but uses the spiky tonality, brilliantly outlined registers, and urbane polish of neoclassicism. One actual folk tune is used in the score: a graceful melody called "Simple Gifts," a favorite of the intensely devoted religious sect known as the Shakers.

A scene from the premiere performance of ***Appalachian Spring.*** The seated woman, in fact, is choreographer-dancer Martha Graham, for whom the work was composed.

Aaron Copland
Appalachian Spring

The orchestra suite consists of eight sections, joined together without pause. As in any suite, and as one might expect in a style heavily influenced by Stravinsky, there are strong contrasts between sections and a vivid, episodic quality to the whole. It might be interesting, in fact, to compare Copland's gentle, homespun Spring with Stravinsky's brutish, prehistoric ***Printemps.*** Although the two ballets are worlds apart in some respects, they are strangely similar in others.

Section 1 begins very slowly. There is great stillness and calm, a series of slowly shifting chords, and a triadic motive (Figure 17.14) outlining a broken A-major chord. The material is thoroughly diatonic, clearly tonal without any chromatic ambivalence (or fussy European "sophistication"). The limited pitch vocabulary evokes a kind of pioneer innocence here. Copland also conveys the ***spaciousness*** of the pioneer landscape with an ingenious use of ***register.*** His slowly moving chords are actually ***polychords,*** created by sounding tonic and dominant (I and V) or tonic and subdominant (I and IV) together in a registral spacing that lets them sound open, shimmering, and resonant. (See Figure 17.15).

Section 2 is suddenly fast, bouncy and strikingly rhythmic. A brisk tune, also stressing triadic skips (Figure 17.16), is fragmented and tossed about the registers and timbres of the orchestra. The ♫ ♩ rhythm dominates the section. As the tiny triadic fragments are imitated at different key levels, the fabric becomes almost polytonal. A slowly moving melody appears against the rhythmic dance, and gradually becomes more intense in its stable, hymnlike harmonization. ***Section 3*** moves at a moderate, gentle tempo; Copland calls it a "Duo for the Bride and her Intended." It features a lyric passage for winds, also built on a triadic contour (as shown in Figure 17.17), and leads directly to ***Section 4:*** "The Revivalist and his Flock. . . . folksy feelings." The tempo is quite fast, and the rhythms are highly synco-

Figure 17.14

Figure 17.15

Figure 17.16

Figure 17.17

pated in the manner of barn dances and country fiddling. As in section 2, Copland creates great energy by the precise, brittle articulation of percussive timbres: piano, xylophone, wood block, and bass drum all contribute to the sonority. After a brief passage of solemn ***polychords,*** we move directly to ***Section 5.*** This is a frenetic dance with unexpected syncopations and changing meters, portraying the "Solo dance of the Bride . . . extremes of joy and fear and wonder."

With ***Section 6,*** the contemplative mood of the opening returns, spacious and still; the landscape itself is the subject. Against this backdrop, ***Section 7*** begins with a gentle statement of "Simple Gifts," shown in Figure 17.18. Copland calls this section "Scenes of daily activity for the Bride and her Farmer Husband." After the initial tune, five variations follow without a break. The melody is slowed down, placed in different registers, combined contrapuntally with itself, boldly heralded against a Stravinskian bass line. (By the way, note that the opening skip and succeeding strong beats of "Simple Gifts" outline a rising major triad. The authentic folk song, then, seems to grow naturally out of the basic material of the composed ballet. Or is it the other way around?) The song itself eloquently sums up the spirit of the entire stage work: "'Tis the gift to be simple, 'Tis the gift to be free . . ."

Section 8 is really an epilogue, a quiet return to the hushed, peaceful atmosphere of the frontier landscape, as the young couple stand alone on the empty stage.

Figure 17.18

* = outlines tonic triad

Although shaped by diverse influences, Copland's style has acquired a unique profile of its own. His chamber works and symphonies retain this quality, even though they belong to the world of absolute music rather than programmatic Americana. And when Copland began to make use of the twelve-tone technique in the 1950s, the musical results remained unmistakably his own: spiky, brilliantly transparent, irrepressibly rhythmic and inventive.

Bartók

Like Copland, Béla Bartók (1881–1945) forged a unique profile from many sources, uniting diverse musical strains under the strong focus of nationalism. He was born in Hungary when that country was still dominated by Austro-German culture, and his first musical idols were Brahms, Liszt, and Wagner. But as a student in Budapest, he was caught up in the great nationalistic movement that was energizing Hungarian literature and politics. With his friend and fellow composer Zoltán Kodály (1882–1967), Bartok went out into the countryside, collecting, recording and analyzing folk songs. They soon discovered that the "Hungarian" melodies used by Brahms and Liszt in their salon pieces had been so altered for Western taste that they bore little resemblance to the real music of the people. The rhythms and melodic patterns of Hungarian folk music were actually more striking than Westerners realized.

Bartók also became captivated by Debussy; an abiding concern for sheer sonority and impressionistic color remained with him all his life. The chromatic dissonance of Schoenberg and the "primitive," brutal energy of Stravinsky contributed to his creative development as well. Bartók certainly enjoyed the driving percussive rhythms of folk dance and the fierce power of dense cluster sonorities. (He even wrote to Henry Cowell in America requesting permission to use piano clusters, as though the device were Cowell's patented invention.) In fact, his *Allegro Barbaro* for piano (1911) was one of the most shocking pieces of pre-war Europe, and gave critics the excuse to apply the unflattering label "barbarism" to his style.

Only after Bartók's death did listeners realize that his style, perhaps more than any other, defies *all* "isms." It results from a unique synthesis of every important strain in Western music: expressive romanticism, chromatic dissonance balanced with triadic tonality, unusual folk scales, delicate impressionistic timbres, new instrumental sonorities, great rhythmic energy, the neoclassic concern for structural clarity and the use of traditional models. He composed music in every genre, from operas, sonatas, concertos, ballets, and a major series of six string quartets, to simple piano pieces for children. Various sets of folk songs and dances testify to Bartók's immersion in Balkan national music. But we can guess that simply by hearing his work: the irregular meters, asymmetrical phrase groups, and odd intervals of East European folk scales are evidence enough.

Béla Bartók

Music for Strings, Percussion and Celesta

R6 S1 B2

This composition displays Bartók's biting tonal language, flair for tightly organized formal structure, and highly sensitive ear for sonority. The work is also a fascinating synthesis of the traditional and the innovative. It is a "symphony" of sorts, with a sonata-form allegro, an evocative slow movement and vigorous dancelike finale. But it is scored for a unique, unsymphonic ensemble of strings and a large percussion battery. Bartók specifies the instruments' placement on the stage, with two string bodies surrounding the percussion forces. He also provides a second slow movement, instead of a scherzo, with a four movement scheme.

The opening movement takes the shape of an elaborate fugue, in which a complex key scheme, in an ever-increasing spiral leading away from the tonic and then gradually returning to it, creates gradual tension and release. The movement that follows, a rhythmically vigorous allegro in sonata form, begins with an arresting first theme that exploits the percussive timbres of piano and timpani, often set against pizzicato strings. The two-note figure (bracketed in Figure 17.19) acquires great motivic force during the movement; it is varied, extended in sequence, heard as a string ***glissando*** or a brutal timpani figure.

A wonderfully evocative, atmospheric slow movement follows. Bartók begins with points and splashes of pure "color": the suggestive sound world of impressionism, perhaps, or of Varèse. A repeated note for xylophone alone, canonic string entrances, and timpani ***glissandi*** provide the opening material. These lead to an extended middle section in which piano, harp, celesta, and string ***glissandi*** are interwoven, followed by a return to the quiet beginning. Bartok was fond of mysterious, hushed sonorities and delicate passages that suggest natural outdoor sounds (insects, distant thunder, birds, the wind). Such passages or movements occur in a number of pieces, and are often referred to as his "night music."

The Finale is also a sectional part form, akin to a Rondo. It begins with a rush of sound, in the tempo of a joyous peasant dance, stressing rhythmic bursts of asymmetric "twos" and "threes." (Note in Figure 17.20 that the 8 ♪ per measure can be grouped as 2 + 3 + 3.) The striking timbres of this movement, alternately delicate and ferocious in their impact, never fail to command our attention.

Figure 17.19

Figure 17.20

Bartók enjoyed great success as a virtuoso pianist and professor at the Budapest Conservatory. He had also been an outspoken opponent of Nazism and the Hitler regime. When the Germans overran Austria and advanced upon Hungary, Bartók realized that he had to leave his country. He came to the United States in 1940, with little money and few contacts, and settled in New York. Columbia University provided him with a research position in folk music, but at modest wages. He was now in his mid-sixties, homesick, financially unsettled, and seriously ill. His last years were spent battling leukemia, shuttling in and out of New York hospitals, and struggling to complete the few commissions that had finally come his way.

Bartók's last work, composed during the final stages of his disease, was the Third Piano Concerto (1945), written for his pianist wife Ditta as a kind of "insurance" that he hoped would provide her with a touring showpiece. He died with the last seventeen measures of the concerto incomplete; they were later filled in from sketches. In this concerto Bartók tried to reconcile his earlier aggressive style with a simpler, more direct tonal lyricism. The slow movement, with its extended fabric of shimmering "night music" is especially lovely. The finale is a relentlessly driving rondo.

Towards the Avant-Garde

Bartók died in the year 1945. So did Anton Webern, accidentally shot by a soldier shortly after the war's end. The Allied victory in Europe ended the Nazi censorship of "modernist" music; young European musicians were eager to re-establish links with their immediate past. The United States, which had gradually assumed a position of musical leadership during the war years, entered the postwar era with confidence. There was a great surge of interest in building, including plans for "arts centers," the first signs of a population boom, and an increase in the size and scope of college and conservatories.

For many composers, tonality was no longer interesting, despite the neoclassic efforts to salvage it. Composers were also convinced, by and large, that ***Gebrauchsmusik*** attempts to bridge the great "schism" had failed. The era of social consciousness was now just past, and in a pluralistic, mobile society, audiences were more fragmented than ever. The newly emerging patrons—universities, dance companies, European radio networks—encouraged composers to explore and experiment freely. And most explorations led *away* from tonality.

Although the tonal assumptions of neoclassicism had lost favor, many composers still endorsed Stravinsky's notion of the artist as someone concerned with "problem solving"—the objective manipulation of materials and processes. The younger composers, however, were interested in radically new materials. They enjoyed extremes of register, articulation, and dynamics, complex rhythmic interaction, and sonorities that could be exquisitely delicate or brutally vulgar. Was there any way of relating the detached, elegant game playing of Stravinsky to *those* interests? Could a composer explore the sensuous, airy sound world of Debussy and discard the impressionistic esthetic that went with it? Could one use Schoenberg's discipline of control, but not his expressionistic gestures?

The answer could be summed up in a single name: Webern. In the many concertos and festivals devoted to twentieth-century music during the early postwar years, the greatest focus of attention was the music of Webern. Just as Wagner had profoundly influenced the first half of our century, Webern dominated the start of the second half. For some composers, another figure was equally important. John Cage, with his all-embracing attitude to the total world of sound and his fascination with accidental, unplanned "processes," exerted an ever-growing influence on both sides of the Atlantic.

Americans finally became aware of the pioneering work of Ives and Varèse. In a similar manner Europeans were influenced by Olivier Messiaen (1908–), a French organist and composer who had spent much of the war in a concentration camp. Messiaen, like Varèse, had long been interested in static, spatial, blocklike sonorities; his work also reflected a deeply religious sense, and serious absorption, on mystical and musical levels, with bird calls. By 1949 Messiaen was beginning to explore the total organization of all musical elements—durations, articulation, dynamics, and pitch—that was to be called ***serialism*** (see Chapter 18).

Behind all this lay two crucial developments in postwar technology, the invention of the long-playing record in 1948 and the mass marketing of tape recorders in the mid-fifties. LP records brought an entire literature of neglected music to public attention: not only Vivaldi, Handel, and Berlioz, but Ives, Webern, Partch, and other twentieth-century composers. Tape became an ideal vehicle for recording, storing, and reproducing musical performances cheaply and efficiently, so that composers all over the world could be aware of what their colleagues were doing. A new piece could be played on a given evening in New York, and within a short time be studied by musicians in Stockholm, London, or Tokyo. This phenomenon has had two immediate results. Stylistic changes which might have taken decades to evolve in the past now whiz by in a few years; the rate of change is unique to our time. Secondly, emerging new styles are more likely to be international than regional.

Changing Styles: Carter, Luening and Ussachevsky

The extraordinary impact of postwar developments can be seen in the fact that many established composers *altered* their styles during the 1950s. Aaron Copland began working with twelve-tone techniques after the war, and the American Roger Sessions, who had strong ties to the German chromatic tradition, began to use the twelve-tone method as well. Lukas Foss (1922–), whose early style had been forged from Hindemith and Copland, became interested in group improvisation and Ivesian collage. (A recent work of his will be discussed in Chapter 18.) Most surprisingly, Stravinsky—the acknowledged spokesman for neoclassic tonality—adopted the twelve-tone method, when past the age of seventy! The ballet *Agon* (1957) is typical of his later work: row forms are used to generate motivic fragments, articulated with Stravinsky's own lean, athletic energy.

The stylistic development of Elliott Carter (1908–) is especially interesting because it took place so gradually. Carter studied with Walter Piston at Harvard and then with Nadia Boulanger in Paris. His early music shows this influence in its tonal "American" flavor. But Carter had also known Charles Ives personally (it was a letter from Ives that had helped send him to Harvard) and had the intellectual curiosity of a true experimental maverick. By the 1950s he had evolved a style in which tonality had all but disappeared. Carter preferred a dense, free chromaticism, highly dissonant but not a Schoenbergian system. He also began to explore the "personalities" of ensemble parts. In the spirit of Ives, Carter creates his chamber pieces as scenarios, plays without words, in which performers act out roles of conflict, confrontation, or agreement. These might be heard at simultaneous levels (as in Ives's *Three Places in New England*), or sharply focused upon a single argument.

Elliott Carter

Sonata for Flute, Oboe, Cello, and Harpsichord *R5 S1 B3*

In this 1953 chamber work Carter exploits four distinctly different timbres, and treats the players as actors in a minidrama. In the first movement, note how the opening flurries overlap and interrupt one another. Soon afterwards, the regular even beats of the harpsichord collide with the lyric, semi-improvisatory gestures of the other instruments. This establishes a pattern for the rest of the movement: simultaneous levels of rhythmic activity (rigid against fluid), and bursts of "commentary" that add unexpected weight to the linear texture.

There is also a unique interaction of pulses in certain passages of the *Sonata,* where one kind of regularity meshes with, or merges into, another kind, very much like clocks ticking at different speeds. Carter, devoting special attention to that particular experience, has perfected an accurate metric modulation

notational technique that would allow one tempo or meter to change to another. This procedure is known as ***metric modulation.***

The superimposition of impulsive rhythms on a regular "beat," and the virtuosic ornamentation of lines, creates an oddly jazz-like effect. Paradoxically, the harpsichord timbre suggests a very different association, that of the baroque. Carter uses both levels of "meaning" to great advantage.

In the later String Quartet no. 2 (1959), Carter expands upon the idea of role-playing "personality" by assigning different musical materials (intervals, rhythms, styles of phrasing) to each of the players, and different moods as well. Violin I presents a virtuosic brashness, Violin II always plays in "strict time" no matter what happens elsewhere, the Viola seems obsessed by expressive ***glissandi,*** and the Cello often makes statements that either speed up or slow down. Carter also has the players seated far apart on the stage, so that these individual traits become underlined. Metric modulation has become an essential component of the ever-changing atonal fabric: an interplay of monologues, dialogues, asides, and group discussions that is highly theatrical yet abstract.

Another major change was taking place during the post-war years, with two Columbia University professors collaborating on experiments that would alter their own styles and the course of music in America. Otto Luening (1900–   ) and Vladimir Ussachevsky (1911–   ) were experienced composers in a neoclassic idiom; both had strong interests in science and technology. Inspired by postwar European composers who were creating music directly for playback on tape, Luening and Ussachevsky began to make their own tape music, using the sounds of traditional instruments as the basic material for manipulation (see Chapter 18). Their efforts were presented at New York's Museum of Modern Art in 1952, the first all-electronic concert in America and an event that drew composers and critics from many countries. Listen to two of these brief 1952 pieces.* Ussachevsky's ***Sonic Contours*** is an introspective collage of piano sounds: chords and melodic fragments, altered by careful tape splicing, changes of speed and echo effects. This is a piece that could not be performed by an actual pianist on stage. It ***uses*** sounds made by a pianist to create a sonic sculpture that only exists as it emerges from loudspeakers.

Similarly, Luening's ***Fantasy in Space*** employs flute material but is not a "flute piece:" its sole performance medium is tape playback. The virtuosic flute patterns are extended into many dimensions by editing, multiple track overlays, reverberation and tape speed changes. Note that Luening, like Ussachevsky, admits familiar gestures to the new idiom; a simple diatonic tune emerges from his web of drifting flute sonority.

John Cage and Edgard Varèse were also drawn to the tape medium during the 1950s. Cage was collecting snippets of noises, street sounds,

*Music from the historic 1952 tape concert can be heard on Desto 6466.

electrical tones, and instrumental fragments, and assembling them into collages as early as 1952. And Varèse had finally found the medium for the "liberation of sound" (as he put it) that had eluded him for thirty years. The elderly composer, now in his seventies, worked with studio engineers to create one of the major tape pieces of the postwar decade: the massive ***Poème Électronique*** of 1958. The ***Poème*** was composed for the 400 loudspeakers ringing the interior of the Phillips Pavilion at the Brussels Worlds Fair; existing entirely on tape, it combines natural sounds (including those of instruments) with electronically generated ones, retaining Varèse's own unique approach to sonority and density.

For Varèse and Cage, of course, the move to tape did not represent a new direction. On the contrary, both of these frankly experimental composers had been anticipating and prophesying electronic music for decades. In 1937 Cage said:

> Wherever we are, what we hear is mostly noise. When we ignore it, it disturbs us. When we listen to it, we find it fascinating. The sound of a truck at fifty miles an hour. Static between the stations. Rain. We want to capture and control these sounds . . . (We could) compose and perform a quartet for explosive motor, wind, heartbeat, and landslide . . .

These words were being realized twenty years later.

Interlude 5
Music and Technology

The preceding chapter ended with a reference to early tape music; more electronic music will be surveyed in the next, and final, chapter. This seems an appropriate moment, then, to consider the relationship of technology to music: first of all, the belief that music "by machines" is somehow lacking in "human" values. This belief has haunted the field of electronic music ever since the first tape and synthesizer pieces. It was fostered by various press releases of the 1950s, with such blazing headlines as "Sinus Tones with Nuts and Bolts" (*Harper's*), "Nothing But Us Speakers" (*New York Times*), or "Union Card for a Tape Recorder" (*Music Journal*)—all rather horrifying prospects to humanists.

The phrase "music by machines" may conjure up images of music *composed* by machines. In fact, such experiments have been very rare. Certain synthesizer circuits and computer programs can generate their own patterns, but they only do so upon human instigation and control. More likely, electronic equipment is used to aid a human composer in the mechanics of *preserving* and / or *manipulating* ideas, very much as a writing desk, pen, or manuscript paper might. (Those are all pretty sophisticated human inventions themselves.) Electronic equipment may also be used as a *performing* medium, an elaborate "instrument" of great versatility. Sometimes the electronic performance takes place in front of an audience, as at a rock concert; we also "perform" in the privacy of an electronic studio, using the tape medium to preserve our work for later playback.

All instruments—xylophone, oboe, tuba, timpani—are masterpieces of technology. People have been making music on carefully engineered sound-producing inventions for centuries. Moreover, these are more than mere neutral helpers; they often exhibit "personalities" of their own which may well lead to new artistic insights. Consider, for example, the direct musical consequences of the following: valves for brass instruments; the metronome; five-line staff notation; the phonograph; music printing; the evolution of the piano.

That last item, the piano, dominated Western music for two centuries. It has been our ideal accompaniment, heroic solo voice, the perfect teaching tool, the reflection of our concern for harmony and tempered tuning. The piano has also reflected the *social* patterns of its time: the salon parties, dances, and drawing-room entertainments of northern Europe. (In the warmer South, musicians were just as likely to stroll out of doors with smaller, portable instruments.) Pianos, along with clarinets and violins, were once found in almost every middle-class home, for informal singing and dancing on occasions that had nothing to do with high culture. Today's homes may have electronic guitars and jazz drum sets instead, or tape decks, or recorders and lutes. This alone speaks volumes about our changing musical habits, and the informal, grass-roots experience that will help shape our future composers.

Other arts have been equally responsive to changing technology. Major style shifts in the visual arts paralleled the growth of printing, oil painting on canvas versus fresco painting, new structural materials such as concrete and steel for sculpture and architecture, and the invention of photography. In many cases musical innovations have reflected other arts: the style of Gothic sacred music exploiting the resonant acoustics of grand cathedrals, or the early twentieth-century fondness for the "quick cut" or "dissolve" influenced by techniques of movie film editing. (Such transitions take place in *Wozzeck* and *Appalachian Spring,* for example. They were also essential to the editing techniques of early tape music.)

On another level, all technology influences

art, simply because machines change the way human beings live. General improvements in communication permit greater mutual interaction of many artists. Style changes have often grown out of a pool of talent, a "community" upon which the creative imagination feeds. Early in this century, the phonograph and radio made more works available to more musicians than ever before. They were as crucial to the evolution of music as the printing press had been hundreds of years before. And since the 1950s, the tape recorder has added another resource of enormous potential. The modern jet plane has brought the world's musicians closer together; we find Americans in Tokyo, Swedes in Ghana, or Germans in Bali, studying new cultures and traditions. Composers, performers, and scholars all have access to a great fund of information.

In earlier times, however, information was often spotty and erratic. A century or so ago, when European travel had become moderately efficient, Liszt, Chopin, Schumann, Mendelssohn, Wagner, and Berlioz knew one another personally. A few decades earlier, the friendship of Haydn and Mozart had profound consequences for both. But it is disconcerting to read that, while going through Germany in 1794 on the way to his second London visit, Haydn decided to call on C.P.E. Bach—only to discover that Bach had been dead for years. Looking backward to the early eighteenth century, we might be surprised to note that J. S. Bach and Handel never met. They came very close on one occasion; Handel was visiting his mother in Germany, and Bach made a special trip in hopes of seeing him. According to legend, Bach missed Handel by a matter of days, there being no telephone or telegraph, of course, to relay travel plans. (Whether Handel would have cared to meet a stodgy provincial organist named Bach is another question.)

Consider, too, changes in medical technology over the centuries. "Wonder drugs" might have prolonged the lives of Purcell, Schubert, and Mozart; moreover, many researchers believe that Beethoven's deafness was of a distinctly correctable nature, and would have been eased with a modern hearing aid.

It seems, then, that art and technology are intimately related. We cannot reasonably expect twentieth-century composers to work with eighteenth-century tools; on the contrary, the creative imagination will use the resources of our society, from microphones to videotapes to plastics to laser beams, in an unforeseen and exciting way. Recent styles have already been changing in response to the great musical fact of the century, *sound recording*. Recording technology has opened up entire worlds of music for many listeners; it has brought Beethoven's work to the "millions" he envisioned in his lifetime. It has taught us the musical traditions of distant lands and peoples. Most important, recording has altered our basic assumptions about music: music as social ritual, as acoustic phenomenon, as "performance," as personal expression, as humanistic literature. Recording technology has made a difference in our lives that we have not yet begun to understand. In their own way, the composers of the eighties are trying to tell us about it.

18

The New Music

There is no avant garde. There are only people who are a little late.

Edgard Varèse

Is it art? Depends on how it's done. Art is turning it out.

Andy Warhol

Babbitt and Cage: "Order" and "Chaos" of the Sixties

Musical styles and interests have changed drastically since the 1950s, and in a bewildering variety of directions. Not all composers adopt the most radical new styles. Just as the early eighteenth century saw the conflicting approaches of Bach, Handel, and Scarlatti, and the early twentieth century those of Mahler, Puccini, Satie, and Schoenberg, our own era nurtures "radical" and "conservative" approaches to music. Although this chapter stresses the striking innovations of recent years, these have coexisted with many significant works in a tonal, expressively neoromantic idiom: symphonies, concertos, and operas by such composers as Shostakovitch, Benjamin Britten, and Samuel Barber.

In the 1960s, the phrase "New Music" was frequently used to distinguish the most radical directions from traditional approaches. And clearly there is a difference between today's new view of art and the music of the past—even the immediate past of Schoenberg, Bartók, Hindemith, or Shostakovitch. Most earlier twentieth-century music represents the final development of the Western tonal tradition. By contrast, many features of the

"New Music" have been anti-Western, anti-tonal, or both. Many of today's experimental composers question such hallowed notions as "responsibility," "interest," and "personality."

For the first postwar decades, the chief focus of New Music was the question of *control.* How controlled should the art of music be? Is music a carefully structured rational argument in time, or is it a spontaneous activity of immediate theatrical impact? Music of the past has always related to both extremes: it speaks to our love of precise order *and* to our response to sound as an irrational, magical force. During the early postwar years of New Music, the twin aspects of music appeared to split off from each other, each drawing upon musical tradition in its own way. Milton Babbitt and John Cage became known as chief spokesmen for the extreme positions at either end of the spectrum, advocating respectively the "order" of ***serialism*** and the "chaos" of ***indeterminacy.***

Babbitt and Serialism

Many postwar composers were fascinated by Webern's music, for its precision and its jewel-like sonorities. Webern seemed to have split a musical "atom" in a way, focusing our attention upon the qualities of single tones—register, dynamic level, articulation—with intense, concentrated energy. Some composers envisioned "rows" of durations or dynamics, which could organize those musical dimensions just as Schoenberg and Webern had organized pitch. In 1949 Olivier Messiaen composed a piano piece built on a plan of twenty-four different durations, a dynamic "row" of seven levels and a series of seven kinds of articulation. Messiaen's student Pierre Boulez created a piece called ***Structures I*** in 1952 using "rows" of twelve durations, twelve dynamic levels and twelve articulation levels as well as a twelve-note pitch series. Boulez further tightened this organization by relating one series to another in the course of the work. (See Figure 18.1). In the United States, Milton Babbitt explored similar ideas, and by

Figure 18.1

1	2	3	4	5	6	7	8	9	10	11	12
pppp	*ppp*	*pp*	(*p*)	*quasi p*	*mp*	*mf*	*quasi f*	*f*	(*ff*)	*fff*	*ffff*

1	2	3	4	5	6	7	8	9	10	11	12
>	>	·		*normal*	⌒	!	*sfz* ^	> !		−	⌒

The title of this sculpture, ***Maze Music*** by Michael Ayrton, may articulate the dilemma many listeners confront in our age of contradictions.

1948 had composed the first totally "controlled" music in which *every* aspect of a work was strictly derived from a single premise. This approach to music is called ***serialism.*** It treats all aspects of musical language in ways analogous to the twelve-tone treatment of pitch, so that a work is organized as a network of tightly interlocked "series."

serialism

Serial music often delights in extremes of register, complex rhythmic interaction, and sudden changes of dynamics and articulation as well. It provides a Webernian sound world of fleeting points and colors, arrived at by articulating precise relationships. Serialists generally prefer Webern's esthetic to the late romantic Wagnerian rhetoric of Schoenberg. In fact, many works of the 1950s and '60s were referred to by critics as ***"post-Webernian"*** to indicate their very special approach to texture and kaleidoscopic color.

post-Webernian style

As one of the leading serialists, Milton Babbitt has had a strong influence upon younger composers. In his teaching and writing, Babbitt stresses a concern for the rational, logical properties of music: the art "object"—a fixed relationship of building blocks, laid out in a written score—is primary. As virtually every detail has been specified, his music is often quite difficult. Performers must be absolutely precise, perhaps more so than with a traditional style, since a missed note or incorrect dynamic would misrepresent an entire network of relationships. Since the advent of electronic music, it is possible for a composer to bypass these difficulties by "performing" the work himself in an electronic studio and fixing an ideal realization permanently on tape. Babbitt has created a number of electronic works, such as the ***Composition for Synthesizer*** discussed in Part I of this book.

Serial music presents a unique situation to the listener: its most important "facts" are usually ***not*** heard, and probably not meant to be heard even by the best of ears. On the other hand, the serial composer may create a distinctive "surface" to hold the listener's interest. One composer who uses serial technique in a dramatic, intense language of his own is Charles Wuorinen (1938–   ). Like most composers who came to maturity in the postwar era, Wuorinen has forged a personal style from many diverse influences: Webern, Stravinsky, medieval music, Babbitt, Varèse. His ***String Trio**** (1968) is a taut one-movement work that unfolds gradually, stating only six pitches of its twelve-note series at first (Figure 18.2). During the opening minutes of the work, a drone on G functions as a springboard and backdrop for the other five pitches (C, A♭, B♭, B, A). The pedal G remains prominent, even after the other 5 pitches of the series make their entrance (most clearly heard in an arching violin solo line). That persistent G, now alternating with a drone C♯, provides a curiously "tonal" fabric of momentum and rest.

The Wuorinen excerpt may sound spontaneous, and even improvisatory. But a glance at the score will confirm its precision, and its difficulty for

*Recorded on Nonesuch 71319.

Figure 18.2

to the Potomac String Trio

TRIO

CHARLES WUORINEN

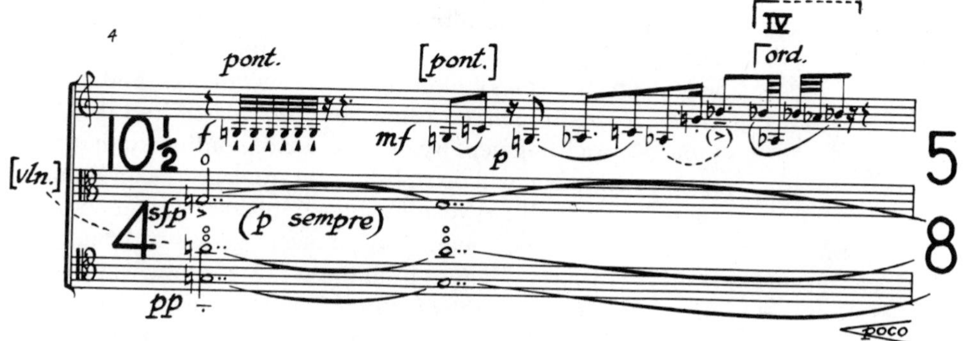

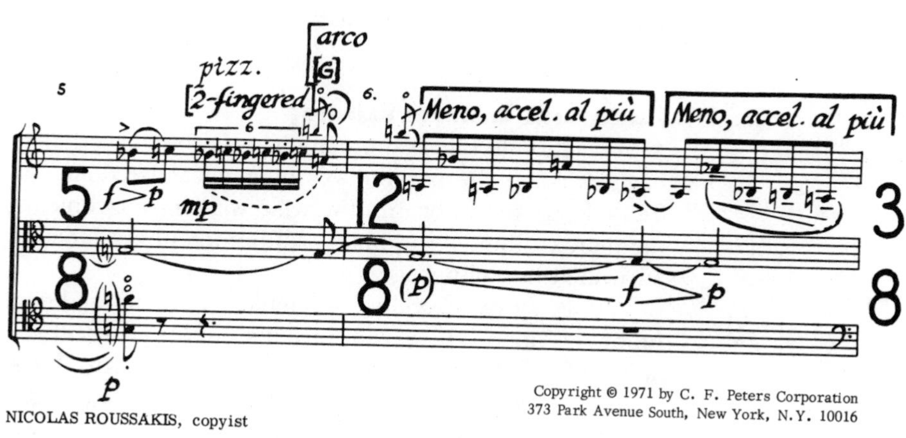

NICOLAS ROUSSAKIS, copyist

performers. Wuorinen is himself a skilled virtuoso pianist, used to stretching the limits of technique. Moreover, his esthetic gives a higher priority to the musical *object* (coherent structure) than to the temporal activity of performing. In this sense, Wuorinen, Boulez and Babbitt are heirs to a grand Western tradition, with roots in Beethoven's contemptuous treatment of weak performers, or the problems players had with Wagner, or Schoenberg's comment to an irate violinist claiming a certain passage would be unplayable for a hundred years: "I can wait." The "grand tradition" is apparent in other aspects of total serialism as well:

1. the manipulation of pitches—specifically the twelve pitches of the tempered octave—to generate forward motion;
2. developing material by varying and extending a few ideas, anticipating and encouraging relationships that gradually unfold in time;
3. the notion that great or important music is "difficult," revealing its secrets only after careful study, and that these secrets have more to do with structure than with the sounds of any single performance.

Apart from the ultra-logical structure of serial music, listeners may simply enjoy responding to the sounds themselves. These may appear as a kaleidoscopic array of pitches, durations, attacks, and dynamics. Even register and instrumentation may be "serialized," so that they, too, appear atomized and fragmentary. The sense of continuity that we associate with traditional music will often be absent, replaced by an "inner" continuity of tight (but inaudible) relationships. Still, serial composers' styles remain distinctive and personal. The intense, aggressive language of Wuorinen's string trio is very different from the delicate, exotic world of Boulez's equally serial ***Le Marteau sans Maitre*** ("The Hammer without a Master"). In the latter work Boulez uses voice and instruments to evoke images of Debussy, Messiaen, Balinese gamelan, and African drumming. Neither work has the spiky, extroverted, almost jazzy quality of Babbitt's ***Composition for Synthesizer.***

Cage and Indeterminacy

As a reaction to the total order advanced by the serialists, other composers have explored the possibilities of musical freedom. Many works call for limited improvisation in otherwise written-out contexts, and some adopt the more extreme position of total randomness ("chaos," for some critics) advocated by John Cage.

Cage's new "freedom" of chance, accident, and random assemblage is uniquely American: we can trace his interest in sheer sound, simultaneous layers of colliding material and his gentle Eastern philosophy to such pioneers as Ives, Cowell, Partch, and Varèse. In fact, Cage's emergence as an important figure by the 1950s marks the coming of age of the American experimental "tradition," no longer a little band of mavericks, but an influential force on the world music scene.

John Cage
Aria and Fontana Mix (1958)

This performance* reveals important aspects of Cage's work. We say "performance" rather than "piece," because Cage has created a situation—a do-it-yourself kit—which might result in any number of vastly different realizations. The ***Fontana Mix*** is a wild crazy-quilt tape collage: bits of electronic sound, musical fragments, and amplified everyday sounds (swallowing, scraping on glass), spliced together to form a rapid succession of discontinuous images. There are a number of such tapes which can be played simultaneously in various combinations. In addition, the ***Fontana Mix*** may be performed simultaneously with a wholly different work, the ***Aria*** for improvising solo voice. In fact, we have not one piece here, but two heard as one.

In Cage's score for the ***Aria,*** the words are clearly given, but pitch and rhythm are only approximated. An entire phrase may be notated as a general contour: or for example. Compare that with the detailed, carefully calibrated markings of traditional, especially serial, music! Cage is concerned only with the large-scale gesture. He prefers to write an "ideogram" visualizing an entire concept, rather than an alphabetical construction of component parts: that is, rather than F A C E. He therefore forfeits the opportunity to recombine and "develop" internal details (FA, ACE, CAF) in the Western tradition, but he has gained great flexibility and a refreshing unpredictability in performance. ***Colors*** are used throughout the printed ***Aria*** score to suggest styles of singing. Cathy Berberian, the soloist of the recorded example, interpreted the colors so that blue = jazz, green = folk, brown = nasal, and so on. Other singers are free to realize the color distinctions differently.

In listening to this performance, remember that any other performance would probably sound very different in its details. Nevertheless, an impulsive, irreverent exuberance would probably emerge from any realization. The tape noises and the singer's words or nonsense syllables, have a curious affinity, as though they were intended for each other. But they weren't; Cage has suggested that the ***Aria*** be sung with other tapes, or with any instrumental parts from another piece of his.

The Western tradition assumes that the composer's efforts are directed toward a finished musical "product," that he or she controls the performance we hear. Cage, by supplying general outlines for players to assemble in kit format, has relinquished this control. ***That*** is actually more revolutionary than his fondness for noise and nonsense syllables! It raises the issue of "responsibility:" What is the composer's responsibility? What role does the performer or the listener play in shaping the experience? For Cage, the very idea of "responsibility" implies that music making is an act of will and

*A complete Aria and Fontana Mix can be heard on Mainstream Records S8003.

purpose. In his work, he has often tried to deny both, creating music by the throw of dice, the use of a random numbers table, or exploiting the imperfections of his writing paper. By such means he arrives at a music which consists of "sounds, not purposes."

indeterminacy

aleatory

Cage often speaks of ***indeterminacy***—the use of chance operations to arrive at the composition or performance of a piece. Other composers may use the term ***aleatory,*** or ***aleatoric*** music to indicate the same phenomenon (the Latin word "alea" meaning dice). ***Improvisation*** is a related, but really very different, concept: when musicians improvise in jazz or baroque realizations, they have a known context (usually a tonal grammar) as a constant reference point. ***Indeterminacy*** avoids the known context. Performers and listeners alike, and the composer, too, must explore uncharted territory. Improvisation and indeterminacy do share one important quality, though; they stress the spontaneity of performance as an immediate, unique experience. Those composers who create flexible performance situations—either the indeterminate "chaos" of Cage or more controlled improvisation—want to emphasize that sense of immediacy. For them, music is a sonic activity, a ritual celebration that occurs in real time and space, and not a fixed "art object" bounded by its relationships.

Chance may be used to determine the *form* of a work in performance, the order in which events succeed one another. The material for Barney Childs's ***Take Five*** is written on cards which are shuffled just prior to performance, and then dealt to five players. In ***Klavierstücke XI*** for piano (1957) by the German composer Karlheinz Stockhausen, there are nineteen fragments on a single sheet. (Two of them are given in Figure 18.3.) The pianist plays any fragment, and then chooses the tempo, dynamics, and articulation (at our arrows) for use in the next randomly selected fragment. The same fragment might sound totally different if played again during the piece. The American composer Earle Brown has also encouraged a flexible succession of events. In Brown's ***Available Forms*** for orchestra (1962), the conductor selects the order and duration of specified gestures and textures during the performance, "shaping" the work as it occurs. Incidentally, Brown's interest in the random arrangement and rearrangement of a few shapes was stimulated by the free-floating sculptural mobiles of Alexander Calder. Brown, Morton Feldman (see Chapter 7), and Cage worked closely together during the 1950s in New York; significantly, they were all strongly influenced by developments *outside* the field of music, notably modern art, theater, philosophy and dance.

The Electronic Revolution

Another important factor emerged during the 1950s: musical composition for direct playback on tape recorders. Shortly after the war, French radio engineers had used phonograph recordings of noises and musical sounds to

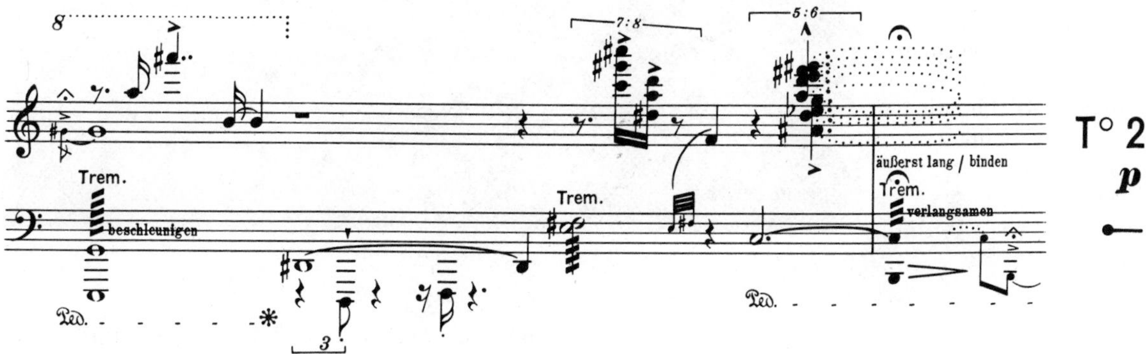

Figure 18.3

make brief montages of distorted, repeated fragments. These works were played over the French Radio network and led to the installation of a Paris studio, dedicated to further exploration of the new medium. In America, Luening and Ussachevsky began their collaborative work (see Chapter 17), and John Cage had started creating tape collage "mixes."

German composers also began working in studios of their own, with an approach to the tape medium very different from that of the French. Work in the German studios focused upon electronically produced sounds created by oscillators, noise generators, and filters—with the objective of greater "control" over articulation, duration, and timbre than could be achieved by any live performer. A composer anxious to explore four precise varieties of staccato, or three dynamic levels between *mp* and *mf* or a complex polyrhythm of thirteen beats against nine could realize such concepts electronically on tape. The twin issues of "chaos" and "order," then, were as pronounced in the early postwar studios as in the concert halls. For example, compare Cage's ***Fontana Mix*** with the Babbitt ***Composition for Synthesizer*** discussed in Part 1. Cage has built a collage of random sound snippets, delighting in their unpredictability and the magic of sound itself. Babbitt's

synthesizer

music, on the contrary, was created on an elaborate device called a *synthesizer*. By using this machine, he could produce carefully calibrated succes-

A view of the Bregman Electronic Music Studio at Dartmouth College, containing synthesizers, tape decks and loudspeakers.

sions of sound, and transform these with great precision and flexibility. The studio provided Babbitt with a medium for control: a way of "performing" highly complex serial patterns.

Today's composers still bring a variety of esthetic attitudes to the studio. The technology itself has changed a good deal since the 1950s and '60s. Synthesizers have become smaller, more portable and much less expensive, allowing many more people throughout the world to create and process electronic sound. Composers may now use high-speed digital computers as well; these can automate the operation of synthesizers, or generate sounds directly onto tape. The sound material can also come from the world of musical instruments and the everyday environment, just as it did in the earliest tape experiments. Here are a few examples of tape compositions created during the last few decades.

Electronic Compositions (excerpts)* *R6 S1 B4 B5 B6*

1. Ilhan Mimaroglu's ***Bowery Bum*** is a highly sophisticated example of tape technique, using speed changes, tape reversal, echo, repeated fragments, and multi-tracked overlays. These are all applied to a single sound source: a twanging rubber band.

2. In ***Thema*** (***Omaggio a Joyce***) by Luciano Berio, the same techniques are used to fragment a vocal text drawn from James Joyce, breaking

*The Mimaroglu work is available on Turnabout TV40045, and the Berio on Mercury SR2–9123.

it down into an evocative sensuous fabric. (In fact, we could say that Berio does to Joyce's language what Joyce does to everyday language.)

3. Jon Appleton's ***Chef d'Oeuvre*** is the first example on this list to use the modern synthesizer. Pre-recorded material (a television jingle for frozen pizza!) was "processed" by the synthesizer and edited into a concise study.

4. Charles Dodge is highly active in computer-generated music. His ***Speech Songs*** (1973) make use of a computer system developed at Bell Telephone Laboratories for the synthesis of human speech, here adapted for musical use. The sounds of this piece were not made by any living voice. Rather, the syllables have all been constructed and manipulated through the computer program. Listen to the fourth song, set to a poem by Mark Strand:

> The days are ahead
> 1,926,346 to 1,926,345
> Later the nights will catch up.

The quasi-canonic imitation, and the sliding "chorus" of downward ***glissando*** voices near the end, make for a telling deadpan commentary on the whimsical text.

5. Our final example is an excerpt from ***Touch*** by Morton Subotnick, one of the most imaginative American composers using electronics. Subotnick has explored new formats for the "performance" of electronic music: some highly theatrical multi-media ventures, and the performance medium of the phonograph record. In fact, he was among the very first composers to be commissioned by a record company for an electronic piece.

Subotnick's synthesizer technique often stresses elegant control of timbre and articulation, as well as repetitive, but infinitely varied, sequential patterns. In this opening fragment of ***Touch*** we hear an amazing range of timbres and gestures: these may approximate the colors of traditional instruments (taut strings, deep bells, xylophones), or the phonemes of human speech, or insect-like buzzings. The sounds have all been created on a synthesizer, in an electronic studio, and shaped further by editing and the multitrack capabilities of recorders.

In our excerpt, sonic fragments are at first etched against a background of silence, and then combine and grow in a multi-level fabric of repetitive ostinato patterns. At the peak of activity, the music becomes abrupt and jagged again. In its novel timbres and its alternating waves of tonal motion, the excerpt may resemble an Indian raga or African drumming at times. Throughout, Subotnick delights in airy textures and resonant electronic colors.

These compositions all share one important feature: they were intended to be heard through loudspeakers. Their recorded form is their ***only*** form. Composers are usually motivated to create music for loudspeakers (or earphones) because they enjoy sound effects beyond the powers of acoustic instruments, or because their ideas involve difficulty beyond the capability of the human hand. Perhaps they want to distort familiar material for ex-

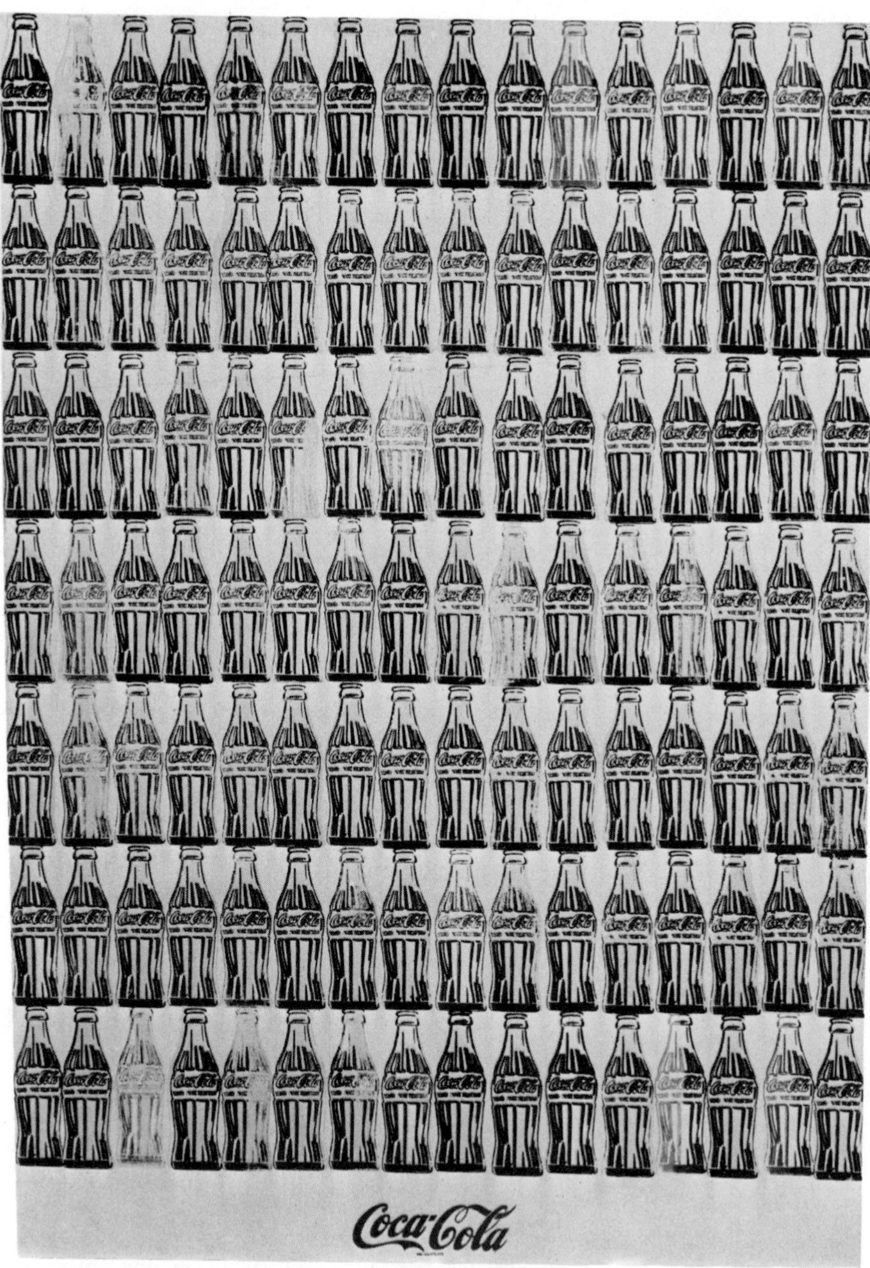

Andy Warhol, ***Green Coca-Cola Bottles.*** Warhol's painting of gently repetitive bottles shares a certain single-mindedness with some "process"-music. By taking a familiar visual symbol, and a printing technique, from advertising, and adapting both to the domain of Fine Art, Warhol also reminds us of some tape music and collage-quotations. Collection of the Whitney Museum of American Art, New York. Gift of the Friends of the Whitney Museum of American Art.

pressive purposes. In some instances they may simply delight in the loudspeakers themselves: the theatrical and acoustic possibilities of these "magical," inhuman boxes from which sounds miraculously flow. The ***placement*** of speakers within the performance space also concerns many composers. Having loudspeakers standing on a concert stage is not always satisfactory. Many other spaces are more attractive and appropriate: lobbies or outdoor gardens or cathedrals, depending upon individual works, their acoustic qualities, and listening demands.

Of course, not all electronic music is restricted to loudspeaker performance. As anyone who follows rock groups knows, live performances can be amplified and distorted by electronic equipment. Even in a traditional concert setting, human performers and electronic tapes can be brought together in a unique interaction. Two such works, with strikingly different approaches, are Mario Davidovsky's ***Synchronisms no. 1*** for flute and tape and Jacob Druckman's ***Animus I*** for trombone and tape. Davidovsky uses an elegant post-Webernian language, whith a fine ear for graceful gesture amidst serial atomization of pitch and rhythm. In the best tradition of chamber music, the imitative dialogue between flute and electronic counterpart is blended in a single fabric. The Druckman ***Animus I*** is much more highly charged; the performer seems to be pitted against the tape, itself a sinister mesh of electronic sound and distorted trombone fragments, in a spirit of concerto-like confrontation.

Density and Process

Although Babbitt's "order" and Cage's "chaos" have influenced many composers, there are other musical approaches that bypass issues of control and freedom. Recent works often concentrate on texture, creating music in which ***density*** plays a prominent role. In a sense, such music is "about" density, just as traditional Western music is "about" pitch. Listeners are immediately aware of broad bands of sound—delicate washes, thick clusters or scattered points—which emerge, recede, undergo changes, and create their own "form." ***De Natura Sonoris I*** by Penderecki, studied in the early chapters of this book, presents a brilliant orchestral unfolding of mass, volume, register, and articulation; these seem to dictate specific pitches and rhythms, rather than the other way around. Penderecki frequently uses such massed sound clusters: in fact, this technique has been an important feature of many East European, especially Polish, compositions since the 1960s. (The revolt of 1956 gave Poland a chance to absorb radical Western influences. Almost overnight, Warsaw became a major center for experimental music, and has remained so ever since.) Another East European, the Hungarian Gyorgy Ligeti (1923–   ) also enjoys working with clusters and instrumental masses. His orchestral ***Atmospheres*** and ***Volumina*** for organ convey utter absorption in overall "fabric" rather than internal detail.

The Greek composer Yannis Xenakis is yet another who explores density levels. Xenakis studied engineering in Athens and then lived for many years in Paris, working with Messiaen in music and Le Corbusier in architecture. Like Varèse, whom he also knew well, Xenakis was fascinated by the relationship of music and science. In the 1950s he began composing a music of ever-shifting density, analogous to such natural phenomena as sand storms or swarms of insects: powerful masses emerging from collections of tiny particles.

process music

Process Music

Much of Xenakis's work relates to natural processes. Since the 1960s many composers have become interested in other sorts of "processes." In some instances, they are fascinated by scientific data which are basically unpredictable (except statistically); in other cases, composers begin with a single musical premise and then follow it through in a clearly marked direction. Here the results ***are*** predictable and, in fact, the listener can hear the process slowly unfolding. Terry Riley's ***In C,*** discussed in Part 1, represents the latter sort of process in its straightforward ground plan and its faithful adherence to that plan.

In a work created from a ***process,*** virtually all details emerge from a single idea. The composer's chief concern may be the logical unfolding of this ***idea,*** rather than any individual sound-by-sound details (such as the pitches of the bassoon part in measure 37). The serialist creating from a row, or the Cage-inspired composer using the random throw of dice, may also enjoy "following through" on a predetermined scheme. But ***In C*** is different in that its pre-compositional scheme is completely audible. Its process is out in the open. In this vein, composer Steve Reich (1936–) has written: "I am interested in perceptible processes. I want to be able to hear the process happening throughout the sounding music . . . (determining) all the note-to-note details and the overall form simultaneously."

Reich's earliest process pieces were tape works constructed from loops—fragments of tape with head and tail joined to create an endlessly repeated cycle—running slightly out of "sync" with each other. By 1970 he had transferred his interest in out-of-sync phase shifts to instrumental, live performance situations, involving simple ostinato figures that are repeated continuously for many seconds or minutes. As the figurations repeat, some performers gradually move ahead of others; timbres may also change, as new instruments fade in or out of the ensemble.

Another American composer, Philip Glass, also works with accumulating cells, devoid of Western "development" or "climax" but rich in additive variety. His best-known work is the experimental opera ***Einstein on the Beach*** which, in its staging, words, and music, attempts a suspension of time and space—concentrating instead upon the immediate, lingering "present" of static repeating cycles.

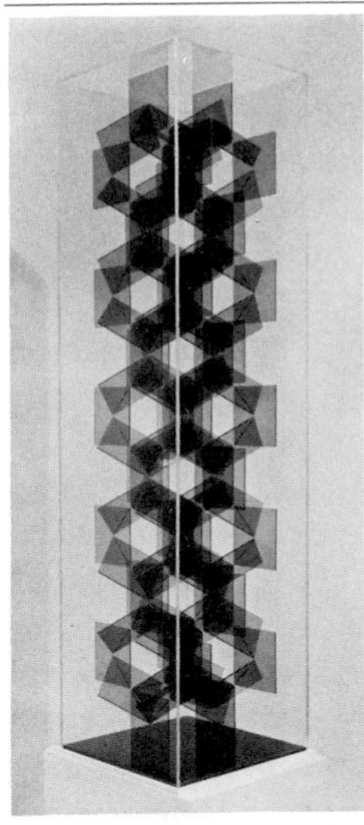

Steve Reich, Philip Glass, Frederic Rzewski "Process" Pieces (excerpts)

R6 S1 B7
R6 S2 B1

1. Steve Reich's *Violin Phase* of the mid-1960s is scored for solo violinist and a tape that the violinist has prepared in advance. There are no electronic sounds; in fact, the entire work consists of an extended melodic shape for violin—in live performance and on tape tracks—heard at many levels which overlap and imitate each other in various phase-shift relationships. The single phrase is recorded on different tape channels, separated by an interval of time. In this excerpt (the very opening), the live soloist is asked to synchronize with one of the tape channels, and then, by gradually moving forward, out of "sync" with the tape, arrive at a point where he is synchronized with a *different* channel. At every canonic level, live and recorded, the single phrase is being repeated as a continuous ostinato figure.

2. The beginning of Philip Glass's ***Einstein on the Beach*** consists of three low tones.* As these repeat, we hear major triads superimposed upon them, a basically simple chord progression treated as a static ostinato "object." A small chorus articulates the chord series by simply singing the number of beats through which each chord is held. Eventually another level of activity appears, a speaking voice, superimposed upon the repeated chord series; then a second voice overlaps the first, maintaining a quiet, understated quality throughout. Occasionally some of the words come through ("Oh these are the days my friend . . . will we get some wind for the sailboat . . ."), but more likely the listener notices the total fabric. Also listen to a later section of the opera: here a chord series is arpeggiated in various ways, with a steady ostinato pulse but many simultaneous additive meters and changing timbres. Listen for flutes, organ, different keyboard instruments, and voices, using the numbers of rhythmic structure or the names of pitches as the words of text.

3. *Les Moutons de Panurge* by Frederic Rzewski is, like Riley's *In C,* composed for flexible, indeterminate body of melody instruments. All players in the ensemble perform a single melodic line in tight synchronization. The line itself consists of 65 pitches in an undulating, repetitive contour and complex additive rhythm; it would be very difficult to maintain precise coordination of such a tune for very long. Rzewski complicates the players' job even further, by requiring that the line be played in an additive sequence of pitches:

121231234123451234561234567123456 78 . . . . etc.

until all the notes are performed. At this point the entire melody is played *minus* pitch 1 (that is 2 through 65), and then repeated again minus 1 and 2 . . . until only the last note is sounded as a final "tonic" pedal tone. The

*In the opera production, these low tones were repeated again and again, as the audience entered the hall.

process is laden with pitfalls and booby-traps. Inevitably, the single line breaks up into prisms, fragments, and overlapping canons during performance. In the recorded performance, the ensemble is made up entirely of tuned percussion.*

For all three works, an extraordinarily complex texture results from minute changes applied to ostinato figures. The rate of unfolding may be so slow, as in the Reich or Glass examples, that time seems "frozen." We seem to observe a pattern of sound as though it were a visual object in space. The effect is hypnotic, and often joyously so: the unswerving pitch centers, simple contours and semi-canonic imitation are reminiscent of African ritual drumming, or the ecstatic organum of the medieval church (see Chapter 8, especially Perotin). In the music of Reich and Glass, there is ***no*** improvisation; on the contrary, every detail of performance is carefully rehearsed. The Rzewski example, though, deals with a process in which distortions and "error" play an important role, as they do in the physical universe.

In other circumstances or for other composers, ***process*** may mean the natural working of any machine—human or artificial. Pauline Oliveros and David Rosenboom have used the rhythms and changes of our bio-feedback mechanisms to trigger electronic sound equipment, or amplified pulses and heartbeats for musical purposes. In many ways, each of these approaches to "process" is influenced by technology. Note how different the ***late*** twentieth-century view of technology is from the earlier romanticized image of the Jazz Age. Artists are no longer excited by the sleek beauty, speed, or raw brutal power of machines, at least not as they were fifty years ago. Today they may be more fascinated by the efficiency, or the perverse randomness, of machines' internal workings, or by the cyclical, throbbing hum of their motorized sounds. Reich's term "pulse music" is especially apt: we live in a world surrounded by drones, pulses and steady-state frequencies: automobiles, refrigerator motors, vacuum cleaners, our own body rhythms, beating against each other.

Collage and the Return to Tonality

In listening to the music of Riley, Reich, Glass or Rzewski, we notice a strong sense of key center, owing to the restricted pitch selection and emphatic repetition. This may resemble non-Western or medieval pitch centering, rather than the major-minor "tonality" of Bach and Mozart. However, traditional tonality has also been used more frequently by many composers ever since the late 1960s. Chord progressions and fragments of earlier styles may occur in works that are otherwise non-tonal; such tonal references often have a dramatic function, rather than a structural (key or goal-related) one. They may sound curiously restless, precisely because their context is

*The Rzewski piece is available on Opus One, No. 20 Records.

Robert Rauschenberg, ***Tracer.*** This painting combines images of past and present, and forces us to reconsider history and "art"; note the fragment of a Venetian Old Master at the upper right.

unclear. They may provide momentary stability in an atonal fabric, or nostalgic, stylized jogging of cultural "memory" for expressive purposes.

A number of composers deliberately quote fragments of earlier music, such as a hymn tune or Chopin nocturne. This creates an extroverted focus for their work, reaching beyond traditional boundaries to a larger world outside, including the world of "other music." Such a piece might be conceived as a form of commentary ***about*** music, an essay on history, taste, perception, and memory. The practice of using other people's music in this way is frequently referred to as ***collage,*** a term derived from the analogous use of cloth, wallpaper, newsprint and other found objects by visual artists.

collage

Why would a composer refer to familiar music in a newly created work? Some may feel that "originality" in the late twentieth century is a matter of syntax and grammar, the rearrangement of existing material. The Danish composer Karl Aage Rasmussen, who builds impressive large-scale works from nineteenth-century symphonic fragments, quotes the philosopher Pascal: "There are no new thoughts. There are only new ways of combining the thoughts we know." For other composers, collage is an evaluation of the past—a way of confirming the vitality of tradition, or a nostalgic look backward at an elusive past that cannot be recaptured, or (if one is pessimistic) sifting through the ruins of a shattered tradition, picking up an isolated brick here and there. Finally, collage technique can be a way of commenting upon modern ***listening*** habits: the fact that, (thanks to the long playing record) twentieth-century audiences have more varied tastes and experiences than any comparable group in history. Since Webern, Vivaldi, Tibetan chant, and Dixieland jazz are all available in record shops, and all inescapably part of our century, why not use them all?

Listen to a well-known example of collage technique: the third section of Luciano Berio's ***Sinfonia*** (1968) for large orchestra and chamber chorus.

Luciano Berio
Sinfonia: section III

R6 S2 B2

During the Scherzo movement of Berio's quasi-symphonic work, fragments of material previously composed by others (Bach, Beethoven, Debussy, and Ives, for example) form a fabric of free association, set against ***another*** Scherzo, that of the Mahler Second Symphony. The Mahler excerpt is a lengthy one; Berio treats it as a swiftly moving vessel upon which the other fragments ride. At times the Mahler dominates the free-association material, and at other times it is overwhelmed by the barrage of shorter quotes. Generally, we must be prepared to hear the music as the interaction and collision of simultaneous levels, very much as we hear the music of Ives.

There is another level of quotation as well: the words sung, spoken, whispered, cried out by the vocalists. Just as the music centers about Mahler, Berio's text centers about an excerpt from Samuel Beckett—from which we get the urgently shouted refrain, "Keep going." In addition, there are references to James Joyce, notations from Berio's own diary, and graffiti found on the walls of Paris during the 1968 student riots. From the very beginning of this section, Berio's deep involvement with Mahler is evident. The overpowering sense of foreboding that often attaches to Mahler—the sense of time running out and "style" itself at a crossroads—is only heightened by the other snippets of telescoped music history. Consider, too, the relation of the explosive, often angry wall writings to the musical "graffiti" of quoted fragments, in which the repeated "Keep going" takes on new meaning.

In his own music, Berio has worked through a variety of styles, from strict serialism to open-form improvisatory theater. A number of composers, like Berio, have embraced a wide variety of styles during their careers, with a special interest in tonality and stylistic collage in recent decades. Here are three such composers:

1. George Rochberg (1918–) was for many years a staunch champion of twelve-tone music, and abandoned strict pitch control for a more flexible free association of seemingly unrelated languages. His earliest pieces in the new style, dating from the 1960s, used many quotations, from Ives and Varèse to Bach and Chopin. In recent years he has preferred to create original statements in the style of other composers who have moved him deeply, often playing these styles against one another as though they were themes or key centers. Rochberg's String Quartet no. 3 (1972) uses the language of Beethoven, Mahler, and a biting Stravinskian primitivism virtually side by side. These different worlds merge, overlap, repel and collide in the process of coexisting.

2. George Crumb (1929–) is known for his sensuously ravishing *sounds,* ranging from the delicate to the brutal, often with roots in the influences of Debussy, Bartók or Webern. He also works from strong dramatic premises, including vividly theatrical elements of ritual ceremony: he may ask performers to move about on stage, whisper quietly, or assume the costumes of solemn symbolic mystery. Within this context, tonal fragments take on great psychological or associative value. There may be actual quotes in Crumb's music as well—Schubert, Chopin, flamenco dance, courtly minuet—most likely in a distant, fleeting dreamlike state.

Crumb's 1971 *Vox Balanae* ("Voice of the Whale") is based upon the recorded sounds of whales. It is scored for electronically amplified flute, cello, and piano: the amplification makes whispered sonorities audible, and reinforces piercing sounds at the other end of the spectrum. The three musicians are masked, and bathed in a dark blue spotlight. The work begins with an extended flute solo, eventually leading to a vibrant climax based on a distorted version of the opening of Richard Strauss's *Also Sprach Zarathustra* (the famous phrase for horn, orchestra, and pounding timpani that was used in the film *2001*). The pianist's brilliant chords mimic those of Strauss's orchestra; a muted piano timbre provides an eerie analog of Strauss's mighty kettledrums. The cello enters shortly afterwards with a quiet motive that serves as the "theme" for five variations, also symbolizing five great ages of history (such as the Archeozoic and Proterozoic). The entire work fades out with the cello motive enveloped in an ethereal, shimmering B-major triad.

Crumb always aims for heightened expressivity in the romantic sense. His written instructions to performers are quite revealing: "dramatic . . . fateful . . . with solemn majesty . . . transfigured . . . dying," and so on. They show a concern for fine shades of traditional ***affection*** unmatched since the era of Debussy and impressionism, linked now to the sonorities of our own age.

3. Lukas Foss (1922–) began his career in the neoclassic tradition of Hindemith and Copland. But during the 1960s he began to direct an improvisation ensemble, and found aspects of chance and free choice entering his compositional style. The dreamlike aspects of Ivesian collage interested him, and he was also attracted by the "time-warp" possibilities of electronic technique: tape delays, loops, and echo effects. His new concerns led to a three-movement orchestral work entitled ***Baroque Variations*** (1967), a surrealistic montage of dream images and unfocused fragments drawn from Handel, Scarlatti, and Bach. Here Foss makes use of dense textures in the manner of Penderecki, improvisation for orchestral players, and the visual shock of radical "theater." He aims not to compose a crisp neoclassic work in baroque style, but to transform familiar material into a surprising late-twentieth-century context.

The first movement is drawn from a piece by Handel; the original notes are retained, but curiously obscured. For much of the movement the musicians play the Handel *silently.* Sound emerges at unpredictable beats, or perhaps only on an inner line of Handel's texture; strings, trumpets and

Figure 18.4

electric organ create a fragmented, Webernian series of colors. In the second movement, a harpsichord sonata by Scarlatti is surrounded and obscured by orchestral clusters, *glissandi* and overlapping rhythmic distortions.

The final movement, the most elaborate of the three, is based on a well-known Bach prelude for solo violin. Foss had originally composed this movement as a separate orchestral piece, and gave it the name "Phorion," translated from the Greek as "stolen goods."

Lukas Foss
Baroque Variations, Movement III ("Phorion") *R6 S2 B3*

The movement begins with a bang (see the score excerpt of Figure 18.4), and the solo violinist plunges into an extended statement of the original Bach. This is reinforced by the other violins, but only in fragmentary, unpredictable bursts. As the music continues, the steadily driving rhythms of the Bach are always present, filtered by sudden timbral changes and canonic overlapping new rhythms against old. A fairly intense climax is reached, only to subside. Rhythms have gone askew (many of them now being chosen by the players), and the sonority is non-directional, motionless. Brief outbursts of Bach fragments, alternate with a romanticized cello phrase derived from the Bach at very slow speed. These are sounded against a very high, distant organ cluster which gradually descends as the performer's arms slide slowly down the keyboard.

The stillness is shattered by a sudden burst of noise: rude percussion instruments in unpredictable fits and starts, garbled random fragments of Bach, and an obsessive repeated note in the brasses. The texture becomes even bolder, louder and more insistent, and the repeated trumpet notes ever more manic, as the work advances to its angry conclusion.

Each of these composers views the contemporary musical condition as an interaction between past and future: confrontation, merging, and reconciliation. In the words of George Rochberg:

> . . . My search has led to an ongoing reconsideration of what the "past" (musical or otherwise) means. Current biological research corroborates Darwin: we bear the past in us . . . We are filaments of a universal mind; we dream each other's dreams and those of our ancestors . . .

or those of Lukas Foss:

> What I did in the *Baroque Variations* was to present my own nightmare—Adam and Eve driven out of paradise. My home is Bach, Beethoven, Mozart, etc. But you see: man has a double need, to return to his past, which is home, and to discover the future. Then he feels that he is living in the present.

Experimental techniques and novel sounds pose no problems for young people. Here are some British schoolchildren "preparing" a piano interior, perhaps in advance of an improvisatory performance game.

The Future

The study of new music is truly unique: even as we examine stylistic directions, they are constantly changing, making it impossible to predict the future. On the other hand, certain areas of musical thinking have become important in recent decades, and should be considered in any exploration of the musical future. Here are four such areas: ***grammar, ritual, game playing,*** and the relation of music to ***society.***

Grammar

As we hear music, we perceive a number of pitches, durations, and timbres over a period of time. Usually some sort of continuity holds these tiny events together: a regular meter, or the gentle curve of dynamics. In fact, we often comprehend large-scale forms by distinctive changes in one or more of these continuities (such as a new tempo). The thread of continuities and connections, linking sounds to each other over time, constitutes musical ***grammar.*** Many composers of recent decades wish to redefine the familiar grammar of the Western tradition. Those who conceive of music as "thought"—Schoenberg, Elliott Carter, the later serialists—create works whose subject matter ***is*** grammar itself. Others, like Cage, may conceive of music as "sound," and focus attention upon individual moments rather

I GLOTZ	YOU GLOTZ	THEY GLOTZED	WE ARE GLOTZING

Figure 18.5

Figure 18.6

colorless green ideas sleep furiously

than connections. Composers of minimal "process' music, perhaps influenced by non-Western traditions, define grammar in still other ways.

In listening to a brand-new piece, we are faced with a situation unique in the history of music. There are so many style options and varieties of grammar that we must assume, at least for the first few moments of a work, that *any* event is just as likely to follow a given sound as any other event! Only gradually will a work's particular grammar, or lack of it, become apparent. Some works will attack time in a straight line forward thrust ⟶; in other kinds of music, time may be perceived as a static, frozen block. Some kinds of music establish priorities of interest, while in others every instant is equally meaningful (or meaningless). In some grammars, there are easy reference contexts, repetition and redundancy, against which we measure and relate events; in others, very little.

We might ask ourselves: do events seem to ***cause*** other events? Do sounds have a *function* with regard to each other and the total complex? The relation of function to grammar is an important feature of all language. Students of linguistics claim that we all have an ingrained sense of function, even with regard to nonsense words. (See Figure 18.5). Moreover, the degree of grammatical structure in any arrangement of events can be related to function. In Figure 18.6, created by a famous linguistics scholar, the sentence is perfectly grammatical although its meaning is obscure. (One might consider this a model for complex linear music, perhaps of the twelve-tone variety.) If the functional links in that sentence are weakened we may become absorbed in the sounds and shapes of individual words and syllables. (Perhaps we have in Figure 18.7 a model for certain kinds of Cage-ian indeterminacy.) Finally, relationships may become apparent only gradually;

Figure 18.7

furiously sleep ideas green colorless

col col col col col color color color color colorless colorless colorless lorless green lorless gre... (etc.)

Figure 18.8

not words, but particles that coalesce into words, as in Figure 18.8. (Perhaps we comprehend certain minimal process pieces of music in this way.)

Some composers would protest that any combination of sound events in time generates its own unique grammar. Nowhere is this more apparent than in collage technique. Composers who build works from ready-made fragments hope to create striking new connections between them. In assembling and recombining familiar gestures, they too are working with grammar—the grammar of memory.

Ritual

Since the 1950s many composers have concentrated upon the "theatrical" dimension of music: the use of performance space, ceremony, and audience interaction. The grammar of sounds may not be as crucial for them as the placement of performers or a special lighting effect. Such composers can trace their roots back to the "role-playing" chamber music of Ives, but the greatest influence has been that of John Cage—on all the arts, not only music. In fact, this influence has often led creative people in related arts to collaborate on joint projects.

The postwar development of the long-playing record and tape recording also contributed to the growth of "theater" music. Many composers enjoy creating music that could ***not*** be recorded, music which is too spontaneous, or too visual, to be "canned" and packaged. If a composer willingly chooses the option of live performance by creating a piece for woodwind quintet rather than a synthesized work on tape, it makes sense to exploit those qualities which are in fact most "alive." We might compare these tendencies to developments in nineteenth and twentieth-century painting after the growth of photography.

Much new music, then, is conceived as a total ***ritual,*** designed for the unique experience of live performance. Crumb's *Vox Balanae* and the Foss *Baroque Variations* both contain strong ritual and theatrical elements, although neither one uses text: sight, sound, physical space, and activity all contribute to the total experience, in a tightly focused, controlled way. Other composers enjoy working with the diffuse, jumbled multiplicity of real-life experience. Here, too, John Cage has been a strong influence. When once asked why he composed music, he answered,

> Well, the first thing you have to do is not ask the question "why." Look at your environment, which you are enjoying, and see if it asks why . . . it doesn't.

Cage draws music or theater from ***his*** environment, from his openness to varieties of experience. A similar merging of environment, performance and ceremonial is found in the work of Pauline Oliveros (1932–   ). Her students collect sounds of the Pacific Ocean or San Diego Zoo on tape and create collage pieces from them; she has created performances for the desert, or for town squares and campus quadrangles, often quite solemnly ritualistic. In her ***Bonn Feier,*** an entire city is used as a performance area in such a way that city residents become aware of an altered environment only very gradually over a period of days.

Max Neuhaus (1936–   ) also uses unexpected settings for the performance, usually through loudspeakers, of his music: the bottom of a swimming pool, a sidewalk grating near New York's Times Square, a telephone receiver. The sounds of his ***Drive-In Music*** can only be heard on an automobile radio, as the driver travels along a specially prepared route, with sound generators placed in trees and lighting fixtures. On a less drastic level, composers are creating more and more works specifically for performance in courtyards, parks, or churches, just as their predecessors did centuries ago. Electronic music may be heard in lobbies, gardens, private living rooms, or cathedrals. And as we know, rock concerts are held anywhere that electronic gear can be set up, from park to field to open beach to campus gymnasium.

Games

Another environment where we find more and more new music is the classroom. Students are composing and performing works that use controlled improvisation, minimal processes, theatrical ritual, and new sound resources. English schools pioneered in this area during the mid-1960s and are still highly active in developing experimental classroom music. Their efforts range from simple games designed for small children (such as Figure 18.9, by Trevor Wishart) to the elaborate eight-part polyphony of David

Figure 18.9

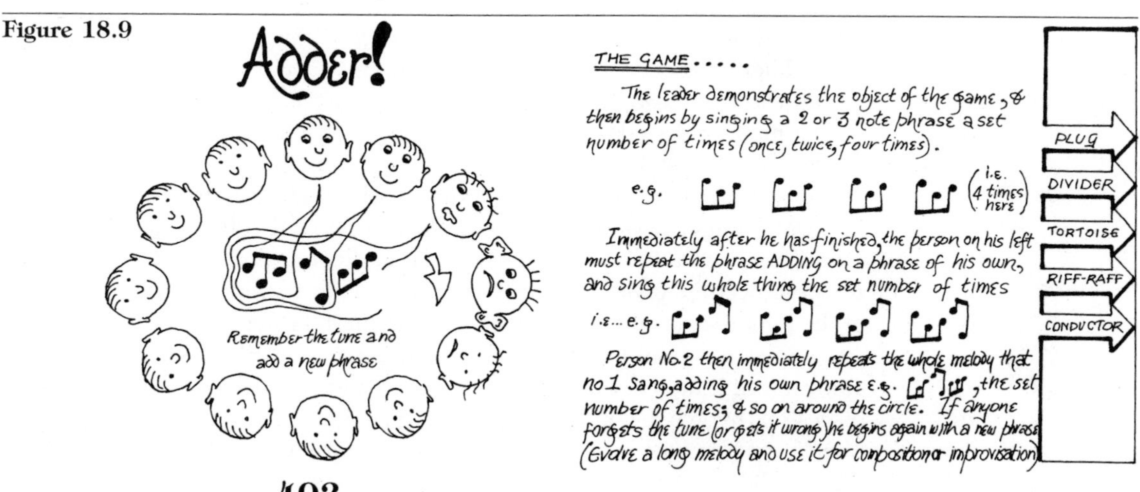

Figure 18.10

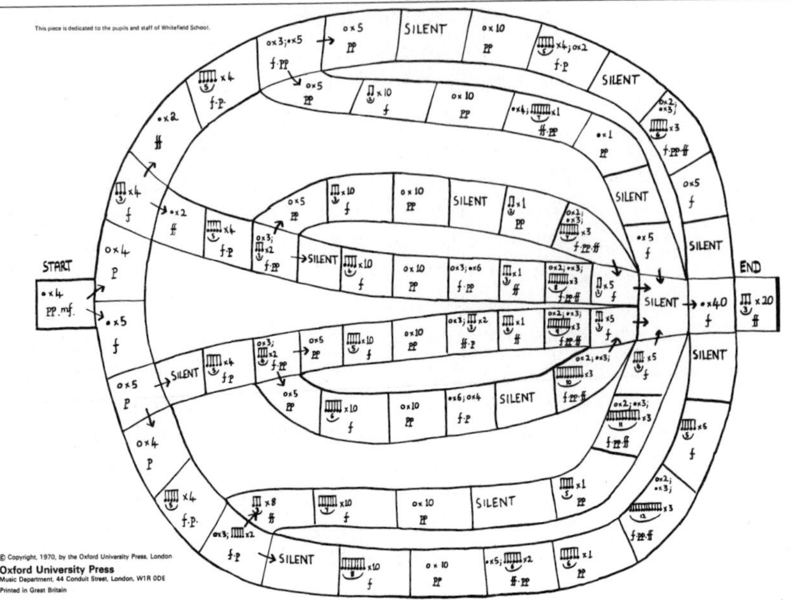

Bedford's ***Fun for All the Family.*** In the Bedford piece (Figure 18.10), all players begin on the same square, marked "Start"; each player makes four short sounds, either *pp* or *mf* during the twenty-second duration of the square. Note that the performers gradually split off into two groups, then four, and finally eight distinct parts, eventually joining again at the very end.

Bedford's written score and title suggest a board game, and perhaps the music should be approached in that spirit. The game-playing aspects grow out of the very nature of performance: materials, skills, goals, the pressures of time, and coordination. Whereas these are always present in the traditional realization of a musical "object," they can now ***be*** that "object." There is a certain anti-romanticism in this view. Music is conceived not as the expression of grand feelings, but as the immediate activity of people making sounds, testing their responses, reflexes, skill, and intelligence.

How would an ***audience*** respond to all this? Perhaps they might not find game music as much fun as the players do. Of course, many of these pieces don't assume the existence of an audience. They were intended for performance in a classroom or living room. That puts them in the tradition of the Renaissance madrigal, or the string quartet of Haydn's day: performers' music, first and foremost. We may happen to overhear such music and enjoy it, but that is not why the music was created. In any event, many game pieces ***do*** involve the audience directly. Xenakis's ***Strategie*** for two orchestras (1964) creates a competition for the conductors according to a set of

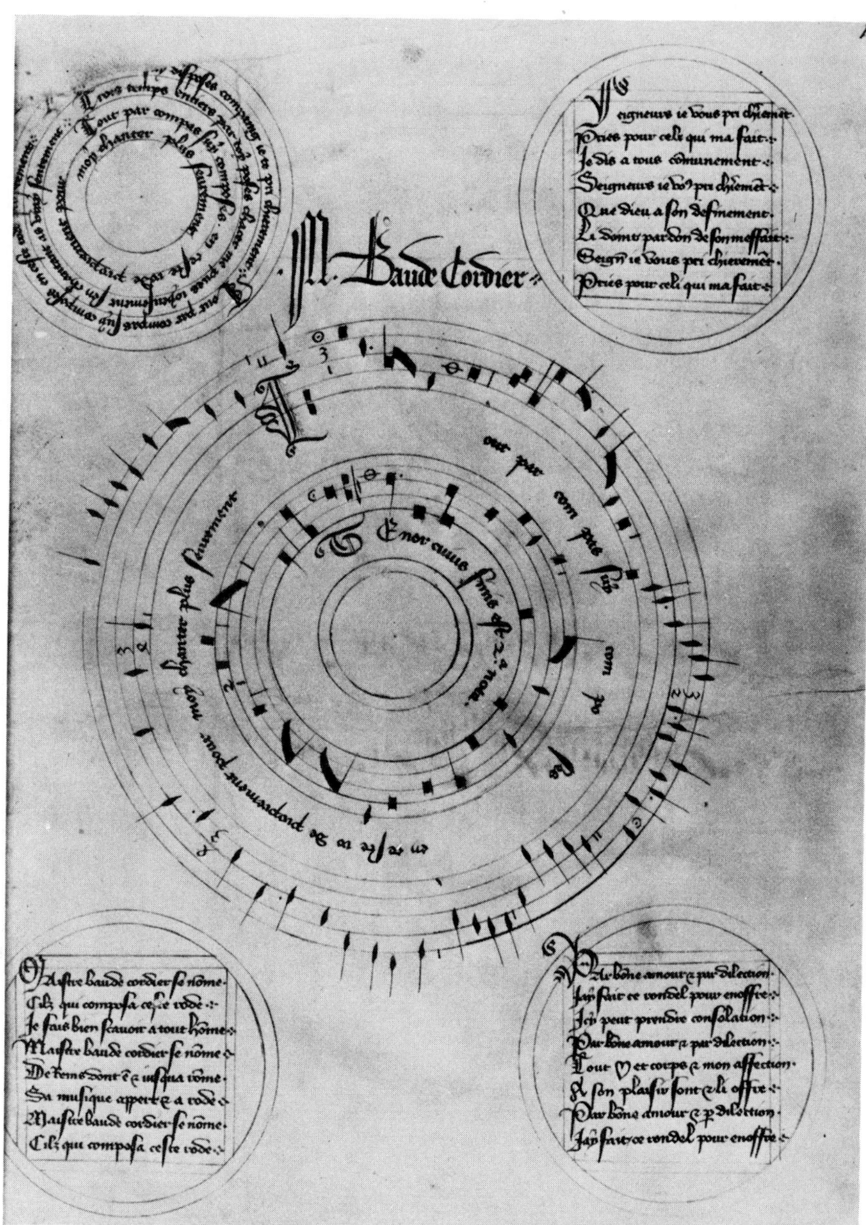

Baude Cordier, manuscript of a medieval canonic song. Game-playing performance is not solely the province of the recent avant-garde! Compare this score with our contemporary examples by Wishart and Bedford.

ground rules; the audience follows the results on a scoreboard. The Belgian composer Henri Pousseur has created his opera *Votre Faust* (1967) so that the ending is decided upon by audience vote.

Tom Johnson
Failing, A Very Difficult Piece for Doublebass *R6 S2 B4*

Composer Tom Johnson is active in areas of ***theater, process*** and ***game*** music. His works are characterized by a deliberately spare use of pitch and density, and a keen sense for ingenious processes of all kinds. In many of his pieces, performers sing or speak directly to the audience, describing the processes taking place—thus moving into the broader domain of theater and, ultimately, game playing (since the processes often involve unusual challenges).

For one piece, Johnson has devised a game plan so formidable that the work is entitled ***Failing.*** We will immediately recognize the challenge by looking at the opening pages of the score (Figure 18.11), or by listening to the recorded performance; Johnson's game requires the player to tell us everything that's happening as it occurs. Further comment here would be superfluous. Listen to the music, which in this instance really does "speak for itself."

Figure 18.11

♩=72, 6-7 seconds per stave, about one minute per page.

mf

In "Failing" I am required to read a long text while playing music written above the text.

The text must be read out loud at a more or less normal pace, and I must not allow the music

to slow me down. The task is fairly easy for a while, because there is not much music, and

p

most of it comes at the ends of clauses and sentences, almost like normal punctuation.

f

Later on, there is more music, and the task becomes more difficult - so difficult, in fact

that I will probably not be able to do it without either slowing down my reading speed or

mf

else making mistakes in the music. At least the composer feels confident that I will eventu-

ally begin to run into trouble, which is why he called the piece "Failing." So far, the task

The Artist and Society

Many contemporary composers are concerned with social issues. The aloof distance between artist and public is diminishing; both realizing that music grows out of its environment, and that it can, in turn, help shape that environment. There are strong social concerns in the following areas:

1. The growing interest in game pieces for children and amateurs indicates a sincere desire to have the language of new music accessible to all. Amateurs are being encouraged to build instruments and to compose. The study of world music has led many to question the traditional Western roles of composer, performer, and listener. Why can't each individual be all three? As Barney Childs has remaked, "Hearing a performance isn't much of anything. Music is to *do*." Sophisticated technique for all is not the goal, either. Stravinsky once asserted that only a highly developed style could produce masterpieces; but a "masterpiece" may be the very last thing one wants to create in a civilization trying to shed its egocentricity! Some composers would rather work with communally produced statements and rituals and unique instruments fashioned out of materials at hand. Forms and processes can be designed for the enjoyment of performers, and not audiences, so that—to use an analogy of composer Christian Wolff—playing in an ensemble piece might be like taking a walk with friends, observing the scenery along the paths.

2. Traditional classifications of music, especially "serious" and "popular," are being abandoned in many quarters. There are too many artists who constantly cross the lines between concert music, jazz, and rock: Frank Zappa, Stanley Silverman, Anthony Braxton, Marion Brown, William Bolcom, Sun Ra, and Joshua Rifkin, to name a few. In a society that is pluralistic, fragmented and overly commercialized, none of these artists are really "popular" anyway. There are other ways of classifying music, if we need classification at all. For example, is the music meant for attentive listening, or motor response? Is it to be performed by professionals or amateurs? Is it designed for loudspeakers, or for human players and acoustic instruments? Will we hear it in our everyday environment or do we go to a special place for a special ritual? Every one of these distinctions has a legitimate place in our experience.

3. Composers are writing politically committed music, drawing upon their own convictions and beliefs. Steve Reich's early tape phase-shift work *Come Out* drew its vocal sound source from the Harlem riots of the sixties. Christian Wolff has built music out of the workers' protest songs of the 1930s, and Frederic Rzewski used the Attica prison uprising as the stimulus for his 1972 *Attica* and *Coming Together*. In a less direct way, Crumb's *Vox Balanae* reflects a concern for the plight of endangered creatures; Glass's *Einstein on the Beach* relates images of atomic devastation (even referring to the famous antiwar novel *On the Beach* in its title), a trial, and telescoped history to its scientist-hero.

4. On another level of commitment, creative artists are exploring their own identification with different cultural groups, particularly minorities with a long history of oppression. Apart from American popular culture, the history of Western music has been basically that of white males, reflecting the power of that subgroup over the rest of society and the strong ties of "art music" to economic power. That situation has changed during the past decades: there is now a growing number of Afro-American composers drawing upon the Black experience in distinctively personal ways. Among the most imaginative are T. J. Anderson (1928–), who uses jazz elements, as well as programmatic material taken from the literature of the South and the urban ghetto, in a fluent international style; Carman Moore (1936–), who integrates pop culture and his commitment to the Harlem community with an eclectic "art music" language; Olly Wilson (1937–), who is highly active in the world of electronic music; and Talib Rasul Hakim (1940–), who was born in North Carolina as Steve Chambers, now works in New York, and fuses many influences (Ives, Cage, African ritual, Webern, jazz) into a remarkably strong style.

Similarly, the role of women in music has grown enormously. A number of women composers have been directly active in the political struggle for equal rights: for example, Pauline Oliveros organized an all-female performing group during the 1960s, known as the ♀ensemble. Surprisingly (or perhaps *not* surprisingly), many women have excelled in electronic music, dispelling the myth of musical "technology" as a male preserve. Jean Eichelberger Ivey (1923–) was one of the pioneers of postwar tape studio composition, and Priscilla McLean (1942–) has established an excellent reputation with her works using synthesizer, computer generated sound, and acoustic instruments. Joan Tower (1938–) is known for her striking compositions in a controlled, non-tonal idiom, and is also quite active as a pianist. Thea Musgrave (1928–) is a truly international figure, born in Scotland, trained in Paris, and now resident in the United States. Musgrave uses space and texture in a dramatic, Ivesian way; her operas and concertos have been praised throughout the world.

5. Finally, musicians are voicing their concern for the sound-world we live in and its ominous future. The most articulate opponent of "noise pollution" is a Canadian composer named R. Murray Schafer, who has accepted Cage's definition of music as "sounds around us, whether we're in or out of concert halls." Schafer maintains that "the most vital 'musical' composition of our time is being played on a world stage." What he perceives in the sonic landscape (the "soundscape," as he calls it) is grim: the loud, piercing, and boring sound of motors, the roar of loudspeakers, heavy machinery, street traffic.

> I once drew a picture of a city of the future on the blackboard for a group of architecture students and asked them what the salient features of the environment appeared to be. There were seven helicopters in the sky of

> my drawing; yet no student found this particularly salient. I (exasperatedly) asked, "Have you ever ***heard*** seven helicopters?"
>
> Portions of the world symphony have already been played and will not be repeated: the steam engine, the horse-drawn carriage . . . the coal-oil lamp. Yes, what did the coal-oil lamp sound like? . . .

Schafer suggests that the musician's most important task of the future may well be actively campaigning for the ***suppression,*** rather than the creation, of sounds: mufflers for motorized lawnmowers, so that we might hear the birds again. He also wants to celebrate the infinite variety of sounds—a shovel in sand, the flag flapping in the wind—by collecting various "soundscapes" on tape, preserving them against the day when, he fears, horses' hooves on cobblestones, trolley cars, or the churning of butter will no longer be sounding.

In all of these ways, the art and activity of music will grow, develop, stumble, falter, revive, and confound its prophets, just as it has for centuries. It is really impossible to predict new directions. Each new piece or performance may influence the future in some unseen way—and inevitably influence the past as well, since the total picture of all music is constantly being reinterpreted through the present. There has never been a better time to explore music.

Coda: Listening to Music

We have come a long way since the opening chapter: many pieces have been heard, many concepts and styles discussed. We hope you will continue listening to music, all kinds of music. With that in mind, here are a few final suggestions.

Try to isolate style and form. See if individual elements, such as melody or rhythm, can be related to the large style categories we have studied. Take a long-range view of musical events, using memory and expectation to get a sense of form as it emerges.

At a concert, compare works to each other. Surely the pieces played on a given program don't sound alike. Try to grasp the distinctions, the areas of similarity and difference. This may be easiest when hearing a mixed program, for example, one classic and one romantic piece, but the effort is worth making under any circumstances.

Enjoy the sounds themselves. Although it is important to listen structurally for style and design, that does not negate a sensual response to sonority, density, and rhythms of each moment. In Chapter 5 we likened musical form to a landscape driven through in one's car. A driver needs to glance in the rearview mirror, and scan the horizon ahead, to see how a given location relates to the entire journey. You might even like to look at a "map:" the score. But you should *also* savor the marvelous sights (sounds) along the way as they occur. Both types of response are legitimate; in fact, both are necessary.

Let a concert stimulate further thinking on a number of topics. Music is an activity that goes beyond its sounds. It may be a communal ritual, a personal statement, a grammatical argument, a series of physical actions occurring within a prescribed space. How do concertgiving and concertgoing vary from one society to another? Why do programs take the shape they do; for example, could the order of pieces be reversed? Why is there often a printed program? Can we draw parallels with performances in other arts?

Consider amplifiers and loudspeakers. They have transformed the way we listen and the performance spaces we can use for listening. In many ways the recorded version of a Brahms concerto or the Rolling Stones is profoundly different from the corresponding performance. Do ***all*** recordings, no matter how superficially different, relate to each other, and evoke similar listening responses, in subtle ways? How do we control musical shape and dramatic "program" when we choose a stack of phonograph records or a sequence of tapes?

Recognize the different functions of music. There are pieces for familiar places and for special rituals. There is music for young people and music for other generations. Certain styles demand attention (a symphony or fugue); others defeat our attention by immersing us in a sensually gratifying "present" (some minimal process music, rock, ritual theater). A good deal of music can be perceived ***both*** ways, as foreground subject or as backdrop for a larger ceremonial (a Bach cantata, or 1940s be-bop dance music). Let any event in which music plays a part—civic parade, supermarket shopping, television commercial—trigger thoughts about musical and social relationships.

Trust your ears and the intentions of composers. Once surface sounds, speeds, and colors are placed in some perspective, it should be apparent that most important musical patterns are ***audible.*** The average listener is capable of understanding almost any piece, given a basic awareness of styles and traditions. If a composition appears to be an incomprehensible jumble or a great bore, perhaps the composer is (a) intentionally setting you up for some later section, or (b) deliberately creating boredom or confusion, so that a positive experience of another kind will result. If you have gone this far with the music and it still fails to hold the ear, discard it for awhile and come back to it later, perhaps years later. A new set of experiences may have altered your perceptions.

Be adventurous; expand your tastes in whatever direction your listening leads you. If you wish to investigate the music of one composer—Handel, or Berlioz—in depth, go ahead. That consuming interest will eventually lead to other musical concerns. Do ***not*** assume that we have covered every interesting style or piece in this book. Far from it: the range is so vast, just in the world of Western "art" music, that we have only skimmed the surface. In fact, we regret not having mentioned many of our own favorites: the Mozart ***Requiem,*** Schubert ***Octet,*** Verdi's ***Otello,*** Britten's ***War Requiem,*** the Bartók ***Concerto for Orchestra,*** and many others.

Nor are the composers mentioned in this book the only composers worth exploring. On the contrary, one of the great pleasures of listening is the first encounter with a provocative new style: the music of Franz Berwald, perhaps, or Gustav Holst, or Amy Beach. By all means, pursue unexplored paths. And don't forget the worlds of non-Western music, jazz, folk styles, Western music before 1600, and the twentieth-century postwar avant-garde.

Finally, ***go beyond the "familiar" and the "beautiful."*** There has never been a single definition of beauty that satisfied everyone. Usually critics find "beauty" in art works that are most congenial, sympathetic, outgoing, or inoffensive. But there is also value in art that offends and provokes and jars the sensibility, or in other-worldly art that keeps its distance. "Beauty" might not be present, but honesty, strength, and the ability to arouse our thinking are ample compensations. As we mentioned earlier, trust the creator. Most composers ***are*** sincerely trying to communicate with you, although they may not say what you expect to hear. They may not always be concerned with beauty; sculptor Henry Moore once wrote, "I am not interested in the expression of beauty, but in the power of expression."

Just draw upon your knowledge and experience, trust your ears, let your tastes lead you in new directions. Keep listening and thinking. The results will be as exciting as you make them. Good luck!

Appendix

A. Elements of Western Notation

The Staffs: Clefs

The musical staff consists of five lines and four spaces. In moving from line to space up the staff, the pitches associated with these lines and spaces become higher in alphabetical order. A *clef* assigns a specific register to the staff, and thereby places specific pitches on its spaces and lines. The ***treble clef*** is also called ***G clef*** because it fixes a particular line as G-above-middle-C. Similarly, the ***bass clef*** is referred to as the ***F clef:*** it assigns F-below-middle-C to a certain line. Note that middle-C itself is not found on either staff, but just beyond: on an extra line, or ***ledger line,*** below the treble staff or above the bass staff.

Placing the two staves together, with middle-C assumed to be in the space between them, produces a dual staff of substantial range, called the ***great staff*** (see Figure A.1). It is commonly used in the notation of keyboard music.

Another clef is used regularly in Western music, for those instruments with a predominantly middle register. This clef assigns a fixed position to middle-C, and is therefore called the ***C clef.*** If it places middle-C on the middle line, it is called the ***alto clef.*** This is most often used in writing for the viola. In the Haydn quartet score excerpt, shown in Chapter 7, first and second violins play from staves using the treble clef. The viola plays in the middle 𝄡 register of the alto clef, and the cello in the lower 𝄢 region dictated by the bass clef.

Figure A.1

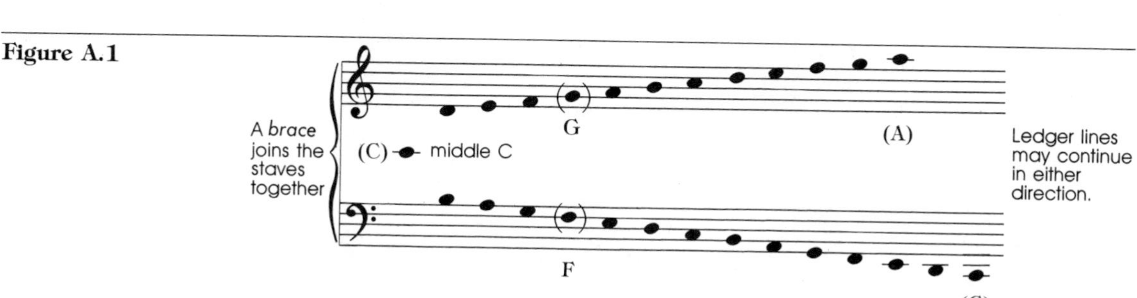

Accidentals and Key Signatures

Symbols which inflect pitches higher or lower are called *accidentals.* The three most frequently used accidentals are the ***sharp*** (♯), which raises pitch one half step, the ***flat*** (♭) lowering pitch one half step, and the ***natural*** (♮), which cancels or neutralizes a previous sharp or flat. There are also the double-sharp (𝄪) and double-flat (𝄫), which raise or lower a pitch two half steps; these are found much less frequently.

In traditional notation, a sharp or flat introduced within a measure remains in effect for the rest of that measure, unless cancelled by a natural sign. When a new measure is reached, the sharp or flat is automatically cancelled anyway. In the Haydn quartet excerpt of Chapter 7 (Figure 7.1), note the C♯ introduced in measure 12. Although the note is repeated during that measure, the ♯ sign is only used once: it remains in force throughout the measure. On the other hand, observe the note C♯ (cello part) at measure 7. When the note C returns for the cello at measure 10, it is C natural. The new measures have cancelled the preceding accidental.

Some accidentals appear consistently throughout a piece of music, because they belong to the diatonic scale of the composition. A ***key signature*** at the left of the staff, next to the clef, will list such accidentals. Some familiar key signatures for major keys are shown in Figure A.2. Key signatures and clefs are placed at the extreme left of ***each*** staff of a composition, just after the clef. The tempo indication and meter, however, appear only at the very beginning. They are not written again, unless they change during the course of the music.

Symbols Related to Form

Western music is traditionally read from left to right along the staff, and from highest staff to lowest on the page. Bar lines mark the movement of metric units. A ***double bar*** indicates either a complete stop (such as the end of each Haydn string quartet variation), or an important change: a new tempo, perhaps a new key signature. A double bar with two dots :‖ functions as a ***repeat*** sign. It instructs the performer to go back to the beginning, or to another repeat sign with dots facing the opposite way, and play the music again. We would find this symbol in Baroque or early classic dance forms, such as the movements of a suite or the minuet of a symphony.

Rhythm, Meter and Articulation

The rhythmic relationships between such symbols as 𝅝, 𝅗𝅥 and ♩ have been described previously, and need not be repeated here. One important rhythmic feature should be added, however: the division of a beat into an "odd"

Figure A.2

number of sub-groups. The ♩ is usually equal to two ♪. But the ♩ can be divided into three units by writing the number 3 above ♪♪♪. This grouping is called a ***triplet.*** Similarly a beat can be divided into five parts. Since there are usually four 𝅘𝅥𝅯 to the ♩, a quintuplet pattern is indicated by writing the number 5 above 𝅘𝅥𝅯𝅘𝅥𝅯𝅘𝅥𝅯𝅘𝅥𝅯𝅘𝅥𝅯.

If a piece uses triplet patterns consistently, it may be notated in one of the compound meters: $\frac{6}{8}$, $\frac{9}{8}$, or $\frac{12}{8}$, rather than the simple $\frac{2}{4}$, $\frac{3}{4}$, or $\frac{4}{4}$.

Signs for articulation and phrasing include the slur ⌒, which joins the notes under it in a smoothly connected legato line, and various degrees of detached sound: –, ·, ≐ and Y. The symbol > calls for a strong accent, and may occur in a detached or connected context.

B. The Overtone Series, Equal Temperament, and the Circle of 5ths

The Overtone Series

As noted in Chapter 6, a body set in vibration vibrates not only as a whole, but in fractions, or ***partials.*** A violin string vibrates along its full length, and ***simultaneously*** vibrates in halves, thirds, fourths and so on, as well. (See Figure 6.1, Chapter 6.) Each of the secondary vibrations has its own particular frequency, specifically related to the lowest frequency, or ***fundamental,*** of the string's full length. This fundamental is considered the 1st partial. The 2nd partial—that is, the frequency of the string divided into halves—is called the 1st ***overtone*** or 1st ***harmonic.***

Leonard Bernstein, discussing overtones in his Norton Lectures at Harvard University, said: "These are arranged in an order preordained by nature and ruled by universal physical laws. If this is news to you, I hope it's good news." It is certainly not news to scientists: ever since the experiments of the Greek mathematician and philosopher Pythagoras about 500 B.C., the acoustical nature of sound vibration has been the object of serious study. We know that music was included in the curriculum of medieval European universities, primarily as an acoustical discipline.

The frequency ratios of overtones to fundamental are 2 to 1, 3 to 1, 4 to 1, and so on. Assuming that the fundamental ***pitch*** is low C, the 1st overtone, vibrating at twice the frequency, would be the C one octave higher. In Figure A.3, the overtone series is shown in relation to the keyboard. The interval between each pitch and the next grows smaller as the series ascends: octave, 5th, 4th, major 3rd, minor 3rd, and so on. These additional pitches are sounding, even if only faintly, when the fundamental is set into vibration, and contribute a certain richness to the sound.

To ***prove*** that overtones do, indeed, vibrate along with the fundamental, a simple experiment may be performed at the piano. Referring to Figure

Figure A.3

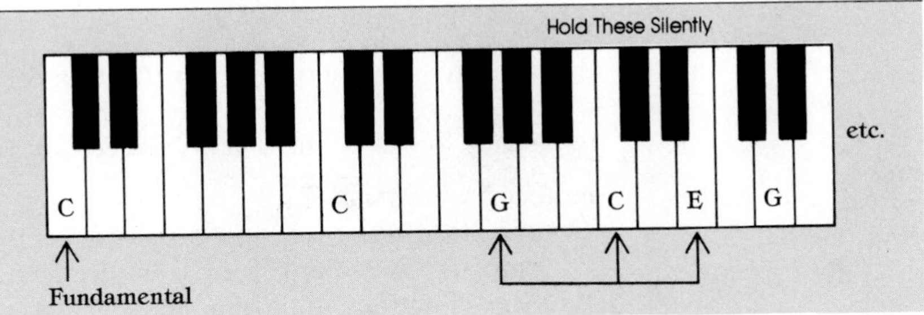

A.3, silently depress the notes of the 2nd, 3rd and 4th overtones, holding the keys down. Then play the low C (the fundamental) as a loud, sharp staccato note. A ghostly C-major triad will be heard, as though from a great distance; this is the result of the 2nd, 3rd and 4th overtones sounding as the strings of the depressed keys vibrate sympathetically with the low C.

Because it is so neat and precise, the overtone series has fascinated musicians for centuries. Some have attempted to relate various musical customs and practices to aspects of the series. For example, the octave relationship between fundamental and 1st overtone may help explain the ease with which people in all societies sing and play in octaves, and the resulting importance of the octave in all cultures. Similarly, the predominance of the 5th and 4th as the next two overtones may offer a clue about the importance of these two different intervals in different musical languages, from Chinese song to Western parallel organum. The acoustical stability of the 5th may be reflected in its widespread acceptance as a restful consonance in both Western and non-Western cultures. (At the opposite end of the spectrum, the most dissonant interval of Western history is located only one half-step away from this consonant 5th. The interval C-F♯, which divides the octave exactly in half, is called the tritone; during the Middle Ages it was referred to as "diabolous in musica"—a symbol of the devil in music!)

Equal Temperament

Before the Baroque era, instruments were often tuned to the natural harmonics of the overtone series, creating pure, resonant 5ths and triads. But the needs of ***tonal*** music—especially those of modulation and key contrast within single works—called for a different intonation system. Our present tonal system, dividing the octave into twelve equal steps, is called ***equal temperament,*** and the scales which use it are considered "tempered." The pitches within a tempered 12-note octave are slightly out-of-tune acoustically, but this is an intentional compromise, leading to fascinating musical results. In the tempered system, for example, the notes G♯ and A♭ are considered equivalent; the pitch F is exactly the same whether it appears as the fourth note in C major, the third note in D minor, or a chromatic note in some other scale. These equivalences make the variety of Western harmony and tonal music possible.

Equal temperament was not widely practiced before the eighteenth century. Before this period, one would have to re-tune a harpsichord to play a piece in a different key. J. S. Bach's first book of ***The Well Tempered Clavier,*** composed in 1722, presents a certain turning point in the tonal tradition—a coming of age of the major-minor tonal system. Bach included 24 preludes and 24 fugues in the collection: one prelude-fugue set for ***each*** of the 12 major and 12 minor keys. The important point was that, by using the system of equal temperament, a performer could play any or all of these at one sitting without re-tuning.

The Circle of 5ths

Because of equal temperament, one could also explore successive pitch (or key) relationships a 5th apart. In fact, one important feature of Western intonation is known as the ***circle of 5ths.*** In Figure A.4 it is shown with reference to the major scales and their key signatures.

The strongest pitch or key relationships of tonal music are those of tonic-dominant, and tonic-subdominant: tonalities that lie only a 5th apart (such as C major and G major). That is, the key represented by any point on the circle is most closely related to those points on either side of it.

Note, too, that the circle is "closed:" we can begin at any point and, by moving in 5ths, reach the same point (pitch or key) again. If it were not for the ***tempered*** scale, this would be impossible. Beginning on C and tuning each successive 5th as a "pure" natural harmonic, for example, would produce a C—at the twelfth stage of the cycle—out of tune with the starting C. In other words, the compromises of equal temperament have created the circle.

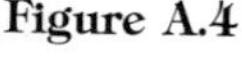
Figure A.4

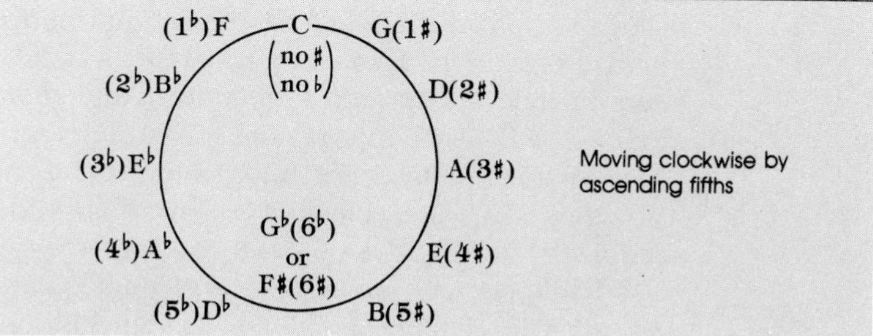

C. Instruments Outside the Western Orchestral Tradition

Early and Non-Western Instruments

Distinguished members of the family of plucked strings, the Middle-Eastern ***oud*** and Indian ***sitar*** have their origins in ancient traditions. The oud was influential in the development of the Western lute; we have already heard an eloquent example of the sitar. Plucked strings also include the increasingly familiar Japanese ***koto,*** which has its strings running the entire length of the soundbox; it rests on a floor or other surface without need for support by the player, in the manner of a zither.

The violin family is not the only group of bowed strings in existence. Bowed fiddles can be found in all parts of the globe, from the simple folk instruments of Turkey and Mongolia to the elaborately carved ones of India and China. Before the emergence of the Western violin around 1550, there were medieval and Renaissance bowed fiddles. An important precursor of the violin was the sixteenth century ***viol.*** This instrument had six strings, frets, and a relatively flat (rather than arched) bridge that enabled a player to bow full chords.

The ***recorder*** is an early ancestor of the modern flute. Like the flute, it makes use of air blown directly into the instrument, but it has a whistle-like mouthpiece, and is held vertically (down) rather than horizontally. Recorders exist in all sizes and ranges, forming a complete family from soprano to bass. They were extremely popular during the sixteenth and seventeenth centuries, and are now enjoying a widespread revival, owing not only to the renewed interest in early Western music, but to the relative simplicity of the instruments themselves. Bamboo flutes, especially the Japanese ***shakuhachi,*** are well known in Asia. There are also various kinds of multiple flutes—double and triple flutes, played together in one breath—found in South America, Eastern Europe, and other areas. ***Panpipes*** are truly ''multiple,'' as they may consist of ten or more flutes joined together, played very much like a large harmonica.

The ***harmonica*** is, in fact, a single-reed panpipe: a family of many tiny clarinets. (The ***accordion*** is also in the single-reed ''family,'' using a bellows to force air through its reeds, and buttons or a keyboard to vary pitch.) Double-reed European instruments of the Middle Ages and Renaissance include the ***rackett, krummhorn,*** and ***shawm,*** derived from the folk shawms of Eastern Europe and parts of Asia. These early double reeds produced a harsh buzzing sound, making them suitable for outdoor playing. The ***aulos*** was a multiple double oboe of ancient Greece; its image may be seen in the decorations of vases and bowls.

Trumpets were known to the ancient Greeks, Egyptians, and Assyrians; we read of them, of course, in the Bible. Ancient horns include the ***shofar,*** made of an animal's horn, and used in Jewish synagogue services.

There are many other horns constructed of shell or hide, and elaborate metal horns native to India and Nepal. The European hunting horns of the Renaissance led directly to our modern musical version. Present-day trombones were preceded by the fifteenth century ***sackbut,*** with a slide mechanism for lengthening its tube, and the wood ***serpent,*** a large cup-mouthpiece instrument with fingerholes like those of a recorder.

The percussion instruments of the world include many stampers, shakers, and rattles (some beautifully carved and decorated), and a great variety of bells and gongs. There are also the steel drums of the Caribbean and the hollowed-out logs of Africa known as slit drums. Drums use material stretched tautly over a resonating body; these bodies come in a staggering variety of shapes, and may be made of materials such as sonorous wood, gourd, ivory, or pottery.

Mechanical and Electric Instruments

Virtually every instrument makes use of complicated gadgetry. Certain instruments, though, are actually motorized, producing sound by rotating wheels, cylinders or rolls. These include the ***Hurdy-Gurdy*** (a motorized violin), ***Player-piano,*** and such familiar folk objects as music boxes, street organs, and humming tops.

Electric instruments are familiar on the contemporary musical scene. We have already noted the vibraphone, a tuned keyboard of metal plates whose sounds are extended and modified with an electric motor. The ***electric guitar,*** mainstay of the modern rock group, uses electronic devices to amplify and resonate its sounds. The traditional need for an acoustical soundbox is thereby eliminated: compare the body of a violin or the rounded back of a lute with the flat, almost two-dimensional shape of the electric guitar. ***Electric pianos*** are also found in jazz or rock ensembles. They have no strings, and rely instead upon electronic oscillations.

The musical use of electronic oscillations has fascinated composers throughout the century. As noted in Chapters 17 and 18, composers began using the newly invented ***tape recorder*** after World War II, to mix, alter and combine pre-recorded sounds in ***tape studios.*** By the '50s the electronic ***synthesizer*** had been developed. During that era Milton Babbitt created his ***Composition for Synthesizer,*** discussed in Part 1, on the largest and most famous of the early synthesizers—a room-sized assemblage of vacuum tubes, dials, and paper key-punch called the RCA Synthesizer. Today's synthesizers are much smaller and more portable, thanks to micro-circuitry. Present developments in ***electronic music,*** as noted in Chapter 18, also stress the many uses of computers.

D. Style Comparison Charts

Style	Element	Characteristics
Medieval Style (c. 500–1450)	Melody	Limited range, smooth singable lines. Based on church modes.
	Rhythm	Not indicated in chant; metric feeling in secular songs and dance. In Gothic era, triple rhythms; duple introduced in fourteenth century.
	Texture and Density	Chants and early songs monophonic. Later: polyphony up to four or even five voices. Strong dissonances.
	Form	Verbal music related to texts; some strophic. In Gothic, use of a known ***cantus firmus*** for ***variation.***
	Vocal Genres	Chant, organum, motet, parts of Mass. Secular songs.
	Instrumental Genres	Dances, Arrangements of vocal pieces.
	Prominent Instruments	Plucked strings such as lute, to accompany songs. Reeds and brass for outdoor performance; organs in sacred music.

Style	Element	Characteristics
Renaissance Style (1450–1600)	Melody	Wider range; lines smooth and singable. Uses church modes. ***Word-painting*** in late madrigals.
	Rhythm	Metric feeling in secular music. In sacred music, measured rhythms but not strongly emphasized. Steady tempo.
	Texture and Density	Imitative polyphony; chords (***triads***) becoming important. Dissonance used very carefully, consonance predominates. Cadences on central pitch of the mode.
	Form	***Variations*** upon ***cantus firmus.*** Dances have part-forms. Imitative textures in smoothly connected sections.
	Vocal Genres	Polyphonic Mass, sacred motet; chanson, madrigal, frottola.
	Instrumental Genres	Dances; short keyboard pieces such as ricercars and fantasias.
	Prominent Instruments	Lute, keyboard, organ, recorder, viol; consorts of families.

Style	Element	Characteristics
Baroque Style (1600–1750)	Melody	More angularity; virtuosic at times. Highly ornamented and embellished. Sequences used frequently. Major-minor tonality replaces the use of modes. Distinction between ***recitative, arioso,*** and ***aria*** melodic styles.
	Rhythm	Steady, relentlessly driving rhythm. Strong, regular meter and tempo. Slow movements and fast movements may alternate. Free, less regular rhythm in recitatives and keyboard fantasias and preludes.
	Texture and Density	Early Baroque: strong interest in solo line against chordal accompaniment (homophony). Later: imitative polyphony and homophony, both controlled by logic of tonal chord progres-

Baroque Style (1600–1750) (*continued*)		sions. Much more dissonance, driving forward to tonal goals. Continuo and figured bass; importance of bass line. Dynamics feature sudden changes in level, especially in keyboard music (terraced dynamics). Strong contrasts of density in concertato style.
	Form	Forms make use of tonality: modulations to related keys, return to the tonic. ***Ritornello*** form; variations on a ground; two-part dance and three-part aria forms; imitative process, such as fugue or canon. Each movement or piece creates a single mood or gesture ("affection"). Multi-movement formats, such as the sonata. Two movements are often joined together: slow-fast sections of French overture, or prelude and fugue. Larger dimensions.
	Vocal Genres	Opera, oratorio, cantata, Passion, Mass.
	Instrumental Genres	Sonata, concerto, suite (large); fugue, fantasia, passacaglia (small); many for keyboard instruments.
	Prominent Instruments	Harpsichord and organ; violin family; improvements in woodwinds. Instrumental style exploits the idiomatic features of different families. Instruments now tuned according to equal temperament.
Classic Style (1760–1830)	Melody	Short balanced phrases, often contrasting. Idiomatic writing for instruments; less ornamentation. Major-minor tonality important. Melodies often conceived harmonically, frequently built on the notes of a chord.
	Rhythm	A variety of rhythms in succession, but maintaining steady tempo and meter. By the end of the period (Beethoven), tempo is altered for expressive or structural purposes.
	Texture and Density	Mostly homophonic, with a variety of accompaniment patterns. The continuo (figured bass) disappears well before the end of the period. Great interest in crescendo-diminuendo dynamics. Sudden changes within a piece or movement (especially with Beethoven). Generally more transparent than baroque style.
	Form	Multi-movement sonata cycle. Individual forms include rondo, sonata, theme and variations; two-part and three-part song and dance forms. Double exposition and cadenza unique to concertos. With Beethoven, cyclic form becomes important in multi-movement works.
	Vocal Genres	Oratorio, opera, Mass.
	Instrumental Genres	Sonata, string quartet, symphony, concerto (all based on sonata cycle).
	Prominent Instruments	Piano replaces harpsichord in importance. String quartet dominates chamber music. The orchestra becoming more standardized; instruments such as clarinet and trombone have been added to the orchestra by the end of this period.

Romantic Style (1800–1900)	Melody	Chromatic, sweeping melody; unusual phrase lengths, and cadences often delayed. Expressive qualities (lyric, tragic, grotesque, and so forth) often stressed. Greatly expanded range. Tonality present, but the sense of key center is weakened by chromaticism.
	Rhythm	Tempo changes used for structural and expressive purposes: ***rubato*** in performance. Rhythms often irregular, avoiding simple pulses. Great variety of patterns. Slower, more deliberate sense of motion in many works (perhaps owing to complex harmony).
	Texture and Density	Density generally fuller than in eighteenth century styles. Texture basically homophonic; chords used for their expressive power. Chord progressions chromatic, with frequent modulations to distant keys, often to the point of obscuring tonality. Sudden, dramatic changes of density and/or dynamics, creating a wide range and great swings of mood.
	Form	Cyclic form (or thematic transformation/character variation) important in sonata cycle, suite, and even opera. Classic forms altered and expanded, using melody and tempo-mood contrast as organizing elements. Experiments in fusion of absolute forms with programmatic narrative or depiction. Many very long, diffuse works; also many brief, concise miniatures.
	Vocal Genres	Lied (art song), opera/music drama, oratorio.
	Instrumental Genres	All the classic sonata-cycle genres, plus symphonic poem, brief lyric pieces, "character" pieces (perhaps combined in suite format). Great differences between works composed for virtuoso performers and those written for amateurs.
	Prominent Instruments	The piano is predominant. Enlarged orchestra, with greater stress on expressivity of woodwinds and brilliant brass and percussion. Timbre and color distinctive features of each composer's style.
Twentieth Century Style (1900–)	Melody	Not necessarily derived from the tonal system, or tied to vocal range. There may be unusual intervals, wide skips, lack of key center. Other twentieth century styles stress repetition, narrow intervals, and reinforced key center (in part drawn from non-Western models). Scales vary: twelve-tone rows, medieval modes, folk scales.
	Rhythm	Often changing meters, and/or asymmetric rhythms. Complex rhythmic patterns, or non-Western ***additive*** rhythms, may also be present. A regular pulse or beat may be quite pronounced, or obscure. In certain experimental styles, silence is as prominent as sound.
	Texture and Density	Counterpoint important again, especially in neoclassic styles. Balance between homophony and polyphony; great variety in density and texture. New approaches include: Webernian

Twentieth Century Style (1900–) (*continued*)		***Klangfarbenmelodie,*** minimal processes of overlapping ***ostinati,*** Ivesian juxtaposition of layers. Harmony may stress atonality, or various ways of stating key center (triads, other chord structures; functional progressions, or repeated ***ostinati***). Great range from extreme dissonance to total, virtually static, consonance.
	Form	All previous forms, transformed in context of atonality or altered tonality. Form, or details of form, may be dictated by a ***process:*** a tone row, or improvisatory game plan, or minimal working out of gradual change. Form may reflect the composer's interest in total control, or random spontaneity, or some position between those extremes.
	Vocal Genres Instrumental Genres	Same as the nineteenth century, plus important literature for mixed chamber ensembles, including voice. The place of performance becoming increasingly important to composers: works specifically created for concert halls, recordings, video, or "mixed media," unusual indoor or outdoor spaces.
	Prominent Instruments	Percussion instruments have new importance. New playing techniques for all instruments, exploiting unusual sonorities; ***Sprechstimme*** and other new techniques for singers. Electronic media: the use of tape, amplification, loudspeakers, and/or electronically generated sound.

E. Texts of Purcell Aria and Schubert Song

Purcell

When I am laid in earth, may my wrongs create
No trouble in my breast.
Remember me, but ah! forget my fate.

Schubert

Gretchen am Spinnrade	*Gretchen at the Spinning Wheel*
Meine Ruh is hin, Mein Herz ist schwer Ich finde sie nimmer Und nimmermehr.	*My peace is gone,* *My heart is heavy;* *And I will never again,* *Ever find calm.*
Wo ich ihn nicht hab Ist mir das Grab, Die ganze Welt Ist mir vergällt.	*Anywhere without him* *Is my grave,* *All joy in life* *Is lost forever.*

Mein armer Kopf Ist mir verrückt, Mein armer Sinn Ist mir zerstückt.	*My poor head* *Is truly confused,* *My poor mind* *Is totally distracted.*
Meine Ruh ist hin Mein Herz ist schwer, Ich finde sie nimmer Und nimmermehr.	*My peace is gone,* *My heart is heavy;* *And I will never again,* *Ever find calm.*
Nach ihm nur schau ich Zum Fenster hinaus, Nach ihm nur geh ich Aus dem Haus.	*It is only him I seek,* *When I look from my window,* *It is only him I seek when* *I leave the house.*
Sein hoher Gang, Sein' edle Gestalt, Seines Mundes Lächeln, Seiner Augen Gewalt,	*His manly gait,* *His noble bearing,* *His lips' smile,* *His eyes' power,*
Und seiner Rede Zauberfluss, Sein Händedruck, Und ach, sein Kuss!	*And his speech,* *A magic flow,* *The touch of his hand,* *And, oh, his kiss!*
Meine Ruh ist hin, Mein Herz ist schwer, Ich finde sie nimmer Und nimmermehr.	*My peace is gone,* *My heart is heavy;* *And I will never again,* *Ever find calm.*
Mein Busen drängt Sich nach ihm hin. Ach dürft ich fassen Und halten ihn,	*My heart longs so* *For him.* *Oh, if I could grasp* *And hold him,*
Und küssen ihn, So wie ich wollt, An seinen Küssen Vergehen sollt!	*And kiss him,* *All I wanted;* *From his kisses* *I should die!*
[Meine Ruh ist hin, Mein Herz ist schwer . . .]	[*My peace is gone,* *My heart is heavy . . .*]

Glossary

a cappella performed by voices without instrumental accompaniment.

accelerando speeding up.

accent stress upon one beat more than others.

accidentals symbols used to modify a written pitch: sharps, flats, and naturals.

additive rhythm method used in non-Western music, in which patterns are built by taking a small durational unit and adding such units together.

aerophone: instrument whose sounds are produced by the vibration of a column of air.

aleatory see *indeterminacy.*

antiphonal involving widely separated performing forces.

aria solo song in opera, oratorio, or other large scale vocal genre.

ario de capo an aria in A-B-A form; usually associated with Italian opera of the late Baroque.

Ars Nova French polyphonic style of the 14th century, characterized by complex rhythmic patterns and meters.

atonality music without a tonal center.

bar line vertical line drawn just to the left of each principal accented beat, thus marking off measures.

bel canto operatic vocal style with expansive, heavily embellished melodies emphasizing beauty of sound.

brass instruments a family of instruments, made of metal and producing sound by lip vibration against a metal mouthpiece. Important orchestral brasses are trumpet, french horn, trombone, and tuba.

cadence point at which a phrase, or complete tonal melody, comes to rest.

canon strict polyphonic imitation, in which each melodic line exactly duplicates that of its neighbors.

cantata musical genre for voices and instruments, consisting of a collection of arias, recitatives, and instrumental interludes.

cantus firmus chant (or other borrowed melody) used as a basis for a polyphonic composition.

canzona late Renaissance instrumental piece derived from the French chanson.

character piece a brief piano piece that depicts a mood, possibly programmatic in nature as well.

chorale hymn tune, generally harmonized in four parts, written for the German Protestant church during the Reformation.

chord one sound made up of three or more pitches stated simultaneously.

chordophone instrument whose sounds are produced by the vibration of strings.

chromatic term used to describe the "extra" pitches which are not included in a diatonic Western scale.

chromatic scale the complete Western collection of twelve pitches within the octave.

clef symbol at the far left of the staff, which assigns lines and spaces to a specific register.

collage the practice of quoting fragments of pre-existing music and using them as a focus for composition; a feature of some recent post-1950 styles, and also of Ives, Mahler, and Stravinsky.

concert overture single orchestral movement, not meant to be the introduction to anything; possibly programmatic in nature.

concertino small solo group in a Baroque concerto grosso.

concerto sonata cycle for one or more solo instruments with orchestra, usually in three movements.

concerto grosso concerto format using a small group of soloists, who also play with the full orchestra during interludes.

consonance an interval or chord which creates a feeling of harmonic resolution or release.

consort a group of instruments of similar timbre; often associated with Renaissance style.

continuo bass line and improvised keyboard chords in a Baroque composition; also called basso continuo. See *figured bass.*

counterpoint a technique for placing distinctive musical lines against each other simultaneously. See *polyphony.*

cyclic form form in which an entire multi-movement work is generated from a few ideas; associated with the sonata-cycle works of Beethoven and later composers.

density the thickness or heaviness of the total sound of a passage or piece; related to concepts of "mass", weight. Also see *texture.*

diatonic term used to describe the seven pitches of the Western major or minor scale.

dissonance an unstable interval or chord which generates a feeling of increased harmonic tension.

dominant pitch number 5 of the Western scale.

dot symbol placed directly to the right of a note head, increasing the relative value of that note by one half.

downbeat the accented beat at the beginning of a measure.

duration the length of a sound.

dynamics musical volume.

exoticism use of distant foreign cultures as material for composition.

expressionism movement which explores inner drives, dreams, and fantasies, and depicts these psychological states in art or music.

figured bass numbers written under the bass notes in Baroque music, indicating chords to be filled in by an improvising keyboard player.

flat notational sign which lowers a written pitch by one half step.

form the architecture of music; the shape given to the passage of time by the organization of the musical events within it.

free polyphony texture in which the different parts are independent, nonimitative, and equally active.

frequency speed of vibration of a sound wave. Frequency determines pitch.

frottola straightforward syllabic text setting without interweaving rhythmically different lines.

fugue imitative polyphonic texture, featuring many passages in strict imitation and others in free counterpoint. The technique is less strict than that of canon.

gagaku ensemble classical Japanese orchestra.

gamelan Indonesian orchestra, consisting of bells, gongs, and other percussion instruments.

Gebrauchsmusik German for "music for use"; term used by Hindemith to indicate works written for specific occasions and needs.

Gesamtkunstwerk German for "total work of art". Wagner's term for his idea of merging music with all other aspects of operatic production to create a unified work of art.

graphic notation notation which is visually related to the "sound" of the music.

Gregorian chant early Christian liturgical literature, with monophonic texture and unaccompanied vocal timbre.

half step in standard Western tuning, the smallest interval between two tones.

harmony an ordering of successive chords, creating a sense of motion toward a goal.

heterophony texture in which a single melodic line is elaborated upon by a group of performers, independently and simultaneously.

homophony texture dominated by a single melody with harmonic background.

idée fixe theme representing a programmatic idea, which recurs in various transformations throughout an entire work; usually associated with Berlioz. See also *leitmotif.*

idiophone instrument producing sounds by virtue of its entire body being set into vibration (for example, a rattle or gong).

imitation polyphonic texture in which variants or duplicates of the same melodic line have their entrances staggered to begin at different points in time.

impressionism esthetic movement which explores the "impressions" of the natural environment on the senses.

improvisation spontaneous performance, without written music, but with reference to a known context (such as a familiar chord progression or tune).

incidental music music intended as background or interlude in a stage production.

indeterminacy the use of chance operations to arrive at the composition or performance of a piece; less dependent upon a known context than improvisation.

interval distance between two pitches.

intonation tuning of a voice or instrument with regard to pitch frequencies.

intonation system any method of tuning or dividing the octave, creating specific pitches and intervals.

key the tonality, and (major or minor) scale, of a passage.

key signature the accidentals needed for a particular scale, listed directly to the right of the clef at the beginning of a staff.

Klangfarbenmelodie German for "tone-color melody". Technique of creating melody by sounding tones on different instruments in turn, devised by Schoenberg but most often associated with Webern.

leitmotif a recurring melodic fragment or chord, used by Wagner to stand for specific themes or characters in his music dramas.

libretto script for an opera or oratorio.

lied German for "song" (plural: lieder).

madrigal secular vocal composition first appearing in fourteenth century Italy and taken up in England at the end of the sixteenth century.

major scale a seven-tone scale with half-steps between notes 3 and 4 and between notes 7 and 8.

mass central act of worship of the Roman Catholic Church; liturgical music written for that service.

measure a group of accented and unaccented beats set of by bar lines.

melismatic setting setting of text in which a single syllable is given a whole series of notes.

membranophone instrument whose sounds are produced by the vibration of a stretched membrane (for example, a drum).

meter grouping of pulses into regular accents and beats.

metric modulation notational technique which allows one tempo or meter to change to another; associated with the rhythmic style of Elliott Carter.

microtones intervals smaller than a half step.

Minnesinger German troubadour of the Middle Ages.

minor scale seven-tone scale characterized by the interval of a minor third between pitches 1 and 3.

minuet Baroque dance, later used for the third movement of the symphony and string quartet.

mode seven-tone scale commonly used in music before 1600, and in folk music.

modulation the process of switching tonalities; changing from one key center to another.

monophony texture consisting of one single unaccompanied melodic line.

motet in the Medieval era, a vocal genre in which new texts were added above a chant tune. Later, a Renaissance polyphonic choral genre on a sacred text.

motive a single phrase, or fragment of phrase, that recurs many times in original or altered form.

music drama Wagner's preferred term for his operas.

nationalism the cultivation of national ideas and idioms, especially prevalent in the nineteenth century.

natural notational sign which cancels a previous sharp or flat.

neoclassicism twentieth century movement that dominated Western music between the two World wars, stressing tonality, clarity of texture, older genres and forms.

non-functional harmony series of chords used in ways which are illogical or "ungrammatical" by the standards of tonality.

octave two notes with the same letter name, twelve half-steps apart. The frequencies of pitches an octave apart are related by doubling or halving.

opera drama set to music; form using a libretto with solo voices, chorus, and orchestra, with a full stage setting.

oratorio a dramatic, religious work for voices and orchestra, using many of the techniques of opera, but not staged.

orchestra a large group of string, wind, and percussion instrumentalists.

ordinary invariable portions of the mass: Kyrie, Gloria, Credo, Sanctus, and Agnus Dei.

organum early form of polyphony in which a chant is sung by one voice with one or more contrapuntal voices added above and below it.

ostinato a fixed, continuously repeated contour, against which a melody may be set.

overture a brief orchestral number at the beginning of an opera, oratorio, or other lengthy genre. A *French overture* consists of a slow section followed by a rapid section in imitative style; associated with Baroque style.

parallel harmony a chord series in which the same chord color moves up and down on successive pitch levels; often associated with Medieval music, non-Western styles, and impressionism.

part form form in which there are contrasting sections occurring one after the other.

percussion instruments a family of instruments creating sound by being struck or shaken. *Tuned percussion* instruments produce a definite musical pitch (tympani, tuned bells, chimes, xylophone, marimba, glockenspiel, vibraphone, celesta), while *untuned percussion* instruments produce complex sounds of indefinite frequency (triangle, snare drum, wood block, cymbal, tambourine, castanets).

pentatonic scale scale having five pitches, analogous to the black keys of the piano.

phrase a group of notes that ends with a cadence.

pitch exact high or low placement of a sound, determined by its frequency.

pizzicato plucking the strings of a stringed instrument.

polyphony texture featuring two or more independent, active melodic lines stated simultaneously.

polyrhythm two or more rhythmic profiles heard simultaneously.

polytonality music with more than one tonal center stated simultaneously.

process music work in which all details emerge from a single idea, i.e., the audible unfolding of the compositional scheme *is* the work. Other avant-garde styles may be related to a variety of "processes" (biological, statistical, etc.).

program music music which expresses a non-musical idea, visual image, or story.

proper parts of the mass which vary according to the particular day of the church year.

pulse periodic beat, creating a standard unit of movement against which surface rhythms occur.

raga in the music of India, a collection of pitches drawn from a twenty-two part division of the octave, which forms the framework for improvised melodic variations.

range distribution of pitch, defined by the high and low points of a passage or piece.

recitative vocal style with no set meter, representing the rhythms and inflections of speech.

register a portion of an instrument's total pitch range, i.e., the clarinet's "low register".

rest a symbol representing silence.

rhythm the pattern formed by the successive durations of sounds (and silences) in a piece of music.

ripieno full orchestra in a Baroque concerto grosso.

ritard (ritardando) slowing down.

ritornello recurrent orchestral passage or theme, especially in Baroque opera and concerto.

rondo part form in which one main theme alternates with a series of contrasting tunes.

round a variety of canon, with imitation at the interval of the unison or octave.

rubato the stretching and contracting of rhythms; often associated with the performance of Romantic music.

scale a collection of particular pitches, grouped in succession from one pitch to its octave.

scherzo Italian for "joke". A fast movement which generally replaced the minuet in the nineteenth century symphony.

sequence a melodic or harmonic pattern that is re-stated at different pitch levels.

serialism total organization of all musical elements; the extension of twelve-tone pitch control to other parameters, such as rhythm or register.

series see *tone row.*

set see *tone row.*

sharp notational sign which raises a written pitch by one half step.

sonata instrumental genre of individual movements played in succession, providing contrasts of tempo and mood; after the Baroque period, associated with the sonata cycle.

sonata cycle musical form consisting of three movements in order fast—slow—fast; and added fourth movement (minuet or scherzo) might occur after the slow movement. See *symphony, concerto, string quartet, sonata.*

sonata da chiesa Baroque trio sonata in a serious mood, or in "church" style.

sonata form also called sonata-allegro form; used for the opening movement of most sonata cycles. Two or more themes are presented (exposition), modulated and varied (development), and restated (recapitulation).

song cycle a group of songs combined in a collection.

Sprechstimme vocal delivery which is half song, half speech; devised by Schoenberg.

staff a group of five horizontal lines on and around which symbols for pitches are written.

string instruments a family of instruments constructed of a sounding box over which strings are stretched. The tone is produced by drawing a bow across the strings or by plucking. The modern orchestral strings are violin, viola, cello, and doublebass.

string quartet (1) sonata cycle for string quartet, with a minuet inserted between the slow movement and the rapid finale: (2) chamber music ensemble made up of four string instruments: two violins, viola, and cello.

strophic form form in which different stanzas of a poem are set to identical music.

style the individual qualities of a piece of music, and their mutual interaction to form a language or manner.

subject the theme of a fugue.

suite in Baroque music, a group of four or more dance-derived movements; in later periods, any collection of excerpts from a larger work, or a group of related programmatic movements.

suspension when one or more voices are held over during a change of chords, creating dissonances which are then resolved.

syllabic setting setting of text which assigns one pitch to each syllable.

symbolic notation use of symbols to represent musical events or relationships.

symphonic poem single-movement orchestral piece with programmatic content.

symphony sonata cycle for orchestra, with a minuet movement inserted between the slow movement and the rapid finale.

syncopation a strong accent at a normally weak spot in the meter.

synthesizer an electronic musical instrument made up of various individual circuits, controlling aspects of the resulting sound; associated with post-1950 electronic music.

tablature writing for plucked stringed instruments, which indicates finger positions by use of a diagram.

tempo the speed at which music moves.

terraced dynamics feature of Baroque instrumental style in which dynamic levels are sharply alternated and contrasted.

texture the way in which different sounds are combined, simultaneously and successively, in a "fabric". See *homophony, heterophony, monophony, polyphony.*

thematic transformation cyclical return of a theme with altered surface characteristics; often a feature of nineteenth century music.

theme a distinctive musical statement that serves as a basis for part or all of a longer composition.

theme and variations form in which a theme is followed by a series of variations on it.

through-composed form in which sections are arranged successively in a straight time line, with none repeated.

tie a curved line extended between two note heads, used to add two rhythmic values together.

timbre the unique sound quality of each instrument or voice.

tonal center the one preeminent pitch in a piece of tonal music, about which the other pitches group themselves.

tonality a system of pitch organization dominated by a tonal center, or tonic, and a hierarchy of pitches and chords around the tonic.

tone cluster several adjacent pitches played simultaneously, such as a sound made by playing a keyboard with palms, fists, or arms; composers who use clusters include Bartók, Cowell, and Penderecki.

tone color see *timbre*.

tone poem see *symphonic poem*.

tone row collection of pitches used in twelve-tone technique, with each of the twelve pitches within the octave appearing only once and in a prescribed order.

tonic pitch number 1 of the Western scale, the tonal center.

transposition performing a passage in a different key or pitch level.

triad a chord consisting of three tones.

trio (1) composition for three instruments; (2) ensemble of three instruments; (3) second part (B section) of a minuet movement within the sonata cycle.

trio sonata Baroque sonata for two solo instruments and continuo.

troubadour Southern French singer of secular song, 1100–1300.

trouvère Northern French troubadour.

tune a symetrically balanced collection of phase groups. See also *theme, motive, subject.*

twelve-tone technique systematic procedure for organizing atonal chromatic material, based upon the continuous varied repetition of a pitch pattern called a tone row.

upbeat weak beat of the measure, just before the bar line.

variation repetition of a theme in changing contexts and situations.

verismo extreme form of realism in opera, especially late nineteenth century Italian opera.

vibrato rapid, slight variations in pitch, used to add richness or brilliance to tone.

virtuoso a performer with extraordinary technical skill.

whole step the interval of two half steps, also called a 2nd.

whole-tone scale a six-tone scale made up exclusively of whole steps.

woodwind instruments a family of instruments producing sounds by causing a column of air to vibrate through a pipe. The vibrations are activated by the player's breath directly (flute), by a reed vibrating against a mouthpiece (clarinet, saxophone), or by vibration of two reeds (oboe, english horn, bassoon).

woodwind quintet (1) chamber music ensemble made up of five instruments: flute, oboe, clarinet, bassoon, and french horn; (2) sonata-cycle work played by this ensemble.

Illustration Credits

Overture: Ways of Listening
4 William Hogarth, ***The Enraged Musician,*** 1741. Engraving. Prints Division. The New York Public Library. Astor, Lenox, and Tilden Foundations. 7 Thomas Eakins, ***A Youth Playing Pipes,*** 1883. Bronze relief. Hirshhorn Museum and Sculpture Garden, Smithsonian Institution.

Chapter 1
11 ***Cycladic Syrinx Player,*** 2600–2000 B.C. Yellowish marble. The Detroit Institute of Arts, Bequest of Dr. Lester W. Cameron. 15 Giacomo Balla, ***Plastic Construction of Noise and Speed,*** 1968. Reconstruction of original, 1914–15. Aluminum and steel relief. Hirshhorn Museum and Sculpture Garden, Smithsonian Institution.

Chapter 2
28 Ravi Shanker playing the sitar. Courtesy of CBS. 30 Milton Babbitt seated at the RCA Synthesizer. 34 Mbunde man from Angola playing a drum. Courtesy Field Museum of Natural History, Chicago.

Chapter 3
44 Ethiopian priests. Courtesy of Unesco/Carraud.

Chapter 4
48 Ben Shahn, ***Silent Music,*** 1951. Philadelphia Museum of Art. Purchased: Harrison Fund. 49 Henri Fantin-Latour. ***A Piece by Schumann.*** Etching, 19th century. Prints Division. The New York Public Library. Astor, Lenox, and Tilden Foundations. 54 Pootagook. ***Woman with Musical Instrument.*** 1958. Stonecut. Prints Division. The New York Public Library. Astor, Lenox, and Tilden Foundations. 55 (top) Lesson in ***koto*** and ***shakuhachi.*** Japan National Tourist Organization. 55 (bottom) Sequoia String Quartet. Sheldon Soffer Management, Inc. 57 A kenong player. Indonesian Gamelan orchestra. UNESCO/Cart.

Chapter 5
66 Merle Freund, ***Musical Instrument.*** Stone and brass. Courtesy of the artist. 68 Giovanni del Biondo, ***Madonna and Child Enthroned with Angels.*** 14th century. Tempera on wood panel. Permission of the Fine Arts Museums of San Francisco.

Chapter 6
76 ***Dog Orchestra.*** English porcelain. Wadsworth Atheneum, Hartford, Ct. 78 Whistle, made from the phalanx bone of a reindeer. France. Courtesy of the Pitt Rivers Museum, Oxford. 78 Egyptian harpist, 19th dynasty. Painted wood. Reproduced by courtesy of the Trustees of the British Museum. 78 Indian tom-tom. Victoria and Albert Museum. Crown copyright. 79 Gong Ageng, from Raffles Gamelan. Reproduced by Courtesy of the Trustees of the British Museum. 81 Tobias Stimmer, ***Woman Playing the Psaltery,*** and ***Woman Playing Viola,*** c. 1570. Woodcut. Prints Division. The New York Public Library. Astor, Lenox, and Tilden Foundations. 83 Richard Hartshone, double bass, and Beth Pearson, cello of the Apple Hill Chamber Players. 85 Hirschfield, ***Benny Goodman.*** Courtesy of Benny Goodman. 88 Catholic University Percussion Ensemble, Garwood Whaley, Director. 89 Wenceslaus Hollar, ***Lady Playing the Virginals,*** 1635. Etching. Prints Division. The New York Public Library. Astor, Lenox, and Tilden Foundations. 89 Grand Pianoforte by John Broadwood, 1883. Decorated with silver and gilt gesso by William Morris and Company. Victoria and Albert Museum, Crown copyright. 89 Thomas Richner and Aeolian Skinner Organ. 91 Lorenzo Costa, ***A Concert.*** 16th century. Ferrarese School. Wood. Reproduced by courtesy of the Trustees, The National Gallery, London. 94 (top) New York Chamber soloists. Courtesy Melvin Kaplan Concert Management. 94 The Canadian Brass. David Haber Artists Management, Inc. 95 Laurie Appleby, oboe; Lesley Bell, flute; Stephen Quint, horn; Paul Stebbins, bassoon; and Larry Tietze, clarinet of the Hancock Woodwind Quintet. 96 Lyre, Sumerian, 3rd millenium B.C. Royal Cemetary of Ur. Courtesy of the Trustees of the British Museum. 98 Rudolf Kempe conducting the BBC Symphony Orchestra, 1975. BBC Copyright Photograph. 99 BBC Symphony Orchestra conducted by Pierre Boulez. BBC Copyright Photograph. 99 Doug Skinner, from ***35 Instrumental Designs*** and Rich Gold, "Georgeo of the Suburbs." Reprinted from the Sept./Oct., 1978 issue of ***EAR*** (306 Fair Oaks Street #4, San Francisco, Ca 94110). © 1978 by ***EAR*** and the authors. All rights reserved. By permission of the artist.

Chapter 7
102 Abraham Bosse, ***Family Concert,*** 1636. Engraving. Prints Division. The New York Public Library. Astor, Lenox and Tilden Foundations, 102 A Choral Rehearsal. Courtesy of Bowdoin College News Service. 104 Pieter Bruegel the Elder, ***The Wedding Dance.*** 16th century. The Detroit Institute of Arts. Purchase, City appreciation. 105 Chou Fang, ***Tuning the Lute and Drinking Tea.*** Handscroll in ink and color on silk. Nelson Gallery—Atkins Museum, Kansas City, Missouri, (Nelson Fund). 105 Vincent M. Langlois, ***Music Party,*** 18th century. Engraving. Prints Division. The New York Public Library. Astor, Lenox, and Tilden Foundations. 120 Edo de Waart, Music Director and conductor of the San Francisco Symphony Orchestra. Courtesy of the San Francisco Symphony Orchestra.

Chapter 8
130 Etruscan frieze. Woman playing kithara, panpipes, and aulos. Ashmolean Musem of Art and Archeology, Oxford. 131 Blind harpist. Egyptian. Courtesy of the Rijksmuseum van Oudheden, Leiden (Holland). 136 13th century

Antiphonary, detail. Walters Art Gallery, Baltimore. 138 Chartres Cathedral, Rose window. 14th century. French Government Tourist Office. 140 Hans Memling, ***Angels,*** 15th century. Oil on panel. Koninklijk Museum voor Schone Kunsten, Antwerp. 135, 139, 144 Detail from a Psalter, English, c. 1170 (Fol. 21 verso, ms Hunter 229). Courtesy of University of Glasgow. 148 Hans V. deVries, ***Palace with Musicians.*** 16th century. Kunsthistorische Museum, Vienna, Austria. 150 Israhel Van Meckenem, ***Dance of Herodias.*** Detail from the engraving. Prints Division. The New York Public Library. Astor, Lenox, and Tilden Foundations. 152 Giovanni del Biondo, ***Madonna and Child with Angels,*** detail. 14th century. Permission of the Fine Arts Museums of San Francisco. 153 Rose Opening of Queen Elizabeth's Virginal, 1570 detail. Prints Division. The New York Public Library. Astor, Lenox, and Tilden Foundations. 156 Crispin DePasse, ***Terra,*** detail. Engraving. Prints Division. The New York Public Library. Astor, Lenox, and Tilden Foundations. 161 ***Henry VIII Playing a Harp.*** From an Elizabethan manuscript. By permission of the British Library. 161 Henry VIII, ***Pastime and Good Company.*** By permission of the British Library. 163 Evaristo Baschenis. ***Musical Instruments,*** 17th century. Oil on canvas. Accademia Carrara di Belle Arti, Pinacoteca, Bergamo, Italy.

Chapter 9

166 Bernini, Colonnade in St. Peter's Square. 17th century. Rome. Italian State Tourist Office. 168 Jean Garnier, ***Louis XIV in an Oval with Musical Instruments, Flowers, and Fruits.*** Musée Versailles. Cliche des Musées Nationaux—Paris. 169 Gerrit Honthorst, ***Musical Group on a Balcony,*** detail. The J. Paul Getty Museum. 171 Canaletto, ***Venice: The Basin of S. Marco on Ascension Day.*** 18th century. Reproduced by courtesy of the Trustees, The National Gallery, London. 171 Canaletto, ***Musician's Gallery, St. Mark's Cathedral.*** 18th century. Hamburger Kunsthalle, Hamburg. 175 Bernardo Strozzi, ***Portrait of Claudio Monteverdi.*** Tiroler Landesmuseum Ferdinandeum, Innsbruck, Austria. 172 ***Musicians in the Court of Christian IV,*** detail, ceiling of Rosenberg Castle. De danske Kongers Kronologiske pa Rosenborg. 179 Jean Le Pautre, ***Versailles Palace during a Performance of Lully's Alceste,*** 17th century. Engraving. The Metropolitan Museum of Art, Harris Brisbane Dick Fund, 1930. 180 Instrument-makers' Workshop, from Diderot's ***Encyclopedia,*** 18th century. Engraving. By permission of the British Library. 181 G. Fentzel, ***The Sense of Hearing.*** Etching. Detail. The New York Public Library. 185 J. Closterman, Portrait of Henry Purcell, 1695. National Portrait Gallery, London.

Chapter 10

192, 201, and 204 Martin Engelbrecht, ***The Organist,*** detail, c. 1720–30. Engraving. Prints Division. The New York Public Library. Astor, Lenox, and Tilden Foundations. 195 Gabriel Metsue, ***Reverie.*** Wood panel. The Fine Arts Museums of San Francisco. Gift of Roscoe and Margaret Oakes. 196 Martin Engelbrecht, Woodwinds, detail, c. 1720–30. Engraving. Prints Division. The New York Public Library. Astor, Lenox, and Tilden Foundations. 199 T. Hudson, ***George Frederick Handel,*** 18th century. National Portrait Gallery, London. 200 William Daniel, ***London,*** 1804. Engraving. Victoria and Albert Museum, Crown Copyright. 202 ***Handel Conducting an Oratorio Rehearsal,*** 18th century. Ink drawing. Reproduced by Courtesy of the Trustees of the British Museum. 203 Rowlandson, ***John Bull at the Italian Opera,*** 18th century. Engraving. Victoria and Albert Museum, Crown Copyright. 209 E. G. Haussmann, ***Johann Sebastian Bach,*** 1746. Museum fur Geschichte der Stadt Leipzig. 222 English Violin, carved tuners and finial, c. 1675. Victoria and Albert Museum, Crown Copyright.

Chapter 11

226 Le Pantheon, Paris. French Embassy Press and Information Division. 227 Antoine Jean Duclos, ***The Concert,*** 18th century. Engraving after Augustin de St. Aubin. Prints Division. The New York Public Library. Astor, Lenox, and Tilden Foundations. 232 ***A Performance*** by Hayden's Orchestra at Esterhaza, 1775. Theater-Museum, Munich. 236 Square piano by Christopher Gainer, 1775. Victoria and Albert Museum, Crown Copyright. 239 Matthias Greischer, View of Esterhaza Palace, 1697. Engraving. Magyar Nemzeti Múzeum, Musée National de Hongrie. 240 Thomas Hardy, ***Haydn,*** 1791. Royal College of Music. 244 Gainsborough, Music Party, 18th century. Chalk drawing. Reproduced by courtesy of the Trustees of the British Museum. 246 Carmontelle, ***Mozart with His Father and Sister,*** from a design of 1763. Watercolor on paper. Reproduced by courtesy of the Trustees, The National Gallery, London. 247 Mozart, ***God is our Refuge,*** autograph by the composer, 1765. By permission of the British Library. 249 J. Lange, ***Portrait of Mozart,*** unfinished, 1789. Original in the Mozart Museum, Salzburg, Austria. 257 Act III, ***Don Giovanni,*** New York City Opera. Photograph by Fred Fehl. Music Division Performing Arts Research Center, The New York Public Library at Lincoln Center. Astor, Lenox and Tilden Foundations. 258 Dora Stock, ***Last Portrait of Mozart.*** Musikbibliothek der Stadt Leipzig.

Chapter 12

266 and 274 Silhouette of Ludwig van Beethoven, detail. Osterreichische Nationalbibliothek, Austria. 266 Beethoven's piano. With permission of the Beethoven House, Bonn. 286 Beethoven's house, Bonn. With permission of the Beethoven House, Bonn. 270 Beethoven's hearing aids. With permission of the Beethoven House, Bonn. 278 Klein, ***Life mask of Beethoven.*** With permission of the Beethoven House, Bonn. 281 and 287 Henri de Toulouse-Lautrec, Six Sketches of Hands on a Contrabass, 1900. Pencil drawing. Courtesy Musée Toulouse-Lautrec, Albi, France. 289 Lyser, ***Beethoven in the Streets of Vienna,*** drawing. With permission of the Beethoven House, Bonn. 290 Stober, ***Beethoven's Funeral,*** March 29, 1827. With permission of the Beethoven House, Bonn.

Chapter 13

295 Brighton Pavillion. The British Tourist Authority. 300 Felix Vallotton, ***La Symphonia,*** 19th century. Woodcut. Stadelsches Kunstinstitut und Stadtische Galerie, Frankfurt. 301 Thomas Eakins, ***The Violinist,*** 1904. Oil on canvas. Hirshhorn Museum and Sculpture Garden, Smithsonian Institution. 303 Metzmacher, Portrait of Hector Berlioz. Engraving. Muller Collection. Performing Arts Research Center. The New York Public Library at Lincoln

Center. Astor, Lenox and Tilden Foundations. 308 and 311 Moritz von Schwind, ***A Schubert Evening at Josef von Spaun's house,*** detail, 1868. Historisches Museum der Stadt Wien. Vienna, Austria. 309 Portrait of Franz Schubert. Gesellschaft der Musikfreunde in Wien-Archiv. Vienna, Austria. 312 Franz Schubert. Lithograph. Deutsche Staatsbibliothek, Berlin. 316 Georges Sand, ***Frederick Chopin.*** Drawing. Music Division. Performing Arts Research Center. The New York Public Library at Lincoln Center. Astor, Lenox, and Tilden Foundations. 317 Chopin, ***Polonnaise No. 1.*** Autograph of the composer (Eg3040f2). By permission of the British Library. 318 Eugene Delacroix, ***Frederick Chopin,*** 1838. Louvre, Paris. The Bettmann Archive, Inc.

Chapter 14

324 John Singleton Copley, ***Watson and the Shark,*** Oil on canvas. The Detroit Institute of Arts. Purchase, The Dexter M. Ferry, Jr. Fund. 327 Felix Mendelssohn-Bartholdy. Deutsche Staatsbibliothek, Berlin/DDR. 329 Henri Toulouse-Lautrec, Six Sketches of Hands on a Contrabass, 1900. Pencil drawing. Courtesy Musée Toulouse-Lautrec, Albi, France. 332 and 335 Clara and Robert Schumann. Gesellschaft der Musilfreunde in Wien-Archiv, Vienna, Austria. 339 F. Lenbach, ***Franz Liszt.*** Oil painting. Hamburger Kunsthalle, Hamburg, FRG. 345 A. F. Pecht, ***Portrait of Richard Wagner,*** detail. The Metropolitan Museum of Art, Gift of Frederick Loeser, 1889. 348 Engraving from an original sketch for scenery used at Bayreuth, by J. Hoffmann, Detail. Victoria and Albert Museum, Crown Copyright. 350 ***Wotan's Farewell to Brunhilde.*** Engraving, from a painting by Konrad Dielitz. Music Division. Performing Arts Research Center. The New York Public Library at Lincoln Center. Astor, Lenox, and Tilden Foundations. 350 Rigoletto and his daughter. Photograph by Fred Fehl. Music Division. Performing Arts Research Center. The New York Public Library at Lincoln Center. Astor, Lenox, and Tilden Foundations. 351 (top) The curse from ***Rigoletto.*** Photograph by Fred Fehl. Music Division. Performing Arts Research Center. The New York Public Library at Lincoln Center. Astor, Lenox, and Tilden Foundations. 351 (bottom) The wall scene from ***Rigoletto.*** Photograph by Fred Fehl. Music Division. Performing Arts Center. The New York Public Library at Lincoln Center. Astor, Lenox, and Tilden Foundations. 354 G. Boldini, ***Giuseppe Verdi.*** Foto Soprintendenza Speciale alla Galleria Nazionale d'Arte Moderna e Contemporanea, Rome, Italy. 356 Aquatint, after L. Boilly. Victoria and Albert Museum, Crown Copyright.

Chapter 15

361 ***A Soirée with Franz Liszt at the Piano.*** Deutsche Staatsbibliothek, Berlin/DDR. 364 Johann Strauss II with Johannes Brahms. Osterreichisches Nationalbibliothek, Vienna, Austria. 365 (top) R. Cruikshank. ***The English Spy.*** Vol. II, 1826. Engraving. Victoria and Albert Museum, Crown Copyright. 365 (bottom) Opera House and Karntner Street, Vienna. Courtesy of the Trustees of the British Museum. 367 Johannes Brahms. Theatersammlung, Hamburg, FRG. 369 Portable piano, "Chapell," 19th century, English. Victoria and Albert Museum, Crown Copyright. 374 Gala opening performance at the Vienna Opera House, May 25, 1869, Detail. Osterreichesche Nationalbibliotek, Vienna, Austria. 376 Honore Daumier, ***The Orchestra during the Performance of a Tragedy.*** Lithograph. Prints Division. The New York Public Library. Astor, Lenox, and Tilden Foundations. 377 Aubrey Beardsley. ***The Wagnerites,*** 19th century. Ink drawing. Victoria and Albert Museum, Crown Copyright. 381 Portrait of Antonin Dvorak. Bibliothèque Nationale, Paris, France. 384 Victor Hartmann, ***The Great Door of Kiev.*** Drawing. The Bettmann Archive, Inc. 385 Portrait of a Modest Mussorgsky. Tretyakov Gallery, Moscow, USSR. 388 Peter Ilyich Tchaikovsky. Press Photoagency, USSR.

Chapter 16

397 Mahler Conducting. Gesellschaft der Musikfreunde in Wien-Archiv, Vienna, Austria. 398 Gustav Mahler at 30. Osterreichische Nationalbibliothek, Vienna, Austria. 400 Arnold Schoenberg. ***Self-Portrait,*** 1921. Grayon. Osterreichesche Nationalbibliothek, Vienna, Austria. 401 Arnold Schoenberg, ***Der Rote Blick,*** 1910. Staatische Galerie im Lenbachhaus, Munich, FRG. Used by permission of Belmont Music Publishers, Los Angeles, Ca. 402 Henri Laurens, ***Guitar and Clarinet,*** 1920. Stone. Hirshhorn Museum and Sculpture Garden, Smithsonian. 408 Leon Bakst, ***Nijinsky in L'Apres Midi d'un Faun,*** Watercolor. Wadsworth Atheneum, Hartford, Ct. 409 M. A. Baschet, ***Claude Debussy.*** Musée Versailles. Versailles, France. 411 Claude Monet, ***River Scene.*** Reproduced by courtesy of the Trustees, The National Gallery, London. 461 Jean Cocteau, ***Stravinsky Playing 'The Rite of Spring'.*** Drawing. Castello Sforzesco, Milan, Italy. 417 Igor Stravinsky. Photo by Columbia Records, Courtesy of Boosey and Hawkes. 420 A scene from the ballet ***Rites of Spring*** by Igor Stravinsky, staged at the Bolshoi Theater, 1965. Fotokhronika TASS, Photo by E. Kassin. Sovfoto. 421 Arthur B. Davies, ***Dancers.*** Oil on canvas. The Detroit Institute of Arts. Gift of Ralph H. Booth. 422 Henry Cowell and Charles Ives. BMI Archives. 424 Charles Ives. CBS Records. 426 Edgard Varese. Detail. Music Division. Performing Arts Research Center. The New York Public Library at Lincoln Center. Astor, Lenox, and Tilden Foundation.

Chapter 17

432 N. A. Udaltsova, ***At the Piano.*** Oil on canvas. Yale University Art Gallery, gift of Collection Societe Anonyme. 438 Composer Alban Berg at the window, above a portrait of himself by Arnold Schoenberg. The Bettmann Archive, Inc. 438 Leo Schutzendorf as Wozzeck, in the first performance, Berlin 1925. The Bettmann Archive, Inc. 439 Portrait of Alban Berg. The Bettmann Archive, Inc. 441 H. F. Taylor, ***Figure with Guitar I,*** 1914. Oil on canvas. Hirshhorn Museum and Sculpture Garden, Smithsonian Institution. 442 Alexander Calder, ***Effect of Red,*** 1967. Painted sheet metal, metal rods and wire. Hirshhorn Museum and Sculpture Garden, Smithsonian Institution. 444 Wassily Kandinsky, ***Opera Green No. 263,*** 1923. Oil on canvas. The Norton Simon Foundation, Los Angeles. 445 Piet Mondrian, ***Composition with Blue and Yellow,*** 1935. Oil on canvas. Hirshhorn Museum and Sculpture Garden, Smithsonian Institution. 447 Juan Gris, Le Canigou, 1921. Oil on canvas. Albright-Knox Art Gallery, Buffalo, New York. Room of Contemporary Art Fund. 452 Duke Ellington. ASCAP. 457 Martha Graham in ***Appalachian Spring.*** Dance Division. Performing Arts Research Center. The New York Public

Library at Lincoln Center. Astor, Lenox and Tilden Foundations. 458 Aaron Copeland. Photo by John Ardous. Boosey and Hawkes, N.Y. 461 Bela Bartok. Photo by Fritz Reiner. Boosey and Hawkes, N.Y. 464 Elliott Carter, 1970. BMI Archives.

Chapter 18

472 Michael Ayrton, ***Maze Music,*** 1972. Bronze. Reproduced by permission of the Portsmouth City Museum and Art Gallery. 475 John Cage, 1940s. Culver Pictures. 478 Roy Lichtenstein, ***Little Big Painting,*** 1965. Collection of Whitney Museum of American Art, New York. Gift of the Friends of the Whitney Museum of American Art. 478 The Bregman Electronic Music Studio, Dartmouth College, Courtesy of Dartmouth College. 480 Andy Warhol, ***Green Coca-Cola Bottles,*** 1962. Oil on canvas. Collection of the Whitney Museum of American Art. Gift of the Friends of the Whitney Musem of American Art. 483 Francisco Solerino, ***Structure Permutationelle,*** 1963–66. Albright-Knox Art Gallery, Buffalo, New York. Gift of Symour H. Know. 485 Robert Rauschenberg, ***Tracer,*** 1964. Oil on canvas. Collection of Mr. and Mrs. Frank Titelman. Photo courtesy of Leo Castelli Gallery, New York. 486 Luciano Berio. Photo courtesy of G. Schirmer, Inc. 489 Lukas Foss. Photo by Warren Brandt, courtesy of Carl Fisher Music Co. 490 English children preparing a piano. Universal Edition (London) Ltd. 495 ***Baude Cordier.*** Manuscripts of 14th century songs. Musée Conde de Chantilly, France. GIRAUDON. 496 Tom Johnson. Photo courtesy of 218 Press.

Music Credits

Cover
Schwartz, *Music for Napoleon and Beethoven on Their 200th Birthdays.* Used by permission of the President and Trustees of Bowdoin College. Bowdoin College Music Press.

Part Openers
1 and 126 Schwartz, *Music for Prince Albert on His 150th Birthday.* Used by permission of the President and Trustees of Bowdoin College. Bowdoin College Music Press.

Chapter 4
112 Missal/Sarum, XIV century, M. 107, plate 112, folio 139. Used by permission of The Pierpont Morgan Library, New York, New York. 116 Childs, *Nine Choral Fragments.* Used by permission; Berandol Music Limited. 11 St. Joseph Street, Toronto, Ontario, Canada M4Y1J8 (416-924-8121). 124 Riley, *In C.* Used by permission of Terry Riley.

Chapter 16
398 Mahler, *Kindertotenlieder.* Printed by Universal Edition, Vienna. Used by permission of European American Music Distributors Corp., sole U.S. agent for Universal Edition, Vienna. 403 Schoenberg, *Pierrot Lunaire.* Used by permission of Belmont Music Publishers, Los Angeles, California 90049. 409 Debussy, *Prelude to the Afternoon of a Faun* (8 measures). From Édition Eulenburg. By permission of C.F. Peters Corporation, sole selling agents for the Western Hemisphere. 412 Debussy, *La Cathedral Engloutie.* Copyright 1910. Durand et Cie. Used by permission of the Publisher, Theodore Presser Company. Sole Representative U.S.A. 414 Milhaud, *Saudades do Brasil.* Reproduced by permission of Éditions Max Eschig, Paris, propriétaires de l'oeuvre. 417 Stravinsky, *Le Sacre du Printemps: Part I.* Used by permission of Boosey and Hawkes, Inc. New York, New York.

Chapter 17
435 Schoenberg, *String Quartet no. 4.* Used by permission of G. Schirmer, Inc. and Belmont Music Publishers. 439 Berg, *Wozzeck.* Full Score copyright 1926 by Universal Edition, A.G., Vienna. Copyright renewed. Used by permission of European American Music Distributors Corp., sole U.S. agent for Universal Edition, A.G., Vienna. 441 Berg, *Violin Concerto.* Copyright 1936 by Universal Edition, A.G., Vienna. Copyright renewed. Used by permission of European American Music Distributors Corp., sole agent for Universal Edition, A.G., Vienna. 447 Stravinsky, *Symphony of Psalms.* Used by Permission of Boosey and Hawkes, Inc., New York, New York. 458 Copland, *Appalachian Spring.* Used by permission of Boosey and Hawkes, Inc., New York, New York. 461 Bartók, *Music for Strings, Percussion and Celesta.* Used by permission of Boosey and Hawkes, Inc., New York, New York.

Chapter 18
473 Wuorinen, *String Trio.* Copyright 1971 by C.F. Peters Corporation. By permission. 477 Stockhausen, *Klavierstücke XII.* Copyright © 1954 by Universal Edition Ltd., London. Used by permission of European American Music Distributors Corp., sole U.S. agent for Universal Edition, Ltd., London. 488 Foss, *Baroque Variations.* Used by permission of Carl Fischer, Inc./ Pembroke Music Co., Inc. 493 Wishart, *Sounds Fun.* Reproduced by permission of Schools Council Publications. 494 Bedford, *Fun for All the Family.* Reprinted by permission of Oxford University Press. 496 Johnson, *Failing.* © 1976 by Tom Johnson. Published by 218 Press, P.O. Box 218, Village Station, New York, N.Y. 10014.

Index